[redacted]

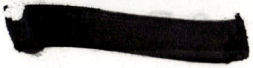

"Information through Innovation"

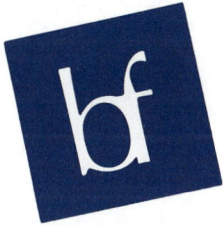

Database

Management

ELIAS M. AWAD

McIntire School of Commerce
University of Virginia

MALCOLM H. GOTTERER

Professor Emeritus
Florida International University

BOYD & FRASER PUBLISHING COMPANY
DANVERS, MASSACHUSETTS

CREDITS:

Senior Acquisitions Editor: James H. Edwards
Production Coordinator: Patty Stephan
Marketing Manager: Christopher Will
Cover Design: Michael Fender
Interior Design: Jennie Bush, Designworks
Composition: Alexander Graphics
Cover Illustration: Ed Scarisbrick, The Image Bank

A Division of South-Western Publishing Company
Danvers, Massachusetts 01923

Manufactured in the United States of America.

Library of Congress Cataloging-in-Publication Data

Awad, Elias M.
Database Management / Elias M. Awad, Malcolm H. Gotterer.
p. cm.
Includes index.
1. Data base management. I. Gotterer, Malcolm H., 1924-
II. Title.
QA76.9.D3A985 1992
005.74— 91-45654
CIP

2 3 4 5 6 7 8 D 5 4 3 2

DEDICATION

To our spouses, Sandy Awad and Shirley Gotterer, without whose patience and support this work would not have been possible.

CONTENTS

Chapter 2 *The Database Systems Life Cycle* 30

Chapter 3 *Database Management Systems* 64

PART VI *DIRECTIONS IN DATABASE MANAGEMENT* 481

Chapter 17 *Expert Systems and Databases* 482

Chapter 18 *Database Management and the Future* 512

APPENDIX A *EXCELERATOR/IS: A TUTORIAL* 533

PREFACE

To the Student

You are already part of a rapidly growing society committed to the use of information for decision making in industry and government. Organizations are increasingly dependent on databases to organize files, access and update records, or query the database on an ad hoc basis. The growing performance and availability of personal computers as workstations in a networked environment has made it convenient for users to tap all kinds of information on a daily basis.

Database systems are part of our everyday affairs. For example, consider these questions:

- How many students are preregistered in the systems analysis and design course?
- What percentage of the graduates accepted full-time positions in 1991?
- What was the average amount of financial aid awarded to in-state students in 1991?
- List all students in the business school who are in their fourth year, are majoring in information systems, and earned a grade of "A" in BUS 425 (database course).
- List all products with annual sales less than $185,000 and a profit margin of less than three percent.

To answer these questions using conventional file systems would take hours and would be quite tedious. Using a database system, the response could be generated in less than five seconds, depending on the size of the files and the demands on the system. Obviously, there is more to database systems than answering basic questions. The point is that a database environment has the distinctiveness of promoting efficiency, accuracy, and integrity, and assuring prompt response to inquiries.

With this in mind, it is almost mandatory that you have an understanding of database development, which is the focus of this book. It is a foundation book whose scope is broader than learning a database software product such as dBASE, SQL, Informix, or ORACLE. The text will introduce you to the concepts of database management, how a database is used in business, and how the resulting information can affect you.

In your first course in database management, you are probably anxious to learn about a number of approaches and applications that involve a database system. Based on our years of experience teaching this subject and on the demands of industry, we feel a database course should focus on the broader view of database *development*, a term that emphasizes data modeling, database design, and database implementation. Each of these three stages needs to be emphasized by examples and robust illustrations to simplify the understanding of this important technical area.

In this book, you will find a plentitude of examples and scenarios addressing the roles and applications of database systems in business. The material is highly readable and simplifies complex concepts and procedures through examples. It is designed for students with no technical background other than a basic course in information systems, which is required in almost all business programs.

In this text, we offer several useful topics:

- The systems approach to developing database applications.
- The importance of logical design, using Excelerator software as a design tool.
- Developing skills in modeling users' data requirements by means of tools such as the entity-relationship diagram.
- Transforming the data model into a normalized design.
- Easy-to-learn chapters on SQL and relational databases.
- Comprehensive coverage of distributed database processing in the context of networking technology.
- How to plan for a database application.
- What to look for in choosing a database management system.
- The role of the database administrator (DBA).
- The growing importance of the interface between expert systems and database systems.

In our years of practical experience, the most crucial aspect of developing a database application has been building the user's data model. The seemingly simplistic process of interviewing the user and transforming ideas, procedures, forms, and so on, into a working data model is more an art than a science. The quality and integrity of the resulting database application depends heavily on the accuracy of the data model. For that reason, we have included separate chapters on assessing user requirements and on data modeling.

Our teaching experience in the information systems area suggests that database and systems development courses overlap considerably. There is certain similarity between database design covered in a database course and application design covered in a systems analysis and design course. Data structure is determined by the structure of the forms as well as the structure of the application program. Students can benefit from the awareness of the relationship between database design and application design.

It is assumed that you, the reader, are likely to be a user of a database management system. This book is written with the end-user in mind; it also covers technical features and procedures that will help you build basic systems. To ensure readability and ease of learning, each chapter contains many examples and practical applications. Several important aids are also included. For example, each chapter opens with a chapter outline to guide your reading followed by an article from a popular database journal that addresses key features of the chapter. Following each article is an At a Glance capsule that highlights chapter contents. Each chapter ends with the following:

- A **chapter summary** that reviews the main points of the chapter.
- **Key words** to improve your vocabulary in database systems.
- **Review questions** that reinforce your understanding of the key points of the chapter.
- **Minicases** based on real-life business situations that illustrate the concepts covered in the chapter. Questions at the end of the cases ask you to identify the problem and prescribe solutions based on your reading.

In preparing this book, we have kept in mind that people, not databases, are the final decision makers. Database systems *support* human decision making. Although the underlying technology continues to provide more "intelligence" to improve the quality of decision making, humans have the final say in the way businesses, and society in general, must perform. Our hope is that you will make best use of this technology and of the contents of this book throughout your career.

Before the manuscript entered final production, it was tested in the classroom over a two-year period, with successive revisions resulting from student feedback and rapid changes in technology. To those students whose suggestions are reflected in the final draft, we are deeply indebted. Because no database management book is ever complete, future revisions are inevitable. After our thorough review and polishing of this material, we invite you to share your experience, ideas, or thoughts with us by writing to:

Elias M. Awad
McIntire School of Commerce
University of Virginia
Charlottesville, Virginia 22903

To the Instructor

Since the mid-1980s, we have witnessed a number of dramatic developments in database management for organizations, large and small. Improvements in the efficiency of the microcomputer, the availability of commercial relational modeling systems, the networking of database processing within and across organizations, and the integration of database software with other types of software such as spreadsheets, graphics, and expert systems—all have contributed to the rising prominence of database management.

This book was developed within the framework of these events. In addition, our years of teaching experience in database management have convinced us that a first course in this area should consist of a broad coverage of database *development*, independent of a specific database product such as dBASE IV, SQL, ORACLE, or Informix. Our emphasis on development addresses data modeling, database design, and database implementation as the three main stages of database management. We have approached this project using the systems development life cycle as a way to promote discipline, order, and control in developing a database application.

Determining the scope of the book posed concerns in terms of the overlaps between database technology and other areas such as systems analysis and design, strategic planning, systems development, and systems architecture. Given the nature of each area, it is difficult to view database management in isolation. Over time we have seen that to do a credible job in database design, you need a reliable data model based on accurate assessment of users' requirements. Even users' requirements are best met when the organization has a master plan, in which the database application in question falls in line with other applications in the plan. This book subscribes to such a top-down strategy.

Distinguishing Features Here is a foundation text on database management—the concepts, procedures, design, implementation, and management of database applications. We feel this edition is well illustrated and highly readable, presenting database terms and technology for a first-time student in a business curriculum or management information systems program. The book offers several important features. It:

- *Stresses the systems development life cycle approach to designing database systems.* Such a view promotes order and discipline in the way applications are managed. This approach is in line with other courses in the MIS field, which include systems analysis and design and building expert systems.
- *Simplifies complex concepts and procedures using numerous examples.* To illustrate, in Chapter 8, we have made an attempt to simplify normalization and how the third normal form is derived. Likewise, Chapters 9 and 10 explain SQL through illustrations. Ample application problems are included at the end of each chapter.
- *Shows in Chapter 16 how to choose a database management system.* Although our main target is database development, we feel a database course should include topics on selecting database management systems and negotiating software contracts. This type of background ties in with the managerial aspects of database development and is covered in the chapter.
- *Introduces in Chapter 17 how and why knowledge-based systems interface with database systems.* The chapter covers the basics of expert systems, followed by a discussion of the basis for and the importance of the interface between the two technologies.
- *Summarizes in Chapter 18 today's database technology and directions for future developments.* This chapter puts a finishing touch on the mechanics and procedures covered in the first 17 chapters. It offers ideas related to potential advances in the field.
- *Includes short problems and case situations at the end of each chapter for easy application of chapter material.* The problems will help students apply what they have learned.
- *Contains a tutorial on Excelerator in Appendix A.* It shows how this CASE tool is used for drawing E-R diagrams and data flow diagrams, developing a data dictionary, and constructing a structure chart. A summary and a list of key words are available at the end of each chapter. A comprehensive glossary of terms is presented in Appendix B.
- *Is organized around several "modules."* Chapters 1 through 3 are prefatory details that set the tone for the whole text. Chapters 4 through 11 cover the technical aspects of database management. Chapters 12 through 14 focus on implementation; Chapters 15 through 17 emphasize managerial topics.

Ancillary Materials A comprehensive instructor's support package accompanies *Database Management*. Its ancillaries are available from the publisher upon instructors' request.

Instructor's Manual The Instructor's Manual follows the sequence of material in the text. The entire manual is available in hard copy or on a diskette, using WordPerfect 5.1. It includes the following:

- A course syllabus that may be used on a semester plan and another syllabus designed for a quarter system
- Individual chapter objectives
- A summary of each chapter
- Lecture outlines (keyed to transparency masters available at the end of the manual)
- Answers to Review Questions for each chapter
- Answers to Application Problems at the end of each chapter
- Objective questions representing materials in each chapter
- Solution to Island Jumpers, Inc. (IJI) project, which is segmented throughout the text. A ready-to-use diskette has a menu-driven, operational version of the project. The diskette and a hard copy of the code are included in the manual.

Transparency Masters An extensive set of over 200 transparency masters is included at the end of the Instructor's Manual. These masters represent figures, illustrations, tables, and so on, that are highlighted in the text.

Test Bank A compilation of objective-type questions and selected application problems are prepared for a mid-term exam and a final exam. Also, all the objective-type items that are tagged to each chapter are included on the diskette.

dBASE Programming, by Robert A. Wray and Philip J. Pratt

Instructors who plan to include dBASE programming as part of the course should find this text useful. It is available through boyd & fraser publishing company.

Organization of the Book

This text contains 18 chapters and two appendices. It is organized as follows:

- **Part I—The Database Approach** encompasses Chapters 1 through 3. Chapter 1 is an introduction to database management, with emphasis on the growing importance and use of database management systems, the value of data in a database environment, and why organizations adopt a database system. Chapter 2 identifies the components and procedures of the database development life cycle and the makeup of logical design. Chapter 3 highlights the key activities and functions of a DBMS and the database facilities needed to support a multiuser environment.
- **Part II—Database Design** is represented by Chapters 4 through 6. Chapter 4 discusses data models, with emphasis on the tools for data modeling. Chapter 5 discusses the steps in database design, the makeup of user requirements, the function of a data dictionary, and the roles of data definition language and data manipulation language. Chapter 6 reviews the models for representing relationships—the tree, network, and relational models.
- **Part III—Database Tools and Procedures** are covered in Chapters 7 through 11. In Chapter 7, we review the basic functions and components of a data dictionary and how to evaluate data dictionary products. Chapter 8 focuses on normalization. Chapters 9 and 10 cover SQL—data definition, data control, and data manipulation commands, use of queries and joins, and a discussion of embedded and dynamic SQL. Chapter 11 addresses distributed databases and networking, with a focus on design criteria.
- **Part IV—Database Implementation** is covered in Chapters 12 through 14. In Chapter 12, we discuss the planning of a database application. Chapter 13 illustrates the main tools that express the logical design. Chapter 14 shows how to create, test, and debug a program.
- **Part V—Management of the Database Environment** centers around the managerial and organizational functions of the database administrator (Chapter 15) and choosing a database management system (Chapter 16). In Chapter 16, we also cover the basics of negotiating the software contract.
- **Part VI—Directions in Database Management** includes Chapter 17 on expert systems and the expert system-database system interface. In Chapter 18, we review the role of CASE tools and object-oriented programming, the status of cooperative processing, and legal issues in database management.
- **Appendix A** is a tutorial on Excelerator.
- **Appendix B** is a comprehensive glossary of database terms.

ACKNOWLEDGMENTS

A book of this magnitude could not have been completed without team support. The authors wish to acknowledge a number of people whose efforts influenced the content and direction of this project. We want to thank the following reviewers for their helpful recommendations and comments:

Robert Brown, University of Georgia
Thomas Case, Georgia Southern University
Mohammed Dadashzadeh, Wichita State University
Martin D. Goslar, University of South Carolina
Timothy Heintz, Marquette University
Ranjan Kini, Indiana University Northwest
Jerry Sawyer, Kennesaw State College

We thank our colleagues Robert H. Trent (McIntire School of Commerce, University of Virginia) and Don Burkhard (Price Waterhouse) for permission to use Island Jumpers, Inc. (IJI) in the text. We also thank R. Ryan Nelson (McIntire School of Commerce) and Robert H. Trent for permission to use the Excelerator tutorial in Appendix A. K. C. Buckley, Christy Hyatt, Matt Shumaker, and Jennifer Wakelin (Class of 1991, McIntire School of Commerce) deserve special credit for contributing the coding part of IJI. Poppy Lumanau and Susan Tien (Graduate Class of 1990, McIntire School of Commerce) contributed to the coding of the Worker's Compensation project included in Chapter 13.

A number of other individuals have contributed in special ways to the completion of this text. We greatly appreciate the input of David G. Smith (McIntire School of Commerce) who served as a sounding board on various matters; of Michele Romani (McIntire School of Commerce) for untold hours spent in reviewing the entire manuscript; and of Carol Stillman for her developmental effort in the early phase of the work.

The authors owe a debt of gratitude to a team of professionals at boyd & fraser publishing company, who have been models of talent, motivation, and quality assurance. We salute Jim Edwards, senior acquisitions editor, who provided unwavering support throughout the project. From copy editors to compositors, we recognize with appreciation their dedication to quality work.

We are deeply indebted to Patty Stephan, production coordinator, for a first-class job managing the entire project. During the authors' 26 years of publishing experience, we have found no match to Patty's talent and commitment to quality work.

Elias M. Awad
Malcolm H. Gotterer

PART I

THE DATABASE APPROACH

C H A P T

The Idea of Databases and Database Management

E R 1

Databases and the Value of Data

AT A GLANCE

Databases and the Value of Data

Gone are the days when aspiring young office workers went to secretarial schools to learn the intricacies of manual filing systems. Today, we use computers, not filing clerks, and it's all too easy for prospective computer users to be seduced by the siren song of user-friendly database management systems: If only they had it in a database, they could get the answers to their questions just by pressing a few keys.

Like all good come-ons, there's a lot of truth in that. But the benefits of databases are neither universal nor automatic. As computer professionals who consult with end-users, we have the obligation to throw cold water on unrealistic plans and expectations as well as to encourage applications that have the greatest chance of being valuable to our organizations.

As computer professionals, we know computers don't build or manage files, people do. So we must make sure our users recognize that every file needs a builder to create the original file and a keeper to maintain the file if it is to be of any value. The cost of compensation for these people must be compared to the value derived from the system. Files retained solely on the basis of storage and processing costs are likely to languish and die if they are more trouble to maintain than they are worth to the people who are supposed to be using them. This is only common sense, of course, but it's easy to underestimate the cost or inconvenience of data entry and overestimate the value of the data retrieved.

What's the Value of the Data?

Data entry costs can often be estimated with fair accuracy, but the real problem in balancing the database equation is estimating the value of the data to its users. Some data is extremely valuable: your company's receivables, for example. Some data is invaluable, such as the poison database available to doctors. Other data is of questionable value, like last year's crop forecasts or a passenger list for a flight that occurred a year ago.

There are many characteristics of data which give it value. Here are some:

- *Adequacy*—Completeness or, at least, sufficiency.
- *Comprehensibility*—Freedom from obscurity and ambiguity.
- *Conciseness*—Freedom from irrelevancy and redundancy.
- *Credibility*—Authenticity, authority, and reasonableness.
- *Durability*—Rate of decay into obsolescence.
- *Exclusiveness*—There's no advantage in common knowledge.
- *Novelty*—Stale news is no news.
- *Precision*—Tall may be accurate, but 6′8″ is better.

• *Significance*—Importance, uniqueness, timeliness.
• *Validity*—Errors always creep in; accuracy is never absolute.

Unless we're selling access to our data, we don't know how all this relates to dollars. Usually, we assume the value of information can be measured by the increase in productivity (or, better, effectiveness) that can be attributed to having the information, where productivity is defined in terms of units of output per work period and effectiveness is defined in terms of progress toward stated goals. But objective measurements of productivity and effectiveness are often difficult to make, so database cost-benefit analyses must typically be supplemented with subjective judgment of intangible benefits. Our users are likely to be the best judges.

More Is Not Necessarily Better

While some data may have value to the user, more is not necessarily better. When data increases, the end-user may eventually suffer information overload, which can be a real problem. For example, a U.S. Air Force study of Vietnam fighter pilots showed that the most successful had learned, contrary to regulations, to shut off irrelevant channels of information during combat situations.

Another important aspect of the value of data to an organization is how its validity varies over time, depending on the way the data is maintained. Over the long term, the validity of any database will come to depend entirely on the ratio of corrections to mistakes that are applied to it, regardless of its initial validity.

Value, as we have also seen, deals with durability. Assuming a static database, with no updating or maintenance, how long would it take to reach the point where the effort of inquiring into the database exceeds the value of the results? In some cases, this time is measured in seconds; in other cases, in years.

Raising these kinds of issues with your users should give them some insight into the expected value and ongoing costs of database updating and maintenance, which need to be included among the factors they should consider before beginning a new database project.

Based on Shaw, Chris, "To file or not to file." *Information Center, November 1987, 36-37. Reprinted with permission from* Information Center.

AT A GLANCE

In today's competitive world, accessing a variety of information for ad hoc decision making as well as day-to-day management is essential. When the application software is appropriate, database processing makes quick and useful access possible. The software designer's main focus, then, must be on the needs of the user rather than on the requirements of the computer and the program.

Database processing was preceded by manual filing and file processing. The manual approach was inflexible, slow, and error-prone. File processing was faster and more accurate than manual systems, but it generated a high level of data redundancy, data inconsistency, and integrity problems. Database processing overcomes most of these problems and provides data and program independence.

There are two major database processing system modes in use: menu-driven and command-driven. The command-driven mode requires that users have greater technical experience than users of the menu-driven mode. In either mode, most database management systems have a HELP facility to assist the user in understanding various commands, syntax problems, and the like.

Today's database management systems may be mainframe-based, microcomputer-based, networked, or distributed database. Each system offers unique features and serves a variety of applications.

By the end of this chapter, you should be able to

- distinguish between database and file processing systems,
- understand the growing importance and use of database management systems,
- understand the value of data in a database environment, and
- understand why organizations adopt a database system.

The Value of Data

In our complex, information-based society, we continually produce and consume data as individuals, as institutions, and as businesses. Significant segments of our society—government, the media, commerce, and industry—cannot function without a continuous flow of data. This data must be organized into a DATABASE in which it can be classified, collated, and compared in order to be used for assessment and decision-making.

It has long been recognized that data is an important company resource, as are employees, capital, property, equipment, and goods and services produced or sold. Data resources incur costs when data is developed and entered into the firm's database, and it provides value to the organization when data is used to implement decisions. Yet the value of data is somewhat different from the value of other resources because the entire organization depends on data to manage the human, financial, and material resources.

Data and Information

It is important that we distinguish between data and information. DATA is facts about objects, people, or entities. Data can come from strange places: For example, a long distance call generates duration data for billing purposes. Data may originate within the organization or outside the organization. Data can be quantitative or qualitative, historical or predictive. For example, payroll and general ledger data is quantitative and internal to the organization, while employee evaluation or job description data is qualitative and internal. Examples of external quantitative data are government tax statistics and market survey data.

INFORMATION is the product of the analysis and synthesis of data. Information is data that has been organized in a form suitable for use by a clerk, staff person, manager, or other member of an organization. For example, a list of loans and their values by name of debtor is data, but the same list arranged by auto loan, home improvement loan, and commercial loan is information to the vice president who needs to determine trends in the demand for loans.

Information plays an important role in decision making. It reduces uncertainty and makes decisions easier. As we gain information about a problem, our certainty about a solution increases accordingly. A database system can provide meaningful information when and in the format needed.

Databases

Databases are so widely used that they can be found in virtually every organization with a computer system, large or small. Here are some examples of database use.

- A state highway patrol officer can enter your car's license plate number in the patrol car's on-board computer. The information is transmitted to the Department of Motor Vehicles database for verification. In less than 5 seconds the officer receives a response, displayed on the screen, including the legal owner of the car, whether it has been reported as stolen, and whether it has been involved in an accident.
- When you call your broker with a question about the last trade of a stock, the broker accesses a securities database that is continually updated to reflect, within seconds, current quotations on stocks, bonds, or commodities. (See Figure 1-1.)
- When you charge a purchase using a credit card, the clerk inserts your card in a scanner and enters the amount of the purchase. The information is transmitted to the sponsoring bank's database, which determines the legality of the card and approves (or does not approve) the purchase. Your account balance is automatically updated to reflect the new purchase. (See Figure 1-2.)

Figure 1–1 Database-oriented stock exchange

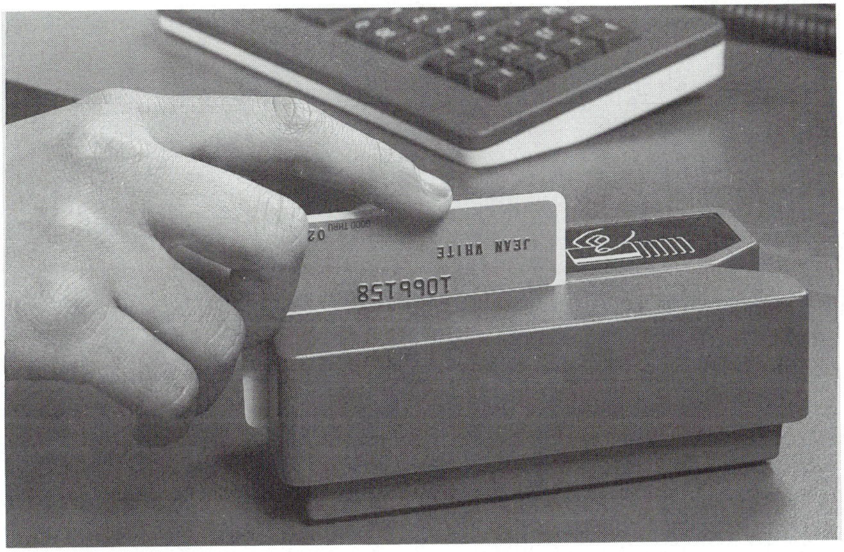

Figure 1-2 Processing a credit card purchase

• In a prescription drug-interaction system, the pharmacist enters the patient's name or ID number and the prescribed drug. The computer scans the drug interaction database, matches the prescribed drug against drugs the patient is presently taking, and alerts the pharmacist to possible adverse reactions. (See Figure 1-3.)

• When you visit a certain middle eastern country, an official at passport control enters your name in the government's massive database

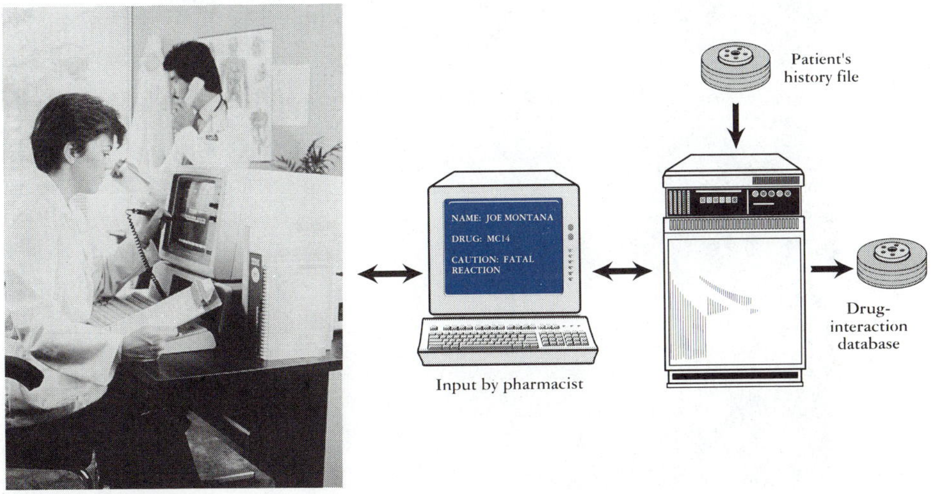

Figure 1-3 Drug interaction tracking system

system to determine if there is any information about you that might raise suspicion about your motives for entering the country.

• Many university libraries are converting their massive card catalogs to computer database systems, which virtually eliminate data redundancy and provide students and faculty access to book titles, authors' names, and subject indexes in a matter of seconds. (See Figure 1-4.)

In today's competitive markets, where a company's key objective is to maintain its position and even gain a competitive edge, database processing has become an important tool. Personnel managers access the employee database; marketing research firms organize demographics into databases; and the Internal Revenue Service stores tax return data in databases. So prevalent is the use of this technology that in most college management information systems (MIS) programs, database processing is a required course.

When the application software is appropriate, database processing offers a business great advantages. To develop such an application, the software designer must focus on the needs of the user rather than on the requirements of the computer.

A USER is anyone who employs a database to solve a problem or compile information. Users may be anyone from stockroom clerks who must enter inventory fluctuations into the database to managers who must maintain a master schedule for the entire workforce.

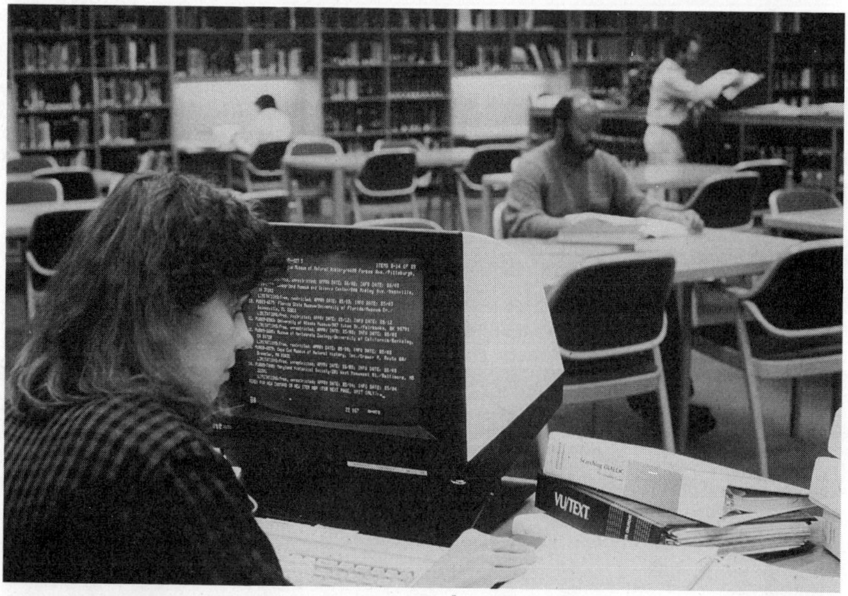

Figure 1-4 Database use in libraries

The Value of Databases

An organization may adopt a database system for one or more of several reasons.

- *High-volume applications*. A database can store large volumes of data vital to operating the business. Business applications such as inventory control and order tracking are commonly handled by a database system quickly, accurately, and efficiently. With the decreasing cost and improved power of database software, more and more corporations have been converting their file processing systems to database systems.
- *Ease of use*. The availability of the microcomputer has made it possible for virtually any size business to implement database applications. The ease of using database packages in general has shortened the time it takes to train users. Most database packages offer the user simple choices such as editing a record, browsing, or printing a report.
- *Access to data*. The user can query a database on an ad hoc (on-the-spot) basis. This is an especially useful feature for decision makers who may need to make spontaneous or unusual requests of the database. How valuable the system is to the user depends on how quickly the user can access and process information. A database system is invariably more responsive to such requests than a conventional file system. The user can go directly to the file without any assistance from the programmer, analyst, or other professionals.
- *Timely availability of data*. Database systems are particularly valued for making data available when it is needed. Users of a database system do not have to wait for data to be collected from several sources and brought together. Data is there when the user needs it.

Case Scenario 1-1: Fund Raising for the New Computer Center

Eastern Business School secured $250,000 in pledges from 14,200 active alumni to build a new wing to house its computer center. The builder contract specified building costs plus 10 percent markup. Toward the end of the project, increasing costs of building materials and design changes required an additional $100,000 to complete the wing. The funds had to be raised within two weeks for the project to remain on schedule.

The dean of the business school had to decide how best to raise the additional funds quickly. He needed information. One available source was the data from the last fund-raising campaign. Somewhere in this massive file, he hoped to find a pattern that could provide an approach to the problem.

The dean reviewed a listing of the alumni contributions and data such as name, age, and position (see Table 1-1). Looking at the list, he could find no noticeable pattern, except that executives and professionals were heavier donors than other alumni. The dean decided to concentrate on the alumni who had contributed $2000 or more to the annual pledge campaign, on the assumption that they might contribute the additional funds needed to complete the project. The dean asked his staff to sort the file by annual pledge.

The dean now had information. The partial list in Table 1-1 had been narrowed to four donors (Table 1-2) who had contributed $15,000 out of the $20,000 raised in annual pledges. He noticed that 40 percent of the alumni pledged 75 percent of the total for the year, and that professionals such as physicians and executives contributed substantially more than nonprofessionals.

The analysis reduced uncertainty by converting the volume of data to meaningful information. Now the dean could contact the heavy donors, hoping to raise the remaining funds within the two-week period.

Alumnus Code	Alumnus Name	Position	Age	Annual Pledge	Building Pledge
14	Howard	Physician	40	$ 3,000	$1,500
16	Kenney	Engineer	30	600	50
19	Sibley	Teller	35	400	50
11	MacArthur	Plumber	48	800	500
27	Kennedy	Librarian	64	500	500
17	Burkhard	Barber	46	1,100	0
20	Solomon	Developer	38	5,000	2,000
12	Garrard	Mayor	40	1,600	600
29	Tremaine	Professor	35	2,000	300
30	Diaz	Executive	54	5,000	2,500
				$20,000	$8,000

Table 1–1 A partial list of alumni and their pledges

Alumnus Code	Alumnus Name	Position	Age	Annual Pledge	Building Pledge
29	Tremaine	Professor	35	$ 2,000	$ 300
14	Howard	Physician	40	3,000	1,500
20	Solomon	Developer	38	5,000	2,000
30	Diaz	Executive	54	5,000	2,500
				$15,000	$6,300

Table 1–2 Donor list sorted by building pledge of $2000 or more

Types of Processing Systems

Obviously, where the data to be analyzed is complex and vast, a database system is helpful for handling it in a timely manner. A database system makes exploring the alternatives and coming to a decision possible. Case Scenario 1-1 is an example of using a basic, simplistic database. Database systems have evolved from just such a process, passing through three transition stages: manual, file, and database processing systems.

Manual Processing Systems

A MANUAL PROCESSING SYSTEM is simply a collection of records stored in filing cabinets or similar containers. Figure 1-5 illustrates a manual

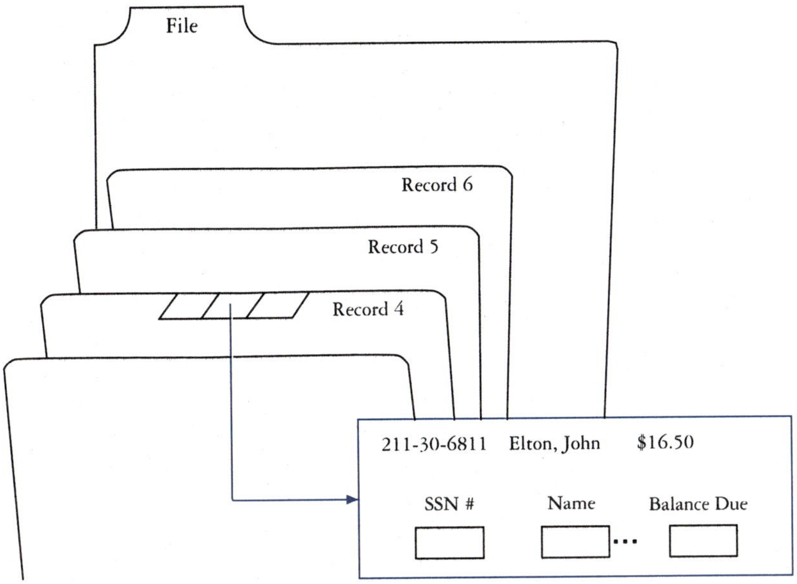

Figure 1–5 A manual processing system

processing system—a manila file folder containing sheets of paper. Each sheet is a record in a file. When tabs are used to organize the folders, the file is said to be INDEXED. The index helps to identify the location of the records in the file. (See Figure 1-6.)

Another example of a manual processing system is the pocket telephone and address book, which stores the names, addresses, and telephone numbers of people we know or associates we deal with, generally in alphabetical order. But such an arrangement is INFLEXIBLE. We cannot very easily rearrange the book by telephone number, by area code, by city, or by state. To do so would require rewriting the entire book manually for each alternative arrangement.

File Processing Systems

Early computer systems stored groups of records in separate files, so they were called FILE PROCESSING SYSTEMS. They were much faster and more accurate than manual systems, but their design was more complex and flexibility was still limited. System design focused on the individual needs of the user in the organization. Each new type of user request had to be translated into a new computer program. File processing systems applications included accounts receivable, inventory control, and demand deposit systems. Each new computer application was designed with its own set of data files, even though some of these data files may already have been available in existing files for other applications. File processing applications could not access other application files.

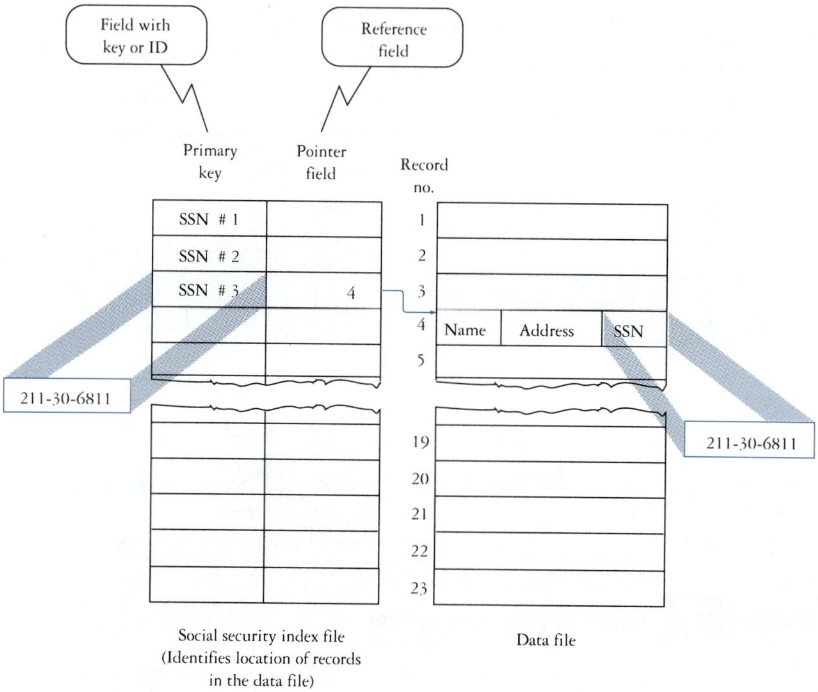

Figure 1-6 An indexing system

Figure 1-7 shows three file processing systems for the business school's fund-raising project. The first system processes the membership file; the second system processes the annual pledge file; and the third system processes the building pledge file. Each file contains several DATA FIELDS, which are predefined data elements such as name, address, and pledge amount.

A file processing system, because it is automated, has definite advantages over a manual processing system. It is quick, accurate, and provides good file organization. But, it has definite drawbacks.

Data redundancy A file system can generate a high level of REDUNDANCY or DATA DUPLICATION because the same data is stored in different files. For example, if the annual pledge file contained the name, address, and telephone number of a donor who also donated to the building pledge, the building pledge file would also contain the donor's name, address, and telephone number. Obviously, this redundancy is a waste of valuable storage space.

Limitations in data sharing In a file processing system, each user has his or her own application files and programs. It is difficult for users to share common data, contributing to data redundancy and inefficiency in general. Furthermore, in this "decentralized" environment, it is difficult to establish standards for and control over how data is processed.

Data inconsistency and lack of integrity When different versions of the same data are in various stages of update or a change is made in one file but not in the remaining files, the result is DATA INCONSISTENCY. In our fund-raising example, alumni names and addresses are stored separately in each of the three files. If a change of address is made in the annual pledge file alone, mail about alumni activities would continue to go to the old address, and the alumnus might begin to feel neglected.

Data inconsistency is related to DATA INTEGRITY, or its reliability. Data that is logically inconsistent lacks integrity because it cannot be depended on. In the case of changing an address in the pledge file but not in the membership file, a report based on the latter will include the old address. In such a case, the integrity of the data comes into question.

Inflexibility User inquiries that require information to be grouped in new ways cannot be done quickly in a file processing system. This means most ad hoc inquiries cannot be accommodated by file processing systems. The data cannot be processed in new ways without tedious restructuring. Using our fund-raising example, if the dean wanted a list of members whose annual pledge was over $2000 and who also contributed over $500 to the building fund, he would have to search both the annual pledge file and the building pledge file. Finally, he would have to compare the two files manually in order to determine which alumni were on both lists.

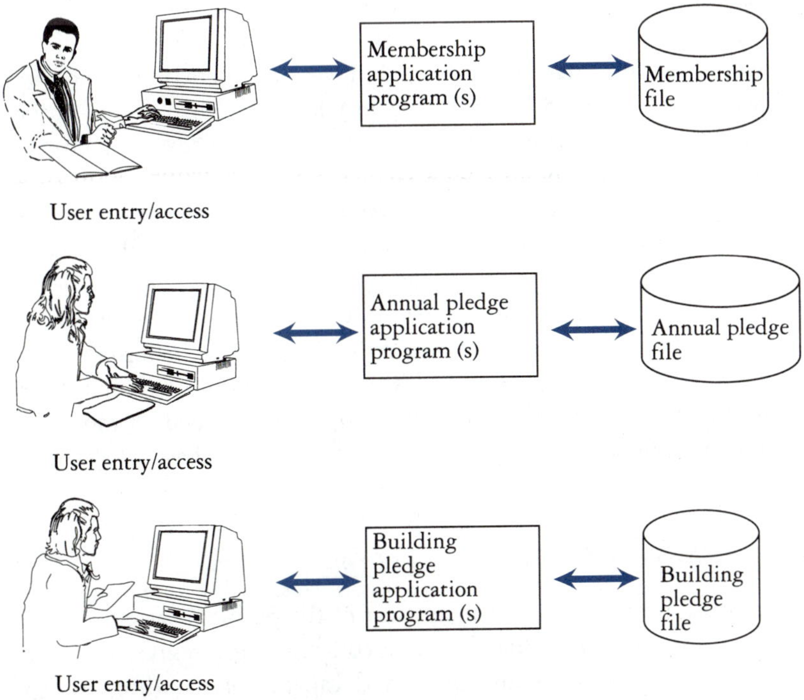

Figure 1–7 File processing system for Eastern Business School.

This problem is compounded if the search involves fifteen or twenty large files rather than just two files. Again, inefficiency stems from the fact that data is isolated and not integrated.

Expense In a file processing system, the application programs that process the data must contain the physical format of the files. That is, each program contains the data definitions for each file that it accesses and the commands for handling the files. Changes in database file formats are costly because each program must be individually reworked. For example, if a business phone field were to be added to the annual pledge file in Figure 1-7, all the programs that use the annual pledge file would have to be modified, even though they might have no use for the business phone field. Modifying application programs is both time-consuming and error-prone, since the update procedure is manual. It could also have implications for programmer productivity.

Because file processing involves creating each file to serve specific requirements—usually a single application—both the data and the system are inflexible. When the same underlying data is required in another application, the data often needs extensive modification. The programmer must

- reorganize the files,
- restructure the file (actually develop a new file with a new sets of fields),
- duplicate data, or
- perform a combination of the above.

A set of files developed around the dictates of a single application will work well for that application, but very frequently will not work well when we try to make that data provide us with different sorts of information. Modifications can be done easily, but they are inefficient, time-consuming, and quite expensive.

The problems of file processing systems were prevalent in first- and second-generation applications. Later on, in the early- to mid-1970s, the introduction of software support packages such as data dictionaries and generalized file management and report writers cushioned some of these drawbacks. But the problems of data redundancy, data inconsistency and lack of integrity, and the time-consuming programming maintenance resulting from frequent file and program update remained. A much more desirable alternative to file processing systems is database processing.

Database Processing Systems

Database processing overcomes most of the problems associated with file processing systems. A database is a collection of integrated (logically related) files shared by many users and capable of handling multiple applications. A DATABASE MANAGEMENT SYSTEM (DBMS) is a set of powerful, comprehensive programs that make it possible to access information quickly and easily. A database management system reduces cumbersome manual tasks to the simple pressing of a few keys.

There are countless examples illustrating the benefits of databases. For example, you may set up a database program to print reports of all employees who must be evaluated monthly. After the user enters dates of employment, the system searches for and prints the names of all employees who match that date. Think of the alternative: searching each employee file each month to decide who should be evaluated.

In addition to file search and data selection, a database management system can do all kinds of calculations. It can compute accrued interest, generate up-to-date balances, and customize reports quickly and easily. Suppose a college department chairperson wanted a report of all juniors majoring in information systems who have taken the basic database course in the fall semester of their second year with Dr. Elam. The chairperson (or the department secretary) could spend all week going through each of the 1500 student files. Depending on the type of hardware and database processing environment available, the chairperson could instead use a database system to produce the same information in less than ten seconds.

DATABASE MANAGEMENT SYSTEMS CHARACTERISTICS

A database management system has four main advantages over manual and file processing systems:

- *data integration*—Pooling the files in a centralized location
- *data sharing*—Allowing all users access through data integration
- *minimum data duplication or redundancy*—Maintaining system integrity, efficiency, and reliability
- *independence of physical file structure*—Allowing programs to be modified without affecting the file structure, and vice versa

Data Integration

DATA INTEGRATION means that data in a DBMS is pooled to cut down on data redundancy. Removing data redundancy is a step toward effective and efficient data shareability and consistency. When we organize data files as a central repository independent of specific users, we minimize data redundancy. In our fund-raising example (see Figure 1-8), names and addresses are stored once. When they are modified, only one update is necessary.

Data Shareability

DATA SHAREABILITY means that a database, as a single repository of data, can be shared by many people, each of whom may use it for different reasons. Sales order entry data, for example, may include

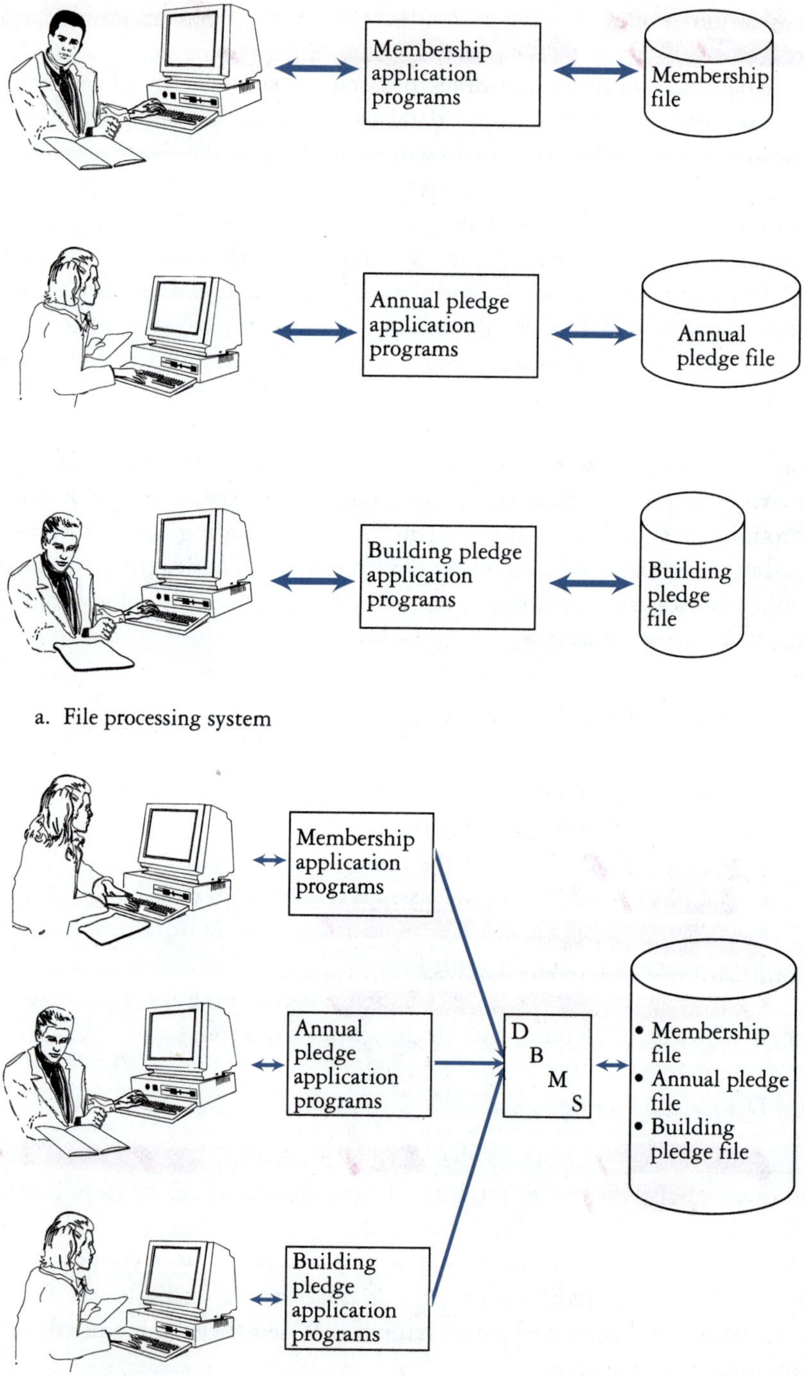

a. File processing system

b. Database processing system

Figure 1-8 File processing and database processing systems compared application programs written for the sales department and application programs written for the purchasing department. The DBMS acts as an interface between users and the physical database.

In a file processing system, the application program directly accesses the records in the file. In a database processing system, the application program no longer interacts directly with data files. It calls the DBMS (the liaison, so to speak) to access the stored records. For example, in our fund-raising scenario, the application program can instruct the DBMS to access either alumni membership data, annual pledge data, building pledge data, or all of the above. If data from more than one file is needed, all the application program needs to do is to specify the logical format of the data and how it is to be used. The DBMS, in turn, manipulates the physical data. In contrast, in a file processing system the application program must handle the physical as well as the logical activities of data processing.

On the surface, programs communicating via DBMS seem to add an extra layer of complexity to the process. But this complexity is invisible to the user and improves the user's ability to access data files. This is analogous to driving an automobile with automatic, as opposed to manual, transmission. An automatic transmission contains more complex parts, but requires less effort to use (especially in stop-and-go traffic) than manual drive.

Data Independence

In database processing, different application programs use the central resource so that all users get the information that suits them best. Application programs no longer depend on file formats that are stored along with the data in the database. All the application program needs to do is define the type and length of the data items from the database. The DBMS locates and retrieves the data requested, apart from the application program. This is referred to as program or DATA INDEPENDENCE. Figure 1-8 illustrates the efficiency of moving from a file processing environment with independent data resources to a database processing environment that emphasizes shared data resources.

Data Hierarchy

Each information system has a hierarchy of data organization, where each level in the hierarchy contains elements of the preceding level. Figure 1-9 illustrates the structure of a database organization. Note that a database is an integrated set of files that handles a number of queries—employee information, employee skills, vacation privileges, and schedules, for example. The hierarchy makes it possible to ensure order and remove redundancy in the database processing environment.

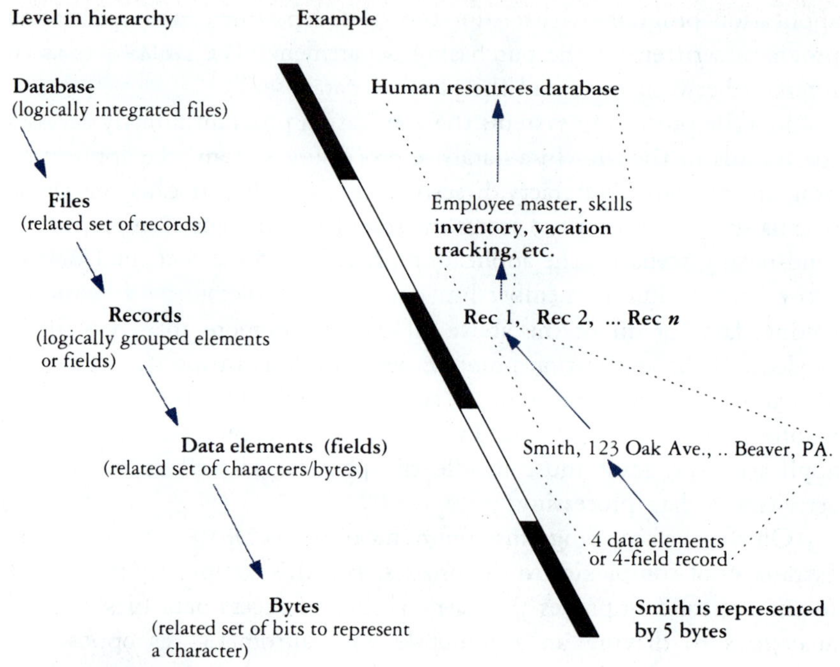

Figure 1-9 Hierarchy of data organization

Database Modes

Database management systems, although they differ by computer configuration (that is, mainframe, microcomputer, or network), have several common operations modes that distinguish them from manual or file processing. The two key modes are menu-driven and command-driven.

Menu-driven mode The MENU-DRIVEN MODE is ideal for novice users or those with a clearly defined set of database applications and options to choose from. In this environment, a list of applications is displayed on the screen. The user selects an application, such as accounts receivable or general ledger. Next, a detailed list of options for the selected application appears. The user selects one option at a time, such as enter data, revise a record, or print a report. (See Figure 1-10). The listed procedure is easy to use and understand. The user can run the database with virtually no prior knowledge of computers or database management systems, because all the instructions are displayed on the screen. However, a database system operating in a menu-driven environment suffers from the fact that the user can select only what the menu offers—no more, no less.

Command-driven mode The COMMAND-DRIVEN MODE allows users with some technical background to enter commands to the database management system interactively. In this mode, the user has a variety of special options, and the flexibility achieved is not normally available in a

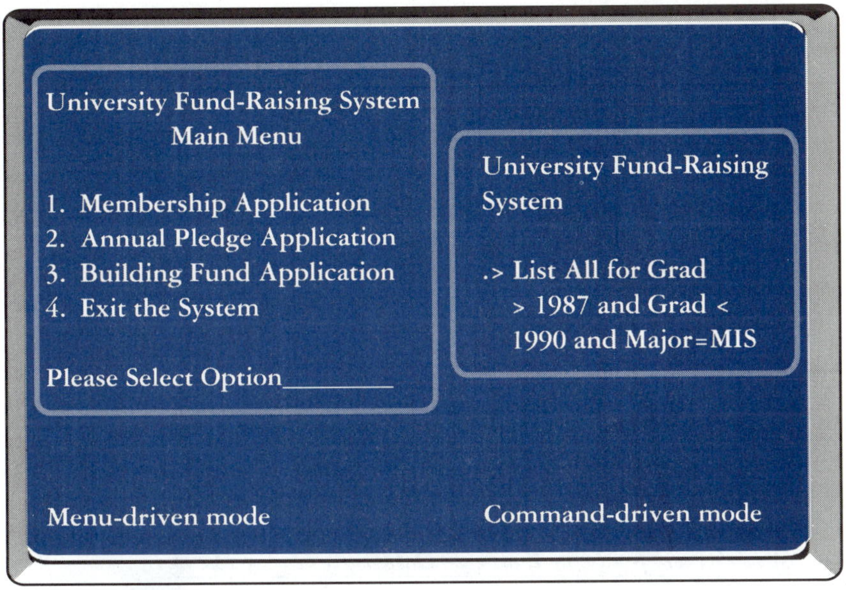

Figure 1–10 Database modes

menu-driven system. For example, in our fund-raising scenario, the dean may ask Professor Jones, who teaches the database course, to solicit funds from alumni who have taken his course. Jones may ask the DBMS to list the names and telephone numbers of all alumni who graduated between 1987 and 1990 and whose major was management information systems (MIS). Since the database course is required for majors in MIS and Professor Jones was the only database instructor between 1987 and 1990, he then would contact the alumni (hopefully he was a well-liked teacher) to solicit donations.

Help In either mode, most DBMSs offer on-line "help" facilities which allow the user to seek assistance about the command features or DBMS instructions. Normally, pressing a special key (such as F1) on the keyboard, allows the user to interrupt the ongoing application and access the HELP menu, which essentially replaces the user's manual—an important time-saving feature.

Database Management Systems Environments

Database management systems and database applications operate in a variety of computer-based environments. Early systems ran on large mainframe computers in the late 1960s, which were followed by microcomputer-based systems in the late 1970s, networked systems in the mid-1980s, and distributed databases in the early 1990s. Let's briefly elaborate on each database system. Later in the text, we should be able to decide on the proper computer configuration that a given database application should use.

Mainframe-Based Database Systems

MAINFRAME-BASED DATABASE SYSTEMS were designed to run on large computers for large firms. These systems require large storage capacities and an environment dedicated to serving multiple users in a real-time mode, that is, immediately. With their highly complex database applications, the design, implementation, and maintenance of such systems require huge budgets. A typical DBMS software package alone can run as high as $250,000, and requires a full-time professional staff for programming and support. (See Figure 1-11a.)

Under the general category of mainframe-based database management systems are public-access information retrieval systems for public users. Examples include the stock market exchange monitor and CompuServe, both of which have multiple databases, depending on the information requested, and require public dial-up lines.

Microcomputer-Based Database Systems

Since the early 1980s, major efforts have been made to bring the power of a database management system to the microcomputer level. These software programs are easy to use and easy to learn. Users have been known to navigate through the process with one or two days of training.

MICROCOMPUTER-BASED DATABASE SYSTEMS are designed to run on microcomputers for medium-sized and small firms (Figure 1-11b). They have made it possible for thousands of smaller firms and nonprofessional users to adopt an enormous range of applications that were nonexistent only 15 years ago. The total cost of installing such databases can be as low as $1500 and as high as $30,000, depending on the requirements of the DBMS. Unlike mainframe DBMSs, micro-based database systems tend to be easy to use and easy to learn. Even a novice user can become skilled after a week's study of the commands and syntax.

One factor that we need to consider in database design for the microcomputer is the growing size of main storage or random-access memory (RAM) and the capacity of secondary storage of the microcomputer. For example, it is not unusual to acquire the high end of a microcomputer with 16 megabytes (MB) of RAM and 300 MB of secondary storage on hard disk—all for under $8000. As the microcomputer DBMS has provided more and more features that were once unique to the mainframe-based DBMS, the additional storage has become necessary. This means greater reliance on available database applications that can also be linked to the corporate mainframe for accessing larger, more complex database applications. This interactive interface is the basis for today's move toward networking corporate applications.

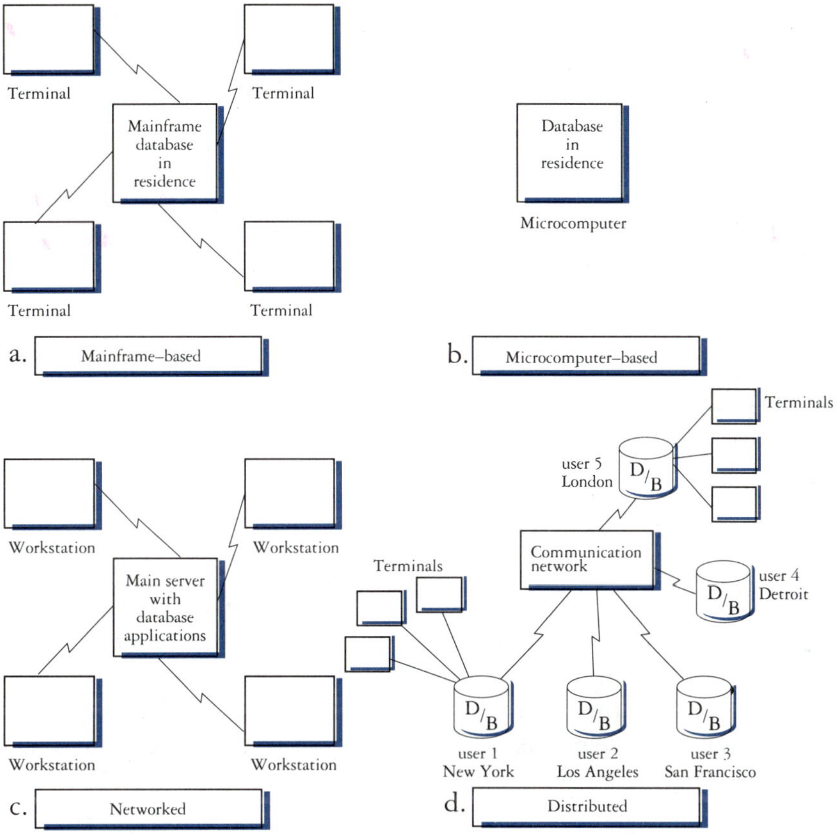

Figure 1–11 Database systems

Network-Based Database Systems

NETWORK-BASED DATABASE SYSTEMS involve physically linking two or more computers so that users can share common resources such as software packages and printers, as well as databases (Figure 1-11c). Networking design requires obtaining a license to use a software package for multiple users rather than purchasing one package for each user. Not only is this more efficient, but it also promotes security and makes it possible to protect the software from unauthorized copying.

Distributed Database Systems

DISTRIBUTED DATABASE SYSTEMS are usually portions of a database maintained at remote physical locations or sites (Figure 1-11d). Each site is responsible for maintaining the part of the database that is proprietary to its users. The design allows users at any site to access databases anywhere in the network as if the data were all stored at their own sites. A good example of a distributed database system is a multilocation auto dealership, where each branch maintains its own database for local business. When a customer requests a car that is not in the local inventory, a search of other branches' databases is initiated to locate the car in question.

With distributed systems, one important issue is CONCURRENCY CONTROL or the ability of the DBMS to deal with several users as they modify the same data at the same time. For example, one user might be trying to modify information that other users are trying to read. Worse yet, one user could be deleting a record, while another user is trying to read it. These concurrency conflicts create a challenge for the DBMS, as it tries to satisfy the needs of different users. Concurrency and other issues are covered in Chapters 3 and 11.

IMPLICATIONS FOR MANAGEMENT

In small businesses, databases are easily created and operated by the user. In larger organizations with extensive computer systems, the corporate database is created by specialists—database designers and database administrators. In such an environment, the user accesses data stored by the database management system just as easily as he or she does in a smaller database environment.

The database concept is both powerful and simple, yet it can be oversold or misunderstood. Not all of an organization's data is kept in the database, nor is a database the ultimate reservoir from which all users can access information. In fact, the reservoir notion—that a database stores all the organization's data—can affect the quality of decision making. A data-oriented rather than decision-making emphasis can lead to serious problems when too much of the wrong data is a part of the database.

Although the notion of a corporate database capable of meeting all users' needs is not yet a reality, the database concept has many attractive features and uses, as long as the problems it raises are overcome at the outset. For example, the fact that a database assumes that data relationships do not respect departmental boundaries means there must also be management policies and security controls to protect the data resources from abuse. Management is responsible for directing database development, participating in the design process, and ensuring quality database administration.

SUMMARY

1 Database processing trades computer power for human resources. The database design orientation should be toward the needs of the user rather than the requirements of the computer.

2 An organization adopts a database system for several reasons:

a. A database system can store large volumes of vital data.
b. Most database packages are menu-driven, offering the user simple choices.
c. The user can query a database on an ad hoc basis.
d. Database systems make information available when needed.

3 Data is facts about objects, people, or entities. The analysis and synthesis of data is information for decision making.

4 A manual processing system is a collection of records with common attributes stored in file cabinets or other storage devices. Manual systems are inflexible and unwieldy. In contrast, a file processing system stores groups of records in separate computer files. It is faster and more accurate than a manual system. Yet, it has drawbacks: Data redundancy, data inconsistency and lack of integrity, inflexibility, and high costs.

5 Database processing is a response to the limitations of file processing systems. It offers four key features:

a. data integrity
b. data shareability
c. minimum data redundancy
d. data or program independence

6 A database management system has a hierarchy of data organization, where each level in the hierarchy includes elements of the preceding level. The highest level is the database (logically integrated files), while the lowest level is the byte (a set of bits to represent a character). The hierarchy ensures order and removes redundancy in a database processing environment.

7 Database management systems have two main operations modes: menu-driven and command-driven. The menu-driven mode is more user-friendly, but less flexible, than the command-driven mode.

8 Database applications operate in a variety of computer-based environments: mainframe-based, microcomputer-based, network-based, and distributed systems. With distributed database systems, an important issue is concurrency control, since multiple users may be modifying the same data at the same time.

KEY WORDS

Command-driven mode
Data
Database
Database management system (DBMS)
Data field
Data independence
Data integration
Data integrity
Data redundancy
Data shareability
Distributed database systems
File processing system
Information
Mainframe-based database systems
Manual processing system
Menu-driven mode
Microcomputer-based database systems
Network-based database systems
User

REVIEW QUESTIONS

1 Define each of the following terms.
   a. database
   b. data integrity
   c. data shareability
   d. information

2 What is the purpose of database processing? Review last Sunday's newspaper and summarize three cases of database use.

3 Why would an organization develop a database management system? Discuss.

4 Do all business firms need a database system? Discuss.

5 Determine whether each of the following is data or information.
   a. automobile license plate AI264M
   b. a list of students and their grades in random order
   c. the balance sheet of a small business
   d. your textbook (so far)
   e. the payroll of a small bank

6 In what way(s) does a file processing system differ from a manual processing system? What type of application might be attractive to each system? Why?

7 How does data inconsistency contribute to data integrity? Illustrate.

8 When we say that files are inflexible, what do we mean? Give an example.

9 "Database processing overcomes most of the problems associated with file processing systems." Do you agree? Explain in detail.

10 Elaborate on the main advantages of a database management system. Which do you think is the most important advantage? Why?

11 What is unique about a DBMS? Can a database processing system function without it? Why?

12 What is the difference between the following pairs:
   a. data and information
   b. database and file
   c. menu-driven and command-driven modes

13 Explain briefly the levels of hierarchy of data organization. Why do we need to understand such a hierarchy?

14 How do mainframe-based systems differ from network-based systems?

15 What is unique about distributed database systems? In what way do they differ from network-based systems? Illustrate.

APPLICATION PROBLEMS

1 Of all the problems associated with file processing systems, which do you consider to be the most devastating for a business? Why? In giving your answer, consider the tangibles, such as hardware, programmer time, and costs, as well as the intangibles, such as user satisfaction.

2 Do you receive separate statements for your checking and savings accounts or an integrated statement for all accounts at your bank? In either case, what clues do you get about whether a database environment exists at the bank? Explain.

3 A typical supermarket carries a variety of products: fruits and vegetables, meats, canned goods, and so forth. How can a database management system improve the efficiency of the market's operations and the quality of the manager's decision making?

4 A lumber yard hired you to assess its information requirements. During the investigation, you discovered that the firm has an inventory file management system that is updated each Saturday. The yard sells lumber daily. All orders are placed on Saturdays and are delivered the following Monday.
   a. What is distinctive about the yard's file management system?
   b. What additional benefits or improvements might be derived from installing a database processing system? What about drawbacks?

5 Is it possible for an organization to be too dependent on database processing? If so, should the firm always keep some processing manual? Explain.

6 *Island Jumpers, Inc. (IJI)*[1]

Island Jumpers, Inc. (IJI) is being formed by a group of recent college graduates. During the spring break of their fourth year, they had all visited a remote group of islands in the Caribbean. They fell in love with the islands and the natives. The only unfavorable experience they encountered was the inaccessibility of the islands from one another. The largest of the islands,

[1] This case is adapted with permission from Dr. Donald L. Burkhard (Price Waterhouse) and Dr. Robert H. Trent (University of Virginia).

Hialathe (which means long and thin) has an airport which is serviced by one commercial flight a day. This is the only public access to the group of islands. Transportation to the five neighboring islands is provided by the natives, if and when they are going to the specific island themselves. This arrangement has made it virtually impossible for vacationers to plan their days on the islands.

The founders of IJI decided to form a company that would provide transportation to the islands. IJI would use three boats and two helicopters to access the islands. All of the islands except Bumpa have a suitable site for a helicopter pad. Bumpa is a very small and mountainous island, which IJI initially considered not serving, but which offers many isolated hiking

Trip No.	From	To	Time	Craft
101	Hialathe	Bork	8:00 AM	B-2
101	Bork	Bodacious	9:00 AM	B-2
101	Bodacious	Kookey	10:30 AM	B-2
101	Kookey	Hialathe	11:30 AM	B-2
105	Hialathe	Kookey	8:00 AM	B-3
105	Kookey	Bork	9:30 AM	B-3
105	Bork	Hialathe	10:30 AM	B-3
106	Hialathe	Bodacious	11:30 AM	B-3
107	Bodacious	Hialathe	1:00 PM	B-3
111	Hialathe	Bumpa	7:30 AM	B-1
111	Bumpa	Gilligan's	9:30 AM	B-1
111	Gilligan's	Hialathe	10:30 AM	B-1
201	Hialathe	Kookey	2:30 PM	B-3
201	Kookey	Bodacious	3:30 PM	B-3
201	Bodacious	Bork	4:30 PM	B-3
201	Bork	Hialathe	4:30 PM	B-3
205	Bork	Kookey	1:30 PM	B-2
205	Kookey	Hialathe	2:30 PM	B-2
205	Hialathe	Bork	12:30 PM	B-2
206	Hialathe	Bodacious	3:30 PM	B-2
207	Bodacious	Hialathe	5:00 PM	B-2
211	Hialathe	Gilligan's	4:00 PM	B-1
211	Gilligan's	Bumpa	6:00 PM	B-1
211	Bumpa	Hialathe	7:00 PM	B-1
301	Hialathe	Gilligan's	10:00 AM	A-2
302	Gilligan's	Hialathe	7:00 PM	A-2
306	Hialathe	Kookey	9:00 AM	A-2
307	Kookey	Hialathe	9:30 AM	A-2
311	Hialathe	Bork	10:00 AM	A-1
312	Bork	Hialathe	10:30 AM	A-1
315	Hialathe	Bodacious	8:30 AM	A-1
316	Bodacious	Hialathe	9:15 AM	A-1
401	Hialathe	Gilligan's	4:30 PM	A-2
402	Gilligan's	Hialathe	5:00 PM	A-2
406	Hialathe	Kookey	5:30 PM	A-2
407	Kookey	Hialathe	6:00 PM	A-2
411	Hialathe	Bork	5:00 PM	A-1
412	Bork	Hialathe	5:30 PM	A-1
415	Hialathe	Bodacious	4:00 PM	A-1
416	Bodacious	Hialathe	4:30 PM	A-1

Craft Capacity

Helicopter A-1	4 persons	Boat B-1	8 persons
Helicopter A-2	4 persons	Boat B-2	12 persons

Table 1–3 Trip schedule for Island Jumpers, Inc

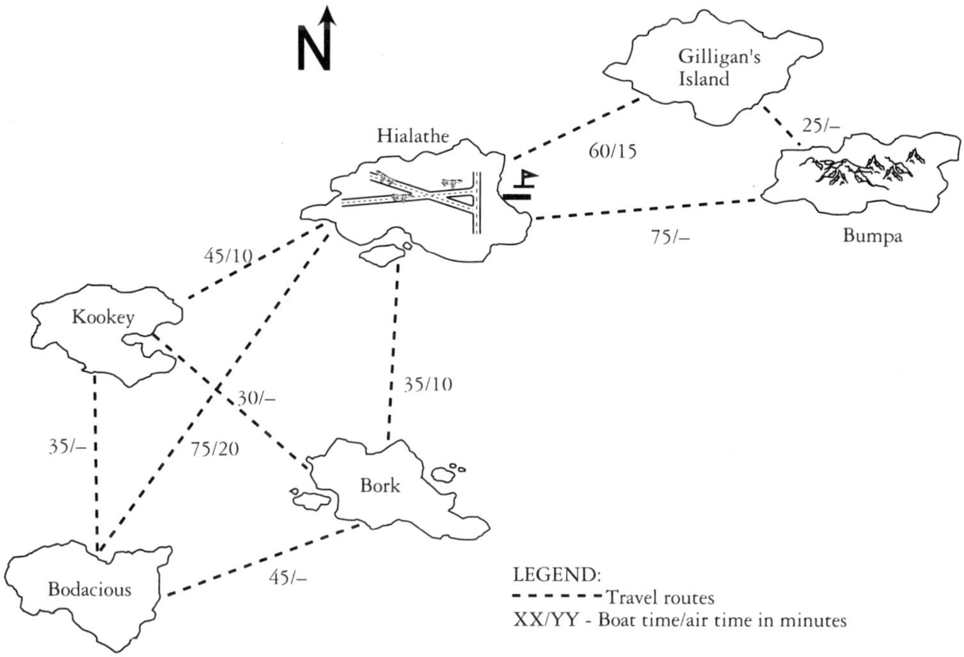

Figure 1-12 Island Jumpers, Inc. transport map

paths with terrific scenery and an opportunity to pick a multitude of tropical fruits (it is also considered the most romantic of the islands).

Service to the islands will include two air schedules and at least two boat schedules per day (except Bumpa, which will have only boat service). Air services will be point-to-point from Hialathe. Boat services may involve a series of stops at different islands. Table 1-3 is a trip schedule for IJI. Figure 1-12 is a map, showing travel times by boat and by helicopter between the islands.

Generally, tourists do not know about IJI services until they arrive at Hialathe. So, reservations typically are not made more than a few days in advance. At the moment, payment is made in cash or by check.

IJI needs a reservation system. At a minimum, this system should provide availability information for a flight or a boat, make reservations, print tickets, and provide management with operating information for planning and control purposes.

1 Explain in your own words just what size business IJI is.

2 How much do you think IJI needs a reservation system? Would you recommend a manual or automated system? If the latter, would it be a mainframe or a microcomputer system? Justify your position.

3 Do you think IJI has use for a database environment? What would be the benefits? The drawbacks?

C H A P T

The Database Systems Life Cycle

E R 2

The Political Role of the Database Specialist

AT A GLANCE

Case Scenario: *Florida Commercial Bank Safe Deposit Department*

The Database Environment

The Functional Components

- Menu
- Report
- Update
- Application Program

The Application Development Life Cycle

- Database Planning
- Study of User Requirements
- Evaluation
- Database Design
- Database Implementation
- Post-Implementation Review

Implications for Management

The Political Role of the Database Specialist

Database analysts, designers, and administrators, collectively referred to here as database specialists, translate clerical activities into the form of a database for the benefit of a user. In developing applications, a database specialist has opportunities for both technical and political performance. Translating a user's requirements into a new form and working within a relationship of mutual trust are examples of political performance.

The following is an example of how one database specialist succeeded in establishing the user's trust. He was representing a time-sharing service bureau, which had assembled some management information databases for one of the Bell telephone companies. In an effort to promote further use of the databases, the specialist had worked with a personnel department to develop a graph comparing planned staffing levels with actual assignments.

When this graph was presented to the user, the user saw that actual assignments fell well below planned levels. Quite disturbed at his poor performance, the user requested that the existence of this graphics capability not be revealed to any managers above him for two months. And he trusted the specialist not to reveal it.

Two months later, the same graph was produced and it showed the progressive improvement in actual personnel assignments. So the user and the database specialist had the pleasure of carrying the new graph upstairs to the user's manager.

Even before he showed the results to his management, the user was using the database as justification for his own political actions—actions that had consequences in his personnel staffing decisions.

Negotiating Tools

In practice, negotiation has become a primary tool. The process of negotiating is stepwise, from the general to the specific. The negotiations at the beginning of the database project start with the user's expectations, the database specialist's reputation for good work, and industry conventions and precedents with respect to how much control the database team needs to get started.

As development proceeds, he will need more control. The logical model of a database (or external functional specification) is a significant political bargaining, or negotiating, tool. The database design team must use this tool to ensure that they will gain sufficient control in the next phases of development.

In addition to control, the database analyst needs knowledge about the user's business activities and records in order to develop specifications and system designs. Like negotiation for control, the process of transforming user requirements into database design is stepwise, from the general to the specific. Periodically, the database design team demonstrates to the user their understanding of the requirements and how these requirements appear to fit into the design. Then it is agreed to proceed to more detailed design, programming, or whatever is the next step.

Performance Opportunities

Besides a degree of control and a knowledge of user requirements, the specialist needs his own skill in order to develop or maintain a database. Political qualifications are hinted at in phrases like "communication skills" or "service-oriented."

The political role of technical skill always exists in relation to other people. A database administrator's technical skills have a political role in relationsip to many different groups: With users, with DP personnel, with computer operators, and with vendors.

Reconciling the difference between the old form and the newer form presented by the database is a political activity comprised of, at least in part, the points discussed above. They can be summarized as follows:

1 Technical skills service the political interest of a database specialist by justifying the trust of the user, by advancing the specialist's career, and by enhancing the reputation of the DBMS.

2 A database design is developed after an analyst has obtained clear and complete user requirements.

3 A negotiation for control of a database is gained by an exchange of accountability for the degree of control acceptable to both parties.

4 An implementation depends on the user's acceptance of the database content as fact.

Grant Wiswell, Computerworld, *February 14, 1986, 49-53. Reprinted with permission from* Computerworld.

AT A GLANCE

The most important goal of designing a database is meeting the user requirements. We design databases by following a development life cycle that begins with scoping the project and ends with reviewing the final product. Database design is conducted in the context of a database environment consisting of the end-user, hardware, software, data, and personnel. In addition, there is a functional way to look at a design which includes the menus, programs, and various reports. Most of these reports are produced using a DBMS report generator.

The database application development life cycle centers around five major steps:

1 Planning, which focuses on forming a planning team and deciding on planning tools.
2 A study of the user requirements, with emphasis on scoping the project and problem definition.
3 Design, which incorporates logical design, program structure design, user/operator procedure, and physical design. In logical design, the data flow diagram and E-R diagram are important tools.
4 Implementation, which involves testing the hardware, program coding and testing, data conversion, user training, and parallel run.
5 Post implementation review, which assesses how well the system meets the user's requirements.

Transforming logical design into a data model begins with transforming the E-R diagram into relations, followed by normalizing the relations and developing the schema. Physical design includes ordering records; loading the full-scale database; satisfying security, integrity, and access control requirements; and testing the performance requirements.

The product of this process is a highly maintainable, effective database environment that best meets the user's requirements.

By the end of this chapter, you should be able to

- determine the makeup of a database environment,
- identify the components and procedures of the database development life cycle,
- understand the makeup of logical design, and
- realize the importance of logical design tools.

INTRODUCTION

In Chapter 1, we established that a database contains the information required for conducting the business of an organization. The data is stored in a logical format and is available for retrieval as needed. Ideally, the database should provide only the information the user needs to conduct day-to-day business, in addition to planning long- and short-range objectives. But the true performance of a database depends mainly on the quality of the design.

Understanding the database development life cycle, from scoping the project to post-implementation review, helps us gain a perspective on important database concepts. This chapter is an overview of how a database system originates, how it is designed, and the steps taken in coding, testing, and converting the files to meet user requirements. Not every step and every component will be immediately clear; later chapters build on the fundamental concepts introduced here.

In this chapter, we concentrate on database applications: what they are and how they are developed. The many components of an application work together to produce the kind of information that users require for decision making. There is also a procedure for developing an application. The major steps of one that is commonly used in business are as follows:

1 database planning
2 study of user requirements
3 database design
4 database implementation
5 post-implementation review

The first three steps are covered in detail in this chapter. The remaining steps are described briefly, since the major part of this text focuses on design and implementation of database systems.

Case Scenario 2-1:

Florida Commercial Bank Safe Deposit Department

A medium-sized, Florida-based commercial bank operates a safe deposit department which has 4000 boxes of various sizes and rates. Bank customers, local jewelers, and retailers rent them on an annual basis. A recent increase in demand has prompted the bank to install 4000 additional boxes, doubling the capacity to 8000. The increase required hiring two additional staff members, bringing the total staff to five employees.

The rental procedure is simple. A customer applies for a box and pays the year's rent in cash or through a debit to his or her checking account. Once a box is rented, the clerk generates a transaction for billing purposes. Bills are mailed to over 5500 customers, some of whom have two or more boxes. Bills are also processed manually on a billing cycle of six days, beginning with the first of each month. Customers also receive renewal notices one month prior to the expiration date of the box.

To access the box, a customer signs an activity sheet. The safe deposit attendant verifies the customer's signature by comparing it against the signature on the master card, which is the original application. The attendant also checks to make sure the customer is requesting access to an authorized box. The customer is escorted to the box by another attendant whose key must be used simultaneously with the customer's key to open the box.

Despite full-time security, several months ago a safe deposit box was accessed by an unauthorized person, and more than $50,000 worth of jewelry was stolen. The customer in whose name the box was rented sued the bank for the missing jewelry and won.

Because of the lawsuit, manual bookkeeping problems, and information access defects, Dave Tremaine, the chief operations officer of the bank, decided something must be done. He asked Professor Smith, a database instructor at a local university, to look into the situation and provide a solution.

Smith has been a MIS consultant for over ten years, with expertise in database applications and user training. Her investigation went beyond the security problem of the safe deposit department. It actually brought up two information systems requirements for the safe deposit department:

1 Keeping track of the number of boxes rented and the number vacant by size and location.

2 Determining how frequently certain boxes are accessed and by whom. The present procedure is lax and informal. The clerk often recognizes a customer and lets the customer into the safe deposit area without verifying the signature.

In discussing these problems with Smith, Tremaine realized that a database system must also produce certain reports. This could be the solution to the whole problem.

In the safe deposit department, Smith foresaw four practical applications for a database management system:

1 BOX_OCCUPANCY application

2 CUSTOMER_TRACKING application

3 USAGE application

4 BILLING application

The BOX_OCCUPANCY application would keep track of safe deposit boxes. This includes storing data and providing status information on each box number, size, expiration date, and so forth. It would also report the number of boxes rented as a percentage of the total boxes available. Table 2-1 shows the box occupancy report, produced monthly for the board of directors of the bank.

The CUSTOMER_TRACKING application would control customer access to safe deposit boxes. After a customer signed an activity sheet, the signature would be verified against a signature on the master card to make sure he or she was an authorized customer to the designated box. Figure 2-1 is a data flow diagram, showing the decision flow for this application.

FLORIDA COMMERCIAL BANK
Safe Deposit Department
BOX-OCCUPANCY Report

Box Number	Box Size	Annual Rent($)	Customer Name	Expiration Date
1213	3 × 5	10	Arnold	8/12
1614	5 × 7	15	Gotterer	9/14
3001	8 × 6	20	Stark	6/10
4614	8 × 6	20	Bush	5/04
*	×	*	*	*
*	×	*	*	*
*	×	*	*	*
7894	3 × 5	10	Kling	7/30

SUMMARY

Number of boxes rented

Box size	Number	Percent of total
3 × 5	2114	85
5 × 7	810	70
8 × 6	1812	62
*	*	*
*	*	*
*	*	*
12 × 12	413	72
	5149	64%

Table 2-1 BOX_OCCUPANCY partial report

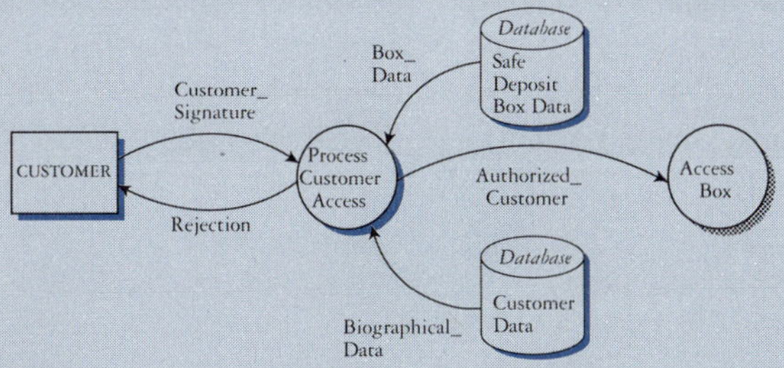

Figure 2-1 Process in CUSTOMER_TRACKING application

The USAGE application would produce two reports: box use by customer name and by box number. Table 2-2a illustrates a partial report of usage by customer name. Table 2-2b shows a partial report of usage by box number. These reports would be generated daily as a security check.

The BILLING application would be used to bill customers when the box rental contract expired. The database would store box rates and customer payments, and would prepare box renewal notices based on a billing cycle. For example, all customers whose box rental contracts expired during the first billing cycle (first five days of the month) would be sent renewal notices one month prior to the expiration date.

All four applications share common data. For example, box number, box size, and customer name are common data items (fields) in each report. Considering the overlap in data and the waste of memory storage if data is stored in separate databases, it would be most efficient to build a single database capable of handling these applications, which will be generated at different times and for different purposes. The database could be installed on a microcomputer system, using a DBMS such as dBASE IV or Oracle, as we discuss in Chapter 3.

FLORIDA COMMERCIAL BANK
Safe Deposit Department
CUSTOMER_USAGE Report

Customer Name	Safe Deposit Area	Box Number	Attendant Name	Date Accessed
Bundy	A	5141	Mattes	8/02, 6/01
Hutchison	A	6214	Weber	9/04
Jones	C	1236	Mattes	11/10
MacArthur	B	5123	Weber	5/01
Keen	A	7400	Weber	6/04

a. CUSTOMER_USAGE report by name

FLORIDA COMMERCIAL BANK
Safe Deposit Department
CUSTOMER_USAGE Report

Safe Deposit Box Number	Box Area	Customer Name	Attendant Name	Date Accessed
1236	C	Jones	Mattes	11/10
5123	B	MacArthur	Weber	5/01
5141	A	Bundy	Mattes	8/02,6/01
6214	A	Hutchison	Weber	9/04
7400	A	Keen	Weber	6/04

b. CUSTOMER_USAGE report by box number

Table 2-2 USAGE application examples

A DATABASE ENVIRONMENT generally includes the database software, the computer that operates the database, and the staff in charge of maintaining the database on a regular basis. Considering the scope and feasibility of the bank application, the database environment will consist of the end-user, the hardware, the software, the data, and bank personnel.

The END-USER is the person (in this case the bank attendant) who enters and accesses data (such as customer ID, name, and box number). Additional users in our scenario are Tremaine (the supervisor) and the board of directors. Each is a user in a different capacity. The attendant is the most frequent user of the system, while the supervisor and the board of directors are casual users with an interest in summarized information via reports.

Computer HARDWARE consists of the devices and equipment that drive the DBMS. Part of the hard disk of a computer system is reserved for storing the DBMS on a permanent basis. A microcomputer-based DBMS has its own particular memory requirements, which range from 512 kilobytes (KB) of main memory storage to over 3 megabytes (MB) of hard disk storage and at least one floppy disk drive. More hardware might be required in a multiuser networked system, in which communication lines link each user's workstation to the main server. Networking within a company or building is commonly carried out via a Local Area Network (LAN), which is a software package that allows users to link workstations to the main server. Figure 2-2 shows two popular alternative database hardware environments.

Database SOFTWARE includes the DBMS, an operating system, and one or more application programs. If the database is shared by multiple users, then a networking configuration is required, including a communication control program (CCP) or a multiuser package. In a mainframe environment, the CCP is a separate software program. With a microcomputer, it is part of the operating system.

Except for the application programs, all other software is provided by the vendor. In our safe deposit application, the software includes a dBASE IV package and an application program written in Structured English—a language that conforms to the dBASE IV syntax.

The physical database is a repository of the safe deposit data: customer names, box types, number of boxes not rented, and so forth. In addition, a data dictionary that defines the structure of the database is also stored on hard disk. Data dictionaries are discussed in Chapter 7.

Our safe deposit database system involves a single user accessing multiple applications through a stand-alone microcomputer system. This configuration would involve minimal security problems, as compared to a multiuser, multi-application database. In either case, the potential

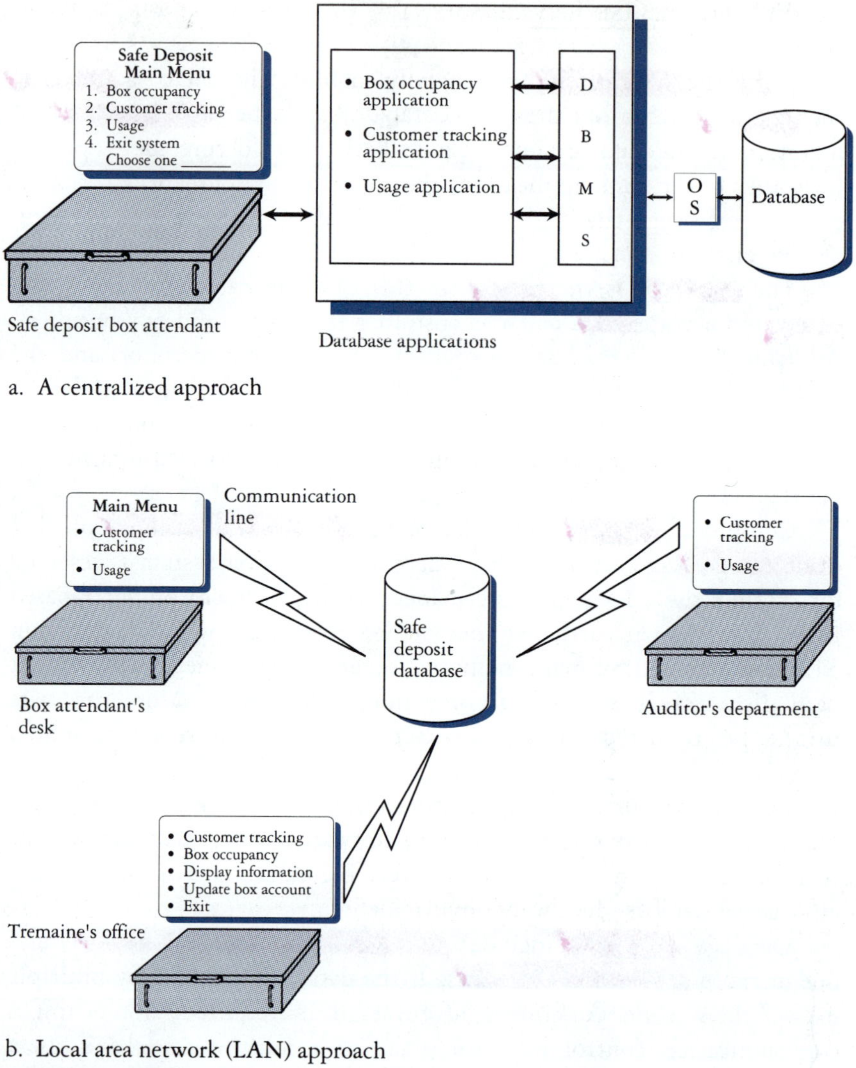

Figure 2–2 Alternative database designs

conflict across application views—different perspectives or samplings of the database—must be assessed against potential threats to data security and integrity. This can be addressed when the application program is written. For example, we can design a program to prevent certain changes. In our safe deposit database, the attendant may display any information available in the database, but cannot delete box numbers, box availability, or customer names whose rent has not expired. Even if he or she did delete data, there are backup files that the auditor examines for discrepancies.

Database design involves the joint efforts of the database designer, the operations staff, and the database administrator (DBA). (These jobs are explained in detail in Chapter 15.) In our safe deposit database, Smith is the database designer and also assumes the role of DBA. In designing the system, she would spend much of her time scoping the problem and evaluating the user's requirements for data. All conflicts or complaints would go to her for resolution.

The Functional Components

In addition to the database system environment, user-oriented applications include functional components such as menus, reports, updates, and programs. In fact, these components are the end products of the database development life cycle.

Menu

A MENU is a list of options from which a user may select a function. For example, after verifying a customer's signature, the safe deposit attendant may choose option 2 of the menu shown in Figure 2-3a. The response is a customer tracking submenu, shown in Figure 2-3b.

The customer tracking menu offers four choices: set up new box account, process customer access, print special reports, or exit back to the main menu. The attendant selects option 2 to process customer access. The system displays information on the screen about the customer and the safe deposit box(es) held in the customer's name. In addition, the attendant enters the date and the time of entry to the safe deposit box

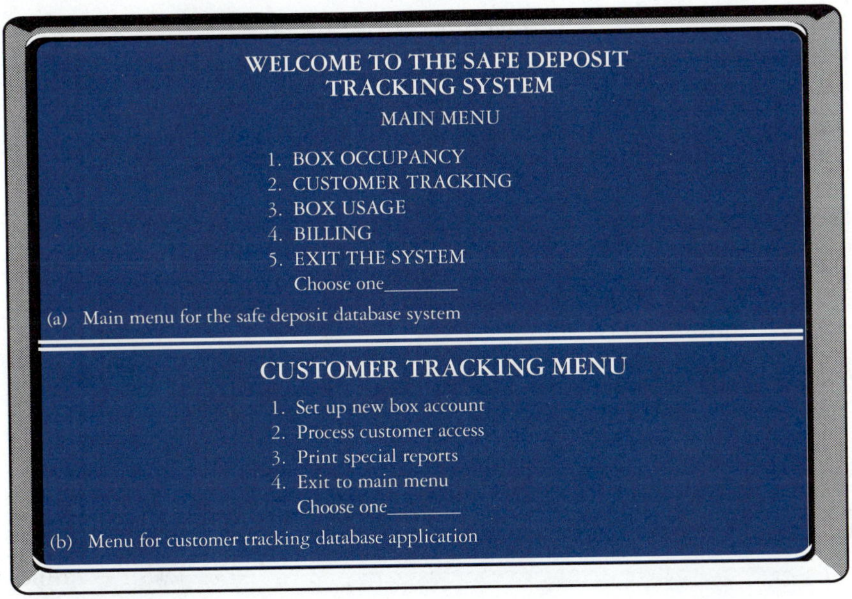

WELCOME TO THE SAFE DEPOSIT
TRACKING SYSTEM
MAIN MENU
1. BOX OCCUPANCY
2. CUSTOMER TRACKING
3. BOX USAGE
4. BILLING
5. EXIT THE SYSTEM
Choose one________
(a) Main menu for the safe deposit database system
CUSTOMER TRACKING MENU
1. Set up new box account
2. Process customer access
3. Print special reports
4. Exit to main menu
Choose one________
(b) Menu for customer tracking database application

Figure 2-3 Menu-submenu format for the safe deposit database system

and, later, the time the customer departed. As the attendant enters the data, the application program asks the DBMS to match customer name and box number in the database, look for other box numbers that the customer rents, display previous entry dates, or update a rental contract.

Report

Processing customer access involves two functions: displaying and updating data. There are two ways to display data: as hard copy or on a screen. Both are reports.

A REPORT is a formal function that is useful for documentation purposes. Reports on paper can be generated on a daily basis, on an ad hoc (when requested) basis, or when exceptions to a routine occur (for example, a customer accessing a box six times in one morning). Figure 2-4 shows a report giving a partial list of safe deposit customer tracking activities.

Currently, most reports are generated using a DBMS report generator, which lays out the column headings, format, and content. The summary section at the bottom of the report is generated through simple, easy-to-learn programming instructions. More sophisticated reports may be generated by an application program, which require professional programming skills to build and take much longer to prepare than a report generator report.

SAFE DEPOSIT DATABASE SYSTEM
Customer Report
September 9, 19XX

Date	Time	Customer ID	Box number accessed	Attendant ID
9/4	8:05 AM	461A	6140	7
9/4	8:05 AM	4674	1256	3
9/4	8:26 AM	1600	7241	3
•	•	•	•	•
•	•	•	•	•
•	•	•	•	•
9/4/XX	4:31 PM	3489	6128	3

Summary of Access Activities

Number of customers	Number of boxes accessed
64	72

Figure 2-4 A partial report produced by a DBMS report generator

Another way to display data, or generate a report, is via a database query language. A popular query language, which became a national standard late in 1986, is Structured Query Language (SQL). We discuss SQL in depth in Chapters 9 and 10.

To illustrate SQL's straightforward nature and simplicity, let us suppose that Mr. Tremaine wants a report listing all box numbers greater than 4000 that have been accessed in a given time period. In SQL, he enters the following commands:

```
SELECT *
FROM   CUSTOMER_TRACKING
WHERE  BOX_NUMBER GT 4000
```

In response he gets a screen display of all the fields in the CUSTOMER_TRACKING file for boxes with numbers higher than 4000. Unlike general reports of daily access, this query requests specific information on only a portion of the daily customer access activities, by box numbers, beginning with number 4001.

Update

Unlike reports or data displays, which are relatively passive, data updates are interactive. The term UPDATE refers to any changes made in existing files. This includes adding data to, deleting data from, or changing existing data in the database. For example, a safe deposit box customer might announce a change of address, telephone number, or the name of the person to contact in an emergency. This requires editing the existing record, which is easily done via the computer screen.

Updating data is carried out in three ways: by form, by columnar format, or by a query/update command language.

The *form* method is probably the most popular. A DBMS-generated form is displayed on the screen with all data items properly laid out in an easy-to-follow sequence. Following each data item is a reserved area indicating the maximum length, or number of characters which may be entered. The user simply enters the change in the space provided. The cursor moves from one space to another either automatically or on user command. (See Figure 2-5.) When the update is completed, the user enters a command or presses a special key (such as F10 = Save a file) to write in the change, which becomes a permanent part of the record.

The *columnar format* method for entering data is also simple. The end-user calls for a listing of customer records, scrolls up and down the screen to the designated record, and adds, deletes, or makes changes. The DBMS incorporates all updates into the record(s) as part of a SAVE procedure, which is activated by depressing the ENTER key or a special key used for this purpose. (See Figure 2-6.)

In the *query/update command language* method, the user issues a query (command) to make a specific change in an existing record. For example,

SAFE DEPOSIT DATABASE SYSTEM
Process Customer Access

DATE ______________ TIME OF ACCESS ____________
CUSTOMER NAME ______________________ PHONE ____________
ADDRESS ____
BOX NUMBER ______________
SIGNATURE VERIFIED (Y,N) _____
ATTENDANT CODE ____________
DO YOU WANT HARD COPY (Y,N) ? _______

PRESS F10 WHEN FINISHED

Figure 2-5 A form approach to entering data

in dBASE IV, a LIST command could be: LIST ALL FOR BOX > 3000 AND AREA = C. An example such of an update is

```
MOVE "SECOND" TO NOTICE_3
SAVE
```

This method is faster and more direct than other access methods.

Application Program

The third key functional component is the APPLICATION PROGRAM. There are a variety of application programs, any one of which may be appropriate depending on whether the database environment is stand-alone or networked. Application programs are invariably written by a programmer, hardware vendor, or a software house.

SAFE DEPOSIT DATABASE SYSTEM
Process Customer Access

Date	Time	Customer Name	Box #	Attendant Code
8/19	10:04 A	Arnold	4213	7
8/19	10:15 A	Weinstein	7201	7
8/19	12:16 P	Sibley	6900	3
8/19	1:31 P	Harold	7010	3
•	•	•	•	•
•	•	•	•	•
•	•	•	•	•
8/19	4:17 P	Jones	1216	3

Figure 2-6 The columnar format method for entering data

The menu, the screen forms, the application program, and the DBMS represent the customer tracking application. Together they make the user-machine interface quite simple. All the attendant needs to do is follow easy instructions, from the main menu to the exit option in the submenu.

A summary of the functional components and their key characteristics follows.

1 Menus
- easy to use, easy to learn, user-friendly
- database capability limited by menu options

2 Reports
- on-screen for ad hoc queries and decision making
- hard copy for documentation

3 Updates
- allow data to be added to an existing record or file
- allow data in an existing record to be changed
- allow data to be deleted from a record

4 Programs
- vital to the full operation of DBMS
- written by in-house programmers, hardware vendors, or software houses

The Application Development Life Cycle

So far, we have discussed the environmental and functional components of a database application. Now we need to explore how a database application is developed. This is an involved process, normally covered in a systems analysis and design course. The steps in both areas are essentially the same, although database application development can be complex in situations involving multiple applications and multiple users.

Although there are several approaches to database design, we propose a life cycle based on five major steps:

1 database planning
2 a study of user requirements
3 database design
4 database implementation
5 post-implementation review (see Figure 2-7)

Database Planning

In database design, planning focuses on defining the user requirements and scoping (determining the boundary of) the database or

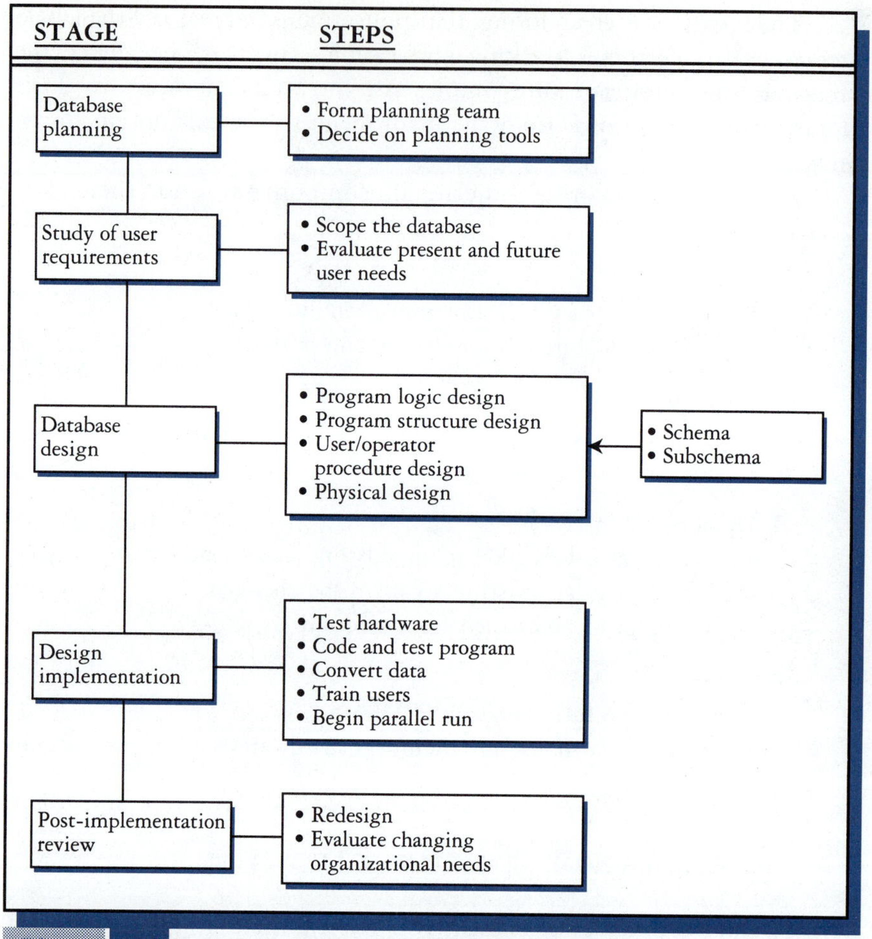

Figure 2–7 Stages of the application development life cycle

levels of involvement in the project. Unless this critical step is successful, projects could fall by the wayside, with serious consequences for the client or users.

Before the planning process begins, two important steps must be taken:

1 *Form a planning team.* For most large database projects, a team consisting of a user representative, a database designer, and an information systems specialist should be agreed on in advance with full top-management support. Some of the best-mapped-out projects phase out midway into the life cycle when top management withdraws or wavers in its support.

2 *Decide on planning tools.* Once a team is selected, its members must decide which planning tools to use, in line with the corporate MIS environment and preferably supported by computer-aided software engineering (CASE) tools. The use of one important CASE tool, Excelerator, is covered in Appendix A.

CASE tools are time-saving, efficiency-intensive programs that are tremendously helpful in database planning. Among the benefits of CASE tools are the following:

- They simplify the database plan updating over time as conditions require.
- They assist in answering "what if" queries in an interactive mode.
- They allow different users to work on different phases of the project, and provide the necessary integration.
- They provide a standard user interface and a standard vocabulary using a common database.

Study of User Requirements

The next critical phase is determining what the user wants the system to do. The key questions are "What is the problem or opportunity?" and "What is the scope of the project?" The designers and users must agree on what must be done as a basis for database design.

An important step in determining user requirements is scoping (determining the level of involvement of) the project. Scoping a project involves determining the level of complexity of the problem and the various constraints that will affect the final design. There are limits, of course, to what can be done. It is impractical to incorporate every single feature a user wants, and constraints can be prohibitive. Trying to solve everything at the outset can be self-defeating, involving too many people, difficulty in controlling costs, design and test problems, and the like. But scoping the proposed database carefully should mean fewer surprises for the users when the system is finally delivered.

In our safe deposit database project, Smith defined the scope of the project to include box occupancy, customer tracking, usage, and billing applications. If you recall, the initial user requirement stipulated by Tremaine, the chief operations officer, was customer tracking, as a reaction to the lawsuit. Smith expanded the scope of the project to include the other three applications, which eventually would be integrated under a master menu.

User requirements often are not so easy to finalize, for the following reasons:

- System requirements change. Applications must be modified to account for these changes.
- Users often have difficulty articulating their problems or system requirements. Functions and processes are not easy to describe. For example, when a first-time user is asked "What information do you want to get from your database?" the user often draws a blank. The user needs to be coached and coaxed into a new way of thinking.
- The system developer must educate the user. A user may have no concept of what a database is or does, what a file is, or how the new technology may affect the way the user does business.

• The developer often does not understand the user's work environment. As a result, he or she may have difficulty identifying the user's requirements. The database developer must establish rapport and try to understand the business of the user early in the application development process.

Related to a study of user requirements is evaluating, justifying, and selecting the areas that will be served by the proposed database. Evaluation involves learning whether there is a new and better way to do the job that the user requires, and deciding whether such an improvement is technologically feasible. Justification means asking what the costs and benefits of the alternative are, and whether the database project can be cost-justified. Finally, the selection phase covers reviewing the recommendations and choosing the one that will bring the database project in on schedule.

Database Design Team With large, complex database projects, it is common to form a project team to assume ongoing responsibilities for the development of the database design. Organizing a project team involves

1 picking users to participate in the early phase of the design,
2 selecting a database administrator to resolve user problems and coordinate database activities, and
3 establishing regular meetings and periodic management reporting during the design phase.

The senior designer is generally appointed as project leader. This role lasts through implementation.

Following these activities, the project team develops an implementation plan which

1 identifies the files that will be converted,
2 specifies the program(s) to do the physical design,
3 estimates various costs and expenditures, and
4 develops a preliminary implementation schedule.

These steps can be extremely important for database design. They are part of the overall planning that guides the life cycle of a database project.

Data Flow Diagram (DFD) Learning about user requirements entails careful review of the user's present system through interviews, observations, and review of the documentation available. A database designer often clarifies the system requirements by using graphic tools such as data flow diagrams to describe the system for user acceptance. A DATA FLOW DIAGRAM (DFD) is a picture of how data moves through a system, usually a series of "bubbles" joined by lines. The bubbles represent data transformations, such as verifying a report or calculating net pay, and the lines represent data that flows from one process symbol to another.

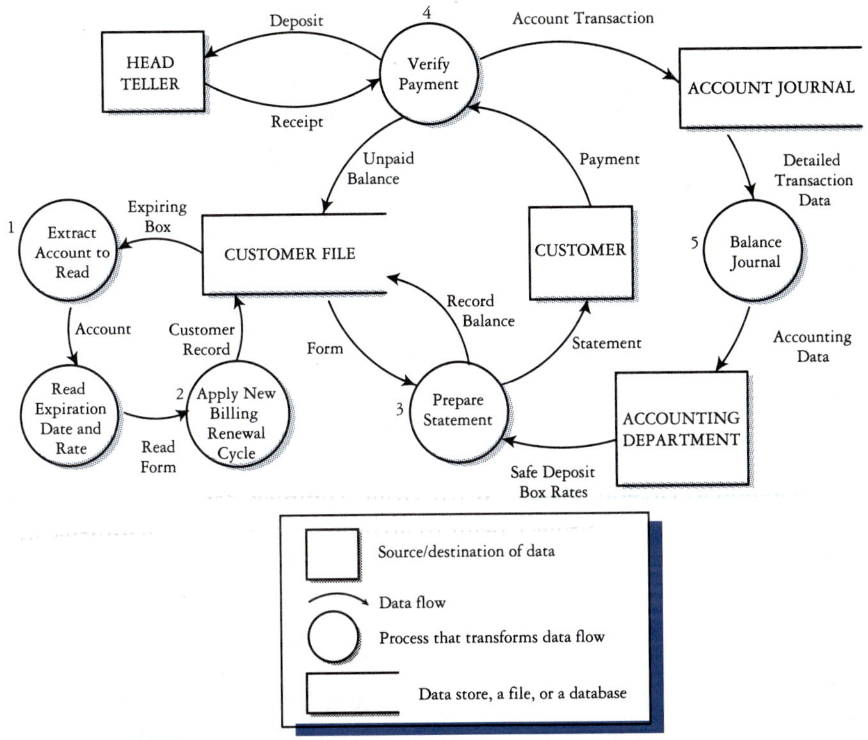

Figure 2-8 Data flow diagram for the safe deposit billing application

Figure 2-8 is a simplified DFD of the existing safe deposit billing system. The processes include extracting the customer's account, applying the renewal cycle, preparing the bill, verifying and processing the payment, and accounting for cash receipts.

As the DFD for our case scenario was developed, several drawbacks to the existing system were identified:

- The manual record-keeping procedure was labor-intensive.
- Manual filing and record retrieval often caused delinquent accounts to go unbilled.
- One out of every 15 bills had errors.
- Documentation was incomplete and inaccurate. Some boxes could not be matched with a contract, and some contracts were missing altogether.
- Similar documents were not filed together, and standard forms were not prenumbered for easy access.
- No documentation existed to describe which file was being updated.
- Records of the number of boxes rented were inaccurate.

Smith then documented the problems and began to identify where this system worked well and where it didn't. She concluded that a database system must satisfy the following user requirements:

- *Improved collection schedule.* The database system must improve collection by billing 30 days in advance of the expiration date, and by automatically generating a second notice two weeks later for mailing.

• *Cost reduction*. The new system must reduce labor by at least one employee. Under the current system, an employee spends six hours each day on billing.

• *Physical space reduction requirements*. The proposed system must occupy no more than a standard desktop. The existing file cabinet containing the data cards would be removed, allowing more space for customer use.

• *Improved customer service*. Master cards and box rental information must be placed in a database, and data entry time reduced from 2 minutes to under 30 seconds.

With these requirements in mind, Smith then listed several specific objectives for the candidate system:

• Mail customers a reminder no later than 25 days prior to the box renewal date and again two weeks after the initial statement.

• Speed rental collections by 40 percent.

• Examine box availability by size, rental charges, and location.

• Evaluate the ratio of rented to available boxes on a daily basis so that management can decide on promotional campaigns to improve box rentals.

• Produce periodic reports to management on the performance of the safe deposit department.

Data Dictionary In the DFDs, data flows (arrows), processes, and data stores (files) are given names which are descriptive of the data, but offer no details. To give the DFD meaning, these items must be defined in a data dictionary. The DATA DICTIONARY (DD) is basically a set of definitions of all DFD data elements and data structures (represented by arrows). It lists all the fields in the database. For each field, it lists the data types, their meanings, and the files. Sample data dictionary entries for the data flow diagram in Figure 2-8 are shown in Table 2-3.

A data dictionary provides documentation and improves designer/user communication by establishing consistent definitions of various elements, terms, and procedures. In constructing a data dictionary, we should consider several points:

• Each data flow in the DFD must have only one entry in the data dictionary.

• Definitions must be easy to access by name.

• The procedure for writing definitions should be uniform and precise.

In addition, the logic of each process (bubble) in the DFD must be delineated by methods such as pseudocode or Structured English. For example, the processing of box renewals would appear in Structured English as follows.

For each expired box, do the following:

1 Get expired box number from customer file
2 Read expired customer account
3 Do new billing renewal procedure
4 Process payment

Data Item	*Data Dictionary Entry*
Receipt	IS Customer name + customer number + REPETITIONS OF Box number + Box location + Box expiration date
Deposit	IS Customer name + Customer number + Box dues
Expiring Box	IS Customer name + customer number + REPETITIONS OF Box number + Expiration date + Amount due
Customer Form	IS Customer name + Box number + Expiration date + Rate due

Table 2–3 Sample data dictionary entries

5 If payment is good
   5.1 Mark renewal "OK"
         Return renewal notice to customer file
6 Send renewal notice to accounting file

Evaluation

Evaluating the proposed database means identifying alternative systems, selecting the best alternative, and producing a feasibility plan. Identifying alternative systems requires technical familiarity with hardware and software—that is, knowing what each candidate system can and cannot do. Selecting the best alternative involves evaluating each system's performance against predefined criteria and the relative cost of each system.

In our safe deposit project, Smith found that, for the volume and scope of the application, virtually any microcomputer with more than 256KB of memory and a dual disk drive would do the job. She also learned that a microcomputer could be installed to interface with the bank's mainframe for billing purposes. The question remaining was which microcomputer to select. Since the system requirements were met by a large selection of microcomputers, she made her decision on the basis of cost.

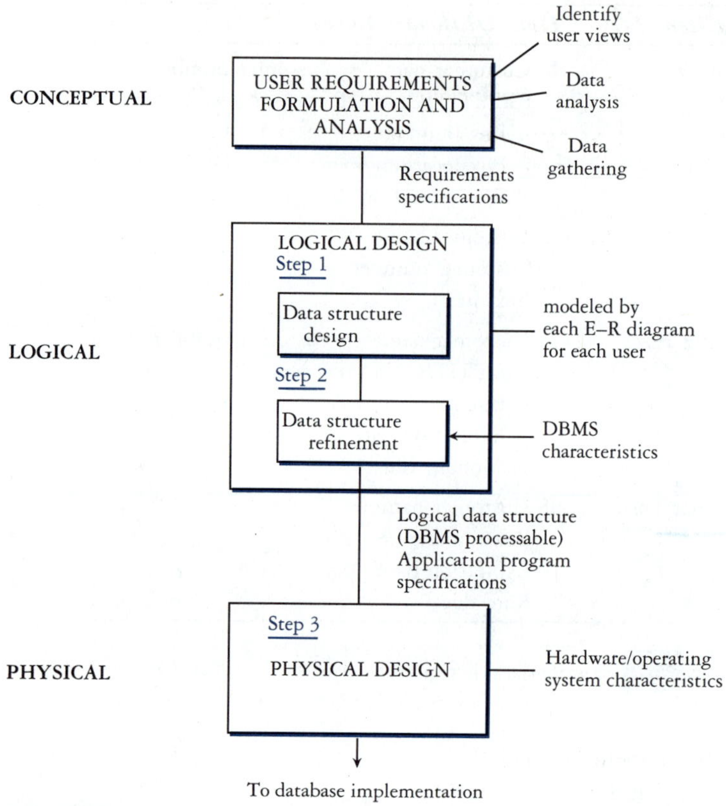

Figure 2-9 Major steps in database design

Database Design

DATABASE DESIGN involves identifying user data requirements and determining how the data should be structured from the requirements. It entails transforming unstructured information and the processing requirements of an application into representations that define the functional specifications. One objective of database design is ensuring that the database elements represent the user's data requirements. Another objective is to improve system performance and produce a flexible database structure adaptive to a changing user environment.

The three major steps in database design appear in Figure 2-9.

Data analysis The database design starts with data analysis and collecting information about present and future user requirements for data in a technology-independent manner. DATA ANALYSIS involves two types of data:

1 data describing data structures such as entities, attributes, and relationships (discussed in Chapter 5), and

2 data depicting rules or constraints that ensure data integrity.

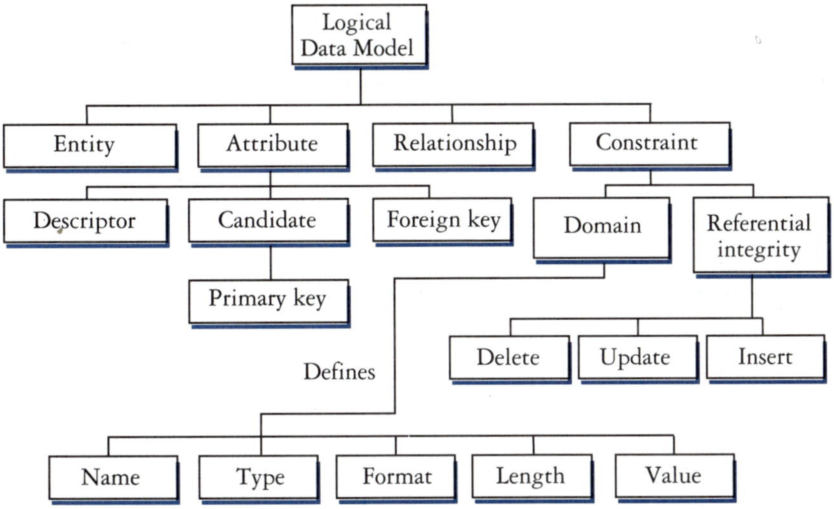

Figure 2–10 Components of the logical data model

These types of data are the basis for the logical design. The components of the logical data model are shown in Figure 2-10.

Entities, attributes, and relationships pretty much make up the data structure. The rules and constraints serve to protect data integrity. Two main types of constraints are used in formulating a database structure: domain and referential integrity. The DOMAIN constraint defines the name, type, format, length, and value(s) for each data item. REFERENTIAL INTEGRITY means accurate relationships or matches between the rows of one table and the rows of another. An example of referential integrity is a database system that will not allow a freshman student to enroll in a seniors-only course or in a course that does not exist. Constraints are designed to protect the database from errors in data entry. These concepts and constraints are covered in Chapter 15.

Logical design LOGICAL DESIGN, the first step in actually designing a database, is a way of identifying and quantifying the key features of a database processing system. Logical design simplifies the existing system to the point where it can be transformed into a database. The objectives of logical design are to make a graphic representation first of the organization's entities and then of the relationships among them, independent of both the DBMS and the hardware. This is the technology-independent approach mentioned at the outset of this section.

There are two fundamental phases in logical design: data structure design and data structure refinement.

Data structure design In DATA STRUCTURE DESIGN, we develop the conceptual schema of the database, a DBMS-independent structure derived from the user requirement specifications.

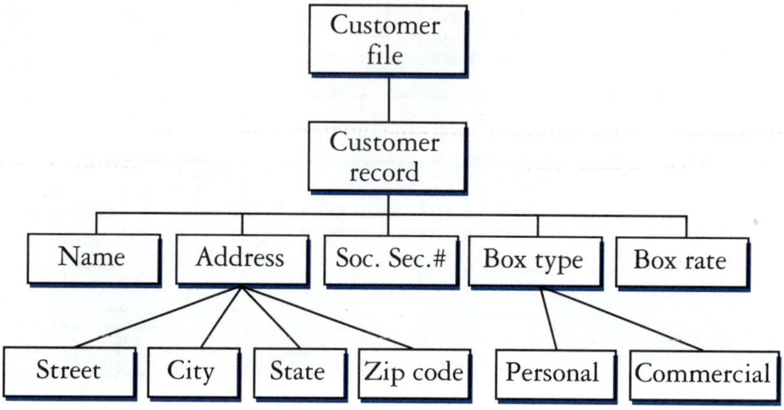

Figure 2–11 Data structure diagram for safe deposit system

One way of representing logical design is through the DATA STRUCTURE DIAGRAM. Figure 2-11 shows a partial data structure diagram for our safe deposit system. Note that it focuses more on relationships among records than on record content. The content of each record (field type, length, and so on), or the data description is documented in the data dictionary.

Data structure diagrams, being somewhat technical, are not the best choice for initial diagrams of the proposed database structure, especially if they are to be understood by the nontechnical members of the design team. An easier way to display the database structure is the ENTITY-RELATIONSHIP (E-R) DIAGRAM. The E-R diagram shown in Figure 2-12 uses a diamond to represent a relationship—in this case defined as "rents"—between two entities. The notation "1:M" indicates that the relationship

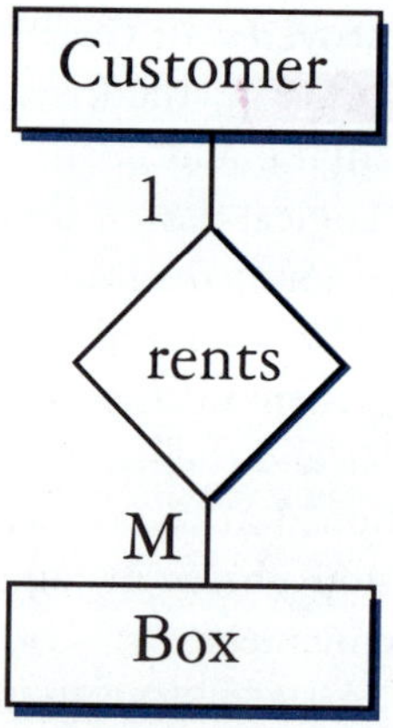

Figure 2–12 E-R Diagram

between "Customer" and "Box" is "one-to-many"—that is, each customer may rent more than one box.

The E-R diagram emphasizes two constructs—entities and relationships—that help the designer analyze the data and organize his or her ideas. Other key constructs are entity-types, attributes, and constraints. The following is a brief description of each construct.

- *Entity-type* A group of similar objects or events. In our safe deposit application, the CUSTOMER and BOX are entity-types.
- *Attribute* A particular quality associated with an entity-type. Customer's name, address, and amount owed are attributes of entity-type CUSTOMER.
- *Relationship* An association between entity-types, objects, or other data items. For example, the relationship between CUSTOMER and BOX is "rents."
- *Constraint* A limit placed on entities or their attributes. For example, a constraint might be placed on a range of values for a numerical attribute, when the BOX_NUMBER attribute is limited to the numbers 1 to 8000. A constraint may also be set to specific values. For example, a MONTH attribute in the safe deposit billing cycle is limited to the values January through December.

A complete logical design is the composite of entities, attributes, relationships among entities, and the constraints imposed on these relationships. The list of entities and their attributes is described in various formats. Relationships among the various entity-types are listed in table format or are shown in data structure diagrams.

Data structure refinement The second major phase of logical database design is transforming the DBMS-independent logical design into a data model compatible with the chosen DBMS. This procedure, called DATA STRUCTURE REFINEMENT, includes the following three steps:

1 *Transforming the E-R diagram to a DBMS-processable model.* The models available are hierarchical, network, or relational. (These models are discussed in Chapter 6.) The relational model is the most popular today. The transformation step is a prerequisite to normalization.

2 *Normalizing the relations.* The resulting relations are normalized, that is, grouped into logically simple data structures with the goal of minimum redundancy. Normalization was developed by E.F. Codd, the creator of the relational database model, and is covered in detail in Chapter 8.

3 *Developing the logical model.* This final step involves merging individual user views into an integrated data structure. Once we derive the logical model, called a schema, we use a data-oriented diagram to define the logical database operations that will implement and operationalize the database. The action diagram is a popular tool for such a representation.

Physical design In the PHYSICAL DESIGN, the logical model is mapped to physical storage, normally on hard disk. The physical allocation of records is also determined. This is all done through programming the database. Programs must be tested before the system can be released to the user. The key decisions of physical design include the following:

1 ordering records and access methods;
2 identifying the records to be placed in physical storage;
3 loading the full-scale database;
4 satisfying security, integrity, and access control requirements; and
5 testing the performance requirements.

While the database design is being developed, any final changes needed in the hardware, peripherals, or facility should be made. In a multiuser environment, where data security is crucial, security and control protocols are also designed at this time. Finally, the role, functions, and responsibilities of the database administrator (DBA) and the database personnel are documented.

Database Implementation

The next phase in the database application development life cycle is implementation. IMPLEMENTATION includes the actual testing and installation of the database, developing a conversion plan, converting the existing application, converting the existing data to the new database environment, writing documentation, and training users.

The main activity in testing and installing the database is coding the logical design, using a special language provided by the vendor. This also involves modifying representative programs for application program testing. A test database is constructed to check the accuracy of the data description and application programs. Testing is a rigorous procedure, especially when a large number of programs are involved. In such a case, programs are tested individually (unit tests), then together (integrated or system test). The program tests, and recovery procedures for bringing up the system after failure, become a part of the final documentation to be used later during database maintenance.

A conversion plan involves scheduling users to verify file contents and reserving computer time for final testing. This step is often overlooked when database applications are behind schedule or when the designer is anxious to get right into testing and conversion.

Converting the existing applications usually means bringing up the application, updating the database as required, and beginning to use the new database. A common approach to system testing is called a PARALLEL

RUN, which means running the old system concurrently with the new system and comparing the two. This ensures that the old system is available while changes are being made to the new system. The parallel-run procedure is costly, and it can be months before the old system can be abandoned. A new database application also produces new kinds of information, which cannot be compared to the old system. Consequently, the new application has to be evaluated on its own merit.

While the database application is being tested, writing documentation and training the user become prime activities. The key documentation is the user's manual, which describes how to operate the system. In most cases, such a manual is incorporated into training where questions regarding the manual can be answered.

Post-Implementation Review

Database applications are quickly taken for granted, but every application requires periodic evaluation after implementation. A post-implementation review is an evaluation of a system to decide how well it meets predefined requirements. It usually involves assessing major problems that surfaced during the implementation phase.

The types of changes facing the review team fall under two categories: maintenance and enhancement.

The MAINTENANCE function entails monitoring the database application and making the necessary modifications to ensure that the system meets the initial user requirements. Database ENHANCEMENT means incorporating changes into the database application to reflect new user requirements. It involves modifying the programs to respond to the user's additional or changing needs. Whether it involves enhancement or maintenance, post-implementation review usually requires a certain amount of fine-tuning the database.

These functions certainly are not for neophyte database programmers. Doing an effective job requires considerable skill and experience, plus an ability to identify user needs. Post-implementation review also demands familiarity with the operational environment and an understanding of what the user wishes to accomplish with the database application.

IMPLICATIONS FOR MANAGEMENT

Three behavioral issues are relevant to developing database applications:

1 *Narrowing user-developer differences.* Ignoring user suggestions and producing developer-oriented database applications has been a frequent

source of system failure. At the root of this problem are fundamental differences in the ways users and developers process information. Variations in the way each sees an application develop has a lot to do with how well it is received by the user. Many of these differences can be alleviated by having the user and the developer learn more about each other's business.

2 *Establishing user motivation*. How much the user values the new database applications determines the user's willingness to use the database when it is installed. A willing user is crucial to system acceptance and implementation.

3 *Neutralizing political factors*. Acquiring a database management system or developing a database application is often viewed as a way of acquiring power or improving leverage in the organization. To neutralize political implications, the database developer must understand the motives behind a new user request before initiating design.

The database developer's main function is designing database applications. This role carries considerable responsibility, high status, and attractive pay. It is important that management keep a close watch on and reward successful developers so as to promote stability in the work environment.

SUMMARY

1 The database environment consists of several components: the end-user, hardware, software, data, and personnel.

   a. The *end-user* is anyone who enters and accesses data from the database system, as well as managers or supervisors who receive reports and act on that information.
   b. The *hardware* is the equipment—the computer processor, monitor, modem, and so forth—that drives the database application.
   c. The *software* includes the DBMS, an operating system, and one or more application programs.
   d. The *data* component includes all the data in the database as well the data dictionary, which defines the structure of the database.
   e. The *personnel* include the database designer, the operations staff, and the database administrator (DBA) who supervises the database system.

2 The functional components of a database application, which make the user-machine interface quite simple, include the following:

   a. *Menu*: a list of options that simplifies database access and entry
   b. *Report*: the outcome of processed database information, which may be presented in the form of hard copy or on a screen. DBMS report generators or a database query language are used to create reports.

c. *Application program*: the software that supports a database application. It is usually written by the hardware vendor or a software house.
d. *Update*: the process of adding to, deleting, or changing data in records.

3 Database application development consists of five steps:
   a. *Database planning*, which involves formation of a planning team and deciding on the appropriate planning tools.
   b. *Study of user requirements*. Data flow diagrams can be helpful tools for showing how the data moves through a system. Data flows are defined in the data dictionary.
   c. *Database design*, which involves identifying data requirements, determining data structures, and completing design specifications.
   d. *Implementation*, which includes testing and installing the database system.
   e. *Post-implementation review*, which includes an assessment of any problems that surfaced during the implementation phase.

4 Logical design is the first step of database design. The two fundamental phases of logical design are data structure design and data structure refinement. In data structure design, we develop the logical model of the database. During data structure refinement, we transform the DBMS-independent logical design into a data model compatible with the chosen database management system.

5 The two key tools used in logical design are the data structure diagram and the E-R diagram. The data structure diagram focuses on the relationships among records, while the E-R diagram displays relationships among entities.

6 The major steps of physical design include
   a. ordering records and access methods;
   b. identifying the records to be placed in physical storage;
   c. loading the full-scale database;
   d. satisfying security, integrity, and access control requirements; and
   e. testing the performance requirements.

KEY WORDS

Application program
Data analysis
Database design
Database environment
Data dictionary
Data flow diagram
Data structure design
Data structure diagram
Data structure refinement
Domain
End-user
Enhancement

- Entity-relationship diagram
- Hardware
- Implementation
- Logical design
- Maintenance
- Menu
- Parallel run
- Physical design
- Referential integrity
- Report
- Software
- Update

REVIEW QUESTIONS

1 "The most important goal of designing a database is meeting user requirements." Do you agree? Discuss.

2 In the database application for the safe deposit department, two information systems problems were specified. What were they? Do you agree with them? Why?

3 What are the components of our safe deposit application database environment?

4 Distinguish between the centralized and networked alternatives to database design.

5 List and define three key database application design personnel.

6 Summarize the system components of a database application. How do they differ from the functional components?

7 Why are menus developed? Since most users are somewhat computer literate today, why are menus still preferred over using a query language?

8 What is normally included in a data update? How is a data update carried out?

9 What is the difference between the form and columnar format methods of updating data?

10 How would you define an application program? How involved is the vendor in writing such a program?

11 Why are user requirements hard to define?

12 Explain the difference between the following pairs of terms:
  a. data flow diagram and E-R diagram
  b. application program and database management system
  c. logical and physical database design

13 What is involved in computing the return on investment in database application development?

14 How does data structure design differ from data structure refinement?

15 "The main activity in testing and installing the database is coding the DBMS." Do you agree? Elaborate.

16 What is involved in the post-implementation phase of database application development? Where does enhancement fit in? Illustrate by giving an example.

APPLICATION PROBLEMS

1 The steering committee for the information system of a large savings and loan bank is evaluating a request from the mortgage loan department to build a database system for all branches. The bank's mainframe is operating at 55 percent of capacity, and has adequate memory to handle the new application. The only equipment needed are on-line terminals in each of the bank's 27 branches and a database package that can be installed in five weeks using the existing telecommunication network. The terminals are available through the vendor, within the week, at $1400 each. Branch tellers could be trained in less than four working days. The database package costs $18,000.

Currently, mortgage loan applications are handled in batch mode. At the end of the day, each branch sends the mortgage payments and documents to the computer center, located 18 miles away. Upon receipt of the documents, data entry operators enter each payment and account number on disk. When all transactions have been entered, they are processed. All accounts are updated, and the resulting report (1400 pages long) is sent to various branches for reference. In a batch environment, all information is based on the previous day's activities.

The bank is an industry leader in introducing new labor-saving and income-generating programs. In the past, when a new program was implemented, the bank set the standard for other banks. The database design group is highly motivated, well paid, and works closely with management on a regular basis.

In the proposal, the vice president of mortgage loans reasons that, by using a database mortgage system, tellers can answer customer mortgage inquiries in seconds. Within the year, she expects more and more customers to call the branch for all information regarding their respective loans. This means a savings in human resources and a more efficient use of branch facilities.

a. Based on the information provided, is this database proposal feasible? Should it be pursued? Why?
b. What other information does the steering committee need to do a thorough investigation? What sources would the information come from? Be specific.

2 The manager of a jewelry store in Coral Gables, Florida, is considering installing a database system to handle sales analysis and inventory control. The system would profile sales activities by sales item and salesperson, and analyze sales fluctuations. It would also provide an on-line update of the inventory. As items are sold, they would be deleted from the inventory file. At the same time, the system would generate orders to replenish stock items and show the dates of arrival. The jewelry store has a good reputation among tourists during the winter season (November 1 to February 1). Almost two-thirds of the business is done during that time. Obviously, if various items are not available, the store risks losing sales. To date, inventory and reordering have been done by two employees on a full-time basis, a job that is tedious and frustrating because errors are easy to make.

It is now June 1, well into the off-season for tourism. Assume that hardware and software are available within 60 days, and that it would take one week to test and install the system, and one week to train the stockroom clerks. Loading data on the entire inventory is estimated to take about seven working days.

Show the database application development life cycle for this project.

3 Consider the following two entity designs:

```
CUSTOMER(NAME, ADDRESS, PHONE)
ACCOUNTS_RECEIVABLE(CUSTOMER_NAME, AMOUNT_OWED)
```

a. What type of relationships exist between the entities?
b. How would you incorporate the two entities into a single entity?

4 List the entities in a typical pharmacy and draw a data structure diagram based on these entities.

5 Your family may be viewed as a small business organization. List the family entities and represent them in a E-R diagram.

6 Using the case of Island Jumpers, Inc. (IJI), presented at the end of Chapter 1, complete the following assignments.
   a. Write a report summarizing the development life cycle of a proposed reservation tracking system. Use this chapter's material to help you organize your report.
   b. What type of planning is involved in designing a database application for IJI?
   c. Should a design team be formed for a project this size? Discuss.
   d. We know it is too early to decide on hardware, but what type of computer do you feel would be ideal for this project? Justify your answer.

C H A P T

Database Management Systems

E R 3

The Age of Friendly DBMSs Draws Closer for Micro Users

AT A GLANCE

Introduction

The Database Management System as Middleman

The Evolution of Database Management Systems
- CODASYL
- Relational-Based Database Management Systems

The Database Management System Components
- Schemas and Subschemas
- Data Definition Language (DDL)
- Data Manipulation Language (DML)
- Host Language Interface
- Query Language
- Data Dictionary

How the Database Management System Works

The Primary Database Management System Functions
- Natural User Interface
- Support of Logical Transactions
- Data Integrity
- Concurrent Processing Controls
- Recovery from Failure
- Database Security

Database Management Systems for the Microcomputer
- R:BASE
- dBASE
- Oracle

Database Management Systems for the Macintosh
- dBASE MAC
- 4th Dimension

Implications for Management
- Size Considerations
- Security Considerations
- User Considerations

The Age of Friendly DBMSs Draws Closer for Micro Users

The PC revolution of the past few years has given database management software vendors a whole new territory to conquer. So far, the action seems to center on extending DBMS programs from the mainframe arena into the PC area without sacrificing substance for simplicity.

Traditional large system vendors such as Oracle Corp. (Belmont, Calif.) and Informix Corp. (Menlo Park, Calif.) have begun to establish base camps in micro territory, trying to stake their claim to the highly lucrative—if volatile—market.

Last year, Informix introduced the Datasheet Add-In, a relational database management system that merges with Lotus 1-2-3 and basically adds more functionality to the spreadsheet programs, making 1-2-3 more of a DBMS. At some point in the near future, Informix will begin to merge some of its largeframe, higher-language products with the product lines from Innovative, according to Susan Nurse, product manager for MS/DOS and OS/2 products at Informix. "One of the benefits of the merger is that . . . we'll get some very nice integration of office automation tools and database tools, as well as some strong user interfaces at the PC level," she says.

The Informix-Innovative merge is a typical example of what appears to be a growing trend in the industry, according to Jamie Reifsnyder, assistant editor for Faulkner Technical Report Inc.'s (Pennsauken, N.J.) *Microcomputers and Software* report. "They're moving toward each other. From the large-scale systems side, they're trying to make themselves more easy to use."

Computer Power to Managers

Giving DBMSs a menu-driven interface is one of the more popular solutions to spreading DBMSs down to the PC level. In September 1986, Alpha Software Corp., Burlington, Mass., introduced its menu-driven Alpha/Three program, which operates as a standalone database and is also compatible with Ashton-Tate's dBASE III.

Meanwhile, in the Apple world, no clear leader has emerged. Ashton-Tate, in fact, has developed a dBASE Mac, but it bears little resemblance to the IBM PC product and doesn't allow Apple-based database systems (Los Angeles based Nantucket Corp.'s McMax among them) to communicate with MS/DOS systems.

Ease of use has always been king in the Mac world, but, in some ways, it's only now that the many years of effort are paying off in the form of DBMS systems that are not needlessly complex for an average user, according to Dash Chang, president of Chang Laboratories, San Jose. Chang Laboratories has developed for the Macintosh a product called CAT (for Contractors, Activities, and Time), a relational database management system designed to aid executives in managing their time.

"Sometimes innovation is not a matter of looking over a fence, but often just looking right in front of us," Chang says. "CAT works the way people work, only it speeds the process along. The biggest challenge in the industry is to get software to be as close as possible to what people do anyway."

Memory Problems Addressed

As traditional mainframe vendors begin their initial push toward the PC market, there inevitably have been some less-than-auspicious debuts. According to Reifsnyder, the first PC version of a mainframe product traditionally is somewhat lacking, usually eating up too much memory and slow to hit its marks, "But the second version is usually greatly improved," she adds.

That was certainly the case when brewmeister Anheuser-Busch Inc., St. Louis, decided to move its Nomad-based mainframe database into the PC arena. It received one of the early issues of PC Nomad, introduced last spring. "The biggest problem we had was (with the) memory (which led to) system crashes," says Peggy Harter, information systems analyst at Anheuser. "We worked around it by suggesting our managers do one group of products at a time."

The food and brew conglomerate uses the system as a relational database to do its budget. In 1987, as a beta site for version 2.0 of PC Nomad, its budget process went considerably smoother because of product improvements, Harter says. "We saw significant improvements in the system with the new version, particularly in terms of memory," she says.

AT A GLANCE

A major component of the database environment is the database management system (DBMS). This powerful software is the middleman between the user and the physical database. It allows the user to store, access, and modify data on demand.

A DBMS is characterized by its data dictionary (DD), data definition language (DDL), data manipulation language (DML), host language interface, query language, and schema and subschema. These important components ensure proper functioning of the DBMS.

The primary functions of a DBMS include the natural user interface, support of logical transactions, data integrity, concurrent processing controls, recovery from failure, and database security.

Powerful DBMSs are readily available for all computers. Most of them are command-driven and menu-driven, easy to use and learn, and affordable for almost every type of application. Some of these DBMSs were once unique to minicomputers and mainframes, but they have been "ported down" to run on the microcomputer, providing similar power and sophistication.

By the end of this chapter, you should

- understand the nature of a DBMS;
- know the primary DBMS functions;
- be able to distinguish among integrity, security, and concurrent processing control; and
- appreciate the potential use of DBMS for microcomputer applications.

Introduction

The database management system (DBMS) is the most significant tool software engineering has yet developed to serve multiple users in a database environment. It improves productivity in terms of faster application development, increased control of the data resources, better information, and greater responsiveness to users. In many ways, the DBMS is a service that allows the user to store, access, and update data. In a multiuser environment, it provides unique user functions and interfaces.

To qualify as a DBMS, a database system must provide several capabilities:

- a natural interface of user data views, independent of the physical database structure
- a multiuser environment where each user can access the same database, using his or her own user view
- the ability to make changes in the physical database without affecting programs that make no use of the change
- control of multiuser access to the database to promote privacy and integrity of stored data
- recovery from failure to ensure no loss of stored files

In this chapter, we highlight the evolution of database management systems, the key activities and functions of a DBMS, and the database facilities needed to support a multiuser environment.

The Database Management System as Middleman

One way to understand the role of DBMS is to view it as a middleman. There are many examples of middlemen. Here are two:

1 A stockbroker facilitates the interests of potential buyers of stocks by bringing them together with potential sellers through the stock market. (See Figure 3-1.) The broker provides three interfaces: buyer-broker, seller-broker, and stock market-broker. These interfaces make for greater order, efficiency in handling transactions, and improved overall productivity.

2 A retailer provides goods to customers in a convenient location. The retail store acquires the merchandise from the wholesaler and makes it available (with a markup, of course) to the customer on a regular basis. (See

Figure 3–1 The stockbroker is a human database management system

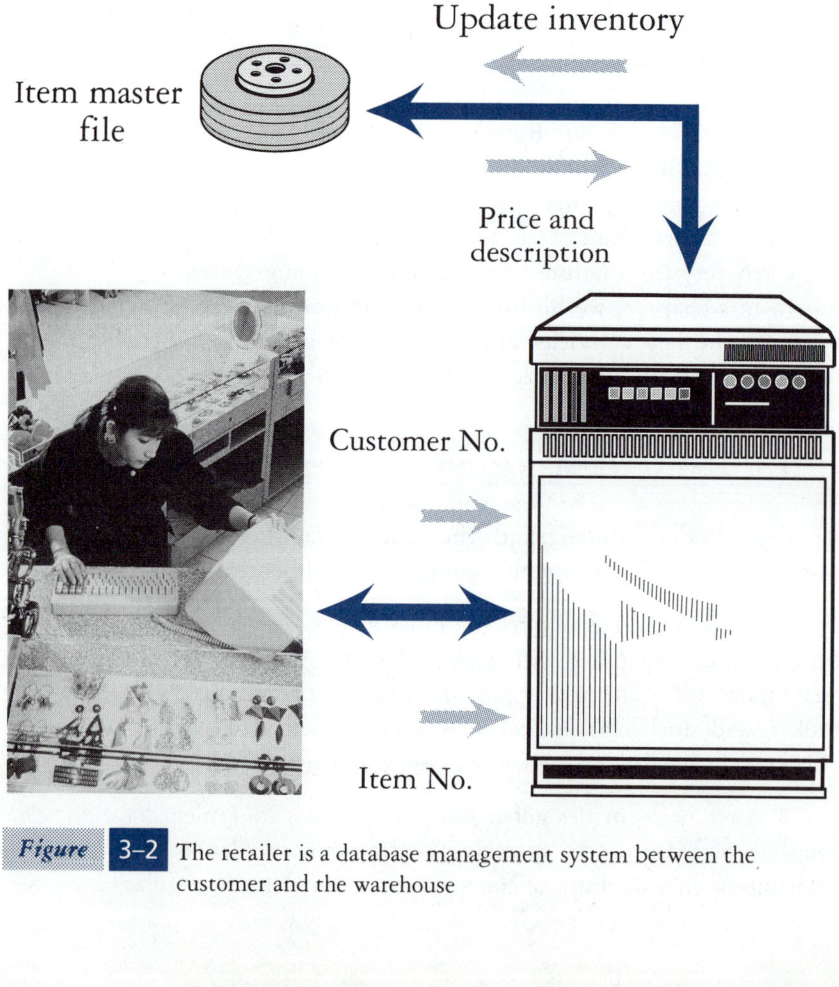

Figure 3–2 The retailer is a database management system between the customer and the warehouse

Figure 3-2.) The sales clerk deals with one customer at a time. The benefits of this arrangement include order in the way customers are accommodated and control over the warehouse inventory. Customers do not deal directly with the warehouse any more than potential stock buyers deal directly with the stock market. All inquiries and transactions are handled through the middleman.

A DBMS is also a "middleman" in that it serves as an interface between the users and the physical database. (See Figure 3-3.) Any ad hoc queries, reports, or updates must go through the DBMS. As a piece of software, the DBMS actually determines who should be served when and in what order, what data access is authorized, and the results to be released. The DBMS also provides security, backup, recovery, and concurrent control of operations.

The Evolution of Database Management Systems

The basic concept of a database management system began in the early days of programming, when file linkage routines were taken out of application programs and placed into common access libraries. An early

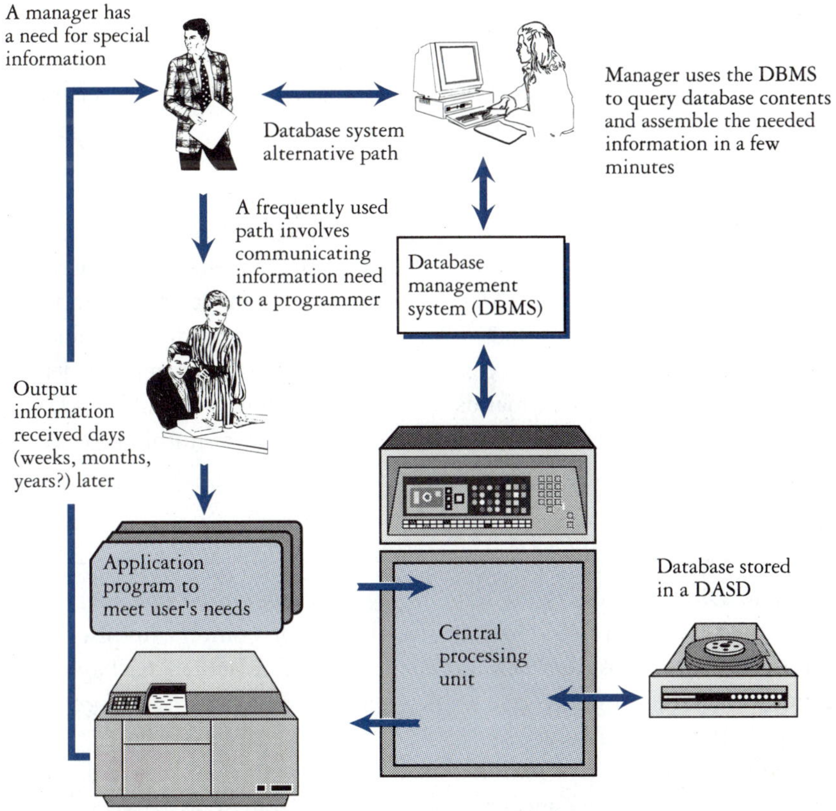
A manager has a need for special information
Database system alternative path
Manager uses the DBMS to query database contents and assemble the needed information in a few minutes
A frequently used path involves communicating information need to a programmer
Database management system (DBMS)
Output information received days (weeks, months, years?) later
Application program to meet user's needs
Central processing unit
Database stored in a DASD

Figure 3-3 The database management system as a middleman in a database processing system

attempt at a DBMS was IBM's Bill of Material Processor (BOMP). A user's call to BOMP caused the application to follow a predefined set of positions through designated data files. A major drawback to this system was that programmers had to know the structure of the data before they could navigate within the structure. Although the data structure at that time was independent of the data, it was still tied directly to the program. This meant the program had to change every time a change was made in the data structure.

In 1967 former IBM engineers created a DBMS called TOTAL. This database software required that the application program know the physical structure of the database. The programmer had to specify the file to be accessed and the appropriate linking paths to navigate around the database.

With these limitations, in the early 1970s IBM, together with Rockwell International Corporation, developed a project called the Information Management System (IMS). The IMS language, called Data Language One (DL/1), featured data independence, which had not previously been available to the programmer. With DL/1, if the physical database changed the program view remained the same.

CODASYL

In 1959, 40 concerned organizations representing government, industry, and computer manufacturers initiated the COnference on DAta SYstems Languages (CODASYL). The focus of the conference was to set specifications for COBOL. In the mid 1960s, a Data Base Task Group of CODASYL (DBTG) began developing specifications for a new database standard. The first report, which came out in 1969, presented the structure and syntax for a data description language (DDL) and data manipulation language (DML). The DDL defines the database and the DML is a host language that manages the data in the database as defined by the DDL. Typical commands in a DML are shown in Table 3-1. The CODASYL DBTG report has been the basis for a number of DBMS products in use today.

Relational-Based Database Management Systems

The DBMS products to date have been networks and hierarchies (explained in Chapter 6) that require the use of pointers (indicators) to set up relationships between data entities. Some DBMS packages still require that the program have knowledge of the physical structure of the database it is trying to access.

These DBMS limitations led to a proposal by E.F. Codd in 1970 which introduced the concept of a relational database as an approach to true data independence. A RELATION is a two-dimensional table in which all entries are single-valued. Codd's relational model is built around two

Command	Description
OPEN	Opens a file or a set of records for an application program
CLOSE	Closes a file or a set of records from an application program
MODIFY	Replaces data item values with values in the application program work area
INSERT	Inserts a record in the work area into one or more specific groups of records
STORE	Stores a new record in the physical database
FIND	Searches for and locates a designated record and makes it available to the application program
GET	Makes record contents available to the application program work area
DELETE	Deletes a record from the database

Table 3–1 Sample Data Manipulation Language commands

concepts: that the logical structure of all relations must be in what is called "third normal form" (the goal of part of the database design process, discussed in Chapter 8) and that the DML is designed to operate on these relationships.

With this model, the user can use the database without interacting directly with the physical database. In this case, all operations involve relations. Among the better-known relational-based DBMS packages in use today are Oracle, DB2, and SQL/DS. Several other relational packages that run on the microcomputer include dBASE IV and R:BASE 5000. These packages are described briefly at the end of this chapter.

The Database Management System Components

The following characteristics or components of a DBMS are important to our understanding of how a DBMS works.

Schemas and Subschemas

The SCHEMA is the overall logical structure of a database. It is the global plan that controls the organization and use of data. A schema can also be viewed as the logical representation of the physical database, or as complete description of all records, fields, and data relationships. The main job of a schema is to describe the structure of the database to the DBMS. From another perspective, it describes the application processing needs of a business.

The SUBSCHEMA is the functional database, or the user's view of the database, and is a subset of a schema. When a user requests a record, for example, the request is expressed in terms of the functional database. The data requested is translated from the declarations of the user (subschema) to that of the declarative structure of the schema. Schemas and subschemas are covered in greater depth in Chapter 5.

Data Definition Language (DDL)

The DATA DEFINITION LANGUAGE (DDL) describes the schema to the DBMS. It converts requests for data generated at terminals or by application programs from the LOGICAL VIEW, the view perceived by the programmer, into the PHYSICAL VIEW, the way data is actually stored on the disk. In other words, the DDL describes logical data structures within a logical framework, called a data model, in preparation for creation of a physical database. (See Figure 3-4.)

Data Manipulation Language (DML)

The DATA MANIPULATION LANGUAGE (DML) is the mechanism used for retrieving data stored on the disk. It contains statements that store, access, modify, update, or retrieve data. There are two ways of accessing data through the DBMS. One way is to sit at a display terminal and enter a command (called a query) to the DBMS to retrieve a record or a piece of information from the database. The other way is to have the application program issue an internal instruction (called an embedded statement) to the DBMS to retrieve certain data and return it to the program. (See Figure 3-4.)

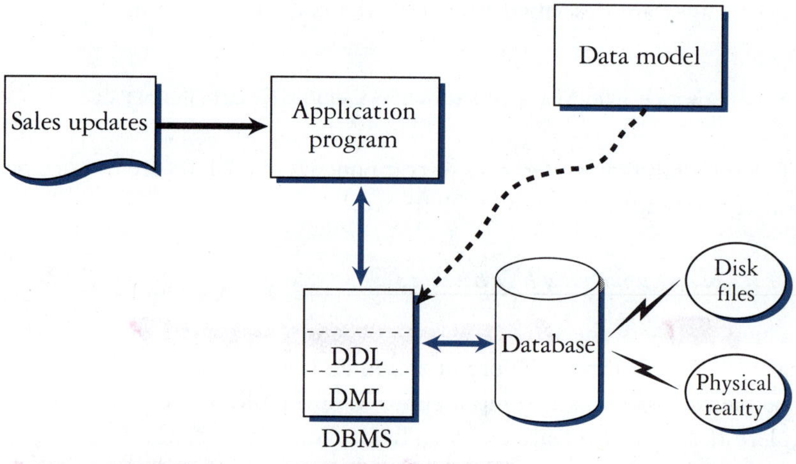

DDL: Interprets the requirements of the application program based on the data model

DML: Retrieves data stored on disk

Figure 3-4 Roles of Data Definition Language and Data Manipulation Language in a database management system environment

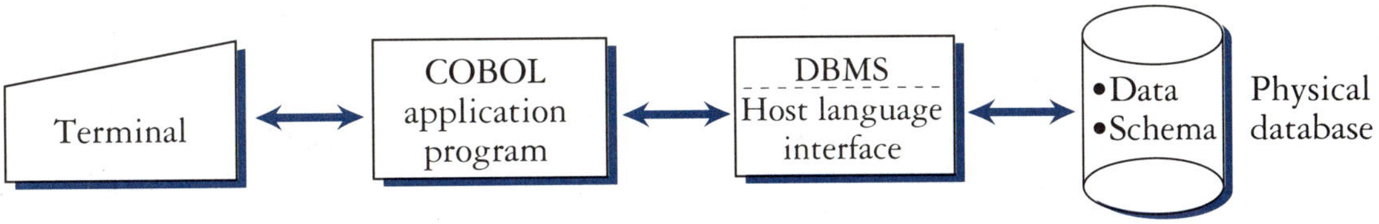

Figure 3-5 Host language interface

Host Language Interface

The HOST LANGUAGE INTERFACE makes it possible for programs written in a high-level language such as COBOL, FORTRAN, or C to manipulate and access data in the database. Instructions that are part of the DML are coded into the program and are converted by the host language interface into chunks of code. This sets up the link between the application program and the DBMS. With the host language interface, programmers do not need to learn a language other than DML to develop DBMS applications. (See Figure 3-5.)

Query Language

A QUERY LANGUAGE is an English-language facility that allows users with limited or no programming language or computer experience to query the database for information via a display terminal. For example, if the user wants a list of customers who bought merchandise on April 1, 1991, he or she would enter the query:

```
LIST CUSTOMER_NAME IF PURCHASE_DATE = 910401
```

The DBMS authorizes the database search and produces a listing of all customers who made purchases on that date.

A query language is more efficient than traditional programming languages, such as COBOL or BASIC, in that fewer instructions are needed. For example, finding the average salary for all senior programmers might require eight lines of code, while in SQL (a query language), the same results could be achieved in one three-line command. (See Figure 3-6.)

Data Dictionary

The DATA DICTIONARY is the portion of the DBMS that stores the schema, subschema, integrity rules, security information, and descriptions of all data items in the database which indicate the application programs that use the data. In essence, the data dictionary stores data about data, called METADATA.

```
BASIC

Open "SALARY. FIL" AS FILE # 1 MAP (SAL)
MAP (SAL) 10=6. FILL=73, POS=8. FILL=11, PAY=4
LET SUM=0
UNTIL EOF(1)
   GET #1
   IF POS= "SRPROG" THEN SUM=SUM + PAY
      NUMBR=NMBR +1
NEXT
PRINT "AVG. SALARY": SUM/NMBR

SQL

   SELECT AVG (PAY)
      FROM PERSONNEL
      WHERE POS= "SRPROG"
```

Figure 3-6 BASIC versus SQL–finding average salary for all senior programmers

How the Database Management System Works

With these DBMS characteristics in mind, let us consider how a DBMS actually works. Suppose the user, through an application program, requests a record for update. This request triggers several activities to be handled by the DBMS. As shown in Figure 3-7, the sequence of activities is as follows:

1 DBMS receives a request from application program 1 to read a record. The program provides the record key (ID or number) and record name for processing.

2 DBMS looks up the record through the application program subschema.

3 DBMS interrogates the schema to determine the record type requested.

4 DBMS taps the physical database description to verify the record to be read.

5 DBMS instructs the operating system to read the record. (The operating system (OS) is a collection of programs that controls and manages the activities of a computer system.)

6 The record is loaded into the system buffers. (A buffer is a temporary storage area designed to speed up the availability of data for processing.)

7 Using the subschema and schema, the DBMS determines the data needed by the application program.

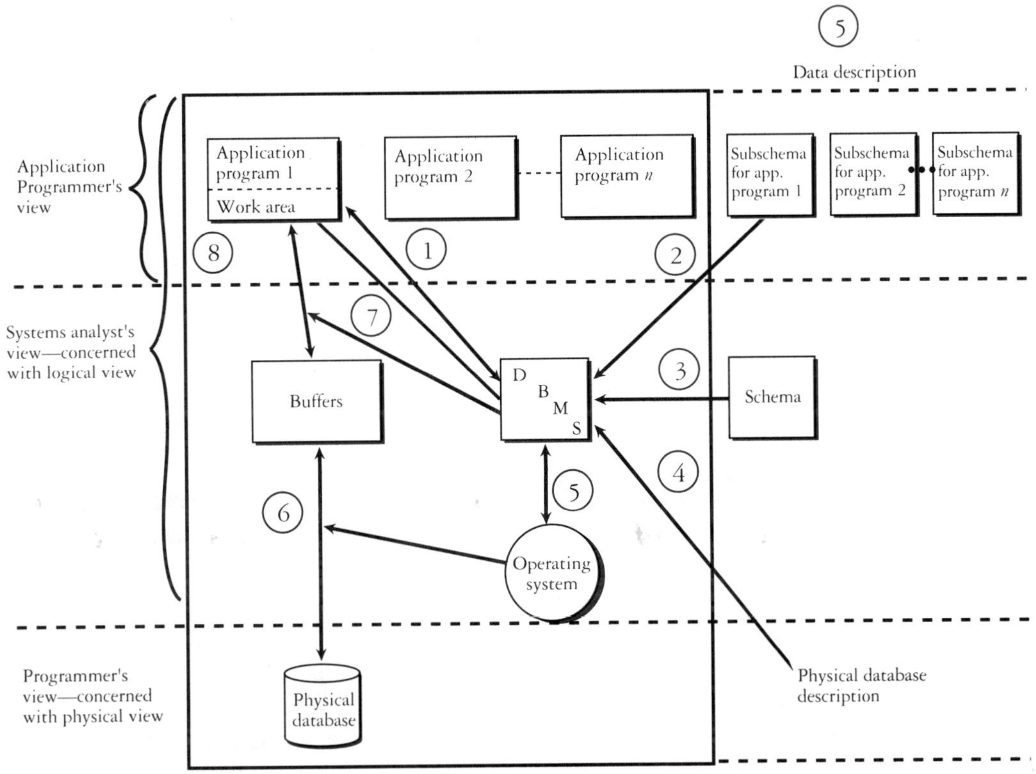

Figure 3–7 Sequence of DBMS activities

8 DBMS authorizes the transfer of data from the system buffers to the application program.

9 The application program operates on the data in the work area. (The work area is the physical file or a named portion of a physical file located in one secondary storage area and currently loaded into memory.)

Once the data becomes available in the work area, the user can easily modify or update it. The application program then automatically issues an instruction to the DBMS to write back the updated record, and the DBMS reverses the sequence of its record-reading activities. A WRITE command prompts the operating system to actuate the physical storage of the data.

Remember that the DBMS can handle multiple data calls at the same time. This means that system buffers have to be organized for all the operations in process. The DBMS should also be organized so as to restrict each application program to its own view (subschema) and work area (the data files or portions of files with which it works). The other two views shown in Figure 3-7 may be changed without changing the application programs or their subschemas.

The Primary Database Management System Functions

A DBMS is distinguished from a file system by the functions it performs. Besides the traditional functions of accessing, updating, and storing records, a DBMS performs other key functions:

- natural user interface of user data
- support of logical transactions
- data integrity
- concurrent processing controls
- recovery from failure
- database security

Natural User Interface

The NATURAL USER INTERFACE function of a DBMS expresses system functions in terms that are natural to an application or a user. For example, a DBMS might provide personnel terms and structures for a personnel information system, and statistical terms for a statistics package. In a multiuser system, natural interface means that each user can have a separate, natural view of the same problem, each emphasizing a different relationship in the database.

The DBMS also maintains data independence among user views and between each user view and the physical database. This means that the DBMS which supports multiuser views also supports logical data independence. And because user views are independent of one another, a change in one view leaves others unaffected.

Interface problems, such as an unclear message or an inconsistency, are often easy to recognize. Yet, many such problems go unfixed, and users learn to live with them. Part of the problem is that the interface portion of the DBMS is tested against software performance rather than user performance criteria. The growing complexity of the DBMS further compounds the problem. This is why software analysts should map the interface to uncover inconsistencies and dead ends.

Support of Logical Transactions

Another important function of the DBMS is to provide ways for the application programmer to manipulate logical transactions that affect the database. A LOGICAL TRANSACTION is a series of specific steps that have to be fully executed; otherwise, the database remains unaltered.

For example, Figure 3-8 shows a transfer of funds from a customer's savings account to a checking account. Both accounts are modified and the new balances are inserted in the database. To execute the transaction, both actions must be taken or both accounts must remain unchanged. Imagine the problems the customer would have if the savings account decreased by an amount not reflected in the checking account balance!

INTEGRITY means that the data in the database is correct at all times. Integrity is important in a single-user as well as a multiuser environment. In a multiuser database system, however, integrity problems become especially critical, because each user is affected by the actions of the other users. Integrity can be threatened in several ways:

SEMANTIC INTEGRITY THREATS result from miskeyed input data, program errors, or user misunderstanding of what is supposed to be entered. Constraints are data definitions that attempt to safeguard the database from some of these threats.

CONCURRENCY THREATS occur when two or more data modification entries work well separately, but produce invalid results when used together, as, for example, when the same airline seat is sold by two travel agents to two different customers. In another example, when a checking account is debited without a corresponding reduction to a loan balance, the database becomes invalid. This is called INTEGRITY VIOLATION, and it plays havoc with the system.

A basic requirement for maintaining database integrity is to ensure that all operations related to a transaction must either be completed or no other changes be allowed. This means the DBMS must know when a transaction begins and when it ends. It must also be able to undo operations when necessary.

Several types of constraints serve to protect data integrity:

Predefined constraints Some constraints are built into the data structure. For example, the data item "weight" may be allowed a

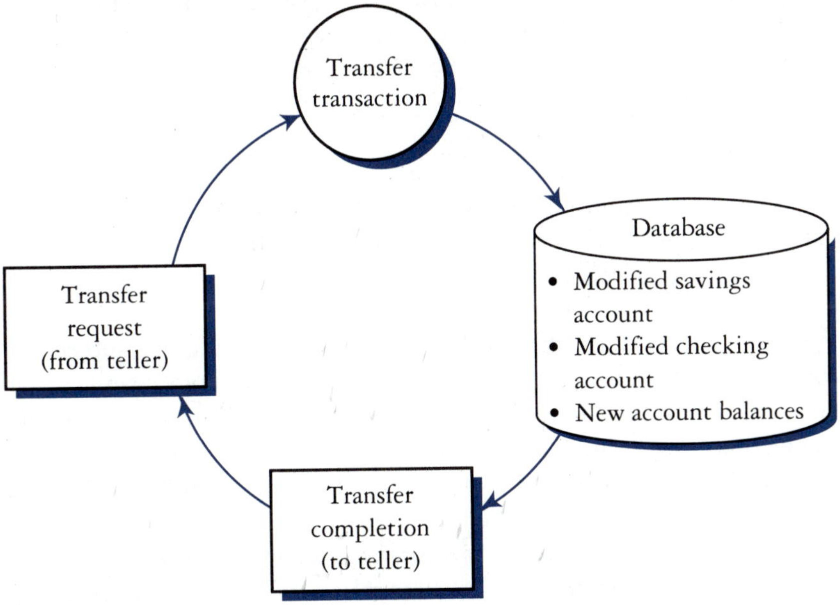

***Figure* 3–8** Transfer of funds transaction

maximum of three numeric characters. A social security number thus assumes the form "digit digit digit hyphen digit digit hyphen digit digit digit digit." These predefined integrity constraints ensure that only valid numerical data is accepted.

Specific value range constraints These constraints define a range of acceptable data. For example, "years on job" may be predefined as greater than 0 and less than 52, assuming minimum employment age is 18 and maximum age at retirement is 70.

Specific data values The stipulation that "hours worked" must be either "regular" or "overtime" is one example of integrity specification based on data values.

Specific associations Some constraints allow only certain types of relationships between record fields or data items. One variation of this form involves relating two data items to each other. For example, if a teacher's rank (data item A) is "assistant professor," his or her salary (data item B) must not exceed $38,500. Other constraints deal with specific activities. For example, a customer loan record may not be deleted from the database if there is an outstanding balance. (This is called referential integrity.) A constraint may be labeled as conditional or unconditional. An example of a conditional constraint is "if employee is a systems analyst, salary must not be less than $35,000." An example of an unconditional constraint is "total hours worked must not exceed 40 hours."

Concurrent Processing Controls

In most database systems, many users access data concurrently. User programs are switched back and forth by the operating system to accommodate high-volume traffic. This interweaving process causes updating errors unless the DBMS provides a protocol for preventing interference between transactions during processing. The DBMS must ensure that concurrent processing does not corrupt the database.

Concurrency control allows many users to access and update the database simultaneously while preventing partially completed updates from being displayed. This technique is essential in a high-performance, multiuser database environment.

Only transactions that affect the database should be subject to concurrency processing control. Multiple simultaneous processing creates no special problems. But when a transaction reads a record while another transaction is updating it, invalid data can result. Database integrity can be easily compromised if more than one program operates on the same record concurrently.

The concurrency problem is illustrated in Figure 3-9. Two travel agents are processing reservations on a Miami flight with 40 available seats. Travel agent A wants to reserve 20 seats, while agent B concurrently reserves 11 seats on the same flight. At the conclusion of

Travel agent A activities

1. Read flight reservation record (balance=40 seats)
2. Reduce seats available by 20
3. Write in flight reservation back to database

Travel agent B activities

1. Read flight reservation record (balance=40 seats)
2. Reduce seats available by 11
3. Write in flight reservation balance back to database

CPU activities

1. Read reservation query by agent A
2. Read reservation query by agent B
3. Reserve 20 seats for agent A
4. Write flight reservation data for agent A
5. Reserve 11 seats for agent B
6. Write flight reservation data for agent B

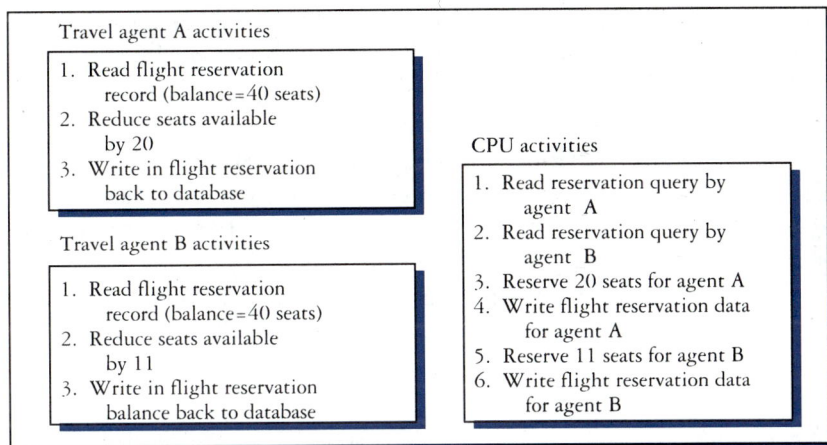

Figure 3–9 Concurrency problems: Loss of integrity

these transactions, there should be 9 seats still available. Agent A reads the flight record into the work area and finds 40 available seats. Agent B reads the same flight record into her work area and finds the same 40 seats available for booking. Again, agent A reserves 20 seats, and agent B reserves 11 seats. The database now shows 29 seats still available. What do you think happened?

Both travel agents accessed the current flight reservation file for booking. But when agent B accessed the flight record, travel agent A was about to update the file, but didn't do so before travel agent B had reserved 11 seats. This left a false balance of 29 (40 − 11) seats rather than 9 (40 − 20 − 11) seats. Clearly, integrity was lost at this point.

Controlling concurrency processing, then, is necessary to ensure database integrity. The final state of the database must be the same as it would be if the programs executed transactions one at a time. Users must be prevented from accessing the same copies of the same record when the record is being updated. So, in our example, the net remaining seats would be 9 if one travel agent executed a transaction before the second.

Recovery from Failure

RECOVERY is an integrity-protecting procedure that reacts to hardware or software malfunction by returning the data to its original condition. The DBMS should be able to manage the damage caused by breakdowns and to return the database to normal operation.

All systems have a probability of failure due to program bugs, disk-head crashes, hardware breakdowns, and personnel incompetence. In today's business, activities must continue regardless of system failures. In retailing, for example, customers won't wait for the store's system to be repaired—they'll simply go elsewhere. Since most businesses depend heavily on their databases, the DBMS must be capable of repairing the system and recovering lost transactions as quickly as possible.

Recovery is a difficult job. Determining how quickly a system can be repaired, let alone knowing when or how often it will fail, is a matter of speculation. System reliability should be seriously considered during the feasibility study and depends largely on factors such as vendor reputation, response time for maintenance, and the performance update record of the system in existing user installations.

Several types of failure can occur in database processing. The most common types are

- incorrect data entry
- aborted transactions
- hardware failures
- database destruction

Incorrect data entry When a database accepts valid but incorrect data, the failure is usually human. For example, a bank teller may enter a cash deposit of $10 as $100 and end up short $90 when he tries to balance his drawer later in the day. Such an error is difficult to trace, especially in a bank that handles thousands of similar transactions each day. Human intervention, such as a letter of explanation or a telephone call to the customer, may be the only chance to recover the difference.

Aborted transactions Occasionally, a transaction in progress terminates prematurely due to human error or system failure. In such a case, the DBMS rolls back the transaction and deletes all changes made prior to transmission. The software requests the user to reenter the transaction.

To illustrate, bank terminals capture each transaction handled by tellers. In the event of an electrical outage, the volatile memory of the computer loses all data in memory. After electric power is restored, the teller has to reenter each transaction manually. A better way is for the teller to generate a subtotal after a given number of entries. This way, the teller would only have to reenter the transactions made after the last subtotal. An ideal alternative to our scenario would be to have an uninterruptible power supply (UPS), which ensures a continuous flow of battery-based electricity in the event of power outage.

Hardware failures Aborted transactions often result from hardware failure, including such mishaps as disk crashes, electric blackouts, telecommunication transmission problems, and human errors. When the system goes down, one or more transactions may be in progress. Each transaction must be looked up and the correct changes made.

Database destruction Disk-head crashes are the most common causes of database destruction. A disk-head crash means the read/write head of the hard disk can no longer function. It can also mean that one or more tracks on the hard disk that hold the data are damaged so that the read/write head can no longer read from or write to sector tracks. When a head crashes, data is impossible to read or update. In this case, the user must go to the backup files for recovery. One DBMS function is to produce regular backups automatically. All activities that took place before the loss and after the last automatic backup must be reentered to restore the database.

Database Security

When an organization centralizes its information resource in a database environment, that information becomes vulnerable to unauthorized access. Security measures must be implemented to enforce authorization of access. Most of today's DBMSs have these measures in one form or another.

Authorization rules Not all users and programmers who access the database have equal authorization. A good security system allows individuals access to the information that relates to their functions—no more. This means the level of authorized access varies with the job.

Authorization rules also specify the actions a user may exercise on the data in the database. To illustrate, in a database representing the activities of a religious group, the menu shows three major applications:

1 *membership* application detailing members' names, addresses, telephone numbers, hobbies, offices held, etc.

2 *accounting* application centered around the general ledger and the pledge file

3 *administrative* application that provides word processing and various utilities

Officers of the organization are provided passwords to access applications 1 and 3. The treasurer is authorized to access all applications, with a special password for application 2. The minister has authorized access to the data in applications 1 and 3, but has only restricted access to the general ledger. He is also authorized to access, but not change, the pledge file.

User	*Application*	*Activity*	*Constraint*
Minister	Pledge file	Read	No update
Minister	Membership file	Modify	None
Treasurer	General ledger	Modify	At end of month
Members	Membership file	Read	Access through a secretary
Board of elders	Pledge file	Read	None
Deacons' chairman	Pledge file	Insert	Enters weekly pledges only

Table 3–2 Authorization matrix

One approach to database security is to set up a model that highlights the user, the application, the activity authorized, and the constraints imposed on the activities. The key question is "What activities is the user authorized to perform on the application under the specified constraints?" The authorization matrix for the church is shown in Table 3-2. It contains several entries pertaining to the major files in the database. For example, the first row specifies that the minister is authorized to read pledge data with a "no update" restriction. The last row authorizes the chairman of the board of deacons to enter the weekly pledges received from members into the pledge file.

Users The term *user* refers to individuals, departments, transactions, terminals, or applications. The main security problem with users is the reliability of identification. A password is the easiest and most common identification security measure, but it is also the most abused. Whenever a person lends his or her password to another person, regardless of the reason, it is no longer a password. Other identification options are fingerprints and voice prints.

In some cases management is more concerned with controlling the activity than with defining the users for authorization. Here, the procedure is to grant access to a specific program rather than to a person. Users wishing to access information would have to go through an authorized program that performs a protocol before they are granted access to the information. For example, a clerk in personnel trained in personnel matters would access an employee skills file, but not other programs such as sales inventory, customer accounts, and so on.

Applications Generally, access control is implemented at the application level rather than at the record or data-item levels. Data is authorized by defining the values of certain attributes. For example, a manager may be able to access employee salaries from the personnel information database, provided that the employee's department code matches the manager's department.

In addition to these features, a security system must determine the GRANULARITY, or size, of objects to be locked. For example, if an entire file of 1000 records is locked, the system is said to have coarse granularity. If individual records are locked, the system is said to have fine granularity. Coarse granularity means fewer locks and better system performance, but less user concurrency access. That is, when a large block of records is locked, many users are locked out of accessing those records. In contrast, when each record is locked individually, the records that were locked as a block are available. Most systems provide a range of locking granularities to promote security but still allow flexibility for multiuser access.

Activity The third component of a security matrix is the activity, or what the user can do to the application. The activity that a user is authorized to use on the application depends on the user's level in the system and the database model. The most commonly used activity words are Read, Retrieve, Insert, Modify, Delete, and Update. The read and retrieve actions are the least powerful, because all they allow the user to do is view information. Insert, modify, delete, and update actions are powerful because they allow users to change information, thereby affecting the contents of the database.

Constraints The last column of the authorization matrix in Table 3-2 specifies the constraints imposed on the security rule. For example, the chairman of the board of deacons can insert only weekly pledges into the pledge file. He or she cannot otherwise modify the data. Implicitly, no other person is authorized to enter the pledge data.

DATABASE MANAGEMENT SYSTEMS FOR THE MICROCOMPUTER

The features and functions discussed so far are typical of DBMSs in general. Most of today's DBMSs are also multiuser, in that multiple users can access a common database at the same time over a local area network (LAN). Some microcomputer DBMSs are worth reviewing, since the trend is more and more toward microcomputer-oriented databases in a networked environment. DBMSs for the microcomputer fall in two categories. In the first are DBMSs that were developed strictly for the microcomputer, such as R:BASE and dBASE. In the second category are DBMSs that have been written for the minicomputer and have been "ported down" to the microcomputer level, such as Oracle.

R:BASE

The R:BASE family is a product of Microrim Corporation. R:BASE was originally developed at Boeing Aircraft Corporation under the name RIM. Recognizing its potential in the then-young but fast-growing microcomputer market, the developer tailored the software to the microcomputer under the label R:BASE 4000. Two other revisions followed, leading to today's R:BASE System V.

R:BASE has a query language for defining database structure, entering, updating, and modifying data, and ensuring database security at all times. The software also provides a powerful facility for the definition of integrity rules. When data is modified, the DBMS checks the data dictionary to make sure no rules have been violated. The basic package can support up to three users in a network environment. With the proper upgrade, an unlimited number of users can be supported. A summary of the key features of R:BASE is shown in Figure 3-10.

dBASE

The dBASE family, introduced by Ashton-Tate (now a part of Borland International) in 1981 as dBASE II, was the first serious attempt

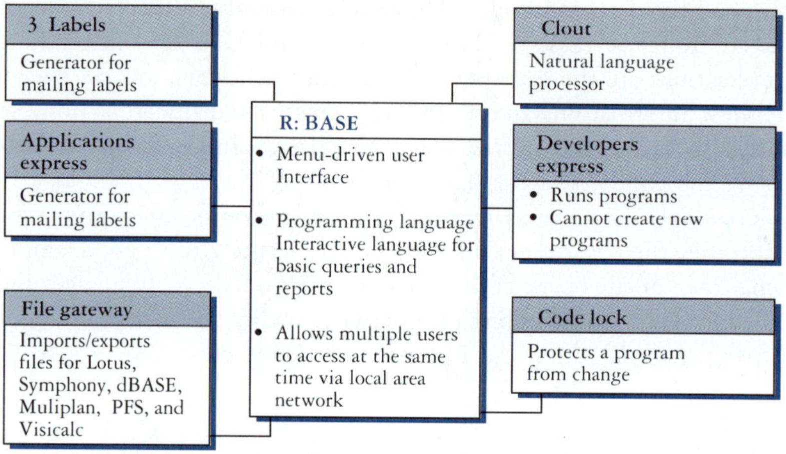

Figure 3–10 R:BASE features

at running a DBMS on the microcomputer. dBASE has gone through several upgrades since then, leading to today's dBASE IV.

Compared to earlier versions, dBASE IV is more task-oriented and has more object-oriented processing. (Object-oriented processing, covered in Chapter 18, treats the program elements as self-sufficient objects that can pass messages to each other.) In dBASE III the programmer had to define procedures and write programs to implement those procedures. dBASE IV has an application generator which virtually automates program development. The programmer spends less time defining procedures and writing programs, and more time determining application and program objectives and the files needed to implement these objectives. This is what makes dBASE IV so task-oriented.

What makes dBASE IV object-oriented programming is that the programmer sees all the parts of the program (for example, menus and reports) as objects. The programmer creates these objects and then lets dBASE IV write the programs that use these objects. Again, the programmer concentrates more on the design of the objects, leaving the procedural chores to the software.

A third feature of dBASE IV is STRUCTURED QUERY LANGUAGE (SQL) support. SQL is a popular relational data manipulation language used in IBM's DB2 and many other DBMSs. Since its first commercial introduction by IBM in 1979, SQL has been adopted by many firms as a database language standard for both the mainframe and minicomputer systems. Introducing SQL to microcomputers means standardizing the development of database applications at all levels of computers. Used in dBASE IV, SQL statements can be embedded in the dBASE programming language without difficulty.

A summary of the key features of dBASE IV is shown in Figure 3-11.

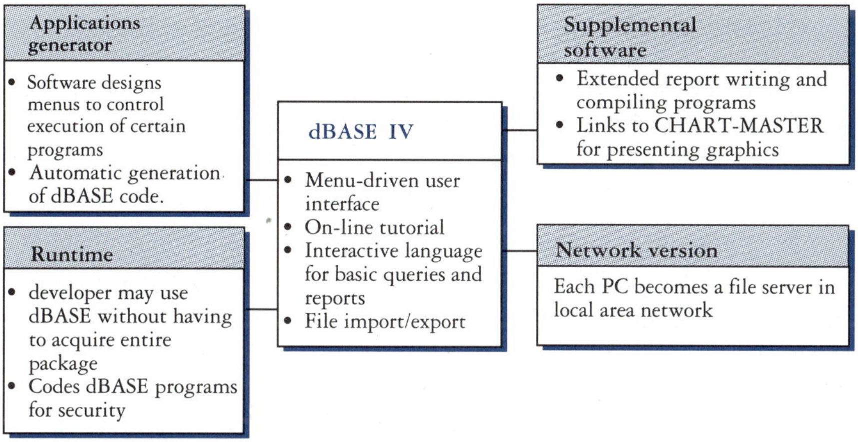

Applications generator
SQL loader
Imports files from dBASE and Lotus
• Software designs menus to control execution of certain programs
• Automatic generation of dBASE code.
Runtime
• developer may use dBASE without having to acquire entire package
• Codes dBASE programs for security
dBASE IV
• Menu-driven user interface
• On-line tutorial
• Interactive language for basic queries and reports
• File import/export
Supplemental software
• Extended report writing and compiling programs
• Links to CHART-MASTER for presenting graphics
Network version
Each PC becomes a file server in local area network

Figure 3–11 dBASE IV features

Allows design of custom report formats
Oracle

As we mentioned earlier, Oracle is known for running on minicomputers. The microcomputer version appeared in 1978 with virtually all the features of the main version. For that reason, Oracle is more powerful and more advanced than either dBASE or R:BASE. Oracle is a production system that deals with stand-alone applications.

Oracle supports an SQL environment, where SQL statements can be embedded in host languages such as Pascal or C. It also maintains a data dictionary which contains integrity rules, the database structure, and details relating to security and protocol. The software has heavier main memory and disk storage demands than either R:BASE or dBASE IV. A summary of Oracle features is shown in Figure 3-12.

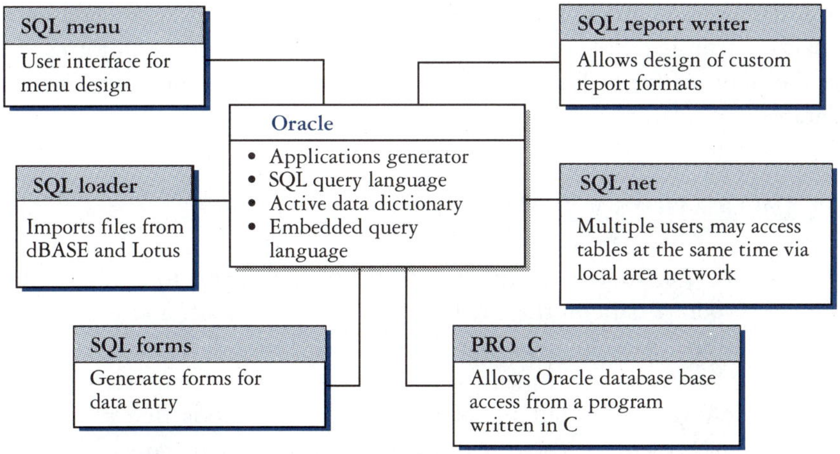

SQL forms
Generates forms for data entry

Allows Oracle database base access from a program written in C

Figure 3–12 Oracle features

There are more DBMSs for MS-DOS than for Apple and Macintosh microcomputers. Two Macintosh products worthy of mention, however, are dBASE MAC and 4th Dimension.

dBASE MAC

Ashton-Tate (now part of Borland International) developed a separate, stand-alone dBASE product for the Macintosh, dBASE MAC. Although dBASE MAC can read dBASE III PLUS and dBASE IV data files, it has extensions for the Macintosh computer that make it incompatible with the MS-DOS version of dBASE. The product has limited integrity rules that have to be written into a program if they affect more than one piece of data.

One nice feature of dBASE MAC is its relationship to the graphic interface. The data structure is defined visually. The specification of search criteria for data access or retrieval is controlled via the mouse or menu options.

The main limitation of dBASE MAC is its lack of multiuser availability. Because of that, its use is limited to users who can manage the database at a single workstation.

4th Dimension

The 4th Dimension software is a French product that uses a variety of graphic screens to define the data structure or to specify how data should be retrieved. Although it has no DDL, DML, or command-driven query language, 4th Dimension can enforce integrity rules that apply to one field. Going beyond the one-field limit requires that the rules be embedded within a program.

4th Dimension is more of a development system than an end-user DBMS. It can handle graphics as data as well as decorations on forms. It is the only software that can generate graphics from data stored in the database.

IMPLICATIONS FOR MANAGEMENT

Adopting a DBMS is often a trade-off between access to accurate and timely corporate data on the one hand and software, staff, and temporary system failure costs on the other. The latter, particularly head crashes, can have disastrous consequences. Many organizations cease to function in the prolonged blackout of information access that is due to such a crash. Management needs to plan for even these extreme contingencies. Nonetheless, many organizations today use DBMS to meet their daily information needs. This trend should continue as vendors improve the reliability of database recovery and security procedures.

Size Considerations

Corporations that need to share large volumes of corporate data daily should consider the mainframe or minicomputer DBMS. Small businesses and departments that need to share only a limited amount of data may want to consider a PC-based DBMS; many are priced at under $1000. Mid-sized businesses may want to link a mainframe DBMS to PC workstations. This concept allows the user to query the DBMS or to use the downloaded information for forecasting and decision making. Communication technology and distributed databases are covered in Chapter 11.

Security Considerations

Security is the basis of DBMS reliability. The DBMS can be programmed to ensure security measures fixed by the vendor. The DBMS can also be programmed to allow the user access to all of the database, to part of it, or to none of it. The advantage of fixed DBMS access is reliability. The disadvantage is inflexibility. The trade-off in security responsibility, then, is reliability versus flexibility.

Certain security over DBMS internal data should be fixed by the vendor. Some security measures should be manipulated by an application program, while other measures should be enforced through user procedures. Overall, DBMS security requires a balance among the components of the database environment. The DBA is a part of the environment and should be a leader in proposing, implementing, and enforcing security standards to ensure effective DBMS performance.

User Considerations

Finally, a DBMS will not bring order out of chaos. It will not correct every flaw in a firm's handling of information and paperwork. When considering a DBMS, management must determine who will interface with the system and which security measures will best suit the user environment. The safeguards and control measures differ with each type of user.

SUMMARY

1 The DBMS receives a request from the application program, looks up the record via the subschema, interrogates the schema to determine the record

type, taps the physical database description to verify the record to be read, instructs the operating system to read the record, determines the data needed by the application program, and authorizes the transfer of data from the system buffer to the application program for processing.

2 To qualify as a DBMS, a database system must provide a natural interface of user data independent of the physical database structure, an operational multiuser environment, program/data independence, control of multiuser access to the database, security, and recovery from failure.

3 Several components of a DBMS are:

a. the schema, which is the logical representation of the physical database;
b. the subschema, which is the user's view of the database;
c. the data definition language (DDL), which describes the logical data structure within a data model;
d. the data manipulation language (DML), which is the mechanism used for retrieving data stored on disk;
e. the host language interface, which allows programs written in high-level languages to manipulate and access data in the database; and
f. the query language, which allows novice users to query the database for information.

4 A natural interface means that each user in a multiuser environment may have a separate, natural view of the same problem and place emphasis on different relationships in the database. The DBMS provides different user views of the same database to multiple users. It also maintains data independence between user views and between each user view and the physical database.

5 Another function of the DBMS is to provide facilities for the application programmer to manipulate logical transactions that affect the database. This is an important function for database integrity.

6 In a database environment, integrity is subject to semantic integrity threats, user error, and system failure, and is protected by concurrency control and recovery operations that react to hardware or software malfunction. Integrity constraints take several forms:

a. predefined by the data structure
b. specified value range on data items
c. specified data values
d. specified associations between record fields or data items

7 In most database systems, several users access data concurrently. Concurrency control makes it possible for multiple users to access and update the database and prevent a user from viewing a partially completed update.

8 A DBMS must provide recovery from the following most common types of failure:

a. incorrect data entry
b. aborted transactions
c. hardware failure
d. database destruction

9 Most DBMSs today are multiuser, with a trend toward microcomputer-based networks. DBMSs for the microcomputer include R:BASE, dBASE, and Oracle. Although there are more DBMSs for MS-DOS, dBASE MAC and 4th Dimension, among others, are available for Apple and Macintosh computers.

KEY WORDS

Concurrency threats
Data definition language (DDL)
Data dictionary
Data manipulation language (DML)
Granularity
Host language interface
Integrity
Integrity violation
Logical transaction
Logical view
Metadata
Natural user interface
Operating system
Physical view
Query language
Recovery
Referential integrity
Relation
Schema and subschema
Semantic integrity threats
Structured Query Language (SQL)

REVIEW QUESTIONS

1 Review briefly the evolution of DBMS. What has been the role of CODASYL in DBMS development?

2 Distinguish between the following pairs:
   a. DDL and DML
   b. schema and subschema
   c. query language and host language interface

3 In your own words, describe how a DBMS works.

4 To qualify as a DBMS, a database system must provide several capabilities. Elaborate on the key capabilities.

5 A DBMS performs several functions. Which three functions do you consider the most important? Why? Elaborate.

6 "Security procedures should be tied to the DBMS, not the application program." Do you agree? Discuss.

7 What does *data integrity* mean? What affects integrity in a database environment? Explain in detail.

8 Distinguish among the various forms of integrity encountered in a database environment.

9 Cite a scenario that illustrates the concurrency problem in database management.

10 What are the most common types of failures encountered in processing a database? Give an example of each.

11 Summarize the security measures used to enforce access authorization.

12 Review several computer journals and describe at least one new DBMS for the microcomputer that has been introduced since 1990. What are the key attributes and limitations of such software?

APPLICATION PROBLEMS

1 Use a microcomputer or a mainframe database product available in your school or lab and develop a prototype for an application of your choice. Would you be able to do the same in COBOL? What are the benefits? Limitations? Be specific.

2 Acme Department Store has a multiuser DBMS linked through a local area network. This DBMS lacks concurrency control. In the accounts receivable file, one customer had a balance of $150. Three adjustments to the account were made at the same time:

a. payment of $150 outstanding balance
b. credit for returned items $15
c. purchases of $50

Without concurrency control, each transaction reads the account with a balance of $150. The balance was stored in the accounts receivable file in the sequence shown above.

a. What was the actual customer account balance after the second transaction was completed? After the third transaction?
b. What should have been the final balance after the third transaction was completed?

3 Visit a local firm that has an established DBMS environment. Evaluate the following:

a. the problems it had when converting to DBMS from the earlier environment
b. the benefits and costs associated with the DBMS installation
c. the procedure followed for concurrency control, security, backup, and recovery

4 Review the literature to find a recent article about computer crime. What kinds of security problems does the article cite? From what you have read in this chapter, what can you prescribe that will improve security? System integrity? Explain.

5 Evaluate a DBMS in your school for the following:

a. key functions as specified in this chapter
b. hardware requirements
c. hard disk memory requirements
d. data dictionary (if any) and how it is queried

e. screen and report generator(s)
f. multiuser capacity

6 Fill out the following authorization tables (Tables 3-3(a) and (b)) for the Acme Department Store, described in Exercise 2, based on the following guidelines.

a. The personnel director is authorized to read and/or update employee records.
b. Employees of the payroll department may do anything with employee salary data only. They may read employee records only.
c. Sales supervisors may read but not modify, insert, or delete employee records.
d. Sales staff may read, insert, and/or modify customer records, but not delete any records. They may not access employee records.

	Payroll Staff	Personnel Director	Sales Supervisor	Sales Staff
READ				
MODIFY				
INSERT				
DELETE				

a. Authorization for employee record

	Product Records	Employee Records	Customer Records
READ			
MODIFY			
INSERT			
DELETE			

Table **3-4** b. Authorization for sales staff

7 Use the Island Jumpers, Inc. (IJI) case presented at the end of Chapter 1 to complete the following assignment:

a. Show the constraints (including integrity constraints) that the DBMS could contribute to the viability of IJI's database application.
b. List the security constraints that should be considered at this time and explain their importance.
c. Since IJI very likely will operate in the Caribbean (tropical climate), what types of failure might occur in IJI's proposed database reservation system? Explain.

d. How important is recovery from failure when it comes to a reservation tracking system such as IJI's? Explain.

e. Now that you have done some work toward IJI's system, what do you think management should consider before selecting a database reservation system? Explain.

PART II

DATABASE DESIGN

C H A P T

Data Models

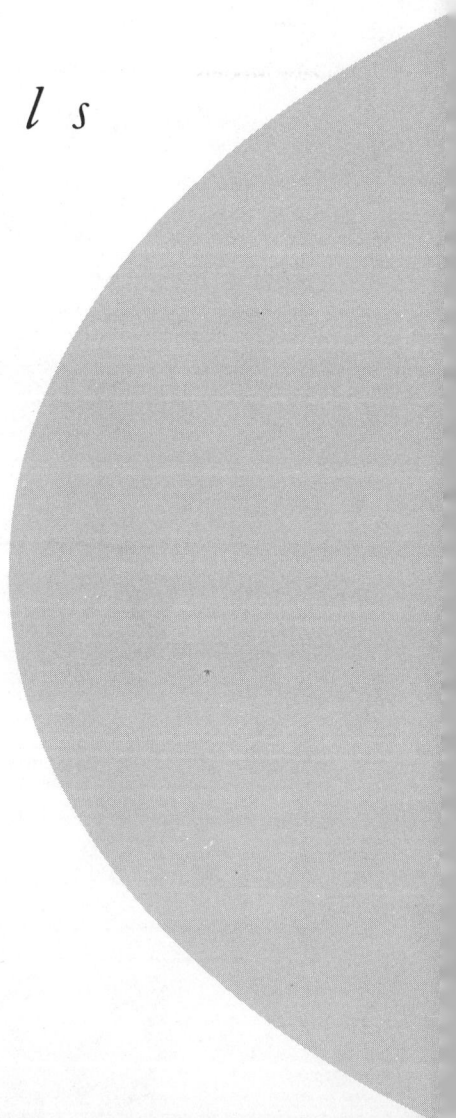

E R 4

A New Era for Data Modeling

AT A GLANCE

A New Era for Data Modeling

The heart of the entity recognition (ER) process is interviews with the people who actually run the business. The data model that emerges should parallel the use of language during those interviews. ER strings the words users actually use to describe their enterprise; the model represented by that sentence, it turns out, will be a fine fit with the relational model. (In terms of language, entities correspond to nouns, relationships are verbs, and attributes are adjectives, adverbs, or prepositional phrases.) When mapped to the relational model, entities are tables, attributes are columns, and relationships are one-to-one, one-to-many, and many-to-many pairings of the tables. The three-step ER process is as follows:

1 *Model the entities*. Discover the entity, determine the scope (is this within the scope of this business?), determine the primary key, and document the entity in table form. Repeat the above steps until you have found all the entities.

2 *Model the relationship*. Discover a relationship by asking people involved in the enterprise. Verify the scope to make sure the relationship is within the scope of the project or application. Determine the type of relationship, that is, whether it is one-to-one, one-to-many, or many-to-many. Then document the relationship in table form.

3 *Model the attributes*. Discover an attribute by asking the people involved in the enterprise. Verify the scope to make sure the attribute is relevant to this phase of the project. Determine the primary key, then document the attribute by adding a column to an existing table. Put in sample data and try out the model.

The best way to find the entities of a business is to discuss that business with the people who run it. The entities are the nouns used in that discussion. A data model for an auto insurance company, for example, might involve the nouns *claim*, *individual*, *policy*, *rate category*, and *vehicle*.

The difficulties you encounter—and you will encounter some, no question of that—will arise in seven guises: homonyms, synonyms, unmentionables, false entities, inflated attributes, isolated subsets, and time.

Homonyms are the words with two meanings. Sometimes this is deliberate, as it is so often in politics; sometimes homonyms are inadvertent, as when two different divisions or departments come up with the same name for two different things. For example, the word *region* is used to model both sales and support regions and is viewed as the same entity. Words that frequently show up as homonyms are *division*, *part*, *region*, *account*, and *order*.

Synonyms are words frequently used to refer to the same real-world person, place, or thing. *Customers*, *clients*, and *accounts* may be synonyms in some contexts. Drawing tables, putting in sample data, and trying out the model will help you avoid synonym problems.

Unmentionables are situations where the users may not mention the entity at all. One reason is that the user has the percept that "it can't be done on a DBMS." Another reason is that the entity is not part of the existing system, which will lead the user to say "we're converting to a relational system, not redesigning the way we do things—there can't be anything new."

False entities are perfectly good words that are indeed nouns and at first blush seem to stand on their own. For example, "Sales, we need to keep track of sales. That must be an entity. And we need to keep track of inventory, that's another entity." The key to uncovering a false entity, such as inventory, is to ask users for a precise definition of the term, rather than accepting the entity at face value.

Inflated attributes—if you can't get a precise definition from the users or if you can't find a primary key for an entity, you may well not have an entity that can stand on its own.

Isolated subsets in the modeling process are entities grouped according to certain roles: engineer, salesperson, manager, and so on. As soon as you think you have discovered an entity, you check the scope, determine the primary key, draw a table, and put in the sample data. If the primary keys are the same for the subentries as for the main entries, there is a strong possibility that you've overlooked a higher level of abstraction. In that case, you'd create a table for the main entry and insert attributes that apply to virtually every entry.

Time behaves like an entity when an attribute or relationship must be tracked across time. For example, in a "patient" table, the attribute "temperature" is dependent on both "patient number" and "time." Temperature, in other words, needs both columns to ensure uniqueness. In this case, "time" behaves like an entity in a many-to-many relationship.

If you define the quality of your database by its utility to the user and the assistance it provides in running the business, your data modelers must demonstrate graphically to users that the model will support their needs. It is possible to get it right the first time. As my friend Miles Coverdale once said, "Data modeling is harder than checkers, but it is not as hard as chess."

Foster, Al, "A new era for data modeling." DBMS, *December 1990, 68ff. Reprinted with permission of* DBMS.

AT A GLANCE

To understand DBMSs, we need to be familiar with the different data models on which they are based. A data model is a map of the entities and their relationships. The main components of the data model are the entities and the relationships between entities.

There are three types of data relationships: one-to-one (1:1), one-to-many (1:M), and many-to-many (M:N). There are also three levels of data models: conceptual, external, and internal. The conceptual model defines all the users' database requirements in a single database description and is the basis for developing the external and internal views. The external data model is the user's view of the data or of a specific processing application. The internal model includes the data structures and file organizations used to store the data on a physical storage device such as a hard disk.

Bubble charts, which describe data items and relationships, involve three types of keys: primary, secondary, and concatenated. Data structure and entity-relationship diagrams are used to identify or represent record relationships.

In drawing a schema, we need to avoid using duplicate names, to specify the primary and secondary keys, to clarify the types of relationships in the schema when data items are gathered into groups, and to write record names outside each box.

User views should be simply drawn, not complex, should properly specify the concatenated keys, and should ensure that the attributes identified by a concatenated key are dependent on the whole key. These rules provide database stability and reflect the actual user's views, which are critical for implementing the physical database.

By the end of this chapter, you should be able to

- understand the difference between conceptual, external, and internal data models;
- identify entities and their attributes;
- distinguish between entities and the relationships among entities;
- draw data structure and entity-relationship diagrams; and
- draw a schema.

INTRODUCTION

The growing use of database products has led to greater emphasis on database design procedures. Early databases could support only one organizational function—one database was needed for a company's accounting system, another for its inventory system, and so forth. Today's "distributed" database environment provides greater flexibility of user functions and supports more than one organizational function.

Such evolution has created a need for better design procedures to control the ever-increasing complexity of databases. Today's database design must

- minimize data redundancy,
- facilitate ad hoc user inquiries,
- ensure stable data structures that can also change with changing user requirements, and
- support a variety of user decision needs.

Obviously, to meet these design requirements, we need proper tools and procedures for applying those tools in a satisfactory manner. *Tools* are the diagrams, computations, documentation methods, and software used in designing the database. The tools for data modeling covered in this chapter are bubble charts, data structure diagrams, and entity-relationship diagrams.

A design procedure is the sequence used in applying these tools, usually involving three major steps: conceptual, logical, and physical design. Each step has unique features and requirements. (See Figure 4-1.)

In this chapter, we focus on data models that represent entities and the relationships between entities, identify the various keys and their role in data models, and show how schemas are formed. In the next chapter, we elaborate on procedures in database design.

One important aspect of a database management system design is how well the proposed software will manage data. Once most database management tools were merely file handlers. In the 1960s, mainframe system developers began to press for more sophisticated tools, which resulted in the development of mainframe database management. DBMSs based on ways of modeling data soon followed.

DBMSs are based on a variety of data models. A DATA MODEL specifies the data structure that represents the user's view of the data. It is made up of entities and relationships. An ENTITY is a conceptual representation

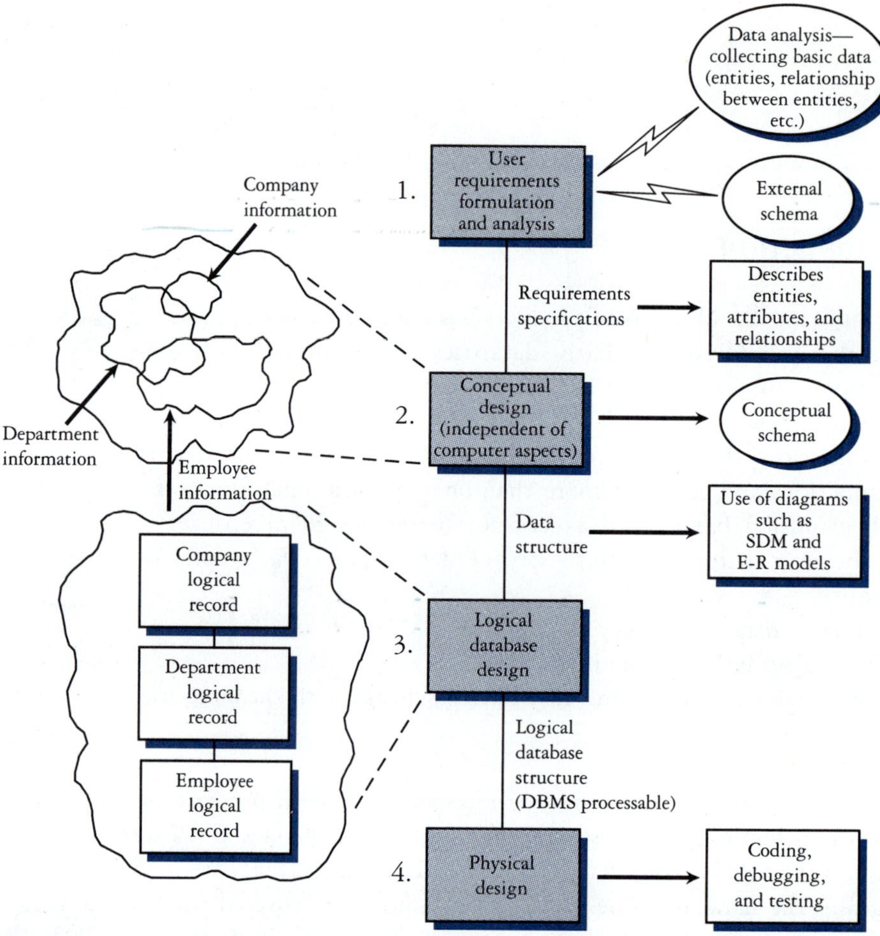

Figure 4–1 Steps in database design

of a thing, event, or person about which data is collected, and is identified by its ATTRIBUTES. For example, "salesclerk" is an entity; the salesclerk attributes might be name, address, telephone number, and gender. Some entities are physical, such as customers and employees, while others are abstract, such as jobs and orders.

DATA RELATIONSHIPS are also important. There are three types of relationships among entities: one-to-one (1:1), one-to-many (1:M), and many-to-many (M:N). Entities and their relationships make up a data model.

Data Models

A data model is a map of the entities and their relationships. A model is the logical representation of the data structure that forms a database. There are three data models or ways of viewing data in a

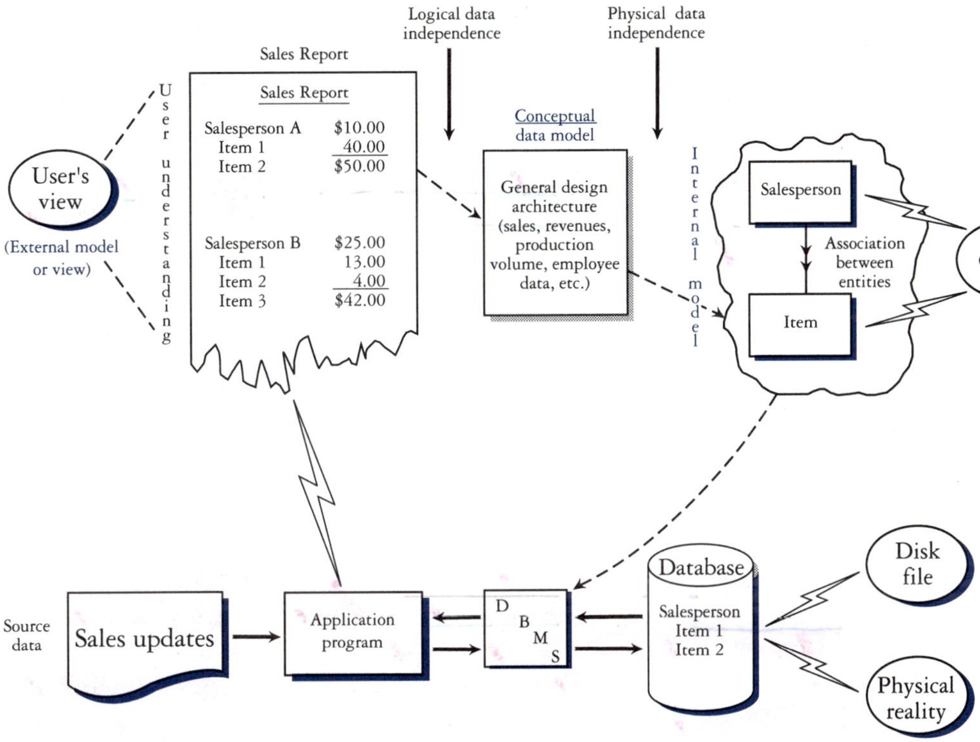

Figure 4–2 Data model

database: conceptual, external, and internal. Figure 4-2 illustrates the three models, or views.

The differences in data models have to do with the way data is logically stored in the computer. How much detail is incorporated into a data model depends on the information required. The more information that is needed, the finer the level of detail in the data model.

Conceptual Data Models

The CONCEPTUAL DATA MODEL, or CONCEPTUAL SCHEMA, defines all the users' database requirements in a single database description. It represents the entire information system structure of the database as seen by the database administrator. Only one conceptual view is maintained in a database system, representing the workings of the organization. (See Figure 4-2.) The database administrator has access to the total conceptual view, while database users have partial access, depending on their needs or predefined requirements. You cannot reference (enter, retrieve, modify, or delete) any entities or attributes in the database system unless they are defined in the conceptual data model.

The conceptual data model is the basis for developing both the external and internal models. The conceptual data model is initially produced through a top-down planning process, then refined when the external data model (the bottom-up design process) is defined. This process links database design to database planning.

External Data Models

The EXTERNAL DATA MODEL is the user's view of the data or of a specific processing application. It actually is a subset of the conceptual data model, necessary for supporting a particular user view. Most information analysts' work is aimed at constructing external data models. In Figure 4-2, the user's view or external model includes an output view (reports and queries) and an input view (screens or forms used to process transactions). The user's view in this illustration is one of many user views that can be derived from the conceptual data model. Each external model is an overlapping subset of the conceptual model.

Internal Data Models

The INTERNAL DATA MODEL shows how the data is internally or physically represented in the database. It includes the data structures and file organizations used to store the data on hard disk or other physical storage devices. The goal of internal design is to make most efficient use of the database, while meeting the user's requirements. In Figure 4-2, the internal data model involves two entities: salesclerk and items. Since the relationship between them is that a salesclerk (one entity) is expected to sell one or more items, the nature of the relationship is one-to-many. In this case, one-to-many describes the relationship in the internal data model.

Models and Data Independence

Placing a conceptual data model between an internal and an external data model provides data independence, which means that upper levels are not affected by changes to lower levels. External views cannot be mapped into the internal data model unless they are part of the conceptual data model. Omitting the conceptual data model provides no assurance that the user's view (represented by the external data model) is represented in the database.

There are two types of data independence: logical and physical. LOGICAL DATA INDEPENDENCE is the capacity to change the conceptual data model without having to change the external data model or the application program. For example, we can add new data items or new relationships to the conceptual model without affecting the existing external view. PHYSICAL DATA INDEPENDENCE is the ability to change the internal data model without having to change the external or conceptual data models. That is, if we make physical changes in record sequence or access method, these alterations should have no effect on the conceptual model.

To understand data models, you need to be more familiar with entities, attributes, and the relationships among attributes. The following case illustrates their role in data modeling.

Case Scenario 4-1:

Dominion Pizza

Dominion Pizza is a small pizza delivery business near a major university. Customers place orders by telephone. A typical order consists of pizza and soft drinks. Pizza is delivered free of charge to customers.

Dominion Pizza uses a DBMS to track inventory (supplies and ingredients), payroll, and sales. Supplies and ingredients are monitored and reordered at specific reorder points. Information concerning the supplies (pizza boxes, napkins, cups, straws, and lids, for example) and the ingredients (pizza dough, sauce, toppings, and soft drinks, for example) are kept in two separate files. Several employees operate the business. They include pizza makers, delivery persons, and a manager. Employee pay is based on an hourly rate. This information is kept in the payroll file. Finally, sales are recorded in the daily sales file at the end of each business day. Figure 4-3 shows the company's layout.

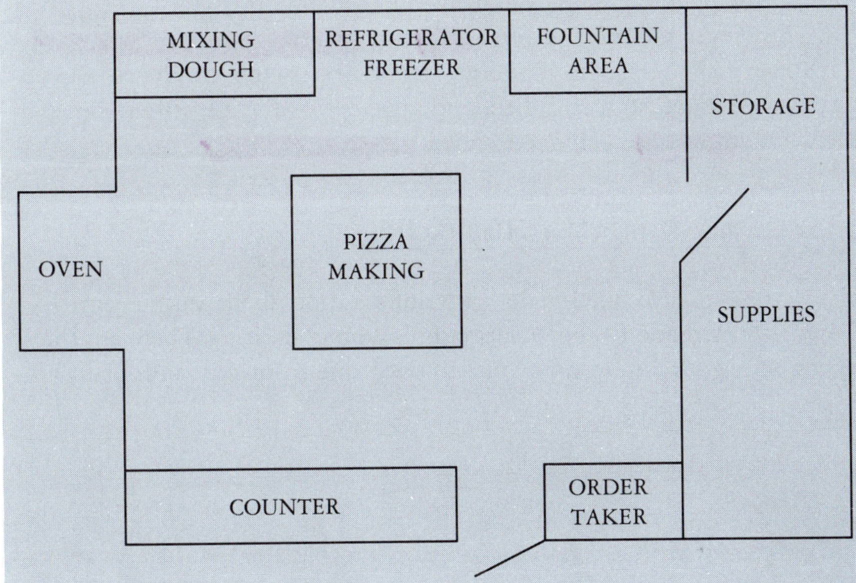

Figure 4-3 General layout of Dominion Pizza

Entities and Attributes

An entity is a conceptual representation of an object. It is something of interest to the user, about which to collect data. In our Dominion Pizza example, employees, customers, and customer orders are entities. An attribute is a property of an entity and can have only one VALUE. In Figure 4-4, an employee number is an attribute of the entity "employee"

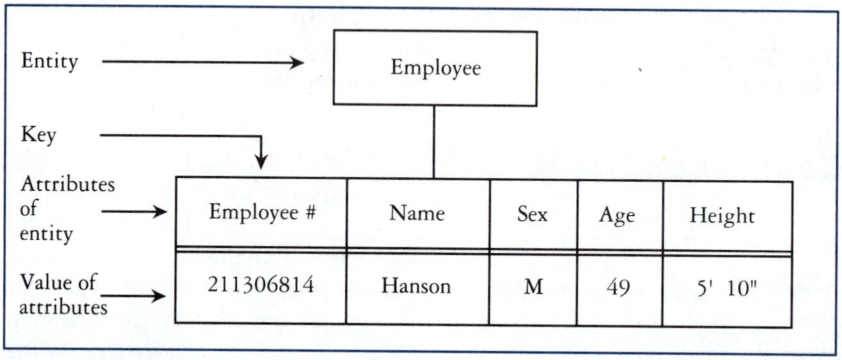

Figure 4–4 Data model showing entities, attributes, and their relationships

and 211306814 (a social security number) is the value of the attribute "employee #."

Note that the entity "employee" determines the attribute value, in this case the employee's social security number. The attribute "employee name," however, does not. But the attribute "social security number" determines both the employee name and the employee entity.

"Employee number" is also a KEY, or a unique identifier of an entity. The key 211306814 is a unique identifier of the employee named Hanson. Gender, age, and height cannot be used as identifiers because they are not unique: They are called NONKEY IDENTIFIERS.

Relationships in a Hierarchy

A data model contains not only information about various entities, but also information about relationships among entities. There are three types of data relationships: one-to-one, one-to-many, and many-to-many.

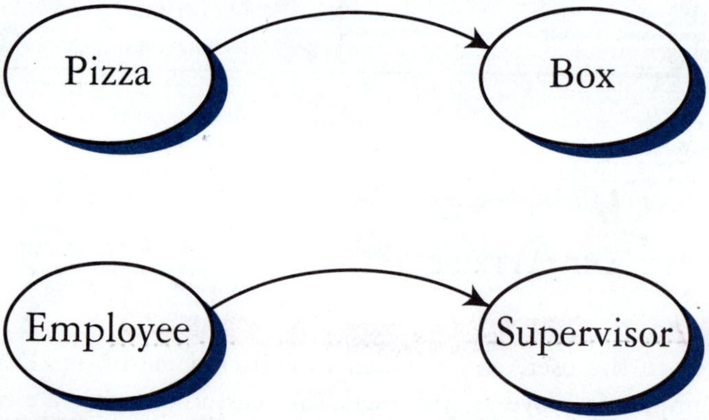

Figure 4–5 One-to-one relationships

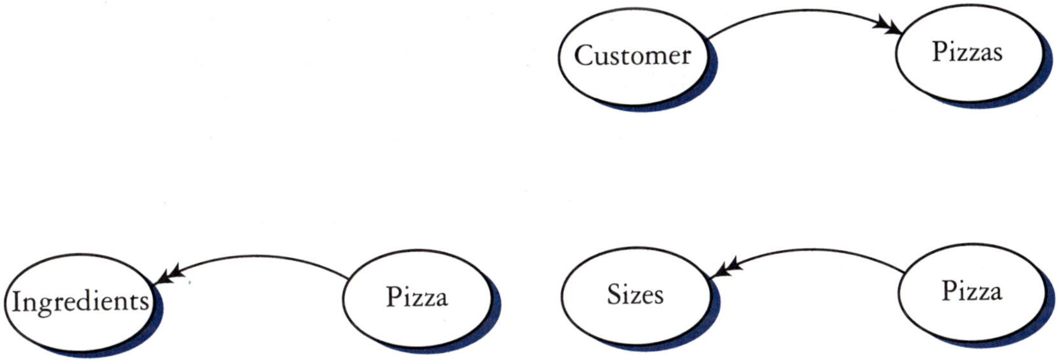

Figure 4–6 One-to-many relationships

One-to-one

A one-to-one (1:1) relationship is an association between two entities, shown in diagrams by a single-headed arrow. It means that every occurrence of a given entity is related to one and only one occurrence of another specific entity. In Figure 4-5, an employee has one and only one supervisor, and a pizza is delivered in one box. The single-headed arrows from employee to supervisor essentially mean "employee identifies supervisor." If we know the employee, we can identify the supervisor. In all one-to-one relationships, if an entity is given one value, the other entity can be easily identified.

One-to-many

A one-to-many (1:M) relationship is an association between two entities, shown by a double-headed arrow. This means every occurrence of entity A is related to many occurrences of entity B, but every occurrence of B is related to one occurrence of A. In Figure 4-6, a pizza holds many ingredients; and a customer orders many pizzas. Note that the double-headed arrow indicates the direction of the 1:M relationship.

The direction of the arrows in a diagram indicates the entity that references another entity. Sometimes an arrow between entities has arrowheads at both ends. Figure 4-7 shows the number of employees that report to a given supervisor. Another way of describing this is to say that a supervisor may have many employees, but an employee can report (at least for payroll purposes) to only one supervisor.

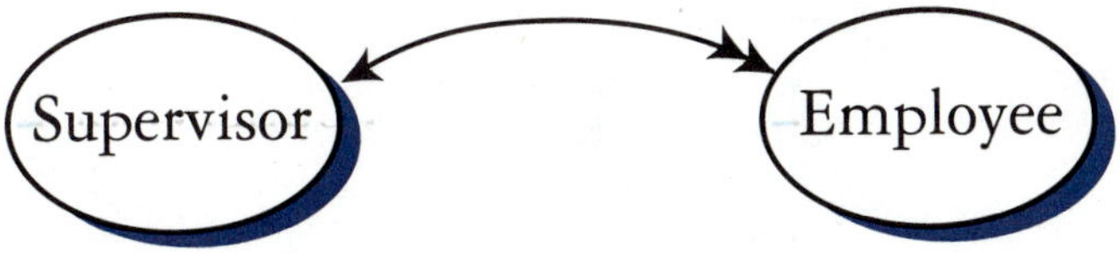

Figure 4–7 One-to-many relationship

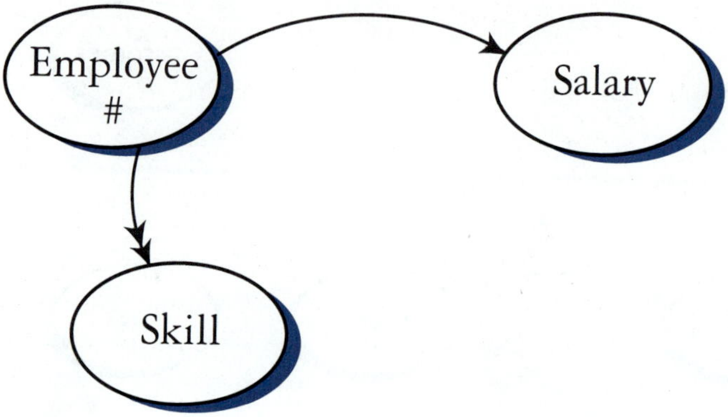

Figure 4-8 Relationships between entities and attributes

One-to-one and one-to-many relationships are also used to show associations between entities and their respective attributes or entity types. Figure 4-8 shows a one-to-one relationship between "employee number" and "salary," and a one-to-many relationship between "employee number" and "skill." In a "salary history" context, this would be a 1:M relationship. Each employee can have many skills but only one salary value.

Many-to-many

A many-to-many relationship (M:N, where N represents a number larger than one) describes entities that may have many relationships in both directions. For example, an employee may have many tools (in our Dominion Pizza example, a pizza maker uses pizza cutter, cheese grater, and other utensils) and a tool may belong to more than one employee (all cooks use the oven). (See Figure 4-9.)

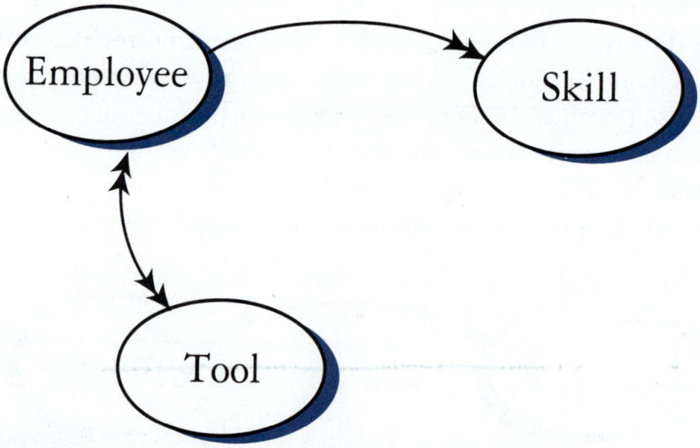

Figure 4-9 Many-to-many relationship

Bubble Charts

Entities, attributes, and their relationships form a data model which can be graphically represented by a BUBBLE CHART, or BUBBLE DIAGRAM. A bubble chart is a useful way for the database administrator to communicate representations of data structures or logical schemas to the end-user. Database designers often use complicated terminology; the simplicity of a bubble chart can make the design understandable to virtually anyone.

Bubble charts are comprised of bubbles, lines, and arrows. The oval-shaped bubbles represent entities or attributes. Lines connecting the bubbles represent relationships between entities, or between an entity and one or more attributes. Arrows indicate the nature or direction of the relationships. For example, in Figure 4-8, "salary" signifies a 1:1 relationship—an employee receives one and only one salary. The double-headed arrow pointing to "skill" indicates a 1:M relationship—an employee may have many skills.

In developing a bubble chart, designers are concerned with a representative number of data items gathered into groups called RECORDS or TUPLES. Associations between records are illustrated the same way relationships between entities are: by lines and arrows.

Figure 4-10 shows a file consisting of four records. Each record contains a set of data items. The value of each data item is also shown. Each column is a unique data item, related to a specific attribute. The name of each attribute appears at the top of the column. "Employee_#" is the primary key that uniquely identifies a record. A bubble chart of each record is shown with the general format in Figure 4-11.

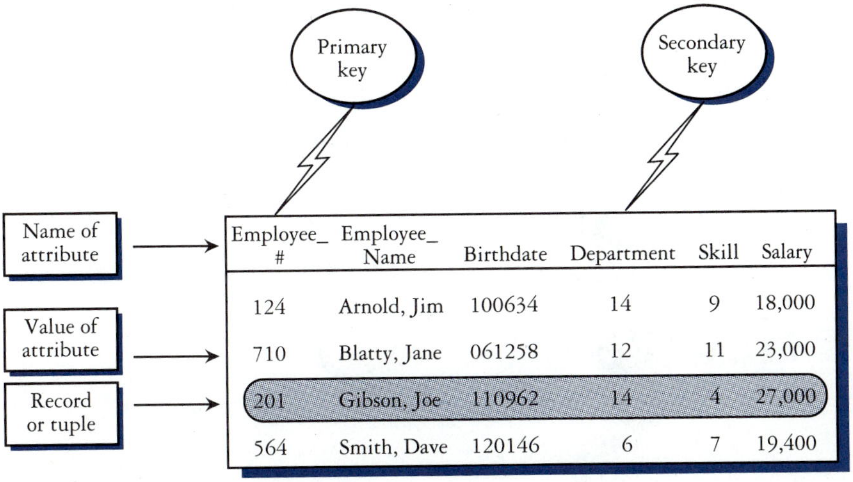

Employee_ #	Employee_ Name	Birthdate	Department	Skill	Salary
124	Arnold, Jim	100634	14	9	18,000
710	Blatty, Jane	061258	12	11	23,000
201	Gibson, Joe	110962	14	4	27,000
564	Smith, Dave	120146	6	7	19,400

***Figure* 4–10** A four-record file with six data items in each record

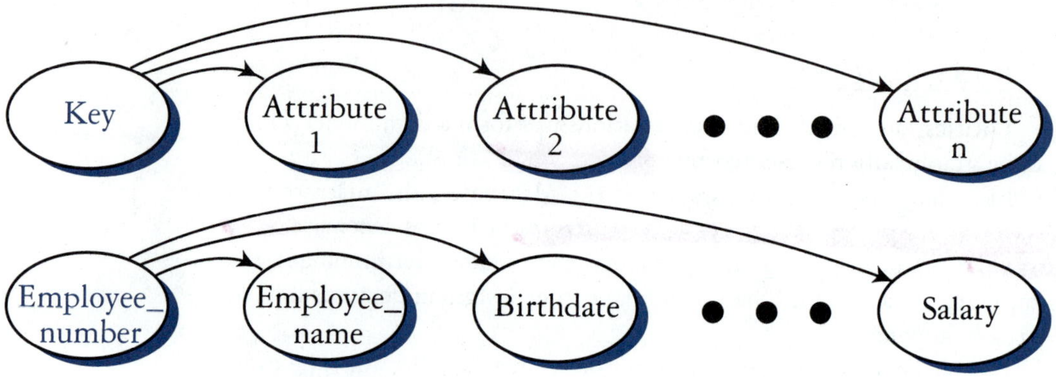

Figure 4–11 Bubble chart of a basic record format

The use of bubble charts for data representation requires that we specify three types of keys: primary, secondary, and concatenated.

Primary keys A PRIMARY KEY uniquely identifies each data element in a group of related elements. In a bubble chart, a primary key is a data item with only single-headed arrows stemming from its bubble to other bubbles in its data group. In Figure 4-11, "Employee_number" is a primary key. The item's value can be used to locate its associated attributes, such as "Employee_name" and "Birthdate."

A related key type is the ALTERNATE KEY, which is a secondary attribute that can also serve as a primary key. For example, "Employee_#" might be the key for the employee record file. If social security number is also stored, it too might be an alternate key.

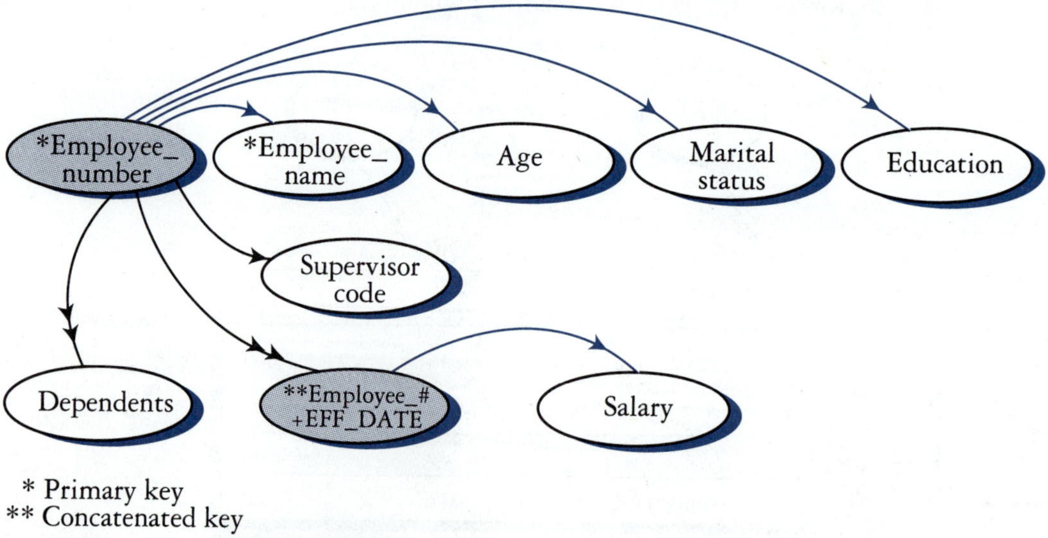

Figure 4–12 Primary and concatenated keys

Secondary keys A SECONDARY KEY is a field that is not unique but is used as an alternative search path. For example, in Figure 4-12, the employee record has a supervisor code. If the supervisor were to leave the company, management would want to know which employees reported to him or her so that continuity could be established. This means that "Supervisor_code" is a secondary employee key.

Concatenated keys Some data items cannot be located using a single data item. They need a primary key that is made up of more than one data element in combination. For example, to retrieve an employee's salary, the payroll clerk needs the employee number and effective payroll date to get to the file that has information about employee salaries and deductions. Two data elements taken together to produce a primary key form a CONCATENATED KEY.

Figure 4-12 shows a user view for an employee report. "Employee_number" is the primary key, denoted by the single-headed arrows leaving it. "Employee_#" plus "EFF_DATE" is a concatenated key. The employee "salary" is obtained through this concatenated key.

Figure 4-13 shows a personnel user's view that utilizes two secondary keys. All employees can be identified through "Department_number", which is a secondary key. "Employee_number" in the diagram is a primary key that helps identify the department where an employee works as well as other employee attributes. "Skill_Num" is another secondary key that identifies all employees with a given skill level. This information is helpful in that it makes it possible to access a record in various ways with various keys. This promotes flexibility and improves system performance.

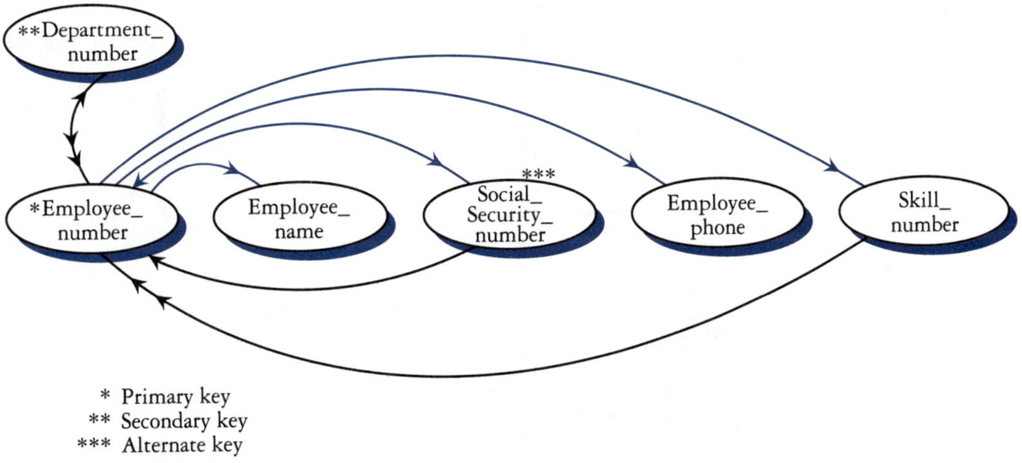

Figure 4-13 Primary and secondary keys

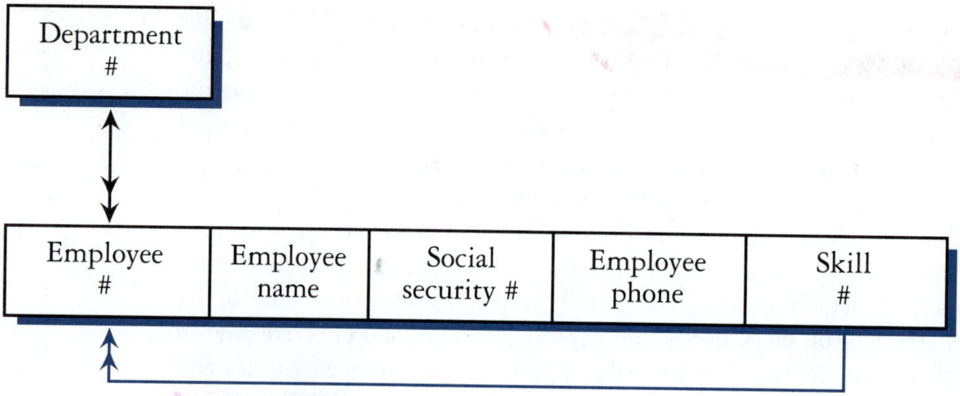

Figure 4–14 Data structure diagram representation of Figure 4-13

Data Structure Diagrams

Another common type of diagram for representing entities and relationships is the data structure diagram (DSD). The DSD is similar to the bubble chart, except that it uses boxes rather than bubbles. The DSD for Figure 4-13 is shown in Figure 4-14.

In addition to record content and format, the database design must identify record relationships. Figure 4-15 shows a DSD illustrating sample record relationships in the Dominion Pizza database. Here, the boxed line segment represents a record, and arrows represent relationships. Single- and double-headed arrows again represent 1:1 and 1:M relationships. The CODASYL approach uses DSDs to display relationships among record types in a database system.

Entity-Relationship (E-R) Diagrams

Another way of illustrating relationships among entities is the entity-relationship (E-R) diagram. The E-R diagram provides a graphic

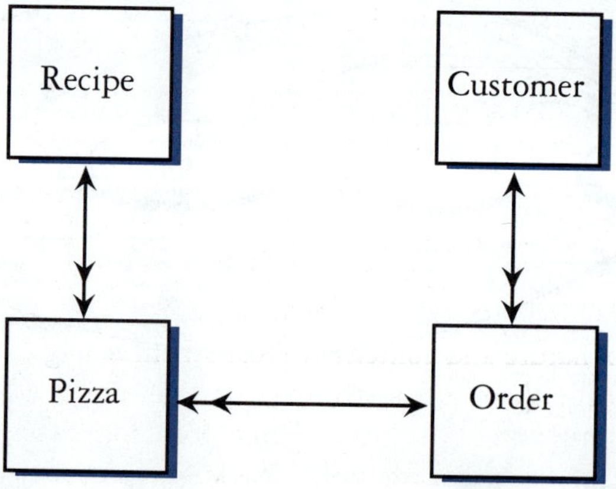

Figure 4–15 Data structure diagram of Dominion Pizza database

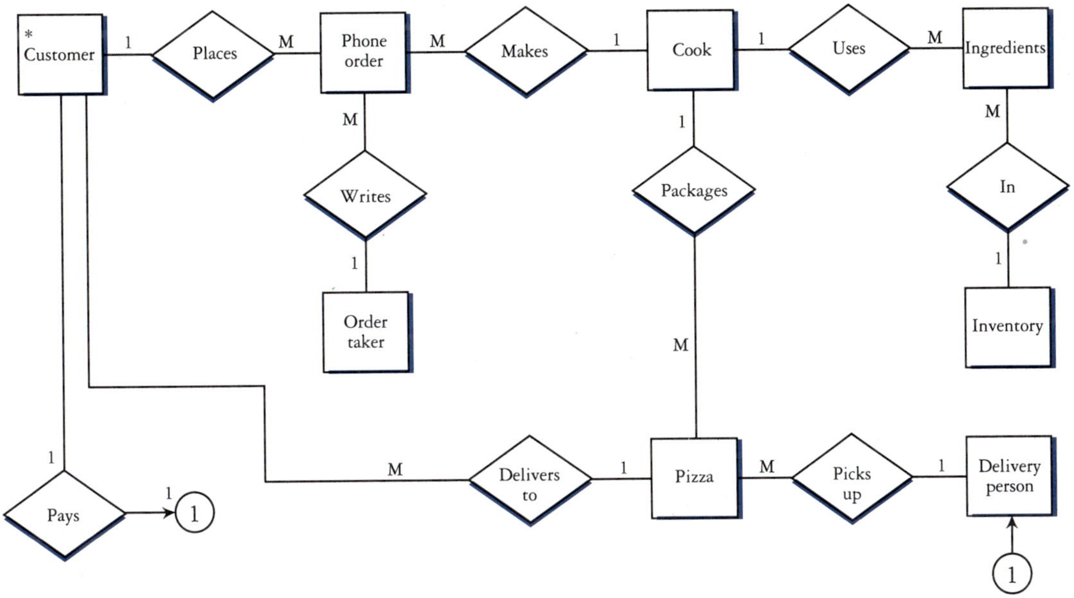

Figure 4–16 E-R diagram for Dominion Pizza

picture of the logical structure, *not* how the model should be represented internally. That is, the E-R diagram describes the conceptual and external data models, not the internal model or physical aspects. In other words, it specifies what is to be represented in the database by incorporating meanings or semantic aspects of data, such as how entities, attributes, and relationships are represented.

Figure 4-16 shows an E-R diagram describing Dominion Pizza entities and their relationships. One way of reading the diagram is as follows: The customer places an order (1:M relationship); the employee writes the order (1:M relationship); the cook prepares the order (1:M relationship); the cook packages completed the order (1:M relationship); and so on until the customer pays the delivery person (1:1 relationship). The E-R diagram can be expanded to reflect as much detail as required to provide the conceptual view of the business.

Drawing Schemas

As we mentioned in the preceding chapter, a schema is a blueprint that puts every part in place. It provides the interface with database management systems, operating system access methods, and other programs. It is DBMS-dependent. Schemas must be clearly laid out due to the complex nature and content of most schemas. Figure 4-17 shows a schema that is not clear, illustrating some of the characteristics and limitations of schemas. First, the schema does not distinguish between data items and records. For example, "NAME" is a data item in the same row as "SKILL," which is not a data item but the name of a group of data items (number and label). Second, the schema does not distinguish

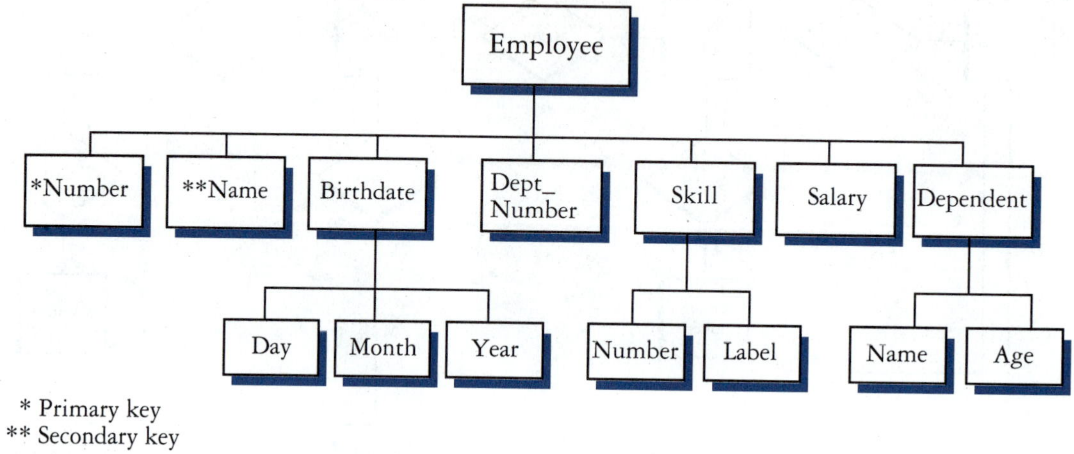

Figure 4–17 A poorly drawn schema

between an attribute and an entity. For example, "BIRTHDATE" is an attribute of "EMPLOYEE," while "DEPENDENT" is an entity. Third, there is no distinction between 1:l, 1:M, and M:N relationships. These are important facts in database design, but the schema offers no information about them.

There are several rules to remember about drawing schemas that enhance clarity and avoid confusion:

- Avoid using duplicate names.
- Specify the primary and secondary keys. Underline primary keys and draw double-arrow links from secondary keys.

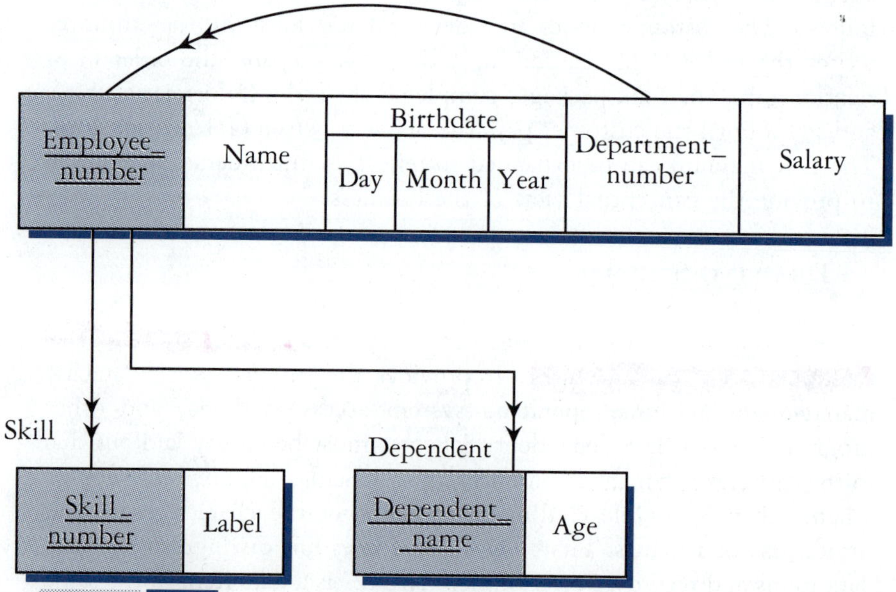

Figure 4–18 A modified schema of Figure 4-17

• Specify where data items are gathered into groups. For example, in Figure 4-18, the data items "SKILL_NUMBER" and "LABEL" are grouped under "SKILL," which shows 1:M relationship with "EMPLOYEE_NUMBER."

• Clarify the types of the relationships in the schema—that is, whether the relationship is 1:1, 1:M, or M:N—by using arrows.

• Write record names outside the box.

Figure 4-18 shows the Figure 4-17 schema redrawn according to these rules. Note the underlined primary keys and the double-arrows leading from the secondary key "DEPARTMENT" to "EMPLOYEE."

Another way to draw a schema is as a list of associations and a list of links in a bubble chart. Figure 4-19 is the modified schema in Figure 4-18 redrawn as a bubble chart, with the links represented as a list of associations. This list is useful in developing the data dictionary.

The User's View in Data Modeling

Many organizations approach database design with limited attention to the end-user. Much more attention is paid to the DBMS

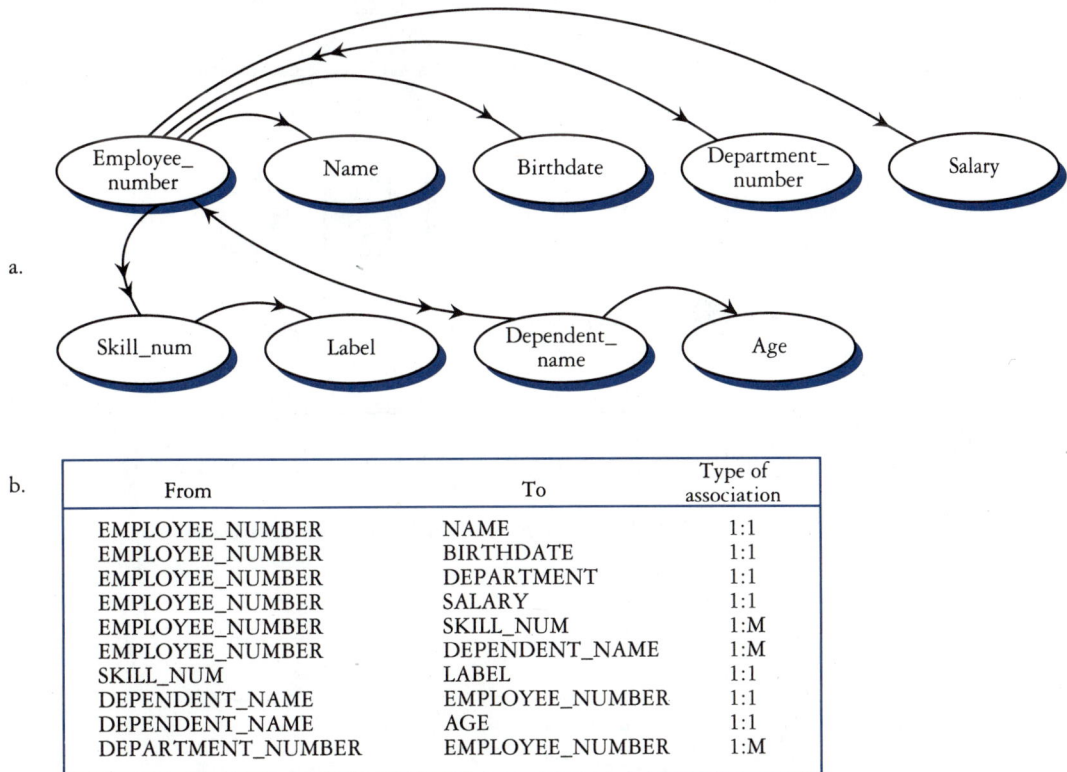

a.

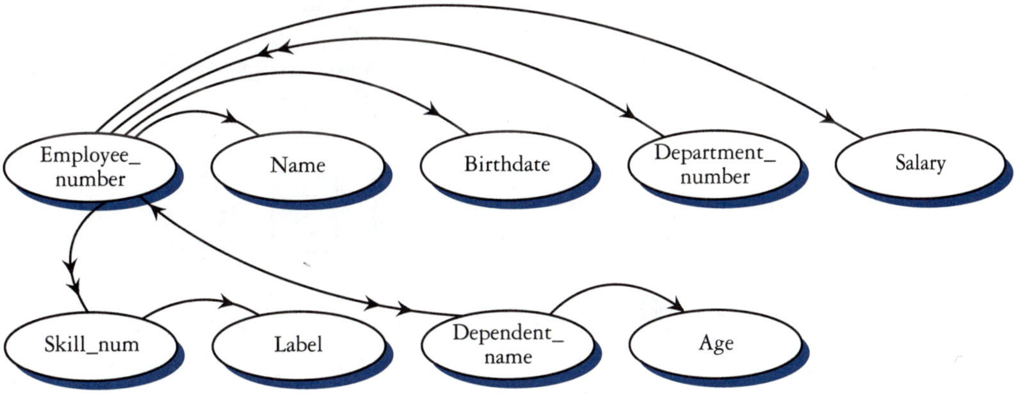

b.

From	To	Type of association
EMPLOYEE_NUMBER	NAME	1:1
EMPLOYEE_NUMBER	BIRTHDATE	1:1
EMPLOYEE_NUMBER	DEPARTMENT	1:1
EMPLOYEE_NUMBER	SALARY	1:1
EMPLOYEE_NUMBER	SKILL_NUM	1:M
EMPLOYEE_NUMBER	DEPENDENT_NAME	1:M
SKILL_NUM	LABEL	1:1
DEPENDENT_NAME	EMPLOYEE_NUMBER	1:1
DEPENDENT_NAME	AGE	1:1
DEPARTMENT_NUMBER	EMPLOYEE_NUMBER	1:M

Figure 4–19 a. Schema represented in a bubble chart
b. A list of associations based on the schema

implementation phase. Figure 4-20 depicts the areas of major concern to database designers, with an emphasis on the DBMS to be used, how it interfaces with host and query languages, and the data that is physically mapped to disk for best performance.

A user view is the logical representation of data the user needs to answer inquiries or to make decisions. A viable database system has many user views. One user may logically have many views, and many

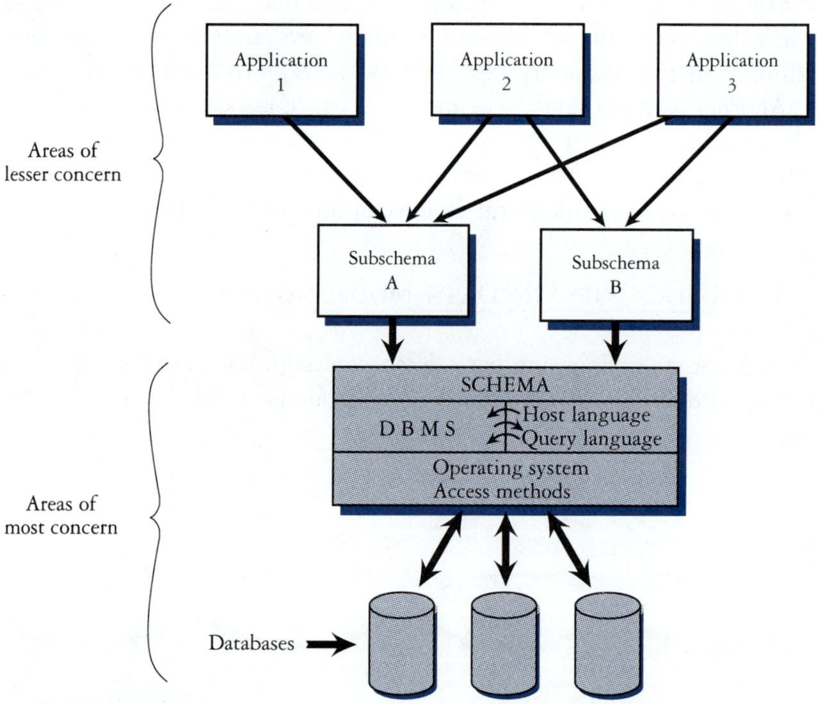

Figure 4-20 Database environment areas of major concern

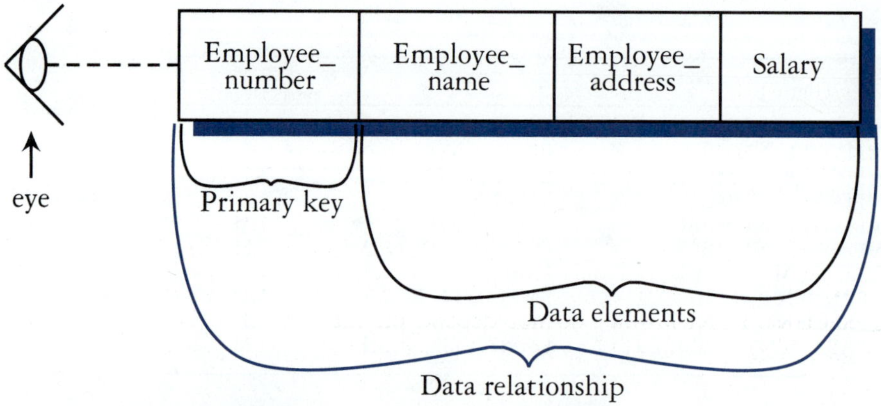

Figure 4-21 User view of data relationships

users with similar job commitments may have the same user view. The purpose of defining a user view is to specify the logical relationships among data elements and synthesize them into an overall database design methodology. In Figure 4-21, the end-user uses "EMPLOYEE_NUMBER" to access "EMPLOYEE_NAME," "EMPLOYEE_ADDRESS," and "SALARY." This group of data items may not represent all the views of the user, but it does represent all the relationships necessary for performing a specific function.

The main design concerns are user education, definition of a user view, and integrating user views into an overall design. Companies that do not properly develop user views stand to expend over 80 percent of their data processing resources on reorganizing, reconstructing, and reloading databases: a costly and needless effort.

There are several guidelines for developing user views:

1 *Draw simple, not complex, user views.* The notion of "great engineering is simple engineering" holds true. Keep user views as simple as possible.

2 *Properly specify the concatenated keys.* For example, in Figure 4-22a, salary queries cannot be answered using "effective date" alone. The user needs the combination of "EFF_DATE" and "EMPLOYEE_NUMBER" (concatenated key) to access "SALARY," as shown in Figure 4-22b.

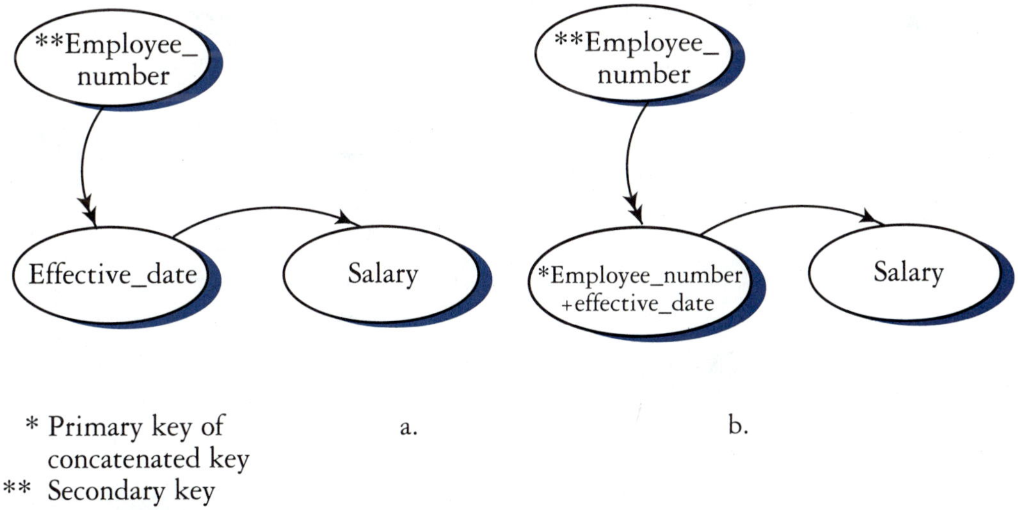

Figure 4-22 Use of a concatenated key

3 *Ensure that the attributes identified by a concatenated key are dependent on the whole key.* For example, in Figure 4-23a, "EMPLOYEE_NAME" and "SOCIAL_SECURITY_NUMBER" do not depend on the "EFF_DATE" of the concatenated key. A better way of drawing the relationship is shown in Figure 4-23b.

4 *Specify all primary keys.* In Figure 4-24a, "EMPLOYEE_NUMBER" is a hidden primary key. It should stand out, as shown in Figure 4-24b.

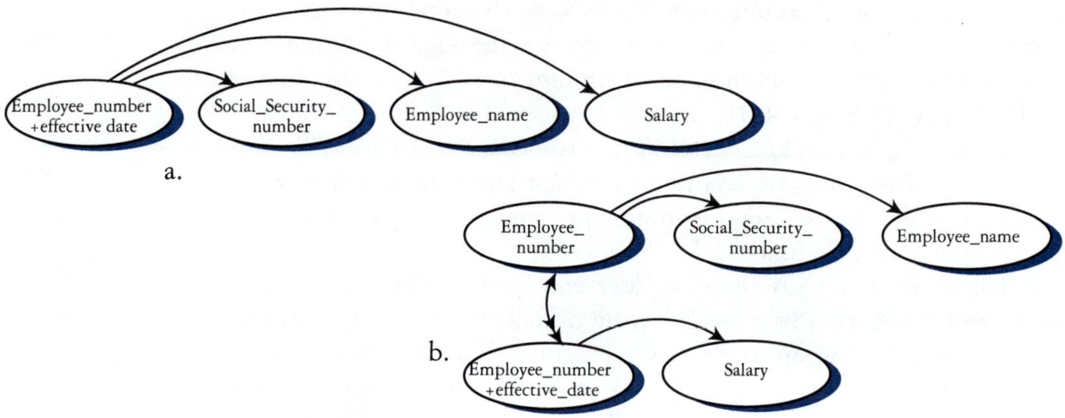

Figure 4–23 Attributes and their dependencies

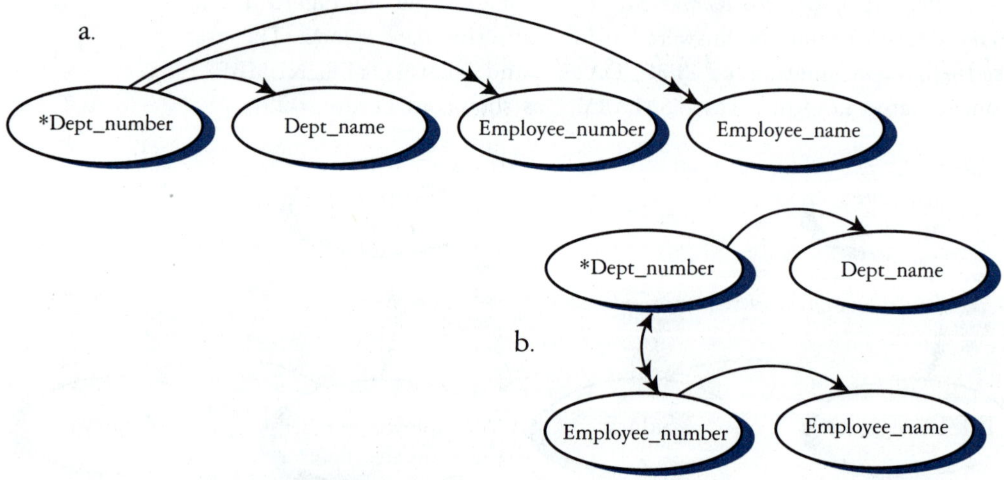

Figure 4–24 Specifying primary keys

These rules should improve the development of data structures, provide stability, and reflect the actual user view(s). Developing the user's view is critical for implementing the physical database and should be taken seriously. More on the procedure to improve the development of data structures (referred to as normalization) is covered in Chapter 8.

SUMMARY

1 Tools for data modeling include diagrams, computations, documentation, and programming. A design procedure specifies the sequence to be used in applying the tools.

2 A data model is a map of entities and their relationships. Such a map gives the logical representation of the data structure that forms a database.

3 There are three data models: conceptual, external, and internal. The conceptual data model defines all the users' database requirements into a single database description. The external data model is the user's view of the data or of a specific processing application. The internal data model shows how the data in the database is internally or physically represented in the database. The three models can be used to explain the concept of data independence, which may be logical or physical. The models allow changes to be made in one model without having to make changes in the other models.

4 An entity is a conceptual representation of an object. An attribute is a property of an entity and can have only one value.

5 There are three types of relationships between entities: one-to-one (1:M), one-to-many (1:M), and many-to-many (M:N).
   a. In a one-to-one relationship a given entity is related to one and only one occurrence of another specific entity.
   b. In a one-to-many relationship entity A is related to many occurrences of entities B but each occurrence of B is related to only one occurrence of A.
   c. In a many-to-many relationship entities have relationships in both directions.

6 Three primary tools for data modeling are the bubble chart, data structure diagram, and entity-relationship diagram.
   a. Bubble charts graphically represent entities and their relationships with bubbles, lines, and arrows. In this chart, we specify primary, secondary, and concatenated keys. Each key serves a useful purpose.
   b. Data structure diagrams are similar to bubble charts, except that they use boxes rather than oval-shaped bubbles.
   c. Entity-relationship diagrams provide a graphic picture of the logical structure, *not* how the model should be represented internally.

7 Schemas have two limitations: They do not distinguish between attributes and entities or among 1:1, 1:M, and M:N relationships. These are important facts in design, but the schema offers no such information.

8 Several rules govern drawing schemas:
   a. Avoid using duplicate names.
   b. Identify the primary and secondary keys.
   c. Specify where data items are gathered into groups.
   d. Clarify the types of relationships in the schema.
   e. Write record names outside the box.

9 The guidelines for developing user views are:

a. Draw simple, not complex, user views.
b. Properly specify the concatenated keys.
c. Ensure that the attributes identified by a concatenated key are dependent on the whole key.
d. Specify all primary keys.

KEY WORDS

Alternate key
Attributes
Bubble chart or diagram
Concatenated key
Conceptual data model (schema)
Data model
Data relationships
Data structure diagram
Entity
Entity-relationship diagram
External data model
Internal data model
Key
Logical data independence
Many-to-many relationship
Nonkey identifier
One-to-one relationship
One-to-many relationship
Physical data independence
Primary key
Records
Secondary key
Tuples
Value

REVIEW QUESTIONS

1 In your opinion, why are data models critical to database design? Explain.

2 Describe the makeup of a data model. Give an example to illustrate.

3 In what way(s) is the conceptual data model different from the internal data model? From the external data model? Explain.

4 Distinguish between the following pairs:

a. primary and concatenated key
b. one-to-many and many-to-many relationships
c. logical and physical data independence

5 What is a nonkey identifier? How does it differ from other keys? Be specific.

6 Data models are represented graphically in various ways. Elaborate on the key tools used for data modeling.

7 What is the benefit of using an E-R diagram? How similar is it to other tools used to represent data models?

8 If you were asked to describe an approach to drawing schemas, what would you say? Be specific.

9 Elaborate on the rules governing the development of user views. In your opinion, how important are these rules?

1 A large organization that does automobile repairs must keep track of its repair facilities or garages, the mechanics, and their qualifications in terms of the courses they have taken, the dates they took the courses, and the grade each earned for each course. Descriptions of these items are as follows:

- Garage: Garage's identification number and manager's name
- Mechanic: Employee number and name
- Course: Number, name, and duration (in weeks)

a. What are the entities (fields) in this situation? What are the attributes of each entity?
b. List the entities and their relationships to other entities or other attributes under 1:1, 1:M, and M:N relationships. For example, "garage" to "manager" (1:1).
c. List the field names to be used in the system. For example, "garage number" is a field name.
d. Which field names have unique values?
e. Describe this situation using an E-R diagram.

2 An automobile dealership has the following entities: owner, buyer, vehicle, sales invoice, and service stop. Develop an entity-relationship diagram to reflect this scenario. Add or invent any data items you need to complete the diagram.

3 The following case situation describes two data environments that might be candidates for a DBMS. Draw a data model for each situation.

a. An inventory system that includes information on items in inventory (item description, selling price, color, size, quantity, and storage location in the warehouse); suppliers from whom items are purchased for resale (names, addresses, and telephone numbers, items purchased, quantity of each item, and cost of each item); customers (including their names, addresses, and telephone numbers).
b. A library system that includes information on books and magazines (file reference number, titles, authors, and number of copies on hand).

4 Draw two E-R diagrams, one for each group of entities, showing entity relationships:

a. students, undergraduate students, foreign students, graduate students
b. bank customer, depositor, estate management user

5 Consider your college as a business enterprise. Identify its entities (professors and courses, for example) and draw an E-R diagram describing it.

6 Use the Island Jumpers, Inc. case presented at the end of Chapter 1 to do the following:

a. draw a data flow diagram
b. list the entities of the system
c. draw an E-R diagram
d. draw a data structure diagram

C H A P T

Database Design and the Conceptual Model

E R 5

Three Steps to Database Design

AT A GLANCE

Three Steps to Database Design

Developing a large database system using traditional methods takes months or even years. Each step of the process—identifying business requirements, general systems design, detailed design, coding and unit testing, systems testing, and user-acceptance testing—is separate and sequential. As the developer proceeds, everything will appear to be going smoothly. Then, suddenly, and long before the system is complete, the clients will invariably ask for enhancements. No matter how hard you try to anticipate requests, users always ask for additional features.

Why? With traditional systems development techniques, the data model is built during the design phase, *after* business data processing requirements have been defined. The data model supports the processing requirements adequately, since these processes were used to define the data. But the same data can support an endless list of processes or functions. When users see the data model, they see the additional information that can be derived from that data. This stimulates requests for additional processes or functions that hadn't been thought of during the requirements definition phase.

Several years ago, I came across a methodology called Extended Relational Analysis (ERA) which is an interview and analysis process that simplifies terminology, allowing both users and analysts to define the data that will produce a set of tables. The tables can then be populated with user-supplied sample data.

One benefit of using ERA methodology is that you can test the data model as you design it. Users learn the data model as you design it. Users learn the data and codes so well that when the tables are populated with sample data, users can spot inconsistencies as they appear. In addition, because ERA methods involve the users in designing the data model, they understand its logical structure, and often feel a sense of ownership of the project.

How does this collaborative effort work? First, a team of key users and systems personnel are given responsibility for the modeling effort. Each team member is taught the basic concepts of what is to take place.

The ERA interview process is led by a facilitator who is familiar with ERA methods and possesses strong data processing and group communications skills. The three-step process defines a set of tables that documents entities, logical relationships between them, and key attributes of these entities and relationships. In other words, the data model is a statement about the business that is constructed by finding all of the important nouns (entities), then the verbs (relations) that associate the nouns with each other, and finally the descriptive adjectives or adverbs (attributes) that complete the business statement.

Synoradzki, Richard L., "Three steps to database design." DBMS, *October 1989, 55ff. Reprinted with permission of* DBMS.

AT A GLANCE

Database design is human-specific, not technology-specific, since it is the user who is affected by the design. Prior to the first design step, an organization should have some type of long-range planning framework within which a database plan can be developed. The database plan should be a top-down view of an overall conceptual model, and should include identification and prioritization of major database application areas.

There are four major steps to database design: formulation of user requirements, conceptual design, logical design, and physical design. The conceptual design, also called a conceptual data model or schema, synthesizes the user's views and information requirements into a global database design, and is expressed in the form of an E-R diagram, semantic data model, or normalized relations. The logical design maps the conceptual design into structures and is where specific data elements are defined and grouped into records. Record relationships are represented by a data structure diagram. Finally, the physical design transforms the logical design into a physical structure through coding or programming.

Physical design is DBMS-dependent, emphasizing two components: the physical schema and the user views. The models used for expressing user views and database constraints focus on data definition language (DDL) and data manipulation language (DML). These languages are DBMS-specific software tools used for implementing the physical design. DDL defines the data model structure chosen for the user's database, while DML manipulates or processes the database.

By the end of this chapter, you should know

- the steps in database design;
- the makeup of user requirements;
- the difference between conceptual, logical, and physical database design;
- what a data dictionary does and where it fits into a database application; and
- the role of data definition language and data manipulation language.

Introduction

Database design is a major first step in developing a database application. The database application is the key interface between humans and machines, and must be designed with the user in mind. The trick in this phase is to match the seemingly fuzzy and qualitative nature of the user's requirements with the technology's demands for precision and accuracy.

The role of the DBMS is to implement the application programs that represent the user's requirements. The DBMS cannot judge whether the design is good or bad, that is, whether it does what the user needs. So the database designer or administrator must work with the user to understand the user's requirements and translate them into an integral design for the database.

The two steps in the design process are logical and physical design. In the logical design phase, we examine the user's requirements and develop a conceptual database structure. Then, we convert the logical design into code geared to a specific DBMS in the physical design phase. The major steps in database design are illustrated in Figure 5-1.

Master Plan

Before taking the first design step, an organization should have some type of long-range planning framework for developing information systems. This is normally a four- to five-year overview of the ultimate organization-wide database. It should specify candidate applications and provide budgets and schedules for database activities during the first year. Each succeeding year should be similarly planned to ensure continuity, consistency, and support for database development.

Using this plan, the designer assesses the functions to be supported, identifies the organization's information requirements, and synthesizes these into a database master plan. Ideally, the master plan should lay out all the database applications by level of priority or importance. Existing applications continue to operate, while new applications are developed based on the plan. One application that has a high probability of success is usually selected for initial conversion. Once that application has been accepted by the user, other applications are put in place. Eventually, a complete set of application programs will be integrated into the existing system.

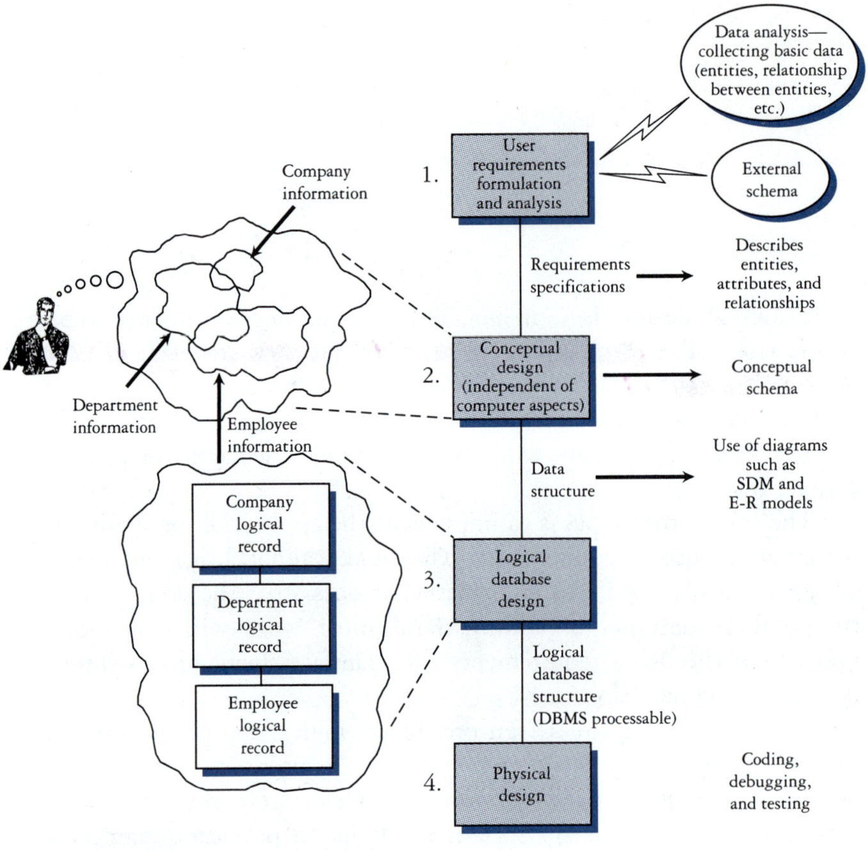

Figure 5–1 Steps in database design

Organizations with a heavy commitment to conventional file-based applications might find this approach confusing or disruptive. For example, this approach may not take into account political considerations, cost justification, and the need to ensure top management support at the outset. To forestall these problems, the designer should take the time to talk to various users in the organization and to understand their informational requirements before beginning database design.

Aggregation and Generalization

In an ongoing retail enterprise, sales are posted and merchandise is ordered, some people are hired while others resign, vendors send invoices, and customers mail payments. At some point, managers are bound to ask questions like, "How are sales compared to what they were a year ago today?" and "What was our turnover rate in bookkeeping?" The managers want answers, not details. Today's database users want a representation of the business.

A database represents a business by aggregation and generalization. Since it is impractical to represent everything, the designer must decide how much detail to incorporate in the design. Thus, the designer's next step is to create a model by aggregating or combining data into a question-answer format. But aggregating information alone tends to leave certain questions unanswered. For example, a car rental agency may total up the number of all rented cars, but in the process lose information about car make or car size.

The designer must also generalize. Generalization combines objects into one category. For example, a store may have men's, women's, and hardware departments. If management did not want to distinguish among sales in these departments, the departments could be grouped together. Like data aggregation, certain information is lost. In either case, the designer faces a dilemma. If data is not aggregated and generalized, the database could duplicate every business detail, and the cost of such detail would outweigh the benefits of the system. On the other hand, this generalized and aggregated arrangement must allow the database to answer the right questions. The designer's key objective, then, is to determine how much detail to incorporate into the design to answer the questions that the user will ask. To do that, the designer must know what the user requires.

Analyzing User Requirements

The first step in database design is to create a statement of user requirements, identifying information flows, the reports to be generated, individual data items, entities and relationships forming the conceptual data model, and performance criteria. User involvement is needed, especially during the requirements-definition step. The database designer works with each user to learn what the user expects the system to do. The designer studies the decisions users make, how they make them, the informational requirements of the business, and so forth. Specifically, the designer assesses the following:

- users' views of data
- required attributes in each view
- primary keys that identify the entities and the associations between entities
- semantic rules (rules concerning the meaning and usage of data)
- secondary requirements related to response time, security, and database integrity

Formulating user requirements is a five-step procedure:

1 Identify the scope of the proposed database.
2 Collect the data.
3 Identify user views.
4 Develop a data dictionary.
5 Specify operational requirements. (See Figure 5-2.)

Identify the Database Scope

Defining the scope, or general goals, of the project with the user can be critical and difficult. Novice users often expect database systems to do wonders. Their high expectations are often beyond the database's abilities. At least for the purpose of managing the project, the designer should set the boundaries or SCOPE of the project.

Explaining the scope of the system to the user promotes cooperation during the development of the database application. In a multiuser/multiapplication environment, each user should understand that the goal of the database system is to satisfy the needs of *all* authorized users, not just one user.

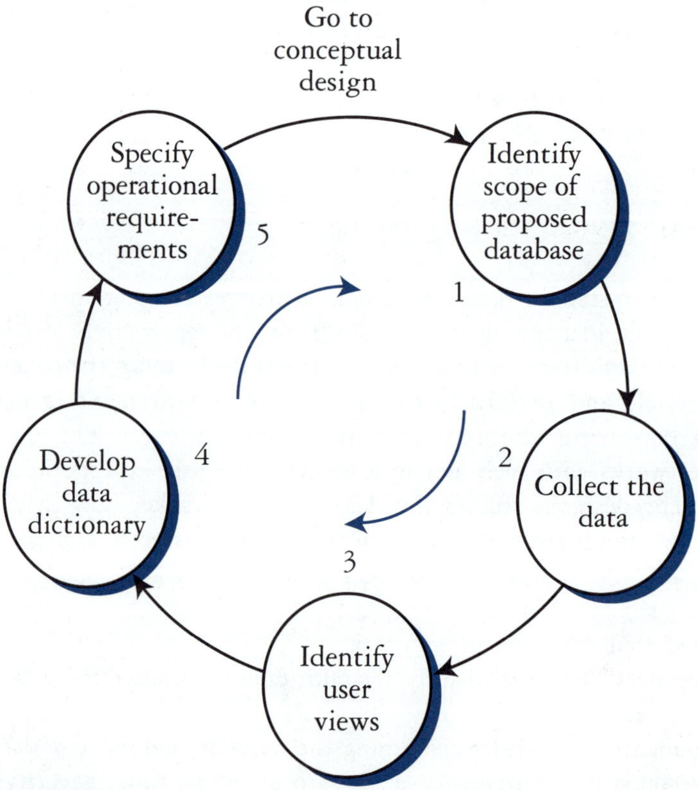

Figure 5–2 Procedure for formulation of user requirements

Collect the Data

After scoping the database project, the designer must gather the data that is relevant to the user views. Data collection tools vary from project to project and include traditional interviews, questionnaires, group discussions with management and staff, and on-site observations. Although there are no standard rules for specifying their use, tools should be chosen that best gather information accurately, methodically, under the right conditions, and with minimum interruption to the user staff. For example, when all needed information is available in existing files or manuals, intensive interviewing would be a backup measure.

The two most popular tools for collecting data about a prospective application area are interviews and questionnaires. Each tool has its own features and limitations.

Interviews The INTERVIEW is a face-to-face situation where the database designer talks to the user or users about the problem and the reasons for developing a database application. The interview has four important advantages:

1 *Verification*. Directly observing what the users say and how they say it makes verifying information easier.

2 *Flexibility*. The database designer can ask questions based on the flow of the interview.

3 *Timeliness*. The designer can elicit information about database proposals and probe sentiments that otherwise might not be uncovered in time to be of use.

4 *Cooperation*. Users, in general, enjoy being interviewed and willingly cooperate when all they have to do is talk.

The major drawback of the interview is the time it takes the designer to prepare and conduct interviews. Interviews range from the highly UNSTRUCTURED, where neither the questions nor the responses are specified in advance, to the highly STRUCTURED, where the questions and responses are fixed. Figure 5-3 cites examples. The designer must decide which approach is appropriate to a given situation.

Questionnaires The interview format is rarely uniform from one interview to the next. In situations where standard information must be gathered from a large group within a short time-frame, the QUESTIONNAIRE is a preferred tool. Because it is a self-administered tool, the questionnaire offers five advantages:

1 *Ease of use*. It requires less skill to administer a questionnaire than an interview.

2 *Efficiency*. It can be administered to a large number of individuals simultaneously.

3 *Uniformity*. Standardized wording and order of the questions and instructions ensure uniformity and consistency of response.

1. Open-ended (unstructured) questions
   a. As a prime user of the corporate computer center, how would you evaluate the changes made in the hardware during the past year?
   b. Now that you have authorized the development of a database system, in what ways do you foresee the role of your staff changing?

2. Closed (structured) questions
   a. Do you personally use a microcomputer in your business?
      _____ YES _____ NO
   b. If not, do you plan to use one in the next twelve months?
      _____ YES _____ NO

3. Closed (ranking) questions
   a. Please rank the five statements in each group on the basis of how well each describes the job mentioned on the front page. Write a "1" by the statement that best describes the job. Write a "2" by the statement that provides the next best description, and continue ranking all five statements, using a "5" for the statement that describes the job least well.
      Programmers on this job...
      _____ are busy all the time
      _____ work for clients
      _____ try out their own ideas
      _____ are paid well in comparison with other programmers
      _____ have opportunities for advancement

4. Closed (scaling) questions

   How satisfied are you with the following aspects of the application in question? (Please circle one for each question.)

	Very Dissatisfied	Dissatisfied	No Opinion	Satisfied	Very Satisfied
a. The way the existing application meets my needs	1	2	3	4	5
b. The way it has been upgraded	1	2	3	4	5
c. The speed of the response	1	2	3	4	5
d. The accuracy of the information received	1	2	3	4	5

Figure 5-3 Examples of different types of questions

4 *Anonymity*. Users often give opinions they might withhold if they feared they might be quoted.

5 *Longer response time*. When they feel less pressured to make an immediate response and have time to think questions over, users may provide more accurate responses.

The main drawbacks of a questionnaire are that users often have difficulty expressing themselves in writing; that impersonal questions may make establishing a rapport with the user difficult; and that, because of their anonymity, users may not feel accountable for sloppy responses.

Data collection approaches We may approach data collection bottom-up or top-down. In the bottom-up approach the designer begins with the existing information system and identifies the data elements used by the business. These elements become entries in the data dictionary. Each entry is a definition of the data element or a specification of its syntax.

In the top-down approach to data collection, the designer begins by identifying the prime users of the organization. This generates a list of users whose information requirements have to be identified. The top-down approach is recommended because of its emphasis on the functions that users intend to perform. In organizations where users have a hard time crystallizing their information requirements, the two approaches can be combined by starting with the existing information and tracing its flow, destination, and use.

Identify User Views

A USER VIEW, synonymous with an external data model or schema, is the summation of data required by the user to make decisions or conduct business. Existing documentation such as reports, files, forms, and the information captured from interviews are good sources for defining the user views. The user view includes all the forms, layouts, updates, reports, and menus. (The menu is viewed here as a processing control mechanism to facilitate access to the database.)

Figure 5-4a illustrates a user view: a basic sales invoice that a customer receives with each sale. Data associations are listed in Figure 5-4b. When determining user views, the designer uses a standard form to capture information about user views. (See Figure 5-4c.) The designer also considers future changes that the user might want to make and builds flexibility into the database so that new applications will not disrupt existing applications.

Develop a Data Dictionary

Once the user view is identified, each data item in the user view is described in a form similar to the one shown in Figure 5-5. This description becomes part of the data dictionary. The data dictionary elements come from the data flow diagram and other sources. Details on the relationship between the data flow diagram and the data dictionary are covered in most systems analysis and design texts.

(a)

LEGGETTS, INC.
Sales Invoice

Date 2/20/91

CUSTOMER # 74267

CUSTOMER NAME Elton Friedman

Item No.	Item Description	Salesclerk Name	Dept. Type	Price
146	Men's socks	Joe	Men's	3.50
210	Men's slacks	Fred	Men's	26.00

(b)

Data Relationships

Customer_No.	1:1	Customer_Name
Customer_Name	M:N	Item_No.
Item_No.	M:1	Item_Description, Salesclerk_Name Dept
Salesclerk_Name	M:1	Dept_Type
(Customer_No, Item_No)	M:1	Price

(c)

USER VIEW
Data Collection Form

USERVIEW_NO 15
USERNAME Sales invoice
DESCRIPTION Given to each customer with merchandise sold
END_USER
NAME Cash customers LOCATION All branches
ORGANIZATION n/a
DATA ELEMENTS

NUMBER	NAME
1	CUSTOMER_NUMBER
2	CUSTOMER_NAME
3	ITEM_NUMBER
4	ITEM_DESCRIPTION
5	SALESCLERK_NAME
6	DEPARTMENT_NUMBER
7	DEPARTMENT_TYPE
8	PRICE

Figure 5-4 a. A sample user view
b. Data associations
c. Sample user view form

When a data element is also an identifier, the name of the entity type that it identifies must also be recorded. For example, if we were to describe data element number 2 (customer number), the description of the entry it identifies would be "sales record." Automated data dictionary systems have preprinted forms on which all the necessary descriptions can be recorded. When such a system is not available, a standard form should be used by the designer every time a system is designed.

Specify Operational Requirements

In addition to these steps, the database designer must consider special operational activities of the database design. They include data security and integrity, backup and recovery, and data migration.

- *Data security* is the procedure that determines who is authorized to access, update, or retrieve data from the database.
- *Data integrity* has to do with the editing rules that ensure data consistency, accuracy, and reliability.
- *Data backup and recovery* specify the range of acceptability for a backup and ensure that the database can be recovered in the event of hardware failure.
- *Data migration* relates to how long data must be stored in memory and how quickly it should be transferred to secondary storage (for example, a hard disk) for future reference.

DATA ELEMENT

DATA ELEMENT_NUMBER 2

NAME Customer name

SYNONYMS CUSNAME

SOURCE Sales record IDENTIFIES n/a

SPECIFICATION:

TYPE Alphanumeric LENGTH 35 characters

CLASSIFICATION Sensitive

USAGE:

FREQUENCY Daily

MODIFY AUTHORITY Sales manager

Figure 5-5 Data item description

The user requirements specifications are translated into a conceptual design model or a conceptual schema. As explained in Chapter 4, a conceptual model is a global, high-level view independent of the computer hardware. The conceptual design describes the entities, attributes, and relationships needed to carry out the functions the user wants to perform. The tools used to describe the conceptual design include the entity-relationship (E-R) diagram, and the semantic data model. A data structure diagram (often referred to as a Bachman diagram) is similar to the E-R diagram, except that the relationship between entities in a data structure diagram is expressed by lines and arrows. (See Figure 5-6.) The semantic data diagram (SDM) describes the meaning of each entity, as illustrated later in the chapter.

The upshot of all this is that we need to rely on charts to show what the system will look like and the way user requirements are represented. This is all necessary before we begin logical database design.

Semantic Data Models (SDM)

As the name implies, the SEMANTIC DATA MODEL (SDM) is another way of classifying data. It is a conceptual modeling tool that uses words rather than graphic symbols. In addition, it is a definitional model with descriptive clauses about entities. Figure 5-7 illustrates the descriptive clauses of the SDM: pizza, soft drinks, employees, and order records. It also includes "value class" which identifies certain values for data items and specifies constraints. The semantic nature of SDM makes it most suitable for logical database design.

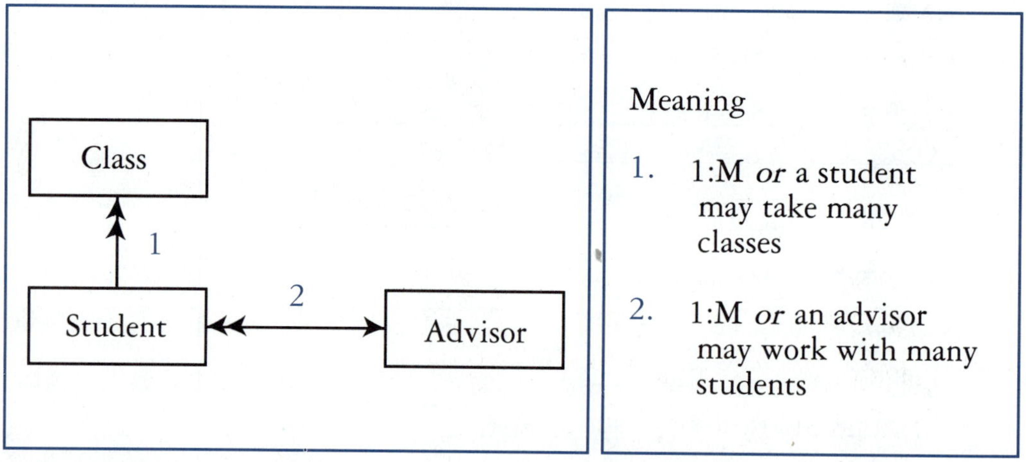

Figure 5-6 Partial data structure diagram showing 1:M relationships between class and student and between advisor and student

Semantic Data Model (SDM)

PIZZA
Description: The date prepared, type, and size of a pizza.
Member attributes:
Date
value class: DATES
Type
value class: TOPPINGS
Size
value class: SIZES
Class attributes:
Total_produced
Description: This attribute contains the sum of pizza sold by Dominion
value class: LARGE
SMALL

SOFT_DRINKS
Description: The date sold and type of soft drink
Member attributes:
Date
value class: DATES
Type
value class: BRANDS
Class attributes:
Total_sold
Description.:This attribute contains the sum of drinks sold by Dominion
value class: BOTTLES

EMPLOYEES
Description: The names of Dominion's delivery people
Member attributes:
Name
description: A unique name
value class: PEOPLES_NAMES
mandatory
Delivery_time
description: Average delivery time
value class: TIME_DELIVERED

ORDERS
Description: The pizzas and soft drinks ordered from a given delivery person.

Member attributes:
Customer
value class: CUSTOMERS
mandatory
Pizza
value class: PIZZA
mandatory
Soft_drinks
value class: BRANDS
Delivery_person
value class: PEOPLES_NAMES
mandatory
Date
value class: DATES
Time
value class: TIME_ORDERED
Size
value class: SIZES
Number
value class: NUMBER
identifiers:
Customer + Date + Time

Figure 5–7 Semantic data model of Dominion Pizza

Logical Design

Logical design is a refinement of the design provided by the conceptual design. It makes it possible to generate the physical schema, subschema, and, later, the physical database.

Design Specifications

A major documentation tool for describing logical design is the data dictionary (DD). The DD is an automated means for defining entities, attributes, and relationships during conceptual design. In logical design development, it can be used to define records and the programs that access the records.

The main step in logical design is to cluster the entities in the conceptual design into records in a logical database. Further analysis determines the attributes associated with each entity, since these attributes will be record keys in the logical database.

After mapping the entities into records, the designer reviews the records to make sure they meet the security requirements of the specific DBMS. (Some DBMSs provide security at the record level, others at the file level, and so forth.) At this time, the designer may also specify the basic approach for accessing the records (adding, deleting, or updating) in the form of a generalized data entry screen.

Case Scenario 5-1:

Dominion Pizza

To illustrate the steps in logical database design, let us return to the case of Dominion Pizza. Remember that orders are phoned in by customers. Pizza is prepared at the shop and delivered free to customers. Delivery is guaranteed within 30 minutes of the receipt of the order.

Supply and ingredient levels are monitored and reordered at specific reorder points. Information concerning the supplies (for example, pizza boxes, napkins, cups, straws, and lids) and the ingredients (for example, pizza dough, sauce, toppings, and soft drinks) are kept in two separate files. Eight employees operate the shop: two pizza makers, three assistants, two delivery persons, and a manager. Except for the manager, who is salaried, employees are paid on an hourly basis. This information is kept in the payroll file. Finally, sales are recorded at the end of each business day. Sales information is kept in the daily sales file.

Incorporation of Detail

The first question a database designer would ask is "How much detail do we need to incorporate into the design in order to answer the questions that the user will ask?" Since it is impractical to represent everything, the designer for Dominion Pizza might decide to measure sales receipts, disbursements, and the number of pizzas and soft drinks produced. But such a model of revenues, expenses, and production units is highly aggregated and generalized. The designer's first practical step should be to improve on the initial model by keeping detailed accounts of the ingredients (pizza dough, sauce, cheese, sausage), records of the phone orders, and the number of soft drink orders filled. The designer could also keep track of the number of pizzas made and soft drinks by size. Such a model is less aggregated and less generalized, and offers more information.

The designer could enhance the model a step further by identifying the various assets and liabilities of the pizza enterprise: the pizza ovens, the dough mixer, the pans, the meat slicer, and the delivery van. The process of reducing aggregation and generalization can go on and on.

Next the designer must decide how much of this information should be represented in the database. This depends largely on the owner's requirements. The statement "all I want is to know how much money I am making" is not detailed enough. The designer needs a set of specific requirements for designing the database system. In addition to the user requirements, the designer must cost-justify the database installation. Economic feasibility must be considered before design, because the business must be able to justify its investment: hardware, workstations, the possibility of networking, operation, and maintenance of the database.

Makeup of the Model

Every customer order constitutes a transaction. Every time a pizza or a soft drink is sold, it will be entered as a sales transaction. Each sale reduces the number of pizzas or soft drinks available for sale and increases the amount of cash in the cash register. Depending on the computer system, entering sales transactions could also be a signal for reordering ingredients for future sale.

Day-to-day business events are reported as transactions that cause data in the database to be modified. The database designer must identify which transactions affect the database and how each transaction should be modeled. Table 5-1 summarizes the key transactions and the data involved. The transactions add, delete, or access data.

An important consideration in designing a database is planning for exceptions. For example, how would Dominion Pizza meet a surge of phone orders following a football game or during parents' day weekend? One way of meeting the demand is to go to the local supermarket and purchase the ingredients. But the supermarket sausage or pepperoni may not taste the same. Dominion Pizza cannot very well go to a competitor and expect support, either. A procedure that provides data for meeting emergencies, then, is extremely important in database design. This means that an arrangement must be made with a reliable vendor who will provide the ingredients on short notice. In many cases, the order and level of urgency are transmitted directly from the customer's computer to the vendor's computer.

Transaction	*Prime Data Affected*
Sell pizza	• Increase cash in cash register • Reduce pizza ingredients • Increase number of pizzas in oven • Generate "buy-ingredients" transactions
Sell soft drinks	• Increase cash in cash register • Reduce number of soft drinks in stock • Generate "buy-soft-drinks" transactions
Purchase ingredients (or supplies)	• Reduce cash in cash register • Increase ingredients (or supplies) on order • Adjust production rate
Receive ingredients (or supplies)	• Increase ingredients (or supplies) • Generate "sell incentive" (through advertising or discounts)
Pay employees	• Reduce cash in cash register

Table 5–1 Partial list of transactions and data for Dominion Pizza

The database design must also consider the different views of the users. Users view data differently, depending on their background, activities, and the nature of the decisions they make. For example, to the owner of Dominion Pizza, "sales" means revenue generated by the number of pizzas and soft drinks sold. The delivery person views sales as the number of pizzas multiplied by a 3-percent commission. Pizza makers look at sales as a measure of their productivity: they get a 10-percent bonus on all pizzas over the first 60 units made.

Differences in meanings and perceptions pose a problem for the database designer. The designer's best approach is to standardize meanings or build a data dictionary that controls the aliases or synonyms used by different users so that words may be properly interpreted.

Defining Records

The database designer now reviews the various diagrams or charts created to analyze the user requirements and then decides which records must be established and what their relationships are. Figure 5-8 shows a data flow diagram (DFD) describing the flow of data, the processes, and the files of Dominion Pizza. Data flow is represented by a line and arrow; a process is represented by a circle; a source or destination is represented by a square; and a file is represented by an open rectangle.

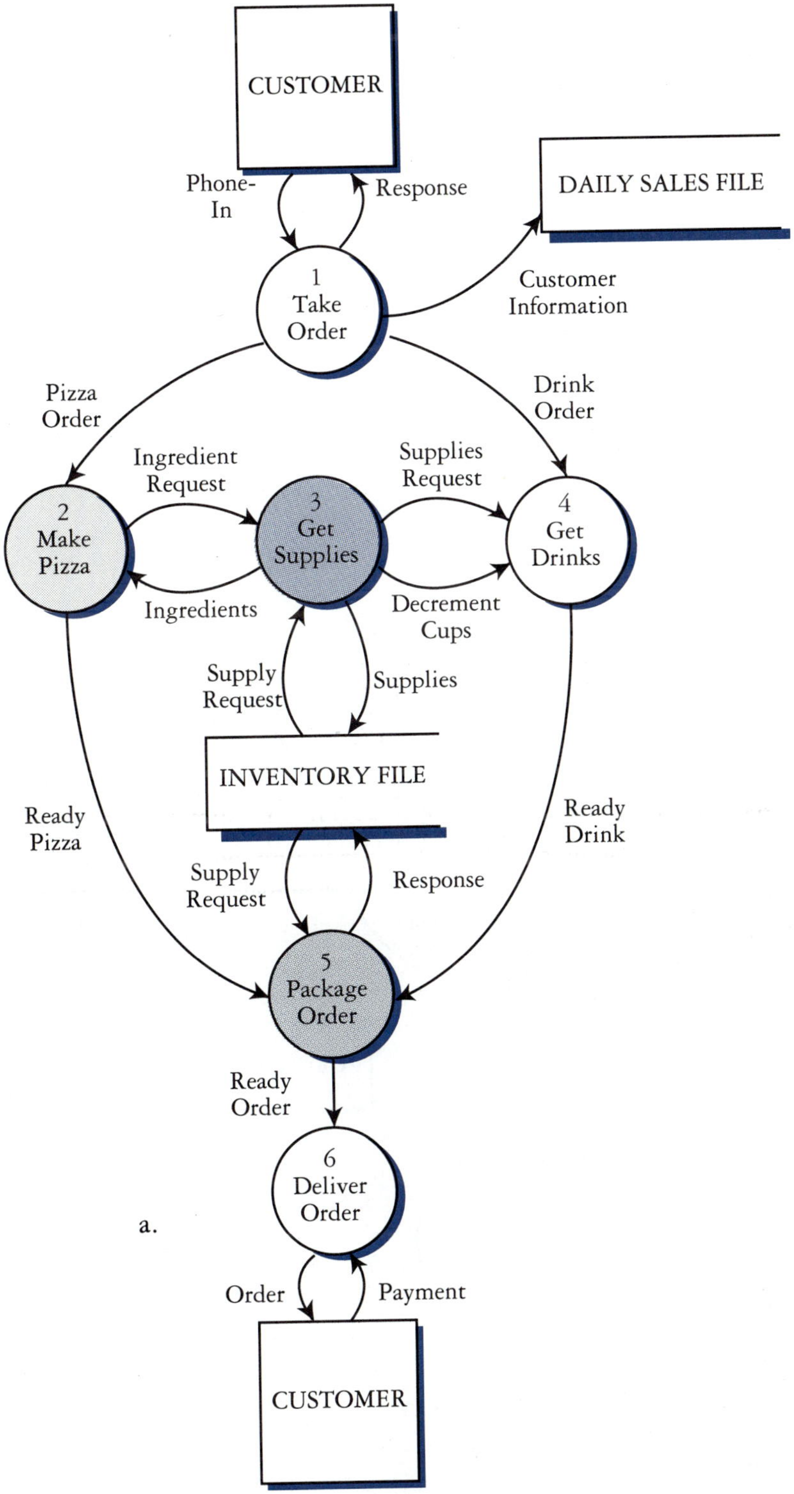

Figure 5–8 Data flow diagram for Dominion Pizza

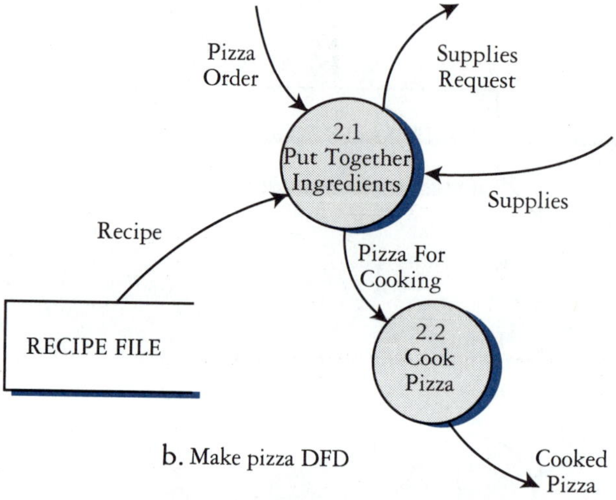

b. Make pizza DFD

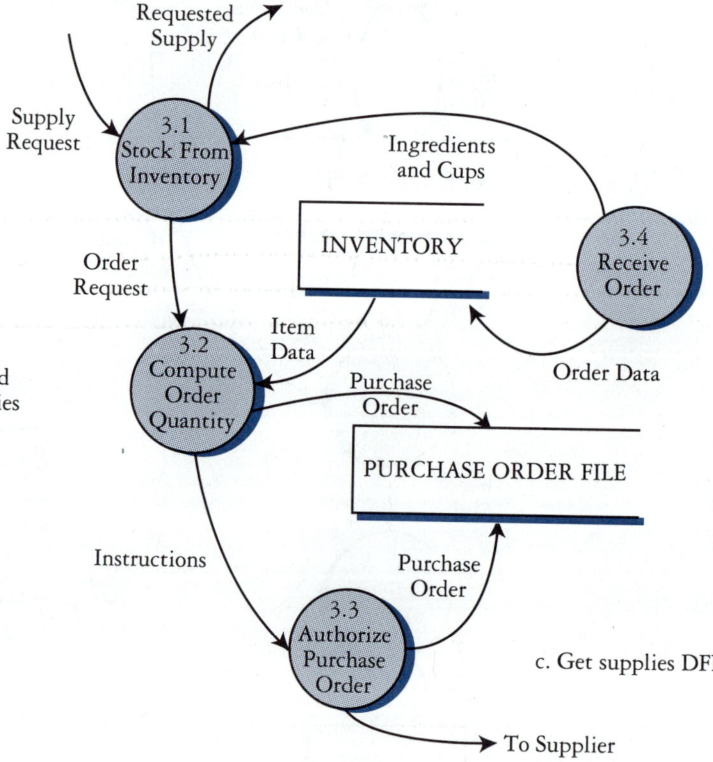

c. Get supplies DFD

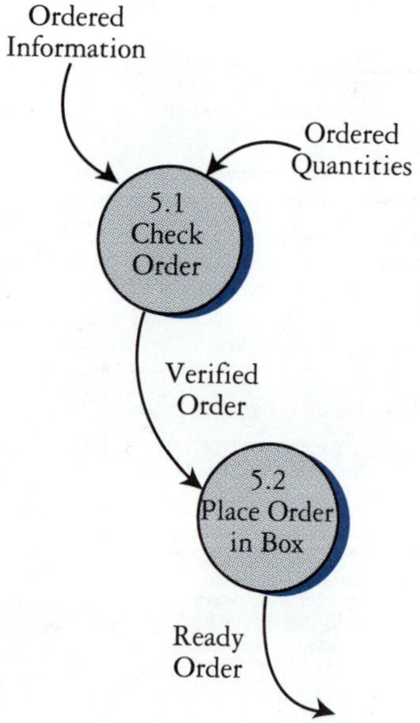

d. Package Order DFD

Figure 5–8 continued

In our DFD, there are four files:

1 inventory file
2 daily sales file
3 recipe file
4 purchase order file

In reviewing the DFD, the database designer considers a number of issues. For example, are there any files that can be merged into one file? Should recipes be separated from supplies? Answers to these and other questions help crystallize user requirements.

After defining the records, the designer must model how the user sees the relationships among records. Possible relationships for Dominion Pizza's records are illustrated in the entity-relationship diagram in Figure 5-9a. Note the relationship between "recipe" and "customer." How necessary is it to establish such a relationship? If the owner wants to know what pizza topping the customer ordered (recipe), then establishing such a relationship will answer the question. The designer can also establish a M:N (many-to-many) relationship between "ingredient" and "order" that describes which customers ordered pizza with specific toppings. Each "ingredient" made by the recipe has a relationship to all orders and their respective customers.

Figure 5-9b shows another E-R diagram describing Dominion Pizza entities and their relationships. Note that the E-R diagram can be expanded to reflect as much detail as required to provide a conceptual view of the firm. Also, the representation changes between Figure 5-9a to Figure 5-9b. The latter diagram elaborates on the nature of the relationship between entities by using the diamond symbol and expands on the total sets of record relationships in the diagram.

Next, the conceptual design must be reviewed against user requirements. One approach to design review is the structured walkthrough. A STRUCTURED WALKTHROUGH is an interchange of ideas among peers who review the conceptual design presented by the designer and who agree on the validity of the design. This step helps the designer anticipate as many design problems as possible before heading into logical and physical design. It is less costly to make changes now than in the implementation phase. The walkthrough helps ensure a maintainable design that is flexible, adaptable, and meets the user's requirements.

Logical Design

Logical design is a detailed review of transactions, reports, screens, and other proposed components to identify the kinds of data to be maintained in the database. Because this is done with user requirements in mind, this step is *DBMS-independent*. Later on the user's view becomes a basis for specifying the DBMS requirements to implement the external view. In physical design, the developer also decides on the organization of the database on hard disk and defines the physical structures of the DBMS.

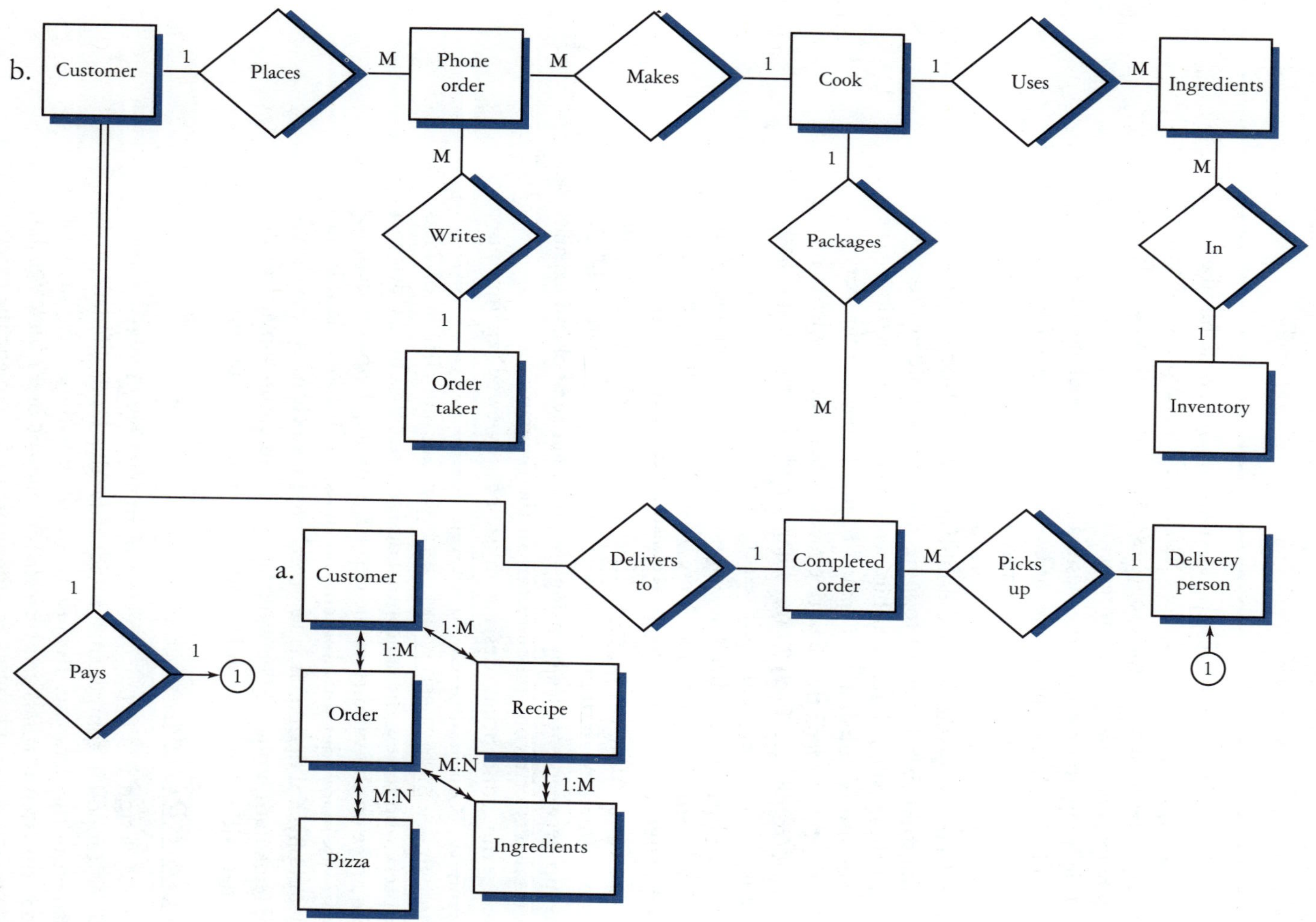

Figure 5–9 Record relationships

Record contents are designed around record fields and their sequence. In the Dominion Pizza example, the designer determines the data about orders and customers, and records about employees. Table 5-2 illustrates the description of the fields for "customer order," and "employee" records.

Field	*Description*
CUSTOMER Record	
Customer_name	alphabetic, 30 characters
Customer_address	alphanumeric, 35 characters
Customer_phone	numeric, 8 digits
ORDER Record	
Order_number	numeric, 5 digits
Customer_name	alphabetic, 30 characters
Order_date	Format: MMDDYY
Time	Format: HHMM
Number of pizzas	numeric, 2 digits
Number of soft drinks	numeric, 2 digits
EMPLOYEE Record	
Employee_name	alphabetic, 30 characters
Employee_address	alphanumeric, 35 characters
Employee_phone	numeric, 7 digits
Date_of_birth	Format: MMDDYY
Employment_date	Format: MMDDYY
Bonus	numeric, 3 digits

Table 5–2 Contents of customer and order records

In addition to specifying logical records and their contents, the database developer specifies various fields and their constraints. For example, MM (month) in "order_date" must not exceed a value of 12, and "customer_phone" must not exceed ten digits. Other constraints limit certain values between data fields within a record. For example, Dominion Pizza pays a bonus of between 5 and 6 percent to employees who have been with the business since 1985. Newer employees receive a 4-percent bonus. A constraint in this case can be represented as follows:

```
IF YY in Employment_date is less than 86
   THEN BONUS must be 5 to 6 percent
   ELSE BONUS must be 4 percent
```

Data structure diagram In addition to record contents and format, the logical database design must identify record relationships. The data structure diagram in Figure 5-10 illustrates sample record relationships in a Dominion Pizza database.

Data dictionary Another tool for expressing relationships in logical design is the data dictionary (DD). As mentioned earlier, the DD contains descriptions of all data flows, input screens, and input details

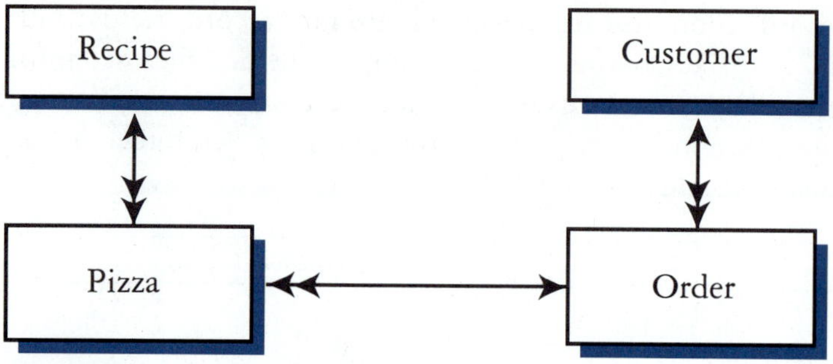

Figure 5-10 Data struction diagram for Dominion Pizza

that relate to the proposed database. A major task in designing a DD is identifying synonyms and aliases to ensure a standard usage. A *synonym* is two or more names used for the same data item. For example, what one Dominion pizza employee calls a "topping" another may call an "ingredient." Ideally, all synonyms should be eliminated and standard names agreed upon by all users. More often, synonyms are recorded as ALIASES or alternate names.

The database design must ensure that the synonyms have the same usage. For example, the data item "bonus" might be a bonus for exceeding a minimum pizza sale, a Christmas bonus, or special payment for exceptional performance. The meaning of the term must be precisely defined in the design.

In summary, the outputs of the logical schema consist of the records to be maintained, their contents, and relationships. On the input side, user requirements must be expressed in forms such as the data flow diagram and must be documented in the data dictionary.

PHYSICAL DESIGN

Physical design follows logical design and is the detailed specification of the database structure. These specifications are compiled by the DBMS. The object format is stored within the database for processing. With this view, we refer to the logical design as DBMS-independent, and physical design as DBMS-dependent (see Figure 5-11).

Physical Schema

The two components of physical database design are the physical schema and the user views. The PHYSICAL SCHEMA defines the physical specifications of the conceptual design. This includes defining the names and formats of records and their fields, laying out the formats of record relationships, identifying the constraints, and specifying the keys of the database records. Once completed, the physical schema becomes available, with the DBMS, for implementation.

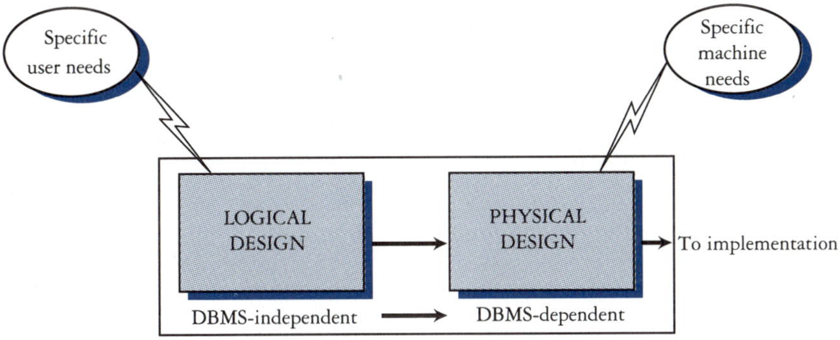

Figure 5-11 Database design–the major steps

User Views and Database Constraints

The user views are defined in the physical design so as to identify authorized users and the portions of the database that they can view. In Dominion Pizza's case, the owner might view sales and revenue data, while the staff might view customer and supplies data only. Each user view may contain information about the names and formats of records and their fields. All synonyms or aliases are also identified.

The process used in designing the physical database should be compatible with the DBMS in residence. In Chapter 9, we discuss physical design for a particular relational DBMS in detail. The important point to consider now is that physical design follows logical design for database implementation.

Models used for expressing user views and database constraints focus on two major DBMS components: Data definition language (DDL) and data manipulation language (DML); both are DBMS-specific software tools used to implement the physical design.

Data Definition Language (DDL)

DDL is a special language that defines the form and structure of the data in the database. It describes the whole logical database. It does not include references to physical organizations or physical media and devices. DDL is executed by a database administrator or a database designer as the system goes into implementation.

An example of one DDL is shown in Figure 5-12. The statements specify the name, physical size, and structure of the files for the database. The system, then, initializes the availability of records in the file. The DDL defines "social security" and "select fields" and their attributes. Once the data is physically allocated and the fields are defined, the database is ready for use.

```
CREATE FILE WORKCOMP
PARAMETER ASIZE+690, BRESERVE-251
PARAMETER BSIZE-72, CSIZE-294
END
OPEN WORKCOMP
INITIALIZE
•
•
•
OPEN WORKCOMP
DEFINE SOC.SEC.NO (KEY, BINARY) NAME (KEY)
DEFINE DIV (KEY, FEW-VALUED) SEX (KEY, CODED)
```

Figure 5-12 Sample of data definition language

Data Manipulation Language (DML)

DML is a set of database access commands in a programming language. The commands are used to access databases through programs written in a high-level language such as COBOL or FORTRAN. So, while DDL defines the data model structure chosen for the users' database, DML commands manipulate or process the database. An example of DML is shown in Figure 5-13.

The DML example uses a procedural language to define the data to be operated on and the steps to be taken. In contrast, a nonprocedural DML simply specifies the desired data without telling the DBMS how to access

```
FIND FIRST WORKCOMP
IF WORKCOMP FOUND
  THEN DOWHILE WORKCOMP LAST
    IF PREMIUM LESS THAN 40
      THEN PRINT ID-NUMBER
    END-IF
    FIND NEXT WORKCOMP
  ELSE PRINT "NOT QUALIFIED"
END-IF
```

Figure 5-13 Sample of data manipulation language

it. A nonprocedural DML for the example in Figure 5-13 would look like this:

```
SELECT WORKCOMP_NAME
FROM WORKCOMP FILE
WHERE PREMIUM LESS THAN 40
```


User Requirements Review

User requirements are the blueprints for designing and building database applications. When the requirements are current and clearly defined, an application can be successfully developed. When they are not, problems will manifest throughout the process. Designers should regularly review the user's requirements and have the user agree on the type of information, format, and completeness of the information desired.

The requirements documentation contains:

- graphic tools as illustrated in Chapter 4;
- a description or illustration of what the system is expected to produce (for example, output reports, forms, and menus); and
- a prototype of the reports, forms, or menus that are required. (Prototypes are useful when the user has trouble visualizing the system from the narratives of the report.)

When the user's review of the requirements document points out deficiencies, the developer might resort to further interviews or discussions. The designer then repeats the review process until all parties are in agreement about the content and goal of the application.

Cooperation, compromise, and trust between the user and the developer are important to database application development. Sometimes trust comes with experience, which means that a first-time user might have suspicions about dealing with a new developer. The graphic approach to design can help the user understand what the system will do and establish a rapport with the developer.

SUMMARY

1 Database design is a turning point in building database applications. There are two major concepts in design: logical and physical. Logical design produces a conceptual database structure which is then converted to physical design—the actual coding that allows the DBMS to do its work.

2 Database design should be done within the framework of a master plan and include four key steps:

a. *Analyze user requirements*: scope the project, collect data, identify user views, develop a data dictionary, and specify operational requirements.
b. *Develop the conceptual model*.
c. *Logical design*: a DBMS-independent refinement of the design provided by the conceptual model.
d. *Physical design*.

3 Conceptual design is a global high-level design independent of the computer hardware. It describes the entities, attributes, and relationships that carry out the business of the organization. Among the tools used to organize the conceptual schema are data structure diagrams and the semantic data model.

4 The first step in logical design is to cluster the entities in the conceptual model into records in a logical database. After mapping entities into records, the designer reviews the records to make sure they meet the security requirements of the specific DBMS.

5 The data dictionary is an important documentation tool in database work. It contains descriptions of all data flows, input screens, and input details that relate to the proposed database application. It also identifies synonyms and aliases to ensure standard usage.

6 In physical design, the user's view is the basis for specifying the requirements of DBMS to implement the external view. The developer also decides on the organization of the database on hard disk and defines the physical structures to the DBMS.

7 Models for expressing user views and database constraints focus on data definition language (DDL) and data manipulation language (DML). DDL describes the whole logical database and is executed by a developer or the database administrator as the system goes into implementation. DML processes the database by defining the data to be operated on and the steps to be taken.

KEY WORDS

Alias
Aggregation and generalization
Data migration
Interview
Logical design
Physical schema
Questionnaire
Scope

Semantic data model	Synonym
Structured interview	Unstructured interview
Structured walkthrough	User view

REVIEW QUESTIONS

1 Write a short essay explaining the steps in database design. Make sure you relate this phase to the life cycle of database application development.

2 What are the prerequisites to database design? Why are they considered prerequisites?

3 Distinguish between:
   a. aggregation and generalization
   b. DBMS-dependent and DBMS-independent
   c. conceptual schema and physical schema
   d. DDL and DML

4 When analyzing user requirements, what assessments does the designer need to make? Why? Be specific.

5 Discuss the procedure followed in formulating user requirements. How important is this phase in database design?

6 What is involved in scoping a database application? Why is it important?

7 Data collection involves the use of interviews and questionnaires. Under what conditions would a designer choose one over the other?

8 Illustrate the difference between a structured and an unstructured interview. How would a designer decide when to use one type of question over another?

9 Why must a data dictionary be part of the database design effort?

10 What is the difference between data security and data integrity? How do they relate to data backup and recovery?

11 How would a designer express conceptual design? Illustrate.

12 How useful is a data flow diagram to database design?

13 Explain the difference between entity-relationship (E-R) diagrams and data structure diagrams. When would you use one over the other? Why?

14 Physical design consists of the physical schema and the user's views. How do the two components relate to design? Explain.

15 When are semantic data models used in database design?

1 Draw a data flow diagram representing the registration system of your school.

2 Consider the user view—a grade report—shown in Figure 5-14. List the logical steps used to create the grade report.

McIntire School
GRADE REPORT
Fall Term 1991

Student_ID: 5726
Student_Name: Al Case **Major:** MIS

Course_Num	Course_Name	Inst_Name	Course_ Location	Grade
COM 425	Database	Edwards	M110	A
COM 427	Sys. Analysis	Stillman	M130	B

Data Relationships

Student_ID <<---------------> Student_name, major
Student_ID <<------------->> Course_Num
Student_ID <<---------------> Grade
Course_Num <<---------------> Course_Name, Inst_Name, Course_Location
Instructor_Name <<----------> Course_Location

Figure 5-14 Grade report

3 Consider the customer order form in Figure 5-15. Develop a data structure diagram for the form.

4 Use the details presented in the Island Jumpers, Inc. case scenario to do the following:

a. identify the scope of the proposed database
b. identify user views
c. specify operational requirements
d. draw a data structure diagram

ORDER FORM

ORDER_NUM	:	6100
CUS_NUM	:	0121
CUS_NAME	:	A.B. JONES
CUS_ADDRESS	:	123 HAPPY LANE
CITY	:	ARLINGTON
STATE	:	VA
ZIP	:	02156

PROD_NUM	PROD_NAME	QUANTITY	UNIT PRICE
A61	Tire	4	69
C29	Battery	1	47

CUS_NUM ←——→→ ORDER_NUM
PROD_NUM ←——→→ PROD_NAME

Figure 5-15 Customer order form

C H A P T

Models for Representing Relationships

E R 6

DBMS: Next Wave Could Be an Easier Ride

AT A GLANCE

DBMS: Next Wave Could Be an Easier Ride

From the hierarchical structure in the 1960s, to the network model in the 1970s, to the relational model in the 1980s, database management system developments have yielded benefits for users—but not without a price.

During the 1970s, users invested in systems such as Cullinet Software, Inc.'s IDMS, whereas before the DBMS of choice had been IBM's IMS. When relational products were introduced in the 1980s, their technology departed completely from the two earlier models.

Because the technology involved in the hierarchical and network models could not be extended to this new relational model, users lost the investment they had made in time as well as technology. Given this history, it would be perfectly understandable if users were apprehensive that a shift toward object-oriented DBMSs might jeopardize the future of their investments in relational technology.

In this case, however, most users can get the gain without the pain—with a little forethought and selectivity.

Object orientation does not have to be a replacement for relational DBMS. As its name implies, it is an orientation rather than a full-blown DBMS model. As such, it can blend with and build on the relational schema. There are no strict rules preventing a relational database management systems vendor from enhancing its product to become an object-oriented DBMS; in fact, many of them are now doing just that.

So, instead of a full-fledged rebuild of the kind that accompanied the evolution to RDBMSs (relational DBMSs), at least this time there will be the option of choosing a smooth and natural glide to the next plateau.

Of course, that assumes object orientation has something real to offer—something that warrants a second look for those who have made the transition or are considering the transition to an RDBMS. In other words, why bother?

First of all, object-oriented DBMSs integrate a variety of real-world data types—such as business procedures and policies, graphics, pictures, voice, and annotated text. Although these data types need to be managed in today's business world, current relational products are not equipped to handle them efficiently. Data types in RDBMSs are more commonly record-oriented and expressed in numbers and text.

Object orientation also makes a contribution to application development efficiency. It makes the data functions, attributes, and relationships an integral part of the objects, just as human attributes are a part of the DNA molecule. In this way, objects can be reused and replicated.

Since the object-oriented approach views and treats not only the data but also the role of the data (see story below), you can query the data on its functions, attributes, and relationships. By contrast, most RDBMSs demand that the knowledge associated with the data be written into and maintained separately in each application program.

Assuming that those features sound enticing, the real trick to making sure you don't buy more change than you want is recognizing that object orientation is basically going to be available in two forms: one for those who need and want a radical change, and one for those who want some of its advantages without going through a major conversion.

From the Vine

What's an illustration of an object-oriented DBMS object? Think of the Fruit of the Loom television commercials.

Remember the person inside the stem of grapes? Like any grape, he has functions in a lunch box or a punch bowl; he also has color variations between his skin and his stem and multiple relationships to other fruits.

The difference in this grape's case is that you can query him about any of these functions, attributes, or relationships, and he will answer all your questions. You can also give him additional information, such as the recipe for how to make himself into a fine wine, and he will be capable of holding onto the recipe and even acting on it. That is called *encapsulation*.

Inheritance gives the object-oriented DBMS user an ability that even the Fruit of the Loom® grape lacks. With an object-oriented DBMS, the user can replicate the grape with all its functions, attributes, and relationships intact. Therefore, the grape can be reused under different circumstances and modified as necessary. Since many objects are almost the same except for slight variations, inheritance enables the DBMS developer to replicate the characteristics of one object to form another.

For example, many of the qualities of a grape would be passed down to any of the juice that is made from it. A new object, "grape juice," could therefore be developed by simply adding the new information.

"Multiple inheritance" extends the concept further so that a new object could be created by combining the characteristics of multiple "parents"—as in the case of "grape soda."

Rybeck, Ted, "DBMS: Next wave could be an easier ride." Computerworld, *March 5, 1990, 67ff. Reprinted with permission from* DBMS.

AT A GLANCE

There are three DBMS implementation models: hierarchical, network, and relational. The hierarchical, or tree, model is based on the rule that an entity can have only one owning entity. A file with hierarchical model relationships among records is a hierarchical file. Data breaks down into hierarchical formats, where one data category becomes a subset of another. The hierarchical model's similarity to data structure in programming languages such as COBOL makes it easy for many programmers to understand. It is an efficient model when data relationships follow a nested 1:M pattern.

There are several ways of representing record relationships with a hierarchical model, including listing, link-listing records, and creating an inverted file using a secondary key. Pointers play an important role in file structure.

Network models are classified as simple or complex. An absence of lines with double-headed arrows in both directions joining records makes a schema a simple network model. The presence of such lines makes it a complex network model. The reason for distinguishing between simple and complex network models is that a complex network needs elaborate methods for physical representation. A network can also be decomposed into hierarchies to simplify all the relationships to 1:M relationships.

Relational models represent all data and relationships in a flat, two-dimensional table (rows and columns) called a relation. Unlike hierarchical or network models where all relationships are predefined, a relational model develops new relations on user commands.

Which model is best in a given situation depends largely on the application and the DBMS in residence. The hierarchical model supports a large number of enterprises on the mainframe. A relational model is easy to use and supplies a high level of data independence.

By the end of this chapter, you should be able to

- distinguish among hierarchical, network, and relational models;
- demonstrate how to represent a hierarchical model in a list and a linked-list format;
- understand how pointers are used to establish logical sequence of records;
- explain how an inverted file works;
- describe the types of network models;
- see how a complex network model is decomposed in trees; and
- understand the concept of the relational model.

Introduction

Virtually all DBMS packages use direct files because of their versatility. Yet, to provide the services required by end-users, specialized data structures are built into DBMS packages. Understanding data structure is an important background for database designers, database administrators, and system programmers when they are confronted with evaluating DBMS packages.

There are three DBMS implementation models: tree structures, network structures, and relational structures. The tree, or hierarchical, model is easy to conceptualize, which means that a schema for a database can be easily understood. But since this structure allows only a parent-child association between records, it cannot adequately represent the semantics among entities that have M:N associations. Showing M:N relationships requires a network model. Finally, the relational model is simpler than the hierarchical and network models, and for this reason is widely used.

Tree Structure

The first widely used DBMS for business applications was IBM's Information Management System (IMS). IMS was based on the hierarchical data model. Compared to today's standards, early versions of IMS were crude and slow. Today's IMS, although unfairly overshadowed in some business areas by the relational data model, is a powerful and highly sophisticated DBMS running on the mini- and mainframe computer.

Hierarchy is a common word for a superior-subordinate relationship in business, the military, and society in general. Conceptually, a hierarchy is represented by a tree that has been turned upside down. A TREE is a hierarchy of nodes or records. A database model is hierarchical when its data structure is a hierarchy or a tree. A NODE is a record in a hierarchical data structure. It contains one or more fields or data items that represent attributes that describe an entity. A tree can describe one entity or many entities.

In hierarchical database models, an entity can have only one owning entity, or higher-level entity to which it reports. The owning entity is called the PARENT; the owned entity, the CHILD. A parent with no owners is a ROOT. A tree may have only one root, but any number of root occurrences. Nodes that have the same parent are called SIBLINGS.

For example, in a family tree, the parent is the owning entity level and the children are the owned entities. Figure 6-1 illustrates a tree structure drawn upside down with the root on top and branches pointing downward. The highest level (level 1) has one node, the root. Every other node is related to only one node at a level higher than itself. A parent can have many children (1:M), whereas a child can have only one parent. As a parent, node 2 has three children (5, 6, 7). Node 3 has two children (8, 9), and node 4 has four children (10-13). Nodes at the end of the branches are called LEAVES. They have no children.

The shaded area connecting nodes 1, 2, and 6 is an example of a PATH. A MAXIMAL PATH originates at the root and picks up one branch of the tree all the way to the leaf. The path concept is important in designing hierarchical and network database models, because it helps us determine how records are accessed.

The HEIGHT of the tree is the number of levels it contains. In Figure 6-1, the tree has a height of 4. The MOMENT is the number of nodes. In Figure 6-1, the MOMENT is 20.

Balanced and Unbalanced Trees

A BALANCED TREE has the same number of branches in each node. The branching capacity of the tree begins with the root and works its way down from left to right in each row. Deviations from this result in an UNBALANCED TREE. (See Figure 6-2.)

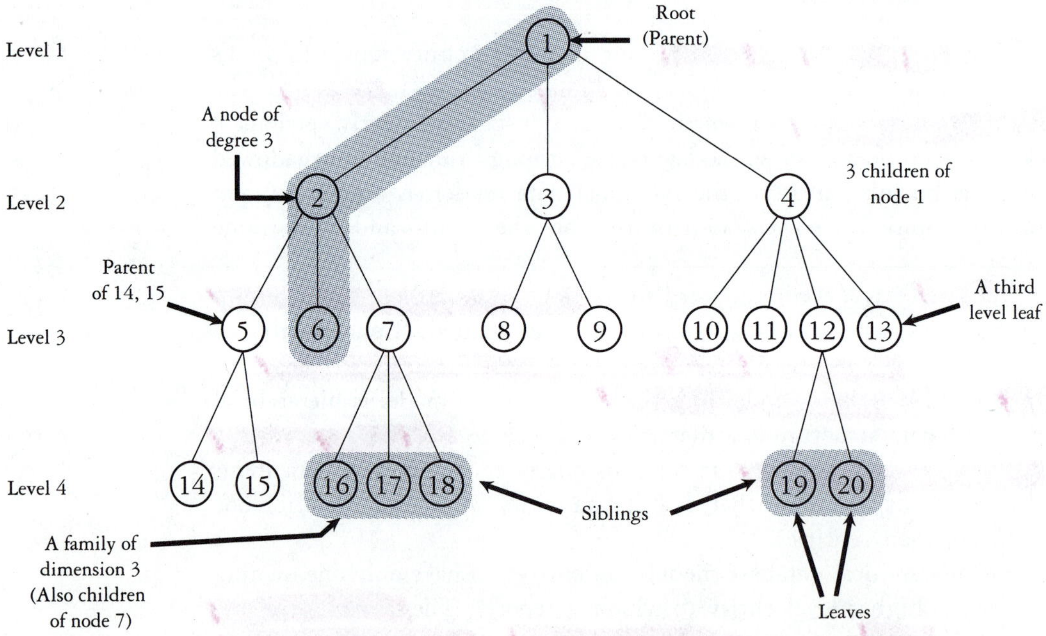

Figure 6–1 Tree structure: root, parent (s), children, and levels

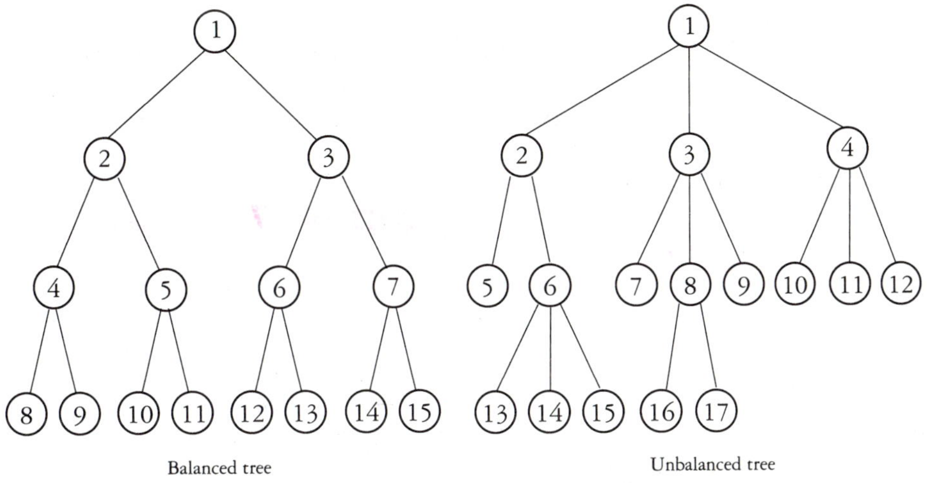

Figure 6–2 Balanced and unbalanced trees

It is often easier to implement a physical data structure with a balanced than with an unbalanced tree. Search procedures also fit well with a balanced tree.

Hierarchical Files

A file with a tree-structure relationship among its records is a HIERARCHICAL FILE. In a hierarchical file, data breaks down into hierarchical formats, where one data category becomes a subset of another. For example, a used-car dealer may stock cars of different makes, such as Chevy, Ford, and Toyota. Each car make comes in many styles: coupe, four-door, and station wagon, for example. Furthermore, each car is classified by year of manufacture. This information can be organized into a hierarchical model, as shown in Figure 6-3.

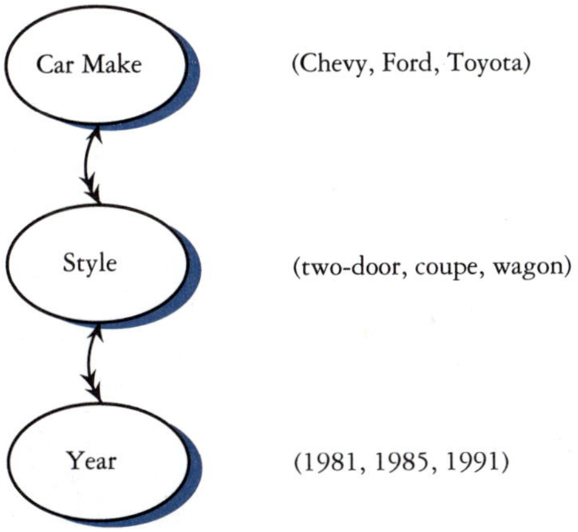

Figure 6–3 Hierarchical model showing automobiles by make, model, and year

The hierarchical model is useful in database management because its similarity to data structures in programming languages such as COBOL makes it easy for many programmers to understand. It is an efficient model when data relationships follow a nested 1:M pattern.

The hierarchical structure allows the user to query the system for information such as what Ford wagons are available, and what was a good year for Toyota wagons. Hierarchical files are easy to access and maintain.

Record Relationships

There are three ways to represent record relationships within a hierarchical model: as a list, as a linked list, and as an inverted list.

List record representation To represent a hierarchical model in a list, we simply decompose the tree. One way to do this is to start with the root and work downward along the extreme left branches of the tree, listing each node on the way. When we get to the bottom, we continue up the next level to the bottom of that level, and so on until we have scanned the rightmost level of branches. This procedure is called PREORDER TRAVERSAL. Preorder traversal is commonly done when a backup copy of a database is desired.

To illustrate, the lines in the tree structure in Figure 6-4 represent hierarchical pointers that link parent to child and nodes in some orderly fashion. The shaded area denotes the first list (ABDIJ). The remaining sequential levels are EKLM, F, CGNO, and H.

Pointers In a disk storage environment, records are not necessarily stored in sequential order. As a result, there has to be a way of tagging

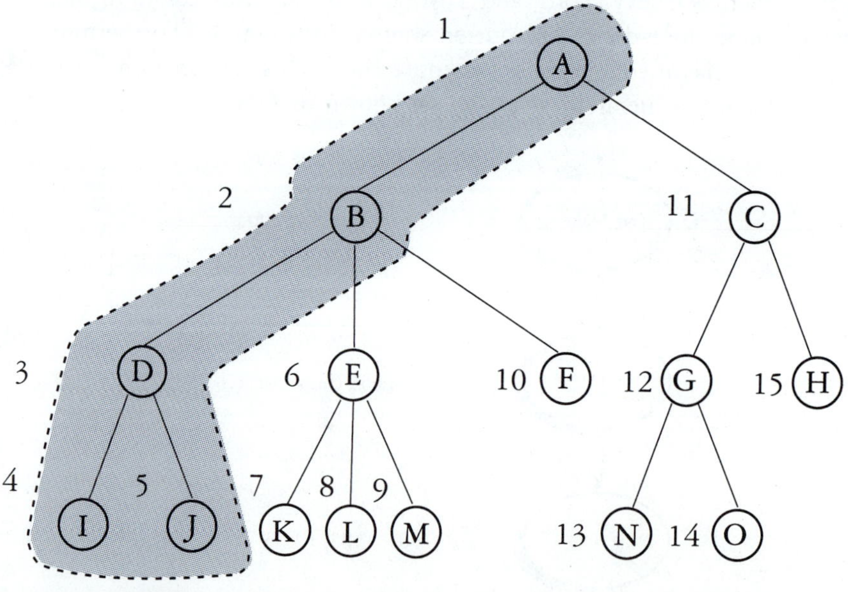

Figure 6–4 Tree structure showing preorder traversal

children to their respective parents. This is done through the use of pointers. A POINTER is used to establish the logical sequence of records and is a field in a record that holds the address of the next record in sequence.

There are two types of pointers: physical and relative. These pointers are part of the way physical and logical records are organized. PHYSICAL RECORDS are etched electronically on designated sectors of the hard disk during the formatting process. They are fixed in size and are separated by evenly spaced interrecord gaps. (See Figure 6-5.) The operating system's file manager generates LOGICAL RECORDS by allowing the user to create a file that is either fixed-sized (relative file) or variable-sized (sequential file). A PHYSICAL POINTER points to the absolute location of the next record in the chain of records by specifying the cylinder, track, and position of that record on the hard disk. A RELATIVE POINTER specifies the relative position of the next record within the file.

a.

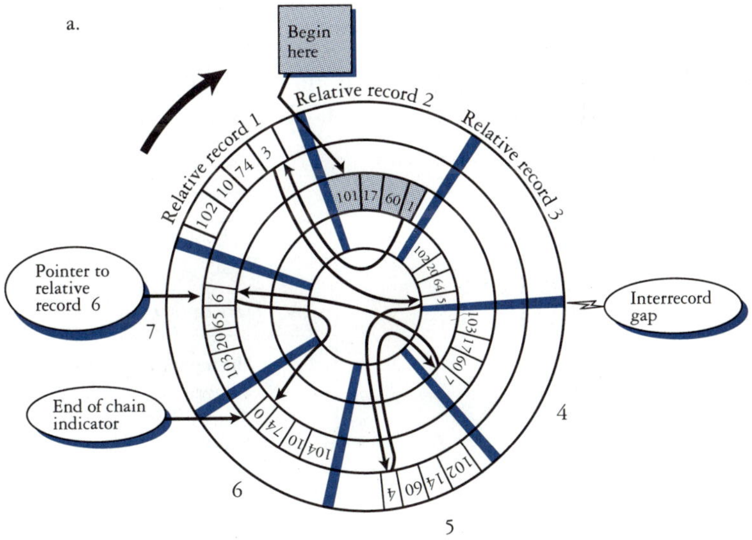

b.

Allows for sequential ordering

Begin here → 2

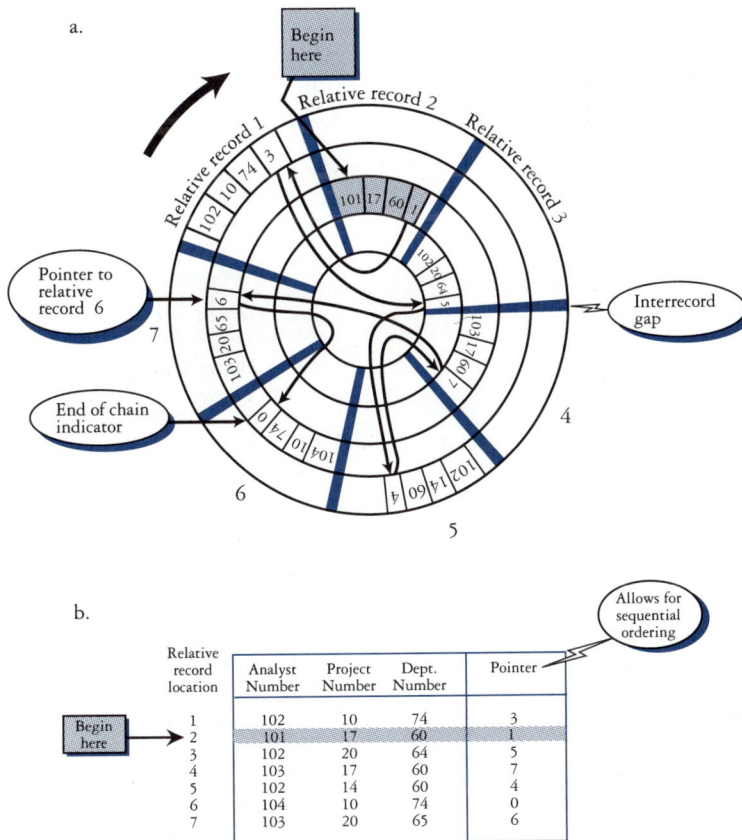

Relative record location	Analyst Number	Project Number	Dept. Number	Pointer
1	102	10	74	3
2	101	17	60	1
3	102	20	64	5
4	103	17	60	7
5	102	14	60	4
6	104	10	74	0
7	103	20	65	6

Beginning of list = 2

Figure 6–5 a. Physical record layout of disk pointers to link relative record locations
b. Using pointers to order records by analyst number

To illustrate the use of pointers, Figure 6-5a shows a disk layout of records. A pointer has been added to each record in Figure 6-5b. The left column specifies the relative location of each record. To process the data by "analyst," we would start at the second record, which contains the first analyst number (101). The pointer in the 101 record sends us to relative record number 1, which contains data about the second analyst, 102. That record points to record 3, and so on until the seventh record is found. The last record, number 7, contains an end-of-chain symbol, in this case 0, indicating that it is the last record in the logical chain. This layout provides a logical ordering by analyst without requiring a specific physical arrangement of the records.

Linked list record representation Trees are not often stored as sequential lists because changing nodes is time-consuming and often confusing. Usually, either a linked list or inverted list is preferred. The following data model will help explain linked list record representation. The structure involves salesclerk records (parents) and items (children). The nature of the association is 1:M. Let us assume we have two salesclerks in the shoe department of a retail store and items they sold. Figure 6-6 shows two "salesclerk_item" tree structure. One represents salesclerk Adams and the other represents salesclerk Jones. The storage layout of the two records is shown in Figure 6-7a. The linked-list structure (ascending and descending) is shown in Figure 6-7b.

Salesclerk Adams		
Item No.	Description	Price
04	Slipper	36.50
14	Wingtip	99.00
17	Oxford	84.10

Salesclerk Jones		
Item No.	Description	Price
01	Hush puppy	40.40
09	Wingtip	96.00
10	Casual	38.50
15	Sandal	15.95

a. Sales records

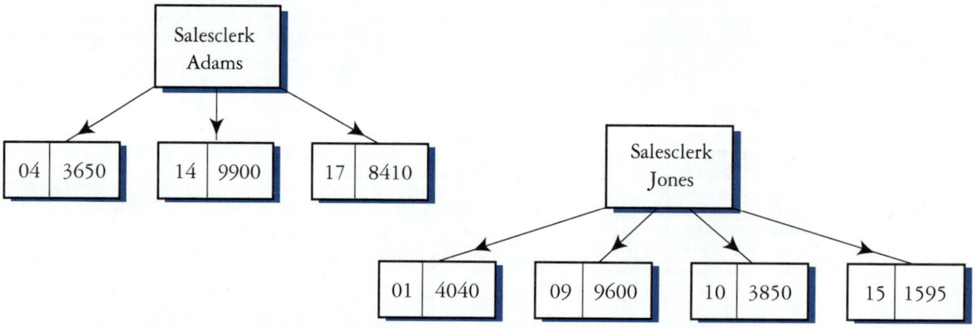

b. Salesclerk_item trees

Figure 6–6 Records (a) and their tree structure (b)

Relative record number	Record data	
1	Salesclerk Adams	
2	Salesclerk Jones	
3	09	96.00
4	15	15.95
5	04	36.50
6	01	40.40
7	14	99.00
8	10	38.50
9	17	84.10

Item # → (first column); Price → (second column)

a. Tree file

Relative record number	Record data		Item pointer	Reverse pointer
1	Salesclerk Adams		5	9
2	Salesclerk Jones		6	4
3	09	96.00	8	6
4	15	15.95	0	8
5	04	36.50	7	0
6	01	40.40	3	0
7	14	99.00	9	5
8	10	38.50	4	3
9	17	84.10	0	7

b. Two-way linked-list file structure

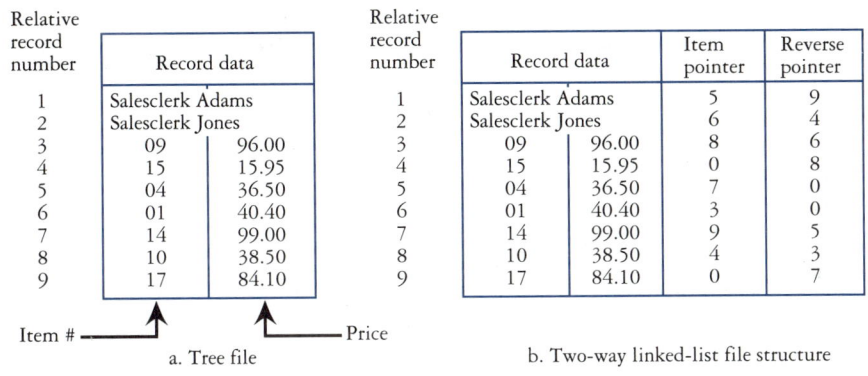

Figure 6–7 Tree file (a) and two-way linked=list file structure (b)

In ascending structure, the first parent (Adams) contains a pointer which means that the first child (item sold) and its price are stored in record location 5. Record 5, in turn, has pointer 7 which links to the second child (item 14). The second item has pointer 9 which leads to the location of the third child (item 17) which has pointer 0. This indicates the end of the children (items) linked to the parent Adams. The same procedure applies to parent Jones. Reverse pointers begin with the last item, and point successively back to the first item.

Adding or deleting records in a linked-list structure is a simple procedure. As illustrated in Figure 6-8b, to add item 05 to the file and also keep it in ascending order, we make item 04 in record 5 point to item 05 in record location 10. Item 05, in turn, points to the next sequential item (14) in record 7. The circled pointers are the only ones affected by the addition.

Relative record number	Record data		Item pointer
1	Salesclerk Adams		5
2	Salesclerk Jones		6
3	09	96.00	8
4	15	15.95	0
5	04	36.50	7
6	01	40.40	3
7	14	99.00	9
8	10	38.50	4
9	17	84.10	0

Item # → (first column); Price → (second column)

a. Linked list file structure

Relative record number	Record Data		Item pointer
1	Salesclerk Adams		5
2	Salesclerk Jones		6
3	09	96.00	8
4	15	15.95	0
5	04	36.50	10
6	01	40.40	3
7	14	99.00	9
8	10	38.50	4
9	17	84.10	0
10	05	64.35	7

Added record → row 10

b. Addition of item 05 to the file

Relative record number	Record data		Item pointer
1	Salesclerk Adams		5
2	Salesclerk Jones		6
3	09	96.00	4
4	15	15.95	0
5	04	36.50	10
6	01	40.40	3
7	14	99.00	9
8	10	38.50	4
9	17	84.10	0
10	05	64.35	7

Deleted record → row 8; Changed pointer → row 3

c. Deletion of record 10 from the file

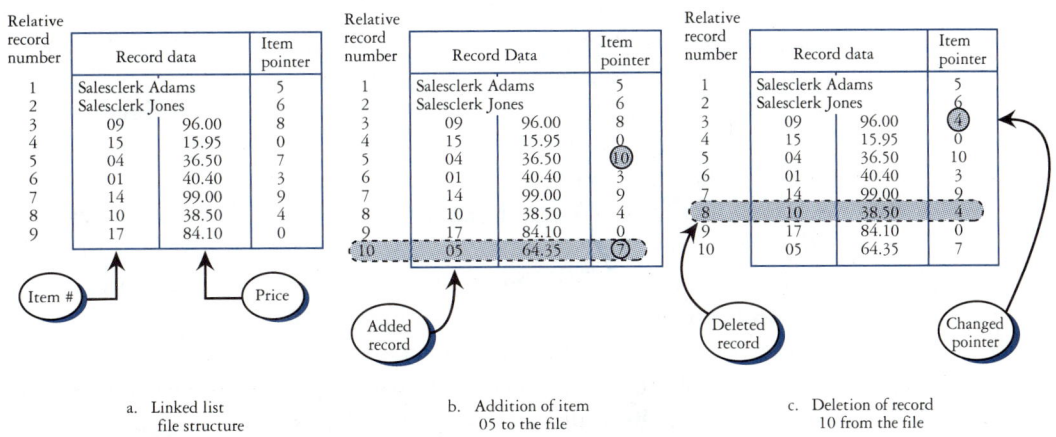

Figure 6–8 Adding or deleting records in a linked-list structure

Relative record number	Record Data		Item Pointer	Reverse Pointer
1	Salesclerk Adams		5	9
2	Salesclerk Jones		6	4
3	09	96.00	8	6
4	15	15.95	0	8
5	04	36.50	7	0
6	01	40.40	3	0
7	14	99.00	9	5
8	10	38.50	4	3
9	17	84.10	0	7

Item # — Price

Relative record number	Record Data		Item Pointer	Reverse Pointer
1	Salesclerk Adams		5	9
2	Salesclerk Jones		6	4
3	09	96.00	8	6
4	15	15.95	2	8
5	04	36.50	7	1
6	01	40.40	3	2
7	14	99.00	9	5
8	10	38.50	4	3
9	17	84.10	1	7

Figure 6–9 Two-way circular linked list

Deleting a record from the tree file is also easy. In our illustration, Figure 6-8c, deleting item 10 in record 8 requires only that we change the pointer in the item that is pointing to record 8, which is item 9 in record 3. The pointer in item 10 will indicate the item to be deleted (item 10). This way, item 9 will point to item 15, bypassing item 10, which is now logically deleted.

Two-way circular linked list representation In addition to the ascending and descending linked lists, we can also develop a one-way or two-way circular linked list by changing pointer 0 to go back to the parent. For example, our two-way linked list structure in Figure 6-7b is converted to a two-way circular list in Figure 6-9. The only difference is changing pointer 0 to go back to the parent.

Direct record representation The illustrations so far have shown the physical relationships in trees with single 1:M relationships. The advanced version of record relationships involves several 1:M relationships. Assume that our two salesclerks now sell items in various departments rather than items in the shoe department only. Each department also sells unique items. The tree structure and illustration of this situation are presented in Figure 6-10.

Figure 6-11 shows a direct record representation of Figure 6-10. Salesclerks Adams and Jones (parents) each have a pointer containing the record location (address) of the first "department" child. In Adams' case, the "department" child has two pointers: One pointer has the address of the first "item" child, and the other pointer has the address of the next "department" sibling. Item records use a single pointer, each containing the address of the next sibling.

Inverted list representation Inverted files are commonly used to allow the DBMS to retrieve records on the basis of a secondary key. For example, if we physically arrange a salesclerk's records by ID, we can easily retrieve records by ID using the sequential access method; but if we want to retrieve the records by last name we need to either sort the

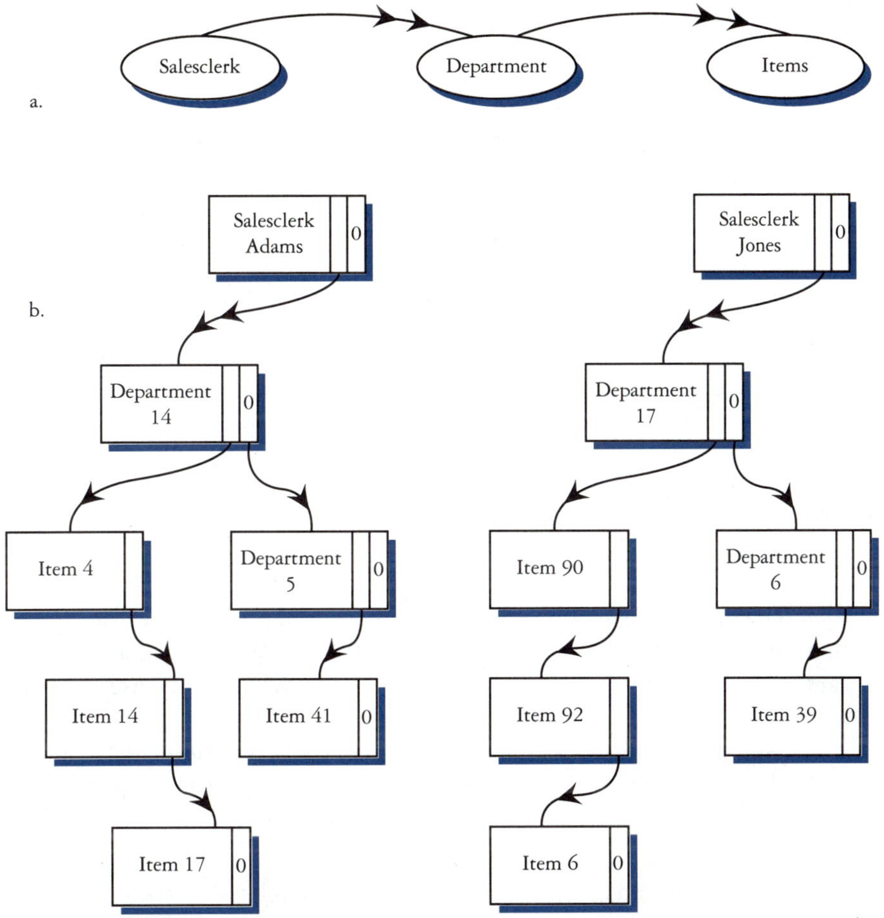

Figure 6–10 a. Salesclerk_department_item tree format
b. Illustration

Relative record number	Record data	Pointer	Pointer
1	Salesclerk Adams	3	0
2	Salesclerk Jones	4	0
3	Dept 14	5	6
4	Dept 17	14	11
5	Item 4		7
6	Dept 5	8	0
7	Item 14		12
8	Item 41		0
9	Item 92		13
10	Item 39		0
11	Dept 6	11	0
12	Item 17		0
13	Item 6		0
14	Item 90		9

Figure 6–11 Direct record representation of tree in Figure 6-10

Relative record number	Record Data		Pointer
1	Salesclerk	Adams	5
2	Salesclerk	Jones	6
3	92	69.00	8
4	15	15.95	0
5	04	36.50	7
6	90	40.00	3
7	14	99.00	9
8	06	38.50	0
9	17	84.10	0

a.

Relative Record	Child Record
Adams	5
Adams	7
Adams	9
Jones	6
Jones	3
Jones	8

b.

Figure 6–12 a. One-way linked=list structure
b. Inverted list of salesclerk_item relationship

file each time (a waste of processing time) or build a second file, arranged in alphabetical order (a waste of database space). To get around this we can index or invert the file on the name field. We actually use relative addresses in this process.

Using an inverted list to represent a tree structure means developing an inverted list for each 1:M relationship. The inverted list can then be used to match parents and children. Figure 6-12 shows the inverted list for the "salesclerk_item" relationship from Figure 6-9. Note that the pointer for each parent record refers to the next relative record number. For example, the record "Adams" (the first line in Figure 6-12b) has pointer 5, which represents relative record number 5 (fifth line in Figure 6-12a) as the next alphabetically sequential record, and so on.

Network Model

The second model found in database relationships is the network model. The network model was standardized in 1971 by the Data Base Task Group (DBTG) and is often called the DBTG model.

In certain situations a child may have more than one parent. Such a relationship cannot be described in a tree structure, but requires a network model. A NETWORK MODEL describes relationships among records in which one item can be linked to any other item. The nature of the relationship is many-to-many or M:N.

A network model allows 1:1, 1:M, or M:N relationships among entities. For example, an auto parts store may have dealings with several automakers (parents). As illustrated in Figure 6-13, the store orders many spare parts from General Motors and Ford, an M:N relationship that can best be supported by a network model. If the automaker sold spare parts to only one shop (say, a new car dealer), their relationship

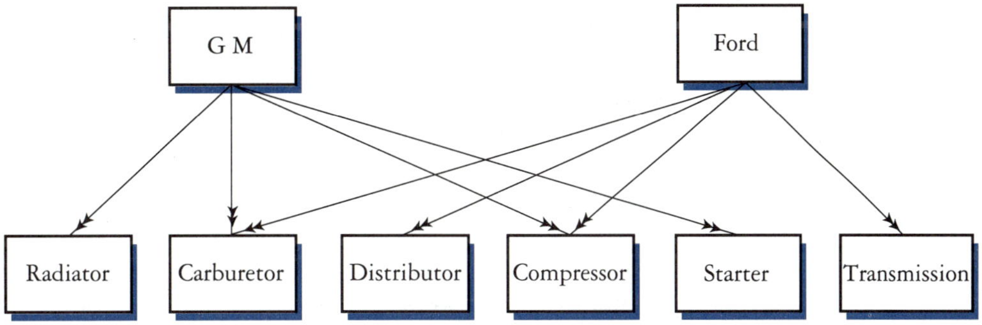

Figure 6–13 Network model for auto parts store

would be 1:1. If the automaker supplied many other dealers, its relationship to the dealers would be 1:M. The 1:1 and 1:M relationships can be represented by a tree structure. However, when many auto parts stores are supplied by many automakers, they have an M:N relationship, which is best described by a network model.

Simple and Complex Models

Network models are classified as simple or complex. The absence of lines with double-headed arrows joining records in both directions makes the model a SIMPLE NETWORK MODEL. The presence of such lines makes it a COMPLEX NETWORK MODEL. Figure 6-14 shows a simple network model: None of the lines joining the record types have double-headed arrows in both directions. If we add double-headed arrows to the "reservation_

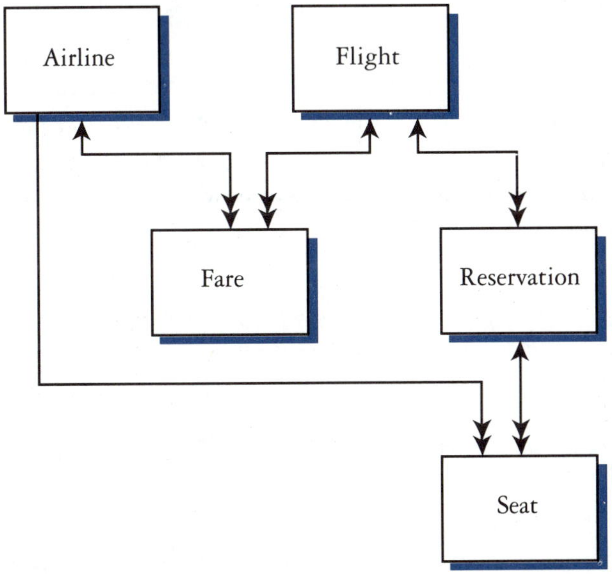

Figure 6–14 A Bachman diagram for a simple network model

flight" relationship, the structure becomes a complex network model. (See Figure 6-15.)

The reason for distinguishing between simple and complex network models is that a complex network needs elaborate physical representation. Some DBMSs can handle simple but not complex network structures, as when, for example, a DBMS data description language (DDL) may describe simple but not complex network models. This should not be a serious drawback, since complex network models can be decomposed into simple network models.

Simple network models are useful primarily at the internal database level, while the complex network models are useful for describing an external or a conceptual database because many types of relationships can be easily depicted and stated. On the other hand, network models can be extremely difficult to use unless the network diagram and procedures are carefully arranged. Whether a network is simple or complex, the purpose of the data model is to portray what is implemented in the database.

Intersection Records

Many-to-many relationships are constructed using the INTERSECTION RECORD—a record that is owned by two different records, which represents a M:N relationship. The fare records in Figure 6-14 are intersection records. Each fare has a relationship with an airline and with a flight. In database design, each such record is strung on two different pointer chains. This means it cannot be associated with an airline record alone or with a flight record alone, only with both types of records.

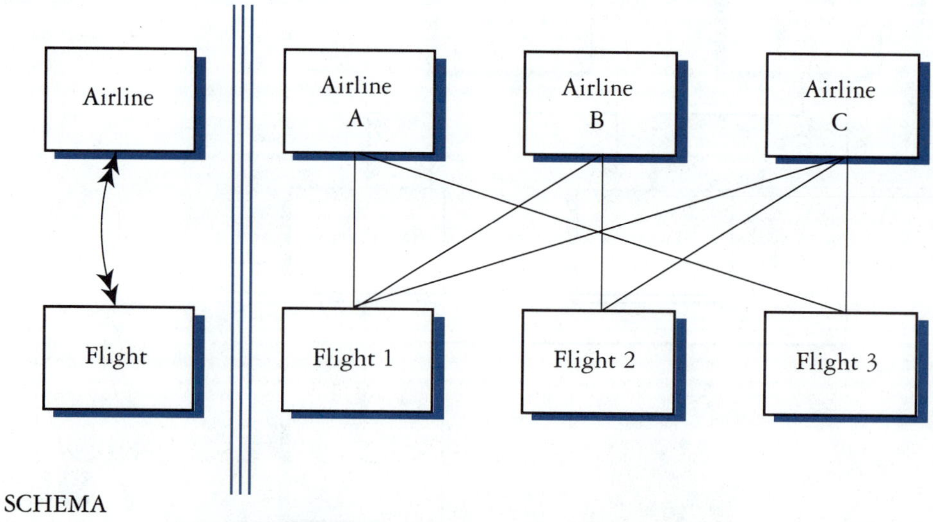

Figure 6–15 A complex (M:N) network model with two entities. Note the complex mapping (double-headed arrows in both directions)

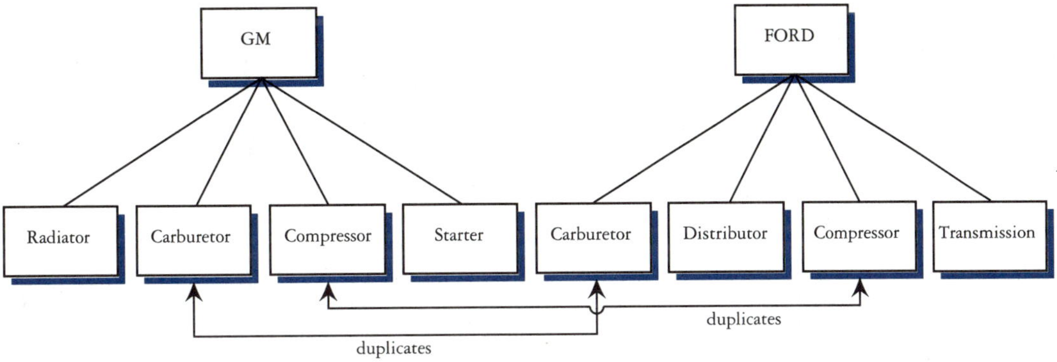

Figure 6–16 Simple network models

Decomposition into Simpler Forms

A practical approach to decomposing a network into hierarchies or trees involves introducing redundancies. This simplifies the relationship to no more than a 1:M relationship. The simplified network model shown in Figure 6-16 has been decomposed from the network in Figure 6-13.

In some cases, redundant elements may be few and can be tolerated; in other cases, they are excessive. Figure 6-17 shows two examples of decomposition.

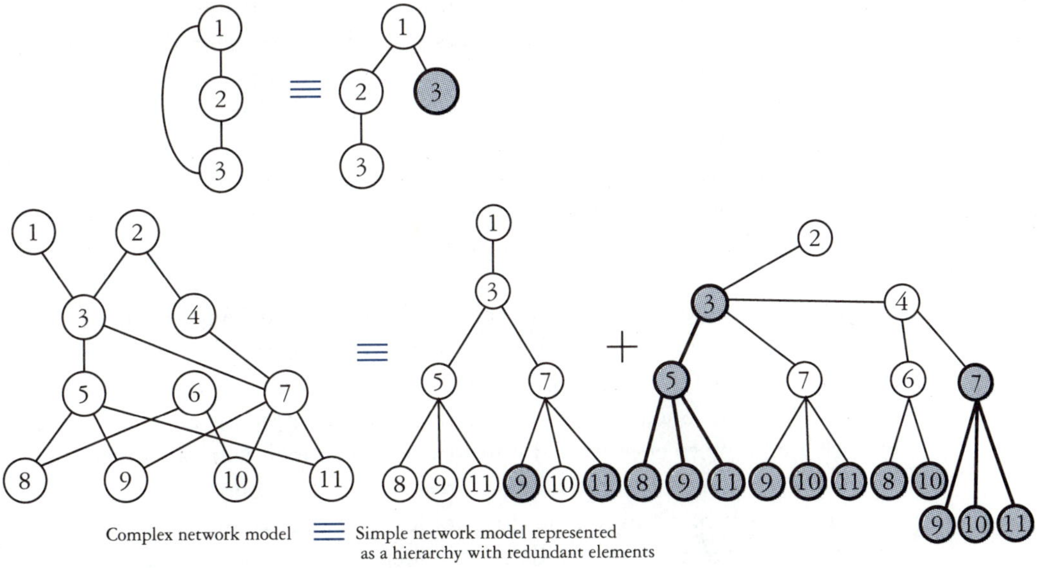

Figure 6–17 Decomposing a network model

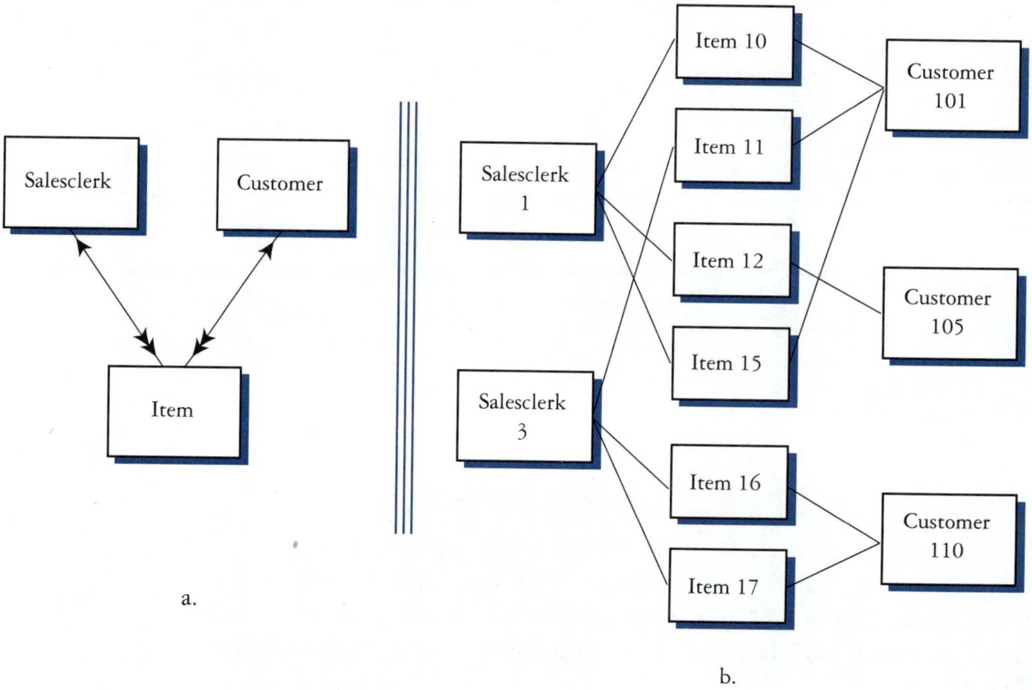

Figure 6–18 a. Simple network model
b. Instance of the model

Representing Simple Network Models

Simple network models can be represented using primarily linked lists or inverted lists. (Sequential lists can be used if the simple network model is first decomposed into trees, each with a sequential list, but this is rare. Linked lists and inverted lists are more common.)

Linked lists with decomposition Let us take our "salesclerk_item" example and add "customer," as shown in Figure 6-18a. We now have one child (item) reporting to two parents (salesclerk and customer.) We also have two 1:M relationships: "salesclerk" to "item" and "customer" to "item." Figure 6-18b shows an instance of the network model with this addition.

To represent this simple network model, we decompose it into two trees, as shown in Figure 6-19a. Using the instance in Figure 6-18b, we produce a simple network decomposition, shown in Figure 6-19b.

As mentioned earlier, every time we decompose a network model, we are likely to encounter duplicates or redundancies. In our illustration, there are several redundancies, represented by the connecting brackets in Figure 6-19b. To overcome this problem, we use pointers. After the data is stored, we refer to the data by pointing to its location. Figure 6-20 shows the same structure with pointers added. Note that there are two types of pointers: One pointer (in the record data column) points to the

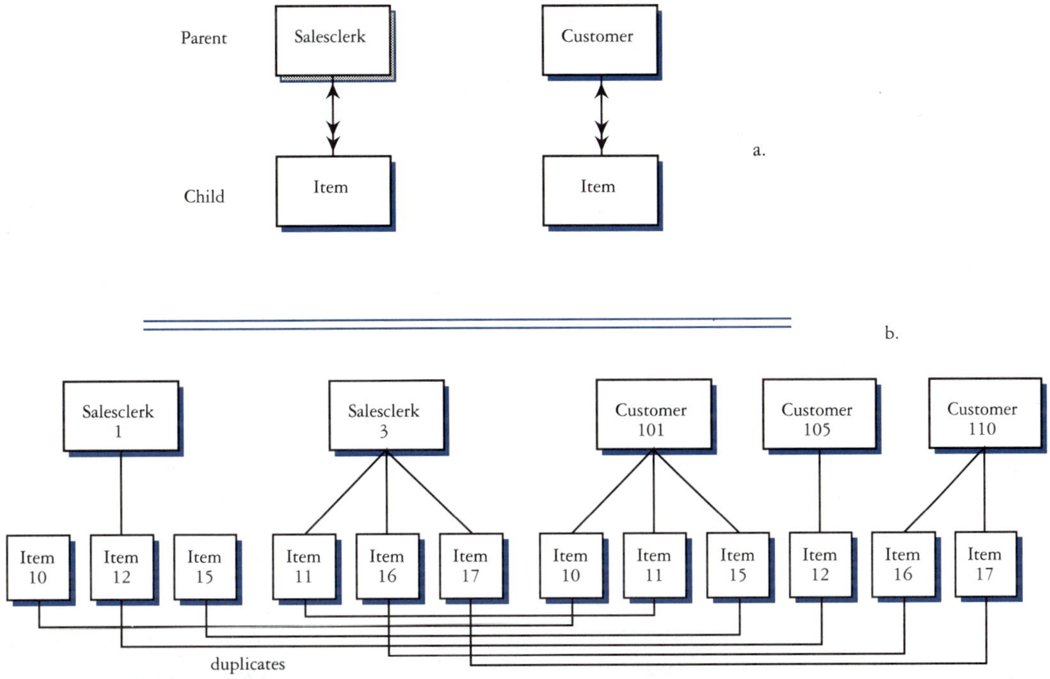

Figure 6–19 a. Decomposing hierachy of simple network model
b. Instance of decomposition

Relative Record Number	Record Data	Pointer
1	Salesclerk 1	6
2	Salesclerk 3	7
3	Customer 101	12
4	Customer 105	14
5	Customer 110	16
6	Item 10	8
7	Item 11	10
8	Item 12	9
9	Item 15	0
10	Item 16	11
11	Item 17	0
12	Pointer to item 10 = 6	13
13	Pointer to item 11 = 7	15
14	Pointer to item 12 = 8	0
15	Pointer to item 15 = 9	0
16	Pointer to item 16 = 10	17
17	Pointer to item 17 = 11	0

Figure 6–20 Tree decomposition with redundancies eliminated

location of the data, while the second (in the pointer column) refers to the location of the next child of the "customer" record.

Linked records without decomposition An alternative to the decomposition procedure is to create a set of pointers for each set of 1:M relationships. This approach is similar to the linked lists used to represent trees. To illustrate, consider our "salesclerk_customer_item" network structure in Figure 6-18. We simply link "salesclerk" to "item" with one set of pointers, and link "customers" to "item" with another set of pointers. This procedure is shown in Figure 6-21.

Inverted list As illustrated earlier, a simple network model consists of two 1:M relationships, each of which can be represented by inverted lists, as for tree structures. In our "salesclerk_customer_item" simple network model, we can create two inverted lists for each 1:M relationship: "salesclerk" to "item," and "customer" to "item," as shown in Figure 6-22.

Representing Complex Network Structures

Complex network structures are most commonly represented through decomposition into trees or by simple network models.

Consider the automaker-auto parts relationship, a 1:M relationship in both directions, as illustrated in Figure 6-23a. Automakers distribute spare parts to various auto parts stores and the stores purchase from different automakers. This complex network has been decomposed into trees in Figure 6-23b. Note that the duplicates resulting from the decomposition S2 and S4 appear twice. Duplicates can be eliminated by replacing them with pointers.

Another alternative to representing a complex network model is to decompose it into a simple network model and then to represent the

Relative record number	Record Data	Sales clerk Pointer	Customer Pointer
1	Salesclerk 1	6	
2	Salesclerk 3	7	
3	Customer 101		6
4	Customer 105		8
5	Customer 110		10
6	Item 10	8	7
7	Item 11	10	9
8	Item 12	9	0
9	Item 15	0	0
10	Item 16	11	11
11	Item 17	0	0

Figure 6–21 Simple network model without decomposition

Relative Record Number	Record Data	Salesclerk Pointer	Customer Pointer
1	Salesclerk 1	6	
2	Salesclerk 3	7	
3	Customer 101		6
4	Customer 105		8
5	Customer 110		10
6	Item 10	8	7
7	Item 11	10	9
8	Item 12	9	0
9	Item 15	0	0
10	Item 16	11	11
11	Item 17	0	0

Salesclerk Record	Item Record	Customer Record	Item Record
1	6	101	6
1	8	101	7
1	9	101	9
3	7	105	8
3	10	110	10
3	11	110	11

Figure 6–22 Representing a simple network model using an inverted list

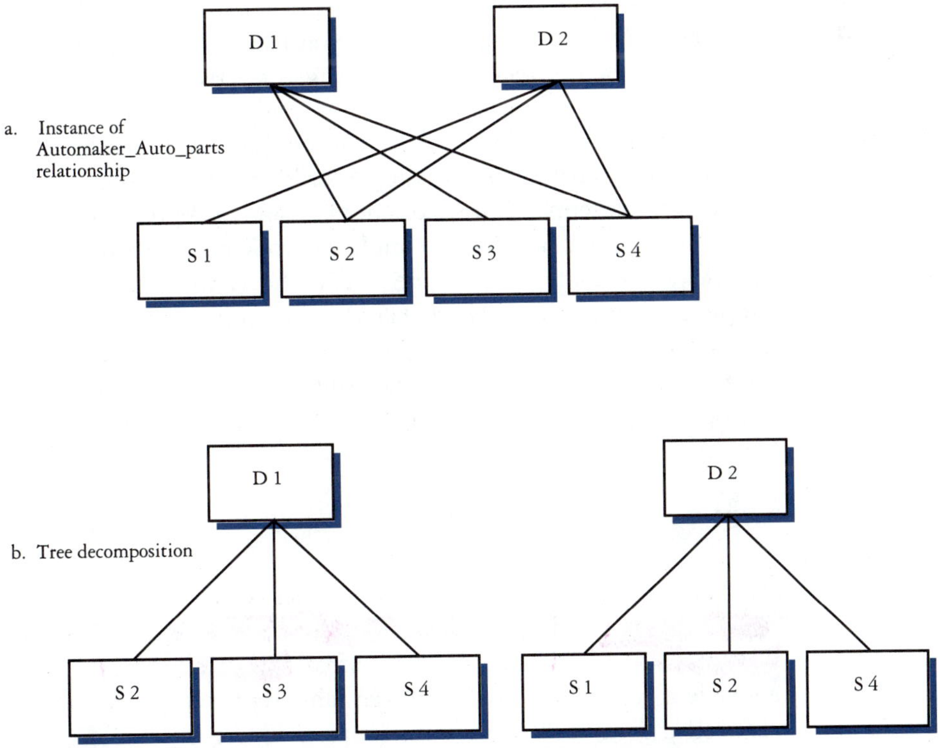

Figure 6–23 a. The automaker-auto parts stores network model
b. The complex network model decomposed into a tree structure

a. Complex network

b. An instance of complex network decomposed to simple network

Figure 6–24 Decomposing a complex network model into a simple network model

simple network model with linked or inverted lists. For example, Figure 6-24 shows a complex network model involving a 1:M relationship between two records. To decompose it to a simple network model, we add a third record, called an intersection record, since a simple network model requires 1:M relationships among three records.

To create an intersection record, we simply take a unique key from the automaker record and tag it to a unique key from the auto parts record. The resulting intersection records are D1S1, D1S2, . . ., D3S4, where D represents "automaker dealer" and S represents "auto parts store." Figure 6-25a shows a simple network model decomposed using intersection records, and Figure 6-25b shows the decomposition of a simple network model. Note that the relationship between dealer and intersection record is 1:M, and the relationship between store and intersection record is also 1:M. The result is a simple network model that can be represented with the linked list or inverted list procedure.

RELATIONAL MODEL

The third DBMS implementation model is the relational model. The RELATIONAL MODEL represents all data and relationships in a flat two-dimensional table (rows and columns) called a RELATION, which is equivalent to a file. Each row in the table represents a record. A row is also called a tuple (rhymes with couple). Figure 6-26 shows a relation describing the entity "employee" using social security number, name, and title.

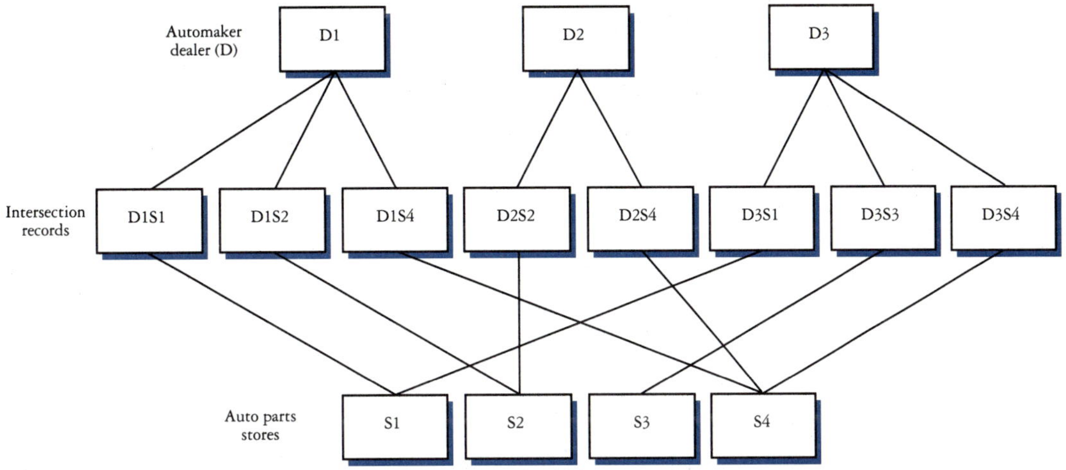

a. Decomposing a simple network with intersection records

Relative Record Number	Record Data	Dealer Pointer	Store Pointer
1	D1	8	
2	D2	11	
3	D3	13	
4	S1		8
5	S2		9
6	S3		14
7	S4		10
8	D1S1	9	13
9	D1S2	10	11
10	D1S4	0	12
11	D2S2	11	0
12	D2S4	0	15
13	D3S1	14	0
14	D3S3	15	0
15	D3S4	0	0

b. Representing a simple network with intersection records

Figure 6–25 Simple network model with intersection records

A relational model has several features:

1 Entries in a table are single-valued (no repeating groups).

2 Entries in any columns are all of the same kind. For example, the "salary" column shows only numbers representing salary.

3 Each column has a unique name. The order of the columns is immaterial.

4 No two rows in the table can be identical. The order of the rows is immaterial.

5 The user can add, delete, or modify a table's contents.

Attributes (4)

ID	Employee	Years with firm	Salary
124	Arnold	2	18,500
241	Davis	14	26,500
362	Elam	7	22,000
180	Mandelbaum	6	21,200
820	Sibley	1	16,000
762	Travis	3	19,000
215	Unger	5	20,010
500	Ziegler	9	23,145

Tuples (8)

Value of "NAME" attribute

Figure 6–26 A relation for "employee"

6 Inquiry capability is easily available to the user. For example, a user may inquire: "How many years has Arnold been with the firm?" The response is "2."

7 Unlike hierarchical and network models where all relationships are predefined, a relational model develops new relations on user command.

To illustrate, suppose we have a relational structure consisting of two relations: The "employee" relation (Table 6-1) and the "employee education" relation (Table 6-2). A query requesting the employees with three or more years with the firm and a bachelor's degree would result in the following routine:

1 A temporary table of employees with three or more years is generated from the "employee" relation and placed in the file. This table is deleted once the query has been answered.

2 The information in the temporary table and the "employee-education" relation are used to answer the query. This results in a second temporary table with the answer "Davis." The two temporary tables are shown in Table 6-2.

Temporary employee relation		*Query response relation*	
ID	*Name*	*ID*	*Name*
241	Davis	241	Davis
362	Elam		
180	Mandelbaum		
762	Travis		
215	Unser		
500	Ziegler		

Table 6-1 Temporary relations for query response

Employee education (EMPED) relation		
ID	***Name***	***Degree***
124	Arnold	BS
241	Davis	BS
362	Elam	PhD
180	Mandelbaum	MBA
820	Sibley	BS
762	Travis	MA

Table 6-2 Employee-education relation

Details of relational databases are covered in Chapters 9 and 10.

Human-Oriented Relation Model

The hierarchical, network, and relational models have been known to be effective for representing organizational data because they are oriented toward machines and machine specifications. Because a wide variety of relationships can be established using these models, such models are appropriate at the internal level. But conceptual and external data models need data description conventions that are technology-independent; that is, oriented to human meaning. The two human-oriented data models are the semantic data model and the entity-relationship model.

Semantic Data Model

"Semantic" is another word for "meaning." As discussed in Chapter 5, a semantic data model (SDM) is a definitional model of descriptive classes. It provides information that gives meaning to entities and relationships. By documenting the meaning of data, the designer can then incorporate the necessary information for structuring the data. Therefore, the SDM can be very useful for logical database design and documentation.

Figure 6-27 shows an example of an SDM. Each entity or class can be defined by a name (such as "client"), a description, and a set of member attributes. The member attributes of the entity are described by a name and by clauses that specify permissible values. For example, the name of the client must come from a set of values called "names," which is defined elsewhere in the model. Also, the meaning of an attribute can be more precisely defined by specifying whether values may change, whether they may be missing or null, or whether they are related to other entities (such as "inverse: client").

CLIENT
Description: All clients who have invested in the Vanguard fund within the last four months
Member attributes
Name
Value class: NAMES
not changeable
may not be null
Address
Value class: ADDRESSES
Contact
Value class: VAN-ORDER
Inverse: Client
•
•
•
CLIENT-ORDER
Description: All orders for investments by clients.
Member attributes:
Contact
Value class: NAMES
not changeable
may not be null
Class attributes
Fund-$-Value
Value class: MONEY

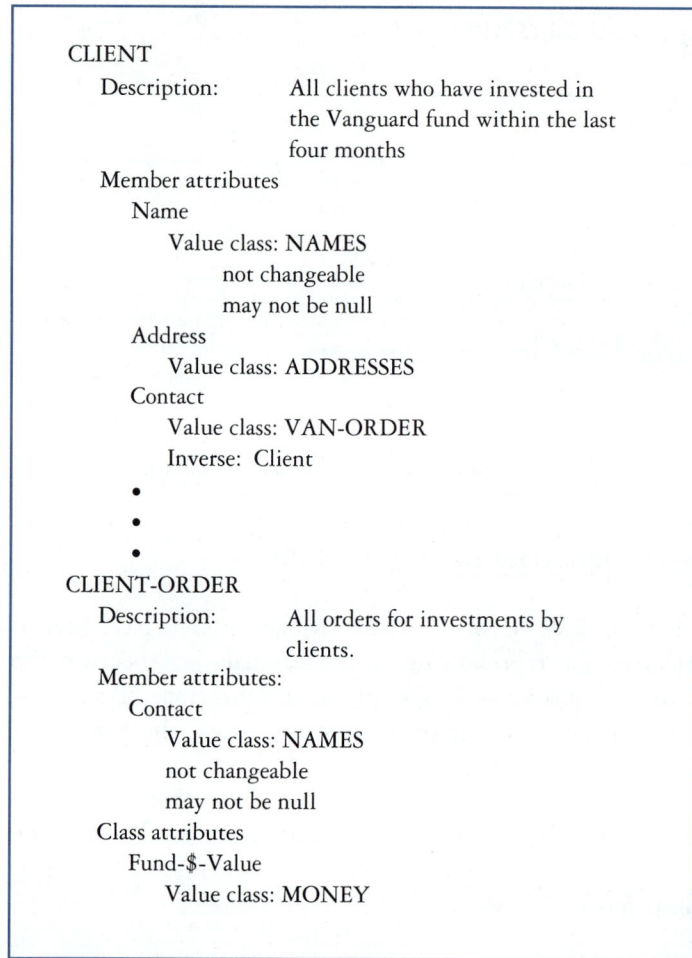

Figure 6-27 Semantic data model

Entity-Relationship (E-R) Model

An entity-relationship (E-R) model is a graphic tool for representing conceptual, logical, or external databases. It focuses on relationships and requires that they be given names. Figure 6-28 shows an E-R diagram of the relationship of the doctor and patient entities, a M:N relationship, including a table of data about the patient entity, another table of data about the doctor entity, and a third table of data about the relationship. Note that the relationship may have data of its own (date of visit and charge).

E-R diagrams are useful in relational database design because they force us to think carefully about the nature of the relationships between entities. Some database developers have argued that for external, logical, or conceptual data models, it is better to use conventions that are DBMS-

E-R diagram

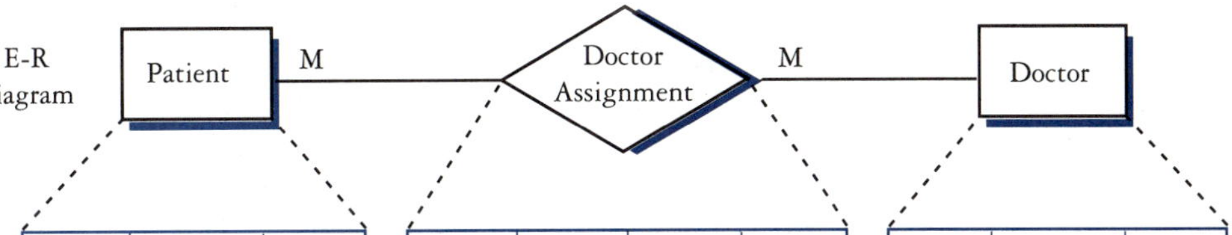

Tables of data

Patient #	Patient	Other data
14	Morgan	•••
19	Parker	•••
81	Yaworski	•••

Patient #	Doctor	Date of visit	Charge
14	Jones	110486	10.00
19	Abel	100286	15.00
19	Thiele	021186	15.00
81	Thiele	020986	20.00

Doctor #	Doctor name	Other data
104	Abel	•••
109	Jones	•••
110	Park	•••
111	Thiele	•••

Patient data

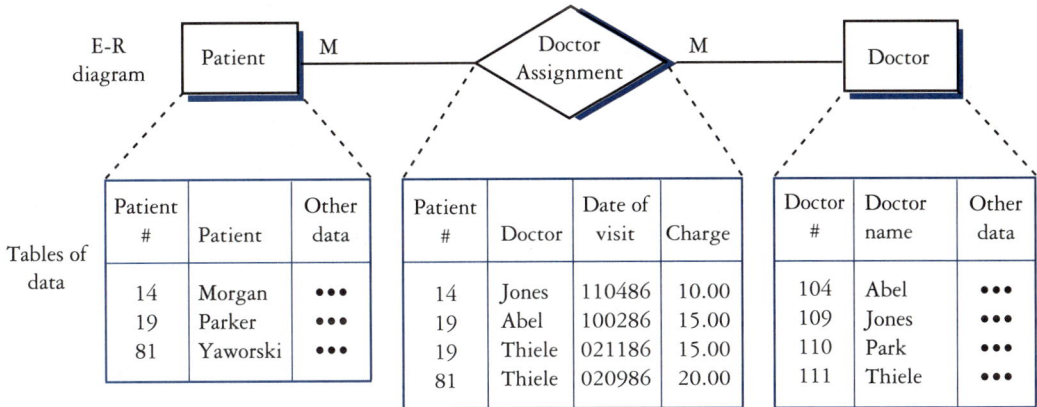

Figure 6-28 E-R diagram of a patient billing system

independent. Doing so means specifying the database requirements without a preference for the use of a particular DBMS. By far, the most widely used data model for conceptual, logical, or external data analysis is the E-R diagram. Much attention has been given to it since the introduction of CASE tools in the mid-1980s. For example, Excelerator can be used to generate an E-R diagram with ease. (Excelerator is covered in Appendix A.)

Comparing Data Models

To decide which data model is the best, the designer must consider the relative strengths and weaknesses of the three relationship models. In the first place, commercially viable relational database systems have been available only in the last 15 years. The general understanding is that the relational structure is superior for its ease of use. For novice users, the hierarchical and network structures are not as easy to use or learn. Interactive and nonprocedural query languages also fit the relational model, because the associations among data in a relational structure are all based on data value rather than on pointer chains.

Perhaps the most important advantage of a relational database is data independence. Data independence means isolating the user's logical view of a database from the hardware's physical storage requirements. This makes modifying the structure and implementing the system easier.

The main limitation of the relational model, however, is possible slower response time compared to the hierarchical or network models. The CPU also has to work longer, and more memory space is required to accommodate the various relations and their linkages. Another limitation is that most related DBMSs do not provide for referential integrity. For example, a table record can be deleted without deleting dependent table records. This is likely to be corrected soon.

In contrast to the relational model, the hierarchical model offers three important advantages:

• *Simplicity:* fewer commands are needed to effectively navigate the database.

• *Programmability:* ideal for applications that have predefined or fixed relationships.

• *Performance:* better than that provided by the relational data model.

The biggest disadvantage of the hierarchical model is that it restricts us to only one parent per child. Another disadvantage is that some of the powerful hierarchical DBMSs (for example, IBM's DL/1) are not easy to learn and use, and must be handled by experienced programmers who are trained in working in this database environment.

The network model offers two major advantages:

• *Flexibility:* Compared to the hierarchical model, there is no limit on the number of data relationships that can be represented.

• *Performance:* generally better than the relational data model and as good as the hierarchical model.

The main disadvantage of the network data model is that it is not as easy to understand and use as the relational model. Most application programs written for network models are complex and are best left to senior database developers to maintain.

SUMMARY

1 A hierarchical database model, or tree structure, is a hierarchy of nodes (records) that resembles an inverted tree. Each node contains one or more fields or data items that represent attributes which describe an entity. An entity in a tree structure can have only one owning entity, called the parent. The owned entity is called the child. A parent with no owners is called a root. There is only one root in a tree structure.

2 A balanced tree has the same number of branches for each node; an unbalanced tree has an unequal number. It is often easier to implement a physical data structure with a balanced than an unbalanced tree.

3 Hierarchical record relationships can be represented by list, linked list, and inverted list representation.

4 A list is a tree structure decomposed from the root downward along each branch. This procedure is called preorder traversal.

5 Records are logically tagged together through the use of pointers. A pointer holds the address of the next record in sequence and may be physical or relative, depending on its function.

6 A linked list has a field or a pointer added to each logical record and has as a value the location of the next logical record in sequence. Adding or deleting records from the tree file is a simple procedure. Two-way circular linked lists can also be used by changing pointer 0 to go back to the parent rather than functioning as the end of the search.

7 Using an inverted list to represent a tree structure involves developing an inverted list for each 1:M relationship. The inverted list is then used to match parents and children.

8 When a child has more than one parent (M:N), the relationship is described in a network model. The network model allows for 1:1, 1:M, or M:N relationships among entities.

9 Network models are either simple or complex. Complex networks need elaborate methods for physical representation while simple network models do not.

10 A complex network model can be reduced to a simpler form by introducing redundancies that simplify the relationships to no more than 1:M.

11 A simple network model can be represented using linked lists or inverted lists. Sequential lists can be used if the simple network model is first decomposed into trees and each tree is then broken down into sequential lists. Linked lists and inverted lists are more common.

12 The relational structure represents all data and relationships in a flat two-dimensional table called a relation. Each row represents a record. Entries in a table are single-valued and, in any single column, are of the same kind. Each column has a unique name. No two rows can be identical. Unlike hierarchical or network models, where all relationships are predefined, a relational model develops new relations on user command.

13 Two human-oriented models are the semantic data model (SDM) and the E-R model. The SDM is a definitional model of descriptive classes. The E-R model is a logical model, where entities are representations of objects.

KEY WORDS

Balanced tree
Child
Complex network model
Height
Hierarchical file
Hierarchical model
Intersection record
Leaf
Logical record
Maximal path
Moment
Network model
Node
Parent
Path
Physical pointer
Physical record
Pointer
Preorder traversal
Relation
Relational model
Relative pointer

Root

Sibling

Simple network model

Tree structure

Unbalanced tree

REVIEW QUESTIONS

1 Explain the concept behind tree structure and give an example.

2 "In hierarchical database models, an entity can have only one owning entity." Do you agree? Could we have a parent with no owners? Illustrate.

3 What is a sibling? How does it relate to child? Parent?

4 Distinguish between the following pairs:
   a. node and leaf
   b. balanced and unbalanced tree
   c. network and hierarchical models
   d. maximal path and preorder traversal

5 Explain briefly the ways in which hierarchical record relationships are represented. Which is the best way? Why?

6 How does list record representation differ from linked-list record representation?

7 How important is the use of pointers for record access and update?

8 How does a physical pointer differ from a relative pointer?

9 Illustrate how records are added and deleted in a linked-list structure.

10 Give an example of direct record representation.

11 What is inverted-list representation? How does it differ from direct record representation?

12 What types of applications would be amenable to a network model? Why?

13 Explain briefly the features of and differences between simple and complex network models.

14 What is an intersection record? Give an example.

15 "A simple network model can be represented using primarily linked lists or inverted lists." Do you agree? Explain.

16 Explain the procedure for decomposing a complex network model into trees.

17 Elaborate on the relational model. What is so distinctive about a relational database?

18 Summarize the key human-oriented models. How do they differ from the relationship models covered in the text?

19 Compare the pros and cons of the models covered in the text. Is there a best model? Why?

1 Invert the "order" file in Table 6-3 on customer number ("Cus-Num").

Order_Number	Date	Cus_Number
746	90192	121
641	90292	702
312	90292	667
124	91092	163
600	91192	431
127	91192	372

Table 6–3 Order file

2 Using the "student" file in Table 6-4, invert

a. the file on "Stu_Name"
b. the file on "Major"
c. the file on "GPA"

Student_ID	Student_Name	Major	Credits	GPA
101	Zmud, Jane	MIS	60	3.58
109	Cheney, Dave	Marketing	49	4.00
123	Kroenke, Bob	Accounting	90	3.61
472	Conrath, Ron	Finance	96	2.74
700	Mattes, Jan	Management	87	3.00
719	Frasier, Joe	Economics	62	3.10

Table 6–4 Student file

3 Table 6-5 shows student records in a linked-list with links arranged in order by student name. Relative addresses are used.

Relative Record Number	Student_ID	Student_Name	Major	Credit	GPA	Pointer
1	571	Atkins, Tom	MIS	61	3.50	5
2	620	Young, Jill	Management	92	3.80	0
3	643	Kluge, Dave	Marketing	78	2.70	4
4	844	Smith, Nancy	Finance	64	3.00	2
5	910	King, Ron	Accounting	80	2.90	3

Table 6–5 Student records

a. Explain how the pointers link (sort) the file in alphabetic order by name.
b. What changes would you make to create a circular linked-list?
c. What pointers would you add (or change) to create a two-way linked-list structure?

4 Use the linked-list from Problem 3 to answer the following questions:

a. What pointers would be used to convert the structure to list employee records using GPA as the ordering field?
b. What pointers would be used in a GPA order field to create a circular linked-list?

c. Suppose we add relative record number 6 to Table 6-5 as follows:

```
6 912 Zmud,Jim Management 90 3.40
```

How would this addition affect the pointers in Problem 4a?

5 Consider the tree in Figure 6-29.

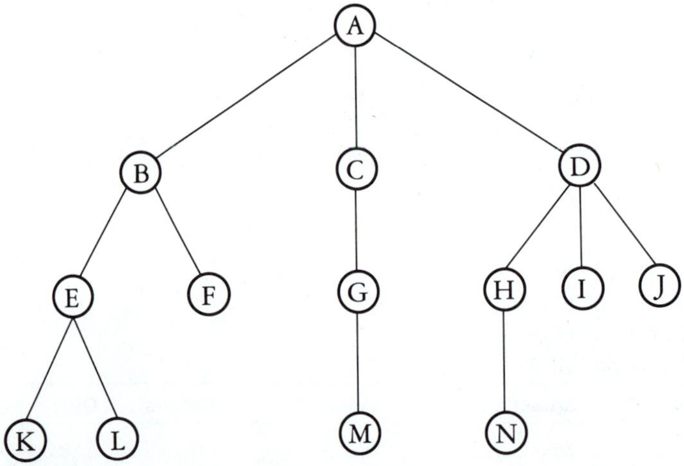

Figure 6-29 Sample tree structure

a. How many levels are there?
b. How many leaves are there?
c. How many children of level-1 nodes are there?
d. Is this a balanced tree? Why?
e. How many lengths does path A to K have? Path A to F?

PART III

DATABASE TOOLS AND PROCEDURES

C H A P T

Data Dictionaries

E R 7

The Times Are Changing

AT A GLANCE

The Times Are Changing

Recently, a speaker at my local Data Administration Management Association (DAMA) meeting compared his company's applications to the Winchester Mystery House. This mansion (located in the heart of California's Silicon Valley) was the home of Sarah Winchester, the eccentric wife of the man who invented the Winchester rifle.

A spiritualist convinced Mrs. Winchester that she wouldn't die prematurely as long as she kept expanding the house. So, for 38 years, she added new rooms to her house—160 in all. Each room supports the individual function for which it was developed—there are beautiful parlors, comfortable bedrooms, and efficient kitchens. However, connections between the rooms are a disaster—doors open to the solid walls of adjoining rooms or to three-story drops, windows are located in the walls between rooms, and stairs lead to dead-end passages. Woe to the unfortunate one who attempts to navigate this maze of hallways and corridors without a map.

A house built without an architect or master plan may have the potential for a great tourist attraction, but I wouldn't want to live in it. If someone asked me to sum up my impressions of the environment that's been foisted upon us by CASE, I'd simply point to the Winchester House. Each CASE tool is like a room in that house—the tool may support the specific analysis methodology or application development function for which it was designed, but moving between separate tools is a challenging proposition. You simply can't integrate the data with ease.

If you believe the current marketing hype, the information repository is the solution to this integration nightmare. These repositories have been elusive, to say the least. We waited for the much-heralded Repository Manager from IBM to replace its aging data dictionary offering. The principal benefit of the repository product will be as a basis for integrated solutions, or tools, used in the efficient development and operation of information systems.

If you have not been initiated into the wonderful world of repositories, let me provide you with some background. An information repository is a knowledge base that contains information about the facts an enterprise must be able to access and the processes it must perform to be successful. An information repository also contains information about how your organization has implemented its applications to support its information processing needs. The description of these business facts and processes and the application components that support them are referred to as *metadata*.

The information maintained in your enterprise's information repository is an important corporate resource and should be managed as such. Most corporations have an information repository that is maintained through a paper-based, distributed, manual system consisting of the documents published during application development. These documents include the business requirements, application design, code, database design, and test specifications. Although some of this information is maintained in a data dictionary, the majority is located in the author's script or word processor files. At best, they are maintained in the application's project libraries. Information maintained in this format is not easily accessed, shared, or updated.

However, some applications provide automated assistance in managing a corporation's metadata. Such an application is known as an IRDS. Generally, whenever you hear people talking about an information repository, they are really talking about an IRDS.

Rearchitecting our CASE strategies around an IRDS is like keeping the rooms in the Winchester House but rebuilding the hallways to allow safe passage. So far, it's been pretty easy for us to sit back and watch the CASE vendors as they attempt to align themselves with a repository-based information management environment.

Perhaps the following questions will help you decide whether or not you're ready for a repository. Have you selected your business requirement analysis methodologies? Are your analysts comfortable with information modeling and structured analysis? Where does your organization stand on application and code generation and automated support for application testing? These questions give us a lot to think about and to prepare for before purchasing those initial repository-based products.

Over the next few months, we will be seeing more information become available about these issues and concerns. If there's a dearth of information today, I believe we'll soon be inundated with repository overload in the form of conferences, seminars, and magazine articles like this one. An IBM Repository user group is already forming across the country. These are exciting times for our industry. The next few years will be extremely challenging for IS developers and CASE tool vendors alike. By sharing our experiences in preparing and implementing repository concepts, I believe we can achieve the benefits of CASE with minimal pain and anxiety.

Moriarty, Terry, "The times are changing." Database Programming and Design, *May 1991, 67–68. Reprinted with permission of* Database Programming and Design.

AT A GLANCE

One problem facing database developers is dealing with inconsistent and redundant data elements. The data dictionary was developed to provide a central repository for information about all entities, attributes, and relationships identified during the development of the conceptual model, and thus is a means of controlling redundancy as well as setting standards.

A data dictionary provides several functions in database design. It helps users identify data elements and provides a way to store, modify, and retrieve information about the data used in the information system of an organization. A data dictionary makes it possible to find and manage data. It treats data as a resource and helps manage and control that resource.

Data dictionary design makes use of four relational operators: sequence, selection, iteration, and optional operators. Aliases and naming conventions are also managed during design.

Independent data dictionaries are simple, easy to implement, and complete. But integrated data dictionaries are more powerful than independent data dictionaries, because both designers and users are forced to respect its definitions.

By the end of this chapter, you should understand

- the basic functions and components of a data dictionary;
- the difference between independent and integrated data dictionaries;
- the makeup of a data dictionary;
- the key data dictionary entries;
- the relationship between the data dictionary and the DBMS; and
- how to evaluate data dictionary products.

Introduction

In the past many computer-based applications were developed without regard to each other. One consequence of this was that data items were used and stored differently in the various systems. At times the functional requirements of the system had suggested certain data item names because the same data was referred to differently in different parts of the company.

Manufacturing might refer to the "part number," for example, while sales used the term "catalog number" to describe the same data item. In another example, an employee number might be stored as 12 characters under the name "EMP_NO" in one application but as an integer named "WORKER" in another. Problems arose when data was transferred from one system to another or when data was modified or deleted.

Excessive duplication of data was another problem. When one application developer did not know that the data required was already stored in the files of another application, he or she duplicated the data.

The data dictionary was developed to deal with the problems of inconsistent and redundant data elements. The data dictionary simply provides a central repository for information about all entities, attributes, and relationships identified during the development of the conceptual model.

Data dictionaries have become important as the size, sophistication, and scope of information systems have increased. Multiple applications and users as well as the size and complexities of information systems have all made it increasingly difficult for analysts to communicate with each other, which in turn has increased the possibility of inconsistent data item names and representations. Without data dictionaries, system development tends to be inconsistent, expensive, and time consuming.

Data Dictionary Functions and Components

A *dictionary* is an ordered set of definitions, a reference book that alphabetically lists the names important to a subject or activity and discusses their meanings and applications. Some dictionaries provide additional information about the subject but the key components are always reference, list, and discuss.

A data dictionary (DD) is a repository of information about data, or data about data, called metadata. A data dictionary is a reference file listing terms or names used in information systems and a discussion of their meanings, sources, and uses. As a dictionary, it provides definitions of data; as a directory it tells the user where to find the data. The DD is used by the database administrator to support design activities and by users to find out what data is available as well as its meaning, usage, format, and means of access.

Functions

The DD is more than a reference document: it is also a tool that performs four major functions.

1 It provides a reliable means of documentation for finding and managing data. It treats data as a resource and helps manage and control that resource.

2 It enables designers and administrators to control the information about the data in the design, implementation, and operational phases of a database.

3 It provides a way to store, modify, and retrieve information about the data. It stores data about data.

4 It helps the user identify data and/or write his or her own programs. The DD contains a description of the data, not the data per se. The data is managed by the database management system, which is stored in the physical database.

To illustrate how a data dictionary works, consider the word "balance," as it is used in a bank. To a customer the "balance" is the amount of money in an account against which he or she can write a check. But to the banker the word "balance" is a broad term with many meanings, such as "opening balance," "closing balance," and "available balance." In fact, in a customer's master account record over 20 data items include the word "balance." The database designer must make the meaning and use of all these terms clear when incorporating them into the data dictionary. This is essential to effective communication among all users of the data dictionary.

Perhaps the most important function of a data dictionary is to enforce data representation standards once they have been subject to review and approval. Management support is necessary to enforce this standardization effort. Managing a data dictionary requires the data administrator and user to construct a practical plan for making all future changes standard as well.

Data dictionaries are organized using a network structure, although they may also be organized using hierarchical or relational structures. A sample dictionary organized using a network structure is illustrated in Figure 7-1.

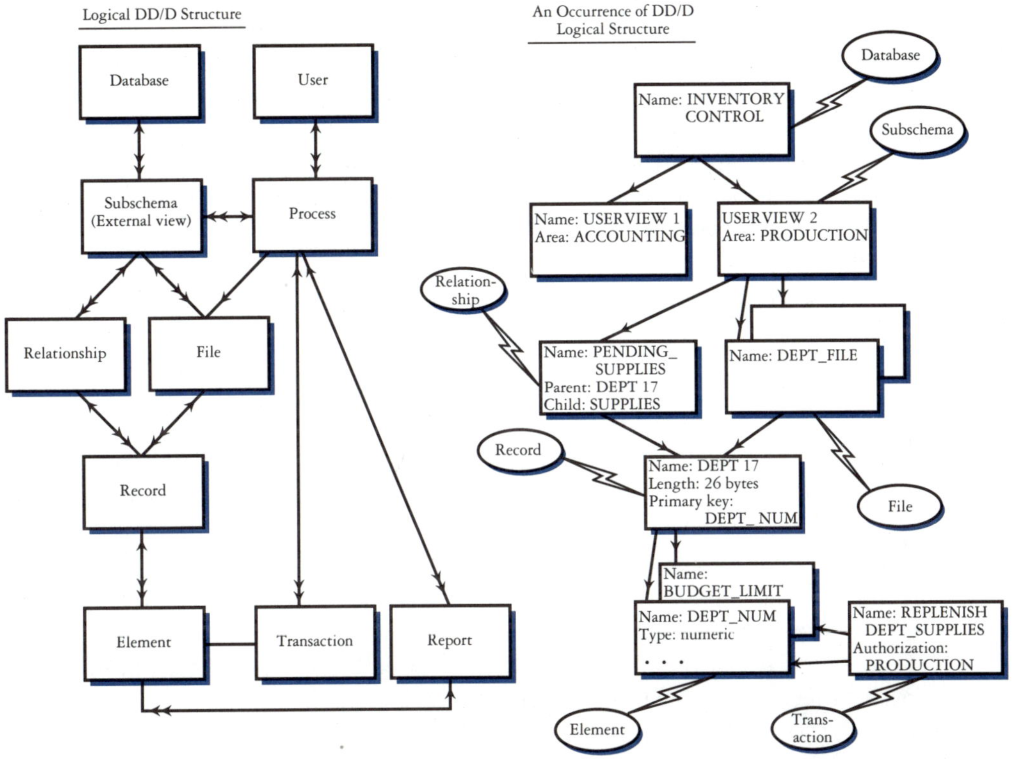

Figure 7–1 Data dictionary organized in network structure

A data dictionary has several beneficial characteristics.

• *System development tool*. The dictionary is extremely useful for capturing, storing, and displaying data when a system is under development.

• *Consistency of data description*. The dictionary is an excellent mechanism for enforcing data standards and for producing centralized, consistent, and up-to-date documentation. Consistent data descriptions can be a part of every program.

• *Efficiency*. Data descriptions are created once and then used by end-users. This means that new data descriptions need not be created every time a piece of data is used in a new program or documentation manual.

• *Cross-referencing*. Cross-referencing data and programs makes it possible to identify where in each program each data item is used. This makes finding programming errors and normal program maintenance and enhancement easier.

• *Commonality*. Commonality ensures that the same data items are represented in the same way across all programs.

• *Control of changes*. Changes in programs are time-consuming and expensive. Using a common data dictionary makes changes easier to control and authorize.

• *Control of synonyms*. It is sometimes desirable to refer to a data item by a name other than the standard name referenced in the dictionary. Such synonyms can be standardized and maintained as a part of the data dictionary.

• *Security*. The data dictionary may also specify the authorized users of the database or individual data items, who is authorized to make changes, and who "owns" the data.

Data Directory Components

The DATA DIRECTORY contains information about where the data defined by the dictionary is stored. Internal schema and programs are also stored in the data directory.

The data dictionary is part of the data dictionary/directory system (DD/DS). The DD/DS has two components: the data dictionary/directory (DD/D) and the data dictionary/manager (DD/M). All data definition and relationship data is maintained in the data dictionary/directory, while the data dictionary/manager is the software module that manages the directory.

The DATA DICTIONARY/DIRECTORY MANAGER performs several vital functions of a DBMS. It provides

• a data definition language (DDL) for describing entities and relationships;

• language facility for updating requests;

• utilities for protecting the dictionary, such as back and recovery facilities; and

• a high-level query language interface for formulating requests for the data dictionary.

Data Dictionary Components

A data dictionary must contain three types of information about data: descriptions, sources, and definitions. It may also contain information about aliases, editing procedures, and allowable values.

Descriptions Descriptions include an ENGLISH-LANGUAGE DESCRIPTION of the data and a MACHINE-ORIENTED DESCRIPTION. In Figure 7-2, "customer number" is defined as "a unique 3-digit identifier assigned to each customer." The machine-oriented description for this item is "PIC X(3)."

Sources Data sources may be end-users or the data processing operations. The dictionary may include a description of how data enters the system (data input), who is responsible for it (authority), and where it comes from. The data processing source explains which program creates the data.

Definitions The DD specifies use of each data item and the programs that access and act on the data.

Customer File		
CUS_NO	CUS_NAME	CUS_ADDRESS
135	Holt	Staunton
461	Tremaine	Chicago

Order File		
ORDER_NO	PART_NO	CUS_NAME
5601	ALE1	Holt
6400	SYS14	Tremaine

Product File		
PART_NO	ACT_COST	INV_ON_HAND
5601	1460.50	60
6400	901.40	110

Data Dictionary					
DATA NAME	ENGLISH NAME	DESCRIPTION	PROGRAM FORMAT	SOURCE	USE
CUS_FILE	Customer file	A listing of customers who have purchased model XL100 during last year	N/A	N/A	Program 14A
CUS_NO	Customer number	Unique 3-digit identifier assigned to each customer	PIC X(3)	Customer's last order	Customer file program 14B
ACT_COST	Actual cost	Based on latest billing from vendors	9999V99	Program A14	Report A product file

Figure 7-2 Relationships between data dictionary and data files

Optional information The data dictionary may list aliases or synonyms, as when "customer number" is also called "customer ID," "CUS_NO," or "buyer."

Data may be subject to examination when it is entered into the system. The set of conditions it must satisfy can be specified in the DD and the process of verifying the data's compliance with these rules is called editing.

Certain data item values may be restricted so that only legal values may be stored. For example, the month portion of "date" is usually restricted to the range 1–12.

Data Dictionary Users and Interfaces

The primary users of the data dictionary are end-users, system developers, information controllers, and system auditors. Each uses the dictionary for a different purpose.

End-Users

The most frequent user of the data dictionary is the end-user. To formulate a data request that conforms to the database system, the end-user must use terms known to the system. The end-user must also know the definitions of the data items that are being processed. Some end-users are also participants in database development or enhancement, and use the data dictionary to determine the potential contributions and impact of proposed changes. Finally, end-users with no prior experience with the data use the dictionary to learn the sources and users of various information and the agents responsible for various related functions.

System Developers

System developers include analysts, database designers, programmers, and all who are responsible for system development, as well as the support staff, such as data entry and computer operators. In the design phase, system developers enter the conceptual data model and information that identifies data entities, attributes, and processes in the data dictionary for verification, and check for compatibility with any existing system. In this respect the dictionary stores all the design specifications, then verifies them and prepares associated reports.

Programmers use the data dictionary to obtain the names and formats of the variables their programs require. In fact, the data definition portions of some programs may be generated from the data dictionary. This improves programmer productivity and ensures that programmers working with the same data use the same definitions for that data.

Information Controllers

Individuals who have responsibility for controlling the database are also frequent users of the data dictionary. Since data definitions are available in machine-readable form, controllers use it as a convenient way to keep up to date. Controllers also use the data dictionary to control user access, since it contains security specifications.

Finally, the dictionary plays a vital role in enforcing database standards. In systems where data definitions are generated from the data dictionary, standards are more easily enforced. In other environments the dictionary can store a standard against which other standards are checked in application programs.

System Auditors

System auditors are playing an increasing role in database environments today, especially when the database is shared. A system auditor is a specialist with a dual background in accounting and information systems whose main job is to examine and assess the reliability and integrity of a database system, or information systems in general. A data dictionary is an ideal way for the auditor to assess information on where data elements and entities are used, who used them, and when they were used.

Interfaces

Software as well as people use the data dictionary. Software that interfaces with the dictionary may include report generators, text editors, the DBMS itself, compilers, and operating systems. Both human and software interfaces with the data dictionary improve the management and control of the database environment.

DATA DICTIONARY STRUCTURE

The data dictionary, like any dictionary, is a set of terms and definitions. Some components of the data flow diagram (DFD) are used in the dictionary, including data flows, data processes, and data elements. A DATA ELEMENT, also called a PRIMITIVE, is the element that cannot be further decomposed into subordinated parts.

Definitions in the dictionary are a top-down partitioning of data. That is, a definition is written in terms of high-level subordinates followed by definitions of those subordinates. For example, if data flow A is composed of B1 and B2, and C is composed of C1, C2, and C3, and D is composed of D1 and D2, we could write the following definition:

```
A = B1 + B2 + C1 + C2 + C3 + D1 + D2
```

Unfortunately such a definition can be unwieldy with complex data flows. To simplify the definitions we use relational operators to define upper-, mid-, and lower-level data.

The relational operators make it possible to define any data dictionary entry as a formula that specifies what is being defined. In the following example the words in capital letters are the relational operators while the lowercased words are data elements:

```
item_identifies IS EQUIVALENT TO: EITHER cat_number
     OR: item_number AND cat_page_number
```

This says that the item can be identified in any of three ways: by the data element "item_identifies," by "cat_number" (catalog number), and by a combination of "item_ number" and a specific page in a catalog ("cat_page_number").

The relational operators and their notations are summarized in Table 7-1.

Relationship	*Operator*	*Notation*
Composed of	IS EQUIVALENT TO	=
Sequence	AND	+
Selection	EITHER/OR	[ ]
Iteration	ITERATION OF	{ }
Optional	OPTIONAL	| |

Table 7–1 Relational operators and their notations

Key Relationships and Operators

Four key relationships describe data and process: sequence, selection, iteration, and optional.

Sequence An instruction that is executed after its predecessor is called a *sequence*. Sequence can also refer to the concatenation of two or more components in a sequence. The "AND" in the "item_identifies" example is called a SEQUENCE OPERATOR.

Selection *Selection* is a choice between two or more alternatives. In the "item_identifies" example "EITHER" and "OR" are SELECTION OPERATORS. Selection options are listed vertically: In the following example an employee's password can be either an employee identification number or a badge number.

```
            ┌              ┐
            │ employee_id  │
Password =  │              │
            │ badge_number │
            └              ┘
```

Iteration *Iteration* is when a component is repeated a number of times. The ITERATION OPERATOR "{" and "}" indicate that the contents of the brackets are to be repeated the designated number of times. For example,

```
Local_extension = First_digit + 3{Digit}3
```

indicates that the local extension is made up of a digit followed by three iterations of the bracketed digit, yielding a four-digit number. A part name specified as

```
Part_name = 1{character}6
```

indicates that the part name is to be made up of from one to six characters.

Optional Some phrases in a data definition may be OPTIONAL. That is, they may or may not be included in the data elements definition. For example, if the password example from above were modified as follows,

```
             | Employee_id |     | Dept_no |
Password  =  |             |  +  |         |
             | Badge_no    |     | SS_no   |
```

the password should be made up of the employee identification number or badge number, with an option to add a second data element, either the employee's department number or social security number. Note that the user can choose one of the two designated data elements.

Redundancy

The level of detail in data definitions is important. Obviously the user must be able to find information—that is the role of a dictionary. But too much detail leads to redundant data, adds little, and can be confusing. Therefore, a procedure that allows no redundancy must be incorporated in the data dictionary. That is, a data dictionary should not have information that is already contained in the primitives of the data flow diagram. For example, in the data dictionary definition

```
Order_line = Quantity_ordered + Unit_price + Item_total
                        * Quantity × Price *
```

the comment portion of the definition (the text between asterisks) specifies the relationship between the basic variables. The comment should not repeat information that is contained in the definition, but only add new information.

ALIASES

An ALIAS is a synonym for an already defined data item. Aliases are generated for two main reasons:

1 Different users have different names for the same item. For example, "purchase order" may be entered by one user as "PO" while another user may call it "Pur_ord."

2 Analysts who work separately with data flow diagrams label data flow differently. It is easier for the analysts to use both names than to settle on one.

Eliminating all aliases is very difficult. When aliases are used they should be explicitly connected to the data item's principal name.

The definition in Figure 7-3 includes an alias, "Travel_Agency_Code" for "BKG_Agent." The definition gives the true meaning of an item, not the name. It is important, then, to identify each alias and specify its meaning or meanings as a part of the data dictionary.

```
Group_Flight_Reservation = Date + Flight_Number +
iteration
                    {Group_Name + Fare_Basis}   ← Iteration
                    = BKG_Agent
BKG_Agent           = Travel_Agency_Code
```

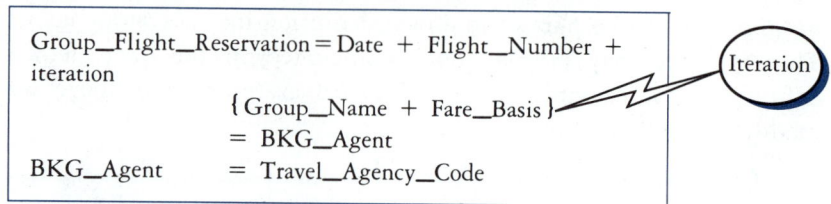

Figure 7–3 Data definition with alias

Naming Conventions

With so many people involved in a database system, agreeing on standard names, including aliases and abbreviations, for each data item in the database is important. Consistency of names requires standard naming conventions, which help people understand and arrive at a similar interpretation for the same data item.

Establishing naming conventions is a three-step process: list, join, and sequence.

List

First, make a list of all English words that might be used to name the data item. Then note which words would be abbreviated and which would not. Carter[1] suggests specific rules for selecting abbreviations:

1 Allow no more than one abbreviation per word. For example "PA," "PENNA," and "PENN" should not all be allowed as abbreviations for "Pennsylvania."

2 Form an abbreviation by dropping at least the last three characters of the word, not characters in the middle. For example, an abbreviation for "NUMBER" would be "NUM," not "NBR."

3 Use an abbreviation consistently as a representation of the word.

4 Do not use an abbreviation for more than one word. For example, "SYN" should not be an abbreviation for "SYNTAX" or "SYNCHRONOUS."

5 Do not use an abbreviation that is another full English word. For example, "MAN" should not be an abbreviation for "MANAGER."

Join

Once abbreviations have been listed, the next step is to form them into data names. Abbreviations may be joined together by underscores or hyphens and then capitalized (first letter only or all capitalized). Whichever style is chosen, it must be consistently used. For example,

[1] Carter, Breck, "On Choosing Identifiers." *ACM SIGPLAN Notices*, May 1982, 54.

names for the data item "item number" might be "ITEM_NUM," "Item_num," "ITEMNUM," "Itemnum," "ITEM-NUM," or "Item-num."

Sequence

Now the terms must be sequenced. Although there are many sequence variations, the most common style starts with the abbreviation containing the broadest context, then adds the one with the next highest context, and so on. For example, the abbreviations for an employee's name might be

```
EMP_NAME_LAST
EMP_NAME_FIRST
EMP_NAME_MIDDLE
```

ENTRIES

The definitions and operators that we have discussed have not distinguished among data flows, data elements, processes, and files. Definitions and entries are not synonymous.

Data Flow Entries

An entry contains more than a definition: It provides detailed information about the element being described. For example, a data flow entry consists of the data flow name, aliases, composition, and notes. The entry is accessed by the data flow name. The alias section contains synonymous data flow names, and the composition section contains the definition. So the entry contains more than just a definition. In addition to the name, aliases, and composition, the data flow entry has a section for explanatory comments. (See Figure 7-4.)

Data Element Entries

Because a data element is not subject to further decomposition, the key components of a data element entry are the values it may assume and their meaning. In Figure 7-5 the data element name is "Booking_Agent," which has three aliases and may assume any one of four values. The notes tell us that two of those values may change without notice. If additional data, such as new aliases or values, are established, then the entry would have to be updated.

Data File Entries

Another type of data dictionary entry is the data file entry. The main difference between a data file entry and a data flow entry is the organization section, which specifies how designated files relate to one another. Such an entry is illustrated in Figure 7-6.

(Synonymous dataflow names) (Definition)

DATAFLOW NAME: STUDENT_GRADE

ALIASES: none

COMPOSITION:

MID_TERM_GRADE
TERM_PAPER_GRADE
FINAL_EXAM_GRADE
PARTICIPATION_GRADE

NOTES:
1. Final exam counts 70% of final grade
2. Other grades are each 10% of final grade

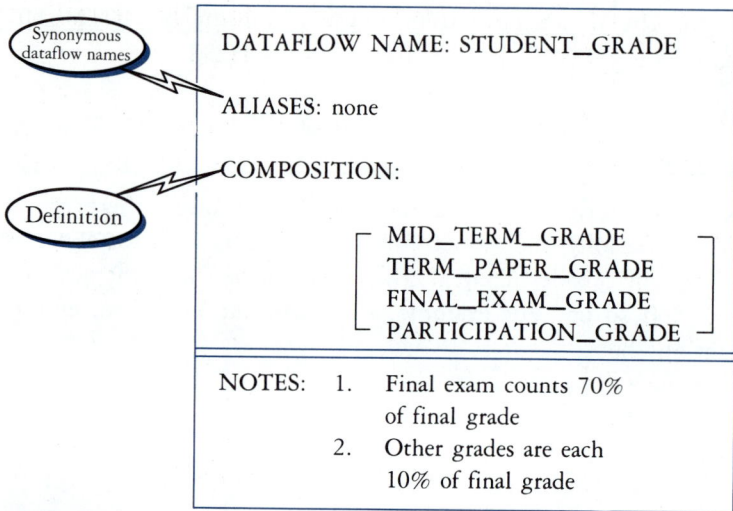

Figure 7-4 Sample data flow entry

(Definition)

DATA ELEMENT NAME: Booking_Agent

ALIASES: BKG_AGENT, BA, TA

VALUES AND THEIR MEANING:

Y	Coach class
M	Super fare basis
F	First class
Q	Super fare; 30-day advance purchase

NOTES: M and Q are subject to change without notice

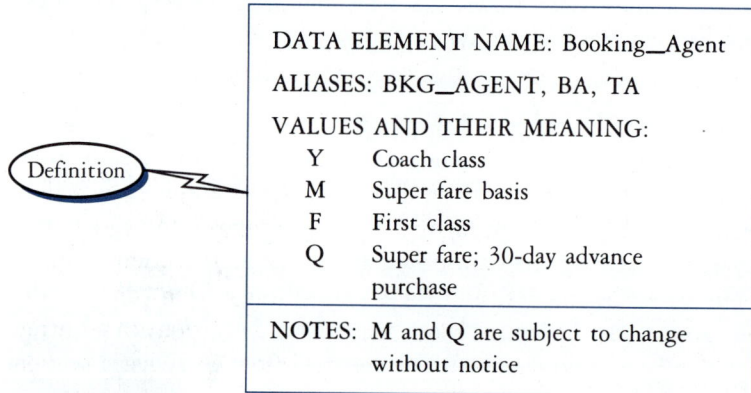

Figure 7-5 Sample data element entry

FILE NAME: Personnel

ALIASES: HUMAN RESOURCES MANAGEMENT

COMPOSITION:

{EMPLOYEE_ID + WORK_EXPERIENCE DESCRIPTION +
PERSONNEL_DATA +
{DEPT_NUMBER + DATE_OF_APPOINTMENT}}

ORGANIZATION:

DIRECT ACCESS BY DEPT_NUMBER

NOTES: Employees with firm less than 90 days, file is by sequential order by EMP_NAME

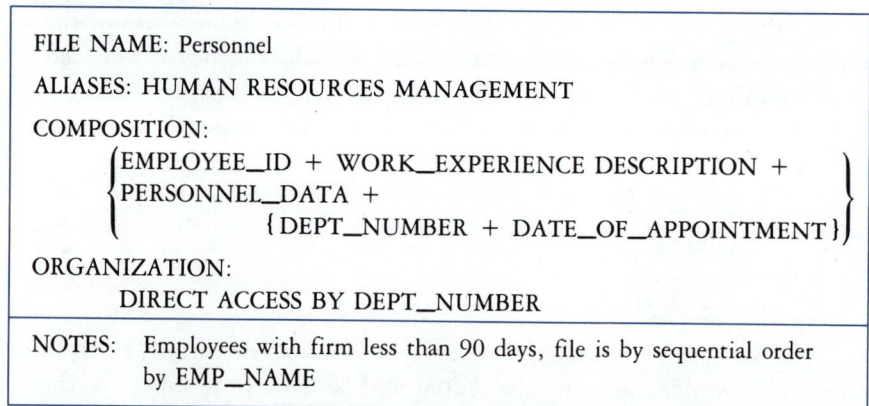

Figure 7-6 Sample file entry

The Data Dictionary/Database Management System Relationship

The relationship between the data dictionary and the database management system may be either independent or fully integrated. That is, the data dictionary may be either a free-standing, independent application—a separate piece of software—or it may be fully integrated into the database management system as one of the DBMS features. (See Figure 7-7.)

Notice that in the first case there are two separate and distinct software systems. In the integrated approach all data descriptions are stored and maintained within the DBMS. The DBMS then can manage the processing, making certain that all processing rules contained within the data dictionary are observed. In a free-standing mode, the DBMS may, or may not, exercise such control.

A viable dictionary must meet the proposed system's hardware and software criteria.

Independent Data Dictionaries

The independent and integrated data dictionaries each have advantages and disadvantages. Among the advantages of an independent data dictionary are the following:

- *Simplicity*. The data dictionary is an independent system and therefore easy to learn and maintain.

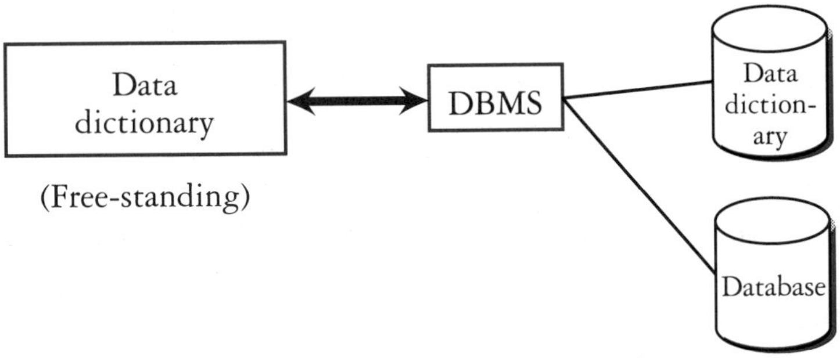

a. Data dictionary as a database management

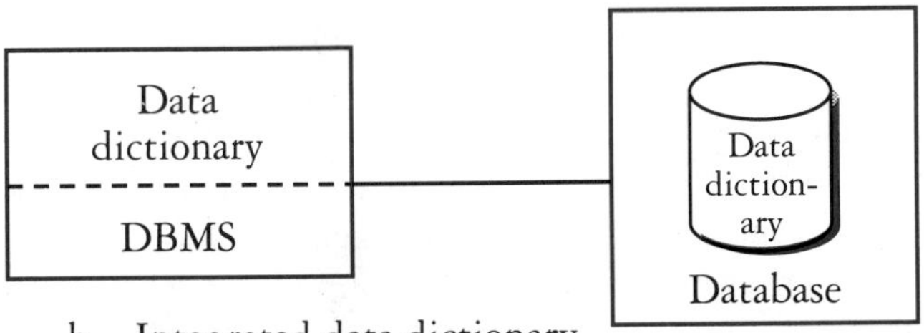

b. Integrated data dictionary

Figure 7-7 DD/DBMS interface

- *Easier implementation*. Since the data dictionary is a limited-function system, it is easier and faster to implement.
- *Incompleteness*. An independent data dictionary need not be fully completed before it is used for an application.

An independent data dictionary has one major disadvantage: its form and content are whatever the user organization wants them to be, not, most likely, the form needed by the DBMS. This can lead to inconsistencies between the data definitions in the data dictionary and those in the DBMS.

Integrated Data Dictionaries

The key advantages of the integrated data dictionary are as follows:

- *Power*. The integrated data dictionary can be more powerful because both designers and users are forced to respect its definitions: The system will not let them do otherwise.
- *Consistency*. Because the database management system enforces the rules specified in the data dictionary, all items are consistent.
- *Singularity*. In an integrated system the data descriptions reside in one, and only one place. Hence redundancy and inconsistency can be controlled.

The principal limitations of the integrated system are as follows:

- *Implementation*. Although integrated, a data dictionary is still a system in and of itself. Thus, two major systems must be implemented at the same time, putting additional stress on an organization.
- *Portability*. Since the data dictionary is an integral part of the database management system, it can be used only with that database management system. It cannot be used in other software environments.

EVALUATING DATA DICTIONARIES

A number of data dictionary products are available. It is therefore necessary to carefully evaluate each of them before making a procurement decision. Ideally, the evaluation procedure adopts objective measurement criteria. This involves preparing a list of the functions that a data dictionary is required to perform and specifying the relative importance of each function. Figure 7-8 identifies the key functions of a data dictionary. In addition to providing evaluation criteria for the data dictionary products, this list serves as a detailed definition of a data dictionary system and, as such, a vehicle for understanding what it can do.

The data dictionary must meet hardware and software criteria. It also must be evaluated on its capability and the degree of vendor support needed and available.

Function	Weight	×	Vendor score	=	Weighted score
Hardware					
Compatible with current hardware	______		______		______
Compatible with future hardware	______		______		______
Software					
Availability of source code	______		______		______
DBMS independence	______		______		______
Modularity	______		______		______
Operating system capability	______		______		______
Source language independence	______		______		______
System Capabilities					
Input flexibility	______		______		______
Standard reports	______		______		______
Cross-reference reports	______		______		______
Query facility	______		______		______
System Operation					
Batch	______		______		______
On-line	______		______		______
Cross-reference maintenance	______		______		______
Vendor Support					
Availability of support	______		______		______
Documentation quality	______		______		______
Enhancements capabilities	______		______		______
Maintenance support	______		______		______
Training availability	______		______		______
Security					
System files and functions	______		______		______

Figure 7–8 DD evaluation checklist

Hardware

The data dictionary system must operate successfully on the organization's current and proposed computer systems. Remember, the computer system is made up of more than just the central processing unit (what users usually refer to as "the computer"). Compatibility must be established with *all* elements of the computer system, such as printers and terminals.

Software

A data dictionary is a collection of computer programs—software. Compatibility with the existing operating system is essential. The software must also be as independent and portable as possible. The importance of software independence in the database environment should be reflected in the weights assigned on the evaluation form (Figure 7-8).

Source code availability and modularity is another software consideration. Will the supplier of the data dictionary system also supply copies of the source code? If so, the designer can customize it to specific system needs and find problems without having to depend on the supplier. This protects the user in the event the supplier goes out of business or stops maintaining the data dictionary system. Modularity is the underlying design of the software. Highly modular software will not load the entire system into memory, only those portions needed for a current operation. This leaves memory available for other activities.

System Capability

Because a data dictionary system is acquired for the functional capabilities it offers, it is necessary to examine the capabilities of each system available. Among the features required should be an entry system that is easy to use (user-friendly). A set of standard reports should be supplemented by a report writer that allows the user to define new reports. Of special importance is a CROSS-REFERENCE REPORT showing where every variable is used in the application system program. This is useful when data problems arise or when data definitions must be changed.

Vendor Support

Several types of support should be available from the system vendor: training, system maintenance and enhancement, documentation, and technical support. Since a data dictionary system is a complex assembly of functions, the vendor should offer training customized for different classes of users. Since no computer software system is static, the supplier should also regularly enhance the data dictionary system with new and improved features. System maintenance, on the other hand, relates to the vendor's responsibility to rapidly remove any "bugs" or ambiguities in the system's operation. Finally, the vendor should provide comprehensive and well-organized documentation and, because the documentation cannot anticipate every user question, technical support available either locally or by telephone.

Rating vendors involves several steps. First the buyer must prioritize the data functions shown in Figure 7-8. Every organization will—and should—weight the factors differently, depending on its needs. Weighting is usually done on a scale of from 1 to 10, 1 denoting least-important functions and 10 denoting highest importance. Next each product must be evaluated function by function. Once again a numeric value from 1 to 10 can be assigned, with a 1 meaning that the system performs that function very poorly and a 10 signifying that it performs the function in an exemplary manner. The weighted score is computed by multiplying importance by performance and then totaling these. The system with the highest score is the one which should be considered the best.

SUMMARY

1 The data dictionary concept was a response to the problem of multiple data element names and differing computer encodings for those data items within data files. The data dictionary system provides a central repository for information about all entities, attributes, and relationships identified during the development of the conceptual model.

2 A data dictionary performs several important functions:

a. It provides a means for finding and managing data.
b. It provides control of information about the data in the design, implementation, and operational phases of a database.
c. It provides a way to store, modify, and retrieve information about the data used in the information systems of an organization.
d. It helps users identify data elements so that they may achieve their goals more effectively.
e. It provides consistent data descriptions.
f. Its data descriptions are created once and then used by all.
g. It provides commonality of data representation.
h. It gives the user a means of controlling changes and synonyms.
i. It provides security by specifying who is authorized to make changes and who "owns" the data.

3 The data dictionary is part of the data dictionary/directory system. It contains definitions of data items, records, relations, and other items of interest to the user. In contrast, the data directory contains information about where the data defined by the data dictionary is stored. Internal schema and programs are also stored in the data dictionary.

4 There is a strong relationship between the data dictionary and the data flow diagram. The data dictionary makes, defines, and documents data flows, processes, and data elements identified by the data flow diagram.

5 The relational operators that may be used to define the data elements and processes are as follows:

a. the sequence operator, which indicates that one instruction is to be executed after another;
b. the selection operator, which indicates two or more components to be selected;
c. the iteration operator, which indicates a component to be repeated a designated number of times; and
d. the optional operator, which indicates an option of using a component or not.

6 An alias is a synonym for an element defined in the data dictionary. Aliases occur when data is referred to in different terms in various components in an organization or when system developers do not have access to a common dictionary of terms.

7 Naming components is a three-step process:

   a. List all possible names for each item.
   b. Join together the names.
   c. Sequence the abbreviations.

8 The data dictionary entries cover data flows, data elements, and data files.

9 The data dictionary may be either independent or fully integrated in the database management system. An independent data dictionary is simpler to use, easier to implement, and capable of being used independent of the database management system, but it requires that two separate systems be implemented and maintained. An integrated data dictionary is more powerful, more consistent, and eliminates the danger of duplicate and inconsistent definitions, but it takes longer to implement and its use is limited to its specific database system.

10 To evaluate competing data dictionary products, first weight each factor according to its importance. Next, rate each data dictionary product on each function. The functions are classified under hardware, software, system capabilities, system operation, vendor support, and security. Finally, multiply weighting by rate for each factor and total the numbers. The product with the highest score may be the best data dictionary for the organization.

KEY WORDS

Alias
Cross-reference report
Data directory
Data element
English-language description
Iteration operator
Machine-oriented description
Optional operator
Primitive
Selection operator
Sequence operator

REVIEW QUESTIONS

1 Explain fully the need for data dictionaries.

2 What is a data dictionary and what are its four major functions? Give an illustration of each.

3 What is the difference between the data dictionary/directory and the data dictionary/manager? What functions does each perform and why?

4 What are the components of a data dictionary? What is the use of each?

5 Who are the principal users of the data dictionary?

6 What is the relationship between the data dictionary and a data flow diagram?

7 What are the relational operators used in defining data? Give examples of each individually and in combination.

8 Are there justifiable uses for aliases? Give some examples of aliases you feel are acceptable.

9 What are the rules for naming? Give an example of their use starting with a English-language definition of the element you are using for your example.

10 What are the four types of entries in a data dictionary? Give an example of each.

11 What are the advantages and disadvantages of independent and integrated data dictionaries?

12 Explain how you would go about deciding which data dictionary you might select for your employer.

APPLICATION PROBLEMS

1 Interpret the following data entries:

a. address = (city) + (state) + (zip)
b. name = (first_name) + (last_name)
c. a = 1{b}
d. a = {b}9
e. a = 9{b}9

2 How logical is it to define "employee_record" as follows?
employee_record = employee_name + mailing_address + 5{zip}

3 What is wrong with each of the following data dictionary definitions?

a. a = b d e
b. a = c + + n
c. a = {c
d. a = 3{b}2
e. a = (z}
f. a = ((b))
g. x = 3{4}6}5

4 Interpret the following data dictionary definition:

`Ship_File = {Ship_Name + Ship_Code}`

5 Write the following data dictionary entries in English:

a. PURCHASE_ORDER = Line_Item
b. Line_Item = Catalog_Number + Quantity + Description (+ Size) (+ Color) + Unit Price + Total Price

6 Write a data dictionary definition for each of the following:

a. Telephone number is made up of location extension, 9 + outside_ number, 8 + WATS_number, 0 *In_House Operator*. All are optional.

b. Invoice line is the summation of item_ID, quantity_ordered, unit_price, item_subtotal *QTY * Price*

7 Write a data dictionary definition representing the information available on

a. your driver's license

b. your passport

c. your credit card

8 Refer to the Island Jumpers, Inc. (IJI) case scenario (Chapter 1) and use the information you generated from the data flow diagram and E-R diagram to develop a data dictionary for IJI. Remember that each entity, process, or file is a candidate for representation in the data dictionary. The sample in Figure 7-9 was generated by Excelerator.

```
DATE:  7-NOV-91              PROCESS - OUTPUT                    PAGE 1
TIME: 13:45                  NAME: 1.0                   Excelerator/IS

TYPE PROCESS-------------------------   NAME 1.0-------------------

 Label        Determine_availability

 Explodes to:      [DFD-STC-PPS-PRG]
 Type DFD Name        diagram_1:Determine_Availability

 Location             -------------------------------

 Process Category     -------------------------------

 Duration Value       -------------------------------
 Duration Type        -------------------------------

 Manual or Computer          C


      Satisfies Requirement:              Associated Entities:
Type Name                              Type Name

                              Description

 This_process_receives_reservation_requests_and_checks_them____
 against_the_reservation_file_to_determine_availability.__It____
 then_receives_the_availability_information_and_sends_the_______
 customer_either_confirmation_information_or_other_suggestions__
 (other_dates,_flights,_vehicles).__If_the_reservation_is_______
 confirmed,_the_reservation_information_is_sent_on_to_be_______
 compiled_with_the_customer's_personal_information.____________

 Modified By    student          Date Modified 911107   # Changes 4
 Added By       student          Date Added    911105
 Last Project   project
 Locked By      _______          Date Locked   0_____
```

Figure 7-9 Excelerator data dictionary entry

C H A P T

Normalization

E R 8

Design Strategies

AT A GLANCE

What Is Normalization?

Record Design

Anomalies

- Update Anomalies
- Deletion and Insertion Anomalies

Normal Forms

- First Normal Form
- Second Normal Form
- Third Normal Form
- Fourth Normal Form

Storage and Performance Considerations

Design Strategies

To develop a smoothly functioning system in a reasonable amount of time, you must start with a correct database design. Yet, in spite of the extensive research and literature on the subject, database design remains more of an art than a science. Most database designers continue to rely on intuition, experience, and trial and error, rather than a rigorous methodology.

Normalization is one popular technique for optimizing table design. It involves breaking information in tables down into smaller tables until each field in each table depends (only) on the key of the table. Theoretically, normalization begins with a single table that contains all data elements in the database. This table is, in essence, all the tables in the database joined into one universal table. Database designers must identify all functional (one-to-one) and join (one-to-many) dependencies and gradually break down the universal table based on these dependencies.

In practice, it is almost impossible to identify all dependencies, especially for large databases that have an overwhelming number of elements. For this reason, designers often begin normalization by taking an educated guess at a few partially decomposed tables and planning to further normalize them later. These tables are smaller and more manageable than one large, comprehensive table, but if the developer's initial guess turns out to be wrong, there's bound to be trouble ahead.

For example, suppose a real estate system has two entities: a building and a tenant. The building contains the following elements: building identifier, address, number of units, building complex number, lot number, and so forth. In the tenant record we track data such as the lease date and employer. From the designer's perspective, the tables and relationships are complete.

Then, during development, we find that building complexes can have multiple addresses and that many include multiple buildings. To accommodate these one-to-many join relationships, we must add two new tables to the database. This impacts all work done up to that point and requires massive redesign and reprogramming.

The Entity-Relationship Method

Many database designers turn to the entity-relationship (E-R) method for help. In fact, most CASE [Computer-Aided Software Engineering] tools are based on the E-R approach. E-R diagrams identify the major entities (objects) in a database and the relationships between them. Entities are then mapped to tables, and attributes (fields) are assigned to each entity.

But the E-R approach has major shortcomings. The first step in E-R is to identify the entities and their relationships. In practice, it is impossible to distinguish between entities, relationships, and attributes. For example, a relationship can become an entity, depending upon how information is used in the database. Many times, you can assign an attribute to two or more entities. Often, what you've designed as an attribute should actually be an entity.

The second weakness is that E-R puts the cart before the horse. The first step of E-R design is to choose entities. Because entities map to tables, this approach essentially asks designers to design tables as their first step. But I believe table design should be the last step, as we shall see.

CASE tools have the weakness of being unable to properly document special types of relationships, such as subtypes. In the aforementioned example, employees can be one of the two subtypes: permanent or temporary. During the physical database design, a designer will map subtypes into one table (with an identifying field) or into separate tables. The actual decision will depend upon how the subtypes are used in the system and their impact on performance. To make the appropriate decisions, designers must be aware of subtypes. CASE tools do have some positive features. For example, they are useful for documenting portions of the data model during development, and designers need all the automated support they can get for preparing documentation. E-R diagrams provide a compact and straightforward way of pictorially representing entities (tables) and relationships as the design progresses, providing designers and users with a quick overview of the database. CASE tools also automate the maintenance of E-R diagrams, which is preferable by far to drawing them by hand.

In conclusion, database design must become more like a science than an art. New tools that take a completely different view of the problem may help us out. DB Software, of Palo Alto, California, for example, is working on a product that will analyze real data using statistical analysis to automatically determine functional dependencies. From this information, the software will generate third normal form tables without any manual intervention. You can use the design as is, or if you are an experienced designer, you can refine it. This approach would allow novice DBMS users to design appropriate tables, and experienced designers to design even better data models faster. As more research is invested in database design, better solutions will emerge.

Finkelstein, Richard, "Design Strategies." *DBMS, January 1991, 22, 24.*
Reprinted with permission of DBMS.

AT A GLANCE

In database system design it is necessary to identify those data elements, or attributes, that must be stored to satisfy the system users. After identification, these attributes must be organized into relations or records and stored in tables or files in the computer. Grouping these attributes into tables is called normalization.

Poor or indifferent database table design can result in inconsistent or redundant data or both. Normalization helps avoid update, insertion, and deletion anomalies by assigning attributes to entities. Normalization also reduces the amount of data to be stored by reducing redundant data.

The organization of data items into records, rows, or tuples is a key issue facing the database designer. If the grouping of fields, or attributes, is well thought out, then we can provide flexibility and efficiency in updating and modifying data while preserving the user view of the data. A formal approach to record design or one that best accommodates change and quick access to data is normalization.

This chapter focuses on the use of normalization as a tool for grouping data items. The basic ideas are simple. The concepts and procedures used in normalization are a fundamental part of the designer's understanding of the data. They are important for designing reliable data structures that minimize the probability of future maintenance problems.

By the end of this chapter you should be able to

- understand the problems of insertion, deletion, and update anomalies;
- understand the significance of functional dependencies among data items;
- convert a table in first normal form into second normal form; and
- convert a table in second normal form into third normal form.

What Is Normalization?

Database designers must group data elements into records (sometimes called rows) and records into files (sometimes called tables) for effective storage in the computer system (see Chapter 6). Even a small database has many possible grouping combinations, and how the groupings are made may have a profound effect on the accuracy and validity of the database.

The technique for organizing data elements into records is called NORMALIZATION. The purpose of normalization is to eliminate possible anomalies of the logical database structure resulting from insertions, updates, and deletions. The design of a database requires an understanding of the functional dependencies among the data elements to be included in the database. This, in turn, requires that the database designer have knowledge of the semantics of the information.

In the normalization process, the designer's objective is to put the right data in the right place; that is, to put data elements into logical records and to order those records in a useful way. When records are poorly designed, data will be inconsistent and highly redundant. When records are well designed, data inconsistency is eliminated and redundancy reduced to a minimum. In addition, when the data elements are combined into records in a meaningful way, certain errors encountered in data entry are eliminated.

As we shall see in this chapter, the process of converting a real world to a model which is understood by the computer is facilitated by normalization. This means we are able to:

- Represent any data relationship as a table.
- Remove unwanted data dependencies and redundancy.
- Minimize the need to modify the data relations as new systems are entered into the database.
- Improve the quality of the information in the database.
- Lower the amount of space needed to store data.

The key to normalization is identifying dependencies between data elements. This requires an understanding of how data elements are interrelated. Without normalization, there are two potential problems:

1 When we update a record, we may not update all redundant copies of the data element.

2 If we delete a record to get rid of unused data, we may lose needed information.

These potential problems are called *anomalies*. The data design process should assign attributes to entities to ensure that the potential problems resulting from adding or deleting existing records do not occur.

To illustrate the importance of normalization, let us assume a local club has a computer-based system that keeps track of members' pledges. Each pledge record has the following format:

```
Name                      Character(35)
Address                   Character(30)
City                      Character(20)
State                     Character(2)
Year_Joined               Character(4)
Amount_Pledged            Money(4.2)
Date_Pledged              Character(12)
```

Some of the records in the file appear as follows:

```
Snyder, N.   123 Elm St Crozet VA 1981  850 Feb 10,1985
Snyder, N.   123 Elm St Crozet VA 1981  300 May 23,1987
Tremaine, A. 461 Oak St Louisa VA 1983 1400 Feb 21,1987
```

Although the record format does not show it, the records themselves clearly demonstrate that this is a poorly designed file. Notice the excessive data redundancy: The first two records repeat the name, address, city, state, and date joined for the member Snyder. Further, in the event Snyder were to move, both records would have to be updated. If only one were updated, each record would show a different address for Snyder, an example of data inconsistency. Further, if the pledge file were purged of all pledge records prior to 1986, one of Snyder's records would be deleted, possibly the one with the correct address.

The obvious solution to the dilemma faced by the club is to provide two files, not one. The first file would contain data about the club member (name, address, city, state, date joined), while the second would contain information about the member's pledges (name, amount pledged, year pledged). Note particularly that the data elements in the first file all relate uniquely to the member, while the data in second file relates to pledges. Now it is possible to make changes in one file without adversely affecting the second. Some, but not all redundancy has been eliminated. The name, or other identifying data, must be repeated in the second file so that its records can be associated with the records in the first file. The new files would now look like this:

```
Member File

Snyder, N      123 Elm St  Crozet  VA  1981
Tremaine, A    461 Oak St  Louisa  VA  1983

Pledge File

Snyder, N       850  Feb 1985
Snyder, N       300  May 1987
Tremaine, A    1400  Feb 1987
```

An ANOMALY is an operation on a database that has unwanted secondary effects, such as loss of data or data inconsistency. Anomalies can be removed through successive levels of normalization of the data. The goal is to ensure that each relationship among data appears only once and that relationships do not depend on one another.

There are three types of anomalies: update, deletion, and insertion.

Update Anomalies

An UPDATE ANOMALY occurs when updating a file becomes unnecessarily complicated due to redundancy, as when updating an attribute of a logical entity occurrence necessitates the updating of several other logical entity occurrences. For example, Figure 8-1a shows a series of records listing dealers, the city in which each operates, the item each has ordered, and the quantity of the ordered item. Dealer Leggett moves from Staunton to Crozet, and Figure 8-1b shows the updated record. But note that the update is reflected only in the first Leggett record; the second Leggett record still shows Staunton as the dealer's city. The data has become inconsistent.

One reason for this is an improperly understood functional dependency. A FUNCTIONAL DEPENDENCY occurs when a unique value of one attribute can always be determined if we know the value of another.

ORDERS

Dealer	City	Item	Qty
Leggett	Staunton	Freezer	6
Michie	Culpeper	Fan	4
Lawson	Madison	Recorder	2
Leggett	Staunton	Fan	2

a. Before update

ORDERS

Dealer	City	Item	Qty
Leggett	Crozet	Freezer	6
Michie	Culpeper	Fan	4
Lawson	Madison	Recorder	2
Leggett	Staunton	Fan	2

b. After update

Figure 8–1 Example of update anomaly

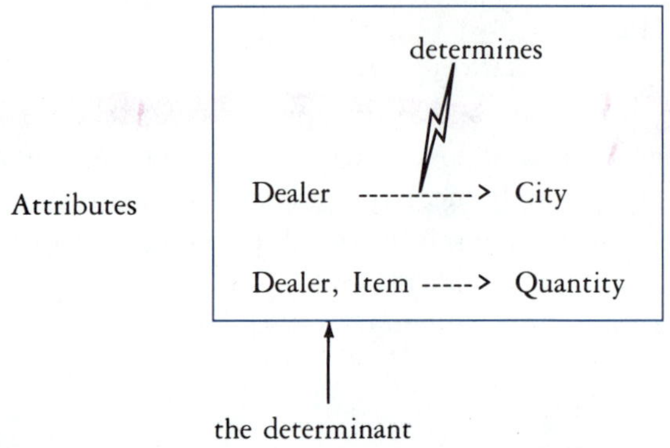

Figure 8–2 Functional dependency diagram of Figure 8-1

A functional dependency between the two attributes "Dealer" and "City" is a one-way relationship such that knowing a value of "Dealer" helps us determine the corresponding value of "City." This is demonstrated in the functional dependency diagram in Figure 8-2. The top relationship reads "Dealer" determines "City," meaning the attribute "Dealer" is the determinant of "City," and that "City" is dependent on "Dealer."

We might be tempted to use the variable "Dealer" as the key for this set of data. But notice that "Dealer" only determines "City," not "Qty." The concatenated key "Dealer, Item" is sufficient to represent all other data attributes in the record. The update anomaly in Figure 8-1b is a violation of the functional dependency "Dealer" determines "City."

Note that the attribute "City" is not dependent on the whole key "Dealer, Item," only on the "Dealer" part of the key. One of the rules for designing databases is that every nonkey variable must be dependent on the whole key.

The update anomaly shown in Figure 8-1b can be eliminated by redesigning the records as shown in Figure 8-3. The functional dependency of the data in Figure 8-3a is now:

```
Dealer, Item ----------> Qty
```

while the dependency in Figure 8-3b is

```
Dealer -----------> City
```

There is no update anomaly in the tables in Figure 8–3 because in each case all nonkey data elements are dependent on the entire key.

Insertion and Deletion Anomalies

An INSERTION ANOMALY occurs when we try to add a record to a file, and it is rejected because it is missing a value or because the data needed for a complete primary key is not available. This problem is often the result of mixing attributes from two or more entities. In contrast, a

ORDERS

a.

Dealer	Item	Qty
LEGGETT	FREEZER	6
MICHIE	FAN	4
LAWSON	RECORDER	2
LEGGETT	FAN	2

b.

Dealer	City
LEGGETT	STAUNTON
MICHIE	CULPEPER
LAWSON	MADISON

Figure **8–3** Update anomaly eliminated by record redesign

DELETION ANOMALY triggers an unintended deletion of data about another record of a different type.

Figure 8-4 shows a series of records subject to insertion and deletion anomalies.

```
Dealer ----------------> Shopping Mall
Shopping Mall --------> City
Dealer ----------------> City
```

Since "Dealer" determines "Shopping Mall" and "Shopping Mall" determines "City," then "Dealer" determines "City," implying that "Dealer" would be an adequate key. But suppose we want to add (insert) the fact that the Westgate shopping mall is in Lynchburg. In the absence of a dealer who is located in Westgate, we have no way to enter this data. Likewise, if we remove dealer "Lawson" from the database, we lose the information that "Cutler" is in "Madison."

These insertion and deletion anomalies can be traced to the TRANSITIVE DEPENDENCY in the data; that is:

```
Dealer ------->Shopping Mall------->City
```

To eliminate the transitivity in functional dependencies, we can decompose the table into the two tables shown in Figure 8-5.

Dealer	Shopping Mall	City
LEGGETT	FASHION SQUARE	STAUNTON
MICHIE	DADELAND	CULPEPER
LAWSON	CUTLER	MADISON

Figure **8–4** Records of dealer locations

Dealer	Shopping Mall
LEGGETT	FASHION SQUARE
MICHIE	DADELAND
LAWSON	CUTLER

Shopping Mall	City
FASHION SQUARE	STAUNTON
DADELAND	CULPEPER
CUTLER	MADISON

Figure **8–5** Redesign of Figure 8-4 records

In Figure 8-5, we have separated the location of a shopping mall from the existence of a dealer in a particular mall. It is now possible to freely insert or delete shopping malls and their associated cities. The deletion of a dealer will not result in the potential loss of data about a shopping mall. The functional dependencies illustrate the independence of the two tables:

```
Dealer -------------->Shopping Mall
Shopping Mall ------->City
```

Normal Forms

Normalization is the process by which data elements are grouped into tables to eliminate anomalies. The stages of normalization—the ways in which attributes can be arranged—are called normal forms. NORMAL FORMS are sets of increasingly stringent rules that govern the design of a table. They are used to successfully examine specific aspects of data relationships in order to reduce the complexity, redundancy, or inconsistency of these relationships.

Normal forms are considered NESTED, by which we mean that each level of normalization is dependent on the previous level. For example, the third normal form depends on the second, and the second normal form on the first normal form. Relations in higher normal forms are considered better than those in lower normal forms, because they are less prone to problems.

First Normal Form

An UNNORMALIZED RELATION is one in which there are repeating fields or fields that are not the key or partial key for the data set. A REPEATING FIELD is a collection of logically related attributes that occur many times within a record or row. When repeating fields are removed, each record in the relation contains the same number of data items or columns. That is, for all records, each column must take a single value. Therefore, we can define a relation in the FIRST NORMAL FORM if and only if every attribute is single-valued for each record.

An unnormalized table is shown in Figure 8-6. Each record contains repeating fields in that the "SKILL"/"YRS" and "PROJ"/"SUPR" columns each contain two values.

EMP* +	POS*	SKILL,	YRS**	PROJ	SUPR**	PAY* (000)	AGE*
AKIN	DESIGNER	PROLOG	2	RESERVATIONS	ODELL	38	26
		dBASE IV	4	BENEFITS	KEHOE		
KING	ANALYST	COBOL	4	PAYROLL	KEHOE	31	34
		PASCAL	3				
TURBAN	PROGRAMMER	COBOL	9	INV.CONTROL	WIRTZ	27	46
		RPG	11	COMPENSATION	KEHOE		
WIRTZ	PROJ.MGR.	ADA	3	SALES ANAL.	WIRTZ	39	41
		UNIX	4				

* = nonrepeating group   + = key
** = repeating group

Figure 8-6 Employee relation unnormalized table

We convert the records in Figure 8-6 to first normal form by reproducing the nonrepeating fields ("EMP," "POS," "PAY," and "AGE") for each combination of values in the repeating fields. As shown in Figure 8-7, this results in more than one record for each employee with more than one skill and assigned to more than one project. Since employee Akin has two language skills (Prolog and dBASE IV) and is assigned to two projects (Reservations and Benefits), there are now four records for this employee. Employee name is no longer a unique key that functionally determines or identifies each record.

An obvious difficulty with the first normal form is that changes made to the data (such as an employee being removed from the relation) may result in an anomaly. The potential update anomaly is present because changes must be made to more than one record. For similar reasons, the deletion anomaly exists. The insertion anomaly is also present because of the potential errors when an employee is added. In this case, multiple records must be added if the employee either has multiple skills or will be assigned to multiple projects or both.

It is important to emphasize at this time the importance of key uniqueness. A key determines or identifies the whole record. If the value of the key were duplicated, then the entire record would be duplicated, which would result in redundancy. The relational model requires that

EMP*	POS*	SKILL*	YRS	PROJ*	SUPR	PAY	AGE
AKIN	DESIGNER	PROLOG	2	RESERVATIONS	ODELL	38	26
AKIN	DESIGNER	PROLOG	2	BENEFITS	KEHOE	38	26
AKIN	DESIGNER	dBASE IV	4	RESERVATIONS	ODELL	38	26
AKIN	DESIGNER	dBASE IV	4	BENEFITS	KEHOE	38	26
KING	ANALYST	COBOL	4	PAYROLL	KEHOE	31	34
KING	ANALYST	PASCAL	3	PAYROLL	KEHOE	31	34
TURBAN	PROGRAMMER	COBOL	9	INV.CONTROL	WIRTZ	27	46
TURBAN	PROGRAMMER	COBOL	9	COMPENSATION	KEHOE	27	46
TURBAN	PROGRAMMER	RPG	11	INV.CONTROL	WIRTZ	27	46
TURBAN	PROGRAMMER	RPG	11	COMPENSATION	KEHOE	27	46
WIRTZ	PROJ.MGR.	ADA	3	SALES ANALYSIS	WIRTZ	39	41
WIRTZ	PROJ.MGR.	UNIX	4	SALES ANALYSIS	WIRTZ	39	41

* = Key

Figure 8–7 Employee relation in first normal form

rows be unique. Therefore, when we say that a given attribute is a key, we mean that the key is unique.

Second Normal Form

The requirements of the first normal form can be satisfied by eliminating repeating nonkey fields. The SECOND NORMAL FORM is defined in terms of functional dependencies—the relationship between nonkey and key fields—and requires that every nonkey field be fully and functionally dependent on the whole key of the record.

In Figure 8-8 the relation shown in Figure 8-7 has been split into two relations. The first (Figure 8-8a), the employee relation, has "EMP" as its key. Note particularly that the employee name uniquely defines a record and that all nonkey fields are functionally dependent on the key "EMP." The skills relation (Figure 8-8b) contains information about the employees' skills. The skills relation has a compound key, "EMP + SKILLS," and the field "YRS" is functionally dependent on the entire key.

The key for a record made up of data items "Employee," "Skill Code," "Skill Desc," and "Date Completed" is made up of "Employee" + "Skill Code," a compound key. To be in second normal form, all nonkey data items must be functionally dependent on the entire key. But "Skill Desc" is dependent on only part of the key, "Skill Code." "Date Completed" is dependent on the entire key, because it tells when a particular person completed the requirements for a particular skill. Two sets of information have been combined in one relation. In this case, the two tables are

```
Skill Code     Skill Desc
Employee       Skill Code     Date Completed
```

EMP	POS	PAY	AGE
AKIN	DESIGNER	38	26
KING	ANALYST	31	34
TURBAN	PROGRAMMER	27	46
WIRTZ	PROJ.MGR.	39	41

a. EMP relation

EMP	SKILLS	YRS
AKIN	PROLOG	2
AKIN	dBASE IV	4
KING	COBOL	4
KING	PASCAL	3
TURBAN	COBOL	9
TURBAN	RPG	11
WIRTZ	ADA	3
WIRTZ	UNIX	4

b. SKILLS relation

Figure **8–8** Personnel database in second normal form

(Underscored words are keys.) Now we have a skill relation in which each "Skill Code" uniquely defines a "Skill Desc." We also have a separate relation in which the combined key of "Employee + Skill Code" functionally determines "Date Completed."

The solution, then, to the problem that some nonkey fields are not dependent on the entire key is to divide the relation into two relations. Each new relation is formed so that all nonkey fields are dependent on the entire key. It follows, therefore, that a relation in first normal form in which all nonkey fields are functionally dependent on the entire key is also in second normal form.

Third Normal Form

A relation is said to be in THIRD NORMAL FORM if every nonkey field is not transitively dependent on the primary key. That is, the third normal form is violated if a nonkey field is dependent on another nonkey field. A transitive dependency, you will recall, is a functional dependency among three attributes such that A determines B, B determines C, and A determines C. A relation is in third normal form when each nonkey field is functionally dependent on the whole key and nothing else, and when there are no transitive dependencies.

For example, in the relation

```
Student    Dept    Building
```

the "Student" field is the key. But the building in which a department is housed is not dependent on the key, "Student," but rather on the "Dept." A relation containing this type of dependency creates data inconsistency and update problems. For example, if the location of a department is changed, then all student records containing that department must be individually updated to show the new building assignment for the department. The relation should be decomposed as

```
Student    Dept
Dept       Building
```

In the personnel example in Figure 8-6, since each employee is working on one or more projects, we could create a separate table to represent the employees and their projects. The data items "EMP" and "PROJ" can become a table called "PROJECT." The key for this table, "EMP," provides the link between this table and the table that contains information about the employee. Since the supervisor of a project is not dependent on the employee but on the project, this relation must also be divided into two tables. The four tables in Figure 8-9 show the employee relation in third normal form.

EMP relation

EMP	POS	PAY	AGE
AKIN	DESIGNER	38	26
KING	ANALYST	31	34
TURBAN	PROGRAMMER	27	46
WIRTZ	PROJ.MGR.	39	41

SKILLS relation

EMP	SKILLS	YRS
AKIN	PROLOG	2
AKIN	dBASE IV	4
KING	COBOL	4
KING	PASCAL	3
TURBAN	COBOL	9
TURBAN	RPG	11
WIRTZ	ADA	3
WIRTZ	UNIX	4

PROJECT relation

EMP	PROJ
AKIN	RESERVATIONS
AKIN	BENEFITS
KING	PAYROLL
TURBAN	INV.CONTROL
TURBAN	COMPENSATION
WIRTZ	SALARY ANALYSIS

SUPR relation

PROJ	SUPR
RESERVATIONS	ODELL
BENEFITS	KEHOE
PAYROLL	KEHOE
INV.CONTROL	WIRTZ
COMPENSATION	KEHOE
SALARY ANALYSIS	WIRTZ

Figure 8–9 Personnel data in third normal form

A relation in third normal form avoids the anomalies found in the first and second normal forms and minimizes, but does not eliminate, data redundancy.

The rules for the first three normal forms are shown in Table 8-1.

Normalization Level	*Rules*	*Comments*
Unnormalized Relations		Records with repeating fields
First normal form	• All attributes of a relation be atomic (single-valued) • No *repeating fields*. Each repeating field element becomes individual row	Repeating fields destroy the natural rectangular structure of a table
Second normal form	• Table must be in first normal form • Removal of anomalies • All nonkey attributes are *fully dependent* on the primary key	Decompose table or split records to produce a second normal form table
Third normal form	• Table must be in second normal form • Remove *transitive* dependencies • Every key is not transitively dependent on the primary key	Place attributes not dependent on the key into a separate table

Table 8–1 Summary of rules for first three normal forms

The normalization process can be accomplished in five steps:

1 List the unique identifiers required for the database. For example, identifiers for an inventory system might be the serial number of a part, a code for the part type, a code for the part's location, etc.

2 Determine the nature of the relationships among the identifiers. That is, are relationships one-to-one, one-to-many, or many-to-many? For example, a part number has a one-to-one relationship between the number and the part, but a location code may have a one-to-many relation to parts stored there.

3 Eliminate the many-to-many relations, since the database system cannot uniquely identify the matching occurrences of the identifiers. This is most commonly accomplished by dividing the many-to-many relations into two or more one-to-many relations.

4 Identify the nonkey fields of each unique identifier and group them accordingly.

5 Check to make certain that the relations are in third normal form: no repeating groups, no functional dependencies, and no transitive dependencies.

Fourth Normal Form

Many database administrators are content to stop at the third normal form. And most of the time, third form will produce an effective database without anomalies. But in some situations further normalization is necessary. The FOURTH NORMAL FORM addresses multivalued determinancies—facts that correspond to many-to-many relations. The relationship between students and courses is a many-to-many relationship, for example, because a student typically enrolls in more than one class and a class contains more than one student.

In order for a relation to be in fourth normal form, it must first be in third normal form and must not contain two or more independent multivalued facts about an entity. The relation

```
Student   Course   Club
```

is in third normal form because it has no repeating fields, all nonkey attributes are dependent on the primary key, and there are no transitive dependencies in the data. But a student may enroll in more than one course and may join more than one club: two many-to-many relations that are independent of each other and, therefore, are not in fourth normal form. The alternative is to create two records:

```
Student   Course          Student   Club
```

Had the original relation not been changed, the relation with some data would have looked like this:

STUDENT	COURSE	CLUB
Hays	BA 110	Psychology
Hays	BS 427	MIS
Hays	CS 159	Delta Chi

The problems inherent in this table are update, insertion, and deletion anomalies. One approach to maintaining independent multivalued facts in one record is to allow a row to contain a course or a club, but not both. This relation would then appear as

STUDENT	COURSE	CLUB
Hays	BA 110	
Hays	BS 427	
Hays	CS 159	
Hays		Psychology
Hays		MIS
Hays		Delta Chi

But this format is unclear because it contains blanks. Does a blank in the "COURSE" column mean that the student is not enrolled, that data about courses is not available, or that data about courses is stored elsewhere?

Another approach to the problem of multivalued dependencies suggests that our sample would look like this:

```
STUDENT   COURSE   CLUB

Hays      BA 110   Psychology
Hays               Legal
Hays      BS 110   MIS
Hays               Delta Chi
```

But with this approach deleting a course may result in the loss of data about a club membership; inserting a course may involve searching for a blank or inserting a new record; and in case of repetition, updating might be necessary in multiple records that, in turn, could become inconsistent.

Finally, we need to stress the negative impact of the independent multiple multivalued determinants in a record. The many-to-many relationships ("STUDENT:COURSE" and "STUDENT:CLUB") are independent of each other, because there is no dependency between course and club. There might be an indirect relationship, in that the student who enrolls in a course in dramatic arts is perhaps more likely to join the drama club, but membership in a club is not a course requirement. This pairing of two or more independent multivalued facts in the record can create data maintenance and integrity problems.

Storage and Performance Considerations

Experience has shown that grouping data items in the third normal form improves system performance because the third normal form ensures that data redundancies are minimized and, therefore, less storage will be required. Although decomposition produces more records, the resulting records almost always occupy less storage space. The reason for this savings is that well normalized relations have minimum or no redundancy in attributes that take on values and are not keys. Normalization often results in reduced machine time, too, because the need for multiple updates, deletions, and insertions has been eliminated.

The normalization process and the desirability of developing third normal forms (fourth normal forms when the data requires it) are extremely important parts of the database design process. Normalization is emphasized in the development of relational databases, but it can be easily applied in other cases as well.

SUMMARY

1 The database designer must identify the data elements to be stored in the database, then group them into logical storage units called tables or files. Grouping data elements into tables or files is called normalization.

2 Normalization deals with the functional dependencies among the data elements. It is, in essence, concerned with logical database design, validating data relationships.

3 The first step in normalization is to identify the keys by which the data may be accessed. The second step is to identify the nature of the relation between the data and the keys. Next, repeating fields must be eliminated from the data. Finally, there must be no functional dependencies or transitive relations between the key and the data elements.

4 There are three types of anomalies: update anomalies, which occur when updating a file becomes unnecessarily complicated; insertion anomalies, which occur when we try to add a record to a file and it is rejected; and deletion anomalies, which occur when a deletion triggers an unintended deletion of data.

5 Normal forms are rules that govern the design of a relation. The first normal form requires that the repeating fields of nonkey items be eliminated. The second normal form requires that every nonkey item is functionally dependent on the primary key. The third normal form requires removal of transitive dependencies.

6 The fourth normal form addresses many-to-many relationships between data or multivalued determinacies. All data in third normal form must be examined to see whether these conditions are present. If so, the fourth normal form is used to eliminate the problem.

KEY WORDS

Anomaly
Deletion anomaly
First normal form
Fourth normal form
Functional dependency
Insertion anomaly
Nested
Normal form
Normalization
Repeating field
Second normal form
Third normal form
Transitive dependency
Unnormalized relation
Update anomaly

REVIEW QUESTIONS

1 What is normalization? What are the main objectives of normalization?

2 "The key to normalization is identifying dependencies among data elements." Do you agree? Explain.

3 Describe a situation that illustrates the importance of normalization.

4 Distinguish the difference between the following pairs:

a. update anomaly and insertion anomaly
b. insertion anomaly and functional dependency
c. functional dependency and transitive dependency

5 When does a deletion anomaly occur? Give an example to illustrate.

6 What characterizes the first normal form? The second normal form?

7 What is a repeating field? Give an example.

8 When is a relation in third normal form? Why do most designers stop at this level of normalization?

9 How practical is it to go beyond the third normal form?

10 What distinguishes fourth from third normal form? Explain briefly.

APPLICATION PROBLEMS

1 The bank's systems analyst has identified the data elements required by the safe deposit management system as

```
Boxholder
     First Name
     Middle Initial
     Last Name
     Address
     City
     State
     Zip Code
     Phone Number
Deputy Boxholder
     Same as for Boxholder
Box
     Box Number
     Box Size
          Length
          Height
          Depth
     Box Category
     Key Number
Date Rented
```

Design a normalized table, or file, system for the safe deposit system. Provide clear documentation and a discussion of your design demonstrating that it meets all the requirements for a good design and does not violate any of the rules for any normal form.

2 The following is a conceptual file containing potential anomalies.

`CUSTOMER (CUSTOMER_NO, TRAN_CODE, CNAME, PHONE, SIZE, UNITS, COST_PER_UNIT, TOTAL)`

A tabular occurence of the conceptual file is shown in Table 8-2.

CUSTOMER_NO	TRAN_CODE	CNAME	PHONE	SIZE	UNITS	COST_PER_UNIT	TOTAL
100	12A	ARNOLD	210-5000	REG	2	16.70	33.40
100	10B	ARNOLD	169-6160	LARGE	1	14.10	14.10
110	12A	FROST	296-6206	SMALL	6	27.00	162.00

Table 8–2 Customer order table on

a. The conceptual file is a poorly designed file. Do you agree? Why?
b. Explain where or in what way the addition, deletion, and update anomalies are suspect.
c. Show three examples of a fully functional dependency.
d. Show a functional dependency that is not fully dependent.

3 What is the normal form of each of the following relations?

a. INVOICE (INVNO, TRANNO, INVDATE, VENDORNO, TRANCOST)

if:

```
INVNO -------------> VENDORNO
INVNO -------------> INVDATE
INVNO, TRANNO------> TRANCOST
```

b. CAR (CARNO, MODELID, COLORID, PRICE, ONHAND)
MODEL (MODELID, MODEL)
COLOR (COLORID, COLOR)

if:

```
CARNO -------> COLORID
CARNO -------> MODELID
CARNO -------> PRICE
CARNO -------> ONHAND
COLORID------> COLOR
MODELID------> MODEL
```

4 Consider the following relation:

BOOK #	TITLE	AUTHOR
146	MIS	ARNOLD
201	DATABASE	NEWCOMB, JOHNSON
146	MIS	ARNOLD

a. What is wrong with this relation?

b. What is the name of the relation?

c. What are the attribute types?

d. Is "database" an attribute type or an attribute value?

5 Review the following relations and state the highest normal form of each with any assumptions to support your answer.

a. JOB1 (EMPNO, EMPNAME, JOB_TITLE, DATE_HIRED)

b. JOB2 (EMPNO, EMPNAME, SSN, DEPENDENT_NAME, DEPENDENT_AGE, DEPENDENT_SEX, DEPENDENT_RELATION_TO_EMP)

c. JOB3 (EMPNO, EMPNAME, PROJ_NO, PROJ_NAME, EMP_SUPR)

d. JOB4 (EMPNO, EMPNAME, DEGREE, ALMA_MATER, DATE_GRADUATED)

6 Examine the following sets of functional dependencies and identify any redundant functional dependencies in each

a.
```
A---------->B
A---------->D
B---------->D
```

b.
```
AC--------->B
A---------->E
E---------->C
```

7 Review the following relation.

INV (INUM, INVENTORY, RESERVE) where:
INUM = item number
INVENTORY = inventory level
RESERVE = minimum inventory before order

An instance of this relation is:

INUM	INVENTORY	RESERVE
101	9320	432
192	7645	235
410	8500	100
533	7565	235
700	8989	455

What normal form is this relation in? Justify your answer.

8 Consider this relation.

```
STUDENT (NUM, NAME, ADVISOR)
```

Assuming that a student may have only one advisor,

a. is "ADVISOR" functionally dependent on "NUM"?
b. is "NUM" functionally dependent on "ADVISOR"?

C H A P T

Structured Query Language and Data Manipulation

E R 9

Database Server Performance

AT A GLANCE

Database Server Performance

"Relational means poor performance." In the early years of the relational era, this statement was a primary reason organizations delayed the move to a relational DBMS. While the last few years have seen such enormous performance improvements in relational DBMSs that the argument rings hollow—and IBM's OS/2EE Database Manager in particular offers very high performance—it cannot be denied that performance is always a consideration when designing database applications.

What follows are "rules of thumb" that apply generally to SQL database performance; most aren't specific to IBM's OS/2EE Database Manager. The reasons for this are several. First, if you use techniques that pertain strictly to the OS/2 Database Manager and not to similar DBMSs, such DB2, SQL/DS, or Oracle, you limit portability. Second, even within Database Manager, many of the more obscure rules of SQL efficiency are release-dependent. It is poor programming practice to rely on release-dependent techniques, because you guarantee your application's obsolescence and the need to rework it at some unspecified point in the future. I strongly recommend against succumbing to fascination with obscure release-dependent efficiency techniques.

Efficient SQL

In basic retrieval statements, there is quite a lot you can do to maximize the Database Manager's efficiency in resolving your query. First, select only columns you need. Overly broad queries consume unnecessary processing time. (This principle also applies to rows—only those rows you need should appear in your result set.)

Where To Index

At the highest level, there are two reasons to build indexes. The first reason is that the index will increase retrieval performance for appropriate queries. The second is that in a relational system like the Database Manager, an index is the mechanism through which you ensure the uniqueness of indexed column(s).

Remember that it is always Database Manager's decision whether to use an index to resolve a query. However, you decide whether to build the index and on what column(s) to build it. It is also important to remember that the benefits of indexing come at a cost.

These include

- The disk space consumed by the index. Numerous indexes on a table significantly increase its space requirement.
- Indexes are transparently updated by the Database Manager in real-time whenever those columns are updated, inserted, or deleted. Numerous indexes on a table slow interactive data maintenance.
- Indexes on very small tables or indexes built on columns that are poor candidates for indexes may rarely be used. In this case, there are costs but no benefits to indexing.

Programming Techniques

A wide variety of programming techniques decrease the execution time required by a program. Some enhance the performance of the program in which they are used; others have little effect on the program in which they are employed but may increase overall performance in a multiuser environment.

Key to the best overall application performance is the distinction between the *designed* or *preprogrammed* application versus that of the ad hoc environment. Programmed applications endeavor to meet all potential user needs by code supplied in the application. Typically, preprogrammed applications are menu-driven and, therefore, they limit the user to menu options that cover all the anticipated user functions.

The benefit of the programmed application is predictability. Since you developed all the code, you control the manner in which all SQL queries are formulated and how and when they are issued. You have a greater knowledge of how to do this efficiently than do users. Moreover, you prevent the disastrously expensive queries those users sometimes create with a powerful set-processing language like SQL.

Structured applications ensure that the efficiency techniques in this article are employed, versus the hit-or-miss techniques that users will employ in the free-form, ad hoc processing environment.

Preprogrammed applications are always more efficient than ad hoc work where relational database management systems are involved.

Excerpted from Fosdick, Howard, "Database server performance." *DBMS, June 1990, 36ff. Reprinted with permission of* DBMS.

AT A GLANCE

SQL is the language used to create, manipulate, and maintain a relational database system. It is used as a standalone language or embedded into other languages such as COBOL or C. The surprisingly few commands in SQL cover three basic groups of activities: data definition statements, data manipulation statements, and data control commands.

The data definition commands are used to create tables or indexes or to eliminate them from the database. Data manipulation commands are used to insert data into a table, change existing data, remove rows from tables, and select data from a table. Data control commands involve access control (identifying which individuals will have access to which data within the database) and data integrity through transaction control.

In a DBMS, each user has a unique picture or view of the database. Because functions of other columns may appear as a column in a particular view, it is possible to further limit access to data. Views, in general, offer several advantages, including data independence, security, and integrity of the database.

Indexing is a special concept in SQL, designed to improve the efficiency with which data is accessed or retrieved from the database. Indexes speed up some database operations, especially joins and insertions, although each additional index slows down processing in general. An index can be removed without removing the table on which it is based.

By the end of this chapter, you should be able to

- use SQL commands and notations;
- create a new table, drop a table, or alter a table;
- work with datatypes and the null clause;
- use the INSERT, UPDATE, DELETE, SELECT, and ACCESS control commands; and
- create and drop views and indexes.

INTRODUCTION

The language for creating, maintaining, and manipulating a relational database system is called Structured Query Language (SQL). This language can be either standalone or embedded into other languages such as C and COBOL. SQL is also an integral part of a number of commercial database systems, including the widely used DB/1, Oracle, and INFORMIX.

SQL has a long and rich history. Its development is generally credited to the database research team at IBM's San Jose Research Laboratory, when they were working on advanced database systems in 1970. SQL is unique among computer languages in that its developers based the language on applied predicate calculus. Its development went through a number of versions, referred to as SQUARE and SEQUEL, before it emerged in its present form.

SQL has been standardized by the American National Standards Institute in its publication *Database Language SQL*,[1] which means it is available to anyone who chooses to use it. The standard contains syntax and semantics of the language. Like all ANSI standards, this one is under constant review by volunteer committees of experts who recommend changes and additions from time to time. After a lengthy review process, new documents are published updating the original standard. The fact that SQL has been standardized is not a minor consideration. When a language complies with a standard, the user knows what it contains and what its capabilities are. Think, for example, of COBOL and BASIC.

NOTATION AND COMMANDS

In this chapter, the SQL commands are capitalized; lowercase letters are used for user-supplied information. For example, the following command specifies that the SQL command DELETE TABLE is to be executed on the table named by the user.

```
DELETE TABLE user-specified-table;
```

Every SQL statement is terminated with a termination symbol. In this and the next chapter we use the semicolon (;) for that purpose.

[1] *Database Language SQL*, (ANSI X3.136-1986) American National Standards Institute, New York, 1986.

Other notations will be introduced when needed throughout these chapters.

There are surprisingly few commands in SQL. The basic commands and their descriptions are contained in Table 9-1. This list of commands is in a constant state of development because the ANSI standard is constantly being reviewed and because individual implementors may add their own commands as extensions to the language. Of course the user is free to ignore these language extensions.

Command	*Explanation*
ALTER	Modify a previously defined file
COMMIT	Post a completed transaction to the database
CREATE	Create files, indexes, or views
DELETE	Remove rows from a table
DROP	Delete the designated table, index, or view from the database
GRANT	Assign designated database privileges to a user or group of users
INSERT	Add a row to a table
REVOKE	Cancel previously granted database privileges
ROLLBACK	In the event a transaction is not completed, return the database to its original state
SELECT	Select specified rows and columns in table(s)
UPDATE	Change the value of data in a row

Table 9–1 Basic SQL commands

The commands cover three basic groups of activities: data definition statements (ALTER, CREATE, and DROP), data manipulation statements (INSERT, UPDATE, DELETE, and SELECT), and data control commands (COMMIT, ROLLBACK, GRANT, and REVOKE).

Data Definition Statements

The data definition commands contained in SQL are used to create tables or indexes, or to eliminate them from the database.

CREATE TABLE

Since a relational database is a collection of one or more tables, creating a table is one of the most basic operations. To create a simple table called "employee_table," which will contain employees' names, addresses, social security numbers, the number of the job to which they are currently assigned, and the department in which each employee works, we can use the CREATE TABLE command as follows:

```
CREATE TABLE employee_table
     (ss_no              CHAR(11),
     first_name          CHAR(12),
     mi                  CHAR(1),
     last_name           CHAR(15),
     address             CHAR(25),
     city                CHAR(15),
     state               CHAR(2),
     zip                 CHAR(5),
     phone_no            CHAR(8),
     date_of_birth       CHAR(8),
     sex                 CHAR(1),
     date_hired          CHAR(8),
     date_terminated     CHAR(8),
     job_no              INTEGER,
     dept_no             INTEGER);
```

Note that this command has created a table named "employee_table" (Table 9-2), which contains 15 columns. All except for the last two, the employee's job number and department number, are of character data with the designated amount of space assigned to each data item. The two exceptions, the job number and department number, are integers. They could have been characters as well: the decision of which datatype to use is based on the nature of the data and the use to which it will be put.

Datatypes The basic datatypes provided by SQL are character, integer, and real; the latter have several variations. While all database operations can be performed with these three datatypes, others are often included in extended SQL. One of the more common, and useful, is the DATE DATATYPE. With date as the datatype it is possible to do very simple date arithmetic. For example, we could define a variable "length_of_service" as equal to "date_terminated − date_hired." In the CREATE TABLE example, the date datatype would be useful for the two date fields and would change the declaration as follows:

```
date_hired          DATE,
date_terminated     DATE,
```

Column specifications Two additional optional specifications that can be used in defining each column are UNIQUE and NOT NULL. NULL means an actual value is either unknown or not applicable. A column that is specified UNIQUE will not be allowed to contain duplicate values. In a column specified NOT NULL a valid value will have to be entered before the data is inserted into the database. In the employee table it would be reasonable to expect that an employee's social security number is unique, and any duplicate is an error; furthermore, a social security number is an essential part of the employee's record, without which the company cannot pay the employee or withhold taxes. Therefore, the social security number column should be specified UNIQUE and NOT NULL. Likewise, we would not want to allow a new employee record to

SS No	First Name	MI	Last Name	Address	City	St	Zip	Phone No	DOB	Sex	Date Hired	Date Term	Job No	Dept
230-76-2438	Mary	F	Barnes	1265 SW 32 Road	New York	NY	10045	102-9384	04/25/65	F	07/21/85		1	1
092-02-0188	John	J	Allison	P O Box 125	Brooklyn	NY	10067	283-7465	07/01/63	M	10/19/84		14	3
320-71-1872	Alice	C	Marks	875 Grand Ave	Newark	NJ	10101	718-0914	10/13/60	F	11/01/81		5	3
543-02-9428	Paul	P	Altman	1954 Riverside Ave	New York	NY	10045	102-3745	01/23/55	M	08/03/83		3	1
193-28-3746	Henry	D	Hirsch	75219 Park Place	Bronx	NY	10054	102-4523	06/27/64	M	04/15/84		4	1
405-96-8776	Bruce	R	Morgan	8543 Maple St	Newark	NJ	10111	729-3782	11/30/70	M	03/05/90		11	2
697-88-9706	Tony	NI	Hunter	R R 45	New York	NY	10034	283-4632	09/06/57	M	02/17/78	06/30/85	13	2
718-29-3041	David	D	Sargent	5673 NE 37 Place	Brooklyn	NY	10012	932-2359	12/18/53	M	05/20/70		5	1
829-10-0192	James	H	Whitehead	743 First Rd	Bayonne	NJ	10121	365-4582	11/15/59	M	09/30/80		6	3
920-11-2031	Larry	Y	Lewis	654 Atlantic St	Hartford	CT	10020	283-1682	08/28/61	M	12/06/82		12	2
294-38-2342	Josephine	L	Marshall	453 Maple Dr	Hartford	CT	10020	718-3484	08/19/50	F	06/27/70		6	3

Table 9–2 Employee table

be created without the person's name, so the name columns must be NOT NULL (but *not* UNIQUE, since the company could employee two Ann Johnsons). The lines specifying name and social security number would look like this:

```
CREATE employee_table
   (ss_no                CHAR(11) UNIQUE NOT NULL,
   first_name            CHAR(12) NOT NULL,
   mi                    CHAR(1)  NOT NULL,
   last_name             CHAR(15) NOT NULL,
   ......                .......);
```

Now the employee's full name and social security number must be present, and the social security number must not be a duplicate.

CREATE INDEX

In his article, "Database Server Performance," excerpted on page 238, Howard Fosdick points out that there are two reasons for indexing a table: Indexing improves performance and guarantees uniqueness of indexed columns. Indexes are also useful for sorting data. For example, if you almost always sort sales data by customer name, then it would be wise to index on the customer name column. This way the data would be in the proper order.

Indexes speed up some database operations but, unfortunately, each additional index slows down processing in general because every time a row is added to or deleted from the table, or the key value of a row is changed, the index must also be updated. Therefore, indexes should be used as needed but not excessively.

For the employee table we can create an index on the employee's name with the statement

```
CREATE INDEX name_index
     ON employee_table(last_name,first_name,mi);
```

In this particular table another index, one for social security numbers, might be very useful because it is likely that queries using "name_index" will produce multiple responses which result in isolating the particular person being sought. A known social security number can narrow the responses to one, and the record can be retrieved rapidly. The specification for a social security number would look like this:

```
CREATE UNIQUE INDEX social_security
     ON employee_table(ss_no);
```

The UNIQUE specification again prevents duplicate social security numbers from entering the table. (If the column had been specified to be UNIQUE and NOT NULL in the CREATE TABLE command, the specification UNIQUE in the index command would not be necessary.) This index ensures that, when a social security number is inserted or updated, the system will check to make certain that the entry is not a duplicate. This index is shown in Table 9-3.

EMPNUM INDEX	
SS_No	Row No
092020188	2
193283746	5
230762438	1

SS No	First Name	MI	Last Name	Address	City	St	Zip	Phone No	DOB	Sex	Date Hired	Date Term	Job No	Dept
230-76-2438	Mary	F	Barnes	1265 SW 32 Road	New York	NY	10045	102-9384	04/25/65	F	07/21/85		1	1
092-02-0188	John	J	Allison	P O Box 125	Brooklyn	NY	10067	283-7465	07/01/63	M	10/19/84		14	3
320-71-1872	Alice	C	Marks	875 Grand Ave	Newark	NJ	10101	718-0914	10/13/60	F	11/01/81		5	3
543-02-9428	Paul	P	Altman	1954 Riverside Ave	New York	NY	10045	102-3745	01/23/55	M	08/03/83		3	1
193-28-3746	Henry	D	Hirsch	75219 Park Place	Bronx	NY	10054	102-4523	06/27/64	M	04/15/84		4	1
405-96-8776	Bruce	R	Morgan	8543 Maple St	Newark	NJ	10111	729-3782	11/30/70	M	03/05/90		11	2
697-88-9706	Tony	NI	Hunter	R R 45	New York	NY	10034	283-4632	09/06/57	M	02/17/78	06/30/85	13	2
718-29-3041	David	D	Sargent	5673 NE 37 Place	Brooklyn	NY	10012	932-2359	12/18/53	M	05/20/70		5	1
829-10-0192	James	H	Whitehead	743 First Rd	Bayonne	NJ	10121	365-4582	11/15/59	M	09/30/80		6	3
920-11-2031	Larry	Y	Lewis	654 Atlantic St	Hartford	CT	10020	283-1682	08/28/61	M	12/06/82		12	2
294-38-2342	Josephine	L	Marshall	453 Maple Dr	Hartford	CT	10020	718-3484	08/19/50	F	06/27/70		6	3

Table 9–3 Indexed employee table

DROP

From time to time a table must be removed from the database, perhaps because it was used to store data temporarily during processing, or because the need for that data no longer exists. The command DROP is used to remove a table:

```
DROP TABLE employee_table;
```

When a table is removed, all associated indexes and views, if any, are also eliminated.

Removing an index without removing the table on which it is based is as simple as removing a table. To get rid of an index, but nothing else, the command is

```
DROP INDEX name_index;
```

If the same index name has been used for indexes on more than one table, then the name of the table must be specified:

```
DROP INDEX name_index
     ON employee_table;
```

ALTER

The command ALTER was not a part of the original SQL standard. However, it is a very useful command and is included in a great number of commercially available database systems.

It is common for changes to be made to a table after it has been created. The command ALTER may be used to add or delete a column or to change the datatype for a column. For example, to add a new column to an employee table in which the marital status of the employee will be stored, we would use the command

```
ALTER TABLE employee_table
     ADD (marital_status CHAR(1));
```

The employee table now contains an extra column—marital_status. Any rows added from this point on will have this extra column. The value marital_status will be assigned as the row is added. For existing rows, some value of marital_status is assigned by assigning the value NULL as a marital_status on all existing rows. This means that marital_status has to accept null values. Any columns added to a table definition *must* accept nulls. To delete the same column from the table, we would use the command

```
ALTER TABLE employee_table
     DROP (marital_status);
```

Datatypes may also be changed. For example, in the employee table 15 characters were specified for the employee's last name. But this does not provide enough space for the name of new employee Mary L.

Tomlinson-Smythe. To change the size of the last-name column in the table from 15 characters to 20 characters, we use the command

```
ALTER TABLE employee_table
     MODIFY(last_name CHAR(20));
```

The MODIFY option of the command ALTER TABLE can be used to change only the datatype for a column. The datatype may be changed to any legal datatype, but the change must be logical and not lead to useless data or unusable columns. For example, changing datatype from character to integer might render a column unusable because the character datatype allows any legal character to be stored while the integer datatype allows only numbers.

DATA CONTROL COMMANDS

There are two basic areas of data control: access control and transaction control. ACCESS CONTROL identifies which individuals may have access to which data, if any, within the database. TRANSACTION CONTROL maintains the accuracy of the database (data integrity) by preventing partial transactions from being posted to the tables.

Access Control

There are many reasons why access to a database should be controlled. When data is confidential, for example, it should be available only to certain users. Certain financial data and research and development information may be considered confidential by a company. The right to change or enter data may also be restricted to certain individuals. Finally, data that is not confidential may be viewed or updated at will by anyone with the proper authorization.

Access to the database tables is controlled by granting privileges to an individual or group of users with the GRANT command. These PRIVILEGES are the right to SELECT, UPDATE, ALTER, INSERT, or DELETE rows in the tables. When a user is allowed to do all of these activities, the ALL privilege is assigned to that individual. The name by which the system recognizes an individual would be the set of characters used by that individual for system access, that is, his or her system password. The GRANT command, therefore, has no relevance on systems without password protection.

The basic GRANT command to give John Jones ALL privileges on the employee table would be

```
GRANT ALL ON employee_table
     TO Jones;
```

The ALTER privilege allows a designated individual to add or delete columns or to modify the datatypes of columns. The INSERT and DELETE privileges allow a user to insert new rows or remove rows from the table. When granted the SELECT option on a table, a user can access any column in the table. But when only certain columns are specified, the user is limited to accessing only those columns: The specification SELECT [col1, col2, . . .] permits the user to retrieve data only from the specified columns. Any of the privileges can be similarly restricted.

For example, if only certain privileges were granted to certain individuals, the following commands would be used:

```
GRANT INSERT ON employee_table
     TO user1, user2,...;
```

In this case the designated employees can only add rows to the table. To expand their privileges, we change the command to

```
GRANT INSERT, DELETE ON employee_table
     TO user1, user2,...;
```

Now the users can both add and delete rows, a normal database maintenance function. Data access control is thus achieved through various combinations of the privileges on different tables.

If all users are to have access to a table, instead of listing the users individually we use the term PUBLIC. PUBLIC means that anyone on the system has the designated privileges:

```
GRANT INSERT, DELETE ON employee_table
     TO PUBLIC;
```

Now anyone with access to the system can add or delete rows in the employee table.

When a table is created, a record may be kept of the person who created it, sometimes called the OWNER. That person may pass along the privileges he or she has on that table to others. Each new owner of the table must still have his or her privileges explicitly specified, as well as the right to pass those privileges to others. For example,

```
GRANT ALL ON employee_table
     TO Jones
     WITH GRANT OPTION;
```

(the "WITH GRANT OPTION") allows Jones to grant his privileges to anyone he desires. Thus when Jones hires Mary Smith, he may give her total access to the table by issuing the command

```
GRANT ALL ON employee_table
     TO Smith;
```

The removal of some or all of a user's privileges is achieved by the use of the REVOKE command. This command is of the same form as the GRANT command and uses the same access privileges. Its form is

```
REVOKE privilege1, privilege2,... ON table name
     FROM user1, user2...;
```

In the last example of the GRANT command, Smith was granted ALL privileges on the employee table. That grant may have been too broad because, perhaps, we do not want Smith to be able to ALTER or INDEX the table. The following command removes these two privileges but leaves Smith with all others:

```
REVOKE alter, index ON employee_table
     FROM Smith;
```

Previously, we granted insert and delete privileges on the employee table to the PUBLIC. We may now want to remove the delete privilege using the command

```
REVOKE delete ON employee_table
     FROM PUBLIC;
```

Transaction Control

A *transaction* is usually a series of steps which must be completed before the transaction is complete. If data is entered into the database before all the steps are completed, the database is in error.

For example, if a company's warehouse staff received merchandise and updated the inventory but did not notify accounts payable, accounts payable might well refuse to pay the supplier's bill, thinking that the supplier was in error. Meanwhile, the purchasing department might call the supplier to ask where the merchandise is. By the time the mess can be straightened out, the company may have incurred late payment fees and lost the services of a reputable supplier—all because the transaction was not completed. In database terms, when the merchandise was received a system should have been in place to:

1 determine that there was a valid purchase order for the merchandise;
2 verify that the number of items received was correct;
3 update the inventory records with the new counts for the items received and with the locations in which the items are stored;
4 add the value of the shipment to the current accounts payable records;
5 change the company's supplier records to reflect the received merchandise; and
6 revise the purchasing department's information to show that the merchandise was received.

Until all of these steps are taken the transaction is not complete.

Let us assume now that the company does have a system, but that the system fails before all the necessary updates take place. (This could be a hardware failure, a software problem, or just an employee who went to lunch and forgot what he'd been doing when he got back.) Now the company is in the same fix it was in without a system: Its tables lack consistency and are inaccurate. Substantial time and effort are required to correct the database. The solution, therefore, is to ensure that only complete transactions affect the data in the database, and incomplete transactions are automatically aborted. This is called transaction control.

Two SQL commands are used to achieve transaction control: COMMIT WORK and ROLLBACK WORK.

The COMMIT WORK command permits the user to control when tables should be updated. Until this command is issued, the database remains unchanged. Therefore this command appears at the end of a series of commands. Next, tests are performed to make certain that each step in the sequence has been properly completed before the work is applied to the tables.

The ROLLBACK WORK command is executed when, in the course of processing, an error occurs in database operations. In this way the integrity of the database is maintained. The form of these two commands are simply

```
COMMIT WORK;
ROLLBACK WORK;
```

Views

The term *view* as used in database processing is a restricted set of columns from one or more tables. Views are typically used to restrict user access to different sets of columns. A view might be considered a virtual table because that is what it looks like to the users. A VIEW is therefore a named collection of columns from a table or tables. When data that appears related to the user is contained in different tables, views permit the user to insert, delete, or update data.

A view can limit users' access to only aggregate data, not the details. Sometimes unauthorized users need to see data derived from data items to which they would normally not be allowed access. Employee salaries are a classic example; a personnel manager may not want her staff to see how much each individual in the company is making, but still wants them to be able to produce reports on salary ranges. A view would allow her staff to review salaries by job description, job location, and job qualifications but not by individual employee.

To create a view we use the CREATE VIEW command. As an example, when access to the employee table needs to be limited to the name and address columns, we could define a view named "mail_view":

```
CREATE VIEW mail_view
     SELECT first_name, mi, last_name,
          address, city, state, zip
     FROM employee_table;
```

"Mail_view" will have the same column names as in the employee table, although new names cannot be specified since that would serve no purpose. The datatypes for the columns in the view are the same as those in the table or tables from which the columns were obtained. The SELECT part of the command can be very simple, as in this example, or more complex, as are those discussed in Chapter 10.

When it is necessary to remove a view, the command DROP VIEW is used. To remove the "mail_view" just defined we would use the command

```
DROP VIEW mail_view;
```

From what we have seen, there are several advantages to using views:

1 With each user having his or her views, the same data can be viewed differently by different users. It is more like customizing the layout or format of the data to the requirements of the users.

2 The view contains only the columns required by the user. This means only a few columns of the entire database are displayed, which should simplify the user's view of the database environment.

3 The limited number of columns displayed has implications for security and integrity of the database in a multiuser environment. What the user cannot see, he or she does not need and cannot tamper with.

4 Views, per se, provide data independence. The user's views can still be derived from existing data which has undergone changes (columns added or updated, etc.) in the database structure. The user accesses the same view as though nothing has changed.

DATA MANIPULATION COMMANDS

It is often necessary to insert data into a table (INSERT), change existing data (UPDATE), remove rows from tables (DELETE), and select data from a table (SELECT).

INSERT

The INSERT command is used to add one or more rows to an existing table. In its simplest form, the INSERT command to add a new employee to the employee table is

```
INSERT INTO employee_table
    VALUES('345-01-0333', 'JOHN', 'K', 'GONZALEZ',
        '1923 SW Park Ave.', 'Staten Island', 'NY',
        '10089', '234-9268', '032351', 'M',
        '082385', '          ', 13, 2);
```

The VALUES clause specifies the data to be added, in the order the columns appear in the table. The value for the column titled "date_terminated" is blank so that the job number for Gonzalez will be placed in the correct column.

Incomplete rows can also be added to a table. Suppose, for example, that we lack some information about Gonzalez which is to be filled in later. Now the command is

```
INSERT INTO employee_table (ss_no, first_name,
     mi, last_name, date_hired, job_no, dept_no)
     VALUES ('345-01-0333', 'John', 'K', ""Gonzalez',
          '032385', 13, 2);
```

This command would add a new row to the employee table, but only the columns "ss_no," "first_name," "mi," "last_name," "date_hired," "job_no," and "dept_no" would contain data. The data to be inserted in the columns is listed in the same order as the columns, but not necessarily in the order the columns appear in the table. If any of the unfilled columns had been designated as NOT NULL, this command would have been rejected.

The datatypes of the values specified for insertion must be compatible with the datatype of the column as specified at the time the table was created or altered. In some cases a transformation can take place: numeric data can be inserted into a character column, but nonnumeric character data cannot be inserted into a numeric column.

The INSERT command can use the SELECT command as its source for the data. If, for example, we wanted to create a table of all currently active employees, perhaps in order to generate a mailing list, we would first create a new table:

```
CREATE TABLE emp_mail_list
     (first_name          CHAR(1),
     mi                   CHAR(1),
     last_name            CHAR(15),
     address              CHAR(25),
     city                 CHAR(15),
     state                CHAR(2),
     zip                  CHAR(6));
```

Then we would instruct the system to complete the table using an already existing table:

```
INSERT INTO emp_mail_list
     SELECT first_name, mi, last_name,
          address, city, state, zip
     FROM employee_table
     WHERE date_terminated > '         '
```

Here the INSERT command includes a SELECT command clause. The mailing information for all current employees (that is, employees whose date of termination column is blank) is to be obtained from the employee table and inserted into the new "emp_mail_list" table. The data now exists in both tables.

UPDATE

The UPDATE command is used to change the values in one or more rows of a table. Its structure is similar to the INSERT command. Assume that one of our employees has moved within the same city and has therefore changed her address and zip code. To update her row we would use the command

```
UPDATE employee_table
     SET address = '404 South Avenue'
         zip     = '10098'
     WHERE ss_no = '320-71-1872';
```

The UPDATE command changes the values stored in all rows that correspond to the selection specification in the WHERE clause. This command will change Alice C. Mark's address and zip code to the values indicated.

In using the UPDATE command, as with all commands, we must be specific about just what rows we want changed. Clauses that specify key items, such as the WHERE clause, can prevent disaster. For example, had no WHERE clause been specified, the update in our example would have been applied to all rows in the table. We must also make sure that the datatype of the data to be stored in the table after the update is compatible with the datatype specified for the column of the table, lest the update be aborted.

The UPDATE command can also be used to update a number of rows that all meet the conditions of the WHERE clause. For example, if we wanted to give all employees with job number 5 a 10-percent raise, we would use the command

```
UPDATE salary_table
     SET salary = 1.1 * salary
     WHERE job_no = 5;
```

The WHERE clause can also contain a SELECT command (see Chapter 10).

DELETE

The DELETE command removes one or more rows from a table. In its simplest form, DELETE removes all rows from a table but leaves the table intact. For example, the following command will remove all the rows from the employee table:

```
DELETE FROM employee_table;
```

The WHERE clause is used to delete rows selectively as it is with the UPDATE command. To delete the rows for all employees working in department number 3, we would use

```
DELETE FROM employee_table
     WHERE dept = 3;
```

Note the risk involved in this type of deletion. If you are deleting a customer's name (say, Brown), and there happens to be another customer with the same last name, that customer would also be deleted in the process. The best time to delete is when the condition involves the primary key. Because it is unique, we do not have to worry about deletions of other rows in the table.

SELECT

The SELECT command is used to extract information from a table. The simplest form of the SELECT command chooses all columns of all records in a table:

```
SELECT *
     FROM employee_table;
```

The asterisk indicates that the query is to return all the columns making up the rows that meet the selection criteria. This query would therefore return all columns and all rows in the employee table.

The SELECT command returns a table to the user containing the data that satisfied the command. This return table is made up of the data contained in the columns specified in the SELECT command for each row. This return table is then available for further processing, according to the needs of the user. It may simply be displayed on the user's terminal, printed, or subject to further processing as input to other programs.

Selecting specific columns requires that they be specified explicitly. In the following command, the name and address columns of the employee table for all rows are returned:

```
SELECT first_name, mi, last_name,
     address, city, state, zip
FROM employee_table;
```

A clause can be used to further specify the selected columns. If, for example, we wish to select only current employees, we would use the command

```
SELECT first_name, mi, last_name,
     address, city, state, zip
FROM employee_table
WHERE date_terminated > '        ';
```

Note that when we use the SELECT command, we must always specify the column and table. The conditions (FROM and WHERE) for the selection are optional.

SUMMARY

1 Structured Query Language (SQL) is used to create and manipulate the tables making up a relational database. SQL has a long history of development, a sound theoretical basis, and has been standardized by the American National Standards Institute. The SQL standard, like all computer language standards, is subject to constant review and modification.

2 SQL commands can be divided into three categories: data definition commands, data control commands, and data manipulation commands.

3 The data definition commands allow the creation and removal of tables, indexes, and views from the database. They also allow the alteration or changing of the structure of a table after it has been created.

4 The data control commands maintain accurate and reliable data by controlling which individuals have access to data as well as by aborting incomplete transactions. Views further control access to data. The key data control commands are:

- COMMIT: Causes a completed transaction to be posted to the database
- ROLLBACK: Returns the database to its original state should a transaction fail to be completely processed
- GRANT: Assigns designated database privileges to a user or a group of users
- REVOKE: Cancels previously GRANTed database privileges

5 The data manipulation commands allow users to insert, delete, and update rows in tables. Further the data can be accessed through the use of a feature-rich command called SELECT. The data manipulation commands are:

- INSERT: Adds a row to a table
- UPDATE: Changes the value of data in a row of a table
- DELETE: Removes rows from a table
- SELECT: Selects specified rows and columns in a table or tables

6 The term NULL or null data value indicates a situation where an actual value is either unknown or not applicable. To support nulls, the programmer must indicate which column(s) contains null values and which cannot. This is done with the NOT NULL clause.

7 A view gives each user a unique picture of the database. It is a restricted vision of the columns in one or more tables. SQL retrieves the contents from data in existing tables every time the user attempts to access his or her view. The manner in which the data is derived is stored as part of the view definition.

A view is created with the CREATE VIEW command. If it is necessary to remove a view, the simple command DROP VIEW is used. For example, DROP VIEW employee_table;

8 Indexing improves the efficiency with which data is accessed or retrieved from the database. One can create an index or remove an index using the CREATE and DROP commands, respectively.

KEY WORDS

Access control
ALTER
COMMIT WORK
CREATE
DELETE
DROP
GRANT
INSERT
NOT NULL
Owner
Privileges
PUBLIC
REVOKE
ROLLBACK WORK

SELECT
Transaction control
UNIQUE
UPDATE
VALUES
View

REVIEW QUESTIONS

1 What are the major components of the SQL language and what does each do?

2 Explain in your own words the characteristics of a relation. Illustrate.

3 Distinguish between:
   a. COMMIT and ROLLBACK
   b. ALTER and INSERT
   c. DROP and REVOKE
   d. GRANT and INSERT

4 What are nulls? How can they be useful in relational database design?

5 Describe briefly the basic data types provided by SQL. Which is the most common data type? Give an example.

6 How would you alter a table? Give an example.

7 Review the basic data manipulation commands and show, by example, how the following commands are used:
   a. INSERT
   b. UPDATE
   c. DELETE
   d. SELECT

8 What does the asterisk in SELECT mean? What would happen if it were absent? Be specific.

9 What are some of the reasons for control access in a database? In what ways do these reasons promote integrity and security in SQL design?

10 Having covered the first eight chapters in the text, is a view similar to a subschema? Why? Explain.

11 What are some of the advantages of using views in SQL? Discuss.

12 Create and remove an index by means of an example. Why are indexes so useful? Explain.

APPLICATION PROBLEMS

1 Write the command to generate a table to contain the mailing and membership status information for the members of a social club.

2 To improve performance, what indexes, if any, would you put on the table in Problem 1? Show the commands you would need to use.

3 Limit access to the table (in Problem 1) to the officers of the club.

4 The president of the club wishes to have the option of allowing some of his

committee heads to access the table. Show the commands that allow him to do this. Consider the effect or implication of Problem 5.

5 Create a view that allows everyone to access the names of the members. What is the effect of specifying this view instead of a table name in the various SQL statements?

6 Ron Martin Appliances, Inc., is a local retail store in a small town in Virginia. Mr. Martin is the president and owner of the store. It is pretty much a family-run business, as the store employs only three sales representatives plus the family, handling various aspects of the business—stocking inventory, answering the phones, and so forth. Martin's store has a database designed to maintain information about the sales force, inventory, and customers as follows:

   a. Each sales rep is represented by name, address, commission rate, and total commission.
   b. The inventory aspect of the database is represented by part number, description of product, number of units in stock, and unit price.
   c. The customer database stores customer name, address, credit limit, balance owed, and the name of the sales rep who sold the appliance to that customer.
   d. The order database stores number, part number, quantity, date, customer number, price, and total order.

   Tables 9-4 through 9-7 contain this information.

SLSREP_Table

SLSNUM	SLSNAME	SLSADDR	COMRATE	TOTCOM
1	Snyder, Jack	123 Oak St.	.10	714.00
2	Snead, Linda	5647 Henry St.	.15	610.00
3	Martin, Bob	711 East Ave.	.18	917.00

Table 9–4 Salesrep table

INVEN_Table

PARTNUM	DESCRIPTION	QUAN	UNITPRICE
12A1	Sony TV	114	540.50
1504	GE stove	25	692.00
1617	Amana freezer	19	314.00
123T	GE microwave	86	167.40
5721	GE refrigerator	71	991.00

Table 9–5 Inventory table

CUST_Table

CUSNUM	CUSNAME	CUSADDR	ORDLIM	BALANCE	SLSNUM
123	Adamski, Ron	174 East Ave.	600	301	1
210	Brown, Joe	601 Main St.	1900	1610	2
094	Kildare, Herb	162 Happ Rd.	700	690	1
111	Levin, Pearl	62 Acadia Ln.	1000	784	3
060	Carr, Dave	500 Park St.	400	360	3

Table 9–6 Customer table

ORDER_Table

ORDNUM	PART_NAME	QUAN	ORDATE	CUSNUM	PRICE	TOTAL
170A	Timer	1	2/2/92	210	72.00	72.00
612B	Circuit bd.	1	1/6/92	123	210.00	210.00
Z210	Tube	1	3/4/92	094	182.00	182.00
7A10	Compressor	1	2/7/92	111	292.00	292.00
62B1	Pump	1	2/9/92	210	61.00	61.00
1767	Belt	2	2/9/92	094	9.00	18.00

Table 9–7 Order table

Use SQL to do the following:

a. Find the names of all customers whose credit limit is over $700.
b. Give the order number placed by customer 123 on 1/6/92.
c. List the names of customers represented by sales representative 3.
d. Find the number and name of all customers whose last name is Kildare.
e. Find out how many customers have a balance over $350.
f. List the total of the balances of sales representatives with at least two customers.
g. Use CREATE TABLE commands to describe each table.
h. List the complete "ORDER_table."
i. List the totals of customers' balances for each sales representative.
j. Change the description of part 1504 to "Amana stove."
k. Add $200 to the credit limit of customer 123.
l. Delete all customers whose sales representative number is 2.
m. Change the address of sales representative 2 to null.
n. Remove the "ORDER_table" from the Ron Martin database.
o. Define a view called "Small_talk." It should include the customer number, name, balance, and credit limit for all customers whose credit limit is over $900.
p. Write SQL commands to grant sales representative 1 the ability to retrieve data from INVEN_Table, and to grant sales representative 3 the ability to delete customers.

C H A P T

Queries, Joins, and Embedded SQL

E R 10

Back to the Basics of Joining

AT A GLANCE

Back to the Basics of Joining

You won't get very far in SQL without a solid understanding of the "join" process. The following should get you started if you're new to SQL. I'll use this database as an example:

```
SQL> SELECT  *  FROM SmallPat;

PATNO
1
2
3

SQL> SELECT  *  FROM SmallProc;

PATNO     PROC
1         A
2         B
3         C
```

In joining two tables, SQL takes all the columns from the first row of the first table and all the columns from the first row of the second table to create the first row of a temporary table. (In theory, that is. In practice the process is much more efficient, but the end result is the same.) The second row of the temporary table contains all the columns from the first row of the first table plus all the columns from the second row of the second table.

The process continues until there are no more rows in the second table to join with the first row of the first table. At that point, SQL directs its attention to the second row of the first table and joins it to each row of the second table, one at a time. Next, it tackles the third row of the first table, and so on through all the rows of the first table. The end result is called the "Cartesian product" of the two tables. It has as many rows as the number of rows in the first table times the number of rows in the second table and contains every possible combination of a row from the first table and a row from the second table. This is the Cartesian product of the two tiny example tables:

```
SQL> SELECT  *
  2    FROM SmallPat, SmallProc;

PATNO     PATNO     PROC
1         1         A
2         1         A
3         1         A
1         1         B
2         1         B
3         1         B
1         2         C
2         2         C
3         2         C
```

The join shown above has made a useless hash of our two tables. Indeed, a Cartesian product works much better as a theoretical construct than as a practical reality. Simply joining two tables by mentioning both of them in the FROM clause (there is no "JOIN" verb in SQL) is only the first step—finding the useful bits in the Cartesian product with an appropriate WHERE clause is the vital second step. The next example shows a "real" join of the two tables:

```
SQL> SELECT  *
     2    FROM SmallPat, SmallProc
     3    WHERE  SmallPat.PatNo =
          SmallProc.PatNo;

PATNO      PATNO      PROC
1          1          A
1          1          B
2          2          C
```

Sometimes, however, you want to see all the rows of the first table, plus some information from the second table for those rows or rows in the second table. In other words, don't eliminate a row in the first table just because it doesn't have a matching row in the second table. This last example shows an Oracle "outer" join (note the parenthetic plus sign in the WHERE clause) that will return all the patients and the dates of their operations if any:

```
SQL> SELECT  *
     2 FROM  SmallPat,  SmallProc
     3 WHERE  SmallPat.PatNo =
       SmallProc.PatNo  (+);

PATNO      PATNO      PROC
1          1          A
1          1          B
2          2          C
3
```

Darling, Charles B., "Back to the basics of joining," DBMS, *July 1991, 79. Reprinted with permission of* DBMS.

AT A GLANCE

SQL can be used as part of a traditional development host language through processes called joins. A join is a process of accessing multiple tables. Joins can be simple, multiple, self-, or outer.

The aggregate functions of a join produce a single value that is a summary of information about the subject rows of a table. These values include data average, minimum, maximum, total, and count.

When it is necessary to use the same table more than once in a SELECT statement, the table must be joined with itself. A self-join requires that the table be declared twice in the FROM clause and that an alias be assigned to each occurrence of the table.

Any number of tables can be joined in a query merely by adding the tables to the FROM clause and the join conditions to the WHERE clause of the SELECT statement. The multiple clauses in the WHERE clause are joined by AND, OR connectors.

Embedded SQL is the SQL statements included in the computer program and converted into the host language by a precompiler. All embedded SQL statements within a COBOL program are specified by the key words EXEC SQL and end with the key words END-EXE, followed by a period. The SELECT statement is still the basic query command in embedded SQL. The simplest form of an embedded SELECT statement is the singleton select.

SQL is assuming an important role in developing client and LAN database applications. Many of today's SQL database servers offer mainframe and minicomputer system advantages at microcomputer prices. Among the client database server products available today are Oracle's Oracle Server, IBM's OS/2 Extended Edition Database Manager, and Gupta SQL Base.

By the end of this chapter, you should be able to

- distinguish among simple, self-, outer, and multiple joins;
- understand the basics of queries and subqueries;
- understand the basic features of embedded SQL; and
- evaluate the key functions and primary products of SQL database servers.

Introduction

In this chapter, we shall see how SQL can be used as part of a traditional development host language, such as COBOL. We shall also deal with queries in SQL—an expansion of the introduction to the SELECT statement contained in Chapter 9. We also elaborate on the function of joins, the power of embedded and dynamic SQL, SQL database servers, and the trend they're setting in the database environment.

Some database system queries can be answered by interrogating a single table. But more often multiple tables must be accessed to provide answers to complex and significant questions. The process of accessing multiple tables is called a JOIN. There are a variety of types of joins: simple joins, multiple joins, self-joins, and outer joins.

Complex queries require that a system collect data from two or more tables in a particular way and summarize that data in a specified way—by adding it up, for example, or figuring its average. These processes are called aggregate functions.

Aggregate Functions

Simple queries always produce a column of results—one for each row in the table being queried. AGGREGATE FUNCTIONS, on the other hand, producc a single value which in some way summarizes the subject rows of the table. The exception is when aggregate functions are used in a SELECT statement, in which case they produce a single row with the results of the function, rather than a value.

The functions available in SQL are AVG (average), MIN (minimum), MAX (maximum), SUM (total), and COUNT (count). With the exception of COUNT, these functions cannot be applied to columns containing character data. Since COUNT counts the number of rows that meet the selection criteria, its contents do not matter. To illustrate these functions, let us use a table called "test" with two columns, "age" and "income," each of which currently contains five rows:

AGE	INCOME
43	23,500
23	32,000
36	43,980
61	65,050
52	51,000

Average

The AVERAGE function (AVG) produces the average for the values contained in the rows selected in the table, ignoring all null values. For example, we could get the average of all income entries for the "test" table with the statement

```
SELECT AVG(income)
       FROM test;
```

This would produce the result 43,106. We could also get the average income for those over 40 years old with the command:

```
SELECT AVG(income)
       FROM test
       WHERE age > 40;
```

This would give the result 46,516.67.

Minimum and Maximum

The MINIMUM aggregate function (MIN) produces the lowest value and the MAXIMUM (MAX) returns the highest value in the specified column of the table. To get the minimum income from table "test," we would use the command

```
SELECT MIN(income)
       FROM test;
```

which would return the value 23,500. To find the highest age in the table, we would use the command

```
SELECT MAX(age)
       FROM test;
```

which would return the value 61.

Total

The TOTAL function (SUM) produces the total for the values in the specified column. The values in the column must, of course, be numbers. The total annual wages for the persons in the "test" table, produced by the command

```
SELECT SUM(income)
       FROM test;
```

would be 215,530.

Count

The COUNT function (COUNT) produces the number of items in the column specified. The count function looks at the rows rather than at the contents of a specified column. Therefore, "COUNT(column_name)" is not allowed; "COUNT(*)" is used instead. Thus, to find the number of persons in the "test" table, we would use the command

```
SELECT COUNT(*)
     FROM test;
```

which would produce the value 5.

Queries and Joins

In most of the previous chapter, we introduced the elementary SELECT clause to extract data from SQL tables. No selection criteria were used—as is sometimes useful. We will enhance the SELECT clause to include the WHERE, GROUP BY, HAVING, and ORDER BY sections of that command.

The WHERE Clause

The WHERE CLAUSE limits the scope of the command to only those rows that meet the conditions specified. The basic syntax is

```
SELECT columns
     FROM tables
     WHERE selection criteria;
```

For example, if we want to retrieve the names and addresses of all employees living in New Jersey from the employee table created in Chapter 9, we would use the SELECT command

```
SELECT first_name, mi, last_name,
          address, city, state, zip
     FROM employee_table
     WHERE state = 'NJ';
```

Multiple selection criteria can also be used in the WHERE clause of the SELECT command. For example, if we want to limit the command to males living in New Jersey or Connecticut, we would use the command

```
SELECT first_name, mi, last_name,
          address, city, state, zip
     FROM employee_table
     WHERE sex = 'M'
               AND
           state = 'NJ'
               OR
           state = 'CT';
```

Notice the equality COMPARISON OPERATOR (=) in the WHERE clause. In addition to equality, other operators are

- greater than (>),
- less than (<),
- not equal (<>),
- greater than or equal (>=),

- less than or equal (<=), and
- BETWEEN, LIKE, IN, or NULL.

The last four operators require explanation. The BETWEEN operator is used to limit a search to within given parameters. For example, to search for employees in certain zip code areas, we might say

```
WHERE zip BETWEEN '10045' AND '10111'
```

The result would be the names and addresses of all employees living within zip code areas between 10045 and 10111. By adding NOT, we can exclude a range from our search. The command

```
WHERE zip NOT BETWEEN '10121' AND '10199'
```

would give us all employees who do not live in areas with zip codes between 10121 and 10199.

The IN (and likewise NOT IN) operator is used to specify the value of data. For example,

```
WHERE job_no IN (1,3,5,14)
```

means we want to see only that data for job numbers 1, 3, 5, and 14, while

```
WHERE job_no NOT IN (2,4,6,7)
```

means we want to see all data *except* that which has job numbers 2, 4, 6, and 7. Note that the job numbers are not sequential; if they were we would use BETWEEN.

LIKE (or NOT LIKE) is used for *pattern matching*. Because pattern matching implies that we know some, but not all, of the information we want, we use the symbols "_" and "%" to represent the missing information. The "_" (underscore) represents one, and only one, missing character; the "%" (percent sign) represents a missing character string. These are sometimes referred to as "wild cards" because, like wild cards, they can assume any legal value for the datatype of the data being retrieved except numerical datatypes. For example, the command

```
SELECT last_name, first_name
     FROM employee_table
     WHERE last_name LIKE '_AR%';
```

would result in

```
MARY BARNES
ALICE MARKS
DAVID SARGENT
JOSEPHINE MARSHALL
```

where each last name starts with any character followed by "AR," which in turn is followed by any string of characters.

LIKE is sometimes used when the spelling of a data item is uncertain or when only partial information is available. For example, to retrieve a table of all employees whose names start with "M," we would use the command

```
WHERE last_name LIKE 'M%'
```

The NULL operator assumes that, when the table was originally defined, NULL values were designated in some column. While it is generally not good policy to have many NULL values in a database, it is, nevertheless, sometimes necessary. For example, a person may be employed but not assigned to a department for a while. During that period the "DEPT" value for that individual would be NULL.

SQL permits only one form of NULL value search:

```
WHERE column_name IS NULL
```

or

```
WHERE column_name IS NOT NULL
```

Subqueries

Sometimes it is necessary to perform a query to obtain a result which will then be used as the basis of the WHERE clause in another query. This is called a SUBQUERY or NESTED QUERY. The general form for a subquery is

```
SELECT column1, column2, ...
     FROM table1, ...
     WHERE condition (operator)
          (SELECT column1
               FROM table3, ...
               WHERE selection criteria);
```

Theoretically, there is no limit to the depth of the nesting. However, each software implementation of SQL provides its own limitations.

The response table from the subquery may include no values, one value, or a set of values, depending on the comparison operator specified in the primary query. But the subquery may only have a single column or expression in its SELECT list. The subquery may not contain an ORDER BY clause.

In the general form for a subquery shown above, the WHERE clause of the initial SELECT statement contains a "condition." The condition is an operator that combines the two queries in a meaningful way. These conditions include ALL and ANY, IN and NOT IN, and EXISTS and NOT EXISTS.

ALL and ANY ALL and ANY operators allow the subquery to return no values, a single value, or multiple values. The WHERE clause is said to be true in the case of ALL if the comparison is true for every value returned by the subquery. If the ANY operator is specified, the comparison is satisfied when it matches any of the values returned by the subquery.

IN and NOT IN The IN and NOT IN operators determine whether the specified value is contained in, or not contained in, the response set from the subquery. We use it when we want to select rows that match one of several listed values. If the row value matches any value in the list of values, then the row is selected. The format for IN or NOT IN is

```
Expression [NOT] IN (value1, value2, ...)
```

For example, to get a list of all employees residing in New York or Brooklyn, we enter the statement

```
SELECT first_name, last_name, city
    FROM employee_table
    WHERE city IN ('New York', 'Brooklyn')
```

The row is retrieved if the employee's city is one of the cities in parentheses.

EXISTS and NOT EXISTS Sometimes only one record will satisfy a specific query. In this case the WHERE clause of the primary query is used to test the existence of rows that result from a subquery. If the subquery returns a value, the conditions specified in the subquery exist.

Conversely, the NOT EXISTS operator requires that the subquery return no value. The form of the WHERE clause that is linked to the subquery is

```
WHERE [NOT] EXISTS (subquery)
```

To illustrate the use of EXISTS, let us add another table to those introduced in Chapter 9. This is the Degree File (Table 10-1), which lists all degrees earned by the staff members who are referenced in the employee_table (Figure 9-4). In this table the employee's major and degree are listed.

SS No.	*Degree*	*Major*
230-76-2438	BS	Business Administration
320-71-1872	BS	Computer Science
543-02-9428	BS	Biology
405-96-8776	BA	History
697-88-9706	BA	Fine Art
829-10-0192	BS	Computer and Information Systems
920-11-2031	AA	Data Processing
294-38-2342	BS	Business Administration

Table 10-1 Degree table

Now let us ask which of our employees does not have a college degree. To answer this we use the NOT EXISTS form of the subquery.

```
SELECT first_name, mi, last_name, ss_no
    FROM employee_table
    WHERE NOT EXISTS
        (SELECT ss_no
        FROM degree_table
    WHERE employee_table.ss_no=degree_table.ss_no);
```

The response table for this query would be:

```
JOHN      J       ALLISON
HENRY     D       HIRSCH
DAVID     D       SARGENT
```

A request for a list of all jobs with a wage grade higher than the average wage grade for all jobs requires a subquery using a simple comparison operator, greater than (>). Note that all comparison operators can be used in this way.

```
SELECT job_no, job_title, wage_grade
     FROM job_table
     WHERE wage_grade >
          (SELECT AVG(wage_grade)
               FROM job_table);
```

This subquery will produce a single value, the average wage grade. The primary query will use that value as the basis for its comparison. The resulting table would be

```
1    COST ACCOUNTANT             12
4    PROGRAMMER B                12
6    SYSTEMS ANALYST              9
7    SYSTEMS ANALYST SENIOR      13
10   COMPUTER OPERATOR B         10
13   DATABASE PROGRAMMER         14
14   DATABASE ADMINISTRATOR      16
```

To obtain a list of all employees in wage grade 12, we would write the query as

```
SELECT first_name, mi, last_name
     FROM employee_table
     WHERE job_no IN
          (SELECT job_table.job_no
               FROM job_table
               WHERE wage_grade = 12);
```

This subquery produces the set of job numbers (1,4), which becomes the basis for the evaluation of the primary query comparison, resulting in the table

```
MARY F BARNES
HENRY D HIRSCH
```

Simple Joins

When it is necessary to retrieve data from more than one table or view, the tables must first be joined. Joining involves logically connecting multiple tables through a column with data common to both and then dealing with the combined data as if it were a column. The basic syntax for a join is

```
SELECT rows from table1, rows from table2
     FROM table1 alias1, table2 alias2
     WHERE condition joining table1 and table2;
```

To illustrate the use of joins, we will add two additional tables to the employee table (Figure 9-1): the job table (Table 10-2) and the supervisor table (Table 10-3).

Job No.	*Job Title*	*Wage Grade*
1	Cost accountant	12
2	Programmer A	7
3	Programmer trainee	5
4	Programmer B	12
5	Systems analysis trainee	5
6	System analyst	9
7	Systems analyst senior	13
8	Computer operator A	4
9	Computer operator B	6
10	Computer operator C	10
11	Control clerk A	3
12	Control clerk B	7
13	Database programmer	14
14	Database administrator	16

Table 10-2 Job table

Dept No.	*Supv No.*	*Dept Name*	*Supv Name*	*Dept Loc.*
1		Programming		2
2	920-11-0231	Data control	Larry Y Lewis	3
3	092-02-0188	Database	John T Allison	3

Table 10-3 Supervisor table

When tables are joined, their column names must be clearly identified. To specify a column whose name appears in more than one of the tables involved in the SELECT statement, we must first specify the table. This qualified notation appears as

```
Table_Name.Column_name
```

Both the employee and job tables in the example contain a column titled "Job_no". To refer to the one in the employee table, we must specify

```
Employee_table.Job_no
```

If the reference is from the job table, the reference would be

```
Job_table.Job_no
```

If the names of the columns are unique, the columns need not be qualified and can be referred to simply by names, as in

```
Last_name
```

In a SIMPLE JOIN, two tables are joined and duplicates of common columns are removed. To list all employees and their job titles, we could write the command

```
SELECT first_name, mi, last_name, job_title
     FROM employee_table, job_table
     WHERE employee_table.job_no = job_table.job_no;
```

to produce the table

```
MARY      F   BARNES      COST ACCOUNTANT
JOHN      J   ALLISON     DATABASE ADMINISTRATOR
ALICE     C   MARKS       SYSTEMS ANALYST TRAINEE
PAUL      P   ALTMAN      PROGRAMMER TRAINEE
HENRY     D   HIRSCH      PROGRAMMER B
BRUCE     R   MORGAN      CONTROL CLERK A
TONY      NI  HUNTER      DATABASE PROGRAMMER
DAVID     D   SARGENT     SYSTEMS ANALYST TRAINEE
JAMES     H   WHITEHALL   SYSTEMS ANALYST
LARRY     Y   LEWIS       CONTROL CLERK B
JOSEPHINE L   MARSHALL    SYSTEMS ANALYST
```

Note that the resulting table includes an employee (Tony Hunter) who has been terminated. But we want only current employees. Since the termination date for all current employees is NULL, the query can be restated as

```
SELECT first_name, mi, last_name, job_title
     FROM employee_table, job_table
     WHERE employee_table.job_no = job_table.job_no
                    AND
               date_term IS NULL;
```

Now only current employees will appear in the resulting table.

Self-Join

Sometimes it is necessary to use the same table more than once in a SELECT statement. Because the query requires that the table be joined with itself, this is called a SELF-JOIN. In the self-join, the combined result consists of two rows from the same table. All that is necessary is that the table be declared twice in the FROM clause, and that an alias be assigned to each occurrence of the table. The tables may be referred to by their aliases from that time on. To declare an alias we use the command

```
FROM table1 alias1, table1 alias2, ...
```

An example of a self-join is a request for a pairwise list of all employees who live in the same zip code. (Such a request might be the first step in a carpool program.) The request requires that the employee table be joined with itself, with the zip code column as the linking field. Since we do not want to show an employee paired with him or herself, we must assign aliases to both instances of table specification in the

FROM clause, then select accordingly. The command might then be written

```
SELECT alias1.first_name, alias1.mi, alias1,last_name
       alias2.first_name, alias2.mi, alias2.last_name
    FROM employee_table alias1, employee_table alias2
    WHERE alias1.zip = alias2.zip
             AND
         alias1.ss_no <> alias2.ss_no;
```

The resulting table would be

MARY	F	BARNES	PAUL	P	ALTMAN
LARRY	Y	LEWIS	JOSEPHINE	L	MARSHALL

Outer Joins

Simple and self-joins produce tables made up of rows from the base tables that meet the selection criteria. If we wanted a list of employees and each employee's supervisor, but did not want the list to show anyone as his or her own supervisor, we would write

```
SELECT  last_name, mi, first_name, supv_name
     FROM employee_table, supervisor_table
     WHERE employee_table.dept_no =
           supervisor_table.dept_no
                AND
           ss_no <> supv_no
                AND
           date_term IS NOT NULL;
```

which would give us the table

ALICE	C	MARKS	JOHN	J ALLISON
PAUL	P	ALTMAN	JOHN	J ALLISON
DAVID	D	SARGENT	LARRY	Y LEWIS
JOSEPHINE	P	MARSHALL	JOHN	J ALLISON

While the query does result in a list of employees and their supervisors, it may not have satisfied the intent of the person requesting the data. Only those employees who currently have an assigned supervisor are listed. But the employees in department 1 are not listed because they have no supervisor; the data item in the supervisor table is NULL and therefore ignored. To provide a more comprehensive list we would use an outer join.

An OUTER JOIN is used when the data required meets one but not both of the conditions specified in the WHERE clause of the SELECT statement. Outer joins were not supported in the original SQL standard, but several leading SQL-based database management systems have provided for outer joins.

In INFORMIX the outer join is specified by placing the key word OUTER before the name of the table in the FROM clause of the SELECT statement. The previous query would be written

```
SELECT first_name, mi, last_name, supv_name
     FROM employee_table, OUTER supervisor_table
     WHERE employee_table.dept_no =
           supervisor_table.dept_no
                AND
           ss_no <> supv_no
                AND
           date_term IS NOT NULL;
```

This query will now give us a list of all employees, as desired, but the values for the supervisor's name for those employees working in department 1 will be NULL. The resulting table will be

```
MARY       F    BARNES    NULL
ALICE      C    MARKS     JOHN J ALLISON
PAUL       P    ALTMAN    JOHN J ALLISON
HENRY      D    HIRSCH    NULL
BRUCE      R    MORGAN    NULL
DAVID      D    SARGENT   LARRY Y LEWIS
JAMES      H    WHITEHEAD NULL
JOSEPHINE  L    MARSHALL  JOHN J ALLISON
```

Multiple Joins

The previous examples have all queried at most two tables. But many queries can only be answered by gathering data from more than two tables. To deal with data from more than two tables we use MULTIPLE JOINS.

Any number of tables can be joined merely by adding the tables to the FROM clause and the join conditions to the WHERE clause of the SELECT statement. The multiple clauses in the WHERE clause are joined by AND, OR connectors.

A simple example of a multiple join would be a list of all current employees who are in job number 5, including their job title and department location:

```
SELECT first_name, mi, last_name, dept_loc, job_title
     FROM employee_table, supervisor_table,
          job_table
     WHERE job_no = 5
               AND
           employee_table.dept_no =
               supervisor_table.dept_no=
               AND
           employee_table.job_no =
               job_table.job_no;
```

The response table would be

```
ALICE      C    MARKS     3    SYSTEMS ANALYST TRAINEE
DAVID      D    SARGENT   2    SYSTEMS ANALYST TRAINEE
```

EMBEDDED SQL

As mentioned earlier, SQL statements can be embedded into a host language in a variety of situations. For example, in on-line transaction processing that uses formatted screens to validate data, interactive SQL is not practical. A host language with embedded SQL can do the job better. Batch transaction applications are also better supported by an embedded SQL. In a payroll application, for example, the number of hours is collected and stored until the end of a pay period. Final processing involves one or more processing runs, each run performing many processing steps. Embedded SQL can be used in the program that processes the payroll.

SQL statements can be included in computer programs written in third-generation programming languages such as COBOL, C, PL/1, and Ada. Embedding SQL makes it possible for the computer program to communicate with and manipulate the relational database tables. For simplicity's sake, we will limit this discussion to the use of SQL in conjunction with the standard business-oriented programming language COBOL.

EMBEDDED SQL is SQL commands that are included in the computer program and converted into the host language by a precompiler. The program can then be compiled using the normal compiler. While embedded SQL commands accomplish the same results as interactive SQL statements, their syntax varies in two ways:

1 All embedded SQL statements in a COBOL program are specified by the key words EXEC SQL and end with the key words END-EXEC followed by a period:

```
EXEC SQL
     sql statement
END-EXEC.
```

2 The INTO clause must follow all SELECT clauses to provide an area to set up the database values for manipulation by the COBOL program.

Variables

The computer program containing embedded SQL commands contains two sets of variables: Those used by the program itself, called HOST VARIABLES, and those used by SQL tables, called COLUMN VARIABLES. Host variables and column variables may have the same name, but programmers must make sure they are referring to the correct variable. In an SQL statement, any host variable is preceded by a colon (:).

The column variables used in a program must be defined by a DECLARE command, as in

```
EXEC SQL
     BEGIN DECLARE SECTION
```

```
END-EXEC.
              01   record description
              05   field description    PICTURE xxx
              05   field description    PICTURE xxxx
              05   field description    PICTURE xxxx
EXEC SQL
END DECLARE SECTION
END-EXEC.
```

The host variables must be defined in the normal way for the program, as is true for any program.

SELECT Statements

In embedded SQL the SELECT statement is still the basic query command. But programming languages are basically sequential processors that deal with a record at a time, whereas SQL deals with sets which may contain more than one record. Furthermore, something must always be done with the table that results from a SELECT command, such as

- display or print the data;
- use the data to make changes in the database;
- move the data to another table of related data; and
- include the data in calculations along with other data furnished by the program.

Singleton selects The simplest form of the embedded SELECT command is the SINGLETON SELECT. In a singleton select, only one row is selected in response to the query and, because something must be done with the row, the column variable data is moved into host variable data. This is done by selecting into suitable host variables. When we know that the response to the query will be only one row, we use the syntax

```
SELECT rows
     INTO host variables
     FROM tables
     WHERE selection conditions;
```

Cursors When a query is likely to produce more than one row a cursor must be defined. A CURSOR is a pointer into the database table. To define a cursor we use the syntax

```
EXEC SQL
     DECLARE cursor_name CURSOR FOR
          SQL statement
END-EXEC.
```

Frequently, the SQL statement referred to in this statement is a SELECT statement with FROM and WHERE clauses as well as any other features needed for that query. Once defined, the cursor must be opened to make it active. This is done with the command

```
EXEC SQL
     OPEN cursor_name
END-EXEC.
```

The next step is to move the cursor through the database table in accordance with the DECLARE cursor statement. This is done with the FETCH command. FETCH also provides for moving the selected column variables into the host variables:

```
EXEC SQL
     FETCH cursor_name
          INTO host_variables
END-EXEC.
```

The FETCH command causes the cursor to point to successive rows. The cursor will not point to any row before the first FETCH is executed. The row retrieved by the most recent FETCH is called the *current row*. Using the FETCH statement requires that one host variable be specified for each column variable specified in the DECLARE cursor statement. In this way, the communication between database variables and program variables is achieved.

When the cursor has moved to the end of the database table, the cursor is normally closed. This is similar to closing a file when you are finished using it in a program, and is done with the CLOSE command:

```
EXEC SQL
     CLOSE cursor_name
END-EXEC.
```

SQL Communications Area

In embedded SQL, all commands must be checked for proper performance. For example, did the FETCH find a row that met the conditions specified in the DECLARE cursor command? SQL provides feedback information in an area called the SQL COMMUNICATIONS AREA (SQLCA). A SQLCODE value indicates the status of the execution of the command. A zero (0) means that the command executed properly with no problem; a value of 100 indicates that a row satisfying the query requirements was not found; and a negative value signifies that an error occurred. Each implementation of SQL provides a full list of return codes which can be tested. To include the SQLCA in the program, we use the command

```
EXEC SQL
     INCLUDE SQLCA
END-EXEC.
```

SQL Embedded in COBOL

We are now ready to look at an example of a COBOL program with embedded SQL. Figure 10-1 shows a program that will display on a terminal the names of all employees and the department in which they work. Notice first that no changes have been made in the database tables, so no COMMIT command is required. If any changes had been made, the work would have had to be either committed or rolled back.

```
IDENTIFICATION DIVISION.
     .
     .
DATA DIVISION.
     WORKING-STORAGE SECTION.
*
(A) * INCLUDE THE SQL COMMUNICATIONS AREA
*
          EXEC SQL
               INCLUDE SQLCA
          END-EXEC.
*
* DECLARE THE EMPLOYEE TABLE
*
          EXEC SQL
               BEGIN DECLARE SECTION
          END-EXEC.
          01 EMPLOYEE-TABLE
               05    SS_NO                   PIC X(11).
               05    FIRST_NAME              PIC X(12).
               05    MI                      PIC X(1).
               05    LAST_NAME               PIC X(15).
               05    ADDRESS                 PIC X(25).
               05    CITY                    PIC X(15).
               05    STATE                   PIC X(2).
               05    ZIP                     PIC X(6).
               05    DATE_OF_BIRTH           PIC X(8).
               05    SEX                     PIC X(1).
               05    DATE_HIRED              PIC X(8).
               05    DATE_TERMINATED         PIC X(8).
               05    JOB_NO                  PIC 99.
               05    DEPT_NO                 PIC 999.
           EXEC SQL
               END DECLARE SECTION
           END-EXEC.
*
* PROGRAM OR HOST VARIABLES ARE NOW DEFINED
*
           01    FIRST-NAME                   PIC X(12).
           01    MI                           PIC X(1).
           01    LAST_NAME                    PIC X(15).
           01    DEPT_NO                      PIC 999.
PROCEDURE DIVISION.
100-BEGIN.
```

```
*
* DEFINE THE CURSOR
*
     EXEC SQL
  (B)    DECLARE SELECTION_CURSOR CURSOR FOR
              SELECT FIRST_NAME, MI, LAST_NAME
                     DEPT_NO
              FROM EMPLOYEE_TABLE
              WHERE DEPT_NO IS NOT NULL
              ORDER BY DEPT_NO, LAST_NAME, FIRST_NAME
     END_EXEC.
*
* OPEN THE CURSOR
*
     EXEC SQL
         OPEN SELECTION_CURSOR
     END_EXEC.
200-FETCH-DATA.
     PERFORM UNTIL (SQLCODE NOT = 0)
         EXEC SQL
  (C)         FETCH SELECTION_CURSOR
                   INTO :FIRST_NAME :MI,
                        :LAST_NAME  :DEPT_NO
         END_EXEC.
         IF (SQLCODE < 0)
              PERFORM 999-ERROR-ROUTINE
         END-IF.
         DISPLAY FIRST_NAME, MI, LAST_NAME, DEPT_NO.
     END-PERFORM.

300-CLOSE-ROUTINE.
     EXEC SQL
         CLOSE SELECTION_CURSOR
     END_EXEC.
     STOP RUN.

999-ERROR-ROUTINE.          (D)
*
* THIS SECTION IS IMPLEMENTATION DEPENDENT BUT THE ERROR
* CONDITION IS CODED IN SQLCODE
*
END PROGRAM.
```

Figure **10-1** COBOL program with embedded SQL

In the example program, the SQLCA is specified in the "Working-Storage Section" (A) along with the definition of the employee table. In the procedure division the cursor is defined (B) and the FETCH (C) is placed with a PERFORM UNTIL control block. When the SQLCODE is no longer 0, indicating an unsuccessful FETCH, the PERFORM loop is terminated. Also note the error-testing in the control block (D). As indicated in the program, the nature of the action to be taken when an error is detected as well as the error codes themselves are implementation-dependent. This ensures that errors are detected and suitable action taken.

Dynamic SQL

In certain applications, the nature of an SQL command is not known in advance. Typical of this type of application are interactive, generalized on-line systems such as an order tracking system. In systems such as these, when a request is entered—usually from a terminal—it is analyzed to determine which SQL command will satisfy the request. Next, the command is formulated and executed, and the results are fed back to the requestor. What makes this interesting is that the program itself is compiled and in object form, while the request is in source code and therefore has to be compiled and bound to the program itself. DYNAMIC SQL is used to satisfy this need. Dynamic SQL is therefore a way in which the system can respond to unanticipated queries.

The PREPARE and EXECUTE statements are used to deal with dynamic SQL requests. When the request is received, it is in the form of a character string. The request must be converted to an SQL command by the database software. The PREPARE command takes that SQL command and compiles it. In the process the command is also bound to the program-executable module. Finally, the EXECUTE statement runs the statement and feeds the results back to the requestor. Note that when the program completes its run, the program generated is no longer available.

SQL Database Servers

Client/server database technology is a front-page story in the computer industry today, and for a good reason. When local area networks became established in the corporate environment, users began to look for more efficient ways to share and access information. This was the basis for client/server computing.

The new evolution in microcomputers began with the introduction of networks and increasingly powerful and fast microcomputers. This means that the user (referred to as CLIENT or requester) can now link PCs to another computer, which will serve as a file server and store common shared data files. A SERVER is a PC with large hard disk capacity used to store common files in a network. A server maintains the data and ships the entire file to each PC on request. But the file server was not designed to deal with large demands and the problems associated with data security, concurrent updates, backup and recovery, and the like. This deficiency prompted the development of client database server technology.

Key Functions

An SQL DATABASE SERVER is a computer that houses an SQL database application. A database server's main tasks are handling multiuser applications, centralized data storage, data security, emergencies such as recovery of the system in case of failure, enforcing data integrity across transactions, and maximum performance within the network. A server processes a client's request, retrieves and updates records, and sends records back and forth to the client's applications at each respective workstation. The workstation application then continues the processing. (See Figure 10-2.)

Many of today's SQL database servers offer the advantages of mainframe and minicomputer systems at microcomputer prices. For this reason, SQL database servers are becoming the first choice for organizations that want to share information stored in databases.

The main function of a client database server is to make best use of the available hardware and software by handling functions as a front-end client computer that runs user applications and a back-end database server where data is stored once and managed at all times. The data may be accessed concurrently by various applications such as order entry, sales, accounting, and so on. Unlike traditional file servers, the database server ships only the data requested from various front-end application(s) running on the client PC(s). The responsibility for running the user

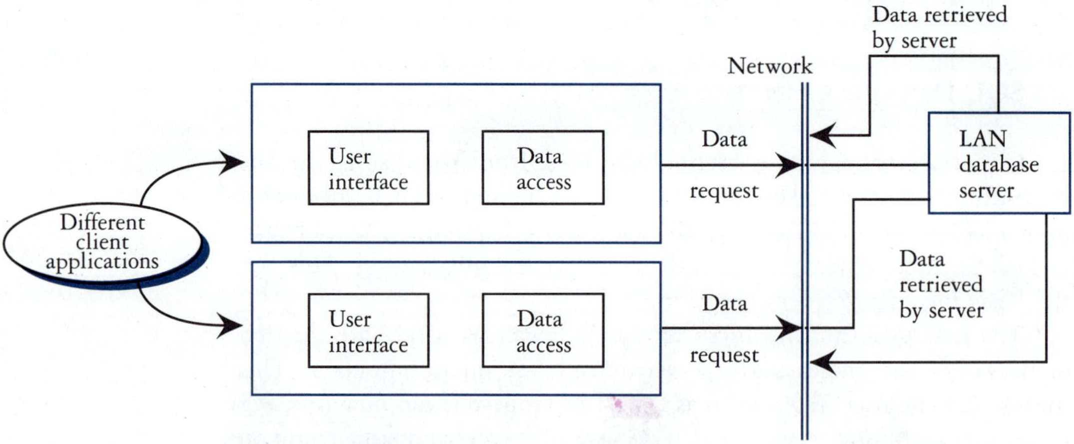

Figure 10-2 SQL database format

application rests with the user's PC. So, instead of concentrating on processing data, the client PC can focus on user applications, leaving the database server to handle database management chores such as data security, recovery, and backup.

Primary Products

There are several client database server products on the market today, including Oracle's Oracle Server, IBM's OS/2 Extended Edition Database Manager, Microsoft/SYBASE SQL Server, and Gupta SQL Base. In each product, requests from front-end applications are made via SQL commands, which provide a precise way for requesting data. For example, a client PC sends a single SQL command to the server, which returns only the requested data to the client.

SQL database servers offer two key advantages:

1 Using SQL as a standard means that different applications can access data stored in the same format. This arrangement makes the task of accessing distributed database servers an easy job.

2 Using SQL also improves the efficiency of the network, since only the data requested is sent to the client server across the network.

As a result of the introduction of SQL database servers, different types of client software have appeared. One type, called decision support products, are ready-to-use, user-oriented query tools and report generators. With a decision support product, all the user has to do is define the application and the data to be retrieved; the software does the rest. On the other hand, custom applications require the development of computer programs to access the server data. For example, dBASE IV Server Edition allows the user to define queries, reports, and a high-level programming language that allows SQL commands to be embedded for accessing server data.

Popular PC products that support direct links with SQL database servers include Paradox, Revelation, Lotus 1-2-3, and Excel. Among the mainframe products are OS/2, UNIX, and VAX platforms. The list is expected to grow, making it convenient for users to migrate to a database server environment. It should be noted that each database server has its own unique features. For example, database servers designed for a client/server environment may offer special features to improve performance over a network or to enforce database security and integrity—both important features to consider.

Another example, Microsoft/SYBASE SQL Server, runs on virtually any network—IBM's LAN Server, Microsoft's LAN Manager, and (via an interface) on netware (a LAN product). The server includes TRIGGERS, which are procedures stored in the server that are automatically executed every time a record is updated. Each of the many database servers available offers unique features that make it suitable for certain applications. Before deciding on a database server, the prospective buyer must understand these features and how well they have been implemented elsewhere in similar environments. Verifying vendor claims and the performance record of the server are also important.

SUMMARY

1 The aggregate functions minimum, maximum, average, total, and count produce a single value which is a summary of information about the subject rows of a table. With the exception of count, these functions cannot be applied to columns containing character data.

2 The average (AVG) function produces the average for the values contained in the rows selected in the table. Null values are ignored by this aggregate function.

3 The minimum (MIN) function produces the lowest value and the maximum (MAX) produces the highest value in the specified column of the table.

4 The total (SUM) function produces the total of the values in the specified column. The values in the column must be numbers.

5 The count (COUNT) function produces the number of items in the specified column.

6 A join is the process of accessing multiple tables by means of the WHERE clause in the SELECT command. The WHERE clause limits the scope of the command to only those rows that meet the conditions specified. Simple joins provide for queries from one or two tables, while multiple joins are used when more tables are involved.

7 The IN or NOT IN operators can be used to specify that the value in a column is contained in a specified set of values. In contrast, pattern matching can be accomplished through the use of the LIKE or NOT LIKE form in the WHERE clause.

8 A self-join is done when it is necessary to use the same table more than once in a SELECT statement. The combined result consists of two rows from the same table.

9 Outer joins are useful when the response table must include rows from a table that satisfy one, but not both, of the join criteria.

10 Some queries are complex and require a subquery to provide the data that satisfies the data request. The response table from a subquery may return no values, one value, or a set of values, depending on the comparison operator specified in the primary query.

11 A multiple join involves adding tables to the FROM clause and the join conditions to the WHERE clause of a SELECT command. The multiple clauses in the WHERE clause are joined by AND, OR connectors.

12 SQL statements can be embedded into traditional programming languages to make the database tables available to those programs. The overall

strategy of embedded SQL is to include the SQL statements in the computer program and convert them into the host language with a precompiler.

13 All embedded SQL statements in a COBOL program are specified by the key words EXEC SQL and end with the key words END-EXEC, followed by a period.

14 A program with embedded SQL commands contains host variables and column variables. Any host variable is preceded by a colon. The column variable must be defined by a DECLARE command. Nondatabase variables must be defined in the normal way.

15 The simplest form of the embedded SELECT statement is the singleton select, where only one row is selected in response to a query. If a query may produce more than one row, a cursor must be defined and moved through the database table by a FETCH command in accordance with the DECLARE cursor statement.

16 The error status resulting from the execution of an SQL command is returned to an area called the SQL communications area. By querying the SQL area, the user can determine whether an error occurred. Dynamic SQL deals with unpredictable data requests.

KEY WORDS

Aggregate functions
Average function (AVG)
Client
Column variables
Comparison operators
Count function (COUNT)
Cursor
Dynamic SQL
Embedded SQL
Host variables
Maximum function (MAX)
Minimum function (MIN)
Multiple join
Outer join
Self-join
Server
Simple join
Singleton select
SQL communications area (SQLCA)
SQL database server
Subquery
Total function (SUM)
Triggers
WHERE clause

REVIEW QUESTIONS

1 What are the aggregate functions and what do they do?

2 What is the purpose of a WHERE clause in a SELECT command?

3 In your own words, explain the difference between simple, self-, outer, and multiple joins. Give examples.

4 Distinguish between the following pairs:
   a. query and subquery
   b. comparison operators and linking operators
   c. singleton select and cursor
   d. host variable and column variable

5 How are aliases used in SQL? Give an example.

6 In your own words, describe a self-join.

7 Describe each class of linking operators briefly. Give an example of each class.

8 Illustrate the use of multiple joins.

9 What is embedded SQL? How does it differ from dynamic SQL? Be specific.

10 How is a cursor used in embedded SQL?

11 How important are SQL database servers? Explain their role in database processing.

12 How would you go about selecting an SQL database server?

APPLICATION PROBLEMS

1 Complete the following using Table 10-4.
   a. Write SQL commands to list the descriptions of all parts that are in warehouse 2 and that have more than 60 units available.
   b. What would the following query result in?

```
SELECT COUNT(PART_NUM)
FROM PART
WHERE CLASS = 'Appliances'
```

   c. Write an SQL query to count the number of parts in item class "Gardening."

PART_NUM	DESC	UNIT_AVAIL	CLASS	WRHS_NUM	PRICE
A16	Freezer	17	Appliances	1	900.00
D62	Rake	4	Gardening	2	8.00
A14	A/C	3	Appliances	1	319.00
A19	Hose	16	Gardening	1	16.00
A10	Mower	21	Gardening	2	160.00
C04	Chainsaw	11	Hardware	1	210.00
C06	Shovel	64	Gardening	2	12.00
B12	Toaster	9	Hardware	2	34.00

Table 10-4 Inventory table

2 Complete the following using Table 10-5.
   a. Write an SQL query to find the number of customers and the sum of their balances.
   b. What is the result of the command

```
SELECT COUNT(CUS_NUM), AVG(BALANCE)
```

c. Write a query (and show the results) to show the maximum balance. Write another to show the minimum balance.

CUST_NUM	CUS_NAME	REPNUM	BALANCE
164	Arens, Joe	3	114.10
192	Pringle, Jim	4	200.00
194	Snyder, Dave	2	320.17
195	Denny, Debbie	2	62.10
210	Smith, Alice	3	72.00
217	Brown, Helen	6	84.00
316	Baker, Art	6	111.00
407	Trent, Bob	3	86.00
514	Daleiden, Bud	2	10.00

Table 10-5 Customer account table

3 Using Tables 10-5 and 10-6, write a query to list the CUS_NUM and CUS_NAME of each customer and his or her respective sales representative (REPNUM and REPNAME). You will need to access both tables with an SQL command.

REPNUM	REPNAME
1	Akins, Gib
2	Parker, Samantha
3	Feinstein, Jerry
4	Daly, Mike
5	Wilder, Bob
6	Gwen, Joan

Table 10-6 Representative table

4 Using Tables 10-5 and 10-6, write a query to list the number and name of each customer whose balance is over $100, along with the name of the sales representative of each customer.

C H A P T

Distributed Databases and Networking

E R 1 1

Distributed Drumbeat Still a Bit Hollow

AT A GLANCE

Distributed Drumbeat Still a Bit Hollow

The MIS director threw his hands up in the air and exclaimed, "Sure, our databases are distributed. If you see any of them, would you please send them home?"

In a sense, distributed databases have been around for a long time. However, technology is just emerging to fit a more contemporary definition: Distributed DBMS systems reside at multiple sites in a network, but appear to the user and applications as one database at the user's own site.

Although the modern definition seems simple, there are many ways to satisfy it, each with trade-offs. "If you're looking to purchase, realize that 'distributed database' is not a binary state of 'have it' or 'don't.'"

Driving Forces

The apocryphal MIS director has already achieved the first step in understanding how to go about implementing a distributed DBMS solution. People, more than technology, distribute data. If technology alone were the answer, probably the most reliable and cost-efficient solution would be huge, centralized, mainframe-based database managers. But the current is running the other way—user demand has spurred the development of low-end and midrange computing.

That trend has brought with it a whole new set of problems. Personal computers, departmental computing, and geographically distributed mainframes led to the need to unify information, but the data's owners are only willing to share it, not give it away. Culturally speaking, Americans hate to depend on anyone else and want control over their own data. For many users, PCs were ego-effective long before they were cost-effective. That is one big reason why we arrived at today's state of affairs.

For many new systems, and many new bodies of data, centralization is clearly the second choice. In the case of distributing systems that five years ago might have been centralized, it's the economics of mid- to low-range computing. Compared to a central site, networks are reliable and economical, although difficult to administer.

Another benefit of distributed databases is that they allow the user to increase computing capacity by adding computers rather than by expanding existing computers. "If your cart becomes too much for your horse to pull, do you trade for a bigger horse, or get a second horse?" asked Umang Gupta, president of Gupta Technologies, Menlo Park, Calif.

DBMS Independence

C. J. Date developed 12 rules for an ideal distributed database system. Today, no software meets all of these criteria. None of the 12 rules states that a distributed system must use one DBMS, but rule 12—DBMS independence—cannot be satisfied with today's technology, Date says.

Enabling different DBMSs to act as equal partners in a distributed system should be possible, but it will certainly be more difficult than using one DBMS product at multiple sites. One reason for this difficulty is the number of different SQL dialects. In the interim, imperfect heterogeneous distributed DBMS implementations may prove to be more valuable than perfect implementations of a homogeneous system because most organizations run multiple DBMSs. Reality always wins.

Another of Date's rules concerns data replication. The advantages of replicated data are fewer remote accesses (due to more local copies), and the availability of another copy if the first is down or locked for update. The major disadvantage of data replication is that when one copy is up-dated, all must be up-dated. Few vendors offer automatic replication. And keeping all replicas synchronized can cause tremendous network traffic tie-ups creating a protocol that ensures consistent updating across multiple copies or, as it is often called, two-phase commit. It is critical to any distributed system. Basically, the protocol must ensure that all copies of an object are updated or none are. If an update fails at one site, the updates at the other sites must be rolled back. This causes updates to fail more frequently, but guarantees the integrity of the database overall. Two-phase commit also requires that numerous messages cross the network between nodes for each update.

What's Missing?

Distributed technology must overcome several hurdles. Distribution across a wide area network increases the network traffic problems tremendously compared to a local area network. And traffic only increases with such desirable capabilities as two-phase commits, data replication, and distributed transaction management.

Other holes that need to be filled include network security support and security administration, and standardized name servers to locate a user or a printer across nodes. Even if problems of performance and interproduct access standards were solved today, the data is often not ready to be joined. What if two databases store pricing information in different currencies? What if one system reflects a one-to-one relationship and another calls it one-to-many?

Work is needed on application deployment—how does one provide a new version of an application to 5000 PCs? With all of these hurdles, is distributed the way to go? "Certainly, it's still in its infancy." "The security, the communications, the networking—all must be so much more advanced. That's why we promote distributed applications more than distributed databases."

Excerpted from Herter, Janis, "Distributed drumbeat still a bit hollow." Reprinted with permission of Software Magazine, *October 1990, Sentry Publishing Co., Inc., 1900 West Park Drive, Westborough, MA 01581, USA.*

AT A GLANCE

Single-site database management systems are gradually being phased out in favor of distributed database management systems (DDBMS) for a variety of reasons, all having to do with improved performance. Whether a DDBMS is part of a local area network or a wide area network, the goal of distribution is to create a single-image, transparent environment where the user can work at the local level and still be able to access or share data with other sites in the network.

DDBMS design criteria focus on local autonomy, location transparency, replication transparency, fragmentation transparency, effective query optimization, transaction transparency, and hardware/network/operating system independence. In addition, security measures and promoting integrity at all levels of the DBMS environment are extremely important. There are also issues in installing a network as well as planning a first-time DBMS environment for an organization.

By the end of this chapter, you should know

- the basic concepts and elements of networking;
- transmission techniques and issues in network installations;
- the basis for implementing a DDBMS;
- DDBMS features and their importance for ensuring a highly reliable DDBMS;
- the importance of referential integrity in a DDBMS; and
- the role of security in designing a DDBMS.

Introduction

Up to this point, we have assumed that the DBMS and the data that represent a database system all reside on a single computer, what is called a centralized database management system. Centralized processing has been prevalent since the early 1970s. It allows multiple users to access a central mainframe computer through terminals, workstations, and PCs. But as mini- and microcomputers became more and more affordable in the early 1980s, decentralized, or distributed processing became popular. Mini- and microcomputers were literally distributed throughout an organization and linked together to form a network so that users at each location, whether near or far, could instantly access data stored at their own or other locations.

Today, most single-site DBMSs are gradually being phased out in favor of distributed database management systems (DDBMS). This is expected to have a profound impact on DBMS clients during the next decade.

Networking software is an integral part of a distributed database environment. Increased network capabilities have contributed in a significant way to the appeal and potential of distributed databases. Software solutions to crash recovery, security, and other major problems are becoming increasingly available. All these developments have contributed to the important role distributed database management systems play in managing today's organizations.

Distributed databases come in two general forms: local area networks (LAN) and wide area networks (WAN). But before we delve into the specifics, we must first understand some basic networking concepts.

Networking Concepts

As a technology, telecommunication, which includes fiber optics, electronic mail, videotext, and satellite transmission, has grown in response to the need to exchange information between locations. Telecommunication is like a highway system for transporting information within and among multiple sites, and as such is a basic ingredient in any networked system.

Key Elements

There are many ways to design a networked system. The basic configuration is shown in Figure 11-1. The key elements in any networked system are as follows.

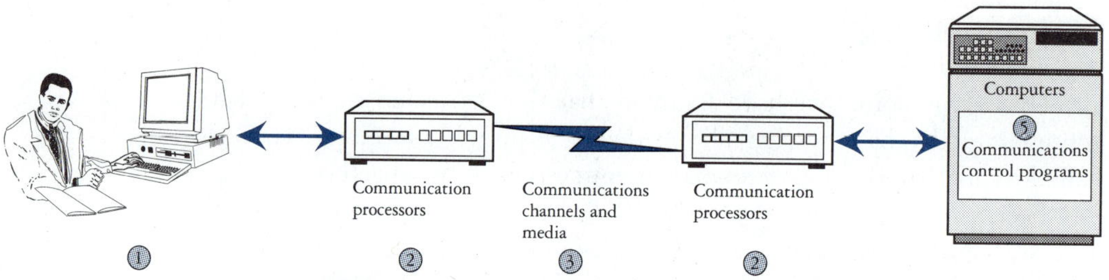

Figure 11-1 Basic components of a telecommunication system

1 The *workstation*—a PC, telephone, video display terminal (VDT), and whatever other hardware the user wants—is where the user enters commands, data, queries, and software into the database.

2 *Communication processors*—modems, multiplexors, front-end processors, and so forth—handle data transmission between the database and the user terminals and vice versa. A communication processor is typically a minicomputer dedicated to handling communications control tasks for a large mainframe. It can code and decode data and messages, detect and correct errors, and poll remote terminals to see whether they are ready to receive or transmit data. The communications processor at each end of the line translates signals from digital to analog (user to computer) and from analog to digital (computer to user). The processor also controls and maximizes the communication flow between computers and workstations. It is more like a messenger manager.

3 *Communications channels* are a combination of media such as telephone lines, coaxial cables, fiber optics, microwave systems, or satellite transmissions. (See Figure 11-2.) The communications channels are the highway down which data travels.

4 *Host computers*, usually large mainframes, execute the system's various processing chores. Most host computers have communications programs that manage the entire communications network.

5 *Communications control programs* control incoming and outgoing activities and essentially manage the communication activities of the network.

Note that software is an integral part of all networked systems. For example, communications control software, called TELEPROCESSING (TP) MONITORS, resides in the host computer or in front-end computers to manage and control communication traffic.

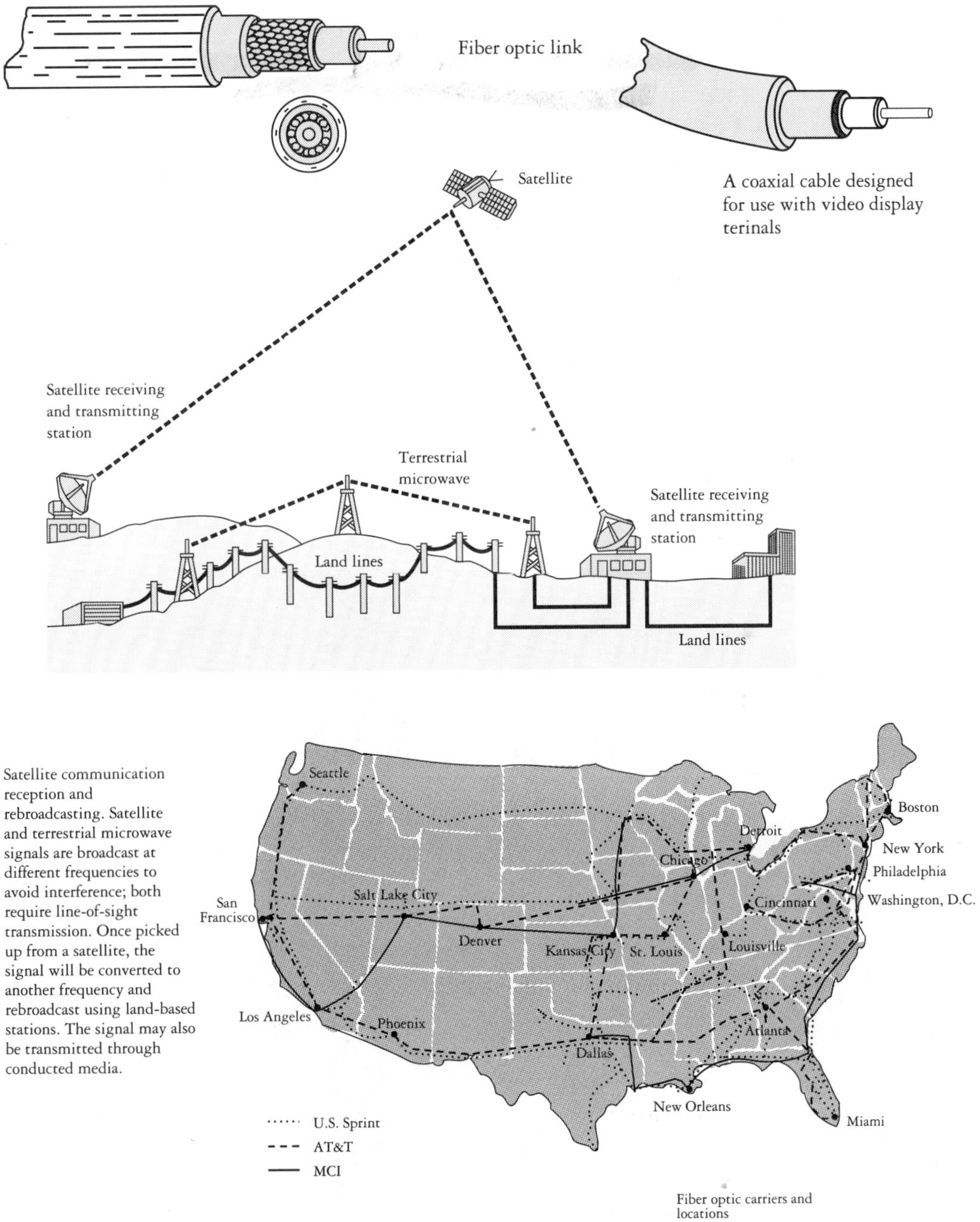

Figure 11-2 Communications media and channels
Source: Awad, E.M., *Management information systems.* Menlo Park, CA: Benjamin Cummings Publishing Co., 1988, p. 209.

Wide Area Networks

A WIDE AREA NETWORK (WAN) covers a large geographic area and is used when branches of an organization are scattered. For example, airline and hotel reservation systems, electronic funds transfer systems in banking, and remote data entry systems in retailing often use WANs.

Satellite transmission is the latest, the fastest, and most efficient way to transmit over long distances, and is the most commonly used communications channel in WANs. The main limitation of WANs is their complex routing and control. To ensure efficiency, a network must employ a complex set of routing and control algorithms. This "distance-insensitive" network can relay messages over the curvature of the earth and in most atmospheric conditions. Satellite communications are illustrated in Figure 11-3.

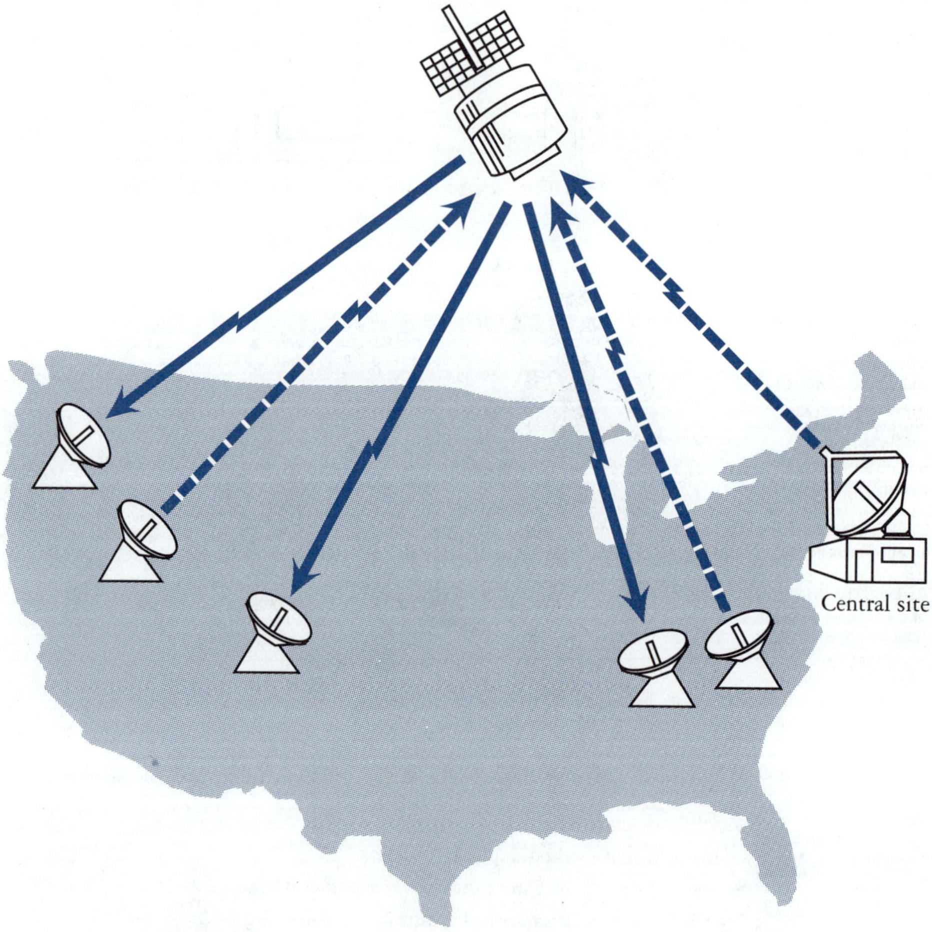

Figure 11-3 A ground station transmits a microwave signal to the satellite, which in turn changes its frequency and transmits the signal back to a receiving station on earth

Local Area Networks

The LOCAL AREA NETWORK (LAN) is distinguished from other networks by the area it covers, its transmission speed, and the ease with which new devices can be added to it. LANs are used for short-haul communication, where multiple users in a local area share hardware, software, and data resources.

Unlike the WAN user, the LAN user is free to choose from a wealth of information and technology through the network, including a powerful PC with a large hard disk capacity called a FILE SERVER. The file server contains the network control program and makes common files and software packages available to LAN users. A PRINT SERVER, another common LAN feature, likewise makes remote printing devices available so that, for example, the user with a short-term need for high-quality graphics may share (at a price) another user's laser printer. A LAN is also connected to other networks via an interface called a GATEWAY. (See Figure 11-4.)

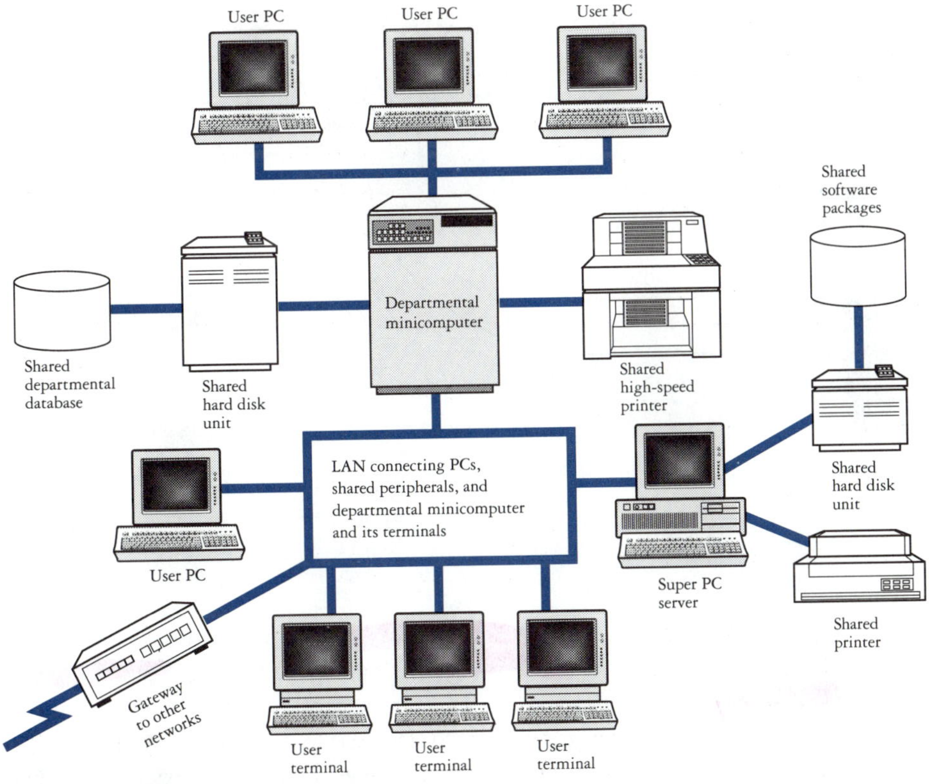

Figure 11-4 Local area network configuration

LANs are described by the small geographic area (within a building or a firm) they occupy, transmitting usually in digital form. They are also classified by the major technologies and types of network control they use to manage communications. The three key technologies are: star networking, token passing, and carrier-sense processing.

Star networking Developed by AT&T, star networking is the simplest configuration and is used for the smaller PCs. In a STAR NETWORK each PC is linked by a telephone line to the host computer. All circuits radiate from a central node, typically a host computer. The network puts the central point in contact with every other location, which makes it easy to control. On the other hand, because all transactions are controlled by the central point, the whole system will fail if the host goes down. (See Figure 11-5.)

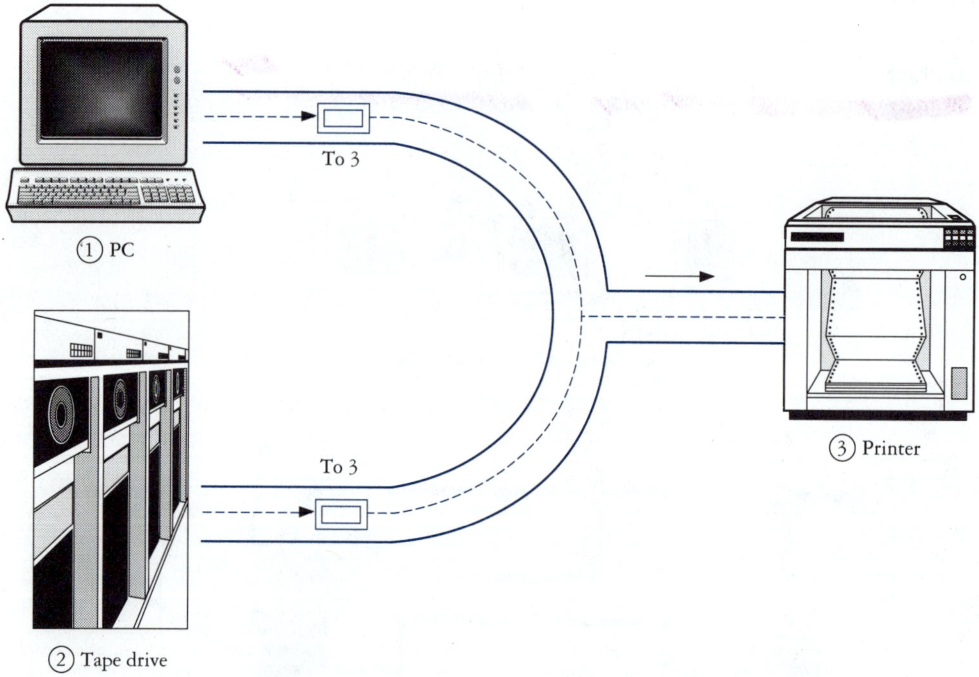

Figure 11-5 Star network

Token passing TOKEN PASSING SYSTEMS, such as those developed by IBM, require that a coded signal, called a token, pass by each workstation. The hardware (the PC, for example) attaches its information to the token, which moves it to the data "highway." Once it has delivered this information, the token passes on to the next device. The major problem with token passing is that, if the token gets lost, no terminal can access the network. (See Figure 11-6.)

Carrier-sense processing THE CARRIER-SENSE AND MULTIPLE ACCESS WITH COLLISION DETECTION (CSMA/CD) system used by Ethernet is like a one-lane highway with traffic going both ways. Computer hardware

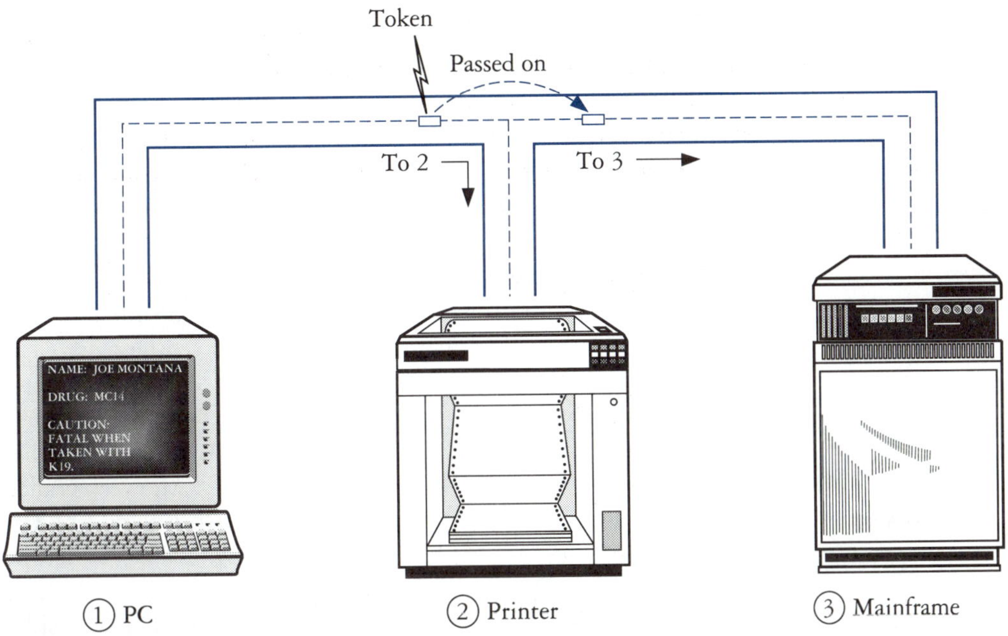

Figure 11-6 Token passing system

monitors the network and sends information whenever the road is clear. If two different packages of data collide, they have to go back and try again. The problem with CSMA/CD is that sending data can become difficult when the traffic is heavy. (See Figure 11-7.)

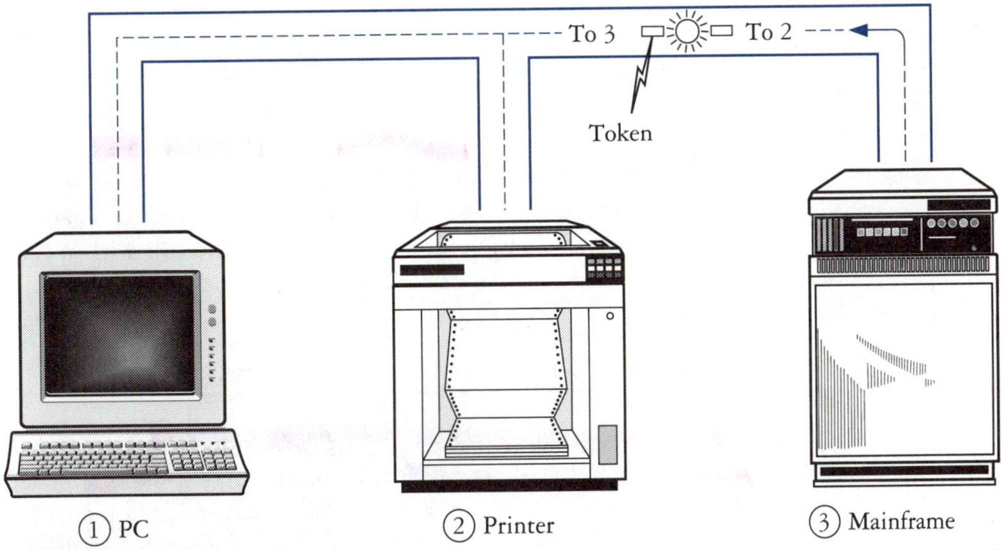

Figure 11-7 CSMA/CD system

Network Planning

Regardless of the type of network, network architecture is an important part of a distributed database environment. Network planning involves procedural details that have important implications for the organization on the network they will serve. A network planner needs to consider integration from logical, physical, and organizational points of view.

The logical view involves the levels of user access that define connectivity access. In contrast, the physical view encompasses the communications channels and hardware that make up the network. The organizational view concerns how well the physical and logical links meet the organization's requirements or affect the organization's structure. Consider, for example, an organization that has 80 branches operating in 20 different countries around the world. With every branch linked to a common network, any change in the network would be felt by everyone in the organization. Therefore, every change must be planned in advance.

To plan a network for a given organization, we need to consider several issues.

- *Number of devices to be attached*. The number and location of PCs, servers, gateways, and so forth that will need to hook up with the system should be considered.
- *Proximity of each device within the network*. This includes distance of the device to the wall plug.
- *Nature and volume of network traffic*. The heavier the load, the more powerful the servers should be. Unless loads are considered, system performance might suffer.
- *Performance requirements*. Overall, network performance is improved by shifting functions from file servers to dedicated communication servers or reconfiguring a network into smaller ones connected with gateways.
- *Bandwidth*. The network BANDWIDTH—the frequency range of the communications channel—determines the maximum transmission rate, measured in bits per second (BPS). A broadband or high-speed channel, for example, allows transmission rates of up to 1 million BPS with special leased lines. Some applications demand more bandwidth than others.

Distributed Database Management Systems

A DISTRIBUTED DATABASE MANAGEMENT SYSTEM (DDBMS) is a system with multiple computer sites within a communication network. Each site (for example, a regional office, branch, and manufacturing plant) has its own database with its own DBMS, CPU, and terminals. Each site communicates through messages. A message sent from one computer site to another can be anything from a data access query to a response that the requested data is unavailable. Each site also manages its own recovery management and logging procedures. The DBMS at each site is assumed to be homogeneous and highly autonomous, but cooperative with DBMSs at the other sites. (See Figure 11-8.)

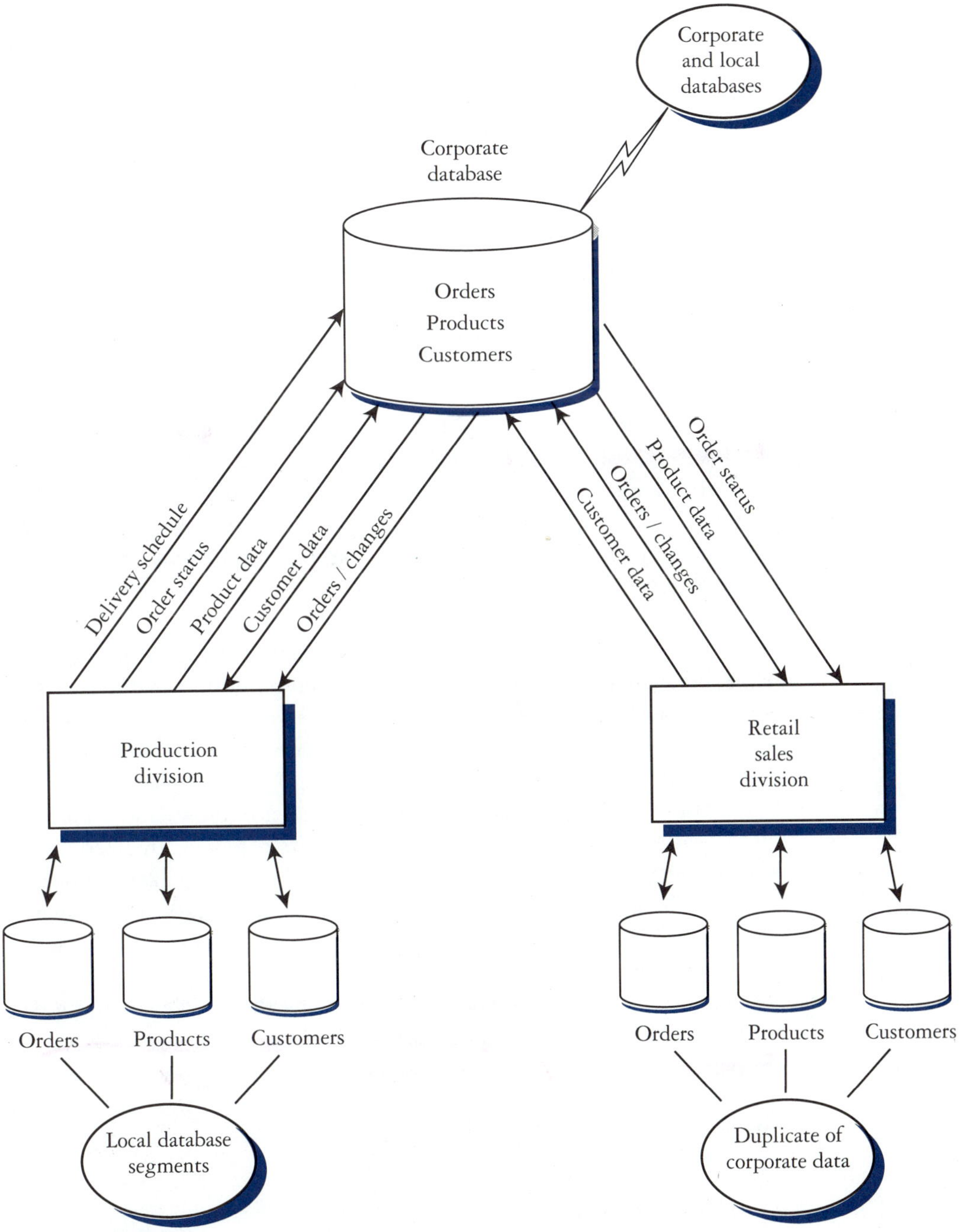

Figure 11-8 Distributed database management system configuration

Since the early 1980s, improved network capabilities, increased availability of software solutions to major problems such as crash recovery, and the growing use of relational DBMS and SQL have all contributed to the impetus for DDBMS. How well this architecture fulfills a real need continues to be debated, as users explore and exploit the possibilities of the technology.

Advantages

DBMSs that communicate with each other offer users a number of advantages. Here are some of the key advantages of a distributed database management system.

Control of data at a particular site In a DDBMS, data entered and stored at a particular site can be directly controlled and regulated at the site. Local users, who are familiar with their own data needs, can ensure greater data integrity and better administration of the data in a network system than in a centralized system, where the database is maintained remotely.

Greater reliability A properly designed DDBMS can be more reliable than a centralized system, although difficult to administer. When a centralized database fails, the whole system fails, but a distributed system failure is not as disastrous because only users at the affected site are unable to proceed. Other users, at other locations, may not be inconvenienced at all.

Greater availability of data In a centralized database, an individual piece of data occurs only once and can only be accessed by one user at a time. In a distributed database, data is often replicated at different sites and thus available to many users. Furthermore, if data is inadvertently deleted or lost due to system failure, it can often be recovered from another site.

Easier system expansion As an organization grows and establishes new locations, it needs to expand access to its database. In a centralized system, an upgrade may require major alterations to the database or even installation of a whole new system in order to handle the increased volume of data. In a DDBMS, the organization can simply add another site to its existing network.

Faster response time and lower communication costs Because data in a distributed system is stored at the site where it is most often used, response time is faster and communication costs are lower. Cheap and powerful computers at local sites make it more economically attractive to process data locally than to transmit it to a central site for processing.

Disadvantages

There are three main disadvantages of a distributed system: updating problems, data dictionary problems, and query problems.

Update problems While replication of data in a distributed database has its advantages, it can also cause update problems and the costs associated with them. For example, let us say a piece of data exists four times in a distributed database system. Instead of updating this data once, as would be done in a centralized system, all four copies must be updated. The cost of transmitting the multiple updates across the data communications network is significantly higher than the cost of the single transmission a centralized system would require. Furthermore, in a distributed system, if one of the four sites is inaccessible at the time of the update (perhaps the specific data is being accessed, or there is a hardware failure at the site), the entire update must wait—a situation that would not occur in a centralized system.

Complexity of the data dictionary Maintenance of a data dictionary in a distributed database is much more complex than in a centralized system, where only one copy of the data dictionary exists. In a distributed system, the data dictionary entries may be stored in one of three ways:

1 in its entirety at a single site (as in a centralized system);
2 as separate copies at each site; or
3 as separate entries distributed among the sites, with some duplication.

Storing the data dictionary at a single site is easily accomplished, but creates retrieval problems. Retrieving dictionary entries is costly for users at all other sites and difficult or impossible when communication with the storage site is blocked by a hardware failure there.

Storing a copy of the entire data dictionary at each site reverses the problems. Retrieval of entries at any given site is easily accomplished, but updates are complicated and storage of all the duplicate entries is costly.

Storing entries at various sites is the preferred method, since the right compromise can result in the greatest efficiency in managing the data dictionary.

Complicated query processing Handling queries in a distributed database system can be complicated and costly when compared to a centralized system. Because data in a distributed system is often duplicated, multiple methods may be needed to handle a query. With each query the user must determine which is the most efficient method (the method that requires communication with the fewest sites is frequently the most cost-efficient) to carry out a particular request for data.

Design Criteria

A DDBMS should shield the user as much as possible from the complexities of distributed database management. That is, it should make transparent the location of the data in the system, as well as other features of a DDBMS. Therefore, in designing a DDBMS, a number of design objectives must be met to make data easy to retrieve.

Location Transparency

Despite being geographically dispersed, the data in a DDBMS appears to users as a single database. In the ideal single-image model, the distributed database appears *transparent* to the user. The transparency assumption is important for exploring the ramifications of actually implementing a DDBMS application.

LOCATION TRANSPARENCY means site data and operations are local, and each site is treated as equal in the distributed database network. Recovery controls, query processing, and the data dictionary are also distributed. This means no logjams and no total crash.

With local transparency, users and programs do not need to know where the data physically resides. The user accesses the data regardless of whether it is stored locally or at another location in the network. The location of the data is therefore transparent to any user of the system, although the location is usually recorded in a table name.

The main idea of tabularity of data is flexibility and autonomy. Whether tables are located on the site's hard disk or on hard disks at different sites should make no difference to user access.

Fragmentation Transparency

DATA FRAGMENTATION involves dividing a group of related data elements into logical units for storage. It also means dividing into chunks certain data to be stored closest to the site where it is used the most. For example, instead of storing all customer savings account data for a national bank at a single location, account data for each customer could be stored at the location where that customer opened an account and does most of his or her banking. The savings account data would thus be fragmented to allow more efficient storage and use of the data. Data fragmentation reduces network traffic.

To illustrate fragmentation transparency, Figure 11-9 shows a global schema which represents an entire pharmacy database as though it were a centralized database. The global schema represents a unified global view of the user's and the programmer's view of the database. Patient and drug tables are fragmented to keep data near to where it is used most often. To keep a drug associated with a patient at the site where that patient buys it, we partition the patient and drug files into FRAGMENTS.

There are two types of fragmentation: horizontal and vertical. HORIZONTAL FRAGMENTATION occurs when a database file is divided "horizontally" to allow storage of data in different locations. That is, a table can be broken up into multiple tables by selecting rows. This can

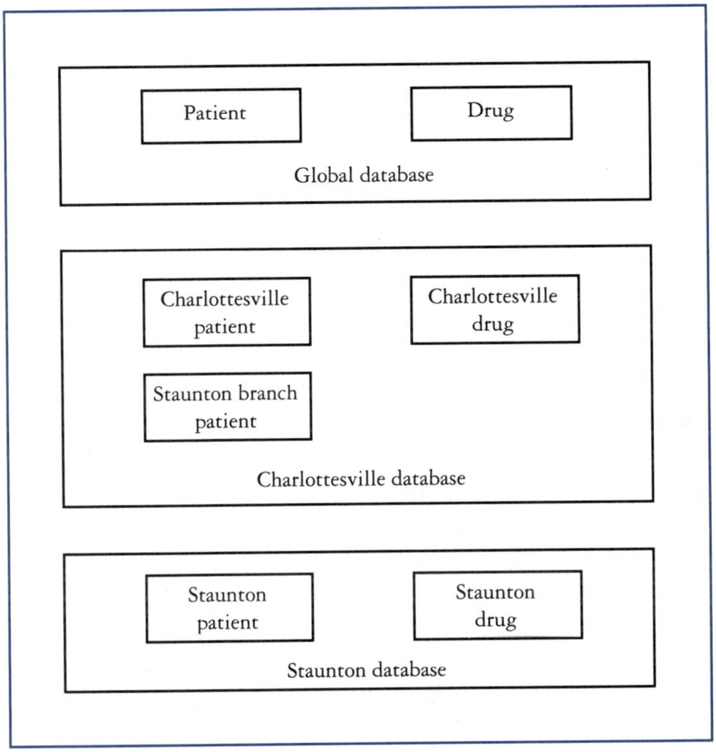

CREATE TABLE patient

(p#	char (5)
name	char (15)
address	char (15)
city	char (20)
state	char (2)
zip code	char (5));

primary key (p#)

CREATE TABLE drug

(d# char (5) not null
p# char (5) not null);

primary key (d#)

foreign key (p#)

Figure 11-9 Distributed prescription entry system

be recombined into the original table using the SQL UNION operator. VERTICAL FRAGMENTATION occurs when a file is split "vertically" and different attributes are stored at different sites. That is, we break up a table into multiple tables by selecting columns. Vertical fragments can be recombined to form the original table by joining the fragments. To support fragments, we need to define how the global schema is split.

In the pharmacy example, the fragments might appear as

```
CHARLOTTESVILLE PATIENTS=
     SELECT *
     FROM PATIENT
     WHERE CITY='CHARLOTTESVILLE'
STAUNTON PATIENTS=
     SELECT *
     FROM CUSTOMER
     WHERE CITY='STAUNTON'
CHARLOTTESVILLE DRUGS=
     SELECT*
     FROM DRUGS
     WHERE P =(SELECT P  FROM PATIENT WHERE CITY=
        'CHARLOTTESVILLE')
```

```
STAUNTON DRUGS=
    SELECT*
    FROM DRUGS
    WHERE P =(SELECT P  FROM PATIENTS WHERE CITY=
       'STAUNTON')
```

Location and fragmentation transparency are interrelated: Fragmentation transparency requires location transparency, because a location can be specified only when fragments are specified, but location transparency does not require fragmentation transparency.

Replication Transparency

REPLICATION TRANSPARENCY means that redundant data is transparently updated. A data object may be duplicated at various sites to minimize traffic, but the duplication, or replication, is transparent to the user. The user should not need to know where replicated data is located, nor even that such replication exists. Selecting the most efficient access method for replicated data should be left to the system, not the user.

Although replication transparency provides improved performance and availability, it also poses certain problems. Retrieval activities must seek the copy closest to the user, and updates must be automatically directed to all copies in order to maintain record integrity. These functions are not easy to maintain.

Referential Integrity

REFERENTIAL INTEGRITY means that the columns in one table that reference a unique identifier of a row in another table should always refer to existing values. Referential integrity ensures that cross-references between tables are always valid. A cross-reference is usually indicated when a foreign key in one table refers to a corresponding primary key in another table. If the two keys don't match, the transaction cannot be completed.

To illustrate, suppose that patient #50000 leaves a prescription to be filled and the clerk mistakenly enters the customer's number as 05000 in the prescription entry system. We have an integrity problem (and confusion) if the drug gets registered to another patient with ID 05000 or if patient 05000 simply does not exist. Validation checks become extremely important.

Local Autonomy

Being able to access data from multiple sites in a transparent fashion, while controlling the data local to the site that actually uses it, is called LOCAL AUTONOMY. For example, the inventory clerk at the Main Street branch of an auto parts chain discovers that a particular item is out of stock, but available at the chain's Rio Road and Park Street stores. The clerk can order a spare part from the Rio Road store, and only the Rio Road store's local database needs to be tapped. With local autonomy, only the sites directly affected are involved and communications performance is improved.

Query Optimization

Processing time for an SQL query in a DDBMS can range from one second to several hours, depending on the size of the database, speed of the network, and the processing power of the user PC. A DDBMS QUERY OPTIMIZER decides on the best route and gets data for processing a query. In a relational database system, performance is dependent on the quality of the system optimizer. In a nonrelational database system, performance is dependent on the quality of the programmer.

Query optimization is especially crucial to DDBMSs, because the order in which operations are handled determines the amount of data that can be communicated from one site to another as well as the number of messages that must pass through the network to process the query. Query optimization should not be centralized, because a hardware failure at that location would bring down the whole system. None of the database server products to date use performance optimization procedures.

Transaction Transparency

Updating a DDBMS is not an easy process. All the different parts of the DDBMS must be in line with one another. In SQL a transaction is a set of SQL statements handled as an atomic unit of work: All the statements have to be executed or all must fail. This is where the two-phase commit (commit or roll back) becomes important.

A TWO-PHASE COMMIT is a coordinating process that ensures that a logical transaction in a physically distributed computer environment is either completely successful or rolled back (aborted). (See Figure 11-10.) Each local DBMS must be able to correctly process the transaction in question. Once a DBMS has signaled it can commit, it must wait for a commit from the coordinating process. While it is waiting, all pertinent resources (tables, pages, etc.) at that site are locked.

The two-phase commit uses twice as much communication capability as an update process running on one centralized computer. Updating a single logical record at several sites is also much more complex than an update process within one computer. Whether the faster response time and improved programming productivity compensate for the increased communication and management costs is up to the individual designer.

To illustrate, suppose you have two accounts, checking and savings,

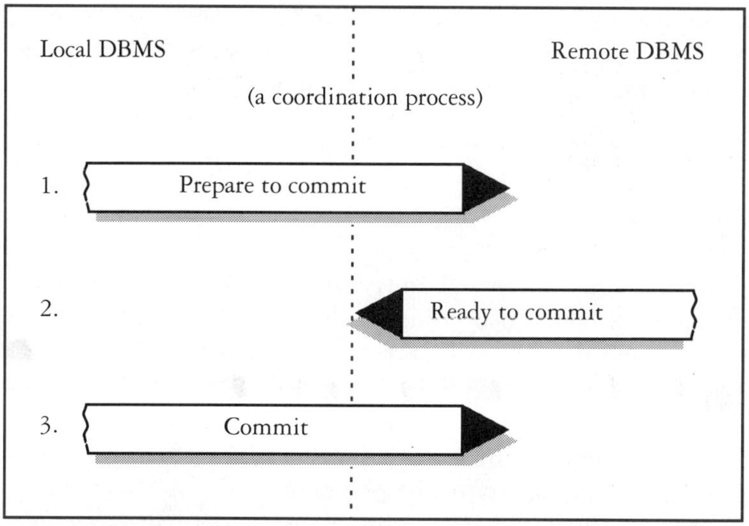

Figure 11-10 Two-phase commit. A logical transaction requires the participant DBMS to look for complete, successful processing of the transaction or to abort

and you wish to transfer $100 from savings to checking. The bank's system must

1 verify that the checking and savings accounts exist;

2 verify that the balance in the savings account is large enough to allow the $100 transfer;

3 subtract $100 from the savings account balance; and

4 add $100 to the checking account balance.

If either of the verifications fails, the whole transfer process must roll back. Suppose further that your savings account is at the bank's main office, and the checking account is at the branch near where you live. When transferring the $100 to checking, the computer at the main office performs the withdrawal and sends its share of the work to the branch. (See Figure 11-11.) A two-phase commit protocol will ensure that the checking account at the branch exists and that the transaction is complete, or the two sites must roll back. Each DBMS must be able to correctly and completely process its share of the transaction.

Hardware/Network/Operating System Independence

A DDBMS runs on different computer systems which must be equal partners in the network. The same DDBMS should also be able to run on different operating systems such as UNIX and PC-DOS, and should be capable of transmitting between network configurations—such as IBM's

Source site

```
select amount
   from savings
where acct_no = 54231
if amount < 100 then rollback
else
   update savings
   set amount = amount-100
   where acct_no = 54231
   create branch site
   send to checking_site
   if no_error
      commit
   else
      rollback
```

Branch site

```
update checking
set amount = amount + 100
where acct_no = 54231
if no_error
   commit
else
   rollback
```

Figure **11-11** A DDBMS where a savings and a checking account are at two separate sites. Two-phase commit ensures that an all-go or all-nogo procedure is followed to promote integrity of operations

System Network Architecture (SNA) and Dec's Decnet—WANs, and LANs.

Finally, we should expect data to be exchanged between two different DBMSs, for example, between IBM's DB2 at one site and Oracle at another site. This is referred to as a HOMOGENEITY ASSUMPTION. A gateway that runs on one DBMS should make that DBMS look like another DBMS in residence. This DDBMS arrangement is the highest level of complexity. Most of today's products fall short of a truly homogeneous DDBMS. A summary of the criteria for a DDBMS is shown in Figure 11-12.

SECURITY

As systems become more distributed, security concerns rise. Although dispersal of processing resources in DDBMS leads to improved

1. Local autonomy—no reliance on a central site
2. Location transparency
3. Fragmentation transparency
4. Replication transparency
5. Query optimization
6. Transaction transparency
7. Hardware/network/operating system independence

Figure 11-12 Key objectives for a DDBMS

access, it also leads to loss of central control. There are two ways to handle basic access security in a DDBMS environment:

1 Let the host machine assume the responsibility for preventing unauthorized access, or

2 Require the user to prove his or her identity for every requested service.

The latter alternative is fundamental to most security plans. That is, users must validate their credibility before accessing any data in residence. If servers are part of the network, users also must prove their identity to prevent illegal emulation of a server device. In the final analysis, users must be validated, devices must be authenticated, and procedures for access and update must be accepted, based on an agreed-upon protocol.

Evolution of Distributed Database Management Systems

Most DDBMS products do not meet all design criteria. To illustrate the evolving nature of DDBMS, consider a three-stage DDBMS IBM is implementing with its mainframe DB2 (DataBase 2): remote request, remote unit of work, and distributed unit of work.

Remote Request

When one application site sends a request (such as SQL query) to a remote site in the network, the request is executed and committed (accepted) or rolled back (rejected) at the remote site. Each query is independent of every other query, and only a single remote site can be specified in the query. In Figure 11-13, site A transmits a single SQL query to site B. Site B decides to commit and execute or roll back the query.

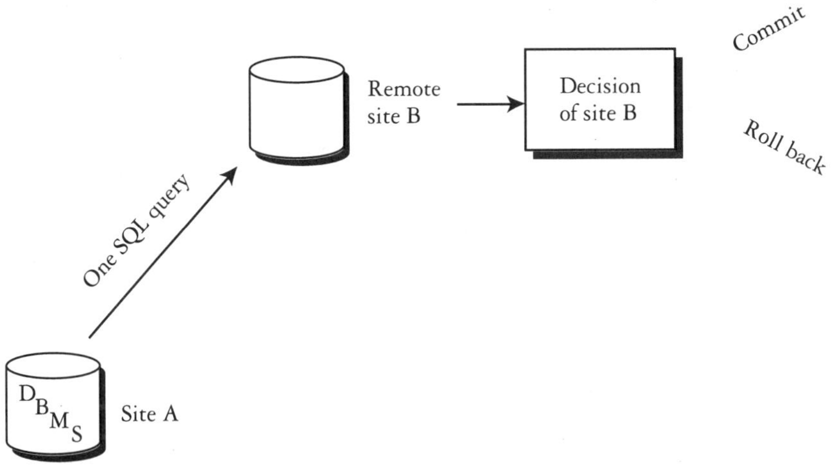

Figure 11-13 Remote request

Remote Unit of Work

When one application site sends all database queries (the group of queries is called a unit of work or transaction) for processing, the decision to commit or roll back rests with site A. In Figure 11-14, site A sends a transaction to site B based on site A's decision to commit the transaction to site B.

Distributed Unit of Work

When one application site sends some or all queries in a transaction to one or more application sites, the originating site decides whether to

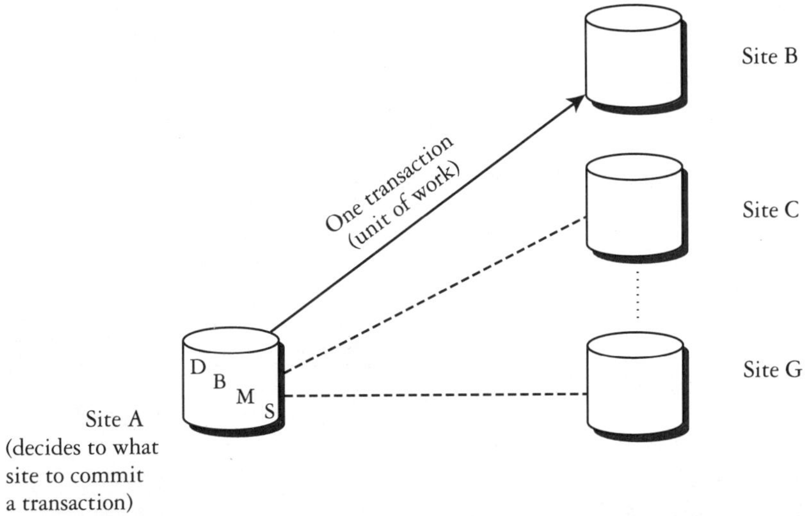

Figure 11-14 Remote unit of work

commit or roll back at the remote site(s). In Figure 11-15, site A splits the total requests regarding the transaction between sites B and D.

Homogeneous networks, although quite diverse in design, provide a single view of security because they have common authority. This is in contrast to heterogeneous DDBMSs, which lack uniformity of access and design. Some systems face severe technical security issues, which suggests that not all vendors have standardized their security protocol. For example, a national network linking more than 180,000 computers at universities and other sites has a host of security problems because of intersubscriber problems that have yet to be resolved.

Ensuring security becomes more complicated in highly distributed systems. Authorization rules can either be fully replicated at each site or individually located at sites as needed, but both ways are expensive because they mean updates must be made at each site. Locating authorization rules at sites where the sensitive data is located is consistent with local autonomy, but when invalidation occurs at some processing stage, rolling back the transaction involves additional communication costs.

At the mainframe level, IBM's System Application Architecture (SAA) has a hierarchy of security levels that are worth noting. The upper levels address

- remote unit of work (RUW),
- distributed unit of work (DUW), and
- distributed request (DR).

At the RUW level, all SQL statements within a unit of work must refer to data stored at a single location. The level of location transparency for RUW is one table per unit of work. At the DUW level, location

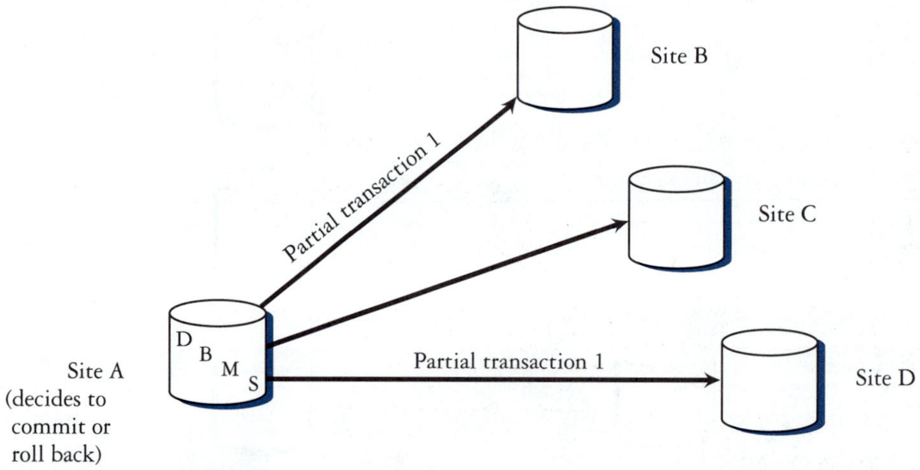

Figure 11-15 Distributed unit of work
Adapted from Bochenski, Barbara, "Coercing DBMSs to cooperate." *Software Magazine*, November 1989, 71.

transparency is one table per statement, and a unit of work may have any number of statements as long as they reference no more than one table. If more than one table is referenced, the programmer must know the physical location of the tables because of the single-site-per-statement restriction.

Finally, at the DR level, all SQL data can be referenced in a single statement. No location restrictions exist, and there is complete location transparency. Files are freely referenced without restrictions.

Planning Considerations

Today's businesses face serious challenges in integrating their data resources. Not only are the volumes of data on the increase, but user requests for data are becoming more complex. This makes database planning critical. Distributed database management with multiple site architecture involves intense advanced planning.

The first decision in building a DDBMS is to determine the level of integration or data distribution the organization needs. Multiple databases may be used to support different branches or divisions for a variety of reasons. The company that decides to distribute data must ensure a viable approach for managing and controlling the data, because today's DBMS software does not readily take care of anomalies that exist in a DDBMS environment.

Implications for Management

If distributed technology is to gain wider adoption, it must overcome several hurdles. For example, distribution across a WAN promotes more serious network traffic problems than distribution across a LAN. Traffic also increases with features such as two-phase commit, replication, transaction management, and query optimization. Another gap in DDBMS technology is network security support and administration. As the DDBMS environment becomes more complex, integrity can become a serious issue, providing even more reason for careful planning.

A major issue for management in instituting a DDBMS is hiring competent personnel. Sad tales of substituting software for talent abound. Corporate database planning must also include career development plans for the technical staff at all levels.

Today's diversification of hardware and software products and services require greater emphasis on distributed databases. To use the technology effectively, an organization must hire top talent for data administration, database design, and management of the distributed network.

In deciding on a DDBMS, management needs to keep in mind alternative approaches to database management systems. As a rule, the more widely distributed corporate database sites are, the more concern there is for data integrity and transmission costs.

Protecting security, privacy, integrity, and auditing functions within a distributed DBMS environment is difficult. Organizations that emphasize a high level of data security and integrity might be better off with a centralized system.

Finally, the need for database stability is extremely important. Users need to know that, regardless of who accesses the database and how often it is accessed, the information they access is reliable at all times. This is, in essence, the ultimate goal of the ideal distributed DBMS.

SUMMARY

1 A telecommunication system consists of five elements: the workstation at the user's site; communication channels to carry data from source to destination; communication processors to handle transmission traffic; computers to handle processing; and communications control programs to execute processing and manage communication activities.

2 Two types of networks are used in data transmission, wide area networks (WANs) for long-haul transmission, and local area networks (LANs) for short-haul transmission. Shareability is made possible via file servers, which are common in many LANs. A LAN is also connected to other networks via an interface called a gateway.

3 Three technologies are available for LAN design: star networks, the simplest configuration, for the assigned smaller PC; token passing, which requires a token to pass by each workstation to accommodate the multiple sites or nodes; and carrier-sense and multiple access with collision detection systems.

4 A network planner needs to consider integration from logical, physical, and organizational views. To plan a network, the designer must consider the number of devices to be attached, the proximity of each device, the nature and volume of traffic, the performance requirements, and the bandwidth requirements.

5 A distributed DBMS (DDBMS) is a system involving multiple computer sites within a communication network. Each site has its own database with its own DBMS, CPU, and terminals. Each site also manages its own recovery management and logging procedure. The DBMS at each site is assumed to be homogeneous and highly autonomous, but cooperative.

6 DDBMS offers control of data at a particular site, greater reliability, greater availability of data, easier system expansion, faster response time, and lower communication costs. Among its limitations are update, data dictionary, and query processing problems.

7 Location transparency, means that site data and operations are local and recovery controls, query processing, and the data dictionary should be distributed.

8 Fragmentation transparency involves dividing groups of related data elements into logical units for storage purposes.

9 Replication transparency is needed when a data object may be duplicated at various sites to minimize traffic.

10 Local autonomy involves accessing data from multiple sites in a transparent fashion, while controlling the data local to the site that actually uses it.

11 Query optimization is that part of software that decides on the best route to handle operations among sites.

12 Transaction transparency means handling a transaction as a unit of work that must be completely executed or rolled back.

13 Hardware/network/operating system independence means the DBMS should run on different operating systems and be able to transmit between network configurations.

14 To maintain security in a DDBMS environment, access to a host must be verified and users must validate their authorization before accessing any data.

15 IBM's SAA hierarchy of security levels includes remote unit of work (RUW), distributed unit of work (DUW), and distributed request (DR). These all use protocols to manage data and ensure integrity at all times.

KEY WORDS

Bandwidth
CSMA/CD
Data fragmentation
Distributed database management system (DDBMS)
Distributed processing
File server
Fragment
Fragmentation transparency
Gateway
Homogeneity assumption
Horizontal fragmentation
Local area network (LAN)
Local autonomy
Location transparency
Print server
Query optimizer
Referential integrity
Replication transparency
Star network
Teleprocessing (TP) monitors
Token passing systems
Transaction
Transaction transparency
Transparency
Two-phase commit
Unit of work
Vertical fragmentation
Wide area network (WAN)

REVIEW QUESTIONS

1 "Increased network capabilities have contributed in a significant way to the appeal and potential of distributed databases." Do you agree? Elaborate on the relationship between networking and DDBMS.

2 Describe in your own words the key elements of a telecommunication system. Why is there a communications processor at each end of the line?

3 What is the difference between the following pairs:

a. WAN and LAN
b. replication transparency and fragmentation transparency
c. referential integrity and two-phase commit
d. star network and token passing process

4 How is a file server used in a LAN?

5 In your own words, describe how a token passing network works. What is the main problem with this arrangement?

6 Why does a network planner need to consider integration from a number of views?

7 In your own words, define a distributed database management system. How does it differ from a centralized DBMS?

8 DDBMS offers certain advantages and limitations. What are they? Under what circumstances do the advantages outweigh the disadvantages?

9 Discuss the homogeneity assumption in DDBMS. How does it relate to transparency?

10 What is the difference between local autonomy and location transparency? Between vertical and horizontal fragmentation?

11 What is referential integrity? How does it relate to two-phase commit?

12 How important is security in DDBMS? Elaborate on the ways in which security measures improve the integrity of the distributed database environment.

13 IBM's SAA has a hierarchy of security levels that are important in DDBMS design. Elaborate on the upper levels of this architecture.

APPLICATION PROBLEMS

1 Review current microcomputer DDBMS literature and identify the features mentioned in this chapter. Summarize each feature and indicate its level of importance.

2 Evaluate a DBMS system in your school lab, local store, or nearby business. Determine

a. the optional features it possesses and
b. to what extent is it distributed. If it is not distributed, what would you do to justify the installation of a distributed DBMS in the facility?

Figure 11-16 Database for parts inventory systems

3 Visit a distributed DBMS environment and identify the following:

a. the commercial distributed DBMS software product in use;

b. how well it provides location, replication, and transaction transparency; and

c. the organization's plan for the future of the system.

4 Consider the distribution database strategies in Figure 11-16.

Indicate the type of transparency (location, replication, transaction) specified by each of the following statements:

a. An end-user in Chicago deletes an item from the Chicago parts list at the Chicago branch. The user does not realize that the same item is automatically deleted from the parts lists in Los Angeles and New York.

b. An end-user in Los Angeles asks for the balance to date for part number 561. He has no idea where this part record is stored. The distributed DBMS looks up the location in the directory and transmits the request to New York.

Write an SQL statement that increases the balance of part 5243 in New York by 5 percent and another SQL statement that decreases the balance of part 6420 in Chicago by 15 percent.

5 Eagle Corporation is a holding company that consists of 15 firms dedicated to the building trade. This includes quarries and truss, precast, building materials, concrete mix, and fuel services. The firms are located within a 150-mile radius from the holding company's headquarters. Eagle maintains a statewide reputation for quality service and continued growth. Much of its success is attributed to the aggressive leadership of its owners and the caliber of management.

Each firm within Eagle has its own president and staff and operates on a decentralized basis. The key personnel at Eagle include the controller and accounting staff, the manager of data processing, and select specialists in charge of areas such as strategic planning and disability insurance. The controller monitors, coordinates, audits, and ensures the viability of the business through various accounting procedures, relying on the information generated via the mainframe. Lotus is used regularly on standalone PCs for tracking accounting and financial applications. The controller also heads the data processing function.

The data processing facility at Eagle centers around a four-year-old minicomputer that runs "bread and butter" applications for a number of firms within Eagle Corporation. The applications include accounts receivable, accounts payable, general ledger, payroll, and sales costing. The minicomputer is estimated to operate at 80 percent utilization. By traditional guidelines, it is operating near or at capacity. If sales continue to grow as anticipated, this computer will take longer to deliver the same information in the future.

The software operating on the existing computer has been "patched" on numerous occasions and for different reasons. Although it is considered "bug-free," it may not be capable of delivering tomorrow's increasingly complex information using the existing hardware.

Some of the technology-specific problems facing Eagle as a holding company are as follows:

- No provisions have been made for backup to the hardware or to data processing personnel. Vendor maintenance has been reported as poor, and computer parts are not easy to locate.
- The present system is on-line, but not interactive. This means that the system continues to produce reports or to display information on a remote terminal, but cannot produce answers to ad hoc requests. This is partly because of the absence of a database environment that requires high-performance hardware, well-conditioned lines, and/or state-of-the-art hardware.
- Different companies have been known to decide on their own which systems they need and, in some case, to place orders through independent contacts. From the viewpoint of Eagle as an entity, independent acquisitions have resulted in the installation of heterogeneous hardware and software. It is estimated that more than six brands of standalone PCs are in operation. Some PCs "talk" to the local minicomputer which, in a sense, is a good beginning for a full-fledged networking operation. There is no established local area network whereby information from one PC can be shared by others within the firm. Furthermore, each brand requires separate maintenance arrangements, which means relatively high fees per contract.

Since Eagle deals with toxic chemicals, it must keep track of the status of these chemicals. At present, no automated information is available regarding underground storage tanks, reports of releases into the environment, or hazard prevention programs.

Eagle Corporation's steady growth has begun to tax the existing systems. As it stands, these computers cannot provide the kind of information that is now needed to operate a growth-oriented enterprise. The existing minicomputers are still capable of handling basic applications (accounts receivable, accounts payable, general ledger, and payroll), but not much more without costly upgrades.

In addition, Eagle must consider

- standardizing data capture and data processing procedures;
- standardizing hardware and software;

- centralizing databases and providing decentralized access and control; and
- networking the PCs to the minicomputer.

a. As a database consultant, would you recommend a distributed database environment for this firm? Provide details with justification for your answer.
b. What needs to be done to plan a distributed database environment for Eagle Corporation? Elaborate.
c. What options does Eagle have in terms of hardware, software, and DBMS packages in line with its potential growth and "global" needs? Be specific.

6 Use the work you have completed on Island Jumpers, Inc. (IJI) to address the following questions:

a. How ideal a candidate is IJI for a distributed database system? Elaborate, using realistic reasons.
b. If your answer to part (a) is yes, what constraints are involved in building a distributed database system for IJI?

PART IV

DATABASE IMPLEMENTATION

C H A P T

Planning a Database Application

E R 1 2

Peeling Back Layers of Quality Equation

AT A GLANCE

Peeling Back Layers of Quality Equation

Companies in search of a silver bullet to put an end to the software development quality and productivity debate will find themselves firing blanks, according to Ed Yourdon, father of Yourdon structured methodologies. "One of the big problems in this country is that we tend to look for one silver-bullet solution to the productivity problem," said Yourdon.

Quality and productivity are tightly linked; the approaches used to address these issues—metrics, methodology, and CASE tools—must be interconnected. Yourdon suggests that simply throwing technology or methodology at the problem is not enough. Information Technology (IT) departments, he says, must also use "peopleware" solutions. (See Figure 1.)

For example, Yourdon says, one way to improve development is to hire better developers. "Rather than spend lots of money trying to bring in a new methodology, why not just bring in better people? . . . If you take a random group of 100 people and put them in a room with a complex programming exercise, one of them will finish 25 times faster than the others," Yourdon says.

The software productivity metric that probably means more than any other is the function-point method. Function points surfaced in the early 1980s as a metric that measured functionality rather than mere lines of code. The function-point metric assesses the functionality of the software development process by first counting the number of external inputs (transaction types), external

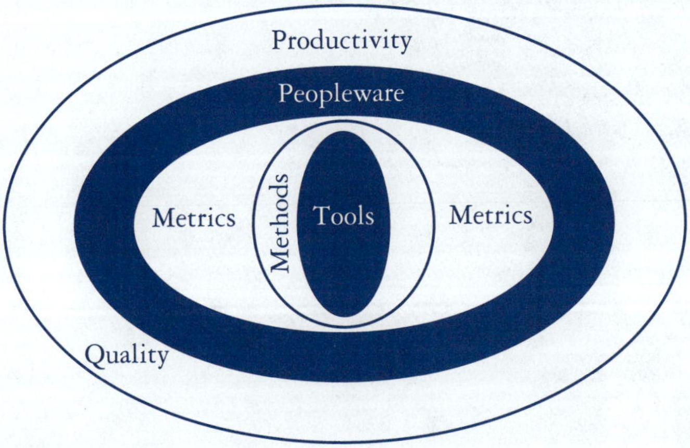

Figure 1 Layers of quality/productivity. Improving systems development quality and productivity requires a multi-layered approach that includes CASE tools, methodology, metrics, and "peopleware."

outputs (report types), logical internal files (nonphysical), external interface files (files accessed by the application but not maintained/ updated by it), and external inquiries.

Using a set of standards for assessing complexity, these components are then classified as relatively low, average, or high. Once the total number of function counts are computed according to a statistical formula, the second step assesses the impact of 14 general system characteristics:

- data communications;
- distributed functions;
- performance;
- heavily used configuration;
- transaction rate;
- on-line data entry;
- end-user efficiency;
- on-line update;
- complex processing;
- reusability;
- installation ease;
- operational ease;
- multiple sites; and
- facilitates change.

These values are then summed to compute what is known as the Value Adjustment Factor (VAF). The VAF is then multiplied by the total function count to create the number of function points.

Even though function points are becoming the most universally used metric, "what is really needed is something that is automatable, something that many call machineable metrics."

Know Thy Business Model

For this type of measurement program to work, the IT organization must fully understand how the company itself measures its business success and how IT performance links to company performance. The companies that will win the competitive battles of the '90s are those that will leverage their technology investments to create new possibilities. But the technology investment is not composed of measurements alone. IT needs "good management, good technical staff, including good estimators and testers, good measurements, good tools, and a good methodology."

IT management can choose from many well-known and well-documented methodologies, the most popular being those developed by Martin, Gane/Sarson and Yourdon. According to Software Productivity Research, "All of the methodologies are basically the same; the key is to use one." Jones offers an analogy of painted houses versus those that are left bare. "These are the ones that get termites; the ones that are painted last a long time. It doesn't matter what color they are. The only thing that matters is the paint." But unfortunately, a small number of IT groups haven't even bought the paint.

Excerpted from Keyes, Jessica, "Peeling back layers of quality equation." Reprinted with permission of Software Magazine*, May 1991, Sentry Publishing Co., Inc., 1900 West Park Drive, Westborough, MA 01581, USA.*

AT A GLANCE

The first step in the database application life cycle is planning. This includes planning the analysis and design, followed by the implementation of the system. Planning the analysis begins with identifying the user's information requirements. The user and the designer compile the hardware and software requirements into the system specifications document, which includes problem identification, cost/benefit analysis, logical design of the current and proposed database, and physical design and implementation considerations.

Planning the design involves preparing a data structure diagram, an entity-relationship diagram, a data model diagram, and a structure chart. These models are part of structured design. Excelerator can be used to produce most of these charts.

The structure chart is an important hierarchical diagram that depicts the overall program structure. It identifies the makeup of a program by showing the program modules and their relationships. The three key components used are the module, the connection, and the couple. A couple represents the data transferred between two modules in either direction.

Prototyping can be extremely important in database design. In prototyping, the system is modeled by building a prototype before committing funds and energy to the final system. Users generally grow wiser as a result of this type of interface. The strongest argument against prototyping, though, is cost.

One of the first tasks in building a file structure is determining what data elements are required. The data elements make up a record, which is part of a file. There is always some redundant data in a file system so that records in different files can be associated.

By the end of this chapter, you should

- appreciate the role of planning in building a database application;
- understand the makeup of a system specifications document;
- understand the function and uses of Excelerator as a tool for generating planning and design diagrams; and
- be familiar with the role of prototyping in database application planning.

Introduction

The main purpose of a database is to answer users' questions. For any given set of circumstances, there are several possible database designs. Deciding which will work best depends on whether the database is to run on a mainframe or a microcomputer, the nature of the user's requirements, and the complexity of the overall application.

A microcomputer database is generally installed either on a stand-alone microcomputer to serve a limited number of users or as part of a network. Depending on the software, database access and processing routines on a microcomputer are informal and provide limited controls. Mainframe or minicomputer databases, on the other hand, provide greater security through limited access control, passwords, and various protocols.

In this chapter, we walk you through a database application running on a microcomputer, emphasizing the planning phase of its life cycle.

The first step in planning a database application is to identify user requirements. Next, using data flow diagrams, we develop a structure chart as a preliminary to the logical design. Finally, we identify the data elements and the file structure required by the new system.

Students of database technology become so engrossed in studying the technical details of data models, data dictionaries, and the like that they often lose sight of the overall goal of database design, which is, after all, to develop real-life, total applications. They need to step back and get a global view of database design that incorporates theory, procedures, and actual coding and testing.

The first activity in designing a database application is identifying the user's information requirements. The outcome of this step is the SYSTEM SPECIFICATIONS DOCUMENT, which identifies the user's problem and details what must be done to solve it properly. In the system specification document, the user and the database designer compile the necessary hardware and software requirements and other information.

System Specifications Document

The system specifications document serves as a reference for designing the database and is used later to measure how closely the newly designed system meets the user's requirements. The system specifications document should include

• a statement identifying the problem and the design objectives;

• a cost-benefit analysis;

• a logical model (design) of the current and proposed database, in the form of data flow diagrams; an outline of the data dictionary; structure charts or action diagrams; and whether the system will use structured English or pseudocode;

• physical design (coding) and implementation considerations, such as implementation specifications and a schedule; test plans; and a list of user documentation that will be needed.

Although the designer should be familiar with the inner workings of the client business, he or she must still validate the problem through interviews, observations, and so forth (see Chapter 5). Next the designer and client agree on costs and financial constraints, and make a preliminary decision on whether the database application should run on a mainframe, minicomputer, or microcomputer. Logical design, coding, and implementation follow from these.

Case Scenario 12-1: *Worker's Compensation*

Until July 1, 1988, the Worker's Compensation Unit in a university with approximately 1600 employees maintained all worker's compensation processing. All injuries and related claims that occurred after July 1, 1988 are now managed by the University Health and Safety Department and sent to Accident Insurance Corporation. Old injuries are defined in the system as all injuries that occurred before July 1, 1988, and new injuries are injuries that happened after July 1, 1988.

Even though Accident Insurance pays compensation on new injuries, claims on old injuries may still be made and, therefore, old injuries information must be maintained. Basically, the university wants the new system to reduce the amount of search time needed to locate information in the physical files. So the university has hired an outside consulting firm to analyze the current system and to design and implement a new system that administers claims on old injuries and meets the user's need for speedy information retrieval.

Project Scope

The current worker's compensation system (WCS) involves mainly the work flows in the Worker's Compensation Unit within the Personnel Department. The other entities affected by this system are employees and their respective departments, doctors, the Industrial Commission, the accounting department, the insurance company, and the university's payroll department. Processes that are within the scope of WCS boundary are the following:

- check claim period
- validate claim
- classify claim type
- prepare invoice
- prepare legal document
- generate quarterly invoice report

Deliverables

The goal of the WCS is to deliver the following:

- Automate claims so that clerks can answer telephone inquiries quickly and to prevent duplicate claims.
- Automate retrieval of compensation (invoice) information to speed up the approval process, invoice production, and quarterly summary.
- Partially automate injury history. Only the physical location of the injury file is to be stored in the computer. This automated file would include the employee ID number, the date of injury, and the physical location of each injury file. Since no new records will be added to the injury file, automating all injury information would not be cost-effective.
- Generate invoices automatically after the worker's compensation administrator enters the amount (or enters the amount in the amount-granted field in the compensation file). For security reasons, only the administrator will have access to the compensation file that contains the amount granted.

When the system becomes operational, several related activities are to continue:

- The file cabinet system where the old injuries information is stored will be reindexed based on employee ID and date of injury.
- Manual tasks such as retrieving injury files that contain doctor's reports and legal documents are still required. However, since the location of each employee's injury file is stored in the database, retrieval time will be drastically reduced.
- At the end of each quarter, the worker's compensation administrator will use the "Prepare Quarterly Invoice Summary" function in the newly automated system and specify the appropriate quarter to produce a quarterly report. The automated program will calculate appropriate summary statistics.
- Inactive files for employees who no longer work for the university will be moved to the university's miscellaneous filing system.

Outcome

After discussing the requirements with the worker's compensation administrator, the designer proposed an efficient, on-line database system for storing accident data with the ability to reference active compensation claimants information. In the proposed system, active files would be assigned an active status, and invoices for covered services would efficiently be tracked. The database would contain records of invoices sent to the accounting department to reduce the chances of anyone issuing two requests for payment on the same invoice. The automated worker's compensation database environment would contain the following commands:

- QUERY, to allow the user to find information about compensation, claims, and injuries.
- ADD, to allow the user to record new claims and compensation.
- EDIT, to allow the user to update claim and compensation files.
- PRODUCE INVOICE, to allow the user to see an invoice on the screen or to print an invoice.
- PRODUCE QUARTERLY SUMMARY to help the administrator to produce quarterly reports.

The proposed system would automatically index the injury files by employee social security number and injury date so that records could be easily found. The designer estimated that the new WCS would reduce file retrieval and filing time from 45 minutes to approximately 5 minutes per file. Likewise, the time needed to prepare a quarterly invoice report would be reduced from 16 hours per semester to approximately 5 minutes.

PLANNING THE DESIGN

After the designer has identified user's requirements, his or her next step is to create a logical design. Several tools can be used to represent the logic of the database design including data model diagrams, entity-relation diagrams, data structure diagrams, and structure charts. A program called Excelerator can help the designer create these diagrams.

Excelerator: An Automated Design Tool

Since the early 1980s, a number of software tools have been developed to help the professional systems analyst in designing database applications. One widely used tool, Excelerator, is a totally integrated system with the ability to design and document almost any software project. Excelerator runs on the IBM System/2, COMPAQ, AT&T, and other IBM-compatible computers.

The Excelerator operation procedure is simple. After the designer enters his or her user ID number, a password, and the name of the project, Excelerator displays a main menu of seven major options: graphics, XL dictionary, screens and reports, documentation, analysis, dictionary interface, and housekeeping. (See Figure 12-1.)

The graphics option is of particular importance in logical database design. Using the graphics function, the designer can draw seven types of diagrams and charts for database design:

1 data flow diagram
2 structure chart
3 data model diagram
4 entity-relationship (E-R) diagram
5 state transition diagram

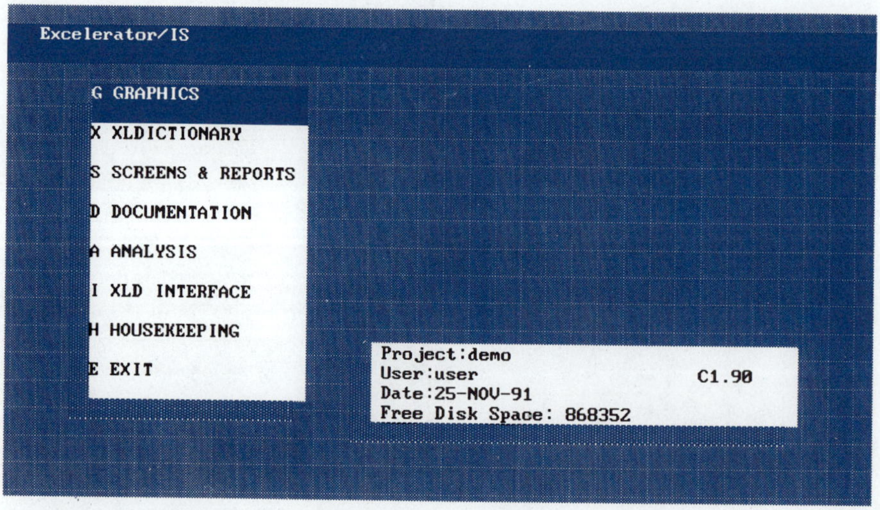

Figure 12-1 Excelerator main menu

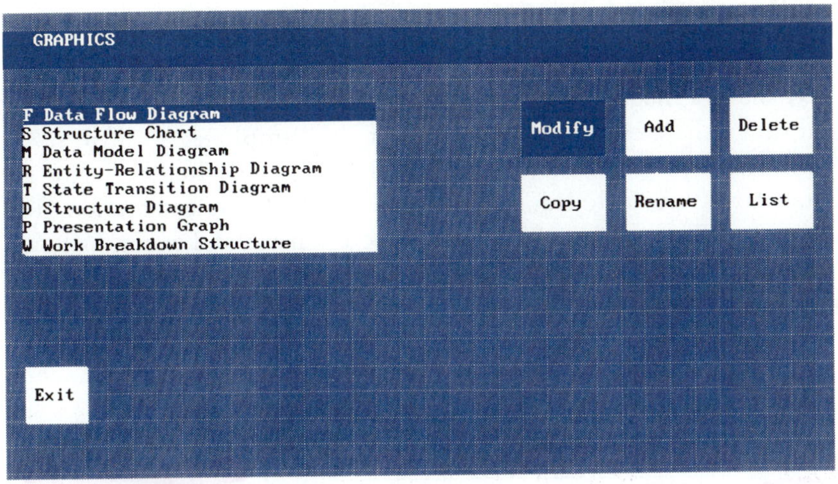

Figure 12-2 The graphics action keypad

6 structure diagram
7 presentation graph

Using a mouse, the designer simply points to the type of graph desired and the action he or she wishes to perform. For example, to update a data flow diagram, the designer points to "Data Flow Diagram" and clicks the mouse. (See Figure 12-2.) When the designer chooses "Modify," the program asks him or her to select the graph. The main data flow diagram representation of the worker's compensation system is shown in Figure 12-3.

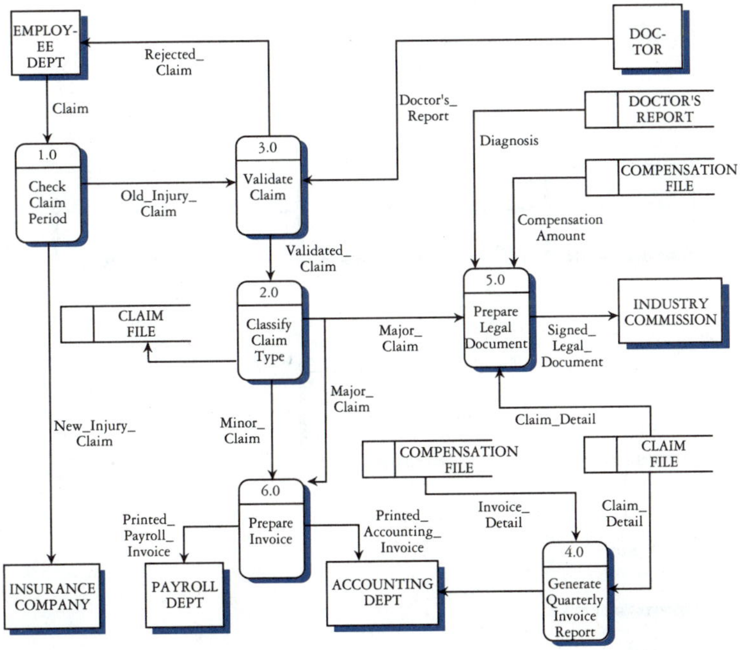

Figure 12-3 Worker's compensation system data flow diagram

Data Model Diagrams

A DATA MODEL DIAGRAM shows entities and their relationships. Figure 12-4 shows a model diagram for the worker's compensation system. The relevant entities are "Department," "Employee," "Injury," "Compensation," "Claim," "Doctor," and "Doctor's Report." Not all data entries are included in the actual physical implementation. For example, "Doctor" and "Doctor's Report" may not be not included because the Worker's Compensation Unit is not responsible for tracking medical information. Figure 12-5 shows an Excelerator-generated description of the WCS entities.

Entity-Relationship (E-R) Diagrams

The ENTITY-RELATIONSHIP (E-R) DIAGRAM is a high-level overview diagram of data used in top-down planning the design of a database application. In top-down planning of data, we identify the entities involved in the design and determine the relationships among them. Figure 12-6 shows an Excelerator-generated E-R diagram of WCS describing all the entities relevant to the WCS and their relationships. Each entity is represented by a rectangle, and each relationship is represented by a diamond. The entities described in the E-R diagram are identical to the ones in the data model diagram, except that the E-R diagram does not show 1:1, 1:M, or M:N relationships. Instead, the name of each relationship is described in a diamond box. In addition to

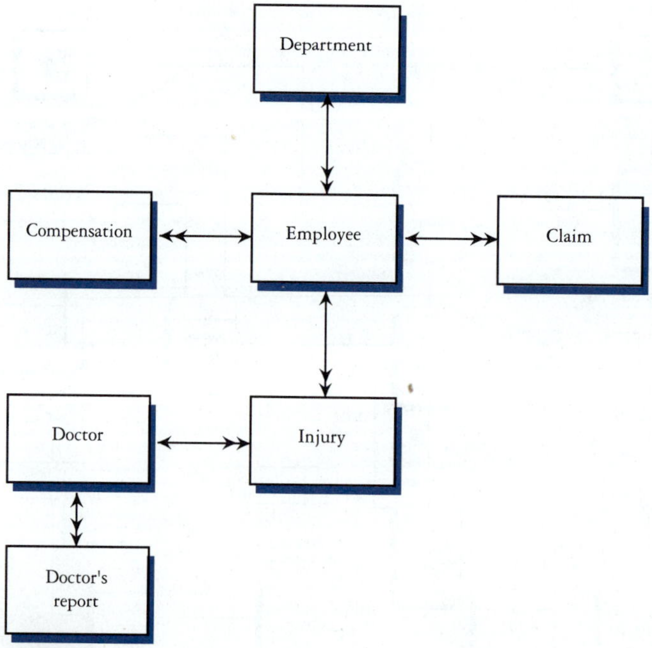

Figure 12-4 Data model diagram of worker's compensation system

```
DATE:  5-DEC-91          DATA MODEL DIAGRAM - OUTPUT          PAGE          1
TIME: 13:55              NAME:  Worker's compensation         EXCELERATOR   1.8

TYPE Data Model Diagram              NAME worker's compensation
   File KRRKMSX.DMD
   Description
  Worker's compensation data model diagram shows the entities
  relevant to the worker's compensation system. The relevant
  entities are: DEPARTMENT, EMPLOYEE, INJURY, COMPENSATION, CLAIM
  DOCTOR, and DOCTOR'S REPORT (i.e. diagnosis). These are the
  conceptual representations of data entities. However, actual
  physical implementation does not involve all entities such as
  DOCTOR and DOCTOR'S REPORT since worker's compensation unit is
  not responsible for keeping track of doctor information. In
  addition, DOCTOR'S REPORT information will be stored within the
  physical injury files. Other entities such as DEPARTMENT and
  EMPLOYEE are also not maintained by the worker's compensation
  unit.

Type Name                               Type Name
 DAE Department                          DAE Compensation
 DAE Employee                            DAE Claim
 DAE Injury                              DAE Doctor's Report
 DAE Doctor                              ---

  Modified By   student          Date Modified 911205   # Changes 10
  Added By      student          Date Added    911204
  Last Project  TARGET CUSTOMER
  Locked By                      Date Locked   0        Lock Status _
```

Figure 12-5 Excelerator-generated description of the data model diagram in Figure 12-4

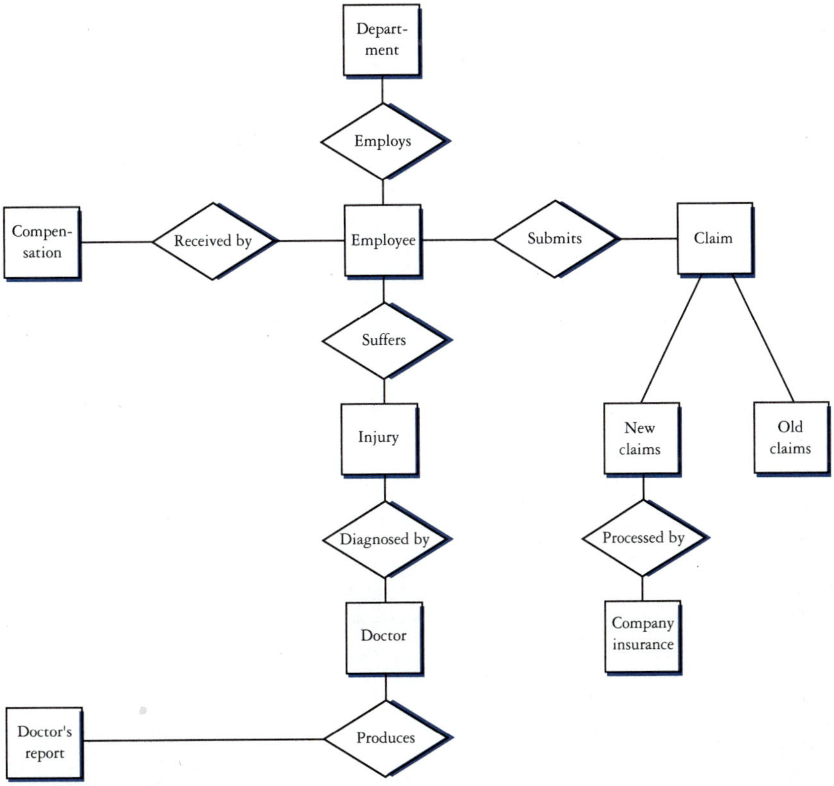

Figure 12-6 Entity-relationship diagram of worker's compensation system

drawing the E-R diagram, Excelerator also allows the designer to describe each entity, as shown in Figure 12-7.

```
DATE:  5-DEC-91      ENTITY-RELATIONSHIP DIAGRAM - OUTPUT             PAGE  1
TIME: 14:05          NAME:  Worker's compensation          EXCELERATOR   1.8

TYPE Entity-relationship diagram  NAME: worker's compensation
   File KZNU4NE.ERA

   Description
  Worker's compensation entity-relationship diagram describes all
  entities that are relevant in the worker's compensation system
  and the relationships between those entities. All entities are
  represented by rectangles and all relationships are represented
  by diamonds. The entities described on the entity-relationship
  diagram are identical to the ones on the data model diagram.
  However, entity-relationship diagram does not show relationships
  as one-to-one, one-to-many, many-to-one. Instead, the name of
  the relationship is described in the diamond box.

Type Name                            Type Name
 DAE Compensation                     DAE Employee
 DAE Claim                            DAE Department
 DAE Injury                           DAE Doctor
 DAE Doctor's Report                  DAE New claims
 DAE Insurance company                DAE Old claims
 DNR Works for                        DNR Receives
 DNR Submit                           DNR Suffers
 DNR Diagnosed                        DNR Produce
 DNR Processed                        ---

 Modified By   student       Date Modified 911205  #Changes  8
 Added By      student       Date Added    911106
 Last Project  TARGET CUSTOMER
 Locked By                   Date Locked   0       Lock Status
```

```
DATE: 30-NOV-91      DATA ENTITY - OUTPUT
TIME: 23:43          NAME:  Claim                          PAGE    1
                                                    EXCELERATOR 1.8

TYPE Data Entity                          NAME Claim
                              EXPLODES TO ONE OF:
 Label                       _Record                  Claim
                              Data Model Diagram
                              ERA Diagram

 Description
Each claim applies to a specific employee.  An employee may submit
many claims.  There are two types of claims--new claims (those
submitted after July 1, 1988) and old claims (those submitted
before July 1, 1988).

 Modified By   student       Date Modified 911130  #Changes 1
 Added By      student       Date Added    911130
 Last Project  TARGET CUSTOMER
 Locked By                   Date Locked   0       Lock Status
```

Figure 12-7 Excelerator-generated description of the entities in Figure 12-6

```
DATE: 30-NOV-91      DATA ENTITY - OUTPUT                   PAGE      1
TIME: 23:46          NAME:  Compensation              EXCELERATOR 1.8

TYPE Data_Entity______________________ NAME  Compensation___________
                                EXPLODES TO ONE OF:
 Label_____________            _Record              Compensation__________
      _____________             Data Model Diagram_____________________
                                ERA Diagram          _____________________

 Description
An_employee_may_receive_one_more_compensations_from_the_company.__
A_compensation_can_only_apply_to_a_specific_employee.____________
Compensation_represents_amount_granted_by_company_to_reimburse_an_
employee's_work-related_injuries.________________________________

  Modified By     student________  Date Modified  911130_ #Changes 3__
  Added By        student________  Date Added     911106_
  Last Project    TARGET_CUSTOMER
  Locked By       _______________  Date Locked    0______  Lock Status _
```

```
DATE: 30-NOV-91      DATA ENTITY - OUTPUT                   PAGE      1
TIME: 23:46          NAME:  Department                EXCELERATOR 1.8

TYPE Data_Entity______________________ NAME  Department_____________
                                EXPLODES TO ONE OF:
 Label_____________            _Record              Department____________
      _____________             Data Model Diagram_____________________
                                ERA Diagram          _____________________

 Description
Department_entity_contains_information_about_each_department.__A__
department_has_many_employees_and_an_employee_can_only_work_for___
one_department.__________________________________________________

  Modified By     student________  Date Modified  911130_ #Changes 2__
  Added By        student________  Date Added     911106_
  Last Project    TARGET_CUSTOMER
  Locked By       _______________  Date Locked    0______  Lock Status _
```

Figure 12-7 continued

```
DATE: 30-NOV-91      DATA ENTITY - OUTPUT                      PAGE      1
TIME: 23:46          NAME:  Doctor                        EXCELERATOR 1.8

TYPE Data_Entity____________________ NAME Doctor__________________

                                  EXPLODES TO ONE OF:
 Label_____________             _Record              Doctor________________
      _____________              Data Model Diagram______________________
                                 ERA Diagram        ______________________

 Description
A_doctor_treats_many_injuries.__An_injury_is_assumed_to_be_treated
by_only_one_doctor._______________________________________________

  Modified By    student________ Date Modified 911130_ #Changes 2__
  Added By       student________ Date Added    911106_
  Last Project   TARGET_CUSTOMER
  Locked By      _______________ Date Locked   0______  Lock Status _
```

```
DATE: 30-NOV-91      DATA ENTITY - OUTPUT                      PAGE      1
TIME: 23:47          NAME:  Doctor's Report               EXCELERATOR 1.8

TYPE Data_Entity____________________ NAME Doctor's_Report________

                                  EXPLODES TO ONE OF:
 Label_____________             _Record              Diagnosis_____________
      _____________              Data Model Diagram______________________
                                 ERA Diagram        ______________________

 Description
A_doctor_writes_up_many_doctor's_reports_on_injuries.__A_doctor's_
report_is_produced_by_only_one_doctor.____________________________

  Modified By    student________ Date Modified 911130_ #Changes 2__
  Added By       student________ Date Added    911106_
  Last Project   TARGET_CUSTOMER
  Locked By      _______________ Date Locked   0______  Lock Status _
```

Figure 12-7 continued

```
DATE: 30-NOV-91      DATA ENTITY - OUTPUT                    PAGE     1
TIME: 23:47          NAME:  Employee                  EXCELERATOR 1.8

TYPE Data_Entity______________________ NAME Employee________________
                            EXPLODES TO ONE OF:
 Label_____________       _Record              Employee______________
      _____________        Data Model Diagram ______________________
                           ERA Diagram         _____________________

 Description
An_employee_works_for_only_one_department.__A_department_has_many_
employees.__An_employee_may_receive_many_compensations.__However,_
a_compensation_may_only_apply_to_a_specific_employee.__An_employee
may_submit_many_claims.__However,_a_claim_may_only_apply_to_a____
particular_employee.__An_employee_may_suffer_many_injuries.__A___
particular_injury_applies_to_a_specific_employee.________________

  Modified By    student________ Date Modified 911130_ #Changes 4__
  Added By       student________ Date Added    911106_
  Last Project   TARGET_CUSTOMER
  Locked By      _______________ Date Locked   0______ Lock Status _
```

```
DATE: 30-NOV-91      DATA ENTITY - OUTPUT                    PAGE     1
TIME: 23:47          NAME:  Injury                    EXCELERATOR 1.8

TYPE Data_Entity______________________ NAME Injury__________________
                            EXPLODES TO ONE OF:
 Label_____________       _Record              Injury________________
      _____________        Data Model Diagram ______________________
                           ERA Diagram         _____________________

 Description
An_injury_applies_to_a_particular_employee.__An_employee_may______
suffer_many_injuries.____________________________________________

  Modified By    student________ Date Modified 911130_ #Changes 2__
  Added By       student________ Date Added    911106_
  Last Project   TARGET_CUSTOMER
  Locked By      _______________ Date Locked   0______ Lock Status _
```

Figure 12-7 continued

```
DATE: 30-NOV-91      DATA ENTITY - OUTPUT                           PAGE     1
TIME: 23:48          NAME:  Insurance Co.                    EXCELERATOR 1.8

TYPE Data_Entity______________________ NAME  Insurance Co.____________

                                 EXPLODES TO ONE OF:
  Label_____________           _Record               ____________________
       _____________            Data Model Diagram___________________
                                ERA Diagram           ____________________

 Description


  Modified By    student_______  Date Modified  911106_ #Changes  1__
  Added By       student_______  Date Added     911106_
  Last Project   TARGET_CUSTOMER
  Locked By      ______________  Date Locked    0______  Lock Status _
```

```
DATE: 30-NOV-91      DATA ENTITY - OUTPUT                           PAGE     1
TIME: 23:48          NAME:  New Claims                       EXCELERATOR 1.8

TYPE Data_Entity____________________ NAME  New Claims_____________
                                 EXPLODES TO ONE OF:
  Label_____________           _Record                Claim
       _____________            Data Model Diagram___________________
                                ERA Diagram           ____________________

 Description
New_claims_are_those_submitted_after_July_1,_1991.__They_are______
processed_by_the_insurance_company._______________________________


  Modified By    student_______  Date Modified  911130_ # Changes  2__
  Added By       student_______  Date Added     911106_
  Last Project   TARGET_CUSTOMER
  Locked By      ______________  Date Locked    0______  Lock Status _
```

Figure 12-7 continued

```
DATE: 30-NOV-91      DATA ENTITY - OUTPUT                          PAGE      1
TIME: 23:49          NAME:  Old Claims                        EXCELERATOR 1.8

TYPE Data_Entity____________________  NAME  Old Claims_____________
                              EXPLODES TO ONE OF:
 Label_____________          _Record              Claim_______________
      _____________           Data Model Diagram ______________________
                              ERA Diagram         ______________________

 Description
Old claims are those submitted before July 1, 1991.  They are_____
processed by the company.__________________________________________

  Modified By     student________ Date Modified 911130_ # Changes   2__
  Added By        student________ Date Added    911106_
  Last Project   TARGET_CUSTOMER
  Locked By      _______________ Date Locked    0______  Lock Status _
```

Figure 12-7 continued

Data Structure Diagrams

A DATA STRUCTURE DIAGRAM (DSD) shows the logical view of data structure. Each rectangle in the diagram represents a data element. A line inside a rectangle indicates that the element is a primary key for the file. The data structure diagram is also a representation of the physical view of a database. Figure 12-8 shows an Excelerator-generated data structure diagram of the WCS. The only new physical implementation of files are the "Claim," "Compensation," and "Injury" files. Figure 12-9 shows an Excelerator-generated list of the entities specified in Figure 12-8.

Structure Charts

A STRUCTURE CHART is a hierarchical diagram that depicts the overall program structure. Each rectangle in the hierarchy is a MODULE—a set of instructions with a single entry point and a single exit point. A module represents essentially a problem-related task to be performed by the program.

The structure chart, in general, identifies the makeup of a program by showing the program modules and their relationships. Modules that involve high-level program tasks are placed in the upper levels of the chart, and modules that perform lower-level, detailed tasks are placed in

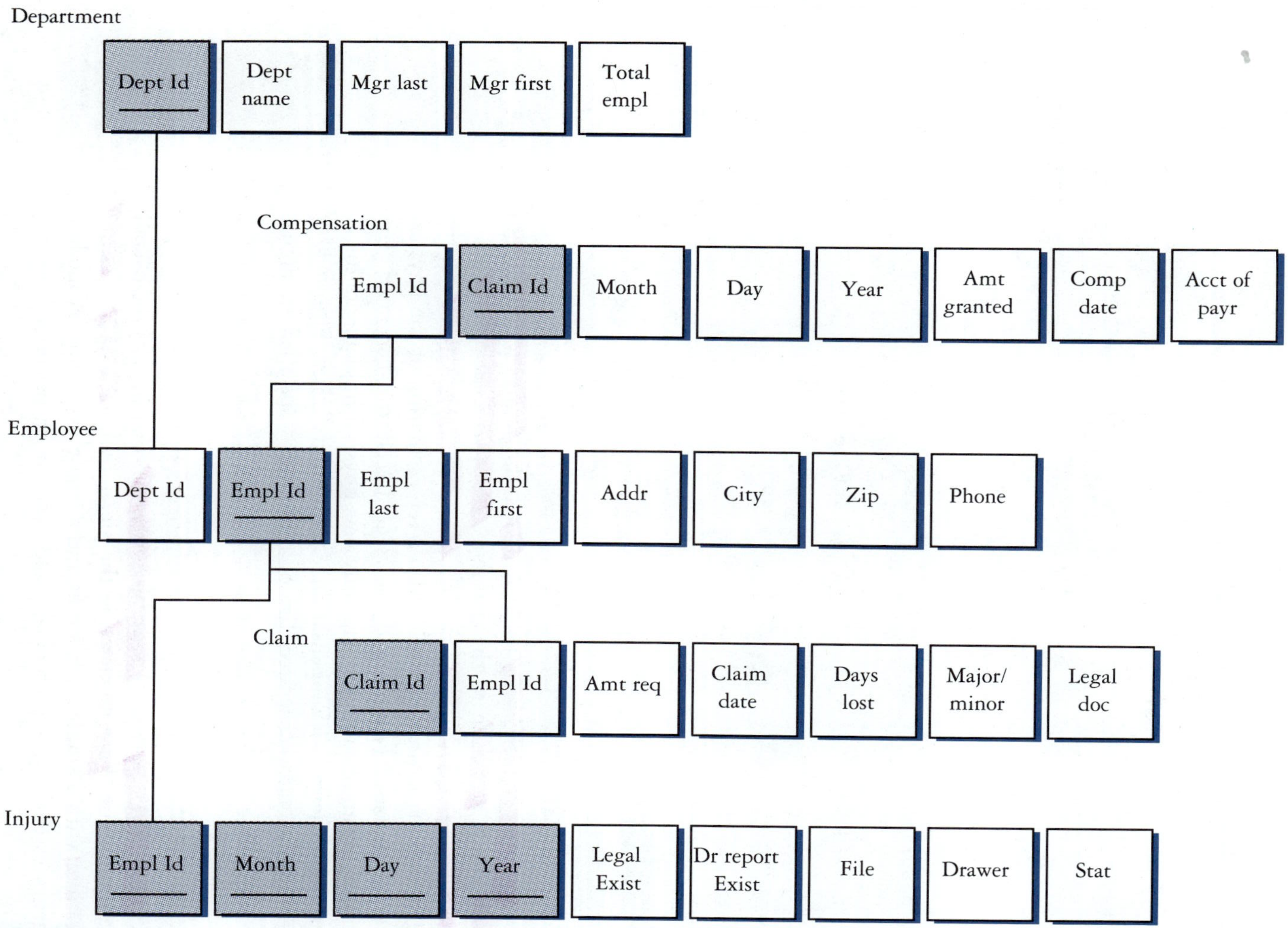

Figure 12-8 Excelerator-generated data structure diagram of the worker's compensation system

```
DATE:  5-DEC-91     STRUCTURE DIAGRAM - OUTPUT              PAGE       1
TIME: 14:24          NAME: worker's compensation         EXCELERATOR 1.8

TYPE Structure_Diagram___________ NAME: worker's_compensation________
   File KZMKAWK.STD_______________

    Description
   Worker's compensation data structure diagram shows the logical_____
   view of data structure.  It is derived from the data model_________
   diagram.  Each rectangle represents data element.  Lines in each___
   rectangle indicate a primary key for each file.  Primary key_______
   uniquely identifies a record in each file.  In this case, the______
   data structure diagram is also a representation of physical view___
   of the database, assuming the university already has a centralized__
   database in place.  The only new physical implementation of files___
   will be claim, compensation, and the injury files._______________

Type Name                                Type Name
 FUN Dept Id_________________             FUN Dept Name_________________
 FUN Mgr Last________________             FUN Mgr First_________________
 FUN Total Empl______________             FUN Empl Id___________________
 FUN Empl Last_______________             FUN Empl First________________
 FUN Addr____________________             FUN City______________________
 FUN Zip_____________________             FUN Phone_____________________
 FUN Emply Id________________             FUN Claim Id__________________
 FUN Amt Granted_____________             FUN Comp Date_________________
 FUN Acctg/Payr______________             FUN Amt Req___________________
 FUN Claim Date______________             FUN Days Lost_________________
 FUN Major/Minor_____________             FUN Legal Doc_________________
 FUN Stat____________________             FUN Month_____________________
 FUN File____________________             FUN Drawer____________________
 FUN Year____________________             FUN Legal Exist_______________
 FUN Doctor Report Exist_____             FUN Day_______________________

  Modified By    student_________  Date Modified 911205__  #Changes  19_
  Added By       student_________  Date Added    911106__
  Last Project  TARGET_CUSTOMER_
  Locked By      ________________  Date Locked   0_______  Lock Status _
```

Figure 12-9 Excelerator-generated list of the entities in the DSD in Figure 12-8

subordinate positions. Modules at successively lower levels in the hierarchy define tasks that are more and more specific in nature. The building blocks of a structure chart are shown in Figure 12-10.

Figure 12-11 shows the structure chart of the WCS. The three key components of a structure chart are

1 the module (rectangular box),
2 the connection (lines connecting modules), and
3 the couple (circle with an arrow).

A module name is written inside the box as a single object that specifies the function of the module. For example, the module "Validate

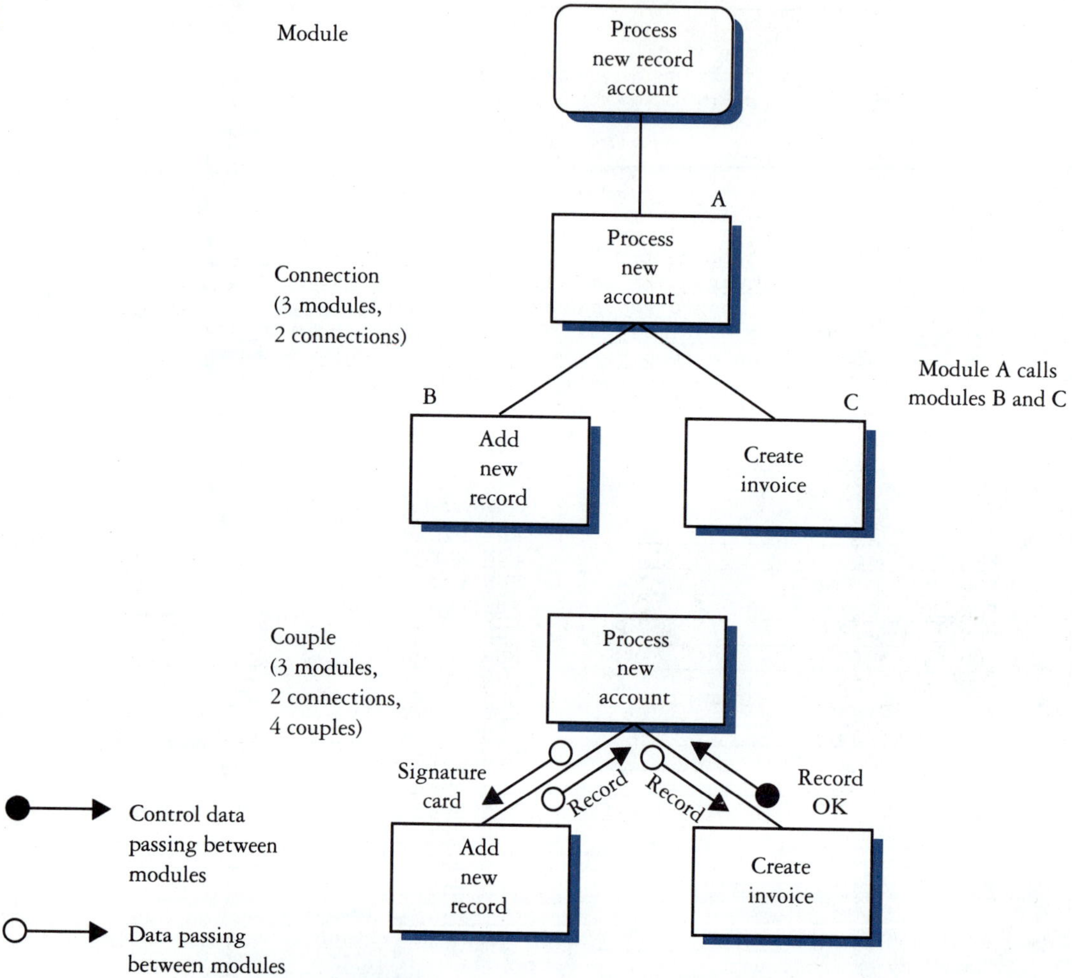

Figure 12-10 Structure chart building blocks

Claim" is specific and self-explanatory. The command "Validate Claim" will call for four sets of tasks (the four lower-level modules): "Read Diagnosis File," "Read Injury File," "Compare Injury_Date and Claim Date," and "Determine Claim by Status." The relationship between these CALLED MODULES and the BOSS MODULE ("Validate Claim") is shown by the four lines or connections from the boss module.

A COUPLE (circle with an arrow) represents the data transferred between two modules in either direction. A data name is written beside each couple to specify what data is being transferred.

PROTOTYPES

It is common practice for database designers to model a proposed system by building a PROTOTYPE before funds and energy are committed

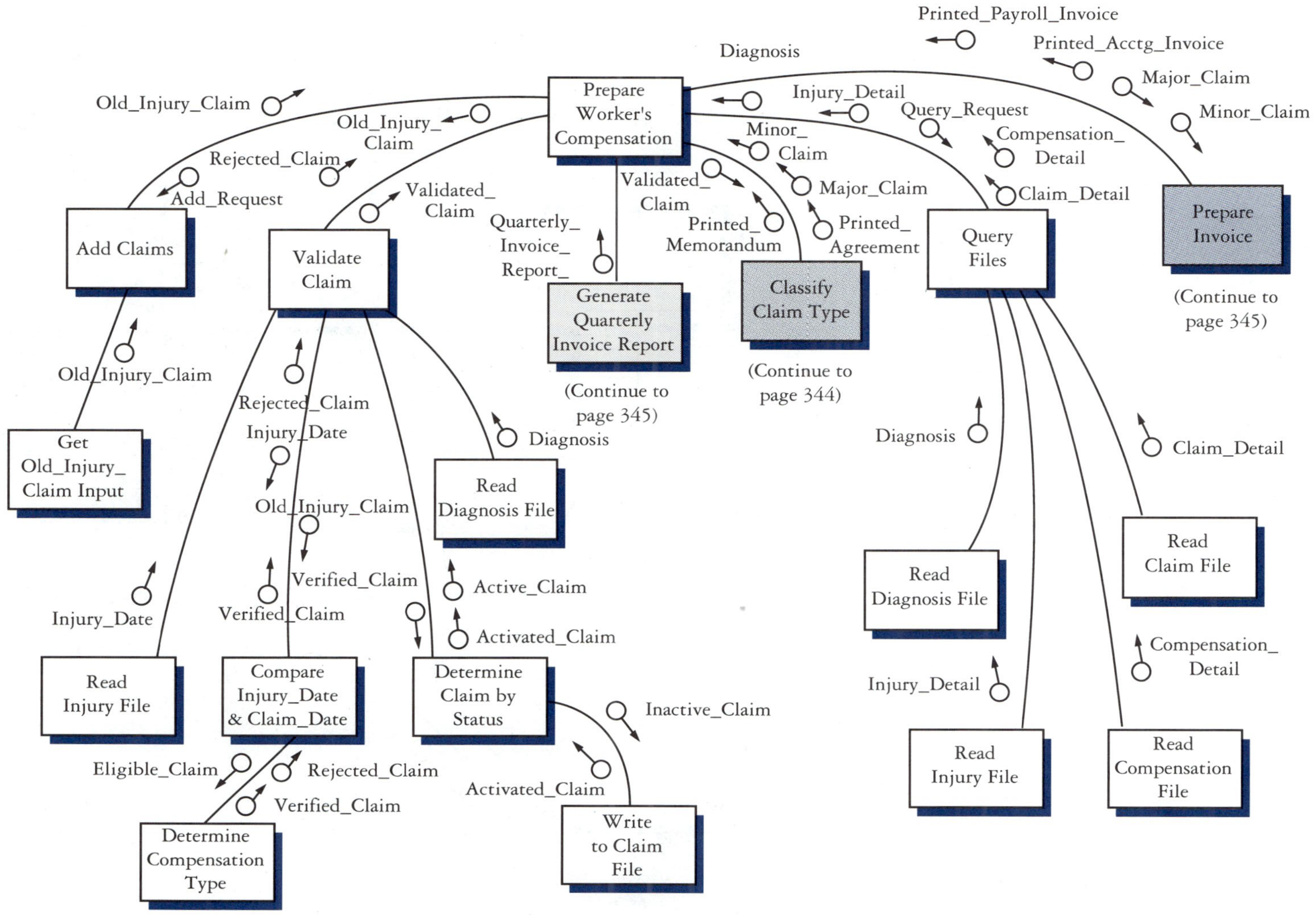

Figure 12-11 Excelerator-generated structure chart of worker's compensation system

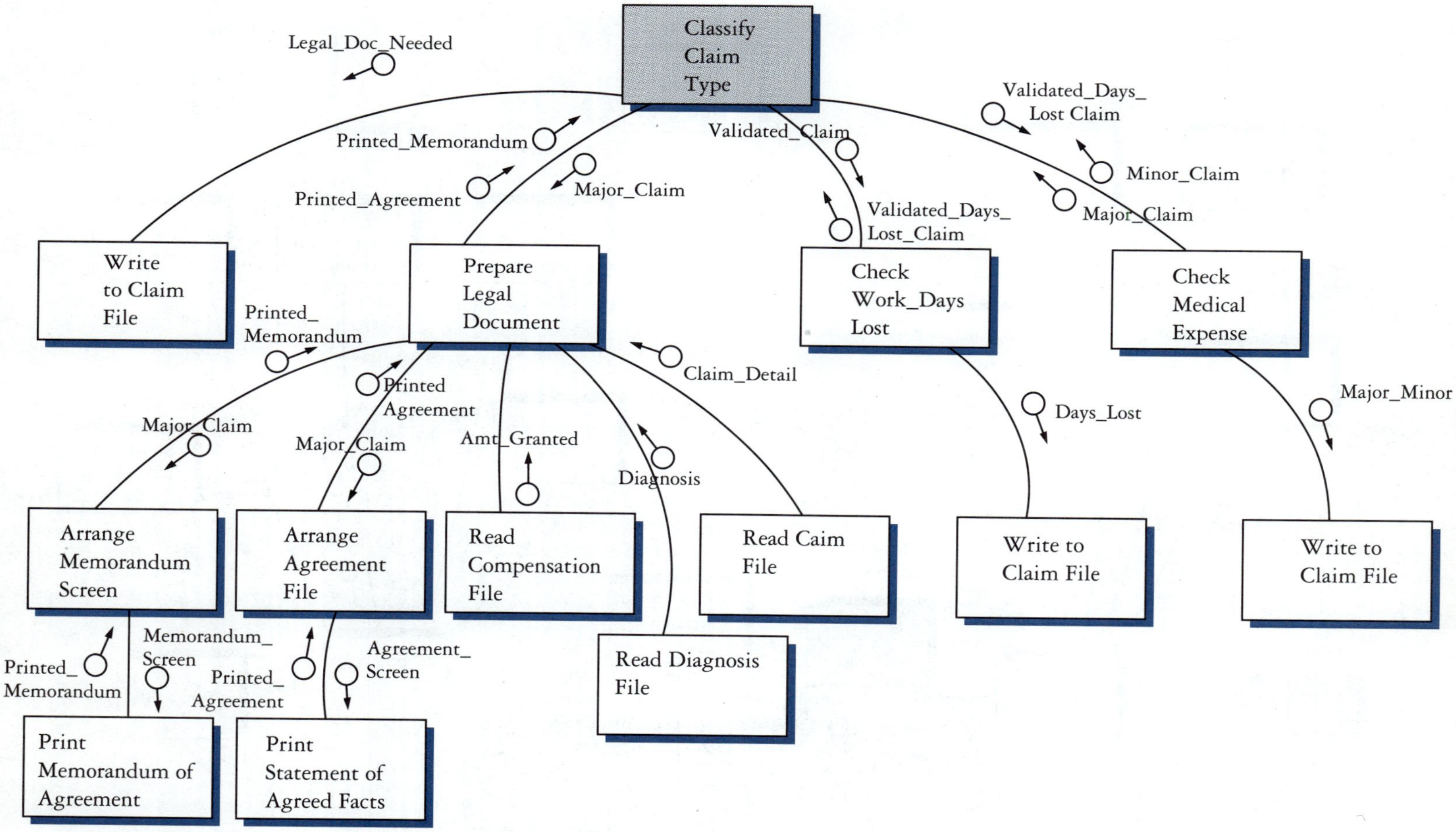

Figure 12-11 continued

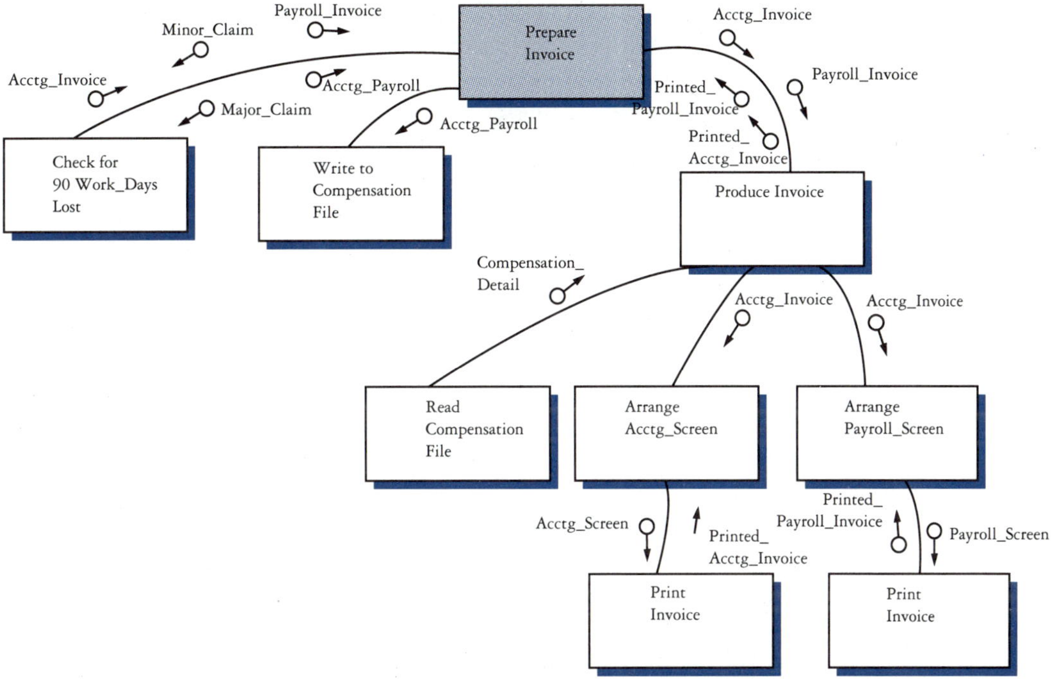

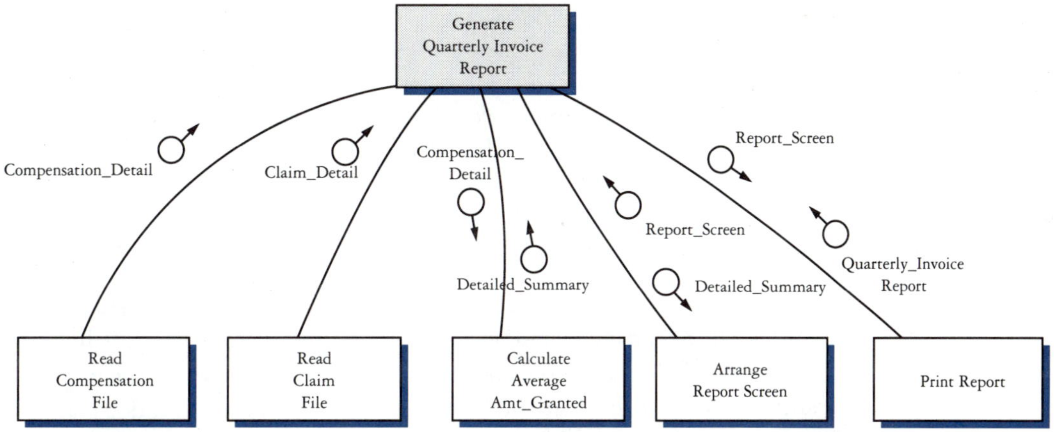

Figure 12-11 continued

to the final system. The client can examine the prototype to determine whether it meets the user's needs.

A database designer working with the user can generate or demonstrate a number of user-system dialogues, queries, and reports. This type of interface helps the designer sell the system to the user and makes it easier to train users and to support implementation.

Users generally grow wiser toward the end of the design process. When they examine prototype menus, reports, and other displays, they often come up with features that enhance the quality of the final system or identify areas of disagreement, which are less costly to fix at the prototype stage. The designer makes changes in the prototype until the client is satisfied with the system. The prototype, in effect, becomes part of the requirements document for the final design of the database.

Prototypes do not need to include all aspects of the proposed system, only those parts of concern to the client. For example, a prototype might simulate a terminal dialogue, allowing the client to see what information will be displayed on the screen and in what format. The user can play with different combinations, suggest changes, and finally sign off on the design. The outcome is an obvious improvement in the user's perception and comprehension of the system.

The principal argument against prototyping is cost. Whether or not a designer decides to create a prototype depends on the complexity of the database application, the user's requirements, and how much time is available. Prototypes can be expensive when they are implemented using the same tools, procedures, and standards as the final system.

File Structure

Now the designer must decide what specific elements are required and how they should be combined into a file structure.

Data Elements

The data elements in the WCS are largely established by the accounting department and the worker's compensation laws of the state. Two types of claims for reimbursement must be dealt with: the employee claim for lost wages resulting from an accident and the vendor claim for medical services rendered to the injured employee. The procedure for the approval of lost wages is provided for in the state's worker's compensation rules. Reimbursement for medical services rendered is based on a certified accident having taken place. Therefore, when a bill is received from a physician, the system must determine that the accident took place and was properly reported. If so, the bill can be paid. To properly pay invoices from medical service providers, the accounting department requires data elements, as shown in Table 12-1.

Data Element	*Use*
Vendor name	To properly prepare checks for payment of services rendered
Employee name	To check that a reimbursement is due to the vendor for the service
Date of service	To identify the service for which payment is being made and to avoid duplicate payments for the service
Date check sent	To ensure that duplicate checks are not issued
Amount	To verify that the amount on the invoice is correct
Invoice identification	To retrieve an invoice
Department	To list accidents by department for statistical analysis

Table 12-1 Data elements required by the accounting department

The state worker's compensation commission requires that certain data be reported periodically. In addition, the accounting department needs similar data to verify that a payment is due. The data elements required to meet these needs appear in Table 12-2.

Data Element	*Use*
Employee name	
Employee social security number	
Date of accident	
Type of accident	To complete state commission requirements and to analyze training needs
Nature of accident	To complete state commission requirements and to analyze training needs
Cause of accident	To complete state commission requirements and to analyze training needs
Part of body affected	
Was there a loss of use?	
Date disability began Date disability ended	To record the claim and dates of disability, and to authorize or deny payment for lost wages
Wages	
Amount of award to employee	To record amount authorized for lost wages
Name of physician	To identify the doctor who certified the disability
Case status	To show whether the case is active

Table 12-2 Data elements required by worker's compensation commission

In designing the data files, the designer remembered that an injured worker might make more than one claim for a single injury. In fact, from discussions with the people in the personnel department, the designer learned that this was a very common occurrence. Therefore, the designer made provisions for multiple claims records against the same injury.

Functional Dependencies

In the case of the example WCS, there is little question about the functional dependencies among data items. The employee name and date of the accident determine all data concerning the accident, which can be shown as

```
Name + Date of Accident ----> all other data concerning
                              the accident
```

An important assumption has been built into this statement of functional dependency: that an employee will have only one accident in a day. While this may appear to be obvious (in this case, reasonable), it is nevertheless important for the designer to state this fundamental assumption to the programmer.

File Layout

The layout of the files for the WCS is shown in Tables 12-3 and 12-4. In Table 12-3 the INVOICE file includes the data needed by the accounting department for payments to medical services providers. Prior to payment the system must establish that the payment is proper using the ACCIDENT file (Table 12-4). Note that the ACCIDENT file contains information about the accident and allows for more than one lost-time claim by the employee. If the file were larger, the repeating fields for these multiple lost-time claims might well have been placed into another file and related to the ACCIDENT file by the employee's social security number.

No.	Name	Field Type	Width	Dec
1	VENDOR	Character	20	
2	EMP_LAST	Character	15	
3	EMP_FIRST	Character	15	
4	SOC_SEC	Character	11	
5	SERVDATE	Date	8	
6	DATE_SENT	Date	8	
7	AMOUNT	Numeric	9	2
8	DEPT	Character	3	
9	INVOICE	Character	9	
Total			99	

Table 12-3 File layout of INVOICE file

No.	Name	Field Type	Width	Dec
1	EMP_LAST	Character	15	
2	EMP_FIRST	Character	15	
3	SOC_SEC	Character	11	
4	ACCDAT	Date	8	
5	TYPE	Character	5	
6	NATURE	Character	5	
7	CAUSE	Character	5	
8	PART	Character	5	
9	LOSSOFUSE	Character	1	
10	COMMENT	Character	32	
11	NUMAWARD	Numeric	1	
12	MEM1	Date	8	
13	FACT1	Date	8	
14	AWARD1	Numeric	9	2
15	WAGE1	Numeric	9	2
16	DOC1	Character	29	
17	MEM2	Date	8	
18	FACT2	Date	8	
19	AWARD2	Numeric	9	
20	WAGE2	Numeric	9	2
21	DOC2	Character	29	
22	MEM3	Date	8	
23	FACT3	Date	8	
24	AWARD3	Numeric	9	2
25	WAGE3	Numeric	9	2
26	DOC3	Character	29	
27	PAYROLL	Date	8	
28	DEPT	Character	3	
29	EMP_STATUS	Character	4	
30	DORMANT	Logical	1	
Total			309	

Table 12-4 File layout of ACCIDENT file

Note that the file INVOICE is made up of nine data items. The datatype for each item is specified in the "Field Type" column. The "Width" column specifies the maximum number of stored characters. The "Dec" column indicates the number of decimal positions within the field size (in this case 2 places to the right of the decimal point). The width of the records in the INVOICE file is 99 characters, as indicated by the total at the bottom of the file layout.

There is some redundancy in this file system. Notice that both files contain the employee's name and social security number. This data is needed to relate the records of the two files. Although the goal of DBMS design is to minimize redundant data, in a relational database there must be enough redundancy so that records in different files can be associated.

SUMMARY

1 The system specifications document identifies the user's information requirements, provides a cost-benefit assessment of the proposed project, lists the logical design tools (diagrams and charts) to be used, and the nature of the coding, testing, and implementation that follows the logical design.

2 A database designer first tries to identify the user's problem, the goals of the project, and the potential outcome of the project up front before attempting logical design.

3 Today's logical design trend is toward automated design tools, such as Excelerator, which take the drudgery out of drawing diagrams and verifying the data elements and entities.

4 A data flow diagram (DFD) is a process diagram that maps out the nature of the data flow of a system under consideration. Data dictionaries can be easily generated from the DFD.

5 An entity-relationship (E-R) diagram is a high-level overview diagram of data which can be decomposed into detailed data models.

6 A data model diagram shows entities and their relationships. These entities are important in structuring the design of the database.

7 A structure chart is a hierarchical diagram that depicts the program structure. Each rectangle in the diagram represents a module, which is later converted into a set of instructions or codes.

8 Prototypes show the client how the proposed system will work and allow the client to make or suggest changes in the design.

9 The file structure of the Worker's Compensation System consists of data elements required by the Worker's Compensation Commission. There are also functional dependencies among data items. There is also some redundancy in the file system, as there must be enough redundancy for records in different files to be associated.

KEY WORDS

Boss module
Called module
Connection
Couple
Data model diagram
Data structure diagram
Entity-relationship (E-R) diagram
Module
Prototype
Structure chart
System specifications document

REVIEW QUESTIONS

1 What is the difference between a database system that runs on a mainframe and one that runs on a microcomputer?

2 Elaborate on the steps involved in planning the logical design of a database application.

3 What is a system specifications document and what is its purpose? Could a designer proceed with logical design without the planning phase? How?

4 Distinguish between the following pairs:

a. data model diagram and entity-relationship diagram
b. structure chart and data structure diagram
c. data element and file structure
d. system specifications document and database planning

5 From what you know about Excelerator, how useful do you think it can be for doing design work? Explain.

6 What is involved in prototyping? What are the pros and cons of developing a prototype? Elaborate.

APPLICATION PROBLEMS

1 Draw data flow diagrams for the following applications:

a. making an auto loan
b. a systems analyst selling professional time by the hour and paying staff salaries
c. ordering supplies for a hair salon

2 Construct a structure chart and show the required couples for the following:

a. top (boss) module: ENTER GRADES
b. Reporting modules: GET RECORD, GET PAST GRADES, ADD NEW GRADES, REPORT DISCREPANCIES, CHECK FOR PROBATION, CHECK FOR DEAN'S LIST

3 Invent a family, with as many members as you like, that owns a local restaurant.

a. Define the major functions, processes, and activities of the family. Draw an organization chart.
b. Define the family entities and draw an appropriate E-R diagram.

4 A professional hockey team is a business enterprise.

a. Define its key functions, processes, and activities.
b. Define the team entities and draw an E-R diagram.

5 Use the work you have completed on Island Jumpers, Inc. (IJI) as a basis for the following:

a. Draw an organization chart for IJI. Consider the scope and other parameters you have drawn for the organization.
b. Draw an E-R diagram of the entities defined.
c. Draw a structure chart to represent logical design of the information system.
d. What deliverables would you say are expected from the system? Elaborate.

C H A P T

Expressing the Logical Design

E R 1 3

Pitfalls in Data Design

AT A GLANCE

Pitfalls in Data Design

"Make data more accessible to management and users." Nowadays, this is one of the most commonly heard phrases in information systems (IS) departments. It is often found as an objective in the IS strategic plan. But experience shows that relying on tools alone often leads to failure. The tools themselves do nothing for data design. This is the crux of the problem. A single application's view is seldom appropriate or sufficient for another application. For the data to be available to all potential users, it must be stored according to a design that reflects the client's use of the data rather than just one application's view. . . .

To this end, we will address three erroneous assumptions leading to the most common data design failures:

- that an existing data design in an established system must be correct;
- that those things called records by initial application designers are, indeed, unique entities and require no further analysis; and
- that response time is the most critical factor for the user.

When such assumptions are made, the resulting data designs usually work well for the problem they were designed to solve, but are often unable to handle changes in the existing application or new applications. Consequently, in most cases new applications are supported by the creation of yet another database or set of files with a data design similar, but not identical, to existing databases or files. The resulting problems of redundancy and integrity are well known.

First, let me stress that the term logical data design refers to a specific methodology aimed at addressing data design from a business perspective. Business analysis and normalization are the keys to the methodology. Data designs that were developed without the benefit of the methodology often demonstrate database design failures.

Let's look at a specific situation. The customer file for a business has a salesperson's name and number as part of each record. (See Figure 1.) The design was developed years ago to meet a batch processing criterion of that era (i.e., to try to have all data required for the application in as few files as possible).

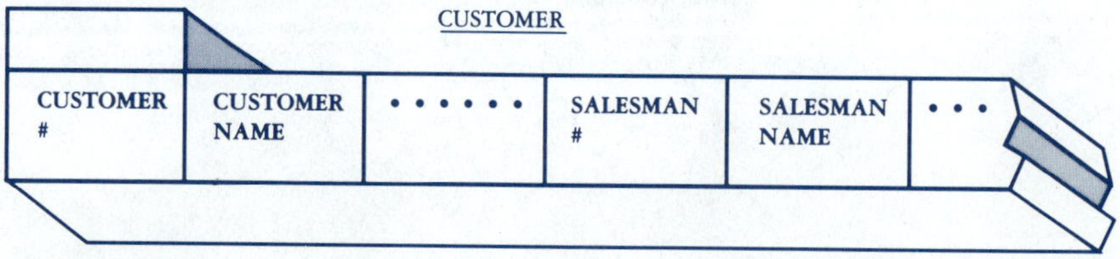

Figure 1 Existing record

Deficient Design Theory

A new request from the user indicates the need to list customers by sales territory as well as by salesperson. The traditional designers' approach (without training in logical data design) is, "The existing record has served in the past. All we need to do is add sales territory to key." This type of inadequate design theory, often resulting in data design failure, also occurs when someone decides that "we don't have time to change the data design, just modify the existing files." The result is simply an extended version of Figure 1, with a "sales territory number" field added. When the salesperson assigned to a territory changes, however, the whole customer file must be reviewed sequentially, changing the salesperson's number and name in each record. To accomplish this task, batch processes and procedures must be set up. They usually must be scheduled overnight, among hundreds of other similar jobs.

On the other hand, if the data designer does not assume that the existing record design is correct and follows good design procedures, the result is very different. This design is shown in Figure 2. It is true that more effort in design may be required initially, but the long-term result is less overall effort.

Let's analyze the design in Figure 2. The benefits are striking. The salesperson's name and number can be altered for the whole customer file using one simple on-line transaction. Only a change to the territory record (by replacing the "responsible employee number" field) is required. Second, territory number is the only field whose data need to be captured for a new customer. There are no problems with determining the salesperson's name and number or recording them incorrectly. In fact, the salesperson's number can be used for data validation (if territory and salesperson's number are entered, they should match those already on file). Finally, the change can be made by an authorized user with a simple on-line transaction. No overnight batch procedures, run books, job control, etc., are needed. Overall work reduction is significant, both in development of the application and in ongoing operation.

Let us now consider the second assumption. The resulting design failure stems from forgetting to continually ask the question, "Am I looking at a business entity or an occurrence of a business entity?" In other words, "Are we looking at different types of records or are they different categories of one record type?" The two are not the same and pose a design problem.

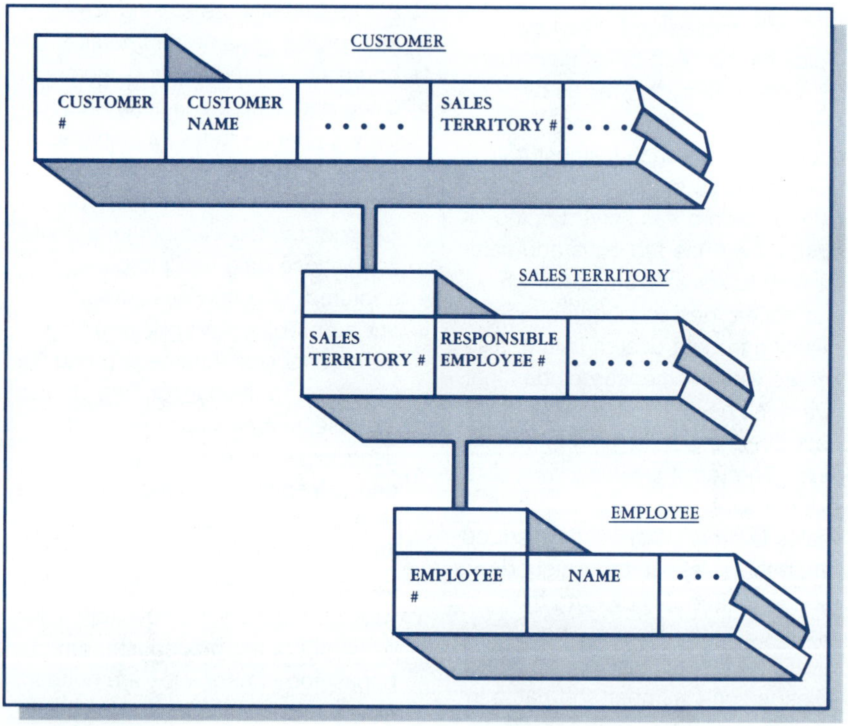

Figure 2 Logical design

. . . In this article, I often referred to records and files rather than record types and databases. This was done deliberately. The reason is that logical data design is independent of a database management system (DBMS). A DBMS is certainly preferable for implementation but is not a consideration in data design.

The tendency to worry about DBMS access paths and structural limitations before the business's functional requirements are understood is another pitfall that cripples the effectiveness of many databases. This is the third problem to be discussed here. I've known applications analysts to start counting the number of I/0 operations as they define the functional requirements. With this concern foremost, data designs are oriented toward the DBMS rather than the business environment. They often result in data designs even less flexible than that shown in Figure 1.

Regarding the third assumption, I agree that response time is important. Users are willing, however, in most cases, to give a bit on this constraint to achieve the flexibility to do what they want when they want, particularly with the advent of end-user, fourth generation tools. Being told that they can't do what they want with data they know exists, or that it will take more than six months for the capability to be built, does not make for happy users. Furthermore, response time can usually be addressed quickly by hardware upgrades.

In any event, response time is a physical design issue. The data design should be modified only if it is determined with certainty that response time will be unacceptable. This should not be done until the logical design is complete. Such a decision is the joint responsibility of the data administrator and the database administrator. They need to agree when flexibility will be reduced in order to deliver an acceptable response time.

Excerpted from Wilson, A. H., "Pitfalls in data design." Reprinted from DATAMATION, *November 15, 1985,*

AT A GLANCE

For implementation, the logical requirements of a system must be represented in a language understandable to the computer. Two types of tools are used to express logic: Structured English and decision trees. Other tools are used, depending on the nature of the problem, the experience of the designer, and the software available.

Structured English is closer to plain English and to COBOL. The vocabulary consists of imperative statements, reserved words for expressing logic, and words defined in the data dictionary. The syntax in a Structured English sentence can be a declarative statement, a closed-end decision, a repetition construct, or some combination of these.

Program logic can be expressed in terms of four basic constructs: sequence, condition, case, and repetition. The sequence construct applies simple top-to-bottom ordering of subordinate descriptions in a logical program. The condition construct specifies that if a specific condition exists, then a certain action must be followed or else a different action must be taken. The case construct is a nested series of conditional constructs that identifies the action to be taken for each possible, and mutually exclusive, set of conditions. Finally, the repetition construct deals with a set of operations that are repeated over and over again until a condition that terminates the repetition is met.

Pseudocode is a tool that does essentially the same job as Structured English. It allows the designer to capture the important elements of the design rapidly. Unlike Structured English, though, this tool uses more formal notation and is geared more to database designers and professionals than to end-users. Because pseudocode is so detailed, there is less margin for error when it is translated into actual code.

A decision tree is a graphic view or model of the decision logic in a program. The values of variables are determined and, based on these values, specific actions are taken. Decision trees can easily be converted into action diagrams or used directly as a step toward program coding. They are seldom used, however, at a high level to show program control structure. They are best used to supplement other design tools.

By the end of this chapter, you should

- understand the main tools that express the logical design;
- know the key features of Structured English and the difference between it and pseudocode;
- recognize the logical constructs used in program logic;
- understand the uses and features of pseudocode; and understand the makeup of decision tables and when they are used.

INTRODUCTION

The logical requirements of a system must be communicated to the user for verification and to the database designer for implementation. In some respects, logical requirements do not all need detailed explanation. For example, the requirement that the month field not exceed 12 needs no explanation, because the calendar year has only 12 months. The user is concerned more with validating the month field than with deciding how to set it up. All the designer needs to know are the validation requirements.

Some logical requirements, however, do need detailed explanation. The analyst often provides these requirements in module narratives that are ambiguous, too detailed, or too brief. A more reliable approach to defining the logical requirements is through logical (graphic) tools that lay out the conditions and actions for implementing the database application.

Two types of tools are generally used to express logic: Structured English and decision trees. Both of these have been used to support or even replace narrative program and system specifications. There are other tools the designer may use, of course—the choice depends on the nature of the problem, the experience of the designer, and the software available.

Structured English is much more detailed than decision trees, but it is closer to plain English and to COBOL. A decision tree, on the other hand, easily lays out the processing specifications, requires a minimum amount of training to use, and can be used directly to develop program logic.

Less important than the tool are the processing requirement specifications. If the specifications are well-written and accurate, the programmer need only concentrate on actually coding and debugging the application.

STRUCTURED ENGLISH

For over two decades, data flow diagrams have been used to express program logic. But, because data flow diagrams are too "physical," they were replaced with Structured English or pseudocode. Choosing which to use depends on which best represents the logic of each module in the structure chart in a format amenable to coding. Structured English or pseudocode usually works better than a simple diagram.

English narrative that describes a program or other specifications is generally tedious to read and understand. For example:

> The servicer shall charge a service fee computed by adding the total DDA transactions to the time deposit transactions and multiplying the sum by .05 (five cents), except when DDA transactions exceed 300,000 during a given month, in which case the fee shall be .01 (one cent) on each DDA transaction at the option of the servicer.

This narrative is time-consuming to write, difficult to follow, and prone to error. We can represent this clause more clearly in Structured English as

```
IF monthly-transactions <= 300000
   Multiply monthly-transactions by .05
ELSE
   Fee = DDA-transactions*.01 + Time-deposit-transaction*.05
```

This illustrates two key attributes of Structured English:

1 The procedure is hierarchically structured, using indentation to make it easy to follow.

2 The structure is similar to the program code that will implement the database.

STRUCTURED ENGLISH is a language based on plain English vocabulary and a limited syntax. It uses a highly orthogonal (not overlapping) set of constructs, which makes it easy for the user to understand and for the programmer to follow.

The vocabulary in Structured English consists of imperative statements, reserved words for expressing logic, and words defined in the data dictionary. Data dictionary words are written as hyphenated names (such as "monthly-transactions"). The syntax in a Structured English sentence may be a declarative statement, a closed-end decision, a repetition construct, or some combination of these. An imperative such as "ADD DDA-transactions TO Time-deposit-transactions," specifies what must be done.

Guidelines for Writing Structured English

Like any procedure, Structured English is written within a set of guidelines. The key rules are as follows:

1 Use concise statements, not rambling sentences with connectors such as "but," "unless," or "except."

2 The verbs must be strong action verbs such as "calculate" and "edit," not "handle," "process," or "proceed."

3 The direct object of the action verb must be clearly stated. For example, "calculate net pay" is clearer than "process pay."

4 Avoid using punctuation, semicolons, question marks, exclamation points, footnotes, or verbs expressing relationships such as "increase" and "improve."

5 The key words and names of program blocks should be capitalized to make them stand out. Every other description should be lower case.

6 Each instruction must have a single starting point and a single ending point.

7 The design layout, in the form of a character diagram, should be included for easy reading.

8 Each system installation must adopt its standards in the choice of key words.

9 Each sequence step should be on a separate line.

10 End words such as ENDIF and EXIT should be used to mark the end of an instruction. A sample Structured English instruction that follows these guidelines is shown in Figure 13-1.

```
AUTO-REPAIR
  FOR ALL autos
    Fill out repair sheet
      IF AUTO is under warranty
        Set up auto details for WARRANTY record;      } Sequence
        Set up estimated time for WARRANTY record;    } construct
        Write WARRANTY RECORD
      ELSE
        Set up customer record
        Write up form for AUTO-REPAIR
      ENDIF
    FOR ALL parts installed
      Obtain PARTS record
      IF PART # is valid
        IF quantity is in stock
          Enter parts details in LINE-ITEM record                 } IF...ELSE
          Enter number of units installed for LINE-ITEM record    } Condition
          Decrease part quantity in-stock by quantity installed   } construct
          Update PART record
          Write LINE-ITEM record
        ELSE
          Set up part details for BACKORDER record
          Record quantity backordered for BACKORDER
            record
        ENDIF
      ELSE
        Enter order message with Dearborn warehouse
      ENDIF
    ENDFOR
  ENDFOR
EXIT AUTOS
```

Figure 13–1 Structured English showing proper use of key words

Program logic can be expressed in terms of four basic constructs: sequence, condition, case, and repetition.

Sequence Construct

A SEQUENCE CONSTRUCT applies simple top-to-bottom ordering of subordinate descriptions in a logical program. For example,

```
           IF AUTO is under WARRANTY
          ┌ Set up auto details for WARRANTY record;
sequence ─┤ Set up extended time for WARRANTY record;
          └ Write WARRANTY record
           Else . . .
```

No key words are necessary to show sequence. The sequence is ended with the word EXIT, followed by an optional sequence title. (See Figure 13-2.)

Condition Construct

A CONDITION CONSTRUCT specifies that IF a specific condition exists, THEN a certain action follows or ELSE a different action must be taken. The key words in a condition construct are IF, THEN, and ELSE. A condition construct must end with ENDIF to indicate the end of the instruction. (See Figure 13-3.) For example,

```
IF customer ID is valid
   THEN cash check
ELSE
   ask for reference
ENDIF
```

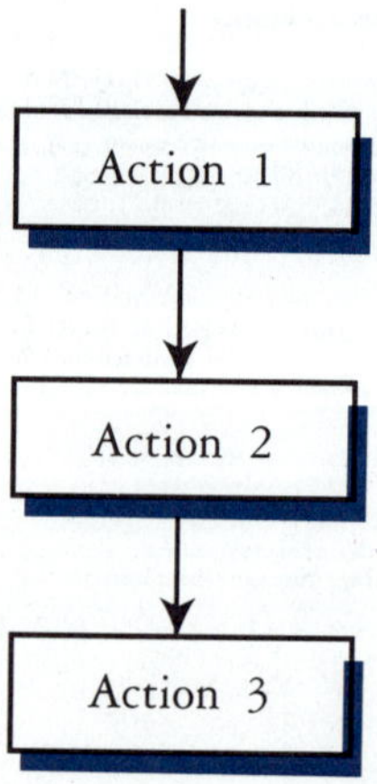

Figure 13–2 The sequence construct

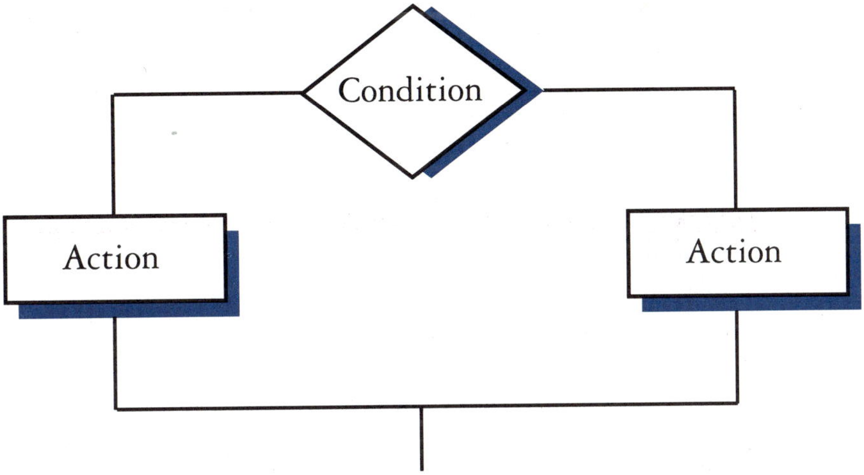

Figure 13–3 Example of condition construct

Case Construct

A CASE CONSTRUCT is a nested series of conditional constructs that identifies the action to be taken for each possible, and mutually exclusive, set of conditions. But where a conditional construct uses IF...ELSEIF...ELSEIF...ELSE, a case construct abbreviates in instruction into CASE statements.

For example, an IF...ELSE structure can be changed to a case construct as follows:

```
     IF...ELSE
IF fresh brewed coffee
   pour a cup
ELSE (no fresh coffee)
   IF instant coffee
      pour a cup
   ELSE
      give me the check
   ENDIF
ENDIF
```

```
        CASE
Case 1 fresh brewed coffee
       pour a cup
Case 2 instant coffee
       pour a cup
Case 3 none of the above
       give me the check
```

Repetition Construct

A REPETITION CONSTRUCT deals with a set of operations that are repeated over and over again until a condition is met that terminates the repetition. There are two key types of repetition constructs, the repeat-until construct and the do-while construct.

Repeat-until The REPEAT-UNTIL CONSTRUCT allows a specific set of operations to be repeated at least once until a condition is met. The key words in a repeat-until construct are REPEAT-UNTIL, IF, and ELSE. (See Figure 13-4.)

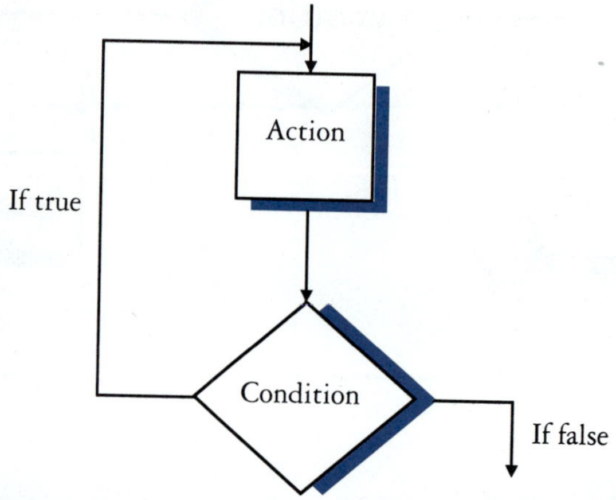

Figure 13–4 Repeat-until construct

For example,

```
REPEAT-UNTIL there are no more OFFICER records
   IF OFFICER has been full-time employee
        for at least 10 years and has not used sick days
     IF OFFICER salary is over $30,000 per year
        compute half-day sick pay for each year of service--
        Example 10 years = 5 days of pay
     ELSE (officer earns $30,000 or less per year)
        do not compute sick pay
   ELSE (not full-time officer for at least 10 years
        or OFFICER has used sick days)
        do not compute sick pay
```

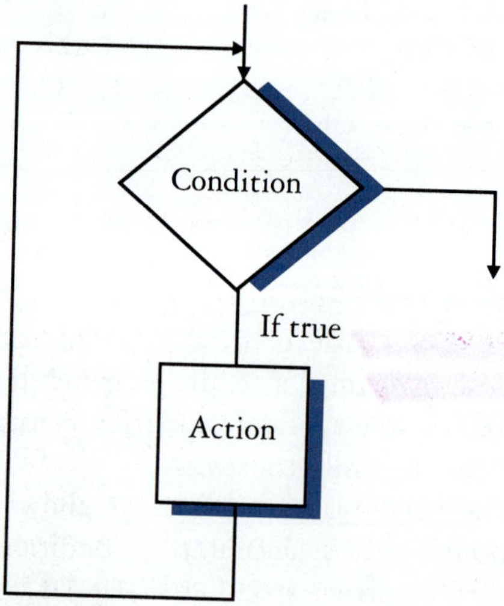

Figure 13–5 Do-While basic format

The condition is tested after the operation is executed. Using our example, the condition is that for an officer's sick pay to be processed, the record must show a salary of $30,000 or more, ten or more years of full-time service, and no sick pay used to date. If this condition is not met, the system will not compute sick pay.

Do-while The DO-WHILE CONSTRUCT is a control structure that executes the statements bracketed between the words DO-WHILE and ENDDO a fixed number of times or for as long as the statement on the DO-WHILE is a repeating IF. (See Figure 13-5.)

The first rule of creating a do-while construct is to place the DO-WHILE...ENDDO loop only around the steps that repeat. For example, planning "run program" within the loop would be technically wrong, because a program cannot be debugged until after it has run for the first time. The correct construct would be

```
Design program
Code program
Run program
DO-WHILE program does not run properly
  Debug program
  Run program again
ENDDO
```

To add the step "write user manual" to the program development cycle, you must place it after (not before) the ENDDO loop, because writing a manual is not subject to a repeated sequence, as is debugging a program.

Preceding the do-while construct is a condition that specifies the number of times the loop is to operate. For example, a partial program that will print "my first try" ten times, would work like this

```
STORE 1 to Loop1
DO-WHILE Loop1 <=10
  ? "My first try"
  STORE 1+Loop1 TO Loop1
ENDDO
```

The first line creates a variable, called LOOP1, and assigns the value "1" to it. The LOOP COUNTER keeps track of the number of times the do-while executes. The variable could be any name, alphabetic or alphanumeric. Mnemonics or variables that aid memory are often chosen, because they are easier to remember than abstract variables, such as *x* or *y*.

The DO-WHILE command in this example simply says "Execute the statements from here to ENDDO ten times." When Loop1 = 10 is false, the software ignores the instructions within the loop and begins executing the commands following ENDDO. In our example, this ends the program.

Structured English for the Worker's Compensation Case

Let us return to our worker's compensation case and see how Structured English can be used to develop the program logic. This WCS application, you will recall, will have a main menu consisting of six options:

1 Query
2 Add
3 Edit
4 Invoice
5 Quarterly invoice
6 Return to dot prompt (exit)

These commands instruct the system to do a routine based on the option the user has chosen. For example, if the user chooses the option "Query," the system will go to the query routine. The Structured English for displaying the menu and acting on the option would provide

WORKER'S COMPENSATION INFORMATION SYSTEM MAIN MENU

```
SET mREPEAT TO TRUE AS FLAG TO END THE SYSTEM EXECUTION
DO WHILE mREPEAT IS TRUE
   SHOW WORKER'S COMPENSATION MAIN MENU
   PROMPT USER TO ENTER THE MENU SELECTION
   DO CASE
      CASE mCHOICE = "1"
         EXECUTE QUERY MODULE
      CASE mCHOICE = "2"
         EXECUTE ADD MODULE
      CASE mCHOICE = "3"
         EXECUTE EDIT MODULE
      CASE mCHOICE = "4"
         EXECUTE INVOICE MODULE
      CASE mCHOICE = "5"
         EXECUTE QRTINVOICE MODULE
      CASE mCHOICE = "6"
         SHOW MESSAGE "RETURN TO THE DOT PROMPT"
         SET mREPEAT TO FALSE TO END SESSION
      OTHERWISE
         SHOW ERROR MESSAGE "INVALID CHOICE"
   ENDCASE
ENDDO
```

The Structured English for each option would appear as

QUERY MODULE

```
SET mREPEAT1 TO TRUE AS A FLAG TO END QUERY MODULE
DO mREPEAT1 IS TRUE
   SHOW QUERY MAIN MENU
   PROMPT USER TO ENTER THE MENU SELECTION
   DO CASE
      CASE mCHOICE1 = "1"
```

```
        OPEN CLAIM FILE
        PROMPT USER TO ENTER CLAIM ID
        FIND RECORD WITH SPECIFIED CLAIM ID
        IF RECORD IS FOUND
           DISPLAY CLAIM RECORD
        ELSE
           SHOW ERROR MESSAGE "THE CLAIM ID NUMBER IS NOT IN THE FILE"
        ENDIF
     CASE mCHOICE1 = "2"
        OPEN INJURY FILE
        PROMPT USER TO ENTER EMPLOYEE SOCIAL SECURITY NUMBER
        FIND RECORD WITH SPECIFIED EMPLOYEE SOCIAL SECURITY NUMBER
        IF RECORD IS FOUND
           DISPLAY INJURY RECORD
        ELSE
           SHOW ERROR MESSAGE "THE EMPLOYEE SOCIAL SECURITY NUMBER IS NOT
           IN THE FILE, PLEASE CHECK THE INPUT AND REENTER"
        ENDIF
     CASE mCHOICE1 = "3"
        OPEN COMPENSATION FILE
        PROMPT USER TO ENTER CLAIM ID
        FIND RECORD WITH SPECIFIED CLAIM ID
        IF RECORD IS FOUND
           DISPLAY COMPENSATION RECORD
        ELSE
           SHOW ERROR MESSAGE "NO RECORD FOUND, PLEASE CHECK THE INPUT AND
           REENTER"
        ENDIF
     CASE mCHOICE1 = "4"
        RETURN TO WORKCOMP MAIN MENU
     OTHERWISE
        SHOW ERROR MESSAGE "INVALID SELECTION"
  ENDCASE
ENDDO
CLOSE ALL FILES
```

ADD MODULE

```
SET mREPEAT TO TRUE AS FLAG TO END ADD MODULE
DO WHILE mREPEAT2 IS TRUE
   SHOW "ADD" MENU
   PROMPT USER TO ENTER ADD MENU SELECTION
   DO CASE
      CASE mCHOICE2 = "1"
         OPEN INJURY FILE
         PROMPT USER TO ENTER EMPLOYEE SOCIAL SECURITY NUMBER
         FIND RECORD WITH SPECIFIED SOCIAL SECURITY NUMBER
         IF SOCIAL SECURITY NUMBER NOT FOUND
            SHOW ERROR MESSAGE "THERE IS NO INJURY FILED FOR THE SPECIFIED
            EMPLOYEE, A CLAIM CAN BE SUBMITTED ONLY IF THERE IS AN INJURY
            FILED BEFORE"
         ELSE
            OPEN CLAIM FILE
            PROMPT USER TO ENTER CLAIM ID
            FIND RECORD WITH THE SPECIFIED CLAIM ID
            IF CLAIM ID IS FOUND
               SHOW ERROR MESSAGE "THE CLAIM ID NUMBER ALREADY EXISTS, NO CLAIMS
               CAN HAVE THE SAME CLAIM ID"
```

```
            RESET VALUE OF WORKING STORAGE VARIABLE mCLAIMID
         ELSE
            SHOW INPUT SCREEN FOR ADDING A NEW CLAIM
            ENTER INFORMATION TO SCREEN
            WRITE NEW INFORMATION INTO CLAIM FILE
            RESET WORKING STORAGE VARIABLES
         ENDIF
      ENDIF
   CASE mCHOICE2 = "2"
      CREATE mCOUNTER AS A FLAG TO END LOOP
      DO WHILE mCOUNTER LESS THAN 3
         SET PASSWORD
         PROMPT USER TO ENTER PASSWORD
         IF PASSWORD IS VALID
            DO WHILE PASSWORD IS VALID
               OPEN CLAIM FILE
               PROMPT USER TO ENTER CLAIM ID
               FIND RECORD WITH SPECIFIED CLAIM ID
               IF CLAIM ID IS NOT FOUND
                  SHOW ERROR MESSAGE "THE CLAIM ID NUMBER DOES NOT EXIST IN
                  THE CLAIM FILE, COMPENSATION WILL NOT BE GRANTED UNLESS
                  THERE IS A CLAIM EXISTING IN THE CLAIM FILE, PLEASE CHECK
                  THE INPUT"
                  RESET WORKING STORAGE VARIABLE
                  END THE PASSWORD LOOP
               ELSE
                  OPEN COMPENSATION FILE
                  FIND RECORD WITH SPECIFIED CLAIM ID
                  IF CLAIM ID IS FOUND
                     SHOW ERROR MESSAGE "THE SPECIFIED CLAIM HAS BEEN
                     COMPENSATED BEFORE"
                  ELSE
                     GOTO BOTTOM OF CLAIM FILE
                     SHOW INPUT SCREEN FOR ADDING A CLAIM
                     ENTER INVOICE INFORMATION TO SCREEN
                     WRITE INFORMATION ENTERED INTO COMPENSATION FILE
                     GO OUT OF LOOP BY SETTING mCOUNTER GREATER THAN 3
                  ENDIF
               ENDIF
            ENDDO
         ELSE
            SHOW ERROR MESSAGE "THE PASSWORD IS INCORRECT"
            INCREASE COUNTER BY 1
         ENDIF
      ENDDO
      IF mCOUNTER = "3"
         SHOW ERROR MESSAGE "ONLY THE MANAGER CAN ACCESS COMPENSATION FILE"
      ENDIF
   CASE mCHOICE2 = "3"
      RETURN TO WORKCOMP MAIN MENU
   OTHERWISE
      SHOW ERROR MESSAGE "INVALID SELECTION, PLEASE TRY AGAIN"
ENDCASE
ENDDO
CLOSE ALL FILES
```

EDIT MODULE

```
SET mREPEAT3 TO FALSE AS FLAG TO END EDIT MODULE
DO WHILE mREPEAT3 IS FALSE
   SHOW "EDIT'' MENU
   ACCEPT MENU SELECTION AND STORE IT TO mCHOICE3
   DO CASE
      CASE mCHOICE3 = "1"
         OPEN CLAIM FILE
         SHOW INPUT MENU SCREEN
         ACCEPT CLAIM ID ENTERED BY USER
         FIND RECORD THAT HAS THE CLAIM ID ENTERED BY USER
         IF NO RECORD FOUND
            SHOW ERROR MESSAGE "THERE IS NO RECORD WITH THE SPECIFIED CLAIM
            ID NUMBER"
         ELSE
            SHOW ALL FIELDS IN CLAIM FILE TO BE EDITED
            REPLACE ALL EDITED FIELDS
         ENDIF
      CASE mCHOICE3 = "2"
         CREATE mCOUNTER AS A FLAG TO END LOOP
         DO WHILE mCOUNTER LESS THAN 3
            SET UP PASSWORD
            PROMPT USER TO ENTER PASSWORD
            IF PASSWORD IS VALID
               PROMPT USER TO ENTER CLAIM ID
               OPEN COMPENSATION FILE
               FIND RECORD WITH CLAIM ID ENTERED BY USER
               IF RECORD NOT FOUND
                  SHOW ERROR MESSAGE "THE RECORD WITH THE SPECIFIED CLAIM ID
                  IS NOT IN THE FILE"
                  RESET VALUE OF WORKING STORAGE VARIABLES
                  GO OUT OF LOOP BY SETTING mCOUNTER GREATER THAN 3
               ELSE
                  SHOW ALL FIELDS IN COMPENSATION FILE TO BE EDITED
                  REPLACE ALL EDITED FIELDS
                  GO OUT OF LOOP BY SETTING mCOUNTER GREATER THAN 3
               ENDIF
            ELSE
               SHOW ERROR MESSAGE "THE PASSWORD IS INCORRECT"
               INCREASE mCOUNTER BY 1
            ENDIF
         ENDDO
         IF mCOUNTER = "3"
            SHOW ERROR MESSAGE "ONLY THE MANAGER CAN ACCESS COMPENSATION FILE"
         ENDIF
      CASE mCHOICE3 = "3"
         GO BACK TO WORKCOMP MAIN MENU
      OTHERWISE
         SHOW ERROR MESSAGE "INVALID SELECTION, PLEASE TRY AGAIN"
   ENDCASE
ENDDO
CLOSE ALL FILES
```

INVOICE MODULE

```
SET mREPEAT4 TO FALSE AS FLAG TO END PRODUCE INVOICE MODULE
DO WHILE mREPEAT4 IS FALSE
   SHOW INVOICE MAIN MENU
   PROMPT USER TO ENTER MENU SELECTION
   DO CASE
      CASE mCHOICE4 = "1"
         OPEN COMPENSATION FILE
         PROMPT USER TO ENTER CLAIM ID
         FIND RECORD WITH SPECIFIED CLAIM ID
         IF RECORD IS NOT FOUND
            SHOW ERROR MESSAGE "THERE IS NO RECORD WITH THE SPECIFIED CLAIM
            ID NUMBER"
         ELSE
            IF INVOICE HAS NOT BEEN PRINTED
               SHOW CLAIM FILE INFORMATION USED IN INVOICE ON SCREEN
               OPEN EMPLOYEE FILE
               FIND RECORD WITH SPECIFIED EMPLOYEE ID
               SHOW EMPLOYEE FILE INFORMATION USED IN INVOICE ON SCREEN
               OPEN DEPARTMENT FILE
               FIND RECORD WITH SPECIFIED DEPARTMENT ID
               SHOW DEPARTMENT FILE INFORMATION USED IN INVOICE ON SCREEN
            ELSE
               SHOW ERROR MESSAGE "THE INVOICE FOR THIS RECORD HAS BEEN PRINTED
               BEFORE, FOR EACH CLAIM THERE IS ONLY ONE INVOICE ALLOWED TO BE
               PRINTED"
            ENDIF
         ENDIF
      CASE mCHOICE4 = "2"
         RETURN TO WORKCOMP MAIN MENU
      CASE mCHOICE4 = "3"
         OPEN COMPENSATION FILE
         PROMPT USER TO ENTER CLAIM ID
         FIND RECORD WITH SPECIFIED CLAIM ID
         IF RECORD NOT FOUND
            SHOW ERROR MESSAGE "THERE IS NO RECORD WITH THE SPECIFIED CLAIM
            ID NUMBER"
         ELSE
            IF INVOICE HAS NOT BEEN PRINTED
               PRINT INVOICE
            ELSE
               SHOW ERROR MESSAGE "THE INVOICE FOR THIS RECORD HAS BEEN PRINTED
               BEFORE, FOR EACH CLAIM THERE IS ONLY ONE INVOICE ALLOWED TO BE
               PRINTED"
            ENDIF
         ENDIF
      OTHERWISE
         SHOW ERROR MESSAGE "INVALID SELECTION"
   ENDCASE
ENDDO
CLOSE ALL FILES
```

QUARTERLY INVOICE MODULE

```
SET mRETURN TO TRUE AS A FLAG TO END THE QUARTERLY INVOICE ERROR TRACKING MODULE
SET mFIRST TO TRUE AS A FLAG TO CHECK FOR FIRST RECORD IN THE FILE
SET mFOUND TO 0 AS A FLAG TO END THE QUARTERLY INVOICE MODULE
DO WHILE mRETURN IS TRUE AND mFOUND EQUAL TO 0
   PROMPT USER TO ENTER STARTING AND ENDING DATE OF A QUARTER
   OPEN COMPENSATION FILE
   LOCATE ALL RECORDS FOR COMPENSATION DATE GREATER THAN EQUAL TO STARTING DATE
   AND COMPENSATION DATE LESS THAN EQUAL TO ENDING DATE
   IF RECORD FOUND()
      SET mFOUND = 1
   ELSE
      SHOW ERROR MESSAGE "QUARTER NOT FOUND!!!"
      ASK USER IF HE OR SHE WOULD LIKE TO TRY AGAIN
      IF mTRYAGAIN = "Y"
         SET mRETURN TO TRUE
      ELSE
         SET mRETURN TO FALSE
      ENDIF
   ENDIF
ENDDO
IF mFOUND = 1
   INITIALIZE THE MAXIMUM ROWS PRINTED PER PAGE
   STORE 0 TO WORKING STORAGE mTOTAL
   STORE .T. TO mFIRST
   OPEN COMPENSATION FILE
   POSITION POINTER AT THE TOP OF COMPENSATION FILE
   PRINT QUARTERLY SUMMARY HEADING
   DO WHILE NOT END OF FILE
      START PRINTING QUARTERLY SUMMARY DETAILS
      IF mFIRST
         LOCATE ALL RECORDS THAT FOR COMPENSATION DATE GREATER THAN EQUAL TO
         STARTING DATE AND COMPENSATION DATE LESS THAN EQUAL TO ENDING DATE
         SET mFIRST TO FALSE
      ELSE
         CONTINUE
         IF END OF FILE
            LOOP
         ENDIF
      ENDIF
      INCREASE mROW BY 1
      @mROW, 11 SAY EMPLID
      @mROW, 32 SAY COMPDATE
      @mROW, 54 SAY AMTGRANTED
      ACCUMULATE mTOTAL
   ENDDO
   @mROW + 2, 25 SAY "TOTAL AMOUNT THIS QUARTER"
   @mROW + 2, 54 SAY mTOTAL PICTURE "9999999.99"
ENDIF
```

The emphasis on indentation, use of delimiters, and the looping concept is not unique to Structured English. The quarterly invoice module is written here in a dBASE IV format to show how similar Structured English is to the actual program.

A tool that does essentially the same job as Structured English is pseudocode. PSEUDOCODE allows the designer to capture the important elements of the design rapidly. Unlike Structured English, pseudocode uses more formal notation and is geared more to database designers and professionals than to end-users. Some pseudocode notations approximate the outline of a final program so closely that they can be translated directly into program code. Because pseudocode is so detailed, there is less margin for error when it is translated into actual code.

Each designer has personal preferences in adopting one form of pseudocode over another. There is no standard pseudocode notation that is equivalent to a standard programming language. However, nearly all pseudocode notations have the following common characteristics:

1 Key words, such as IF-THEN-ELSE, CASE, SELECT, and UNTIL-DO are used to represent specific constructs.

2 Each construct has a delimiter similar to those used in Structured English. The two most common delimiters are ENDIF and ENDDO.

3 The nesting level of pseudocode commands is indicated by indentation at each nesting level.

4 The number of lines of pseudocode used to represent a process or a module is limited.

The basic notational procedure for pseudocode appears in Figure 13-6. For example, pseudocode used to describe the process for determining a customer's net worth might look like this:

```
module find net worth (cus.acct. file: net worth)
  /*find net dollar worth of customers who have
    checking numbers*/
  /*customer account file contains lists of all
    valid account numbers to be scanned*/
  /*net worth is the total balance of all
    customers' checking and savings accounts*/
  /*cus.acct. file is the number of customers*/
  repeat until customer acct number > cus. acct. file
    call retrieve checking(cust. account no: credit bal.)
    call retrieve savings(cust. account no: credit bal.)
    total dollar worth +:=(credit bal.+credit-bal.)
    cus. no. +:=1
  endrepeat
endmodule
```

In addition to module specification, pseudocode can also be applied to module maintenance. Pseudocode is actually ideal as a programming tool, because it gives the programmer a chance to try out ideas at any

```
Fixed indentation   ┌ IF . . . THEN
for each entry      │      IF . . . THEN
                    └   ┌       DO . . . WHILE
                        │
        Do-while loop   │
                        │
                        └       ENDO        ┐ Delimiters
                               ENDIF        │ to indicate
                          ENDIF             ┘ scope of control
```

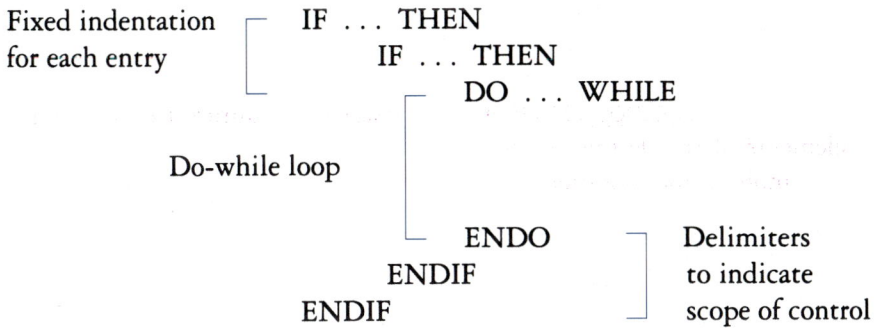

Figure 13–6 Basic notational procedure for pseudocode

level of detail, independent of any programming language. As a documentation tool, it can be included in the listing along with the code.

Decision Trees

Another tool that expresses program logic is the decision tree. A DECISION TREE is a graphic view or a model of the decision logic in a program. The values of a variable are determined and based on these values specific actions are taken. For example, let us suppose that an airline reservation system has three key options: new reservation, flight change, and cancellation. A narrative description of the decision logic might be

> When a reservation transaction is processed, each transaction is first validated. Invalid transactions are rejected with a proper error message. Valid reservations are processed, depending on whether they are new reservations, before a flight ticket is created and an invoice is generated with the amount of the fare. For flight change requests, the initial flight reservation is canceled and a new flight reservation is confirmed. When a reservation is canceled, the flight reservation is deleted and a refund check is issued.

Imagine how tedious it would be for a traveler or an airline agent to have to go through this narrative every time he or she made a flight inquiry. The alternative is to express the logic using a graphic tool such as a decision tree. Figure 13-7 shows the decision tree for the flight reservation system.

Decision trees can easily be converted into action diagrams or used directly as a step toward program coding. Figure 13-8 expresses the same logic in action diagram format.

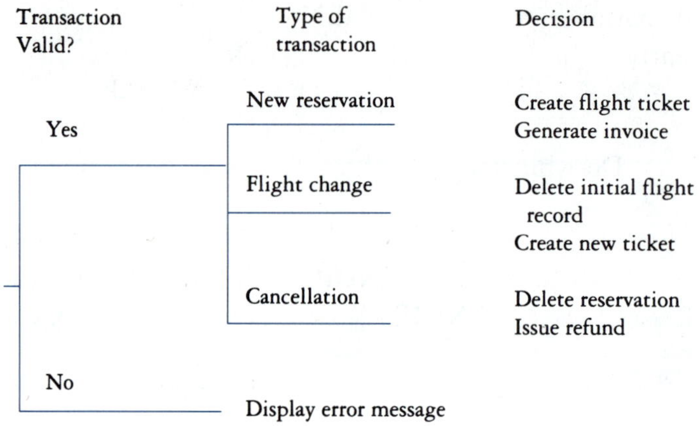

Figure 13–7 Decision tree for airline reservation system

```
IF VALID TRANSACTION
    IF NEW RESERVATION
       CREATE FLIGHT TICKET
       GENERATE INVOICE
    IF FLIGHT CHANGE REQUEST
       DELETE INITIAL FLIGHT RECORD
       CREATE NEW FLIGHT TICKET
    IF CANCELLATION
       DELETE FLIGHT RESERVATION
       ISSUE REFUND
    ELSE
       DISPLAY ERROR MESSAGE
```

Figure 13–8 Action diagram for airline reservation system

Decision trees are easy to read and understand when the number of conditions is small. They are seldom used, however, at a high level to show program control structure. They are best used to supplement other design tools.

SUMMARY

1 Prior to the actual coding of a database program, the logic of each module should be represented in a format amenable to coding. Structured English and pseudocode are recommended alternatives for expressing logical design.

2 Structured English is a language based on English vocabulary and a limited syntax, and is easy for the user to understand. Structured English should be hierarchically structured, and its structure should be similar to the program code that will implement the database.

3 When writing Structured English we must use concise statements and clearly stated action verbs, avoid using punctuation, capitalize key words and names of program blocks, and ensure that each instruction has a single starting point and a single ending point. End words such as ENDIF and EXIT should also be used to mark the end of an instruction.

4 Sequence constructs apply top-to-bottom ordering of subordinate descriptions in a logical program.

5 Condition constructs are based on IF-THEN-ELSE clauses.

6 Case constructs identify action to be taken for each possible, mutually exclusive set of conditions.

7 Repetition constructs are sets of operations that are repeated over and over again until a condition is met that terminates the repetition. Two types of repetition constructs are repeat-until and do-while.

8 The do-while construct executes the statements bracketed between the words DO-WHILE and ENDDO a fixed number of times or for as long as the statement in the DO-WHILE is a repeating IF.

9 Pseudocode allows the designer to capture the key elements of the design rapidly. Some pseudocode notations approximate the outline of a final program so closely that they can be translated directly into code.

10 A decision tree is a graphic view of the logic of a program. It makes the layout or flow of the logic that still has to be coded easier to follow than either Structured English or pseudocode does.

KEY WORDS

Case construct
Condition construct
Decision tree
Do-while construct
Loop counter
Pseudocode
Repeat-until construct
Repetition construct
Sequence construct
Structured English

REVIEW QUESTIONS

1 Explain the difference between the following pairs:

a. do-while and repeat-until
b. Structured English and pseudocode
c. Structured English and decision trees

2 Why are tools important to express logic? That is, why wouldn't a database developer proceed into coding without using tools?

3 "English narrative that describes a program or other specifications is generally tedious to read and understand." Do you agree? Discuss.

4 Elaborate on the key attributes of Structured English. Why are they so important?

5 What makes up the vocabulary of Structured English? Explain each briefly.

6 Distinguish between the following pairs:
   a. condition and sequence constructs
   b. case and sequence constructs
   c. condition and repetition constructs

7 Give an example illustrating the difference between the repeat-until and do-while constructs.

8 Discuss the rules that should be followed in writing Structured English. Which rule do you consider the most important? Why?

9 Explain the key characteristics of pseudocode notations. Is there any characteristic that might be more critical than others? Why?

10 Under what conditions would a designer would use a decision tree over other tools? Explain.

APPLICATION PROBLEMS

1 An international airline initiated a frequent-traveler program designed to encourage passengers to fly regularly and earn free tickets based on the number of miles flown. The airline policy is specified as follows:

> Passengers who fly more than 100,000 miles per calendar year and, in addition, pay cash for tickets or have been flying the airline regularly for more than five years are to receive a free round-trip ticket to anywhere in the world. Passengers who fly less than 100,000 miles per calendar year and have been flying the airline regularly for more than five years also get a free round-trip ticket to anywhere in the world.

   a. Draw a decision tree based on the statement.
   b. Write the Structured English version of the statement.

2 A Virginia-based mail-order house specializes in microcomputers and supplies for various microcomputer models. It offers discounts based on the number of units ordered. When an order is received, an invoice is generated that includes the quantity, unit cost, discount, and shipping and handling charges. The invoice is decomposed into the hierarchy shown in Figure 13-9.

An Invoice_total is computed on each line-item. All line-item totals are then added to get an invoice total. A line-item is extended by multiplying

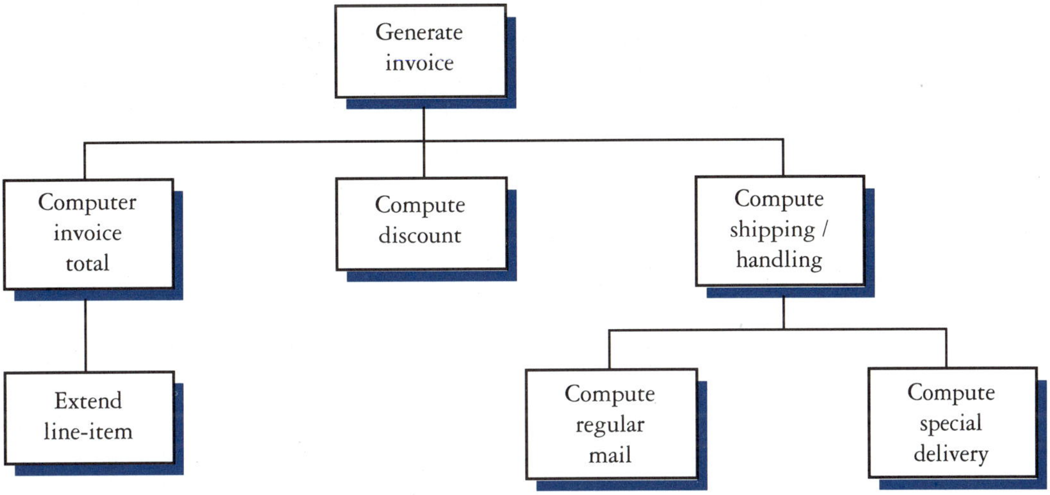

Figure 13–9 Computer supply house invoice system

quantity by unit cost. The product is the line-item total. The discount is computed as follows:

```
If Invoice-total is $3,000 or over, discount is 20
   percent
If Invoice-total is between $2,000 and $2,999, discount
   is 10 percent
If Invoice-total is between $1,000 and $1,999, discount
   is 5 percent
If Invoice-total is under $1,000, no discount allowed
```

Shipping and handling charges depend on whether the item is to go by air or freight. If the order specifies air, the charges are computed as follows:

```
If weight is under 35 pounds, shipping/handling rate is
   $30
If weight is 35 to 55 pounds, shipping/handling rate is
   $45
If weight is over 55 pounds, multiply excess (over 55) by
   $2 and add $45 to get shipping/handling rate
```

If the order specifies freight, each pound of weight is multiplied by $1.85 to get the rate.

a. Develop a decision tree.

b. Represent the information in Structured English.

3 Use the information you have gathered to date on Island Jumpers, Inc. (IJI) and do the following:

a. Write the necessary commands in Structured English to operationalize any of the options in the main menu.

b. Draw a decision table to represent these activities.

C H A P T

Programming the Database

E R 1 4

Code Generators Need Better CASE Relations

AT A GLANCE

Code Generators Need Better CASE Relations

In the world of packaged software, first there were code generators, then there were CASE tools. Developers have come to associate the use of CASE tools with development of structured code. However, the links between the CASE tools and the generators that predated them have been difficult to establish.

This furthering of the principles of CASE and the automation of the software development process is a lofty goal. Programmers generate code directly from one set of design specifications for the desired target platform or platforms. That is the promise of IBM's AD/Cycle, Digital Equipment Corporation's Cohesion, and other comprehensive software development blueprints.

To attain this promise, not only do the CASE tools need to talk to the code generators, but the CASE tools should really be talking to each other as well. Today, developers are employing at least two approaches to the use of CASE tools.

One philosophy is a CASE environment that consists mainly of integrated tools from a single vendor—tools that are built specifically to fit together and that represent different aspects of a single creative idea. Another CASE environment, one that is often considered more prudent, is a mix-and-match or component approach to CASE tool selection.

Both philosophies carry certain problems . . . . While component CASE tools often provide solid solutions to specific problems, developing an application isn't as simple as assembling individual parts. So, the burden of integrating a CASE solution falls on users.

On the other hand, integrated CASE promised to eliminate the need for developers to patch a jumble of unrelated tools into a workable system.

IBM's Solution

IBM, as evidenced by its AD/Cycle blueprint for application development, is a major proponent of the component CASE environment. IBM's plan is to couple high-powered upper-CASE tools with code generators that write efficient, target-specific programs. The idea is to define the strategic interests of a business and then analyze and design applications that will provide a definite competitive edge in that business.

But for those interested in using the upper-CASE tools of IBM's AD/Cycle partners right now, IBM provides an entry into those products with a facility called External Source Format (ESF). The lower level of AD/Cycle is completed with IBM's own code generator, Cross System Product (CSP), as well as those of IBM's AD/Cycle partners Synon, Inc., Larkspur, California, and Easel Corporation, Burlington, Massachusetts.

Focus on Business Needs

One vision for the typical CASE user is for the customer to start by using CSP to develop an application that is built and deployed for a particular business problem. The customer can grow by adding business partners' tools and evolve into more extended users of AD/Cycle features.

The biggest issue for developers is to ensure that people are developing the right application systems in order to put the business ahead. If projects don't handle strategic business needs, then even a 400-percent improvement in productivity is worthless.

Andersen's Generator

Andersen Consulting, of Chicago-based Arthur Andersen & Co., offers an integrated set of development aids with its foundation product, Install/1 code generator. With this package, there is total portability between all platforms of like architectures. The ultimate goal is to port up and down platforms: server between servers and client between clients.

The Department of Transportation, State of North Carolina, used Install/1 to implement a federally mandated commercial driver's license system. Despite the short lead time of one year, the system was designed, coded, and implemented by September 4, 1990, on time and with no major problems.

Along with its powerful code generator features, Install/1 enables the customer to do the remodeling necessary to make good use of cooperative processing without resorting to cosmetic "frontware" changes. Customers do not have to care who wins the client/server battle over who will dominate the client's desk. Andersen's portability will extend over all.

People Are More Important Than Tools

Today, customers have a large selection of code generators from which to choose. Factors such as operating platform, choice of repository, and choice of upper-CASE tools can limit the selection. But in the end, the major criteria for selection are: Will it be used and used properly? Will the programmers and analysts in an information systems department turn to a code generator or to any CASE tool for help in creating and maintaining a system?

This final point is well stated by Aetna Life's John Lee. He said, "A CASE tool will be successful if a person in the shop champions the tools, develops the clear strategy for the product, and provides good support for the product. None of this really has anything to do with the particular tool, it has to do with people."

Excerpted from Hanna, Alice, "Code generators need better CASE relations." Reprinted with permission of Software Magazine, *August 1991, Sentry Publishing Co., Inc., 1900 West Park Drive, Westborough, MA 01581, USA.*

AT A GLANCE

The logic expressed in Structured English must eventually be translated into a language acceptable to a specific DBMS. Good programming habits such as conceptualizing the problem and mapping out the logic to be programmed will make this task easier.

Using dBASE IV as an example of a database management system, we can examine the actual building of an application program. This includes creating a program, developing input and output screens, programming input and output, programming the flow of control, and using multiple databases.

The final phase of programming is program testing and debugging. Programmers must be careful to give themselves adequate time to detect and correct clerical and logical errors. Although there are many ways to test and debug a program, a modular top-down approach is highly recommended. The final tests, called alpha and beta tests, should culminate in user acceptance testing. Good documentation of all phases of programming will ensure that later changes or system updates run smoothly.

By the end of this chapter, you should be able to

- create a basic program;
- create basic screen input and output formats;
- use flow-of-control commands;
- apply the basic multiple database commands; and
- appreciate good programming habits.

INTRODUCTION

In the previous chapter, we illustrated the use of Structured English as a tool for expressing program logic. The next step in database application development is to program the logic in a language acceptable to a specific DBMS. The relational DBMS that we have chosen is dBASE IV, a popular, menu-driven package for the microcomputer. dBASE IV is easy to program and use, and can handle several databases at the same time. In this chapter, we shall discuss programming fundamentals. Specifically, you will learn how to program input, output, and flow of control, and how to use multiple databases.

Programming is an art. No two programs are exactly the same, even those that produce near-identical results. Whether a program is good or bad depends on how well it was thought through and written. The best programs are those written by programmers with good habits—they conceptualize the problem, map out the logic, and *then* begin to do the programming. The commands used in this chapter are dBASE commands.

CREATING A PROGRAM

The first thing to do in programming is to tell the system that you are ready to create a program. So, at the dot prompt, you enter the command

```
CREATE PRGM1
```

"PRGM1" is an arbitrary name that identifies the program for later use or modification. You can use any name you want. This command simply tells the DBMS that you wish to create a program called "PRGM1.PRG." Once you enter this command, the screen clears and the word processor gets ready to store the program in a file called "PRGM1.PRG."

Now you are ready to write the program. After typing each command, enter it by pressing the RETURN or ENTER key. When you have finished writing the program, tell the system to save it by pressing the Ctrl and End keys. If you do not want to save the program, press the Esc (escape) key and respond Y (yes) to the prompt.

To run the program, enter the command

```
DO PRGM1
```

An important step in programming is to give the user easy control of where input, output, or database information is displayed on the screen. User interface is extremely important. The main function is to make using a program easy. Screen forms give the user a way to control program functions.

Before we can control input or output information on the screen, we must be familiar with the screen grid, which is a conceptual view of rows and columns. The SCREEN GRID is an evenly spaced set of horizontal and vertical lines on the VDT screen. (See Figure 14-1.) The intersection of a specific column and row created by these lines is called a COORDINATE. A microcomputer monitor generally has 25 rows and 80 columns, for a total of 2000 coordinates. Each coordinate can be specified to display information. To display a printable character, all you have to do in dBASE IV is specify the character's location. To specify a coordinate, type the row number, a comma, and the column number.

Four key commands control screen input and output:

1 ACCEPT
2 INPUT
3 WAIT
4 @ commands

The first three commands are used for interactive programming or when the user is to respond to an on-line prompt. The @ commands position input and output of information and allow the user to enter information in a blank space.

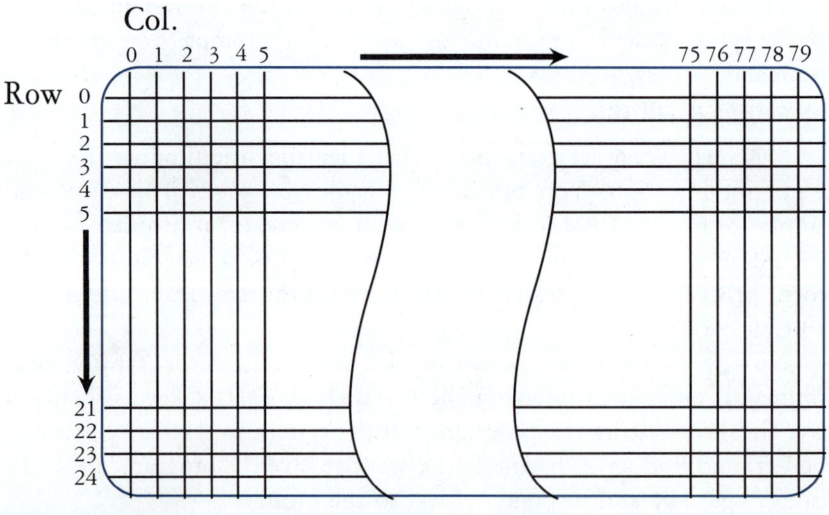

Figure 14-1 Screen layout coordinates

The ACCEPT Command

The ACCEPT command stores an entry as a character variable. For example, if the screen prompt is to ask a user for the name of a firm, wait for a response, and then accept the response, the ACCEPT command would be

```
ACCEPT "Please enter a firm name" TO MFIRM
```

The message in quotes would appear on the screen, and the system would wait for the user's response. When the user enters the response, the system would accept it and place it in a memory variable called MFIRM. A MEMORY VARIABLE is a memory space set aside for specific data.

The INPUT Command

The INPUT command works like the ACCEPT command, except that it stores an entry as either a character or a numeric variable. For example, the command

```
INPUT "Please enter a firm name and phone number" TO MFIRM
```

asks the user for both characters and numbers. The type of memory variable created depends on the information entered by the user. If the entry is "ABCD," for example, the memory variable is automatically character type. The same reasoning applies to numeric data. The ACCEPT and INPUT commands help in retrieving low-volume input from the user during the execution of a program. This is what makes the screen interactive and user friendly.

The WAIT Command

The WAIT command appears at the end of a file to allow the user to view the records selected for display by the program. Without this command, the screen would be cleared immediately by the next command, giving the user no chance to read the information on the screen. In the set of commands

```
ACCEPT "Please enter a firm name" TO MFIRM
USE EMPREC
DISPLAY EMPNO, NAME, SALARY
WAIT
```

the ACCEPT command displays the message in quotes; the USE command opens a file named EMPREC and sets the pointer to the first record; the DISPLAY command asks the database to display employee number, name, and salary of that record; and the WAIT command tells the system to hold the information on the screen until the user touches any key to continue with the program.

The @ COMMANDS allow for precise location of specific input and output information on the screen. The @ commands are

- @ x,y SAY "expression"
- @ x,y GET memvar
- @ x,y SAY "expression" GET memvar

Two commands used with @ commands are STORE TO MEMVAR and READ.

@ x,y SAY "expression" The @...SAY COMMAND asks for row and column coordinates (*x,y*) after the @ command; the information to be displayed (expression) follows SAY. The *x* variable is the row number, counting down from the top of the screen; the *y* variable is the column number, counting right from the left side of the screen.

To illustrate, suppose we want to prompt the user for a new balance. To make the message "NEW BALANCE" appear on line 10 and column 12, we enter the command

```
@ 10,12 SAY "NEW BALANCE"
```

The resulting display is shown in Figure 14-2.

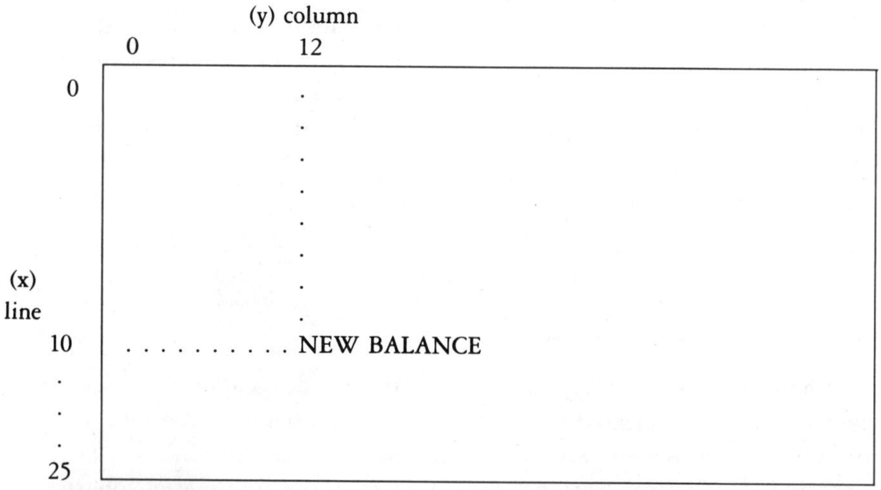

Figure **14-2** Screen display of command @ 10,12 SAY "NEW BALANCE"

@ x,y GET memvar Each @ X,Y GET MEMVAR command displays a blank for user input at the screen location indicated by the variables (*x,y*). The @ GET command works only when the memory variables (memvar) have been previously initialized. The command prompts the user for input. For example,

```
@ 10,12 GET AMT
```

causes the prompt "AMT" to appear at coordinates 10,12.

The READ command The READ command stores screen input into a memory variable. It is used in a program file when a GET form of the @

command is used. dBASE IV can execute many @ commands, but needs only one READ command to get all the variables requested in such commands. For example, suppose we want the user to input his or her full name. First, we initialize the three variables in the program as follows:

```
mfirst= SPACE(12)
minitial= SPACE(2)
mlast= SPACE(15)
```

Next we write the screen commands:

```
CLEAR
@5,1 SAY "ENTER FIRST NAME:"
@5,27 GET mfirst
@8,1 SAY "ENTER MIDDLE INITIAL:"
@8,27 GET minitial
@11,1 SAY "ENTER LAST NAME:"
@11,27 GET mlast
READ
RESPONSE
          ENTER FIRST NAME:
          ENTER MIDDLE INITIAL:
          ENTER LAST NAME:
```

The first command clears the screen. The second command displays "ENTER FIRST NAME:" beginning at row 5 and column 1. The first GET command tells the system to place the memory variable mfirst at row 5 and column 27. When the user has entered the last variable, the READ command stores all the screen input in the designated memory variables.

Note the difference between the GET and the READ commands. The GET command by itself only gets the memory variable to the screen. The READ command puts the value into the memory variable, which is a temporary storage place that exists only during the program execution. If the GET command is used without the READ command, the system will bring the memory variable content to the screen but won't hold it at a specific location on the screen and store it in the memory variable. Instead, it will go ahead and execute the next program instruction.

The STORE TO memvar command The STORE TO MEMVAR command is used to put user input into a memory variable. For example, the command

```
STORE COUNTER+1 TO COUNTER
```

means "add 1 to COUNTER," which would set up the counter as a numeric memory variable. A counter is a space in memory reserved to accumulate numeric values.

Another function of the STORE command is to keep a running total of values, such as

```
STORE TOTSALARY+SALARY TO TOTSALARY
```

The STORE command can also reserve space for later input. For example, the command

```
STORE '   ' TO memvar
```

specifies "memvar" as the name of the memory variable and the number of characters that the variable can hold. In this example, the number of characters is the spaces between the quotes. Thus the commands

```
CLEAR
@ 10,12 SAY "NEW BALANCE"
STORE '    ' TO AMT
@ 10,17 GET AMT
READ
```

cause the amount to be read and displayed at the intersection of column 10 and row 17 on the screen.

PROGRAMMING INPUT AND OUTPUT

Special commands are also needed to input information from a database instead of a user and to output information to a printer instead of to the screen. Three such commands are used with the @ command.

The EJECT Command

The EJECT command causes the paper on the printer to move to the top of the next page and resets the *x,y* positions to zero.

The SET FORMAT TO PRINT Command

The SET FORMAT TO PRINT command sends the results of the @ command to the printer and then resets control to the screen display. This makes it possible to format information on the screen to any location. For example, the commands used to print the balance of an account on line 10 at column 15 would be

```
SET FORMAT TO PRINT
EJECT
@ 10,15 SAY BALANCE
```

The balance of the account would then be printed on line 10 and column 15.

The STORE Command

Once again, the STORE command is useful. The STORE command can specify a value for a memory variable, which can then be used as a part of an @ command. For example, suppose we want to use a preprinted invoice on which a customer's balance must be printed in row 10 and columns 15 through 20. We could type in the *x,y* values every time the balance is printed. But a better way would be to store the values to variables and then use them as *x,y* variables:

```
STORE 10 TO AX
STORE 15 TO BY
@ AX,BY SAY BALANCE
```

Now the *x* and *y* coordinates are variable values which (like row and column numbers) can be used in computations. The *y* values can be incremented for printouts with evenly spaced columns. The *x* values can be incremented to print lines at any spacing.

To illustrate this feature, let us print all the balances for the file called LOAN, using double spacing and a heading. Assuming that the *x* variable is represented by ROW as the memory variable, we use the program commands shown in Table 14-1, which will result in the screen display shown in Figure 14-3.

	Command	*Function*
1.	@ 1,4 SAY "LOAN BALANCE"	Creates the heading for the report
2.	STORE 3 TO ROW	Begins printing balances on row 3, column 6
3.	@ ROW,6 SAY BALANCE	
4.	SKIP	Skips to next record in the file
5.	STORE ROW + 2 TO ROW	Provides double spacing
6.	@ ROW,6 SAY BALANCE	Prints the next balance
7.	SET PRINT TO SCREEN	Displays print on screen and ends the program file
8.	RETURN	

Table 14-1 Commands for printing Loan balance

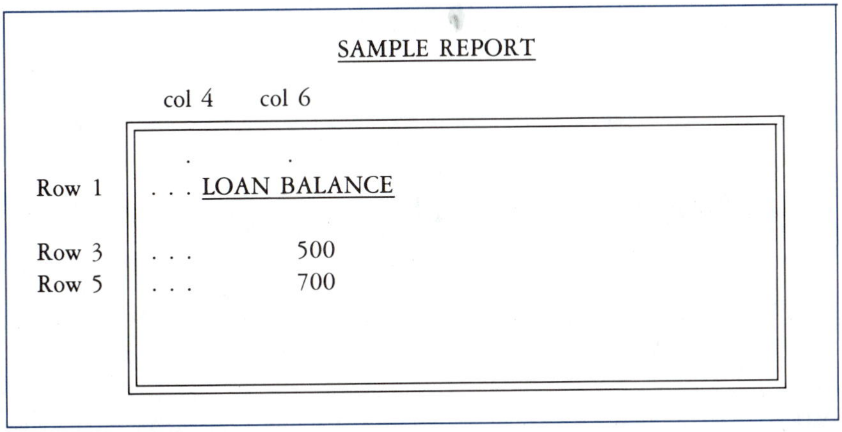

Figure 14-3 Results of commands listed in Table 14-1

Programming input and output emphasized special commands for interactive programming; that is, communicating with the user from a prewritten program. Now we need to control the flow of a program.

There are three parts to a flow-of-control decision:

1 The action to be taken, or **what to do**
2 The time **when** the action should be taken
3 The **next** step to be taken after the action

With these parts, we use three command structures for controlling execution flow (see Table 14-2).

Command Structure	*Function*
IF...ENDIF	Controls a conditional choice
DO CASE...ENDCASE	Controls a multiple-choice option
DOWHILE...ENDDO	Controls a request to repeat a specific action

Table 14-2 Command structures for controlling execution flow

The IF...ENDIF Command Structure

The IF...ENDIF command structure handles a decision between two alternative actions. The action can be a single command or a group of command statements. The IF...ENDIF syntax appears in Table 14-3.

Command		*Function*
IF condition	means	when to take a specific action
. action(s)	means	what specific steps to take
.		
.		
ENDIF	means	end of the IF statement and go on to the following statements

Table 14-3 The IF...ENDIF syntax

For example,

```
IF BALANCE < 1000
   @ 5,10 SAY "LOAN IS LOW-RISK"
ENDIF
```

instructs the program to check the account balance and, if the balance is less than $1000, to display the message "LOAN IS LOW-RISK" on the screen.

The variable in the IF expression can be the name of a field, such as BALANCE, a memory variable, or a specific value entered by the user. Each IF construction must have a corresponding closing command, ENDIF.

A derivation of the IF...ENDIF statement is the IF...ELSE...ENDIF. This statement makes the program choose between two possibilities. That is, if *x* is true, do *y*; if it is not (else), do *z*. Each IF...ENDIF construction may have only one ELSE condition, which must appear on a separate line.

The action in both the IF and ELSE statements can be single or multiple line commands. For example, in

```
IF BALANCE < 1000
   @ 5,10 SAY "LOAN IS LOW-RISK"
   IF BALANCE < 500
      @ 5,10 SAY "LOAN IS VERY LOW-RISK"
   ENDIF
ELSE
      @ 5,10 SAY "INSURE LOAN"
ENDIF
```

multiple conditions are handled by nesting one IF statement within another. The dBASE IV program tests the first condition, then the second. If the balance is found to be less than $1000, the system displays a message "LOAN IS LOW-RISK." The nested IF statement tests to see whether the balance is less than $500. If so, the message displayed is "LOAN IS VERY LOW-RISK." This ends the testing of the two IF statements. The ELSE rule is activated when this balance is $1000 or more. If so, the system displays the message "INSURE LOAN."

The DO CASE...ENDCASE Command Structure

Some situations involve more alternative actions than can be handled efficiently by the IF command. These multiple-choice decisions use the DO CASE...ENDCASE command structure. The general syntax for DO CASE is

```
DO CASE
   CASE (first condition)
        program command(s)
   CASE (second condition)
        program command(s)
        .
        .
        .
   OTHERWISE
        last chance command(s)
ENDCASE
```

A CASE command specifies a condition and the corresponding action to be taken if the condition is met. The last action (following OTHERWISE) is executed if none of the preceding conditions are met. Because DO CASE tells the program that a number of possibilities follow, a DO CASE can contain only one command. Each possibility appears on a separate line after the word CASE. Each CASE sequence must end with an ENDCASE line.

For example, suppose we want to create a menu with the options

```
BILLING INFORMATION OPTIONS:
  1.   ADD NEW RECORD
  2.   EDIT RECORD
  3.   PRINT REPORT

 PLEASE SELECT ONE OPTION:__
```

First, we use the @ x,y SAY commands to display the menu:

```
@ 10,8 SAY "BILLING INFORMATION OPTIONS"
@ 14,12 SAY "1.  ADD NEW RECORD"
@ 16,12 SAY "2.  EDIT RECORD"
@ 18,12 SAY "3.  PRINT REPORT"
```

To get the user's choice and proper response, we use the following commands:

```
STORE 0 TO CHOICE
@ 20,8 SAY "PLEASE SELECT ONE OPTION:" GET CHOICE
READ
```

The STORE command creates a memory variable CHOICE, to be used for storing the user's input. Following these commands, we write the DO CASE commands (MSG is a memory variable that stores a message):

```
DO CASE
  CASE CHOICE = 1
    STORE "ADD NEW RECORD" TO MSG
  CASE CHOICE = 2
    STORE "EDIT RECORD" TO MSG
  CASE CHOICE = 3
    STORE "PRINT REPORT" TO MSG
  OTHERWISE
    STORE "INVALID CHOICE.  TRY AGAIN" TO MSG
ENDCASE
@ 24,10 SAY MSG
```

The response to these commands is shown in Figure 14-4.

Both DO CASE and IF...ENDIF commands accomplish the same thing, but DO CASE determines a number of possible conditions, while IF...ENDIF governs only one or two possible conditions.

```
               12
              .
              .
              .
              .
              .
              .
10  . . . . . . BILLING INFORMATION OPTIONS:
              .
              .
              .
                   1.  ADD NEW RECORD

                   2.  EDIT RECORD

                   3.  PRINT REPORT

        PLEASE SELECT ONE OPTION:_
```

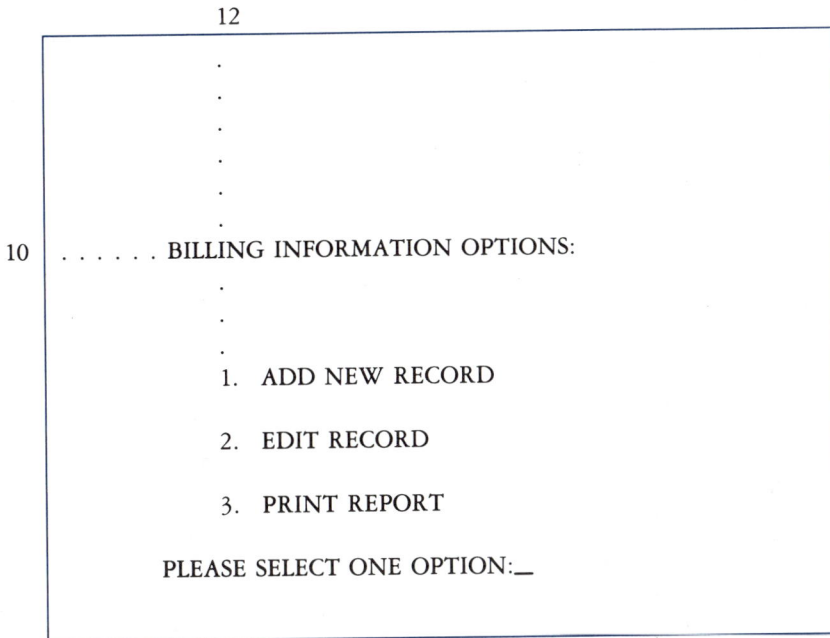

Figure 14-4 Menu development

The DO WHILE...ENDDO Command Structure

The third form of flow of control deals with looping or repetition of commands. In dBASE IV, one or many statements may be repeated any number of times. The structure for manipulating this repetitive routine is the DO WHILE...ENDDO command, which makes the program loop for as long as the condition specified in the DO WHILE command tests as true. The general format for DO WHILE is

```
DO WHILE condition
   program command(s)
ENDDO
```

where DO WHILE specifies when the action should be taken, followed by the action(s) themselves, and finishing with the action that comes next, ENDDO. We need to be careful of the so-called infinite loop. If we do not set a limit on the number of times a condition can be met, the loop will never allow the program to end. That is why we mark the end of every DO WHILE loop with an ENDDO command.

To illustrate the DO WHILE clause, let us take an earlier example:

```
@ 1,4 SAY "LOAN BALANCE"
STORE 3 TO ROW
@ ROW,6 SAY BALANCE
SKIP
```

Here a number of commands have to be repeated for each record in order to complete the printout. We can easily use the DO WHILE command to repeat the @ x,y SAY; SKIP; and STORE commands as follows:

```
@ 1,4 SAY "LOAN BALANCE"
STORE 3 TO ROW
DO WHILE ROW < 7
  @ ROW,6 SAY "BALANCE"
  SKIP
  STORE ROW+1 TO ROW
ENDDO
```

Each time ROW (the counter) goes through the loop, its value is incremented by one, shown by the statement "STORE ROW + 1 TO ROW." The loop is terminated when ROW is less than 7.

In another example, a program must check the credit status field A1 only if the value of BALANCE exceeds $500. The program displays the balance for each record that meets the two IF conditions. The first IF statement is for BALANCE over $500. Only when the statement is true is the second IF statement, "A1 = .F.," executed:

```
STORE 3 TO ROW
@ 1,4 SAY "LOAN BALANCE"
DO WHILE ROW < 7
  IF BALANCE > 500
    IF A1=.F.
      @ ROW,6 SAY BALANCE
    ENDIF
  ENDIF
  STORE ROW+1 TO ROW
ENDDO
```

Notice the difference between DO WHILE...ENDDO and IF...ENDIF. DO WHILE...ENDDO forces the software to continue repeating the loop while the condition is true. In contrast, IF...ENDIF asks the software to decide whether a specific condition is true only once and to perform the commands tagged to the IF...ENDIF construction only once. In summary, there are three key command structures for controlling the flow of execution in a dBASE IV program:

1 The IF...ENDIF and IF...ELSE...ENDIF statements allow basic conditional choices of action in a program.

2 The DO CASE...ENDCASE statement controls execution flow among multiple choices of action.

3 The DO WHILE...ENDDO statement controls looping for repetition of commands.

Any command structure can be nested within the program command of another command structure. In looping, it is important to check the condition specified by the loop so that the program is prevented from making an infinite loop.

Many applications require the use of more than one database at a time. The main commands that control multiple databases are SELECT, JOIN, and UPDATE. The term "database" is used instead of "file" because it is the term used in dBASE IV. The two terms have essentially the same meaning.

The SELECT Command

The SELECT command allows the user to work with information in two or more databases at the same time. First let us set up two databases to illustrate the multiple database commands. (See Table 14-4.) The SELECT command tells dBASE IV which database has the information needed.

Suppose we want to find out which customers have a loan balance over $1000, using the databases in Table 14-4. One approach we could take would be to open the LOAN database and use the DISPLAY command to show balances > $1000:

Command	Meaning
SELECT 1	Label loan file as active file.
USE LOAN	Open the loan file.
DISPLAY NAME FOR BALANCE>1000	Display the first record with balance over $1000.

```
RESPONSE   135  Mary Roth
```

THE LOAN DATABASE

LOAN_NUM	NAME	LOAN	PREMIUM	INTEREST	BALANCE
134	Jim Adams	1000	18	10	802
135	Mary Roth	1550	27	9	1010
136	Paul Licker	900	17	11	866
137	Roger Bennet	3000	56	9	2944

THE NAMADD DATABASE

LOAN_NUM	NAME	CITY	STATE	ZIPCODE
134	Jim Adams	Rochester	NY	13601
135	Mary Roth	Chicago	IL	60611
136	Paul Licker	Hanover	NH	03755
137	Roger Bennet	Miami	FL	33143

Table 14-4 The loan and name-address databases

"SELECT 1" tells the program we want to open a file; "USE LOAN" names the file. The DISPLAY command tells it to display the first record it comes to with a loan balance of $1000 or over. dBASE IV can work with up to ten files simultaneously in ten different work areas. This means that dBASE IV will maintain separate pointers for the current record in each of the work areas.

We can now set up relationships between two databases at a time. For example, if we are dealing with four inventory (INVEN) databases, we can set a relation on record numbers between the active database INVEN1 and the linked database INVEN2, using the following commands:

```
SELECT 1
SET RELATION TO RECNO( ) INTO INVEN2
```

The SELECT 1 command tells dBASE IV that INVEN1 will be the active database and that all commands should be processed against this database unless another SELECT command is given. The second command sets a relation on the record-number field between the active database INVEN1 and the linked database INVEN2. This means that if the record pointer in INVEN1 is moved to record number 7, the record number in the INVEN2 database will also move to record number 7. This setup establishes a one-to-one relationship between the two databases.

To link three databases, we use the commands

```
SELECT 1
SET RELATION TO RECNO ( ) INTO INVEN2
SELECT 2
SET RELATION TO RECNO ( ) INTO INVEN3
SELECT 1
```

The last selection is added to designate INVEN1 as the primary database for the linked arrangement. With this setup, we can move any record in INVEN1 and display or modify the record. When we enter "SELECT 2," dBASE IV automatically transfers control to the same record in the linked database INVEN2, and we can display or modify that record. The command for listing the data from INVEN1 and INVEN2 is

```
LIST PARTNO,INVEN1->ONHAND,INVEN2->ONORDER
```

which will produce the response shown in Table 14-5.

Record #	PARTNO	INVEN1->ONHAND	INVEN2->ONORDER
1	P1	50	50
2	P2	60	70
3	P3	70	80
4	P4	80	80

Table 14-5 Linked-file list response

When there is no more need to maintain a linked relationship, we close the files using the command

```
CLOSE ALL
```

Without this command, the linked databases cannot be used individually, since they remain open.

The JOIN Command

Another way of dealing with multiple databases is the JOIN command. The JOIN command merges data from one database with data from another, based on specific selection criteria, thereby creating a third database. Both databases have to be kept open at the same time.

Suppose, for example, we want to join the contents of the LOAN database in Table 14-4 with the contents of the NAMADD database in Table 14-4 to produce a third database called NOTICE.This requires pulling information from both databases and placing it in a separate database. We designate the LOAN database as the active database and NAMADD as the nonactive database. The commands that identify the databases are

Command	Function
SELECT 1	Label LOAN database as active (primary) database.
USE LOAN	Open the LOAN database.
SELECT 2	Label the NAMADD file as nonactive database.
USE NAMADD	Open the name and address database.
SELECT 1	Return dBASE to the active database.

The command could be also be entered in reverse order:

```
SELECT 2
USE NAMADD
SELECT 1
USE LOAN
```

Joining databases requires that they have a common field. In the case of our LOAN and NAMADD databases, "NAME" is a field common to both. To pull the contents of the two databases together, we use the JOIN command

```
JOIN WITH NAMADD TO NOTICE FOR NAME=NAMADD->NAME
```

This command produces a third database, called NOTICE. We have specified that the only condition for joining the two databases is that the "NAME" from the active (LOAN) database must match the "NAME" from the nonactive (NAMADD) database. The phrase "NAMADD->NAME" means the name from the NAMADD database. The JOIN command procedure is straightforward. The program goes to the first record in the LOAN database and compares it to each of the records in the NAMADD database. If it finds a match based on the selection criteria, it produces the output record in the third database. The program then picks up the second record in the LOAN database and repeats the matching process with each of the records in the NAMADD database, based on the same selection criteria. Each time it finds a match, the program produces an output record in the third file until it has exhausted the LOAN database.

The JOIN command can specify the sequence in which fields from two databases should be stored. For example, the JOIN command

```
JOIN WITH NAMADD TO NOTICE FOR NAME=NAMADD->NAME FIELDS
    LOAN_NUM,NAME,NAMADD->CITY,LOAN,BALANCE
```

is all on one line and instructs the program to place the fields in the following sequence:

```
LOAN_NUM   NAME   CITY   LOAN   BALANCE
```

The resulting NOTICE database will look like Table 14-6.

LOAN_NUM	NAME	CITY	LOAN	BALANCE
134	Jim Adams	Rochester	1000	802
135	Mary Roth	Chicago	1550	1010
136	Paul Licker	Hanover	900	866
137	Roger Bennet	Miami	3000	2944

Table 14-6 NOTICE database created by joined databases

The UPDATE Command

Sometimes we need to update a database rather than produce a new one. The UPDATE command makes changes to existing records in a file. To illustrate, assume we have two databases, CUS_ACCT and ORDER, shown in Table 14-7, and we want to update the quantity field in CUS_ACCT by adding (not replacing) from the ORDER database. We use the UPDATE command sequence

```
USE ORDER
LIST
```

which produces the response

```
1    ADAMS    4
2    BAIRD   20
```

We then enter

```
USE CUS_ACCT
UPDATE FROM ORDER ON NAME ADD QTY
LIST
```

to get the response

```
1    ADAM    54     50
2    WILEY    5     25
3    BAIRD   54    170
4    KURTZ   67    180
```

CUS_ACCT				ORDER		
CUS_NUM	NAME	QTY	PRICE	CUS_NUM	NAME	QTY
1	ADAMS	10	50	1	ADAMS	4
2	WILEY	5	25	3	BAIRD	20
3	BAIRD	34	170			
4	KURTZ	67	185			

Table 14-7 Customer account and order databases

The ADD clause in the UPDATE command causes the value in ORDER "QTY" to be added to the value in the CUS_ACCT "QTY" field. This updates the CUS_ACCT "QTY" field.

Now suppose we wish to update the MASTER database shown in Table 14-8 by replacing the ONHAND field of the MASTER record with the sum of the existing ONHAND units in the MASTER and TRANSACTION databases. We also want to replace the COST data in the MASTER database with that of the TRANSACTION database. First, we set up work areas 1 and 2 for the MASTER and TRANSACTION databases as follows:

```
SELECT 2
USE TRANSACTION
SELECT 1
USE MASTER
```

MASTER				TRANSACTION			
PART_NUM	PART	ONHAND	COST	PART_NUM	PART	ONHAND	COST
10	WRENCH	200	15.00	11	CHISEL	20	3.50
11	CHISEL	75	3.00				
12	HAMMER	62	8.00				

Table 14-8 Master and transaction databases

Next we enter the UPDATE command

```
UPDATE ON PART_NUM FROM TRANS
  REPLACE ONHAND WITH ONHAND+TRANS->ONHAND,COST WITH
    TRANS->COST
```

Note the commas separating the two variables. The result of the UPDATE command is

```
              MASTER
PART_NUM   PART    ONHAND   COST
    10     WRENCH     200   15.00
    11     CHISEL      95    3.50
    12     HAMMER      62    8.00
```

To reduce the existing ONHAND amount by the amount shown in the TRANSACTION record, we would write the command

```
REPLACE ONHAND WITH ONHAND-TRANS->ONHAND,COST WITH TRANS->COST
```

Most, if not all, programs use combinations of all these commands. To illustrate how the various commands combine to form a usable program, let us return to the worker's compensation system (WCS) example used in Chapter 12. The main project menu for WCS consists of the options

1 Query
2 Add
3 Edit
4 Invoice
5 Quarterly invoice
6 Return to dot prompt (exit)

The "Query" option, in turn, leads to the submenu shown in Figure 14-5.

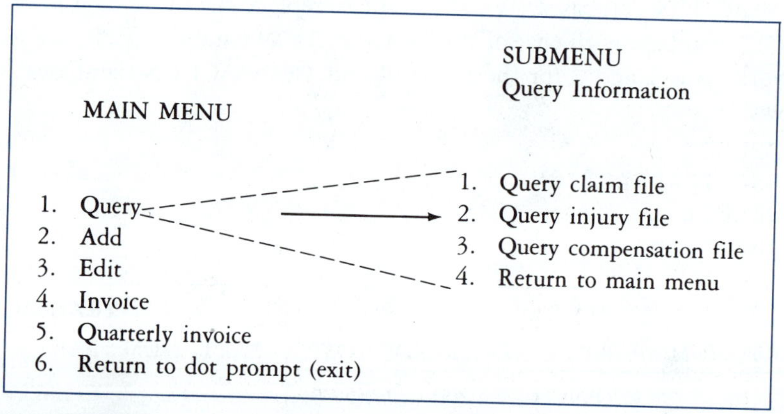

Figure 14-5 "Query" option menu and submenu

Let us choose option 1: "Query claim file." The program for option 1 allows the user to query the file by requesting social security number, claim date, compensation amount requested, workdays lost because of injury, or claim type (major or minor), or to exit to the main menu. The program module for this option is shown in Figure 14-6. The program modules for the remaining main menu options are presented in Figures 14-7 through 14-10, respectively.

```
DO CASE
 CASE mCHOICE1 = "1"
  CLEAR
  USE CLAIM INDEX CLAIM
  REINDEX
  STORE SPACE (5) TO mCLAIMID
  @ 15, 5 SAY "ENTER CLAIM IDENTIFICATION NUMBER:"
  @ 15, 45 GET mCLAIMID PICTURE "XXXXX"
  READ
```

Figure 14-6 Program module for "Query" option

```
SEEK mCLAIMID
IF FOUND ()
 CLEAR
 @ 0, 20 SAY "WORKER'S COMPENSATION INFORMATION SYSTEMS:
 @ 1, 29 SAY "QUERY CLAIM INFORMATION"
 @ 3, 0 SAY "EMPLOYEE"
 @ 3, 63 GET CLAIMID PICTURE "XXXXX"
 @ 4, 0 SAY "SOCIAL SECURITY #:"
 @ 4, 19 GET CLAIM->EMPLID
 @ 4, 51 SAY "CLAIM DATE:"
 @ 4, 63 GET CLAIM->CLAIMDATE
 @ 9, 15 SAY "COMPENSATION AMOUNT REQUESTED:"
 @ 9, 46 GET CLAIM->AMTREQ
 @10, 15 SAY "WORKDAYS LOST BECAUSE OF INJURY:"
 @10, 48 GET CLAIM->DAYSLOST
 @11, 15 SAY "CLAIM TYPE (MAJOR(MJ) OR MINOR(MI)):"
 @11, 52 GET CLAIM->MJ_MI
 @12, 15 SAY "LEGAL DOCUMENT NEEDED:"
 @12, 38 GET CLAIM->LEGAL_DOC
 @ 7, 13 TO 13, 59 DOUBLE
 @18, 15 SAY "  "
 WAIT
ELSE
 CLEAR
 SET COLOR TO RW
 @15,5 SAY "THE CLAIM ID NUMBER IS NOT IN THE FILE"
 WAIT
 SET COLOR TO WB
 STORE SPACE (5) TO mCLAIMID
ENDIF
CASE mCHOICE1 = "2"
 CLEAR
 USE INJURY INDEX INJURY
 REINDEX
 STORE SPACE (9) TO mEMPLID
 @15, 5 SAY "ENTER EMPLOYEE SOCIAL SECURITY NUMBER:"
 @15,45 GET mEMPLID PICTURE "XXXXXXXXX"
 READ
 SEEK mEMPLID
 IF FOUND ()
  CLEAR
  @ 0, 19 TO 3, 52 DOUBLE
  @ 1, 21 SAY "WORKER'S COMPENSATION SYSTEMS"
  @ 2, 25 SAY "INJURY INFORMATION"
  @ 4, 0 SAY "EMPLOYEE ID #:"
  @ 4, 15 GET EMPLID PICTURE "XXXXXXXXX"
  @ 8, 15 SAY "PHYSICAL LOCATION   ADDITIONAL INFORMATION:
  @ 9, 15 SAY "_________      _________"
  @10, 15 SAY "FILE CABINET #:"
  @10, 31 GET INJURY->FILE
  @10, 42 SAY "DOCTOR'S REPORT EXIST:"
  @10, 65 GET INJURY->REPRTEXIST
  @11, 15 SAY "DRAWER #:"
  @11, 25 GET INJURY->DRAWER
  @11, 42 SAY "LEGAL DOCUMENTS EXIST:"
  @11, 65 GET INJURY->LEGALEXIST
  @12, 15 SAY "DATE:"
  @12, 21 GET INJURY->MONTH
```

Figure 14-6 continued

```
  @12, 23 SAY ""
  @12, 24 GET INJURY->DAY
  @12, 26 SAY ""
  @12, 27 GET INJURY->YEAR
  @12, 42 SAY "INJURY FILE STATUS:"
  @12, 65 GET INJURY->STATUS
  WAIT
 ELSE
  SET COLOR TO RW
  CLEAR
  @15, 5 SAY "THE EMPLOYEE SOCIAL SECURITY IS NOT IN THE FILE"
  @16, 5 SAY "PLEASE CHECK THE INPUT AND REENTER"
  WAIT
  SET COLOR TO WB
  STORE SPACE (9) TO mEMPLID
 ENDIF
   mREPEAT1 = .F.
  OTHERWISE
   SET COLOR TO RW
   CLEAR
   @20, 1 SAY "INVALID SELECTION"
   WAIT
   SET COLOR TO WB
  ENDCASE
 ENDDO
 CLOSE ALL
 RETURN
```

Figure **14-6** continued

```
*ADD MODULE
CLEAR
STORE .T. TO mREPEAT2
DO WHILE mREPEAT2
 SET COLOR TO WB
 CLEAR
 @ 1, 18 TO 16, 65 DOUBLE
 @ 2, 22 SAY "WORKER'S COMPENSATION SYSTEMS"
 @ 3, 34 SAY "ADD MAIN MODULE:
 @ 4, 19 TO 4, 64 DOUBLE
 @ 8, 26 SAY "1. ADD NEW RECORD TO CLAIM FILE:
 @ 9, 26 SAY "2. ADD NEW RECORD TO COMPENSATION FILE"
 @10, 26 SAY "3. RETURN TO MAIN MENU"
 @17, 26 SAY "  "
 ACCEPT "PLEASE ENTER THE MENU SELECTION (1-3): " TO mCHOICE2
 DO CASE
  CASE mCHOICE2 = "1"
  CLEAR
  STORE SPACE (9) TO mEMPLID
  USE INJURY INDEX INJURY
  REINDEX
  @15, 5 SAY "ENTER EMPLOYEE SOCIAL SECURITY #:"
  @15, 40 GET mEMPLID PICTURE "XXXXXXXXX"
  READ
  SEEK mEMPLID
  IF .NOT. FOUND ()
   SET TO RW
```

Figure **14-7** Program module for "Add" option

```
 CLEAR
 @15, 5 SAY "THERE IS NO INJURY FILE EXIST FOR THE SPECIFIED EMPLOYEE"
 @16, 1 SAY "A CLAIM CAN BE SUBMITTED ONLY IF THERE IS AN INJURY FILED BEFORE"
 @17, 1 SAY "  "
 @18, 1 SAY "  "
 WAIT
 SET COLOR TO WB
ELSE
 CLEAR
 USE CLAIM INDEX CLAIM
 REINDEX
 STORE SPACE (5) TO mCLAIMID
 @15, 5 SAY "ENTER CLAIM ID #:"
 @15, 40 GET mCLAIMID PICTURE "XXXXX"
 READ
 SEEK mCLAIMID
 IF FOUND ()
  SET COLOR TO RW
  CLEAR
  @15, 5 SAY "THE CLAIM ID NUMBER IS ALREADY EXIST"
  @16, 1 SAY "  "
  @17, 1 SAY "  "
  WAIT
  STORE SPACE (5) TO mCLAIMID
  SET COLOR TO WB
 ELSE
  SET COLOR TO WB
  GOTO BOTTOM
  STORE SPACE (9) TO mEMPLID
  STORE "   " TO mCLAIMDATE
  STORE 0 TO mAMTREQ, mDAYSLOST
  STORE SPACE (2) TO mMJ_MI
  STORE SPACE (1) TO mLEGAL_DOC
  CLEAR
  @ 0, 27 SAY "WORKER'S COMPENSATION SYSTEM"
  @ 1, 27 SAY "ADD NEW CLAIM INFORMATION"
  @ 3, 0 SAY "EMPLOYEE ID #:"
  @ 3, 15 GET mEMPLID PICTURE "XXXXXXXXX"
  @ 3, 49 SAY "CLAIM ID #:"
  @ 3, 61 GET mCLAIMID PICTURE "XXXXX"
  @ 4, 49 SAY "CLAIM DATE:"
  @ 4, 61 GET mCLAIMDATE PICTURE "999999"
  @ 7, 14 SAY "COMPENSATION AMOUNT REQUESTED:"
  @ 7, 45 GET mAMTREQ PICTURE "9999999"
  @ 9, 14 SAY "WORK DAYS LOST BECAUSE OF INJURY:"
  @ 9, 48 GET mDAYSLOST PICTURE "99999999"
  @13, 14 SAY "CLAIM TYPE (MAJOR(MJ) OR MINOR(MI)):"
  @13, 51 GET mMJ_MI PICTURE "XX"
  @15, 14 SAY "LEGAL DOCUMENT NEEDED:"
  @15, 37 GET mLEGAL_DOC PICTURE "X"
  @ 5, 12 TO 16, 59 DOUBLE
  READ
  APPEND BLANK
  REPLACE EMPLID WITH mEMPLID
  REPLACE CLAIMID WITH mCLAIMID
  REPLACE CLAIMDATE WITH CTOD(mCLAIMDATE)
  REPLACE AMTREQ WITH mAMTREQ
  REPLACE DAYSLOST WITH mDAYSLOST
```

Figure 14-7 continued

```
    REPLACE MJ_MI WITH mMJ_MI
    REPLACE LEGAL_DOC WITH mLEGAL_DOC
    STORE SPACE (9) TO mEMPLID
    STORE SPACE (5) TO mCLAIMID
    STORE "   " TO mCLAIMDATE
    STORE 0 TO mAMTREQ, DAYSLOST
    STORE SPACE (2) TO mMJ_MI
    STORE SPACE (1) TO mLEGAL_DOC
   ENDIF
  ENDIF
  CASE mCHOICE2 = "2"
    SET COLOR TO RW
    STORE 1 TO mCOUNTER
    DO WHILE mCOUNTER < 3
     CLEAR
     STORE "XMAS" TO PASS
     STORE SPACE (4) TO mPASS
     @15, 5 SAY "ENTER PASSWORD:"
     @15, 30 GET mPASS PICTURE "XXXX"
     READ
     IF mPASS = PASS
      DO WHILE mPASS = PASS
      CLEAR
      USE CLAIM INDEX CLAIM
      REINDEX
      STORE SPACE (5) TO mCLAIMID
      SET COLOR TO WB
      @15, 5 SAY "ENTER CLAIM ID #:"
      @15,40 GET mCLAIMID PICTURE "XXXXX"
      READ
      SEEK mCLAIMID
      IF .NOT. FOUND ()
       CLEAR
       SET COLOR TO RW
       @15, 5 SAY "THE CLAIM ID NUMBER DOES NOT EXIST IN THE CLAIM FILE"
       @16, 5 SAY "COMPENSATION WILL NOT BE GRANTED UNLESS THERE IS A CLAIM EXIST"
       @17, 5 SAY "IN THE CLAIM FILE, PLEASE CHECK THE INPUT"
       @18, 1 SAY "  "
       @19, 1 SAY "  "
       WAIT
       SET COLOR TO WB
       STORE SPACE (5) TO mCLAIMID
       STORE SPACE (4) TO mPASS
       STORE 4 TO mCOUNTER
      ELSE
       USE COMPEN INDEX COMPEN
       REINDEX
       SEEK mCLAIMID
       IF FOUND ()
        CLEAR
        SET COLOR TO RW
        @15, 5 SAY "THE SPECIFIED CLAIM HAS BEEN COMPENSATED BEFORE"
        WAIT
        SET COLOR TO WB
       ELSE
        GOTO BOTTOM
        STORE SPACE (9) TO mEMPLID
        STORE SPACE (2) TO mMONTH
```

Figure 14-7 continued

```
    STORE SPACE (2) TO mDAY
    STORE SPACE (4) TO mYEAR
    STORE "    " TO mCOMPDATE
    STORE 0 TO mAMTGRANTED
    SET COLOR TO WB
    CLEAR
    @ 2, 17 SAY "WORKER'S COMPENSATION INFORMATION SYSTEMS"
    @ 3, 17 SAY "   INVOICE INFORMATION"
    @ 6, 21 SAY "EMPLOYEE"
    @ 7, 21 SAY "SOCIAL SECURITY #:"
    @ 7, 40 GET mEMPLID PICTURE "XXXXXXXXX"
    @ 9, 21 SAY "INJURY DATE:"
    @ 9, 34 GET mMONTH PICTURE "XX"
    @ 9, 36 SAY ""
    @ 9, 37 GET mDAY PICTURE "XX"
    @ 9, 39 SAY ""
    @ 9, 40 GET mYEAR PICTURE "XXXX"
    @14, 21 SAY "CLAIM ID #:"
    @14, 33 GET mCLAIMID PICTURE "XXXXX"
    @16, 21 SAY "DATE COMPENSATION GRANTED:"
    @16, 48 GET mCOMPDATE PICTURE "999999"
    @18, 21 SAY "COMPENSATION AMOUNT GRANTED: $"
    @18, 52 GET mAMTGRANTED PICTURE "9999999999"
    @ 1, 15 TO 3, 59
    @ 5, 19 TO 19, 62 DOUBLE
    READ
    APPEND BLANK
    REPLACE EMPLID WITH mEMPLID
    REPLACE CLAIMID WITH mCLAIMID
    REPLACE MONTH WITH mMONTH
    REPLACE DAY WITH mDAY
    REPLACE YEAR WITH mYEAR
    REPLACE COMPDATE WITH CTOD(mCOMPDATE)
    REPLACE AMTGRANTED WITH mAMTGRANTED
    STORE SPACE (9) TO mEMPLID
    STORE SPACE (2) TO mMONTH
    STORE SPACE (2) TO mDAY
    STORE SPACE (4) TO mYEAR
    STORE "    " TO mCOMPDATE
    STORE 0 TO mAMTGRANTED
    STORE SPACE (5) TO mCLAIMID
    STORE SPACE (4) TO mPASS
    STORE 5 TO mCOUNTER
   ENDIF
  ENDIF
 ENDDO
ELSE
 CLEAR
 SET COLOR TO RW
 @15, 5 SAY "THE PASSWORD IS INCORRECT"
 WAIT
 mCOUNTER = mCOUNTER + 1
 SET COLOR TO WB
ENDIF
ENDDO
IF mCOUNTER = 3
 CLEAR
 SET COLOR TO RW
```

Figure 14-7 continued

```
     @10, 5 SAY "ONLY THE MANAGER CAN ACCESS COMPENSATION FILE"
     WAIT
     SET COLOR TO WB
    ENDIF
  CASE mCHOICE2 = "3"
   CLEAR
   mREPEAT2 = .F.
  OTHERWISE
   SET COLOR TO RW
   CLEAR
   @20, 1 SAY "INVALID SELECTION, PLEASE TRY AGAIN"
   WAIT
   SET COLOR TO WB
  ENDCASE
 ENDDO
 CLOSE ALL
 RETURN
```

Figure 14-7 continued

```
*EDIT MODULE
CLEAR
STORE .T. TO mREPEAT3
DO WHILE mREPEAT3
 SET COLOR TO WB
 CLEAR
 @ 1, 18 TO 16, 65 DOUBLE
 @ 2, 22 SAY "WORKER'S COMPENSATION SYSTEMS"
 @ 3, 22 SAY " EDIT MAIN MODULE"
 @ 4, 19 TO 4, 64 DOUBLE
 @ 8, 26 SAY "1. EDIT A RECORD IN CLAIM FILE"
 @ 9, 26 SAY "2. EDIT A RECORD IN COMPENSATION FILE"
 @10, 26 SAY "3. RETURN TO MAIN MENU"
 @17, 26 SAY "  "
 ACCEPT "PLEASE ENTER THE MENU SELECTION (1-3):" TO mCHOICE3
 DO CASE
 CASE mCHOICE3 = "1"
 CLEAR
 USE CLAIM INDEX CLAIM
 REINDEX
 STORE SPACE (5) TO mCLAIMID
 @15, 5 SAY "ENTER CLAIM ID #:"
 @15, 40 GET mCLAIMID PICTURE "XXXXX"
 READ
 SEEK mCLAIMID
 IF .NOT. FOUND ()
   SET COLOR TO RW
   CLEAR
   @15, 1 SAY "THERE IS NO RECORD WITH THE SPECIFIED CLAIM ID NUMBER"
   @16, 1 SAY "  "
   @17, 1 SAY "  "
   WAIT
   STORE SPACE (5) TO mCLAIMID
   SET COLOR TO WB
 ELSE
   SET COLOR TO WB
   GOTO BOTTOM
```

Figure 14-8 Program module for "Edit" option

```
 STORE SPACE (9) TO mEMPLID
 STORE "   " TO mCLAIMDATE
 STORE 0 TO mAMTREQ, mDAYSLOST
 STORE SPACE (2) TO mMJ_MI
 STORE SPACE (1) TO mLEGAL_DOC
 CLEAR
 @ 0, 37 SAY "WORKER'S COMPENSATION SYSTEM"
 @ 1, 37 SAY " EDIT CLAIM INFORMATION"
 @ 3,  0 SAY "EMPLOYEE ID #:"
 @ 3, 15 SAY CLAIM->EMPLID
 @ 3, 49 SAY "CLAIM ID #:"
 @ 3, 61 SAY CLAIM->CLAIMID
 @ 4, 49 SAY "CLAIM DATE:"
 @ 4, 61 GET CLAIM->CLAIMDATE
 STORE CLAIMDATE TO mCLAIMDATE
 @ 7, 14 SAY "COMPENSATION AMOUNT REQUESTED:"
 @ 7, 45 GET CLAIM->AMTREQ
 STORE AMTREQ TO mAMTREQ
 @ 9, 14 SAY "WORK DAYS LOST BECAUSE OF INJURY:"
 @ 9, 48 GET CLAIM->DAYSLOST
 STORE DAYSLOST TO mDAYSLOST
 @13, 14 SAY "CLAIM TYPE (MAJOR(MJ) OR MINOR(MI)):"
 @13, 51 GET CLAIM->MJ_MI
 STORE MJ_MI TO mMJ_MI
 @15, 14 SAY "LEGAL DOCUMENT NEEDED:"
 @15, 37 GET CLAIM->LEGAL_DOC
 STORE LEGAL_DOC TO mLEGAL_DOC
 @ 5, 12 TO 16, 59 DOUBLE
 READ
 STORE mCLAIMDATE TO CLAIMDATE
 STORE mAMTREQ TO AMTREQ
 STORE mDAYSLOST TO DAYSLOST
 STORE mMJ_MI TO MJ_MI
 STORE mLEGAL_DOC TO LEGAL_DOC
 STORE SPACE (9) TO mEMPLID
 STORE SPACE (5) to mCLAIMID
 STORE "   " TO mCLAIMDATE
 STORE 0 TO mAMTREQ, DAYSLOST
 STORE SPACE (2) TO mMJ_MI
 STORE SPACE (1) TO mLEGAL_DOC
 WAIT
ENDIF
CASE mCHOICE3 = "2"
 STORE 1 TO mCOUNTER
 DO WHILE mCOUNTER < 3
  CLEAR
  STORE "XMAS" TO PASS
  STORE SPACE (4) TO mPASS
  SET COLOR TO RW
  @15, 5 SAY "ENTER PASSWORD:"
  @15, 30 GET mPASS PICTURE "XXXX"
  READ
  IF mPASS = PASS
   SET COLOR TO WB
   CLEAR
   STORE SPACE (5) TO mCLAIMID
   USE COMPEN INDEX COMPEN
   REINDEX
```

Figure 14-8 continued

```
 CLEAR
 @15, 5 SAY "ENTER THE CLAIM ID #:"
 @15, 35 GET mCLAIMID PICTURE "XXXXX"
 READ
 SEEK mCLAIMID
 IF .NOT. FOUND ()
 CLEAR
 SET COLOR TO RW
 @15, 1 SAY ""THE RECORD WITH THE SPECIFIED CLAIM NUMBER IS NOT IN THE FILE"
 WAIT
 SET COLOR TO WB
 STORE SPACE (5) TO mCLAIMID
 STORE SPACE (4) TO mPASS
 STORE 4 TO mCOUNTER
ELSE
 GOTO BOTTOM
 STORE SPACE (9) TO mEMPLID
 STORE SPACE (2) TO mMONTH
 STORE SPACE (2) TO mDAY
 STORE SPACE (4) TO mYEAR
 STORE "   " TO mCOMPDATE
 STORE 0 TO mAMTGRANTED
 SET COLOR TO WB
 CLEAR
 @ 2, 21 SAY "WORKER'S COMPENSATION INFORMATION SYSTEMS"
 @ 3, 21 SAY "  INVOICE INFORMATION"
 @ 6, 21 SAY "EMPLOYEE"
 @ 7, 21 SAY "SOCIAL SECURITY #:"
 @ 7, 40 SAY COMPEN->EMPLID
 @ 9, 21 SAY "INJURY DATE:"
 @ 9, 34 SAY COMPEN->MONTH
 @ 9, 36 SAY ""
 @ 9, 37 SAY COMPEN->DAY
 @ 9, 39 SAY ""
 @ 9, 40 SAY COMPEN->YEAR
 @14, 21 SAY "CLAIM ID #:"
 @14, 33 SAY COMPEN->CLAIMID
 @16, 21 SAY "DATE COMPENSATION GRANTED:"
 @16, 48 GET COMPEN->COMPDATE
 STORE COMPDATE TO mCOMPDATE
 @18, 21 SAY "COMPENSATION AMOUNT GRANTED: $"
 @18, 52 GET COMPEN->AMTGRANTED
 STORE AMTGRANTED TO mAMTGRANTED
 @ 1, 19 TO 4, 62
 @ 5, 19 TO 19, 62 DOUBLE
 READ
 STORE mCOMPDATE TO COMPDATE
 STORE AMTGRANTED TO AMTGRANTED
 STORE SPACE (9) TO mEMPLID
 STORE SPACE (2) TO mMONTH
 STORE SPACE (2) TO mDAY
 STORE SPACE (4) TO mYEAR
 STORE "   " TO mCOMPDATE
 STORE 0 TO mAMTGRANTED
 STORE SPACE (5) TO mCLAIMID
 STORE SPACE (4) TO mPASS
 STORE 5 TO mCOUNTER
ENDIF
```

Figure **14-8** continued

```
  ELSE
   CLEAR
   SET COLOR TO RW
   @15, 5 SAY "THE PASSWORD IS INCORRECT"
   @16, 1 SAY "  "
   WAIT
   mCOUNTER = mCOUNTER + 1
   SET COLOR TO WB
   ENDIF
 ENDDO
 IF mCOUNTER = 3
   CLEAR
   SET COLOR TO RW
   @10, 5 SAY "ONLY THE MANAGER CAN ACCESS COMPENSATION FILE"
   @11, 1 SAY " "
   WAIT
   SET COLOR TO WB
   ENDIF
 CASE mCHOICE3 = "3"
   CLEAR
   mREPEAT3 = .F.
  OTHERWISE
   SET COLOR TO RW
   CLEAR
   @20, 1 SAY "INVALID SELECTION, PLEASE TRY AGAIN"
   WAIT
   SET COLOR TO WB
  ENDCASE
  ENDDO
  CLOSE ALL
  RETURN
```

Figure 14-8 continued

```
*INVOICE MODULE
STORE .T. TO mREPEAT4
DO WHILE mREPEAT4
CLEAR
 @1, 18 TO 16, 65 DOUBLE
 @2, 22 SAY "WORKER'S COMPENSATION INFORMATION SYSTEMS'
 @3, 22 SAY "  INVOICE MENU'
 @4, 19 TO 4, 64 DOUBLE
 @8, 26 SAY "1. SEE INVOICE ON SCREEN"
 @9, 26 SAY "2. RETURN TO MAIN MENU"
 @10, 26 SAY "3. PRINT INVOICE"
 @17, 26 SAY "  "
 ACCEPT "PLEASE ENTER MENU SELECTION:" TO mCHOICE4
 DO CASE
 CASE mCHOICE4 = "1"
  CLEAR
  STORE SPACE (5) TO mCLAIMID
  CLEAR
  USE COMPEN INDEX COMPEN
  REINDEX
  @15, 5 SAY "ENTER CLAIM ID:"
  @15, 45 GET mCLAIMID PICTURE "XXXXX"
  READ
```

Figure 14-9 Program module for "Invoice" option

```
SEEK mCLAIMID
IF .NOT. FOUND ()
 SET COLOR TO RW
 CLEAR
 @15, 1 SAY "THERE IS NO RECORD WITH THE SPECIFIED CLAIM ID NUMBER"
 @16, 1 SAY "  "
 @17, 1 SAY "  "
 WAIT
 STORE SPACE (5) TO mCLAIMID
 SET COLOR TO WB
ELSE
 IF PRINT_STAT = 0
 SET COLOR TO WB
 CLEAR
 @2, 22 SAY "WORKER'S COMPENSATION INFORMATION"
 @3, 22 SAY "  INVOICE"
 @5, 21 SAY "EMPLOYEE"
 @6, 21 SAY "SOCIAL SECURITY #:"
 @6, 40 SAY COMPEN->EMPLID
 @12, 21 SAY "INJURY DATE:"
 @12, 34 SAY COMPEN->MONTH
 @12, 36 SAY ""
 @12, 37 SAY COMPEN->DAY
 @12, 39 SAY ""
 @12, 40 SAY COMPEN->YEAR
 @14, 21 SAY "CLAIM ID #:"
 @14, 33 SAY COMPEN->CLAIMID
 @16, 21 SAY "DATE COMPENSATION GRANTED"
 @16, 48 SAY COMPEN->COMPDATE
 @18, 21 SAY "COMPENSATION AMOUNT"
 @19, 21 SAY "GRANTED: $"
 @19, 31 SAY COMPEN->AMTGRANTED
 STORE SPACE (9) TO mEMPLID
 STORE EMPLID TO mEMPLID
 USE EMPLOYEE INDEX EMPLOYEE
 SEEK mEMPLID
 @7, 21 "EMPLOYEE NAME:"
 @7, 37 SAY EMPLOYEE->EMPLFIRST
 @8, 37 SAY EMPLOYEE->EMPLLAST
 STORE SPACE (5) TO mDEPTID
 STORE DEPTID TO mDEPTID
 USE DEPARTME INDEX DEPARTME
 SEEK mDEPTID
 @10, 21 SAY "DEPARTMENT:"
 @10, 33 SAY DEPARTME->DEPTNAME
 @1, 19 TO 4, 62
 @4, 19 TO 20, 62 DOUBLE
 @21, 1 SAY "  "
 STORE SPACE (9) TO mEMPLID
 STORE SPACE (5) TO mCLAIMIDM
 STORE SPACE (5) TO mDEPTID
 WAIT
ELSE
 SET COLOR TO RW
 CLEAR
 @15, 1 SAY "THE INVOICE FOR THIS RECORD HAS BEEN PRINTED BEFORE"
 @16, 1 SAY "FOR EACH CLAIM THERE IS ONLY ONE INVOICE ALLOWED TO"
 @17, 1 SAY "BE PRINTED"
```

Figure **14-9** continued

```
    WAIT
    SET COLOR TO WB
   ENDIF
  ENDIF
 CASE mCHOICE4 = "2"
  CLEAR
  mREPEAT4 = .F.
 CASE mCHOICE4 = "3"
  CLEAR
  STORE SPACE (5) TO mCLAIMID
  CLEAR
  USE COMPEN INDEX COMPEN
  REINDEX
  @15, 5 SAY "ENTER CLAIM ID:"
  @15, 45 GET mCLAIMID PICTURE "XXXXX"
  READ
  SEEK mCLAIMID
  IF .NOT. FOUND ()
    SET COLOR TO RW
    CLEAR
    @15, 1 SAY "THERE IS NO RECORD WITH THE SPECIFIED CLAIM ID NUMBER"
    @16, 1 SAY "  "
    @17, 1 SAY "  "
    WAIT
    STORE SPACE (5) TO mCLAIMID
    SET COLOR TO WB
   ELSE
    IF PRINT STAT = 0
     SET DEVICE TO PRINT
     SET PRINT ON
     @1, 21 SAY "_____________"
     @2, 22 SAY "WORKER'S COMPENSATION INFORMATION"
     @3, 22 SAY "  INVOICE"
     @4, 21 SAY "_____________"
     @5, 21 SAY "EMPLOYEE"
     @6, 21 SAY "SOCIAL SECURITY #:"
     @6, 40 SAY COMPEN->EMPLID
     STORE SPACE (9) TO mEMPLID
     STORE EMPLID TO mEMPLID
     USE EMPLOYEE INDEX EMPLOYEE
     SEEK mEMPLID
     @7, 21 SAY "EMPLOYEE NAME:"
     @7, 37 SAY EMPLOYEE->EMPLFIRST
     @8, 37 SAY EMPLOYEE->EMPLLAST
     STORE SPACE (5) TO mDEPTID
     STORE DEPTID TO mDEPTID
     USE DEPARTME INDEX DEPARTME
     SEEK mDEPTID
     @10, 21 SAY "DEPARTMENT:"
     @10, 33 SAY DEPARTME->DEPTNAME
     USE COMPEN INDEX COMPEN
     SEEK mCLAIMID
     @12, 21 SAY "INJURY DATE:"
     @12, 34 SAY COMPEN->MONTH
     @12, 36 SAY ""
     @12, 37 SAY COMPEN->DAY
     @12, 39 SAY ""
     @12, 40 SAY COMPEN->YEAR
```


Figure 14-9 continued

```
      @14, 21 SAY "CLAIM ID #:"
      @14, 33 SAY COMPEN ->CLAIMID     @16, 21 SAY "DATE COMPENSATION GRANTED"
      @16, 48 SAY COMPEN ->COMPDATE
      @18, 21 SAY "COMPENSATION AMOUNT"
      @19, 21 SAY "GRANTED: $"
      @19, 31 SAY COMPEN->AMTGRANTED
      @21, 21 SAY "INVOICE SHOULD BE SENT TO:"
      @21, 47 SAY COMPEN->ACCTG_PAY
      @22, 21 SAY "(PAYROLL (P) ACCOUNTING (A))"
      SET PRINT OFF
      SET DEVICE TO SCREEN
      STORE 0 TO mPRINT_STAT
      STORE 1 TO mPRINT_STAT
      REPLACE PRINT_STAT WITH mPRINT_STAT
      STORE 0 TO mPRINT_STAT
      STORE SPACE (9) TO mEMPLID
      STORE SPACE (5) TO mCLAIMIDM
      STORE SPACE (5) TO mDEPTID
     ELSE
      CLEAR
      @15, 1 SAY "THE INVOICE FOR THIS RECORD HAS BEEN PRINTED BEFORE"
      @16, 1 SAY "FOR EACH CLAIM THERE IS ONLY ONE INVOICE ALLOWED TO"
      @17, 1 SAY "BE PRINTED"
      WAIT
     ENDIF
    ENDIT
   OTHERWISE
    CLEAR
    @20, 1 SAY "INVALID SELECTION"
    WAIT
   ENDCASE
ENDDO
CLOSE ALL
RETURN
```

Figure 14-9 continued

```
*QUARTERLY INVOICE MODULE
SET STATUS OFF
SET TALK OFF
SET BELL OFF
STORE .T. TO mRETURN
STORE .T. TO mFIRST
STORE 0 TO mFOUND
DO WHILE mRETURN .AND. mFOUND = 0
 STORE SPACE (8) TO mSTARTDATE
 STORE SPACE (8) TO mENDDATE
 STORE 0 TO mSTART
 STORE 0 TO mEND
 CLEAR
 @7, 1 SAY "ENTER STARTING DATE OF THE QUARTER"
 @7, 50 GET mSTARTDATE PICTURE "XXXXXX"
 @10, 1 SAY "ENTER ENDING DATE OF THE QUARTER"
 @10, 50 GET mENDDATE PICTURE "XXXXXX"
 READ
 STORE CTOD(mSTARTDATE) TO mSTART
 STORE CTOD(mENDDATE) TO mEND
```

Figure 14-10 Program module for "Quarterly invoice" option

```
 CLOSEALL
 USE COMPEN INDEX COMPEN
 REINDEX
 GOTO TOP
 LOCATE ALL FOR COMPDATE=mSTART .AND. COMPDATE=m END
 mTRYAGAIN = "Y"
 IF FOUND()
  mFOUND = 1
 ELSE
  SET COLOR TO RW
  CLEAR
  @15, 5 SAY "QUARTER NOT FOUND!!!"
  WAIT "WOULD YOU LIKE TO TRY AGAIN?" TO mTRYAGAIN
  IF mTRYAGAIN ="Y"
   STORE .T. TO mRETURN
  ELSE
   STORE .F. TO mRETURN
  SET COLOR TO WB
  ENDIF
 ENDIF
ENDDO

IF mFOUND = 1
STORE 11 TO mROW
STORE 0 TO mTOTAL
STORE .T. TO mFIRST
CLOSE ALL
USE COMPEN INDEX COMPEN
REINDEX
TOTO TOP
CLEAR
SET PRINT ON
SET DEVICE TO PRINT
STORE DTOC(mSTART) TO mSTARTDATE
STORE DTOC(mEND) TO mENDDATE
@ 0, 11 SAY "DATE OF REPORT:"
@ 0, 42 SAY DATE()
@ 1, 11 SAY "START OF QUARTER:"
@ 1, 29 SAY mSTARTDATE
@ 2, 11 SAY "END OF QUARTER:"
@ 2, 29 SAY mENDDATE
@ 4, 11 SAY "WORKER'S COMPENSATION INFORMATION SYSTEMS"
@ 5, 23 SAY "QUARTERLY INVOICE REPORT"
@ 7, 11 SAY "EMPLOYEE ID # COMPENSATION  AMOUNT"
@ 8, 36 SAY "DATE  GRANTED"
@ 9, 11 SAY
"______________________"
DO WHILE .NOT. EOF()
 IF mFIRST
  LOCATE ALL FOR COMPDATE=mSTART .AND. COMPDATE=mEND
  STORE .F. TO mFIRST
 ELSE
  CONTINUE
  IF EOF ()
   LOOP
  ENDIF
 ENDIF
 mROW = mROW + 1
```

Figure 14-10 continued

```
 @mROW, 11 SAY EMPLID
 @mROW, 32 SAY COMPDATE
 @mROW, 54 SAY AMTGRANTED
ENDDO
@mROW +2, 25 SAY "TOTAL AMOUNT THIS QUARTER"
@mROW +2, 54 SAY mTOTAL PICTURE "9999999.99"
ENDIF
SET PRINT OFF
SET DEVICE TO SCREEN
```

Figure 14-10 continued

Testing and Debugging the Program

Once a program has been written, it must be tested, corrected, and retested before it can be put to use. There is no set procedure that will correct all errors in every program, but there are standard ways of deleting and correcting common "bugs," as well as debugging commands that can be built into most programs.

Programming Errors

Programs must be perfect in every detail, or they will not run—because, unlike a person who sees a misspelled word and can guess what the writer meant, a computer is incapable of intuitive jumps. The five most common programming errors are

1 misspelled words
2 syntax errors
3 incomplete commands
4 missing spaces between commands and expressions
5 errors in logic

Spelling errors are the easiest to find. To check for misspelled words, print out the program and proofread it. Syntax errors are incorrectly used or constructed commands. For example, using the command ERASE instead of CLEAR is a syntax error. Incomplete commands and missing spaces between commands can also cause a program to crash. It should be noted that students should not rely on "Spell Checkers," which cannot tell a "friend" from a "fiend."

Logic errors are the most difficult bugs to find because they do not appear until after the program is running. A logic error will not necessarily cause a program to crash; some logic errors simply produce incorrect responses. Frequently made logic errors involve the use of logical operators such as AND and OR.

In programming, as in much else, prevention is the best cure. Good programming habits can reduce errors—if not eliminate them altogether. Here are a few suggestions:

- Use file names, field names, and memory variable names consistently.
- Simple engineering is good engineering. Break down every program

into a series of basic commands and place only one command on a line.

- Allow at least one space between commands.
- Verify the order of the arguments of the command. For example

```
@ 5,4 GET MAMT SAY "ENTER AMOUNT:"
```

should be

```
@ 5,4 SAY "ENTER AMOUNT:" GET MAMT
```

- Use the right word combinations. For example

```
DO UNTIL BRAND="BACARDI"
```

should be

```
DO WHILE BRAND="BACARDI"
```


Testing and Debugging Guidelines

There are many ways to test and debug a program. One recommended procedure is a top-down modular approach with four easy steps:

1 Write one module at a time, beginning with the most basic modules first. Test each module soon after it is written. The example in Figure 14-5 is a program module.

2 After testing a module, work on the module that logically follows. Continue testing modules and building them into units or composite programs. Then test and run one composite program at a time.

3 Link composite programs into larger programs, adding one composite program at a time, then test the total combination.

4 After assembling the entire system, test the system to see how well the entire set of modules work together. The system test in a top-down approach is done in two phases, called alpha and beta. The ALPHA TEST involves giving the program to another person for independent testing. Once it passes the alpha test, the program goes to a limited number of prospective users for a BETA TEST. The beta test is the final test to ensure that the program runs according to specifications.

Even after the program passes all levels of testing, it may still contain errors and require further debugging. Since the system designer or programmer may no longer be around for this (or may have only a hazy memory of the original design implementation), every program should be fully documented.

Built-In Debugging Features

Most database products offer built-in application debugging features. For example, dBASE IV offers a number of debugging aids. The first is a tool controlled by the command SET ECHO ON. This causes each program instruction to appear on the screen as the program is executed. Unfortunately, this command displays instructions as fast as they execute—much too fast for the human eye. The command SET STEP ON tells the software to slow down, to proceed one step at a time. With these two commands, the user can check one instruction at a time as it executes.

As each instruction is displayed on the screen, dBASE IV displays the message "Type any key to step—ESC to cancel," and waits for the user to cancel or continue. The user can press any key to bring up the next instruction, which will be followed again by the same message. But this process often clutters the screen with information, so the SET DEBUG ON command can be used to send the information to the printer. The three commands make it possible to see the program instructions on the printer while checking the results (if any) on the screen. Of course, the side benefit of this approach is documentation of the debugging procedure.

Another debugging tool allows the user to suspend program execution at any point in the program. The command SELECT on a separate line of code at any location in the program terminates program execution and brings up the message "DO SUSPENDED." To resume program execution, enter the command RESUME. To stop, use the CANCEL or RETURN commands.

SUMMARY

1 Database programming begins with a CREATE command. Any name can be used to identify the program.

2 Screen design should make it easier for the user to locate and use the data displayed on the screen. In dBASE IV, there are four basic input and output commands: ACCEPT, INPUT, WAIT, and @ commands.

3 The ACCEPT command is used to display a prompt message and to save the data entered by the user in a character memory variable.

4 The INPUT command is similar to the ACCEPT command, except that it allows for the entry of any type of data into a memory variable. The type of memory variable created depends on the information entered by the user.

5 The WAIT command is used at the end of the file to allow the user to view the records selected for display by the program.

6 The @ command allows for precise input and output information on the screen. There are three forms of the @ command:

a. x,y SAY "expression"
b. x,y get memvariable
c. x,y SAY "expression" GET memvar

7 The READ command stores input into a memory variable. It is used in conjunction with the GET form of the @ command. The GET command by

itself only brings the memory variable to the screen. The READ command places the value into the memory variable, which is a temporary storage place that exists only during program execution.

8 Three input/output commands are used with the @ command: EJECT, SET FORMAT TO PRINT, and STORE. These and other commands are useful for interactive input and output programming.

9 A database management system can control the flow of a program through three command structures: IF...ENDIF, for controlling a conditional choice; DO CASE...END CASE, for controlling a multiple-choice option; and DO WHILE...ENDDO, for controlling a request to repeat a specific action.

10 A DO WHILE...ENDDO command forces the software to continue repeating a loop while the condition is true. In contrast, IF...ENDIF asks the software to decide whether a specific condition is true only once and then to perform the commands tagged to the IF...ENDIF construction only once.

11 The commands used to access or manipulate files are SELECT, JOIN, and UPDATE. Each command offers a unique feature and requires a specific format.

12 Testing and debugging programs is an extremely important step in database application development. Errors are classified as syntactic or logical; logical errors being the most difficult bugs to find. Regardless of the type of errors, however, it is a good idea to practice good programming habits.

KEY WORDS

ACCEPT
Alpha test
@
Beta test
Coordinate
Counter
DO CASE
DO WHILE
EJECT
ENDCASE
ENDDO
ENDIF
Flow of control
GET
IF...ENDIF
INPUT
JOIN
Memory variable
READ
Screen grid
SELECT
SET FORMAT TO PRINT
STORE
UPDATE
WAIT

REVIEW QUESTIONS

1 In what way is programming an art?

2 Explain the differences between the following pairs:
   a. CREATE and DO commands
   b. ACCEPT and INPUT commands
   c. DO WHILE and DO UNTIL commands
   d. alpha and beta tests

3 Define the following terms or parts of commands:
   a. coordinate
   b. ENDCASE
   c. JOIN
   d. SELECT

4 How does the READ command differ from the INPUT command? Illustrate.

5 Explain how the following commands are used with the @ command:
   a. EJECT
   b. SET FORMAT TO PRINT
   c. STORE

6 What are the three parts of a flow-of-control decision and in what way do they contribute to controlling the flow of a database program?

7 Is indentation in programming necessary? Why is it so commonly followed?

8 Why must DO CASE and ENDCASE go together?

9 Explain how DO WHILE and ENDDO commands work together.

10 Write a short scenario or a case situation illustrating the use of the JOIN command.

11 What is the difference between the JOIN and SELECT commands? Be specific.

12 What types of errors would one expect to encounter in program testing? Which errors are the most difficult to detect? Why?

13 What guidelines would you recommend that programmers follow when testing and debugging a program? Explain briefly.

APPLICATION PROBLEMS

Having completed the logical design for IJI (see Chapter 12), it is time to work on the physical design—essentially, coding the system. You must now do the necessary coding to operationalize the system, including creating input and output screens. Use Structured English, dBASE IV, Oracle, SQL, or another language to do the work. The following is an example of the main menu module written in dBASE IV.

```
This is the main module.  All reservation functions are
called from here.  These functions include:
a.   RESERVATION INQUIRY--allows operators to quickly search
     database for customer inquiries.
```

```
b.   RESERVATION INPUT--allows operators to confirm customer
     reservations.
c.   RESERVATION CONFIRMATION--allows operators to confirm
     customer reservations.
d.   RESERVATION CANCELLATION--allows operators to cancel
     reservations.
The reservation system is protected by a password check.  If
the operator enters an incorrect password, he or she is not
allowed access to the system.  In addition, the main menu
only allows proper input choices.
The present password is "AWAD".
mG_TICKET and mG_CUSTNUM are global variables.
  The purpose of making these global has to do with
  generating proper customer numbers and ticket numbers.
Files called from this module are as follows:
  INQUIRY.PRG
  INPUT.PRG
  CONFIRM.PRG
  CANCEL.PRG

SET STATUS OFF
SET TALK OFF
STORE SPACE(1) TO mCHOICE
STORE 0 TO mG_TICKET
STORE 0 TO mG_CUSTNUM

STORE SPACE(4) TO mPASSWORD
STORE .T. TO mREPEAT
STORE .T. TO mBAD_PASS
DO WHILE mBAD_PASS
  CLEAR
  STORE .F. TO mBAD_PASS

  @ 8,20 SAY "ISLAND JUMPERS, INCORPORATED"
  @ 10,25 SAY "RESERVATION SYSTEM"
  @ 18,2 SAY "ENTER YOUR PASSWORD:"
  @ 18,24 GER mPASSWORD PICTURE "AAAA"
  READ
  IF mPASSWORD  "AWAD"
     @ 20, 24 SAY "INVALID PASSWORD, TRY AGAIN"
     STORE .T. TO mBAD_PASS
     WAIT
  ENDIF
ENDDO

DO WHILE mREPEAT
   CLEAR
   @ 3, 15 SAY "MAIN MENU"
   @ 4, 15 SAY "---------"
   @ 8, 10 SAY  "1)  RESERVATION INQUIRY"
   @ 10, 10 SAY "2)  RESERVATION INPUT"
   @ 14, 10 SAY "3)  RESERVATION CONFIRMATION"
   @ 14, 10 SAY "4)  RESERVATION CANCELLATION"
   @ 16, 10 SAY "5)  QUIT"
   @ 18, 12 SAY "Enter menu choice (1-5)  :"
   @ 18, 40 GET mCHOICE PICTURE "9"
   READ
   STORE
   DO CASE
```

```
        CASE mCHOICE = "1"
            DO INQUIRY
        CASE mCHOICE = "2"
            DO INPUT
        CASE mCHOICE = "3"
            DO CONFIRM
        CASE mCHOICE = "4"
            DO CANCEL
        CASE mCHOICE = "5"
            RETURN
        OTHERWISE

            @ 20, 10 SAY "ERROR : PLEASE ENTER A NUMBER BETWEEN 1-4"
                 STORE .T. TO mREPEAT
                 WAIT
            ENDCASE
ENDDO
CLOSE ALL
SET STATUS ON
SET TALK ON
RETURN
```

PART V

MANAGEMENT OF THE DATABASE ENVIRONMENT

C H A P T

Database Administration

E R 1 5

Automating Database Administration

AT A GLANCE

Automating Database Administration

. . . Gone are the days when application programmers could be held accountable for corporate database integrity. Who has assumed that responsibility? Who implements and maintains the corporation's large and sometimes very complex logical data model? In most cases, the DBA. This new responsibility must take its place among the DBA's prerelational duties—physical database design and implementation, database tuning, database reorganization, DBMS software maintenance, and trouble-shooting.

As many DBAs know, this shift in accountability has made the DBMS environment far more complex. How can we meet this challenge, assuming that adding more DBAs is not an option?

View Definition

In a relational environment, programmers define to the DBMS the data required to solve the algorithm they are implementing. They no longer have to be intimately familiar with the data structures and physical navigation required to retrieve the data they'll be using in their programs.

Views are very powerful. Besides simplifying application programs, they enhance the security features of the relational environment by controlling access at both the table and attribute levels. Although they are becoming popular and more widely used, however, views add yet another burden to the DBA staff (which is usually responsible for implementing them).

Let's return to the DBA's problem and examine the workload of a database shop I'm associated with. This shop maintains two major database application systems and is developing a third.

The shop's relational DBMS is Cincom Systems' Supra 1.3.5, which is based on the three-schema architecture. Programs developed in this environment use logical or derived views for access to the logical database. The database administration staff maintains five database environments in support of the three application systems: one test environment for each system, a production-staging environment, and a production environment.

The production-staging environment is used to implement and test the integration of the three logical data models that reside in each test environment. This includes implementing and controlling data sharing among the three application systems.

The production environment consists of a data model based on the production-staging environment (Figure 1). The multiple environments supporting each system force the DBA to be concerned with migration of changes through the environments and to ensure the environments remain in sync.

Supra's Architecture

Supra's three-schema architecture makes some unique demands on the

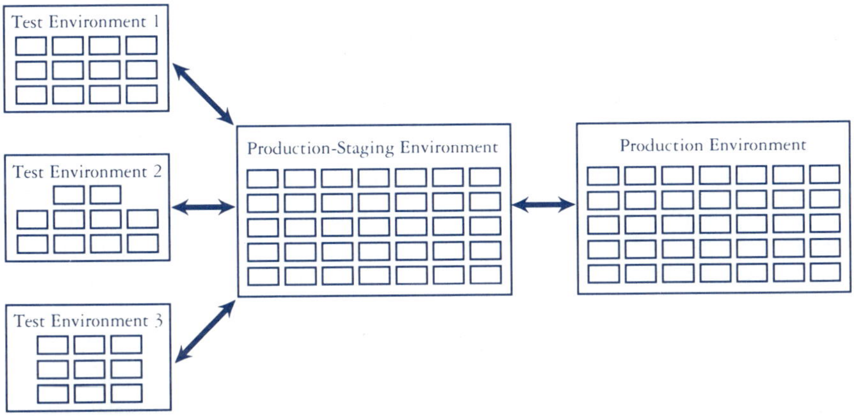

Figure 1 Database environment strategy

DBA's time. The DBA staff is responsible for three levels of database maintenance in each of the five environments: the external schema, the conceptual schema, and the physical schema. The most time-consuming step may be implementing the many logical views required to support the application programs being developed or modified.

The DBA is often forced to prioritize service requests, causing task backlog; database administration becomes a bottleneck rather than a support organization. Definition and maintenance of the complex logical data model are partly responsible for the problem but can also be a major part of the solution.

Relational databases store information about the logical data model in the form of metadata. Depending on the product, this metadatabase is called the dictionary, directory, or catalog. In it resides the key to the relational kingdom.

Metadata can help you automate many database administration tasks, limiting the manual intervention necessary to support entities required by application development. Stored in its own relational database, it is accessed the same way as the data it describes. A shop can use this information to make maintenance responsibilities less overwhelming.

Not every database administration shop can afford the effort required to develop a system on this scale, but our concentration on day-to-day tasks can make us overlook one of our most powerful tools in the relational environment: metadata. Knowing how to access and use metadata is a powerful tool that will increase efficiency—and perhaps loosen the ever-tightening bottleneck.

Excerpted from Gross, Chuck, "Automating database administration." Database Programming & Design, *August 1990, 53ff. © Miller Freeman Inc. Reprinted with permission.*

AT A GLANCE

With multiuser, distributed databases and the growing acceptance of data sharing, the job of the database administrator has become increasingly important. Because data sharing often leads to conflict among users, the database administrator's most important task is to resolve conflict and ensure a smooth-running database environment.

The database administrator sets standards, establishes data ownership, develops backup and recovery procedures, manages the physical database, and evaluates DBMS performance on a regular basis. The administrator's major responsibility is maintaining database integrity procedures and controls, including quality control, concurrency control, and physical data control.

Three managerial issues determine how the database administration function gets organized: staffing, the individual's technical and managerial qualifications, and the location of the database administrator in the organization's structure. There are both professional and political factors to consider when selecting the database administrator.

By the end of this chapter, you should understand

- the functions of the database administrator;
- the managerial and technical considerations in managing a database environment; and
- the various ways the database administration function can be organized.

Introduction

A database is a shared resource, much like the skills of an organization's personnel or a company's finances. But people often find sharing difficult. In a multiuser database environment, many users can access records at the same time, and each user considers his or her own needs a high priority. So someone must coordinate and control this data resource. This person is the database administrator. In this chapter, we also focus on the procedures used and the staff that manages the data, the DBMS, and the overall database system on a regular basis.

The Role of the Database Administrator

When database systems were first developed, data administration was usually delegated by default to users, programmers, and even computer operators. Database integrity did not get the same kind of attention it gets today. But as organizations came to depend more and more on databases, better mechanisms were developed to ensure database integrity. This, in turn, prompted many firms to create the office of database administration to coordinate the whole affair.

Throughout the 1980s, data sharing grew to require a new kind of user cooperation. Deciding who should access what data and who could modify or delete data led to conflicts. An objective, unbiased database administrator was needed to resolve conflicts, sell the change from a nondatabase to a database environment, and guard the database against threats to security and data and software integrity.

Database administration is more than routine management of technology. The database administrator devotes considerable attention to details during design and implementation, including recovery procedures, documentation, and system tuning. Not only must these tasks be performed well, but the entire database must be up and operating on schedule.

Once an organization approves the installation of a database, it must appoint a database administrator (DBA). It is easy to justify the position because, sooner or later, someone is going to have to handle user requests and complaints. Conflict in data sharing is probably one of the most serious problems facing a DBA, such as when

• a user disagrees in the naming conventions adopted in the data dictionary;

• a "high-profile" user complains about worsening response time after new features were added to satisfy another user;

• a comprehensive verification procedure was added to inventory control that slowed the operation of other users; or

• a user needs a local database, which may or may not be compatible with the corporate database.

These kinds of conflicts need a DBA to resolve them. A DBA also authorizes qualified users to access, modify, or delete data based on preestablished criteria and standards. In a multiuser environment, without a strong DBA, a firm can be vulnerable to managerial and technical problems.

Some organizations have both a data administrator and a database administrator. In most organizations, the DATA ADMINISTRATOR (DA) is a high-level manager responsible for maintaining corporate-wide standards, enforcing naming conventions for data elements, and tracking data contents of corporate databases. The DATABASE ADMINISTRATOR (DBA) is a technical person responsible for designing and maintaining the physical database and the DBMS, enforcing security standards, maintaining database performance, and ensuring backup and recovery. (See Figure 15-1.) Both administrators are responsible for making sure

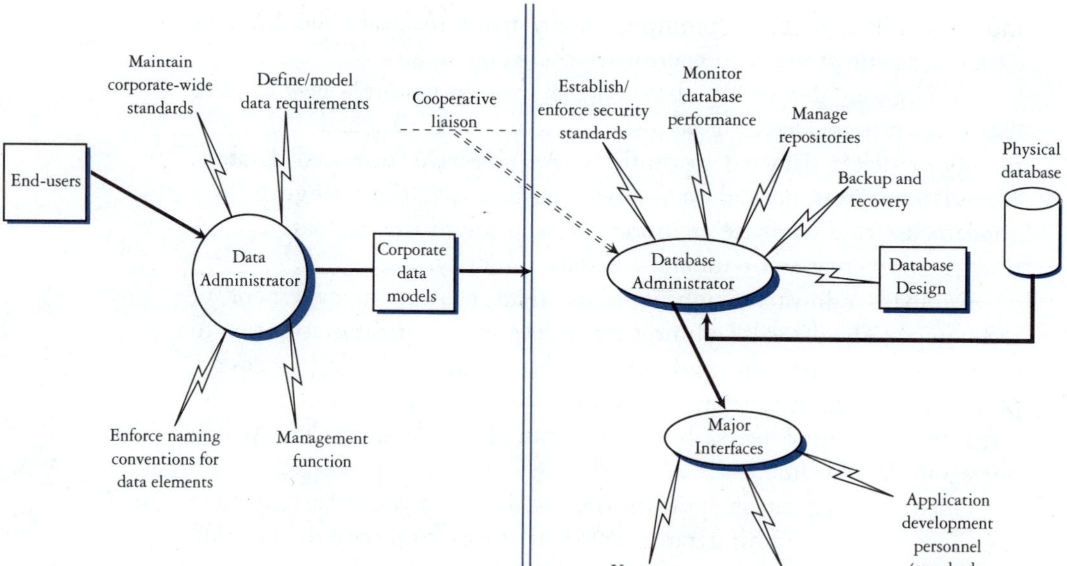

Figure 15-1 The roles of the data administrator and database administrator

the company achieves a highly efficient and effective database environment, but each uses different mechanisms to reach these goals.

A summary contrasting the roles of the DA and DBA is shown in Table 15-1. The DA interface with users focuses on defining their informational requirements. The DA is concerned with the use of data across the organization. Because the DA is concerned with management issues such as lower long-term labor costs of data management, he or she is more directly involved in logical rather than in physical database design.

Area	*Data Administrator (DA)*	*Database Administrator (DBA)*
Primary responsibility	Administrative	Technical
Primary liaisons	Management	Analysts, programmers
Scope	All databases of the organization	Database-specific
Horizon	Long-term data planning	Short-term development and uses of databases
Data design concerns	Logical	Physical
Primary orientation	Metadata (management of information about data)	Data
	Data dictionary	Database
	Data analysis	Database design
	DBMS-independent	DBMS-specific

Table 15-1 Data administrator and database administrator responsibilities

The DBA, on the other hand, is responsible for

- defining and developing databases;
- implementing the technical details of the DBMS;
- monitoring and improving the performance of the corporate database;
- enforcing security standards and protocol; and
- managing information repositories.

The DBA's more technical function focuses on improving the performance of the DBMS. Nonetheless, the DBA does have some managerial functions.

Managerial Functions

The DBA's job has yet to be clearly defined. There is no doubt that the DBA must be a technician, since he or she handles technical problems and must have current technical knowledge about the inner workings of the database. But the job often requires that the DBA be a diplomat as well, persuading users to support common data definitions or access rights, for example.

The DBA deals with three important levels of people in the firm:

1 *Users.* The DBA must manage the user database activity and resolve conflicts.

2 *Information systems personnel.* The DBA must interface with systems designers and other personnel to ensure successful management and support of the database.

3 *Top management.* The DBA must show management that the organization is getting a return on its investment.

The DBA's organizational relationships are diagrammed in Figure 15-2. These relationships help define the DBA's four key managerial function areas: managing database activity, setting standards, establishing ownership and authorization, and informing trainers and users.

Managing Database Activity

Managing a database can be a complicated task. There are several activities involved:

1 designing the physical database;
2 tuning the database for top performance;

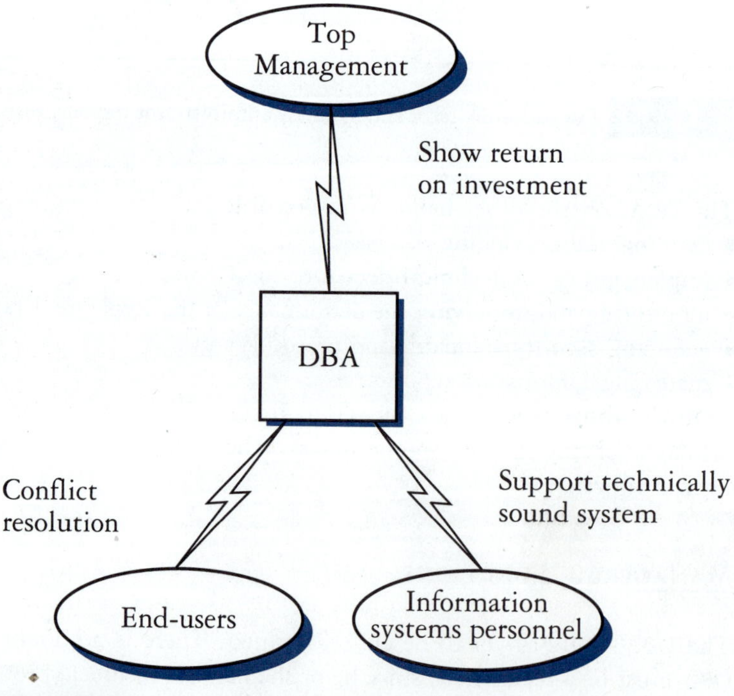

Figure 15-2 The database administrator and organizational relationships

3 evaluating and implementing user needs; and
4 deciding what data will be required in the future.

Note that users manage data—they own the data. The DBA manages data activities, not values. This means the DBA has an interface responsibility with the user. All data activity, through database design and tuning, must be carried out with the user in mind. The goal is to assure easy user access and integrity of the data at all times.

Setting Standards

Standardization is a prime concern in database management. Setting standards, guidelines, or control procedures means making sure that users access only the data they are authorized to access, delete, or update, and that each record has a standard name, format, and access method. Each file should also have a standard name and a standard relationship with other files in the database. Although users often resist it, standardization invariably assures data integrity and system security.

Establishing Data Ownership and Authorization

In a multiuser database environment, establishing who owns what data and who is authorized to access or delete data is important. Ownership does not rest with the DBA; he or she is merely the custodian of the data, just as a bank is the custodian of customers' deposits. The DBA's job is to define data ownership and authorization procedures, arbitrate ownership disputes, and control the use of the data in the collective interests of all users. When two or more users have equal rights to certain files, the DBA should provide a procedure that documents the changes made by each user.

What data ownership is really all about, of course, is authorized access, especially in situations where several users want to access or update the same record at the same time. This concurrency update problem is handled by the DBA, who provides specific instructions for the user to follow. DBAs often assign certain user activities to periods when demand is light. For more on concurrency update problems and authorization rules, see Chapter 3.

Informing and Training Users

The DBA is responsible for informing and training users, top management, and other personnel in the inner workings of the database that are related to other areas of operation.

The level of DBA-user interaction ranges from passive to interactive; that is, from providing easy-to-use documentation to training, assisting, and advising users about application problems. The DBA must be in constant touch with the user. To do a good job, the DBA must

- keep DBMS documentation up to date, including documentation on what data is stored and how it can be accessed, and a data dictionary with cross-references to all data elements;
- make references and user manuals available for successful training; and
- inform users about system problems that could adversely affect user files.

Answering questions and solving user problems, a highly interactive DBA-user interface is part of managing technology and those who use the database for making day-to-day decisions.

A large part of informing users is documentation. The DBA publishes documents and manuals about data ownership, data integrity, data retrieval rights, and data recovery practices.

Technical Functions

Developing Recovery Procedures

The DBA must monitor all database failures and provide for recovery. Failures range from software breakdowns to improper loading of data. For each type of failure, the DBA must make sure a recovery procedure is in place, fully documented, and up to date. The documentation must tell the user how to recreate data, how to use backup copies, and how to regenerate reports. In an environment where customers are involved, the DBA must train the user in backup and recovery procedures that will keep the business in operation. For example, in a banking environment, when a teller is unable to display an account balance on the screen because the computer is down, he or she should be able to access the information by telephoning bookkeeping or by acquiring a hard copy of the previous day's closing balance sheet. Such a procedure should be part of the teller's training.

Managing Repositories

One of the most critical databases in the corporate MIS environment is the INFORMATION REPOSITORY—the metadata that defines the organization's data and processing resources. (See Figure 15-3.) Such a repository is fast replacing the classical data dictionary and is used by the DBA (or DA, in an organization that has both) to manage the total MIS environment. The information repository includes information about the data in the corporate databases as well as the application programs that manage them.

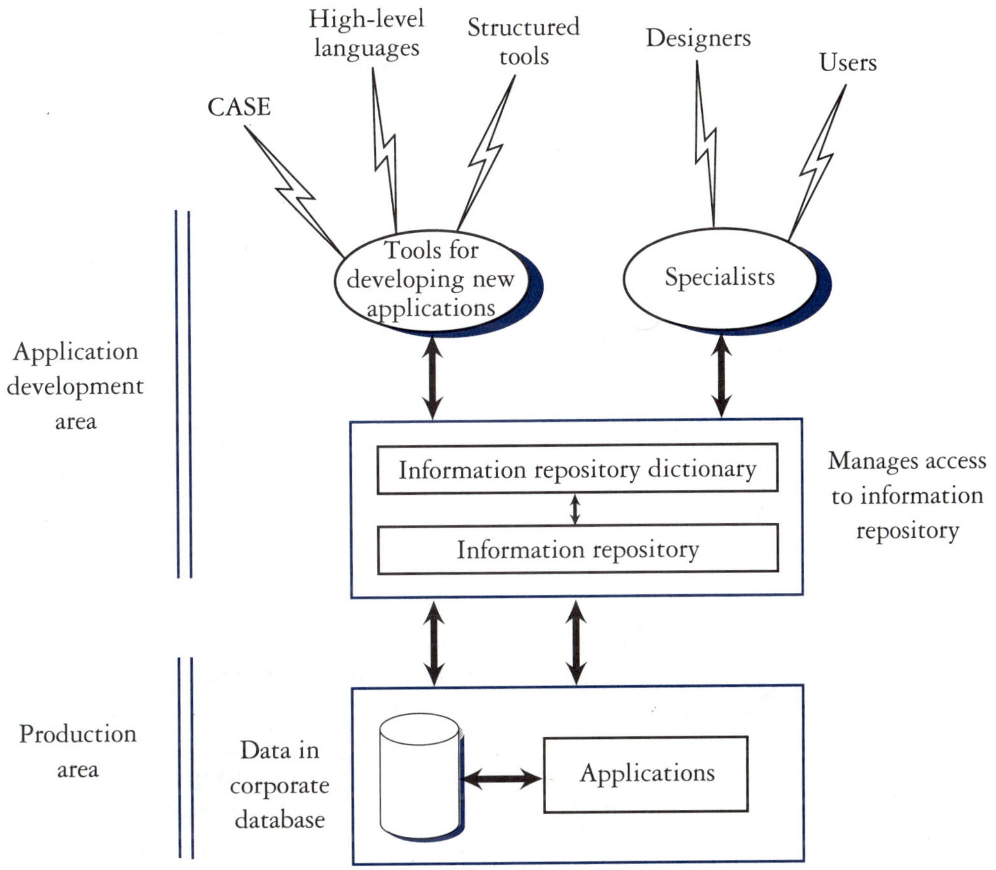

Figure 15-3 General layout of information repository

The information repository consists of two components,

- the APPLICATION DEVELOPMENT ENVIRONMENT, in which specialists use special tools to develop new applications; and
- the PRODUCTION ENVIRONMENT, in which people use applications to build or update databases.

Repositories can be generated using various Computer-Aided Software Engineering (CASE) tools for developing new database applications. For example, the widely used, PC-based product Excelerator allows the designer to draw data structure and entity-relationship diagrams, to generate data dictionaries, to integrate the dictionary with the diagrams, and to check the conceptual design for third normal form. Some CASE products can read DB2, IMS, and other DBMS files and construct the necessary conceptual data models. More and more of these automated products are likely to appear on the market.

Managing the Physical Database

Another important responsibility of the DBA is to see to it that the entire system is well-designed and maintained to standards. The DBA must make sure the physical design focuses on the user's requirements and incorporates all changes or suggestions made by the users prior to testing.

Effective communication is a must in dealing with people. The DBA must keep the users abreast of any change that affects their data. Any new design features or enhancements should have the prior approval of the user before these changes are tested and incorporated into the database.

Managing the Database Management System

The DBA must constantly monitor and evaluate how well the DBMS meets standards. The DBA should monitor such DBMS activities as CPU time (actual computer time needed to process a transaction) and elapsed time (the time it takes to process an activity). These statistics can be captured by simple programs that record the user's overall workload or capture the actual processing times.

The DBA must also investigate performance complaints and oversee all fine-tuning of the database. In the event of DBMS performance problems, the DBA must decide whether or not to modify the database structure to correct the problem. User complaints are normally handled during periodic user meetings or are evaluated on a case-by-case basis. Regardless of the approach, handling user complaints can pay off in terms of user rapport and improved communication between the user and the DBA.

System tuning means optimizing the system for user productivity. The DBMS has a number of built-in timing features that can help the DBA minimize unused memory space and improve communication channels. Buffers can also be used to minimize response time between command executions.

Several tools are available to the DBA for evaluating system performance. Most database systems have built-in PERFORMANCE MONITORING ROUTINES, which are special utilities that keep track of the number of times the disk has been accessed, the CPU time used by each user or workstation, the amount of memory used by each application, and so forth. In addition, the performance of input/output and secondary devices is evaluated by the monitor to ensure a proper match with the performance requirements of the DBMS.

Maintaining Database Integrity

Maintaining database integrity, covered in Chapter 3, means protecting the database against improper access or modification. The DBA is responsible for implementing and maintaining database integrity procedures that control access and reduce the cost of recovery due to integrity problems. Maintaining database integrity also means making sure that the data and software are accurate, reliable, and free of error. Achieving 100 percent integrity is almost impossible, but a resourceful DBA can maintain an adequate level of integrity through physical, quality, concurrency, update and access, and audit control measures.

The DBA must make sure programmers and designers build the required internal controls into every application. Developing a corporate database auditing policy should ensure that future databases meet the security and embezzlement and fraud control requirements of the organization. A summary of the key integrity control measures is shown in Table 15-2.

Control Measures	*Description*
Physical database control	Control for temperature, humidity, back up, etc.
Quality control	Ensure that data is accurate, complete, and consistent
Concurrency control	Users should not have to wait unnecessarily for direct and immediate access to files
Update and access control	Set up access authorization schemes for the users
Audit control	Provide checks and balances on the activities of MIS and DBA staff

Table 15-2 Key integrity control measures

Physical database control Physical database control involves controlling temperature, humidity, and dust to prevent hardware failures. Because physical controls sometimes fail, the DBA must have backup and recovery procedures in place to handle hardware failures. Backup involves copying (sometimes called dumping) the files onto a storage medium such as a floppy disk on a regular basis. In addition, all incoming transactions should be logged before actual processing takes place, so that users will know which transactions must be re-entered in the event of a system failure.

Quality control Quality control means correcting detectable errors to ensure that data is accurate, complete, and consistent with the initial data definition. The DBA is responsible for quality control at all times.

Part of data quality control is validation of incoming, stored, and output data. Dealing with highly sensitive data means checking for consistency. For example, imagine what would happen if a bank's database could not distinguish between account numbers 12-4746 and 127467 when crediting a deposit. The DBA must police the system to ensure that such software problems do not occur and that all monitors work properly.

Concurrency control When two or more users concurrently access the same database (see Figure 15-4), one user may update a record that another user wants to access or delete. Although there are "locks" that protect files or records, most DBMSs do not provide control over how concurrent updates are handled. The DBA must ensure that conflicts such as these are resolved to the satisfaction of all users without creating confusion in the process.

Update and access control Update control involves making sure that all updates are preauthorized. Most systems use two levels of authorization. The first level allows the user to add data to the database but not to change existing records. The second level allows the user to change and delete the files without restriction. The DBA must set stringent program testing requirements for programs that modify the

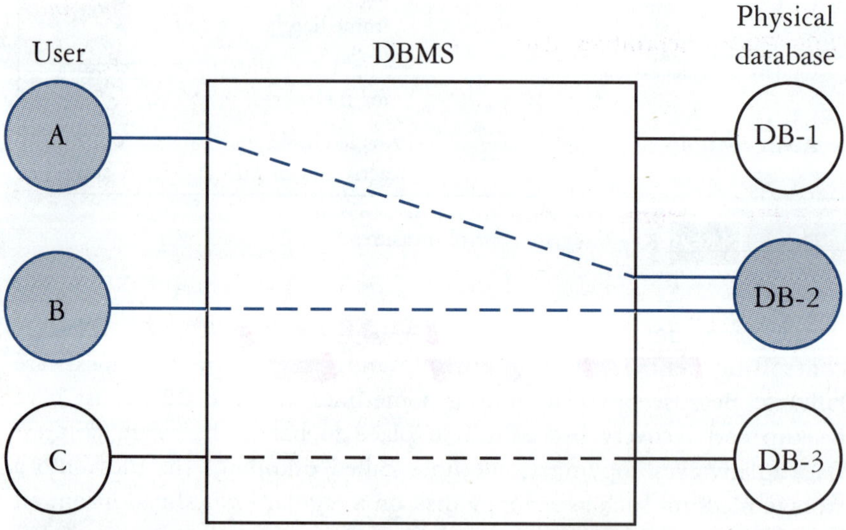

Figure 15-4 Concurrency database access. A and B share a common database, DB2

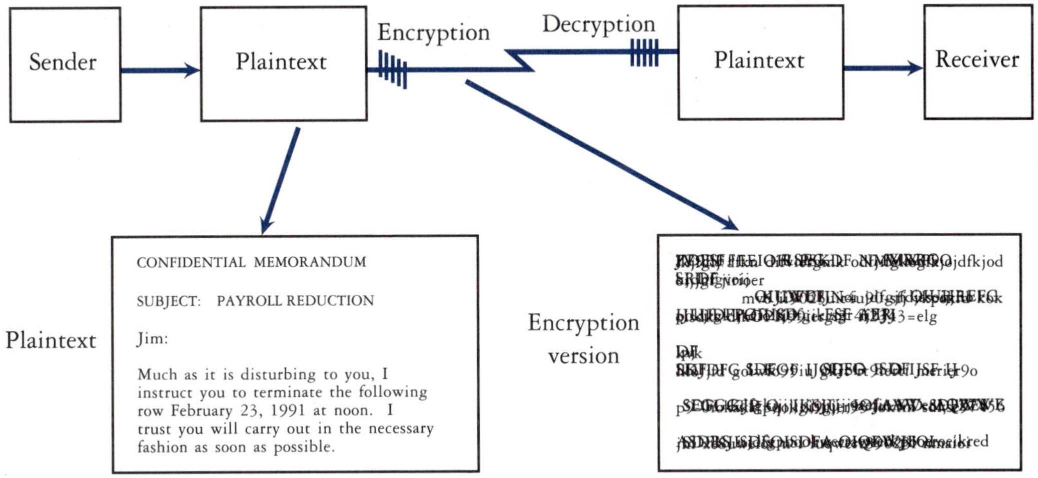

Figure 15-5 Data encryption and decryption

database, to ensure that the authorization system works properly.

Access control means checking for authorized access to the database. The DBA must set up access controls to handle authorization of users, to identify requesters, and to verify their authorization against the request. This is the whole reason behind system security. Imagine how tempting it would be for someone to access a bank's auto loan database and erase a $28,000 outstanding loan balance on a Mercedes. Measures should be incorporated to deter unauthorized access.

In a telecommunication setup where data can be tapped from multiple workstations, a practical access control measure, called DATA ENCRYPTION, scrambles data during transmission from computer to workstation or from computer to computer. This scheme makes the data virtually useless to unauthorized users. For example, the name "Bob" could be encrypted into "[illegible]," which makes it virtually useless because these are nonprintable characters. The inverse process, called DATA DECRYPTION, returns the data to its original form. (See Figure 15-5.)

Most of today's encryption is based on the National Bureau of Standards encryption algorithm, known as the Data Encryption Standard (DES). A system that assures that encryption and decryption (coding and decoding) are done without human intervention is virtually secure from unauthorized access.

Audit control Audit control procedures provide checks and balances on the activities of database administration staff and MIS personnel and manage the effects transactions have on a database. The role of the DBA is to ensure accurate and on going audit control at all times. A DBMS must provide an audit trail of transactions and database changes. One

Time	Update Auto Order	Database Auto Inventory Level (time 0=300 cars)	Audit Trail
1	Lock inventory file		Before image: Inventory = 300 cars
2	Read inventory record		
3	Deduct 2 units		
4	Replace inventory record		
5	Release inventory record	298	After image: Inventory = 298 cars

Table 15-3 Audit trail of before and after images

way to handle this is via a TRANSACTION LOG which keeps track of all transactions processed against the database. A second way is via a CHANGE LOG which captures the before and after images of each transaction on a storage device other than the one that has the database in residence. A BEFORE IMAGE is a copy of the actual record before a modification; only the records being modified are added to the file. An AFTER IMAGE is a copy of the same record after the modification. An example of audit trails reflecting before and after images of an auto dealer inventory file is shown in Table 15-3.

Audit controls protect a database from external security breaches and internal fraud by restoring correct values to the database after a failure makes it inconsistent. This is part of the roll-back and roll-forward procedures was covered in Chapter 3. The DBA must balance the resources invested in audit controls against the sensitivity of the data in question—a difficult task since, like any insurance policy, the worth of audit controls remains intangible until the system has been violated. The complexity of today's databases makes automatic auditing necessary.

Organizing the Database Administration Function

In large organizations with complex database operations, a single DBA cannot perform all these functions. Since database administration practice is not standardized, there are significant differences in database administration functions from organization to organization. Small installations may not even have a DBA, in which case most of the DBA functions are performed by MIS personnel. In large database installations, a staff of specialists makes up the database administration unit.

DBA Role	*Interfaces with*	*Major Responsibilities*
Database administrator	End-users Management Programmers Designers	All database administration managerial and technical functions; supervises staff
Applications expert	End-users Programmers	Applications programming
Database designer	Systems analysts/ designers	Experience in hardware selection and software design
Query languages expert	End-users Programmers Systems designers	Screen formatting for on-line activities, security implementation articulation in the user's business
Data operations expert	MIS operations	Communications between DBA and operations staff

Table 15-4 Database administration functions, interfaces, and key responsibilities

Three managerial issues determine how the database administration function gets organized:

1 staffing the database administration function
2 selecting the DBA
3 location of the DBA in the organization

Staffing and Key Interfaces

The database administration function involves management, users, programmers, systems developers, and computer operators. Table 15-4 summarizes the key database administration roles, their interfaces, and responsibilities. Each position is described according to the three phases of database system development: design, conversion, and operations.

Applications expert APPLICATIONS EXPERTS are programmers proficient in physical database design, conversion, and operations. Their responsibilities involve three phases:

1 *Design.*

- Develops the logical structure of the system in line with the long-term goals of the user or the firm
- Defines the data elements and synonyms
- Supplies data element information, including how it relates to the database designer and the librarian who incorporates elements in the data dictionary

2 *Conversion.*

• Works with the database designer and operations expert to implement security and auditing procedures

3 *Operations.*

• Monitors the consistency and reliability of security, auditing, and access control procedures

Database designer The DATABASE DESIGNER is usually an expert in database languages and procedures. He or she receives the logical structure design from the DBA or the applications expert. The designer's main responsibilities are as follows:

1 *Design.*

• Designs the software schemas

• Develops the physical structure and applies performance criteria against the physical structure

• Designs software configurations, security, and authorization routines for the database

• Designs backup and recovery procedures

• Assists in selecting database hardware and software

2 *Conversion.*

• Works with the applications expert to implement the DBMS package and all applications

• Works with the operations staff to implement backup and recovery procedures

3 *Operations.*

• Projects work loads and notifies the DBA of any performance problems

• Evaluates problem areas and plans appropriate changes or enhancements

• Helps operations staff download the database in the event of abnormal runs

Query languages expert The QUERY LANGUAGES EXPERT is a specialist in on-line query management whose key responsibilities are as follows:

1 *Design.*

• Works with the systems expert to design queries

• Sets up authorization levels and formats for various types of queries

2 *Conversion and operations.*

• Monitors the performance of queries and notifies the DBA of any deviations

• Works with the user in creating query maintenance and update procedures

Data operations expert The DATA OPERATION EXPERT'S main job is to maintain good communications between the database administration and MIS operations personnel. His or her responsibilities include the following:

1 *Design.*

• Evaluates the effectiveness of backup, recovery, and security procedures of the database

• Develops interfaces such that operators can intervene with various applications when necessary

2 *Conversion.*

• Maps out the procedures for implementing the DBMS

• Logs database activities

• Evaluates operator training programs and recommends a program for operating the DBMS

3 *Operations.*

• Supervises logging and recording of hardware malfunctions as well as all restarts and recoveries after failure

• Reviews daily performance reports and reports to the database designer any problems that require attention

• Evaluates the overall database activity to ensure quality performance

• Maintains some control over computer scheduling for database processing

• Controls all periodic data dumps, audit trails, and so on

Selecting the Database Administrator

The DBA's function is both technical and managerial. The DBA must be technically proficient in the mechanics and methodology of database design in order to manage the database administration technical staff. The DBA must also be a good manager, capable of coordinating work, providing leadership and direction, and communicating with users and database specialists.

Placing the Database Administrator

In a large organization, the DBA post is essentially a management position. A suitable candidate must have managerial experience and a broad knowledge of the employing organization. Systems analysts,

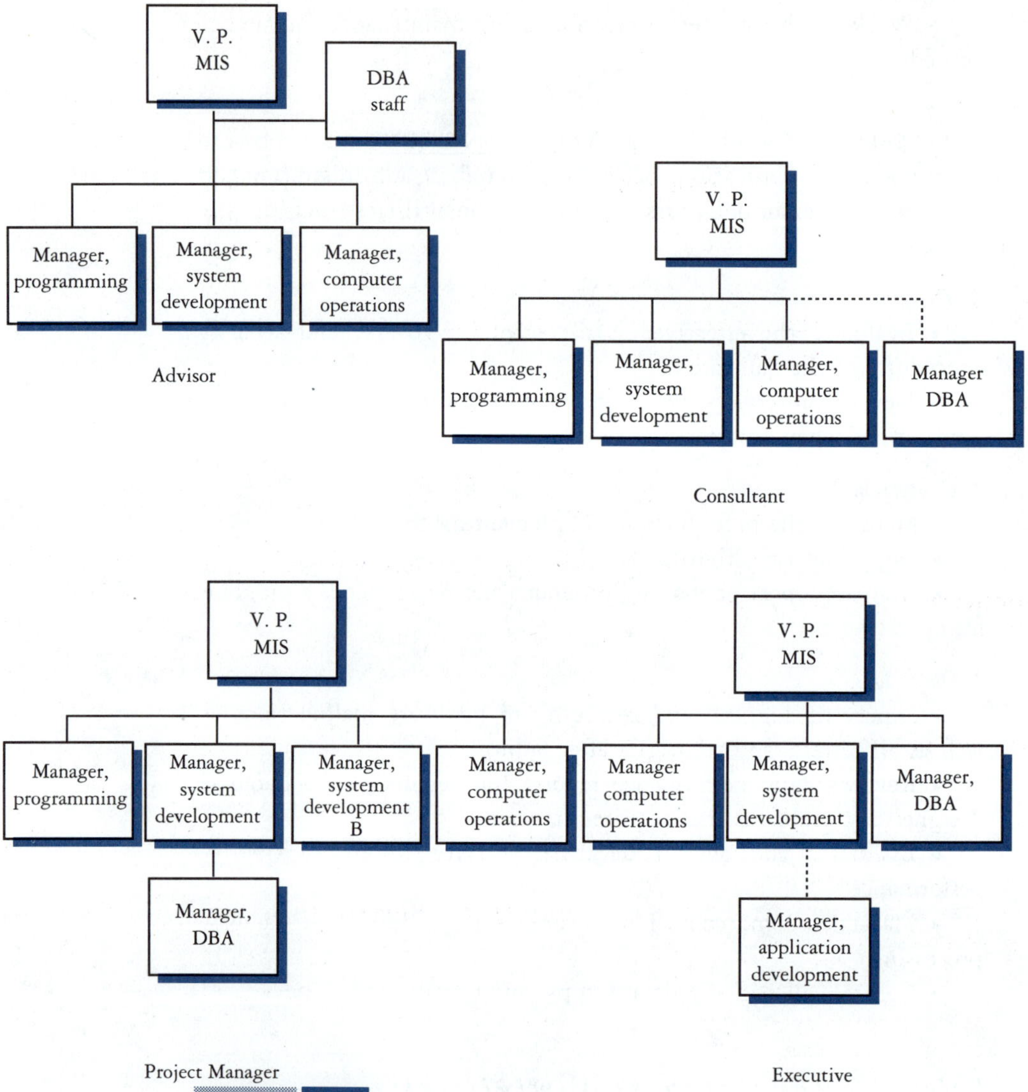

Figure 15-6 Entity-relationship diagrams DBA placement

information specialists, and MIS managers are usually preferred over more technically oriented specialists.

Because the DBA imposes restrictions on users and standards on MIS personnel, he or she must be highly placed in the organization. One school of thought suggests placing the DBA in the organizational structure one step above the departments that the position serves. Another suggests that, because the DBA is in charge of critical shared resources, the position must not be under the control of the corporate groups that compete for use of the resources. The placement of the DBA and DBA interfaces vary from one company to another, depending on how much the organization relies on the database system. But in all cases the DBA should be highly enough placed to be effective, while still staying involved in daily DBMS activities.

The DBA may operate as an advisor, a consultant, a project manager, or an executive. (See Figure 15-6.)

The consultant The consultant DBA is more of a staff position reporting directly to the MIS vice president and consults with application development teams on database matters. This is the most common (and practical) placement category for DBAs in organizations today.

The advisor The advisory DBA is a temporary position set up to accommodate the early planning details of a new database installation. The advisory DBA reports to the user. Once the system has been installed, the DBA's staff is reorganized into a more permanent arrangement. The functions of the advisory DBA include planning and administrative tasks, policy formulation, and standardization procedures.

The project manager The project-oriented DBA reports to an application project leader, a supportive function in application development. The reporting relationship continues until the DBMS is installed. This type of DBA position is typical of small installations that handle a limited number of projects.

The project DBA is usually low in the organizational hierarchy and performs a broader set of tasks than the advisory DBA, but the scope of these tasks is limited to the project. The project DBA has no interaction with other project groups. It is an acceptable role as long as the position is viewed as supportive.

The executive The executive DBA reports directly to a vice president in charge of information systems, which places the DBA on a par with other line officers within the MIS division. This arrangement is common in large organizations with a centralized, multiple-database environment. An executive DBA has high visibility and personal control over enforcing standards. Some executive DBAs, however, are placed too high in the organization to be active in day-to-day database operations.

The consultant and executive DBAs are probably the two most common alternatives. The executive DBA role is on par with line executives. The success of the database administration function depends largely on the attitude of the MIS director and the support that top management gives MIS as an entity.

Data Administration and Management Information Systems

Many companies view data administration as a purely technical position. It is true that managing tools like the data dictionary and

DBMS is the DBA's main priority, but that is not the sole objective of data administration. The DBA only uses these tools to manage quality information within the organization and make its use more uniform and consistent. Data administration is as much a managerial function as it is technical.

Politically, the data administrator is at a disadvantage because his or her accomplishments are difficult to measure by the traditional quantitative means usually applied to MIS personnel. The success of programmers and designers is often gauged by how well they use hardware, software, CPU time, and disk space in developing an application. But it is difficult to measure a reduction in data redundancy or an improvement in data access time achieved by a successful data administrator. It would be wrong to measure a DBA by the number of data elements loaded in a data dictionary or the number of database applications loaded on the company's mainframe.

Another difficulty with evaluating the database administration staff is that their goals and objectives are more long-term and encompassing than the rest of the MIS staff. The success of the data administration staff should be measured in terms of long-term reduction of data redundancy and improved quality of information and user decision making.

Consistency and standardization of data are crucial for managing a multiuser database environment. The DBA must combine intuition and creativity in data design to produce workable and dependable databases. Many database problems are not technical in nature; many are related to problems of organization, lack of coordination, poor communication, or poor planning. Many solutions to data management problems require changes in methodology rather than technology. Changing user work habits requires selling, persuading, and repeated follow-up, which often takes weeks or even months.

The DBA must "sell" the user away from data ownership toward data sharing across applications. This shift is only one aspect of the gradual but steady shift from data-processing-oriented to user-oriented system development, using fourth-generation languages such as dBASE IV. The role of MIS today has become one of controlling and managing data for the user, while allowing the user to determine how the data will be reported and used.

Another likely conflict between data administration and MIS in general concerns technology. Data administration tends to be more business- and management-oriented, emphasizing the relationship between information and the success of the business. In contrast, MIS tends to be more technically oriented, concentrating on how hardware and software can use data most efficiently. MIS management has long associated monetary rewards more with technical expertise than with business expertise. Data administration, on the other hand, relies on understanding the whole business more heavily than on technology, which the MIS staff may perceive as a threat, devaluing their technical expertise. These conflicts can be resolved with regular meetings and cooperation between the data administration and MIS staff on future applications.

Although the database administrator position has become well established in the past decade, there has been higher labor turnover among DBAs than among other traditional professionals, such as programmers and analysts. The main reason for the turnover is industry demand for DBAs. Yet few DBAs leave data administration to return to traditional MIS positions. They usually shift companies, but not roles. Most DBAs are more loyal to the profession than to the employer. Many companies have already established award programs to recognize DBAs for good work.

The DBA has the potential of being a powerful person. Integrating data under the administrative control of the DBA puts the DBA in an influential position in the eyes of users. The combination of technical expertise and top management support makes the DBA function difficult to overlook.

Although the DBA is mostly an advisor and consultant to the user, the DBA's expertise can substantially increase his or her power. Demonstrating strong leadership in database development and an ability to handle uncertainties will also increase a DBA's power. This means that users are likely to compromise and support the DBA in future enhancements. A DBA who fails to establish credibility or who is perceived as weak will lose that power. And a powerless DBA can have an adverse impact on DBMS maintenance, user participation, and management support.

SUMMARY

1 When DBMSs were first developed, database administration was delegated to users, programmers, and even computer operators. Database administration has only became important since the early 1980s when data integration required data sharing among users who once had responsibility for their own data.

2 Because data sharing can lead to conflict, a DBA must be capable of resolving conflicts and managing the database.

3 Data administrators are responsible for the overall management of information as an organizational resource and interfacing with users to

define their informational requirements. In contrast, the database administrator is responsible for designing, implementing, and maintaining the database and the DBMS. Both are responsible for managing and controlling data and maximizing the organization's return on its investment in the database.

4 There are four areas in which the DBA function is most obvious:

   a. *Managing database activity*. The DBA's responsibilities include setting standards, establishing data ownership, informing and training users, publishing documentation, and developing recovery procedures.
   b. *Managing repositories*. The DBA uses the repository to manage the entire MIS environment. The repository includes information about the data in the corporate databases as well as the application programs that manage them.
   c. *Managing the physical database*. The DBA's role is to incorporate all proposed changes to ensure an efficient and an effective database performance.
   d. *Managing the DBMS*. This includes evaluating DBMS performance, investigating performance complaints, tuning the database and the communications software, and implementing new features.

5 The DBA must maintain database integrity through procedures that minimize incidents of failure and reduce the cost of recovery due to integrity problems. Integrity control measures include physical data control, quality control, concurrency control, update and access control, and audit control.

6 The DBA must control the overall operations of the database. This includes ensuring efficient operations by instituting backup and logging procedures.

7 Three managerial issues determine how the DBA function is organized: staffing, selecting, and locating.

   a. *Staffing*. The key DBA staff positions include the applications expert, the database designer, the query languages expert, and the data operation expert. Each staff position has a unique role in the design, conversion, and operation phases of database system development.
   b. *Selecting*. The DBA is expected to be well-versed in technical and managerial protocols and procedures. The DBA must also have strong managerial skills.
   c. *Locating*. The key alternative positions of the DBA within the MIS department are consultative, advisory, project-oriented, and executive.

8 Much of the success of the DBA function depends on the attitude of the MIS director and the support given to the overall MIS effort by top management.

9 The data administrator is at a political disadvantage within the company, because his or her accomplishments are difficult to measure by the traditional quantitative means used in evaluating the accomplishments of data processing personnel. For example, it is difficult to measure the reduction in data redundancy or the improvement in data access time achieved by data administration.

KEY WORDS

After image
Application development environment
Applications expert
Before image
Change log
Data administrator (DA)
Database administrator (DBA)
Database designer
Data decryption
Data encryption
Data operations expert
Information repository
Performance monitoring routines
Production environment
Query languages expert
Transaction log

REVIEW QUESTIONS

1 Make arrangements to interview the DBA of a local firm. Write a report that includes the following.
   a. whether the data dictionary is in use, is active or passive, and is integrated with the DBMS
   b. the DBA's managerial and technical background
   c. the DBA's duties, responsibilities, interfaces, and staff
   d. the DBA's most common problems or conflicts and how he or she resolves them
   e. whether the DBA's position is unique to a large DBMS
   f. the DBA's position in the organization's hierarchy

2 How would a company justify employing a DBA? Be specific.

3 What is the difference between a data administrator and a database administrator? Which one is the more common job title? Why?

4 Why must the DBA have a strong managerial background?

5 "Users manage data; the DBA manages data activities." Do you agree? Explain.

6 What is involved in managing database activity? Illustrate.

7 Choose three key responsibilities of the DBA and elaborate on each, keeping in mind the total commitment of this position to the welfare of the firm.

8 "The DBA's responsibility is defining the concurrent update features of the DBMS and providing details for the user to follow in restarting a transaction should the DBMS ignore it." Do you agree with this statement? Elaborate.

9 Distinguish between passive and interactive communication. How does either level of DBA-user interaction relate to the data dictionary? Be specific.

10 How important are recovery procedures? Discuss.

11 An important responsibility of the DBA is implementing and maintaining database integrity procedures. How is this achieved?

12 Several integrity control measures can be adopted by the DBA. Explain briefly each measure. Which measure (if any) do you consider the most critical for maintaining database integrity on a day-to-day basis? Why?

13 In what way is concurrent control related to update control? Explain.

14 Discuss the managerial issues that determine how the DBA function gets organized.

15 What is involved in staffing the database administration area? What are the pros and cons of having database administration within the MIS division?

16 How does the applications expert's work differ from that of database designer? From the data operations expert?

17 Distinguish between the following pairs:

a. consultant DBA and advisory DBA
b. project-oriented and executive DBA
c. audit control and quality control
d. update and access control
e. quality control and concurrency control

APPLICATION PROBLEMS

1 You are the database administrator for a large pharmaceutical firm that changes the formula for a popular cancer drug. Should a copy of the original formula be saved in case the new one proves unmarketable? What issues are involved? What role should you play if the firm takes no action?

2 Interview a database administrator in your town or area and evaluate how well his or her functions and responsibilities match those covered in the chapter.

3 Draw an organizational chart of your school's computer center or that of a local business and identify the location of the DBA in the structure. If the center does not have one, evaluate the pros and cons of hiring a full-time database administrator.

4 Eagle Corporation is a holding company consisting of 15 small- to medium-sized firms specializing in the construction trade. Annual sales of the holding company are just over $100 million and are growing at a rate of 10 percent each year.

After several years of using a traditional data processing environment (that is, hardware and software managed by a data processing supervisor), the firm's owners have decided to create a database administration position. After advertising the position, they have narrowed the candidates to three finalists:

a. Bill Hall, a project leader with four years' experience with Eagle Corporation. Last year, the company sent him to IBM for a six-week training course in database design and structured design methodology.
b. Debbie Kolb, a senior programmer with a competing firm, who has proven experience in SQL/DS and dBASE IV, which the firm is considering for its IBM AS/400 minicomputer system.
c. Dave Smith, the database administrator for an IBM AS/400 system with a medium-sized firm in a town 20 miles away.

Based on this information, which candidate would you choose as the new database administrator for Eagle? Justify your choice.

5 Based on the work you have completed on Island Jumpers, Inc. (IJI), do you foresee the need for a full-time database administrator for IJI's newly designed system? If your answer is yes, what skills or attributes would you look for in a person occupying this position? Be specific.

C H A P T

Choosing a Database Management System

E R 1 6

Get the Lease with the Most

AT A GLANCE

Get the Lease with the Most

Why do so many sophisticated information systems people use relatively unsophisticated means to select their computer lessors? Because they operate under the misconception that one bidder list, usually containing a small group of lessors, can meet the computer leasing requirements of all of their leased products.

This perception may not take into consideration that there are more than 500 computer lessors in the United States, about 20 categories of computer products, 100 types of products within those 20 categories, and no one leasing company that specializes in even half of the product categories.

To get qualified lessors to bid on each leased product, lessee companies need to understand lessor specialization areas, sort leasing requirements into manageable product groupings, and set the bid process in motion.

Why a Specialist?

What the specialist lessor typically offers a user is a low lease rate and specific product knowledge. Generalists typically base their pricing on residual forecasts supplied by outside forecasting services; forecasts are typically reduced by 10 percent to 30 percent. This gives them a margin of safety. . .

Product specialization With the exception of being aware that lessors tend to specialize in either IBM or non-IBM products, users commonly lump lessors together. But the lessor landscape is much more complex. There are experts in mainframes, minicomputers, printers, and so on.

Beyond these broad product categories, lessors segment themselves further into niches. For example, there are those midrange lessors that deal mostly in one class of machine, such as an IBM Application System/400. While most lessors will arrange leasing for products outside their domain, they will often do so at a higher price than a specialist.

For example, during a recent bid on a large Hitachi Data Systems Corp. CPU, a generalist firm used a forecaster's residual numbers and bid on a 60-month lease, setting payments at $133,300 per month. An HDS mainframe specialist, using its own residual value numbers, quoted $126,500 per month on the same lease, saving the customer $408,000 over the life of the lease. . .

Transaction size specialization Lessors also specialize in the cost of the transaction. Many lessors in the industry are small "niche" lessors that have access to the necessary financing—both equity and debt—to handle a big money lease.

The user must be aware that just as the small-ticket transaction lessor (under $50,000 in cost) may be the wrong lessor for a big-ticket transaction (over $500,000), the big-ticket lessor can be the wrong one for a $50,000 lease. The big-ticket lessor would not make enough money per transaction to handle the overhead costs associated with making a small-ticket deal. In that case, the lessee might get hit with higher prices . . .

Residual risk assumption specialization The lessor that specializes in a product will almost always take the highest residual position in that product because of its intense study of the residual forecast. To get the lowest lease rate, a company needs a lessor that is willing to take the greatest residual risk—that is, willing to recover the lowest amount of the cost over the lease term.

For the lessee, that means the higher the residual exposure taken by the lessor, the lower the monthly rent.

Lease term specialization Many users are surprised that the length of the lease term they want can qualify or disqualify some lessors from their bidder list. Lessors tend to specialize in short-term (two to three years) or long-term (four-plus years) leases based on their investment requirements or the requirements of their equity investors.

Lessors that can use tax benefits . . . will bid most competitively on long-term leases that have the lowest residual exposure. That translates into lower monthly rates. Short-term lease specialists tend not to be tax-oriented and are willing to take significant residual risks with the expectation of substantial gains. While the lease rate may be higher, their value to the user is high flexibility in lease term.

Users' credit specialization Most lessors market to users with a specific class of credit: investment-grade, middle-market, or high-risk. Users that have an investment-grade credit rating will be wasting their efforts if they solicit bids from lessors that specialize in middle- or high-risk credits.

With an understanding of how lessors specialize, customers can begin to sort the products they want to lease into manageable groupings, each with its own leasing criteria.

Selecting Lessors

Once the product groupings are established, the user must determine the number and identity of lessor specialists for the bidder list applicable to each grouping.

To get the most out of its computer leasing operation, the lessee must consciously approach the leasing of each product or product grouping as a separate and unique business. As such, each business transaction requires a discrete bidder list that is designed to meet the requirements of that business only.

The user benefits because the lessor bid process is streamlined, and the user has confidence that his leasing business can be awarded to the most desirable lessor for each lease transaction.

Excerpted from Martin, Tom, "Get the lease with the most." Computerworld, *June 3, 1991, 107-108.*

AT A GLANCE

Selecting a DBMS begins with listing desirable DBMS features and rating available products against the listed criteria, with an eye to ensuring quick and flexible application development at an affordable cost. With the widespread availability of low-cost DBMSs for microcomputers, it is important to keep in mind their limitations and advantages.

- While a mainframe DBMS may handle a large company database well, a microcomputer DBMS is likely to accommodate a small business database just as effectively.
- Microcomputer-based DBMSs are rarely larger than a few hundred thousand characters in size. Mainframe DBMS packages are easily ten times that size.
- DBMSs for micros normally handle fewer than ten users, whereas a mainframe DBMS is capable of serving hundreds of concurrent users with multiple simultaneous access to the database.
- Back-up and recovery for the microcomputer DBMS is not as involved a procedure as that for the mainframe version.

Selecting a DBMS involves identifying the applications to be developed for the user, evaluating available DBMSs against the user's requirements, selecting the DBMS that best meets these requirements, and negotiating a reliable contract to support the DBMS on a regular basis. These steps may involve a steering committee, including a consultant who is a specialist in the selection area.

One of the key questions that comes up during the selection process is whether to lease or make the DBMS. Although there is no clear-cut answer to this question, tax benefits, availability of internal specialists, and cost considerations have an obvious influence on the final decision. In any case, it pays to keep in mind the importance of the user's requirements.

By the end of this chapter, you should be able to

- identify the selection process steps;
- understand the selection criteria in a Request for Proposal (RFP);
- distinguish among the methods for evaluating vendor responses; and
- follow the procedure for negotiating computer contracts.

INTRODUCTION

Users often ask "what is the best database I can get?" They are usually disappointed to hear "it depends." Unfortunately, there is no best program to make the selection easy.

One reason why DBMSs have produced disappointing results is because users know little about selecting a DBMS or have underestimated the importance of matching the capabilities of a DBMS to the total requirements of the organization. For the medium-size and mainframe DBMS, most organizations rely on professional staff or outside consultants to do the selection. But even choosing among microcomputer DBMS packages can be a challenge.

Selecting a DBMS begins with listing desirable DBMS features and rating available products against the listed criteria, with an eye to ensuring quick and flexible application development at an affordable cost. The widespread availability of low-cost DBMSs for microcomputers makes one wonder why the fuss over DBMS selection. In the first place, there are great differences between DBMSs for the micros and DBMSs for the mainframe:

1 While a mainframe DBMS may handle a large company database well, a microcomputer DBMS is likely to accommodate a small business database just as effectively.

2 Microcomputer-based DBMSs are rarely larger than a few hundred thousand characters in size. Mainframe DBMS packages are easily ten times that size.

3 DBMSs for micros normally accommodate fewer than ten users, whereas a mainframe DBMS is capable of serving hundreds of concurrent users with multiple simultaneous access to the database.

4 Backup and recovery for the microcomputer DBMS is not as involved a procedure as that for the mainframe version.

A DBMS is more important than any other piece of software. Its impact will be felt throughout the organization. Installing a new DBMS often means upgrading the hardware and changing users' habits.

In this chapter, we discuss the selection and acquisition of a DBMS for large databases. Later in the chapter, we list selection criteria for a microcomputer-based DBMS. As a process, selection involves:

1 forming an evaluation team,
2 assessing user requirements,

3 preparing a request for proposal (RFP),
4 selecting and weighting criteria,
5 evaluating vendor responses, and
6 finally selecting the product.

Selecting a DBMS is a formal process that requires the joint cooperation of management and the information systems staff. The process can be summarized in four steps:

1 *Identify* the application(s) to be developed on the DBMS.
2 *Evaluate* available DBMSs against the organization's needs.
3 *Select* the best DBMS.
4 *Negotiate* the contract. (See Figure 16-1.)

IDENTIFICATION

The first step in DBMS selection is to identify the database applications that are candidates for design. Since the organization's first experience with a DBMS tends to leave a lasting impression, the first application to be implemented successfully must meet three conditions:

1 It should not be overwhelmingly large. Starting with a manageable project is morale-building, especially when the application could be built in a relatively short time frame.
2 It should be simple enough to ensure a high probability of success.
3 The results should be realized within weeks or months, not years.

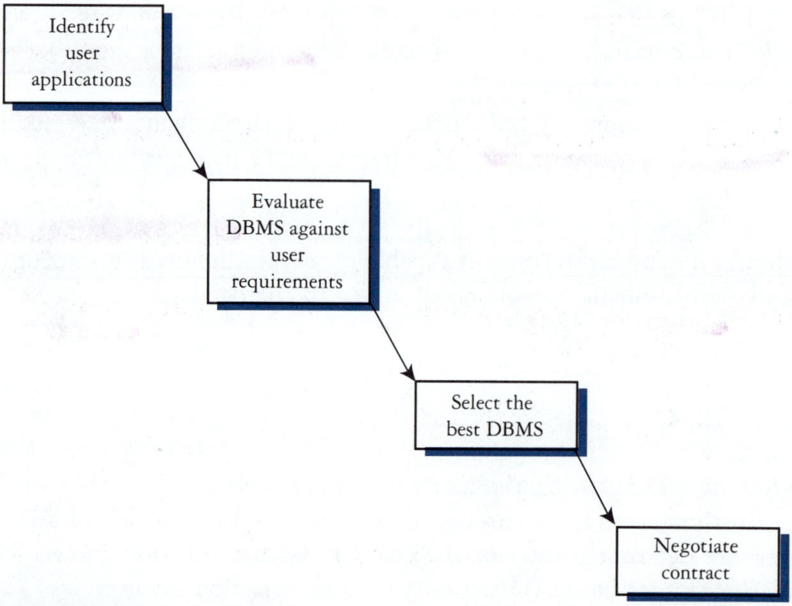

Figure 16-1 The selection process

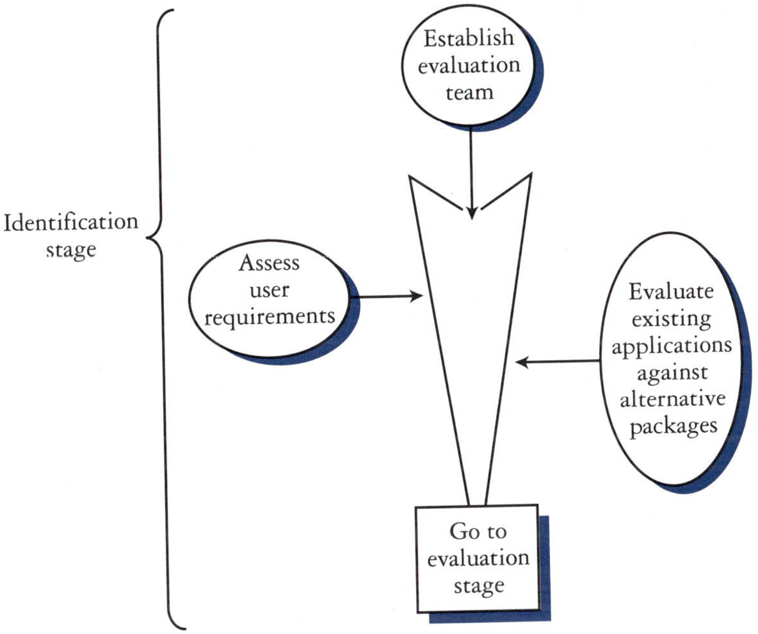

Figure 16-2 Activities of the identification stage

The identification phase involves three steps:

1 establishing an evaluation team,
2 assessing user requirements, and
3 evaluating existing applications against alternative DBMS packages.

(See Figure 16-2.)

The Evaluation Team

Most DBMS selection decisions are made by an evaluation team, which handles a variety of chores. The team reviews user requirements, educates management on DBMS and its impact, and recommends the package that it believes will do the best job. The database administrator usually heads up the evaluation team, which should also include a user representative, a systems analyst, and other software specialists. An outside consultant is often part of the group, despite the added expense.

User Requirements Assessment

A database management system is not a cure for all user problems. The evaluation team must assess user requirements and how ready the users are to change their work habits. There are several features that users should look for in a DBMS package:

- quick response to ad hoc queries
- low program maintenance and operating costs

- prompt response to future changes in the system
- good security
- reliable backup and recovery

The evaluation team should keep in mind that a DBMS is going to be around long past its installation date. The users must live with it. It will change the focus and orientation of both the user and the organization as a whole. It is a shift from standalone application programs to centralized data as a corporate resource and from single-user ownership to multiuser shared data ownership. One of the adjustments that users will have to make is from seeing themselves as autonomous units in the organization who control key applications to team members who willingly relinquish control in the interest of the whole organization.

User education Users need exposure to the technical and managerial uses of the new DBMS, its potential, and the trade-offs they will have to make. Certain habits or expectations will have to be broken and new ones made. User education can be derived from several sources:

- *Software vendors* can, through presentations, explain how data is accessed and how a DBMS addresses user problems. Two or more vendors should be invited to present their DBMS products.
- *Professional literature* or journals such as ACM's (Association for Computing Machinery) *Data Base*, *Datamation*, or *DBMS*.
- *Database specialists* from consulting firms may be hired to conduct workshops for management and staff.
- *Universities*, *conferences*, or *seminars*, where company employees acquire professional education and training.
- *Newly hired college graduates* may be trained to train others in the firm.
- *DBMS users* who have experience with the product can recommend (or advise against) adopting that product. (See Figure 16-3.)

User applications The evaluation team must next consider which should be the first application to be developed, which should be future candidates for development, and to what extent there is going to be continuing management support for this effort.

Once an application has been decided on, the team must determine its requirements:

- the various record types that will make up the database
- transaction volumes such as peak processing times, and average daily volumes
- data volatility or the percentage of the records that will change daily
- the way data will be accessed—whether in real-time processing, by how many users, the extent of on-line query versus real-time processing, and so forth
- security, backup, and the various costs of recreating a database or transactions lost during a system breakdown

Applications can be classified as either static or dynamic. A STATIC APPLICATION usually requires minimum upgrade. For example, a bill of materials application for a lumber yard written closely to the DBMS can

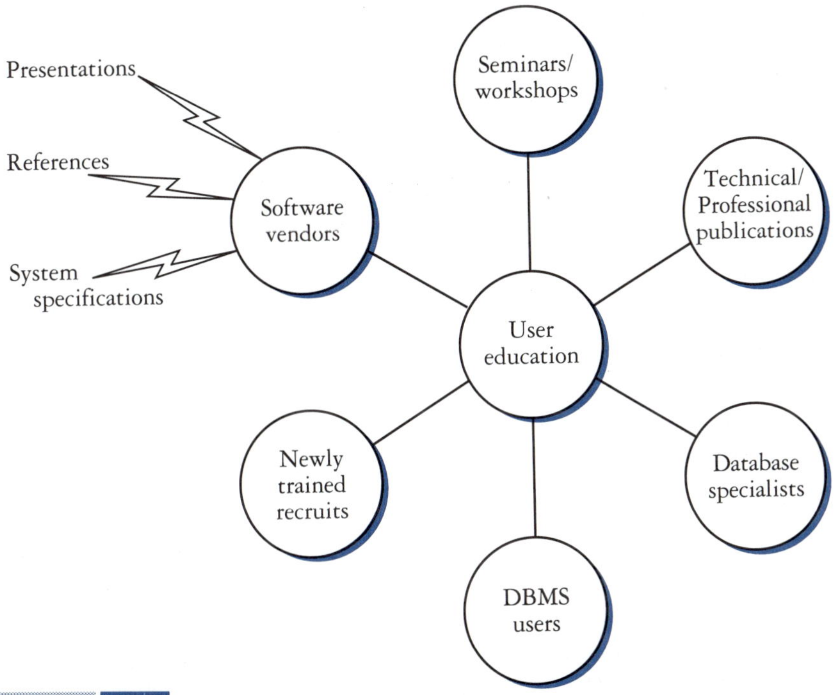

Figure 16-3 Major sources of user education

be expected to run for a long time, requiring only minor changes to keep it up to date. A DYNAMIC APPLICATION requires frequent design changes to keep it up to user standards. These changes come up either because the application is new and evolving or because the user's needs change. In either case, a dynamic DBMS is required to address the change. The key characteristics of static and dynamic applications are shown in Table 16-1.

Application characteristics	*Static*	*Dynamic*
Database design effort	Very significant	Casual
Design change control	Strict	Lax
Design change effects	Significant	Trivial
Frequency of design changes	Low	High
Basic orientation	Corporate-wide	Project
Output requirements	Fixed	Variable
Main interrogative language	COBOL	Query-like

Table 16-1 Static and dynamic application characteristics
Source: German, Michael M.

There are benefits and drawbacks to each DBMS. In a static-relationship DBMS, record types are controlled under a single schema. The DBMS always knows the record types and can easily perform relationship maintenance. But a static DBMS does not perform well when a report has to be generated that does not satisfy the database structure definitions. Such a task requires redesign of individual record types and involves a great amount of computer time and human effort.

In a dynamic-relationship DBMS, record types can operate under a static-relationship DBMS schema without having to be preloaded into a single static-relationship database. For example, an organization may run its applications separately throughout the year, and bring them together under the control of a virtual schema for corporate-wide reporting at year's end. Unfortunately, dynamic-relationship DBMSs perform more slowly than static-relationship DBMSs because they do not follow a predefined pointer-based road map the way a static-relationship DBMS does. Data integrity can also be a problem in a dynamic DBMS, because record types are related through field values, which are under user control.

Make-Lease Considerations

An evaluation team must next consider how to acquire a DBMS: by building its own system or by leasing an off-the-shelf package. When a DBMS is developed in-house, one user's requirement is often emphasized over another's. Politics, foot-dragging, and occasional incompetence inevitably lead to a poorly functioning DBMS, regardless of how technically sound it is. Going outside to acquire off-the-shelf software means searching for qualified vendors, evaluating their packages, and deciding on how well they meet user specifications.

The make alternative Building one's own DBMS requires a highly skilled staff with seasoned knowledge of the technical and procedural aspects of DBMS design, as well as rigorous and exhaustive testing before implementation. Unfortunately, such talent is not that easy to find and developmental costs can be astronomical. For example, building a mainframe configuration can run from $100,000 to several million, requiring strong project leadership and a dependable maintenance program just to keep the DBMS up to date.

An organization that develops its own DBMS can expect to go through an extended period of testing, retesting, and correction before the DBMS can be released for user acceptance. In contrast, ready-to-use software has most of its bugs already under control. The software house also ensures reliability. Compared to today's ready-to-use commercial DBMSs, building an in-house DBMS takes longer, costs more, and incurs high maintenance costs, although it is tailored to the exacting needs of the organization.

Organizations that do not have adequate staff to build a DBMS sometimes hire outside contractors. Having a contractor build the software means passing the responsibility (and the leadership) to the developer, while retaining enough influence over the design to make sure it meets organization standards. The main drawback of using a consultant is cost, which can be reduced by sharing development cost with other firms that might have uses for the same package.

The lease alternative In today's flourishing DBMS market, most organizations opt to lease an off-the-shelf DBMS rather than build it themselves. In addition to mainframe packages, hundreds of easy-to-use database management systems now load on the microcomputer in a matter of hours. Prices for these packages range from $200 to $1200, depending on features and capabilities.

The main advantages of leasing are quicker installation time and lower maintenance, since upgrades are handled by the vendor under a separate contract. The reason leasing involves lower cost is that the vendor spreads the cost of the initial copy over several users and recoups investment through volume sales. For example, a popular DBMS package that costs a software house $460,000 to develop could reap quite a profit at $995 per copy if only 1000 copies were sold.

An obvious drawback to leasing a DBMS is that most packages are less than ideal for many users. Enhancements and compromises must be made, requiring specialized staff and incurring additional costs. (See Table 16-2.)

MAKE	LEASE
Advantages	*Advantages*
• The DBMS fits the requirements of the user exactly • Organization has control over total software • MIS department makes better use of staff time and talent	• Software vendor ensures reliability • Lower overall costs • Quicker installation • Lower maintenance costs • Accommodates significant changes in technology on a regular basis. Risk of obsolescence shifts to the vendor
Disadvantages	*Disadvantages*
• A major user's requirements are often preferred over those of smaller users, causing ill feelings and dissatisfactions • Takes longer than ready-made packages • Possible foot-dragging by management • Requires highly skilled staff • High development costs • Extended period of testing and often unreliable software	• Most DBMSs are less than ideal for every user • Compromised solutions without major changes • User loses residual rights to the DBMS when lease expires • Lease cannot be terminated early without heavy penalty

Table 16-2 The make-lease choice

Evaluating existing database applications takes a lot of time and effort, because there are dozens of DBMS packages to consider and the search can be quite exhausting. During this process, the evaluation team must make every effort to meet the user's requirements. As we shall discuss in the selection process, alternative DBMS packages should be evaluated based on criteria determined in advance to eliminate confusion or bias. The halo of a known DBMS vendor can easily sway the decision away from other packages that provide equal or better performance.

EVALUATION

The second step in the selection process is to evaluate alternative packages based on preset criteria. The evaluation stage involves

- deciding on the selection criteria;
- preparing a request for proposal (RFP);
- evaluating vendor responses to the RFP;
- meeting with representative users; and
- benchmark testing the product. (See Figure 16-4.)

Selection Criteria

The selection criteria should cover both technical details and the administrative details that represent the user's requirements. Technical

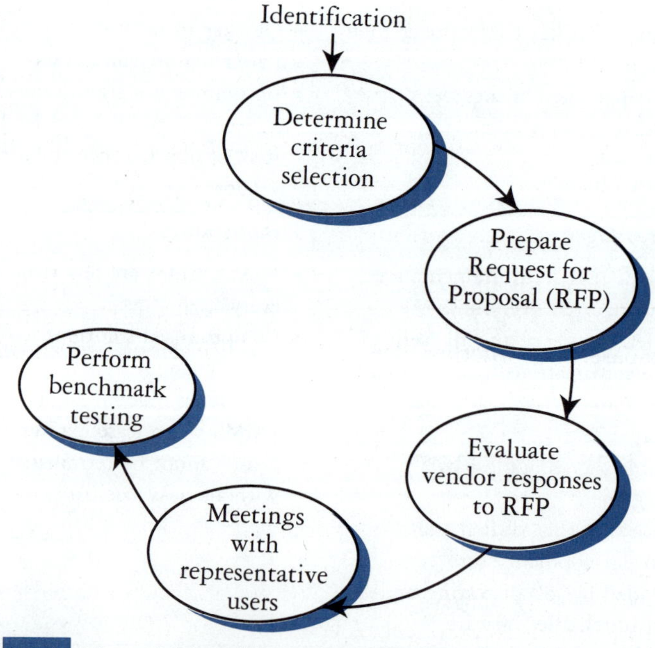

Figure 16-4 The activities of the evaluation stage

criteria focus on the capabilities of a DBMS package, and should include the following:

• *Performance.* The package must perform well, especially for performance-critical applications.

• *Response time.* An application must respond quickly, especially in a performance-driven application such as on-line queries for purchase approval against a credit card.

• *Strong logic and physical storage structure.* The DBMS should be able to handle all the types of data structures the users will need. It must also be able to search efficiently for any data item.

• *Generalized retrieval and update capabilities.* The user must be allowed to ask questions or to add, delete, and modify data in a database.

• *Future portability.* Portability is the ability to move the DBMS to another machine. This is important if the existing hardware will support the first application, but may be replaced by newer hardware in the future.

• *Database evolvability.* EVOLVABILITY makes it easy to modify the system when necessary. It also means new data can be added to an existing record without having to change corresponding programs. Most DBMSs have this feature.

• *User and inquiry language interface.* The query languages, report and graphics generators, and high-level programming languages should be judged by their ease of use and the quality of the reports they generate.

• *Data dictionary facility.* The evaluation team must decide whether they want a standalone or a built-in data dictionary. Each must be evaluated for its comprehensiveness, interactive activities, report-generating features (for data administrative purposes), and ease of use.

• *Security and recovery.* If needed, the DBMS must provide a hierarchy of access control. It should also be evaluated for its recovery capabilities, such as automated system restart, average recovery time, and frequency of system crashes.

• *Database integrity.* The DBMS must be built to ensure user confidence in the information produced by the system. For example, the evaluation team should look for adequate system controls to prevent operators from accidentally or intentionally damaging sensitive data in the database and whether data item modifications are automatically logged for auditors.

The administrative selection criteria should address documentation, ease of use, operation and maintenance costs, vendor support, and the like. The major administrative selection criteria may include the following:

• *Vendor reliability and support.* Vendor reliability can be determined by the product reputation, number of years the vendor has been in operation, number of clients using the product, and the vendor's financial strength. For example, the evaluation team might consider whether the software gives consistent results; what kind of support reputation the vendor has; whether the vendor offers adequate training; and how committed the vendor is to maintenance and enhancement of the DBMS.

• *Ease of learning and use.* The team should look for user-friendly interfaces, clear, complete, and easy-to-understand documentation, availability of on-line help, and features that support enhanced interactions such as flexible formatting of display screens.

• *Maintenance support.* Vendors should provide quality maintenance and prompt response to user complaints and system breakdowns.

• *Ease of implementation.* The team will need to know how long it takes to install the DBMS and what level of user participation is expected during implementation.

• *User training.* User training cannot be overemphasized. Users are interested in quality training classes at reasonable cost. Included in this area is quality documentation with clear graphics.

• *Acquisition costs.* The team must, of course, consider the initial cost of software and testing, as well as future conversion and enhancement costs.

When considering DBMS acquisition costs, it is important to differentiate between one-time and recurring costs, which can add up in a hurry. One-time costs include the cost of

• training users and MIS staff,
• teleprocessing (TP) monitors for on-line database operation,
• installing and testing the DBMS,
• the data dictionary, if it is not included in the package, and
• any hardware upgrades (such as additional main memory or disk drives) required.

Recurring costs include lease and maintenance costs, the salaries of additional MIS or database administration staff, and utilities needed to audit or tune the database.

Table 16-3 summarizes technical and administrative selection criteria.

Technical Criteria	*Administrative Criteria*
• Strong logic and physical storage structure	• Database integrity
• Generalized retrieval and update capabilities	• Vendor reliability and support
• Database evolvability	• Ease of learning and use
• User/inquiry language interface	• Maintenance and support
• Data dictionary facility	• User training
• Security and recovery	• Acquisition costs
	• Ease of implementation

Table 16-3 Selection criteria

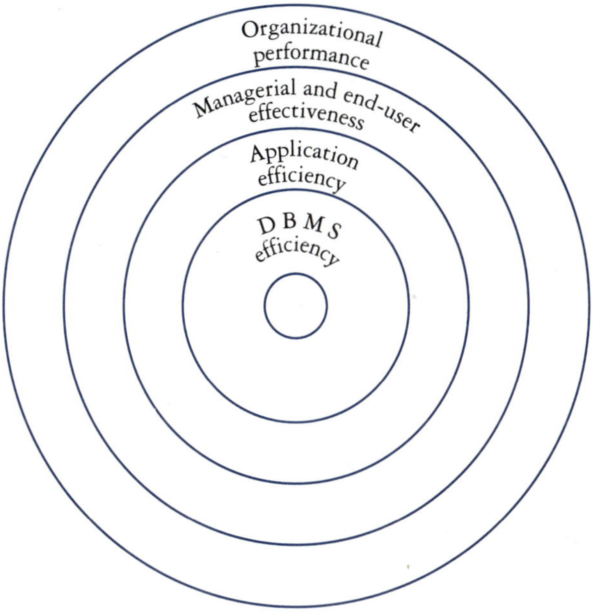

Figure 16-5 Contribution of DBMS to organizational performance

Whatever the criteria, the DBMS will ultimately be judged by its contribution to quality decision making and organizational performance. As shown in Figure 16-5, a DBMS must have capabilities that affect the execution of user applications and respond promptly to user requests.

Request for Proposal (RFP)

User requirements should be translated into a list of technical and administrative criteria that describe what the DBMS package must provide. For medium-size and large DBMS projects, the criteria are presented in a REQUEST FOR PROPOSAL (RFP) to vendors. The RFP is a blueprint for acquiring DBMS software exceeding $50,000 or a monthly lease fee of $1500. The monthly fee is normally one-fourth of the purchase price. At a minimum, the RFP should include the following:

- a complete statement of the DBMS specifications including query or programming language(s), price range, terms, and timeframe
- a list of the vendor's responsibilities for conversion, training, and maintenance
- warranties and terms of license or contractual limitations
- a request for the vendor's financial statement
- the number of staff available for DBMS support
- the vendor demonstration or presentation requirements
- a request to the vendor for current user references
- the proposal due dates

- the awards date
- any general comments unique to the RFP

A sample RFP outlining the prerequisites that vendors must satisfy for a large retail organization is shown in Table 16-4. Note that these requirements are definitive, such as hardware platforms to be supported.

- Hardware. The DBMS must load on an IBM AS/400, model B/60 with 20 Mbytes of memory and must support local area networking.
- Operating system. The DBMS must be executable under VM/CMS as well as MVS under VM/CMS.
- Resource response requirements. The DBMS must handle 8000 transactions/hour from 85 on-line concurrent users with response time average two seconds 95 percent of the time and not exceeding 3 seconds for the other 5 percent.
- Data dictionary. The DBMS must have an integrated data dictionary/directory package.
- Host language interface. The DBMS must support COBOL and RPG/400 interfaces compatible with standard language processors. There should be an interactive query language that interfaces with the DBMS for ad hoc information retrieval by the end-user.
- Restart/recovery. The DBMS must provide a reliable restart/recovery system with at least a rollback feature that backs up invalid or incomplete transactions, records, or files.

Table 16-4 Sample partial Request for Proposal content

Technical considerations In addition to these prerequisites, the RFP must define the technical specifications of the selected DBMS package. This information is derived directly from the vendor and presented in a standard format that makes it easy to compare packages.

Companies looking for a DBMS package to run on their hardware often find the selection limited, especially if their hardware is not up to standard. Organizations looking for new hardware as well as a new DBMS package are likely to have an easier time with the search and decision process.

Role of the consultant For a small organization, evaluating competitive bids can take up too many resources. In this case, outside consultants can be used to give unbiased evaluations based on experience. The problem, though, is finding qualified consultants. A recent survey concluded that 50 percent of respondent users had unfavorable experiences with consultants. Consultants must be screened carefully, and their fees are high. The average rate for database consultants can be between $1000 and $4000 per day, plus expenses.

The past decade has seen a growing use of internal consultants in large organizations, as opposed to outside consultants. Table 16-5 summarizes the pros and cons of external and internal consultants.

EXTERNAL CONSULTANT	INTERNAL CONSULTANT
Pros	***Pros***
• Ideal for short-term, one-time projects • The political atmosphere requires an outsider for an objective opinion • An outside consultant is needed to verify the recommendations of the internal consultant • Internal staff does not have expertise in database selection	• Quick decisions often can be made by internal consultants • The organization already has an internal consultant with good record
Cons	***Cons***
• Outside consultant too costly • Outside consultants do not fully understand the nature of the problem	• Full-time consultant is beyond the organization's budget

Table 16-5 Pros and cons of using consultants

An organization considering a consultant for the first time should define in advance what it is that the consultant must accomplish, the types of skills required, and when and for how long the consulting service will be needed. Only then should the organization contact consulting firms and review the performance record of their consultants. To get the names of reputable firms, the organization can contact companies that have used consultants and ask for recommendations. Next, the organization can request resumes and interview the consultants recommended. Successful consultants are not readily available, so organizations should start looking well in advance of when they need a consultant.

Vendor Response Evaluation

Next the vendor responses to the RFP must be evaluated. One evaluation method is a checklist similar to the one shown in Table 16-6. The lefthand column specifies the weight or relative importance of each function to the user on a scale of 1 to 10, with 10 as most important. The second column rates the vendor level of performance on each function. The third column is the product of multiplying the weight by the vendor score. Weight is an assessment of how important each requirement is to the user. The sum of the weighted score column represents the vendor's total score. The vendor with the highest total score should be awarded the bid.

User Requirements	*Weight (1-10)*	*Vendor score (1-10)*	*Weighted score*
1. Backup and recovery			
2. Costs • one-time price • monthly lease • maintenance charges			
3. Data dictionary/directory			
4. Data integrity and security • interface to present • security software • semantic integrity			
5. Documentation			
6. Hardware support			
7. Host language interface			
8. Micro-mainframe connection			
9. Operating system support			
10. Performance			
11. Query/report capabilities • ad hoc reporting capability • spontaneous queries by end-users • user friendliness			
12. References • satisfied customers • growth in customer base • number of DBMSs installed			
13. Response-time requirements			
14. Terminal support			
15. Vendor support • responsiveness • quality • technical expertise			
Vendor's total score			

Table 16-6 DBMS vendor checklist

Another version of the vendor evaluation checklist is illustrated in Table 16-7, where each requirement is assigned a weight representing its relative level of importance. The weights add up to 100. In addition, each proposed DBMS is assigned a mark for each requirement, based on a scale (in our example, 0 to 1). A mark is a grade that represents how well the DBMS meets the user's requirement. The score of a user requirement is the product of the mark and the weight. The overall score is the sum of the requirements score for a DBMS. In this example, DBMS 1 is the preferred system.

Weight	*User Requirements*	*DBMS 1 Mark*	*DBMS 1 Score*	*DBMS 2 Mark*	*DBMS 2 Score*
40	Backup and recovery	.4	16	.8	32
20	Data dictionary/directory	.8	16	.2	4
40	Vendor support	1.0	40	.5	20
	Total score		72		56

Table 16-7 Evaluation method using weights

An alternative to the evaluation methods using weights is requirements costing. In REQUIREMENTS COSTING, the cost of the DBMS is the vendor's price plus the cost to incorporate features the DBMS does not provide. For each item the vendor does not provide, a specific dollar amount is added to the bid to reflect the cost of acquiring it through a third party. The DBMS with the lowest adjusted cost is selected.

The requirements costs method is not intended to replace the weighted scoring method. For an organization without the time and personnel to perform such a cost analysis, the weighted scoring method may be used alone.

User feedback Vendor response evaluation should result in agreeing on the top vendor and beginning to interview users who use the software. Some of the questions to be asked follow:

- How many remote sites are tied to the database? How many concurrent users are there?
- How many transactions (query, update, etc.) are handled during an eight-hour shift?
- What is the average response time per transaction? How long does it take to access data during peak load?
- How are backup and recovery handled on the site? Is documentation available? How good is it?

Answers to these questions should either reinforce or negate the decision to go with the top vendor.

Benchmark testing In addition to user feedback, a "test drive" of the product, called a benchmark test, is often a good idea. A BENCHMARK TEST is a processing procedure that verifies the performance level of the DBMS under full load. Typically, it consists of loading a file with existing data, performing standard and out-of-the-ordinary queries and update routines, and generating reports.

Database management systems typically have special PERFORMANCE MONITOR ROUTINES, which are utilities that record statistics on activities such as the number of hard disk accesses, the number of records of each type accessed, the amount of time used by the CPU and/or I/O channels, and how much memory was tied up by a given processing query. This indicates how well the system runs, especially during peak times.

Benchmark testing is time-consuming, difficult to cost-justify, and must be done by a qualified person. It also emphasizes machine efficiency, not overall transaction volume. It is mainly useful when quick response time during peak hours and during large-volume transactions will be required on a regular basis.

Final Selection

By now, the evaluation team will have spent several weeks or even months working on the evaluation process. This is time well spent, especially considering that the organization's life-blood is the data available in the centralized database. But often the total weighted scores are too close for a clear decision. In this case less tangible factors come into play, such as the availability of a vendor's Watts line on a 24-hour basis and personal relations between the vendor's vice president and a senior official of the company acquiring the DBMS. If these measures do not firm up the final selection, additional, subjective criteria should be adopted. There is also what is called the "halo" effect to contend with. Clients have been known to favor a DBMS package based on the vendor's name or impressions of what they think it will do. Politics and vendor finesse in pushing for a deal also can determine the final choice.

Contract Negotiation

Virtually all contracts are negotiable; hammering out contract details is probably the riskiest step in DBMS acquisition.

Most vendors have a standard contract. All they do is fill in the blanks. But because vendor contracts are written to protect the vendor, the organization should try to negotiate those items that will affect it the most, such as how much protection it has against system failure and what measures it can take in the event of a failure.

Vendor-User Relationships

Most vendors give buyers accurate information—gross misrepresentation is, fortunately, rare. But even the best vendors hedge when deciding how *much* information to offer, especially when this means informing the buyer about the limitations of the DBMS.

Fortunately, there are laws that protect the buyer even against contingencies not specified in writing. The implied warranty, for example, provides two principles as grounds for litigation: FITNESS and MERCHANTABILITY, both of which are part of the Uniform Commercial Code. If the vendor knows in advance that the product will not fit the user's intended purpose, the user has recourse, meaning that the user has the right to sue for damages in the event of vendor misrepresentations. Merchantability warrants that a DBMS will function for the purpose for which it was intended. Breach of this warranty is evident when a DBMS repeatedly fails during normal use.

Related to the warranty issue is the DISCLAIMER. Most software products have a disclaimer that says the vendor makes no promise about the quality of the software and warns the user of any errors beyond the implied warranty. The vendor specifies the liability to actual replacement of the software or a mere refund of the purchase price. The courts usually support the validity of such a clause, except in cases where it is proven unconscionable.

Negotiation Strategies

Since most vendors try to limit their liabilities, the buyer must learn how to negotiate a software contract. Negotiation is an art that involves sizing up the other party, devising a strategy, and introducing changes or addenda that ensure an equitable and just agreement.

Several strategies have been known to work in negotiating software contracts:

- home turf advantage
- leader role
- "good guy/bad guy" strategy
- use of trade-offs

Home turf advantage Psychologically, it is to the buyer's advantage to negotiate on his or her own turf. Staff support and paperwork is easily available there, and certain courtesies are exchanged when the vendor is on the buyer's turf.

Leader role If an organization is the first in its area to adopt a vendor's DBMS package and could influence others to follow, the vendor should be willing to talk price. On one occasion, the authors represented a commercial bank which other area banks were watching to see which package it would adopt and how well the package would operate. The vendor knew this and was eager to secure a foothold in the area. We negotiated a 40-percent discount and a no-charge, two-year maintenance agreement. In return, the vendor was allowed to bring prospective users into the bank to view the system during the first year of the installation.

"Good guy/bad guy" strategy Experienced consultants can earn their fees during contract negotiation by playing a role. The consultant is usually viewed by the vendor as the shrewd negotiator—the bad guy—while the buyer is perceived as the good guy. Using this strategy, the consultant can "test the water" and make all kinds of offers and counteroffers, subject to the buyer's approval. The buyer, of course, is under no obligation to comply, but offers made by the vendor are usually final, although a sales representative may hedge occasionally. For example, he or she might say, "I'll have to get headquarter's approval on this." In any case, it is to the buyer's advantage to have someone else do the dirty work.

Trade-offs Face-saving is crucial in contract negotiation. If the vendor stands firm on certain issues, the buyer must be prepared to trade-off a few items on the "wish list" to make the vendor feel good about the deal. For example, most vendors won't make changes in the contract, but will agree to make a number of concessions by an exchange of letters.

Early in the negotiation, a common ploy is to rank the less important issues high, leaving the tough ones to the end. Played the other way around, the vendor might decide that the negotiation is going to be an uphill battle, not worth the effort, and walk out. It is also more effective to negotiate over two or more short sessions than one, long, drawn-out session.

Personnel training is an important negotiable item. Even if the buyer has qualified staff to run the software, waiving user training can be used as a "sweetener," because it saves the vendor time and money not to have to train. Training also varies, depending on whether it is conducted on the buyer's premises or at vendor headquarters. It all depends on the nature and duration of the training and the facilities required to conduct it. In microcomputer-based installations, user-friendly software has virtually eliminated the need for vendor training.

Remedies and Responsibilities

A DBMS contract should specify the remedies to the parties in the event of default, nonperformance, or failure of a condition or event. How remedies are provided begins with the list of responsibilities agreed on by both parties. The remedies should be listed in two categories: special remedies and strict damages.

Special remedies are the user's first line of defense. They are practical remedies, spelled out in the agreement, which provide immediate relief to the user without litigation. An example of a special remedy would be, "If the vendor fails to deliver by a certain date, the user has the option of canceling the agreement after notifying the vendor in writing."

When the vendor hesitates to negotiate meaningful remedies, it may be necessary to switch to a demand for strict damage remedies—a fixed amount that will be payable in the event of default. This provides the vendor with a negative financial incentive to perform.

A DBMS contract should stipulate the results to be achieved with the software. Performance criteria must be clearly stated and are usually used as a benchmark when the software is installed.

The major risks inherent in a software agreement are nonperformance, enhancement cost, and bankruptcy of the vendor. The software must perform to buyer standards. When it does not, the contract should be written to allow the buyer to opt out or the vendor to make the necessary corrections at no charge and within a reasonable time frame. As a hedge against vendor bankruptcy, the schemas, subschemas, DFDs, source code, and other specifications must be provided to the user.

Failure of a vendor to meet installation deadlines can be irritating and costly. A contract should specify an installation date, how the software is to be installed, and the remedies provided should the vendor fail to meet the installation schedule. Another provision should describe the tests that must be passed if the software is to meet buyer approval. Most vendors allow the buyer 30 to 90 days of use to meet approval.

Related to DBMS acceptance are guarantees of reliability and responsibility for failure. For example, how long can the DBMS run continuously without necessitating a shutdown? What is the mean time between failures (MTBF)? In the event of a failure, how soon will the vendor correct the problem? All of these should be written into the contract.

Service and support depend on the vendor's experience and reputation. For example, in a microcomputer environment, if the DBMS is acquired through a mail order house and fails within the warranty period, the buyer may have to ship it back to the outlet for replacement, which can be inconvenient and costly. The same applies to off-the-shelf software. This is the more reason for investigating the vendor thoroughly, and incorporating as an addendum to the contract the adjustments that will ensure a satisfactory relationship between the vendor and the user.

PC Database Management System Selection

The process used to select a mainframe DBMS can be used to choose a PC DBMS as well. But selecting a DBMS for a PC environment requires some extra consideration.

First, the types of users who will be dealing with database applications must be considered. Are they novice users, developers, or both? Although many vendors claim that their products are both powerful enough to use for developing and easy to use, this is rarely true because increased power involves more functions, which gives the user more choices and results in complicated user interfaces.

Another important feature to consider is speed. A good DBMS performer supports compiling procedures. In some PC DBMSs, such as Nantucket's CLIPPER, the price is high in terms of ease of use. In addition, in a compiled environment, users have to manage object code and source code libraries and make sure the entire procedure is up to standard.

A third DBMS feature in a PC environment is a query and report writer—a tool used to get information out. Query and report writers involve all kinds of trade-offs between power, speed, and ease-of-use. For example, Paradox has an easier to use query-by-example (QBE) facility than Ashton Tate's dBASE IV, but for handling long text fields, dBASE IV is more powerful. For sophisticated analysis functions, PC/FOCUS is quite powerful, although using it requires reading volumes of documentation.

Finally, a relatively new feature to consider in a PC DBMS is CONNECTIVITY—the ability to connect PC-based database applications to a mainframe database or to a PC acting as a server. SQL is the connectivity language and implies shared access to the files. Related to this interesting feature is the GRAPHIC USER INTERFACE, also known as GUI. This feature, popularized by Apple Computers, offers windows, pull-down menus, and a mouse to "point and shoot." All these features come at a price—a minimum of 1MB of main memory (RAM) and a 386-chip PC.

In conclusion, we go to the opening remark in the introduction: "What is the best database I can get?" The answer is "it depends" on the types of users, whether the emphasis is on power, performance, speed, or special tools, and how important it is that connectivity be part of the total picture. With all this to consider, the user still needs to do cost-justification, to compare and contrast different products, to go through demos, and to decide on "the best database" he or she can get for the money. This requires experience and a plan that has management support.

SUMMARY

1 Selecting a DBMS involves four steps: identification of the application, evaluation of available DBMSs, selection of the best DBMS, and acquisition through contract negotiation.

2 The first application to select for database implementation should be small, simple enough to ensure success, and produce results within weeks or months.

3 There are three steps in the identification stage: establishing an evaluation team of users, analysts, and management; assessing user requirements; and deciding whether to make or lease an application.

4 Users should be educated to understand the pros and cons of installing a DBMS. Software vendors, professional journals, database specialists, conferences, or DBMS users can all provide such education.

5 There are two alternatives to acquisition: make or lease the DBMS. The make alternative has the advantages of fitting the exacting requirements of the user and making better use of the MIS staff's time and talent. The drawbacks include foot-dragging, extended testing, and emphasizing one user's priorities over another's. The advantages of the lease alternative include ensured reliability, lower overall costs, and quicker installation time. Among the drawbacks are compromised solutions without major changes, losing residual rights once the lease expires, and heavy penalties for early termination.

6 The evaluation stage includes determining the selection criteria, preparing the Request for Proposal (RFP), evaluating vendor responses to the RFP, getting user feedback, and benchmark testing.

7 A consultant can be extremely helpful in DBMS selection. The organization should define in advance what it is that a consultant must accomplish, contact a number of consulting firms and review their consultants' records, request resumes, and interview the available consultants well in advance of project start-up.

8 Selection criteria include technical and administrative details. Technical criteria for a DBMS include the following:

a. performance
b. response time
c. strong logic and physical storage structure
d. generalized retrieval and update capabilities
e. availability of high-level languages
f. easy modification in response to changing user requirements
g. user and inquiry language interface
h. data dictionary facility
i. security and recovery
j. database integrity

Administrative criteria include the following:

a. vendor reliability and support
b. ease of learning and use
c. maintenance and support
d. ease of implementation
e. user training
f. acquisition costs

9 In evaluating vendor responses, buyers can use a checklist to rate vendor performance on a number of functions, assigning weights that add up to a total performance score for the vendor's product. An alternative method adds to the vendor's DBMS price the cost of incorporating features that the vendor does not provide and selecting the DBMS with the lowest adjusted cost.

10 Benchmark testing verifies the response time and performance levels of the software under full load. This testing is time-consuming and difficult to cost-justify.

11 Once the DBMS has been selected, the contract should be negotiated. Misrepresentation aside, there are laws that protect the consumer even when the agreement is not in writing. Fitness and merchantability are part of the Uniform Commercial Code that protects consumers from vendor misrepresentations.

12 Several strategies have been known to work in negotiating software contracts: home turf advantage, leader role, "good guy/bad guy" strategy, and trade-offs.

13 A DBMS contract should specify the remedies to the parties in the event of default, nonperformance, or failure of a condition or event. The remedies may be listed as special remedies and strict damages. The contract should also stipulate the results to be achieved by the software and an installation date. Related to user acceptance are guarantees of reliability and responsibility for failure.

KEY WORDS

Benchmark test
Connectivity
Disclaimer
Dynamic application
Evolvability
Fitness
Graphic user interface
Merchantability
Performance monitor routines
Request for Proposal (RFP)
Requirements costing
Static application

REVIEW QUESTIONS

1 Someone once said, "A DBMS is a DBMS. There really isn't much difference between a DBMS for the microcomputer and that for the mainframe." Do you agree? Explain.

2 Elaborate on the four major steps involved in selecting a DBMS. Which step do you consider the most critical for a cost-effective selection decision? Why?

3 Discuss the activities that make up the identification stage of DBMS selection. How important is the role of the evaluation team during this stage?

4 If you were in a position to recommend a first database application for a client, what criteria would you set for the application?

5 What motivates users to consider a DBMS package? Explain.

6 If users wanted to learn more about DBMS packages, what sources or references could they use? Be specific. For a prospective user of a DBMS on a mainframe, which source would be the best?

7 Distinguish between the following pairs:
   a. static and dynamic applications
   b. RFP and a system proposal
   c. PC DBMS and mainframe DBMS

8 How would an organization decide whether to build or lease a DBMS? Explain in detail.

9 What are the steps of the evaluation phase? Which activity is subject to the least bias on the part of the user? Why?

10 What must a Request for Proposal include? List and briefly explain the items.

11 How important is it to have an outside consultant help the evaluation team? Discuss the pros and cons of hiring outside as compared to inside consultants.

12 "A major step in the evaluation process is to identify criteria for evaluating the DBMS." What criteria is this statement referring to? Explain briefly each criterion.

13 Essentially, what is the difference between technical and administrative criteria?

14 In the chapter, two methods are suggested for evaluating vendor responses. Do you agree with these methods? Draw a chart for evaluating a DBMS package for a microcomputer application.

15 What is benchmark testing? How does it differ from system testing in general? Under what circumstances is it important for deciding on a DBMS package?

16 What is the difference between fitness and merchantability? In what way do they relate to contract negotiation? Explain.

17 How is a disclaimer related to product warranty?

18 Elaborate on the strategies that have been known to work in contract negotiation.

19 Explain the difference between special and damage remedies.

APPLICATION PROBLEMS

1 In less than eight years, Cavalier Insurance company has grown through acquisitions and aggressive marketing. Its MIS activity has kept pace with growth in every way. The mainframe has handled applications for all kinds of insurance. New hardware has been added to match increasing requirements for instant information. The company has added 40 percent to the MIS division's budget each year for the past three years.

Decisions on hardware installations, however, have landed the company with three computer makes and five vendors. Software was also acquired through six software houses, and the company's databases were on different media using two database management systems.

The chief executive officer was concerned about the heterogeneity of the hardware. Customers soon began to complain about service. New customers waited at least seven weeks to receive a policy. Likewise, premium billing took weeks to process. In three out of ten cases, customers disagreed on the amount of the premium that they should pay.

A consultant was brought in to review the MIS operation and make recommendations to correct the situation. As can be imagined, the consultant called for sweeping changes in the way the MIS function was managed. MIS was found lacking in control tools or procedures, and the consultant recommended a method of prioritizing application selection and development. The consultant also pointed out the importance of an integrated database to handle all applications. Finally, the consultant recommended developing a long-range plan and forming an executive steering committee to direct and coordinate the MIS function on a regular basis.

The president mulled over the recommendations and, considering the fast-paced nature of the business, could not be sure how much of it to approve and how to implement it. He was afraid that abrupt change could backfire. A way had to be found both to correct the company's problems and simultaneously keep the traffic flowing.

a. What do you think of the president's way of proceeding?
b. How practical is the consultant's approach to the problem? Can all this be corrected? What are the costs?
c. How would you handle the problem? Be specific.

2 Fisher Auto Parts is the largest auto parts dealer in Virginia and Maryland. The firm's headquarters is in Richmond. Fisher operates stores in 17 cities in Virginia and 11 in Maryland. Total annual sales are over $35 million. Net income, however, has been decreasing during the past two years, because of a surge in new car sales and the high cost of used car repairs.

The firm's management team is composed of conservative, old-line managers who were once clerks in various stores. They are not impressed with "fancy" procedures or high-technology "gimmicks" for operating the business. Recently, an auto parts chain began to open stores in various locations, and management decided to fight this new competition by cutting unnecessary costs. All advertising must now be justified and discounts on parts to independent mechanics were dropped to 20 percent from the traditional 30 percent accorded to established garages.

The Fisher MIS organization is run by Al Rubenstein, vice president, who reports directly to Joe Fisher, the president and owner of the chain. Rubenstein has complete MIS responsibility and makes almost all decisions, except those involving major hardware acquisition. The two senior managers are Neil Snyder and Polly Pickering. Snyder manages the applications development area, while Holt is in charge of operations. All MIS work is centralized. Information going to or coming from various stores is transmitted via remote batch mode.

Clerks have been receiving complaints about lack of immediate information on parts availability. For example, when a part is not in the store's stockroom, the clerk sends an inquiry via the terminal. Since this is a remote batch environment, it takes two hours to determine whether the desired part is available in the firm's main warehouse. It also takes another two hours for the part to be delivered to the store for final sale.

a. What are the pros and cons of this MIS system?
b. Specifically, do you recommend installation of a database management system?
c. If the organization can benefit from installation of a database management system, how would you proceed to select the appropriate DBMS? Present a cost-benefit justification for your choice.

3 For nine years, a medium-size commercial bank has been using a service bureau to handle virtually all applications, including checking, savings, installment and commercial loans, and trust activities. Until last month, it has been paying $285,000 a year for this service, which amounts to 10 percent of the bank's net income. The new contract submitted by the service bureau shows an increase in fees to $315,000.

With the steadily decreasing cost of hardware, improvements in computer processing capabilities, and availability of ready-to-use software packages for banking, the senior vice president was curious to know whether the bank should consider having its own system. A computer consultant was hired to explore the matter.

The hardware may also be leased on a three- or five-year basis. The monthly lease fee is $3900, which includes maintenance. The five-year lease provides that, upon expiration of the lease, the bank can acquire the hardware for $1.

a. Which alternative (service bureau versus in-house) would be the most beneficial?
b. Suppose the bank decided to go ahead and process its own applications. Should it purchase or lease? What factors should be considered?
c. Assuming that the bank purchased the equipment, what should be done to protect the system from unauthorized access?

PART VI

DIRECTIONS IN DATABASE MANAGEMENT

C H A P T

Expert Systems and Databases

E R 1 7

CASE and Expert Systems

AT A GLANCE

CASE and Expert Systems

Intelligent Databases

Today's complex business environment requires powerful and flexible tools to meet competitive challenges. In response, a number of intelligent database systems (IDBSs) composed of a combination of computer-aided software engineering (CASE), expert systems (ES), and database management systems (DBMSs) technology are being developed to meet most companies' knowledge-based system development requirements well into the 1990s and the beginning of the twenty-first century.

Currently, the integration of CASE, ES, and DBMS is still an emerging research area. However, recent breakthroughs will soon be making that technology a reality. In fact, by the mid-1990s, IDBSs are expected to become one of the most important application development tools.

Let's begin by reviewing the fundamental objectives of DBMSs, CASE, and ES. An IDBS is defined as a system for developing applications requiring knowledge-directed intelligent processing of shared information. Search is the common underlying function of CASE, ES, and DBMSs. The inappropriate combination of three powerful search engines can lead to a multiplicative explosion in computation time. It is argued that performance is a key challenge in the development of IDBSs.

Now let's look at the principal characteristics of DBMSs, ES, and CASE, and the technical challenges in IDBS design.

Database Systems

A DBMS provides multiuser functions via a high-level transaction specification language. Users generate transactions in this language, and the DBMS assumes the responsibility for managing physical data access, interleaving of overlapped operations, recovery from system failures, and managing access rights. To insulate users from the details of the physical data representations, the DBMS provides a special knowledge representation language called a data model.

Expert Systems

An ES is an application system built around a direct representation of expert knowledge. In general, an ES represents expert knowledge in small discrete chunks as logic rules, production rules, or frames. The attempt is made to preserve a one-to-one correspondence between a separable piece of expert knowledge and a rule or frame in the knowledge representation.

The rationale for ES is that in complex and ill-structured applications, such a knowledge representation makes applications easier to develop, debug, and evolve. In addition, it is argued that interactive messages (explanations) can be made more meaningful for the user.

CASE

Today, the understanding and use of CASE technology has expanded. CASE now incorporates a wide variety of concepts including CASE tools and CASE environments. A CASE tool is a standalone software application that is intended for use by software engineers (and/or their managers), and whose purpose is the automation of some aspects of the software engineer's technical duties. A CASE tool may be placed in a number of different environments, and may or may not be intended to interface with other CASE tools.

Some CASE environments are seamless. A seamless environment is one that provides capabilities as opposed to individual tools. Instead of invoking and quitting specific tools, the software engineer merely uses capabilities. For example, during the process of editing some text, a software engineer may wish to create some graphics. However, instead of quitting a text editor and then invoking a graphics editor, the software engineer merely uses the graphics capabilities provided by the environment.

IDBS

It is most logical to define an IDBS as a tool for developing applications requiring both a DBMS and one or more ES and CASE tools. There are clearly many applications that require such a tool. In fact, the majority of the applications where a DBMS is currently being used would benefit from such a tool. Accordingly, an IDBS is defined here as a system for developing applications requiring knowledge-directed intelligent processing of shared information.

A strawman architecture for an IDBS is shown in Figure 1. There are four kinds of system components between the users and the information: (1) CASE for intelligent software engineering; (2) ES for knowledge-directed intelligent processing; (3) a DBMS for shared information management; and (4) specialized intelligent processors for handling special format data. The number and type of specialized intelligent processors will depend on the application. The pathways between the components reflect a hierarchy of control rather than data or command paths. Any of the components may allow direct access for data or commands to lower-level components. The user will access the IDBS via the ES and CASE interfaces.

The specialized intelligent processors are used for specific data operations such as image enhancement or finite element analysis. These specialized intelligent data processors operate on data stored in particular formats and perform a fixed menu of functions. The structure of this data is of no interest to the user other than its manifestation via the fixed functions. The data structure is therefore not captured in any

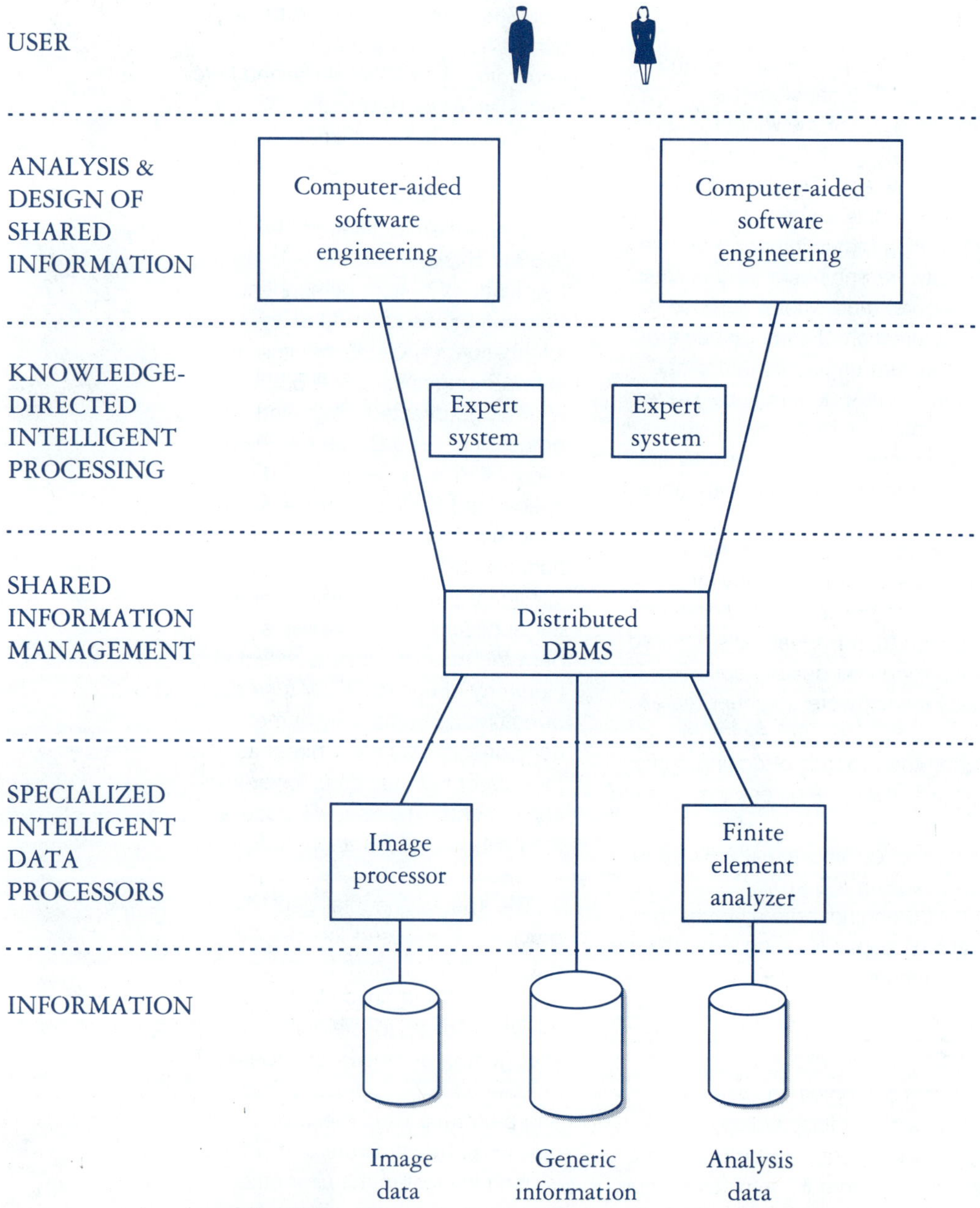
USER
ANALYSIS & DESIGN OF SHARED INFORMATION
Computer-aided software engineering
Computer-aided software engineering
KNOWLEDGE-DIRECTED INTELLIGENT PROCESSING
Expert system
Expert system
SHARED INFORMATION MANAGEMENT
Distributed DBMS
SPECIALIZED INTELLIGENT DATA PROCESSORS
Image processor
Finite element analyzer
INFORMATION
Image data
Generic information
Analysis data

Figure 1 IDBS architecture

knowledge representation language (or data model). The ability to handle specialized data is a requirement in a growing number of ES, CASE, and DBMS applications. It is essential that a general-purpose IDBS have this ability.

The major challenge to developing a general-purpose IDBS will be performance. An IDBS is essentially the composition of three powerful search engines. One engine will be searching knowledge rules to solve an application problem and, in so doing, generating queries over shared information. The second engine will use CASE to analyze and design the shared information. The third engine will be searching the shared information to answer the queries. The result will be a multiplicative explosion in processing time.

The key design criterion for dispersing functionality among ES, CASE, and DBMSs in an IDBS can now be stated. The ES should only be used for those cases of inferencing where the power of its search mechanism is really needed. In other cases, simpler search mechanisms should be used. In particular, the DBMS should be delegated maximum responsibility for searching shared information. The goal is to minimize the amount of knowledge involved in the search cycle of the ES. This goal is entirely compatible with the second goal of giving the DBMS maximum scope for optimization so as to reduce secondary storage costs.

Excerpted from Vacca, John R., "CASE and expert systems." Data Base Management, *May 1991, 12ff. Reprinted with permission from* Data Base Management.

AT A GLANCE

Expert systems represent a major development, advancing user/machine interface and problem solving. The merging of expert systems and database systems in a growing number of business applications is making databases "smarter" when responding to "intelligent" queries from users on an ad hoc basis.

An expert system has several characteristics: reasoning by symbol manipulation, exhibiting intelligent behavior, using rules of thumb or heuristics to emulate the human expert, and reasoning abilities. Expert system developers, called knowledge engineers, build systems by interviewing known experts in a specific domain and representing their knowledge as programs that use popular languages such as PROLOG.

The architecture of an expert system centers around a knowledge base and an inference engine. The knowledge base contains facts and inference rules for determining new facts. The inference engine contains the inference strategies and the controls for managing the facts and rules.

Merging databases and expert systems may have a number of business applications. A higher level of semantic knowledge and deductive capabilities built into the database would make the information system environment more user friendly and more efficient than a conventional database environment. The recent emergence of IBM's SQL, which facilitates access to relational databases, has accelerated the merging of expert systems and database technologies.

An expert system–database interface can facilitate more efficient storage and retrieval of rules in a form amenable to the organization of a database of rules. The interface also means that an expert system, with its rules in its own knowledge base, can access the data in a conventional database in the same way that a programming language does.

By the end of this chapter, you should be able to

- understand why expert systems and databases should merge;
- list the basic elements and attributes of an expert system;
- distinguish between expert systems and conventional programming languages; and
- understand the implications of expert systems for the database environment.

INTRODUCTION

Database management systems technology is restricted and restrictive. Unfortunately, most of the "intelligent" decision making still has to be supplied by the user. Formal query languages have been a barrier for nontechnical users, although user-friendly interfaces such as menu-driven systems have improved the user-machine dialogue for most applications. The answer to this restriction has been natural language, which is part of today's expert systems.

A NATURAL LANGUAGE uses the conceptual structure of English to match the user's conceptualization of the problem. A natural language interface means the user doesn't have to learn computer syntax. An effective communication system for a user-machine interface in complex decision-making tasks, then, is made possible by a procedure that uses a natural language.

Here are some questions that might be asked by a fictitious natural language called "BL":

- What is the name of the vice president of installment loans?
- Give me the names of customers who returned TV model 157V2 after June 17, 1991.
- What is the minimum value of an applicant's assets to qualify for an auto loan?

A large software applications backlog still exists in large firms, and software development technology lags behind advances in hardware. Although relational database technology has made it easier for the user to process data, the difficulties inherent in creating procedural code using, for example, COBOL, are still with us. So, a logical step would be to connect expert system shells (ready-to-use software), which rely on natural language, to the corporate database, with an eye toward developing "intelligent" databases and improving the quality of users' decision making.

To date, the two technologies still go their own ways. For every company that has incorporated expert systems into their database structure, many others are barely assessing the technology. There are structural reasons for this slow pace: DBMSs stress syntax over semantics (structure over meaning), while expert systems stress semantics over structure. For example, today's means of accessing data in a relational database is based on SQL, which is a nonprocedural query language. Most relational database applications use SQL code that is typically embedded in COBOL or C programs—an odd marriage of convenience between procedural and nonprocedural languages.

Since the late 1980s, researchers have begun to see the two technologies as complementary and have sought to use the capabilities of each to enhance the other. More and more corporations are exploring ways to apply expert systems to tasks ranging from robotics to production management. Some success has been achieved by expert systems that use represented knowledge and inference procedures to solve problems that otherwise would require significant human expertise. The key to this kind of problem solving is in knowing the right information rather than in constructing a solution from logical principles. In this chapter, we explain what expert systems are all about and how they can be used to interface with databases to address key applications or improve the intelligence capacity of existing databases.

THE DATABASE MANAGEMENT SYSTEM–EXPERT SYSTEM INTERFACE

An EXPERT SYSTEM is software that performs tasks by using inference to emulate human thinking or decision making. This is supported by a KNOWLEDGE BASE which contains the rules and heuristics that make this possible. In contrast, DBMSs use query matching and emphasize shared access to historical data. Since the late 1980s, industry in general has begun to realize that these two technologies are truly complementary—that they can be used together to solve different parts of the same problem. As a result, research into the integration of database technology and expert systems is under way, with positive results in a number of applications. Knowledge representation (the part of expert systems that represents the rules) is a growing area of research. Knowledge may be graphically represented in the form of semantic nets, linking facts by relations. This approach closely resembles natural language descriptions.

A recommended way of integrating expert systems with database applications is to use an expert system as a FRONT END to a database, asking questions and then initiating a database query. An expert system can also be used as a BACK END to a database. A back-end expert system evaluates the results of a query according to set rules before making a recommendation. The interaction between databases and back-end expert systems is leading to new file structures and refinements in indexing methodology that reduce overall search time.

Key Benefits

Integrating expert systems and database systems could have several benefits. Consider for a moment a typical organization with lower-, middle-, and upper-level management. At the lower level, clerks and office workers use their terminals on an on-line basis as events warrant. At the middle level, managers access data and retrieve reports to handle ad hoc decisions. At the top level, executives use summarized information in the form of reports and graphs to make strategic, company-wide decisions.

Considering how often personnel change and the importance of relating database information to the rules and policies of the firm, expert systems provide a way to make those who access a database follow established rules throughout the three levels of management more consistently and reliably. In this environment, policies are incorporated into an expert system's knowledge base as rules embedded into the kinds of business applications that use the database based on policy. (See Figure 17-1.)

Just as a corporate database is the repository of the firm's data resource, the knowledge base can become the repository of its corporate rules and policies. This means that system functions could be tailored to the evolving experience of the user and tagged to his or her needs. Proactive audit routines could also be triggered by the expert system to guard against a deviation from policy.

Another benefit of merging expert systems with database systems is in the area of user interface. Existing database systems use screens that call for a fill-in-the-blanks approach to data entry and retrieval. With an embedded expert system, an intelligent front end with a visual focus could capture areas of concern and be driven more by events than by preestablished procedures.

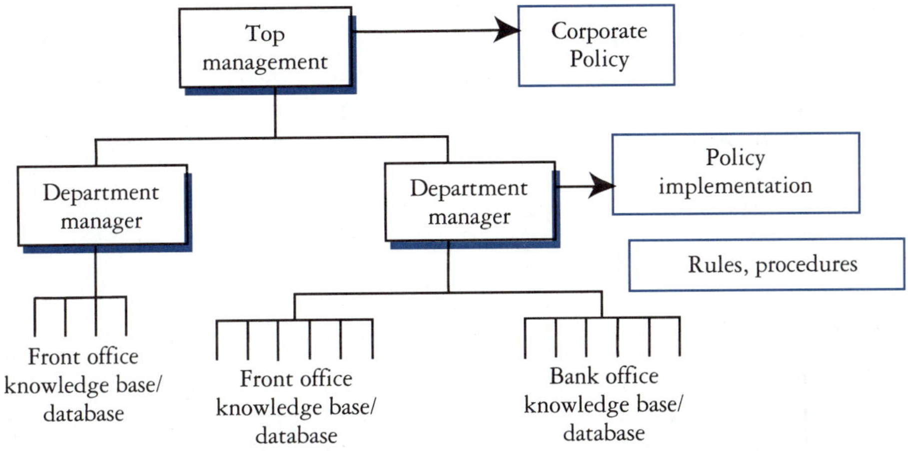

Figure 17-1 Policies and policy enforcement flows down the hierarchy path

Expert systems could also contribute to "intelligent" query management. Database software can efficiently handle data storage and retrieval for multiple users in a networked environment, but it cannot tell which user will make the next request. All a database system offers is historical data, not data based on rules and heuristics designed to emulate human decision making. An intelligent database system should be capable of generating SQL queries and associating queries into logical units called transactions before committing work accordingly.

Seamless integration between a DBMS and an expert system would provide significant benefits when the two technologies share a common interface environment. For example, if a DBMS is written in C and the expert system software is also written in C, one software calling to or calling from the other would know that the call originated within a common environment. Of course, a consistent host language interface would be needed to transport query results from the database to the expert system. This would be part of the logical design.

EXPERT SYSTEMS

Data and Knowledge

In discussing the relationship between expert systems and databases, we need to start at the elemental level of distinguishing between the data that resides in the database and the knowledge that is represented by the knowledge base. As we shall see later in the chapter, the knowledge base is an integral part of the expert system environment.

Knowledge is information at a high level of abstraction. For example, "MIS 101 is a three-hour course" is a fact in a school's database. But "MIS 101 is a basic course" is not a precise fact. This higher level of abstraction implies that knowledge is not so easy to quantify.

Knowledge is generated by experts and is used to define and control data in a database. As such, knowledge comes in various forms. The forms related to a database are structural, intentional, and derived.

Structural knowledge STRUCTURAL KNOWLEDGE deals with constraints and dependencies among data. For example, the statement "insertion into a supersaver fare is subject to reservations 14 days in advance of departure date" contains a familiar constraint, cued by the words "subject to."

Intentional knowledge INTENTIONAL KNOWLEDGE can be fully identified before the database is developed. Expert systems use intentional knowledge in the form of general rules as well as extensional knowledge, or knowledge embedded in facts. EXTENSIONAL KNOWLEDGE represents database systems, since they manage data.

Derived knowledge DERIVED KNOWLEDGE makes use of intentional and extensional knowledge. For example, consider a database with three relations:

- president (president_name, manager_name)
- vice president (vice_president_name, manager_name)
- department head (dept_head_name, title_name)

We can generate a variety of organizational relations from managers to supervisors, which is the job of a knowledge base. Figure 17-2 illustrates the relationship between a database management system and a knowledge base.

Definition

An expert system is a branch of artificial intelligence that allows a novice user to achieve results comparable to those of a human "expert" in a specific decision-making area. It uses a body of knowledge that relates to a specific problem domain and an inferencing component called an INFERENCE ENGINE to produce solutions to complex problems. (See Figure 17-3.)

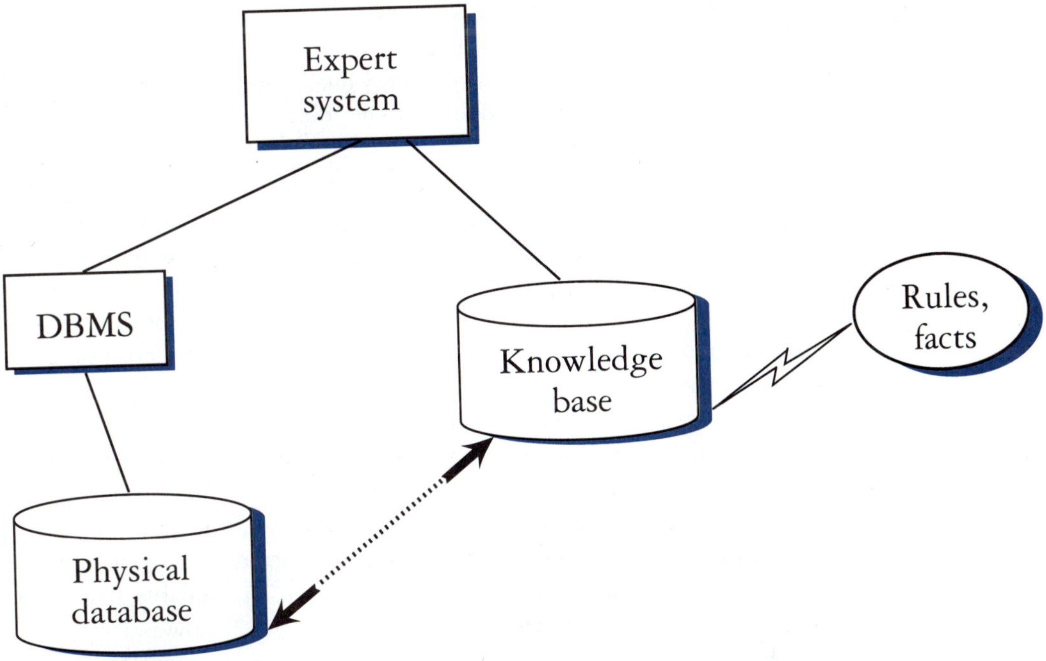

Figure 17-2 Knowledge base and database systems

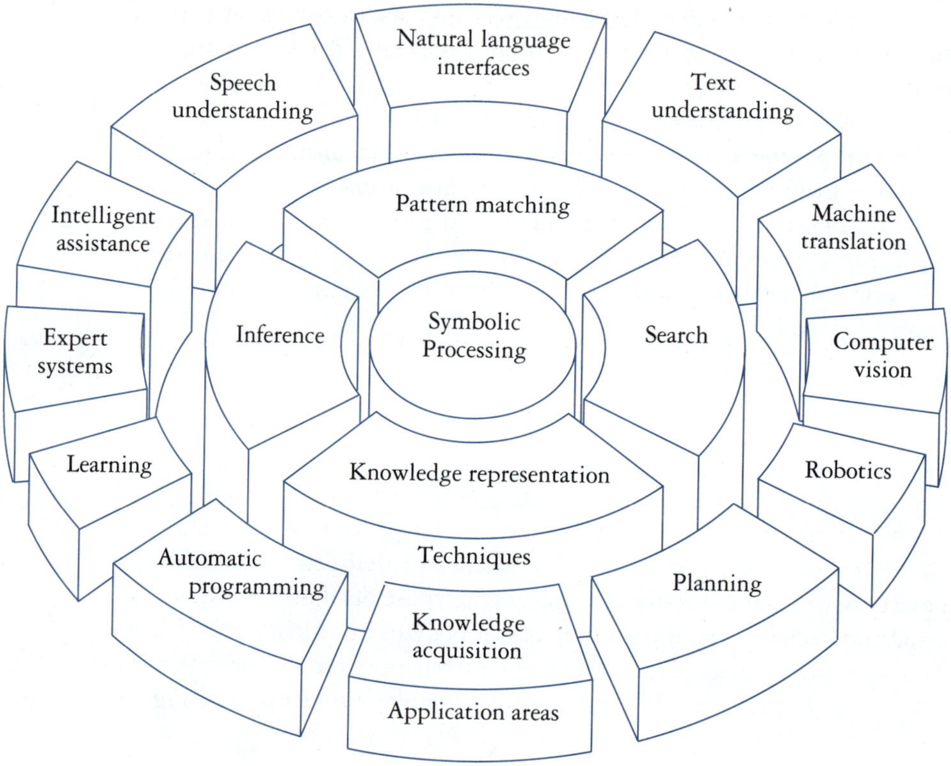

Figure 17-3 Elements of artificial intelligence. The outer circle allows twelve application areas, including expert systems. The inner circle focuses on four symbolic processing techniques. Each technique deals with one or more application areas

In expert systems, the knowledge base contains the decision rules that represent the human expert's thought processes. An expert system is actually a piece of software that sits on top of the knowledge base. To illustrate, an airline passenger submits a list of facts to a reservation expert system, such as "I want to fly to Miami from Boston in the morning, nonstop, on October 9, and stay five days on supersaver. I am diabetic, traveling alone." The system searches the database for various flights, departure times, meals, and fares. Using the knowledge base, an interactive dialogue allows a series of questions and answers concerning a special breakfast, car rental, seat selection, and so on. The initial inquiry is generally unstructured, because of fragmented or incomplete information. Various strategies are then considered for consulting the knowledge base to arrive at the best fit between an available flight and the passenger's requirements. Notice, in Figure 17-2, how practical it is that the knowledge base uses select data in the database before it "fires" the rules that determine the final answer. In a way, the database holds historical data, while the knowledge base holds the logic that decides how or in what way the data can be used to solve the problem.

An expert system can "learn" from each episode and use what it has learned to ask different questions before reaching a final decision. The user's responses are stored for later interaction, just as an alert travel agent would remember the likes and dislikes of a frequent customer.

Expert systems, then, are programs for solving difficult, nontrivial problems requiring expertise. They simulate human reasoning using logical deductions or facts and rules of thumb used by human experts. In *Artificial Intelligence in Business* (John Wiley, 1985) Harmon and King define an expert system as an

> . . . intelligent program that uses knowledge and inference procedures to solve problems that are difficult enough to require significant human expertise for their solution. The knowledge of an expert system consists of facts and heuristics. The "facts" constitute a body of information that is widely shared, publicly available, and generally agreed upon by experts in a field. The "heuristics" are mostly private, little discussed rules of good judgment (rules of plausible reasoning, rules of good guessing) that characterize expert-level decision making in the field. The performance level of an expert system is primarily a function of the size and the quality of a knowledge base it possesses.

This definition implies several ideas:

- expertise
- reasoning by symbol manipulation
- exhibiting generally intelligent behavior
- conversion to expert rules
- reasoning abilities about its own processes

Expertise consists of using high-level rules and high-level inference patterns, or hunches, that come from years of experience at a task. The measure of an expert is that, no matter how fast he or she performs a task, the results are accurate. Speed is also an important factor in expert systems. In a medical expert system, for instance, even the most accurate diagnosis slowly arrived at would be useless if the patient died first.

Reasoning by symbol manipulation means human experts solve problems by choosing symbols to represent the problem situation and apply specific approaches to manipulate these situations. An expert system uses knowledge symbolically, that is, it uses symbols to represent problem situations.

In expert systems, a SYMBOL is a group of characters that stands for a real-life situation, such as being a woman and mother. These symbols can combine to structure relationships between them. The symbol structure

```
(WOMEN mothers)
(MOTHER Ann)
```

may be interpreted as the facts

```
Mothers are women.
Ann is a mother.
```

An expert system can use these two facts to perform deductive reasoning from the two structures:

```
All mothers are women.  Ann is a mother.
Therefore, Ann is a woman.
```

The choice and interpretation of symbols can be very important for fast, efficient responses to inquiries. In this simple example, we refer to knowledge as REPRESENTATIONAL.

Exhibiting a generally intelligent behavior is a product of the principles the system knows and the level of detail at which it knows them. The quality of reasoning depends on how available the facts and principles are and how efficiently the inference procedure is implemented.

Conversion to expert rules is a changeover in which expert knowledge is expressed in the form of expert rules. For example, if we have knowledge about weather, weather conditions, or symptoms, we could state "If the sky is cloudy and the temperature is over 80, then there is a 70-percent certainty it will rain." This is called REFORMULATION.

Reasoning abilities about its own processes means that an expert system must be able to reconstruct the inference paths it has taken to arrive at a given conclusion. Determining how a conclusion was derived requires an ability to link the inference steps with basic expert rules as justifications. This is part of the inference engine, the software that comes with the expert system "shell" or product.

In summary, an expert system uses expert rules, reasons by manipulating symbols, displays on request its line of reasoning in plain English, is in command of fundamental domain principles, and has reasoning abilities about its own processes. It deals with complex or nontrivial problems, takes a problem description in simple terms, and converts it into representation for processing using expert rules.

Knowledge Engineering

Those who build expert systems are called KNOWLEDGE ENGINEERS, in the same way that those who build conventional software applications are called systems analysts. An expert system is built by capturing knowledge from a human expert through interviews or other methods. This expert is someone who is widely recognized for solving a particular type of problem well. This person also has a large amount of domain-specific knowledge. The knowledge engineer attempts to replicate the problem-solving process of the expert, which involves

1 identifying the specific knowledge that an expert uses in solving a problem;

2 determining the facts and HEURISTICS (general guidelines) that the expert uses;

3 specifying the inference strategy that the expert employs in an actual problem situation; and

4 developing a system that employs similar knowledge and inference strategies to simulate the behavior of the human expert—a feature known as TRANSPARENCY.

There are certain distinctive features of knowledge engineering. Expert systems use symbolic programming as opposed to the algorithmic (step-by-step) routines used by conventional programs. Symbolic programming is highly interactive and relies on heuristic search for its structure. With symbolic programming a user can interrupt processing and ask how a conclusion is reached. In contrast, the code and procedure in a conventional program are best known to the programmer or the developer.

Other contrasts between an expert system and a conventional program include the following.

- Conventional programs can be quite complex, understood only by experienced programmers. The knowledge base of an expert system, on the other hand, is easy to read and modify.
- Conventional programmers work with the user, not the expert, to write a program. Knowledge engineers use interactive techniques to develop expert systems. They meet frequently with the expert, produce a first cut at the problem, ask the expert more questions, generate a second version of the proposed system, and so on, developing the expert system in a series of approximations. This is often called RAPID PROTOTYPING.
- In conventional programming, the best possible solution is usually sought. In expert system programming, satisfactory answers are usually acceptable.

Knowledge Representation

As stated earlier, the architecture of an expert system consists of two parts (see Figure 17-4): the knowledge base and the inference engine.

The knowledge base contains the necessary facts and inference rules for coming up with new facts. The knowledge is represented in symbolic form that is used by the inference engine which is the built-in software, similar to a disk operating system (DOS) in a PC. A most common representation is the object. As we will see later, an object is associated with other objects by symbolic references, using links in the memory. A typical associative taxonomy for stating facts is the one known as "is-a" hierarchy. For example, "the parrot *is a* bird" and "the bird *is a* kind of animal that can fly." In this example, the knowledge base can deduce that parrots can fly. The rule, on the other hand, is a collection of "if-then" statements that help in machine decision making.

The inference engine stands between the user and the knowledge base. It contains the inference strategies and controls the processing of facts and rules. It also decides the order in which inferences are made. The inference engine draws logical conclusions based on the data in the knowledge base and general knowledge of the subject domain.

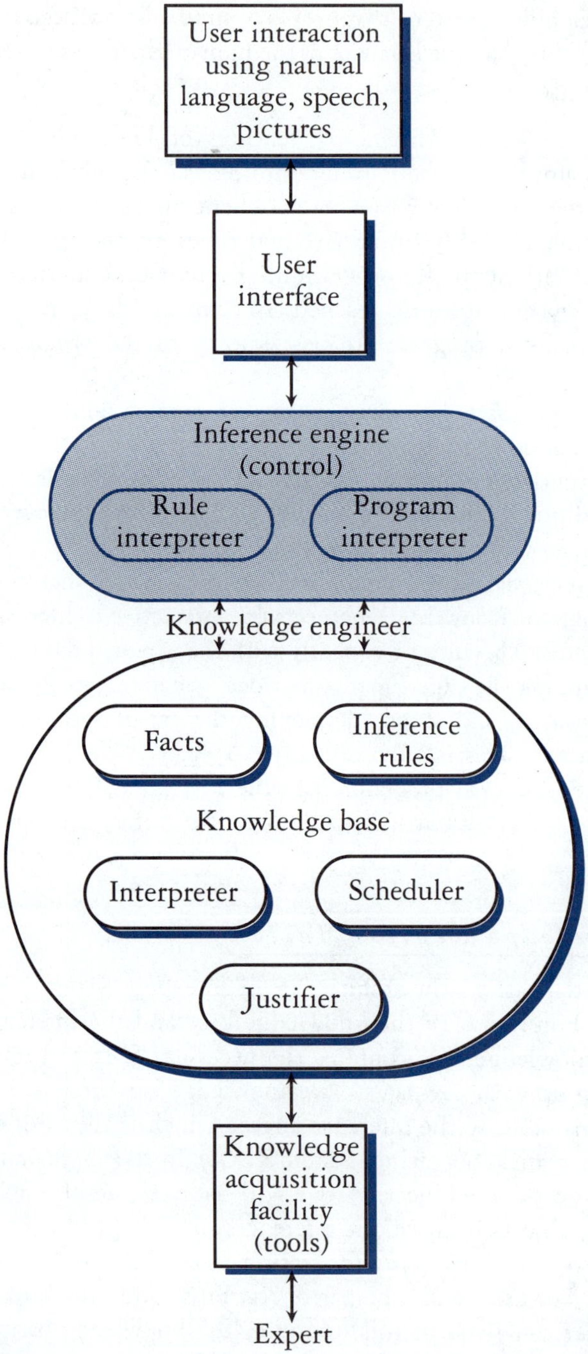

Figure 17-4 The architecture of an expert system. The inference engine stands between the user and the knowledge base. It examines facts and rules and provides the user with advice and explanations

The knowledge base The first step in building an expert system is to capture and evaluate some knowledge. The pattern of interaction between people and expert systems is shown in Figure 17-5.

The knowledge engineer interviews an expert on a specific problem domain. The following is a summary of data an expert (Jim Harding) gathered about a flight instructor (Fred Olesek) for a personnel knowledge base related to specialists in pilot testing:

> It is a fact that Fred Olesek has been a flight instructor for AMERICAN for seven years. The insignia on his shirt sleeve identifies him as a flight instructor. His license certifies him as a specialist in air rescue and emergency landing procedures. (Jim Harding, AMERICAN Personnel Division)

In our example, the expert is Jim Harding. His knowledge about Olesek's job is written in basic elements rather than complex statements. To create a personnel knowledge base, he needs to include elements such as Olesek's license, a list of the characteristics of each element, and a way to link things together. For example, he needs to record the fact that the insignia on Olesek's shirt sleeve signifies that he is a flight instructor.

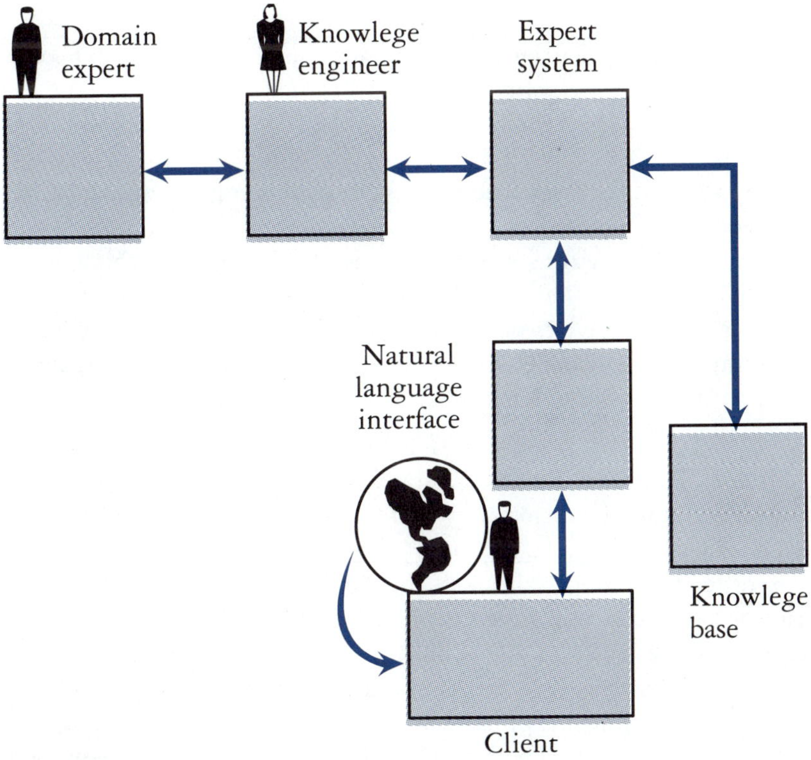

Figure 17-5 How people interact with expert systems

A knowledge base contains the facts and the problem-solving rules. It also uses an interpreter to apply the rules, a scheduler to coordinate processing of the rules, and a justifier to explain how the expert system arrives at the solution (see Figure 17-4).

Facts and relationships can be encoded to represent knowledge in a number of ways. Popular representation schemes include semantic networks, rules, frames, and logic.

Semantic knowledge SEMANTIC KNOWLEDGE is a semantic network or a collection of nodes linked together to form a NET. A NODE is a beginning or an ending point of an activity, represented by a circle. The key elements are the node and the link.

A node may be a physical object (such as a shirt sleeve or insignia) or a conceptual entity, such as the number 2 or the company AMERICAN. It may also be a descriptor that provides additional information such as an insignia.

A LINK connects nodes and descriptors. Links include the following:

- "Is-a" represents the class/instance relationship. In our example, Olesek *is a* male. He is an instance of the large class, male. A male, in turn, is an instance of the larger class, person.
- "Has-a" identifies a node that is a property of another node. For example, a uniform *has a* shirt sleeve. "Has-a" often denotes a subpart relationship.
- "Wear" is a definitional link. In our example, the wear link between person and apparel is a definitional link.
- Some links represent heuristic knowledge, such as "License *certifies* examining. . . ."

Figure 17-6 illustrates the key nodes that represent Harding's knowledge.

One useful aspect of a semantic net is INHERITANCE, which allows for deductive reasoning. This means that instances of one class are assumed to have all the properties of the more general class to which it belongs. For example, the personnel knowledge base in Figure 17-6 lets us answer the question, "Does Olesek wear a uniform?" by determining that Olesek is a male, males are persons, and persons wear apparel.

Rules Rules are conditional statements that specify an action to be taken if a certain condition is true. In expert systems vocabulary, rules are called PREMISE-CONCLUSION or SITUATION-ACTION rules. Expert systems rules differ from the traditional "if-then" programming statement in that they are relatively independent of one another and are based on heuristics rather than on algorithms.

Table 17-1a specifies a rule consisting of a premise and a conclusion. The premise has three expressions, or clauses, each having an attribute, an object, and a value. The conclusion has one expression or clause with an attribute, an object, or value, as shown in Table 17-1b.

Rule		*Expression*		
a. Premise (situation)	If	the look of the clouds is black and the force of the wind is over 35 mph and the height of the waves is over 18 feet,		
Conclusion (action)	Then	it is likely (.8) that the classification of the storm is a hurricane		
		Attribute	*Object*	*Value*
b. Premise	If	site	clouds	black
		force	wind	over 35 mph
		height	waves	over 18 ft
Conclusion	Then	classification	storm	hurricane

Table 17-1 Structure of a rule and its elements

Frames A FRAME associates an object with facts, rules, or values. Each fact or value is stored in a SLOT related to a specific object. So a set of slots and their associated entries represent a frame. Table 17-2 shows a frame of the personnel knowledge base with Olesek's letter as the object. The slots represent the properties of the object.

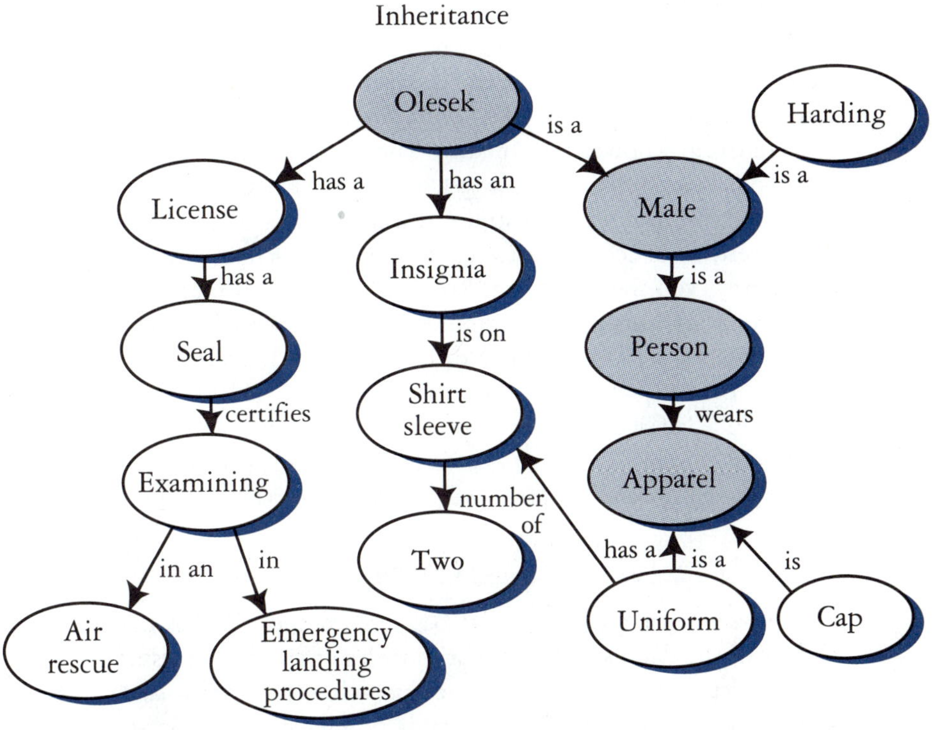

Figure 17-6 Personnel knowledge base

Object: Letter *Slot*	*Entry*
Instructor	Olesek
Verification	Letter
Unique feature of verification	Seal
Teaching certification	Air rescue
Teaching certification	Emergency landing procedures

Table 17-2 A frame representing Olesek's letter

Logic Logic is a system that prescribes rules for manipulating symbols. A widely studied formal language for symbol structures is predicate calculus. A PREDICATE is a statement about an object. An OBJECT is an elementary unit in predicate calculus. For example, "is-instructor (Olesek)" is an assertion that Olesek is an instructor. This assertion may be either true or false. A predicate can address more than one object, however. For example, "instructor-at (Olesek, AMERICAN)" is a two-place predicate. The statement asserts that Olesek is an instructor at AMERICAN.

Drawing Inferences

In order for a system to reason, it must be capable of inferring new facts from what it has already been told. This means creating new symbol structures from old ones. After selecting a method for representing knowledge in the knowledge base, the knowledge engineer's next step is to draw INFERENCES, which are logical conclusions based on the data. To illustrate, Table 17-3 lists the facts and rules about getting to school on time. Rule 1 is "If school is more than two miles away, you should drive." Rule 2 is "If school is more than one mile and you have less than 30 minutes to get to school, you should still drive." Rule 4 is "If school is North Campus and getting to school is by driving, then the action is to ride (drive) a bike." The conclusion that we "ride a bike" if the premise of rule 4 is true results from deriving new facts from existing rules and known facts. It is a rule of inference used in proof procedures and an intuitive way of conducting reasoning.

Making the Database Smarter

The semantic aspect of a database environment makes it possible to embed in the database the heuristics (rules of thumb) necessary to make it "smarter." This involves incorporating heuristics as a way to determine what part of the data must be used to make decisions.

Rule	Premise		Conclusion
	(IF)		(THEN)
1	Distance is > 2 miles	----->	Mode is "drive"
2	Distance is > 1 mile and time < 30 minutes	----->	Mode is "drive"
3	Distance is > 1 mile and time > 20 minutes	----->	Mode is "bus"
4	Mode is "drive" and location is "North Campus"	----->	Action is "ride a bike"
5	Mode is "drive" and location is not "North Campus"	----->	Action is "drive your car"
6	Mode is "bus" and weather is rain	----->	Action is "take an umbrella"
7	Mode is "bus" and weather is "clear"	----->	Action is "bus"

Table 17-3 Rules for getting to school on time

One expert systems language that stresses semantics over syntax is PROLOG (PROgramming in LOGic). This logic programming language uses data to support deduction and computation. PROLOG programs benefit from large numbers of facts, analogous to rows in a relational table, that support reasoning and are used in "IF...THEN" and other logical deductions. PROLOG performs tricks that SQL cannot learn, but at a price: inefficiency. PROLOG cannot access a large amount of information efficiently and quickly when performing large-scale symbolic manipulation.

Fortunately, PROLOG can be viewed as a kind of relational database because it has an equal number of clauses, predicates, and arguments (parameters). The only difference between PROLOG and a relational database is in the type of restriction placed on the arguments. Table 17-4 compares PROLOG and the relational model.

Because SQL-based relational databases and PROLOG knowledge bases are fundamentally information-bearing systems, they may be combined into a new product that takes advantage of their synergy. In addition, PROLOG has a powerful facility for querying. It also permits dynamic data definition of database entities (allowing changes to be made at any time), recursively defined predicates for both data structures and queries, pattern matching, rule-based inferencing, and built-in backtracking and trace facilities. Finally, PROLOG permits functions to appear as arguments, where SQL allows only atomic data elements to appear in fields.

RELATIONAL	PROLOG
Base relation tuple —Constant number of fields	***Ground clause (fact)*** —Same predicate can appear with any number of arguments —Predicate can be defined with facts and rules
Attribute —Type restrictions	***Predicate Argument*** —No type restrictions
View Definition —View updated only when base relation can be updated	***Rules*** —No distinction between relations and view
Query —Queries evaluated over a fixed interpretation	***Theorem*** —Theorems evaluated according to proof theory, making set-oriented queries difficult
Insert/Delete —Semantics of insert/delete operations on relations (facts) are part of data model. Additional operations are required to manipulate table definitions —Consistency is maintained across operations (uniqueness of key values)	***Assert/Retract*** —Assert and retract apply equally to both facts and predicates —No provision for maintaining consistency of facts with respect to existing predicate

Table 17-4 Comparison of PROLOG and the relational model

Implications for the Database Environment

The conjunction of expert systems, database theory, and programming languages may yield a new intelligent relational data manipulation language (DML), one that may become an intelligent database interface. To achieve the integration, logical address space requires a new DML, called PROSQL, which combines the intelligence of PROLOG with the strength of SQL. To the knowledge engineer and the programmer, all database objects now appear within the logical address space of the inference engine and the programming language. PROSQL's ability to implement the extended logical address space, and not its intelligent or efficient data management, is what makes PROSQL so powerful.

Expert systems are a carryover from efforts to extend the manager's ability to understand the business and control its processes. With expert systems, managers can begin to use facts and rules to structure complex human problems, extending the realm of the possible. In many contexts, a small amount of embedded knowledge interfacing with a database facility may drastically relieve the amount of processing needed to produce an answer. This means that managers can begin to tackle badly structured problems for solutions that can give an organization a competitive edge.

The potential uses of combined database management systems/expert systems for modern business applications are tremendous. The large body of facts usually required for large applications can be made available to an expert system through existing DBMSs. The DBMS as part of MIS can also be used more intelligently if it is coupled with expert systems features. A higher level of semantic knowledge and deductive capabilities built into the database would make an MIS more user friendly, user supportive, and efficient than a conventional database environment.

Integrating Expert Systems with Databases

Intelligent Database Interface

Designing database interfaces between human and machine when the human user is not an expert in the use of the database can be difficult. For the inexperienced user, the best possible interface between user and machine is a human intermediary. The intelligent database interface represents the human expert's knowledge of the database, its capabilities, use, and operation on behalf of the user.

There are two facets to an intelligent database interface: the front end and the back end. The front end—what the user sees at a workstation—is concerned mostly with attractive presentation, context-sensitive help, and intuitive operation. This user interface can be implemented in a variety of formats: command line, menu, object-oriented window, natural language interpreter, or in any other way the programmer sees fit. The back end, which controls the database, typically employs a DML like SQL to access the database. It is this database interface, not the user interface, that does most of the thinking for the user. And since the user interface is characteristically a facade fitted on top of the relatively brainy database interface, it seems more worthwhile to focus on developing the database interface's potential first.

The emergence of IBM's SQL, which facilitates access to relational databases, has accelerated the merging of expert system and database technologies. In most products, the developer does not have to know SQL, just how to enter the needed data; the product comes up with the appropriate SQL query.

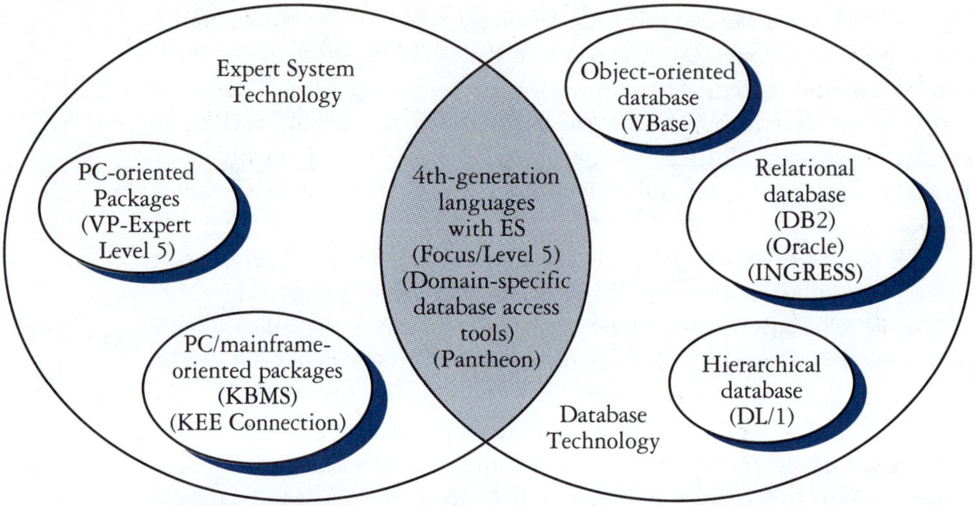

Figure 17-7 The merging of expert systems and databases[1]

Today's trend in building information systems reflects a growing commonality between the two technologies. As shown in Figure 17-7, there are more fourth-generation languages with expert systems than ever before. This means the gap between expert systems and databases may soon be bridged.

Alternative Uses

There are several ways in which expert systems and databases work together: when accessing data in the database, when an expert system is used for intelligent querying or managing data, and when sorting database cases and consultations that have been processed through an expert system.

When data stored in an existing database is accessed using an expert system the integration between the two is loose. An example is IBM's Expert System Environment (ESE). ESE has the ability to access the relational database SQL/DS by creating SQL queries (using a facility called dynamic SQL) and passing data through import/export facilities.

When an expert system is used for intelligent querying, the expert system acts as a front-end tool to provide more efficient access to a database. In most cases, the expert system is used to construct database queries. The system proceeds by asking questions and using rules to reach a final recommendation. Once it reaches a recommendation, it goes back to the database to search for an even more specific (and reliable)

---

[1] Adapted from Harmon, Paul and Sawyer, Bryan, *Creating expert systems for business and industry*. New York: John Wiley & Sons, 236.

recommendation. This is useful in situations where the set of actual recommendations changes, while the logic represented by the rules remains the same.

An example of such a system is INTELLECT, which uses its understanding of English syntax to formulate queries to a database. If INTELLECT comes up with multiple interpretations of the user's meaning, it searches the database in an attempt to discover the intended meaning.

Using expert systems as a front-end tool is popular when users have difficulty formulating queries. The expert system asks the user to state the request, applies the rules to evaluate the feedback, and then generates the database query that will retrieve the necessary record, report, or information from the database. The query is passed to the database program which, in turn, produces the information the user needs.

An expert system can also be used to manage data. The expert system thus becomes an adjunct to the DBMS, often in order to optimize and oversee other DBMS tasks.

An expert system can also act as a back-end tool by taking raw data drawn from a database query as input, evaluating it through the rules, and then making a specific recommendation to the user. For example, in an installment loan application, the expert system goes to the bank's database to inquire about the applicant's checking account balance, past loans, payments history, and so forth. This spares the applicant or loan clerk the tedious task of entering the information afresh. The system might also need to verify some data, such as current address and income, to determine whether the applicant qualifies for a loan.

Using a database to store the cases and consultations that have been processed through an expert system is an attractive way to keep track of the expert system's reasoning and to evaluate the quality of its "advice" during debugging sessions.

Applications and Benefits

In the past few years, the integration of expert systems technology with other systems technology has been one of the hottest areas of development, especially the integration of databases with expert systems. Database access, database intelligence, and data analysis concepts are beginning to find their way out of the research labs and into commercial markets. Companies such as Lotus Development Corporation and Borland International are known to be working on intelligent database software.

Until recently, most expert system shells, especially those built for use on PCs, were built in a vacuum, without regard for other systems. For a shell to be accepted in the marketplace, however, it must allow convenient access to database files. VP-Expert (Paperback Software International, Inc.) is a prime example of a shell. Its main strength is its built-in instructions for obtaining information from database files and modifying the information on the fly. Examples are beginning to appear, however, of tighter integration of expert systems technology with database technology.

One of the primary benefits expected from database-expert system integration is the ability to directly manipulate the semantics of the database. (Currently, the semantics are "hard-wired" into the data model.) Broader database capabilities could extend from such a system, such as the ability to express transitive-closure queries (queries that determine the hierarchy of relationships within a relation) or recursive queries, which are difficult or impossible to express in existing data manipulation languages.

A major point of discussion among researchers in this field is the type of database technology best suited to "tighter" integration with expert system techniques. Some believe that the increasingly prevalent relational database technology should be extended using expert system techniques. Others believe the rigid structure imposed by normalization makes this technology unsuitable and are looking instead to the still-developing object-oriented database technology for a closer fit.

One example of an expert system tightly integrated with a relational database system is the Syntel programming system developed by Syntelligence. This system combines data in relational tables (called extensional data) with intentional data, called equation networks, which are analogous to the rules contained in a knowledge base. The functions contained in this network compute derived value tables, which are updated when the underlying values in the equation change.

An example of an expert system tightly integrated with an object-oriented database is one developed by Peter Gray. Gray began looking at object-oriented database systems when it became apparent that relational databases were not compatible enough with PROLOG, the logic programming language he was using. He wanted to use a frame structure to represent logic, but found that not all frames of the same class need to have the same number of slots (attributes). This is, of course, contrary to relational database theory. Frames have complex metadata. Frames can have other frames attached to them. Slots can have many facets attached. This is difficult to implement in normal-form relations.

The problem with many current approaches is that they involve modifying either the expert system technology or the database technology to achieve a "fit." For example, the MULTILOG language developed by Kauffmann and Grumbach attempts to improve PROLOG's ability to interface with databases. This is difficult to accomplish without violating the design objectives of the underlying system. Some developers are calling for a revolutionary strategy, and predict the development of a completely new paradigm, called knowledge-based management systems, which would be constrained by neither expert system nor database design characteristics.

It will probably be some time before a true knowledge base system becomes a marketable reality, but researchers are trying to find the most appropriate model for such a system. As the volume of information continues to explode, finding more intelligent ways of manipulating and managing information will become essential. Expert systems technology will find broader commercial acceptance when it succeeds in solving problems such as efficient database management. Further research will hopefully uncover a means of merging these technologies.

SUMMARY

1 Solving problems across knowledge bases and databases has become an important function of the knowledge engineer as well as that of the database designer. Two ways of integrating the technologies are to use expert systems as a front end or a back end to a database.

2 Merging expert systems with database management would allow user functions to be tailored to the user's evolving experience and tagged to his or her needs. An intelligent front end with a visual focus can also capture areas of concern and be driven more by events than preestablished procedures. Finally, an intelligent database system should be capable of generating SQL queries and associating queries into logical units called transactions before committing work.

3 Knowledge comes in various forms. Structural knowledge deals with constraints and dependencies among data, while intentional knowledge is that which can be fully identified before the database is developed. Derived knowledge makes use of intentional and extensional knowledge.

4 An expert system allows a novice user to achieve results comparable to those of a human "expert" in a specific decision-making area. The main attributes of an expert system are expertise, reasoning by symbol manipulating, exhibiting generally intelligent behavior, conversion to expert rules, and reasoning abilities about its own processes.

5 Knowledge engineering is the art of building expert systems. The knowledge engineer attempts to replicate the problem-solving process of the expert by identifying the knowledge the expert uses in solving a problem; determining the facts and heuristics; specifying the inference strategy the expert employs in an actual problem situation; and developing transparency.

6 An expert system is made up of a knowledge base and an inference engine. The knowledge base contains facts and inference rules, which are collections of conditional statements that help in machine decision making. The inference engine contains the inference strategies and controls the processing of actions and rules.

7 Facts and relationships can be encoded in semantic networks, rules, frames, and logic. A semantic network is a collection of nodes linked together to form a net. Rules are conditional statements that specify an action to be taken, if a certain condition is true. Frames associate an object with facts, rules, or values. Each value is stored in a slot that is related to a

specific object. Logic is a system that describes rules for manipulating symbols.

8 In an intelligent database interface, the front end is what the user sees at a workstation and the back end is what controls the database.

9 Expert systems have been used to access data stored in an existing database to provide more efficient access to a database through intelligent querying, to manage data as an adjunct to the DBMS, and to produce cases and consultations that can be stored in a database.

10 One of the primary benefits expected from database-expert system integration is the ability to directly manipulate the semantics of the database. Broader database capabilities could extend from such a system.

KEY TERMS

Back end
Derived knowledge
Expert system
Extensional knowledge
Frame
Front end
Heuristics
Inferences
Inference engine
Inheritance
Intentional knowledge
Knowledge acquisition
Knowledge base
Knowledge engineering
Knowledge engineers
Knowledge representation
Link
Natural language
Net
Node
Object
Predicate
Premise-conclusion
PROLOG
Rapid prototyping
Reformulation
Representational knowledge
Rule
Semantic knowledge
Shell
Situation-action rules
Slot
Structural knowledge
Symbol
Transparency

REVIEW QUESTIONS

1 What would be the benefits of integrating an expert system and a DBMS?

2 In what ways are expert systems and DBMS technologies complementary?

3 Distinguish between the following pairs:
   a. knowledge and logic
   b. heuristics and inference engine
   c. knowledge base and database
   d. structural knowledge and derived knowledge

4 What is unique about expert systems technology? Explain.

5 How do the knowledge base and inference engine interact?

6 Illustrate how an expert system reasons through symbol manipulation.

7 How does a knowledge engineer replicate the problem-solving process of the expert?

8 In what ways does an expert system differ from a conventional program?

9 Elaborate on the key components of an expert system.

10 Distinguish between the following pairs:

a. scheduler and justifier
b. node and link
c. front-end and back-end uses of expert systems

APPLICATION PROBLEMS

1 TAXADVISOR was developed in 1982 to perform a tax consultant's role. It uses heuristics to decide on a planning option such as investing in a tax shelter for a client. It actually arranges a client's financial affairs in a way that will minimize income and death taxes, but not at the expense of sound investment or adequate insurance. In doing its work, it considers life insurance, retirement planning, tax shelters, and the like.

The system interacts with a tax consultant as follows:

- The system displays a list to inform the consultant of the questions.
- The system asks questions about the client in need of tax advice. The consultant enters a YES or NO response.
- When the system acquires enough information from the consultant, it displays on the screen a recommendation and produces on a hard copy a summary list of recommendations by order of importance.

TAXADVISOR is built around 275 rules. It generates its recommendations by starting with the system's general goal and moves down the hierarchy of rules in search of the best recommendation for the client.

a. Is TAXADVISOR an expert system or a database system? Explain.
b. If the system proceeds to ask endless questions, does this suggest anything negative about its performance? Elaborate.

2 The Japanese are determined to build a fifth-generation computer by 1995. Since 1988, some 40 computer engineers at Tokyo's Institute for New Generation Computer Technology (ICOT) have already developed an algorithm for the natural recognition of the syntax. Other engineers are close to building a sequential inference machine, a large computer that crunches logic (instead of numbers) at a rate of 20,000 logic inferences per second (lips).

ICOT is heavily subsidized by the Japanese government. One of the project's goals is to achieve a system capable of making inferences, like an artificial brain. So far, it is still working on a relational database management system capable of accepting questions, searching the database, and producing an answer.

a. Search the literature and assess the research being carried out in the U.S. by universities that competes with ICOT's research.
b. How do you foresee this type of research affecting U.S. business? Elaborate.

CHAPT

Database Management and the Future

E R 1 8

Object Orientation

AT A GLANCE

Object Orientation

Not everything in the computer industry is over-hyped. Despite the fact that object orientation (OO) is already a misused term, it does actually offer a model for building software that addresses many old problems. Over the past 20 years or so it has become apparent that the classical model of systems building, which is based around the program/database paradigm, has probably taken us as far as it can. Some software projects are simply not feasible using this model, and many others present huge maintenance problems after they have been built.

The key concept in OO is quite straightforward. Functionality and data are not separated into programs and databases, but are encapsulated into a single whole called an object. So if we want to know any of the attributes that relate to an employee, such as age, sex, or name, or if we want to perform any action on an employee such as "promote," "hire," or "fire," we will find these attributes and functions when we access the employee object. Strictly speaking, a set of similar objects (such as a group of employees) is called an object class. This is similar to a record definition: The actual objects are instances of an object class, just as records are instances of the record definition. The important thing to remember about objects is that they encapsulate what you can know of (attributes) and do to (functions) an entity in a single definition.

The Classical Model

The program/database model of software has served us well over the past 30 or so years. We break applications down into discreet areas of functionality, which we then implement as programs. For example, in a sales order processing system we still have an order entry program, an order cancellation program, maybe an invoicing program, and so on. As such, our programs represent areas of user functionality.

Breaking functionality down in this way tends to result in large pieces of code being written. Unfortunately, human beings do not work well with large, complex structures such as programs, and as time progresses the structures become harder and harder to maintain.

The classical model of software introduces a number of problems that need to be addressed before we can progress any further:

- Programs tend to be large, unmanageable structures because they represent areas of application functionality.
- Duplication of program code is necessary to incorporate the same or similar functionality into different programs.
- Separating data into databases and functionality into programs causes duplication of attribute definitions, which manifests as data dependency.
- The program is not a structure which can be treated in a formal manner, and as such it is difficult to show correctness.

The OO Model

Most of the concepts in OO are not new, and many organizations are already practicing some OO methods without being aware of it. The problems of software reuse, maintainability, correctness, and productivity have been central to the developers of object orientation.

In essence, the OO approach can be characterized by three concepts: encapsulation, information hiding, and inheritance.

Encapsulation of data and functionality is key to the OO approach. This has the side effect of causing functionality to be "normalized" so that each piece of code in a system is written once and can be accessed by all other objects in the system. For example, the "calculate tax" function might be defined with the employee object class. Thereafter, whenever it becomes necessary to calculate tax for an employee, this function in the employee object class will be used.

Information hiding. In the example of the tax calculation, all you want from the "calculate tax" function is a single number. The employee object class should only allow the outside world to see "tax amount," and not all the internal variables and code which are involved in the calculation. This is called information hiding and is a key concept in making software easier to maintain.

Inheritance. Object classes are arranged into a hierarchy. For example, an object class called Employees might be created, and lower in the hierarchy another class called Salespeople might also be created. Clearly, salespeople have the attributes and functions which belong to employees, plus additional ones which are relevant to themselves only. Instead of redefining attributes such as age, sex, name, address, and so on in Salesperson, you can inherit them from Employee instead. The same applies to functions. All employees can be hired, fired, and promoted, and these functions can be inherited by Salesperson from Employee.

The Old and the New

The old should be recognized for what it is: The classical approach with bolt-on functionality. OO is something quite radical and new. It is unlikely that the market will adopt OO rapidly and in a full-blooded manner. OO will be used as enabling technology, as in the creation of graphical user interfaces (GUIs), and existing products will make their way gently down the OO road.

OO will also bring about changes in the way software is developed and how software teams work. One manager involved in the development of OO systems commented that ". . . what I need is fewer people, but better." Creating an object class hierarchy for an application is not a trivial task, but once completed, the application is all but finished.

We can also expect to see the creation of "software supermarkets" that will sell off-the-shelf object classes to application builders. Such an object class may deal with payroll or invoicing. Companies have already been formed to manufacture modularized software of this nature.

The revolution that OO will bring to software will probably be gradual, but far-reaching all the same.

Excerpted from Butler, Martin and Bloor, Robin, "Object orientation." DBMS, *July 1991, 17-18. Reprinted with permission from* DBMS.

AT A GLANCE

In the preceding chapters, we have seen that the database is the foundation of an organization's information system environment and the critical component for building successful systems to assist management in operating the business. For almost a decade, several trends have suggested a definite swing away from traditional, centralized database systems. For example, database mainframes are now linked to minicomputers, PCs, and intelligent workstations in a multiuser environment. Processing has moved away from transaction processing and toward distributed knowledge processing. Data models heavily favor a relational database and knowledge representation. The user interface is increasingly taking the form of screen graphics.

A number of database technology issues are expected to emerge in the next five to ten years. They include the role of CASE tools, cooperative processing, federated DBMS, and object-oriented programming. The role of artificial intelligence will also grow tremendously. Knowledge-based systems are becoming reliable front-end products for complex applications. Likewise, merging CASE tools in the context of DBMS can now be considered in designing databases.

The next generation of database applications is predicted to be more complex and is becoming part of a "federated" DBMS. Another trend is integrating large volumes of data in a heterogeneous distributed database where multiple sites have their own DBMS with respective data already in place. The most recent approach to DBMS disaster recovery is data shadowing, where the entire database is kept on-line at a remote data center. Finally, legal issues related to network growth and an upsurge in the sharing of program code are being re-evaluated to ensure data integrity, the privacy of data, and the right to use database software.

By the end of this chapter, you should be able to

- discuss the role of CASE tools and object-oriented programming,
- understand the concepts and potential of cooperative processing and federated DBMS,
- list the trends in disaster recovery, and
- explain the legal issues surrounding database management system technology and use.

INTRODUCTION

In every field, especially in database management systems, new products appear on the market daily, and research work and productivity may provide even more advanced products before the end of the decade. Table 18-1 is a summary of the key developments since the mid-1960s, in which a number of trends can be seen:

1 The trend in database hardware is away from solo mainframes toward distributed databases that use mainframes and PCs in a network. Likewise, processing has moved away from data and transaction processing toward distributed and cooperative processing.

2 Today's data models are more and more often semantic and object-oriented, and indications are that merging data models will become feasible in the next five years.

3 User interfaces are increasingly handled by screen graphics (graphic user interface or GUI) and by natural language to provide "intelligence" to the interface.

Area	*Mid-1960s to mid-1970s*	*Late 1970s to mid-1980s*	*Late 1980s*	*Mid- to late 1990s*
Database hardware	Mainframes, high end of minis	Mainframes, minis, PCs	Fast PCs, workstations, database machines	Parallel processing
Processing	Data processing	Information/ transaction processing	Transaction processing/ knowledge processing	Distributed/ cooperative processing, Distributed knowledge processing
Data model	Hierarchical, network	Relational	Semantic, object-oriented	Knowledge representation Merging data models
User interface	None	Query languages	Menus Query-by-forms Graphics (GUI)	Natural language

Table 18-1 Trends in database technology

In the next five to ten years, new technologies and new uses for established technologies are expected to emerge, such as knowledge-based systems, CASE tools, cooperative processing, and PC-based DBMSs. These and nontechnical trends, such as the legal issues resulting from vendor alliances and joint software development, will have a major impact on the business environment. (See Figure 18-1.)

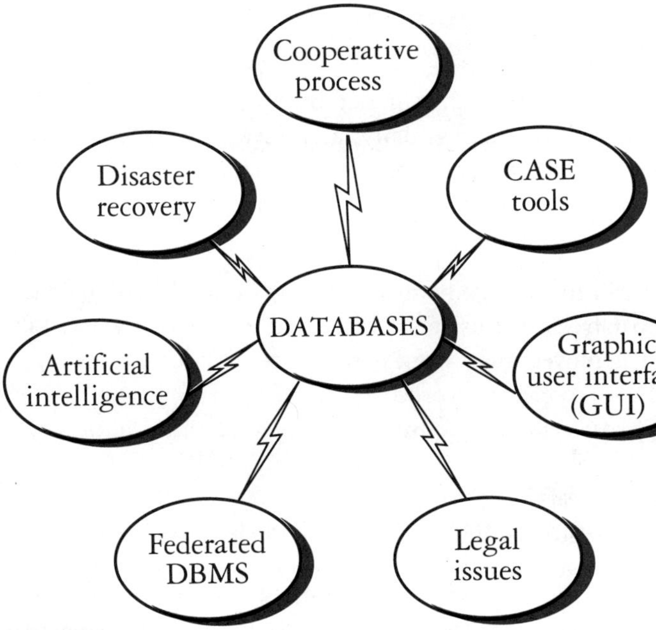

Figure 18-1 Emerging issues in database technology

THE INTELLIGENCE FACTOR

Industry and research sources indicate that database management systems technology is evolving toward ARTIFICIAL INTELLIGENCE (AI), of which expert systems are but one type. One of the best-known operations management systems built around this merger of AI and DBMS is United Airlines' Gate Assignment Display Systems (GADS). This system assists ground managers at key airports to schedule the United Airlines job transport fleet.

Unlike earlier developments in computing, today's state-of-the-art technology deals with specific applications that focus on the operational aspects of an organization. The United Airlines system helps networks of people on the ground manage the allocation of transport services. These are more specific applications than those of the 1980s, which emphasized desktop computing and functionality in general. The adoption of networked systems in the 1990s has made focused applications possible.

The role of AI cannot be over-emphasized. As we have discussed in Chapter 17, knowledge-based systems are becoming integrated elements of complex applications. For example, Ford Motor Company's Service Bay Diagnostic System "knows" the type of car being diagnosed and the kinds of problems that normally arise with that model and year. The service agent can use this knowledge-based system to pinpoint the car's problem and assign the right specialist to correct it. The Ford system uses computing to deal with objects. In this example, the automobile is an object with attributes that are represented in algorithms rather than linear data values. This is where symbolic computing techniques become significant.

One of the largest, most extensive symbolic computing applications was developed in 1990 for the Chicago Board of Trade. This expert system software handles all trades via workstations instead of the old "shout aloud" method. According to one source,[1] it took only 60 days to complete one module of the transaction programming for this system, as compared to a similar exchange, using a conventional workstation and language, which took 14 months.

THE ROLE OF CASE TOOLS

Another trend in database technology is the use of Computer-Aided Software Engineering (CASE) tools, which integrate database and process design. CASE is a collection of software programs designed to improve the performance of the software development process by automating various steps of the application development life cycle, from planning applications to designing databases. The primary end product is application software. Merging CASE tools in the context of DBMS can now be considered in designing databases.

Most CASE tools have a repository (a database about the database) about the database and the application in question. IBM and DEC are building repositories on their own proprietary relational DBMs: IBM's DB2 on MVS and DEC's Rdb on VAXs.

A relatively new product that integrates database and CASE tools is a database design tool that goes beyond the data structure diagrammer and is called a "front end." The "front end" helps the designer create the logical and physical design of a database by handling the detailed procedures of the design process. One example of such a product is the Bachman/Reengineering Product Set, which brings the existing data definition from a stored data model into the design. The software generates a data structure diagram based on relationships among entities and, using graphics and text editors, displays it on a monitor for evaluation.

[1] Peter van Cuylenburg, "Computing into the 90s." *Information Executive*, Sept. 1991, 37.

A relatively new technique in this area is to incorporate an expert system to look for inconsistencies in the data structure and come up with alternative ways of solving a given problem. This design, in turn, generates the new database definition for the DBMS. In essence, the tool helps with the physical database design.

A California-based firm introduced a CASE tool that analyzes the actual data and generates a third-normal-form database design. The database administrator can use this tool to capture functional dependencies in the data—a unique dimension in automating the database development process.

In the next decade, CASE tools are expected to increase system productivity by automating process-oriented design functionality and by providing more automated database expertise.

OBJECT-ORIENTED PROGRAMMING

A new way of thinking about database management programming applications is OBJECT-ORIENTED PROGRAMMING (OOP). In OOP, data abstractions, called OBJECTS, rather than data entities, are the basis of the program. Objects are defined based on how they will be used rather than by what they are. An object is a representation of a real-world entity. Examples of physical objects are customers, products, students, parts; examples of intangible objects are accounts, billing, and production.

The Minuteman Model

The basic concepts behind OOP date back to 1957 and the building of the Minuteman missile. The Minuteman project was divided into a set of discrete components such as nozzle, drag, structural, and trajectory designs. Each component was created by a specialist, because no single person could possibly design the whole system. For example, the drag designer considered aspects of missile flight at various altitudes. The nozzle designer determined the missile's thrust at various speeds and atmospheric conditions. The trajectory designer dealt with problems and procedures when the engines fired and when the fuel was consumed. The computer system passed information between these design components. For example, the program related to the nozzle might be queried by the trajectory component about what thrust levels should be used at a given speed and altitude.

Each program representing the component in question was virtually separate and used its own private data. By sending data and commands between components, the computer program was able to design and simulate the missile flight on the computer.

In today's use of the term, an "object" is like a piece of the design or a component of the missile design program. The object is made up of private data and methods (operations) that communicate with other objects via messages or some actions to be taken. A message is a specific action performed on an object. Object-oriented programming is like a group of experts meeting together to solve a common problem.[2]

Classes and Inheritance

In the 1960s, the concept of class was introduced to refer to the logical grouping of objects that share attributes and methods. A CLASS is a template that permits objects to be created. The concept of class hierarchy was also introduced to allow the inheritance of methods. INHERITANCE is an inference strategy used by object-oriented systems. For example, if you determine that an organization is a bank, then you automatically assume that the bank opens savings and checking accounts to customers. Inheritance, an important property of a hierarchy, allows resources to be shared. Classes can be arranged in a hierarchy from general to specific. Classes that are lower in a hierarchy inherit methods from classes above them.

In object-oriented programming, complex systems can be built as sets of related objects, each of which has ATTRIBUTES (properties of an object) and BEHAVIOR (functions performed by the object). Attributes of an object specify parameters, such as weight (an example of an attribute measured in pounds), and thrust. Messages and methods give the classes the ability to work together. Methods change the value of attributes. For example, the message "change missile course" could be from 30° latitude to 29.8° latitude. (See Figure 18-2.)

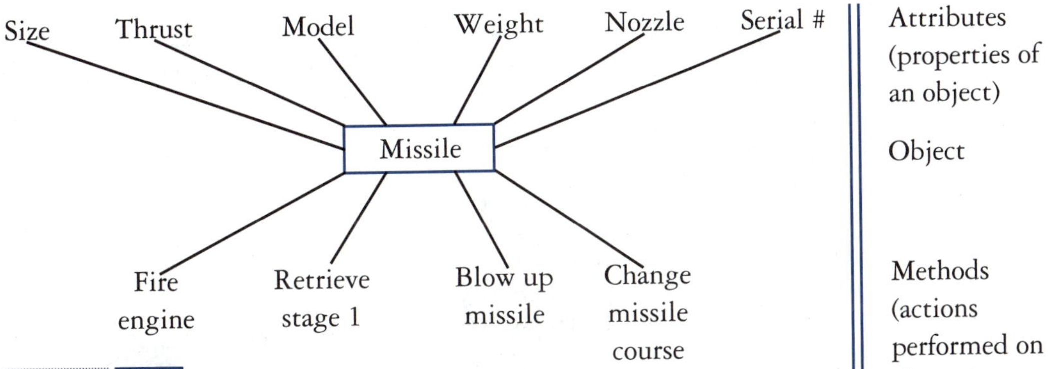

Figure 18-2 Characteristics of objects and their roles in the functioning of the missile

---

[2] Adapted from Ten Dyke, R.P. and Kunz, J.C. "Object-oriented programming." *IBM Journal*, vol. 28 no. 3, 1989, 465-68.

A number of OOP languages, such as Xerox Corporation's Smalltalk and C++, and the Objective C extension of the C programming language, were developed from these concepts. In Smalltalk, for example, integers are viewed as objects that have associated methods. Thus in Smalltalk, the operation "3 + 5" is explained in terms of the "+" message being sent with the argument "5" to the integer object "3". The "+" message is inherited by the integer 3 to do the addition and return the sum 8 to the client (user).

All object classes are arranged in a class hierarchy. A superclass, called "Class," is the root of the class hierarchy tree. In our integer example, the "Integer" class is a subclass of "Number." Subclass "Number" has its own subclass "Float" for floating point. (See Figure 18-3.)

Features of Object-Oriented Programming

As a discipline, OOP can be used in a variety of implementations in virtually any programming language. From the experience of present users, we can cite several unique features:

- The hierarchical structure of OOP makes it possible to create generic components that can be reused in various parts of the system.
- In some large databases, a variety of programs are based on the traditional view of data, while others are object-oriented. OOP can act as a bridge between the two, allowing the data to be temporarily converted to object form then reconverted into its original database form after processing.
- OOP allows for a finer level of object classification and the creation of self-contained, independent components. Each component can be used successfully with other components, based on the specificity of its interface.
- OOP allows efficient management of working storage because OOP languages, such as Smalltalk, reclaim working storage by releasing objects that are no longer referenced.

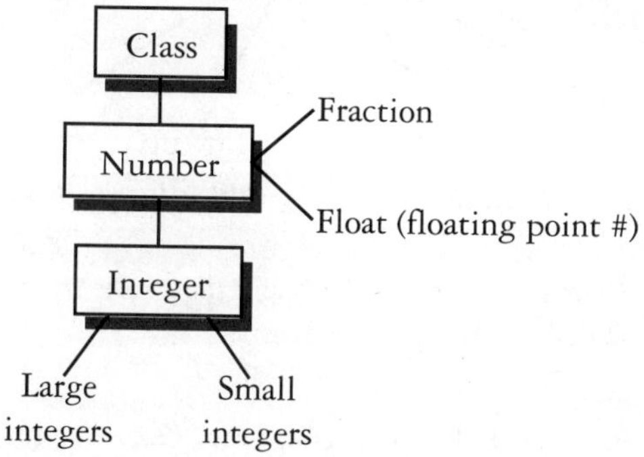

Figure 18-3 Class hierarchy

• OOP has the ability to allow multiple inheritance. Multiple inheritance, as opposed to the single inheritance of traditional hierarchies, means that certain objects can belong to more than one hierarchical structure. Schools, for example, can be classified as colleges or universities, and as private or public. This flexibility makes it possible to use objects and classes in a variety of ways suitable to each application. Object-oriented programming is an honest attempt to promote programming productivity and improved use of computer technology. It is used in a variety of projects, especially in expert systems and in building large, integrated information systems.

COOPERATIVE PROCESSING

One of the hot buzzwords in the DBMS world today is "cooperative processing." In COOPERATIVE PROCESSING, the user interface runs on the client system (PC) and the database operations run on the database server. The data stored on the server responds to SQL queries, performs the processing, and reports the results to the user. This cuts down the amount of network traffic significantly. Likewise, the client might send an SQL query to the mainframe and receive similar results, depending on where the data resides. (See Figure 18-4.)

As we mentioned in Chapter 11, a server is a powerful PC that stores all the data needed for operation. It acts as a bridge between the DBMS and the user, or client. A server is a true "go-fer" in that it handles

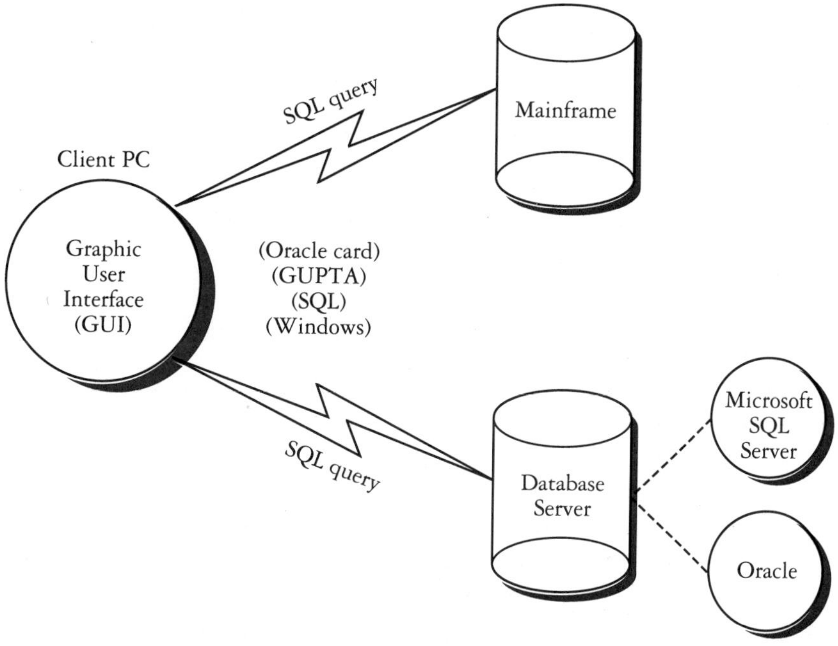

Figure 18-4 Role of server in cooperative processing

recovery procedures, logging, concurrency management activities, database definitions, and the like. It also contains data integrity rules, including referential integrity, to ensure "honest" DBMS management.

Cooperative processing offers several benefits:

- *More effective use of the existing network.* A single SQL command, for example, can request data from many tables, while an "intelligent" server transfers only selected information over the network. For example, if a user needs a list of the top ten salespersons ranked by volume of sales in dollars, the server can do a significant amount of the processing (which would normally occur at a host) so that only selected information—the list—would be transferred over the network.
- *More efficient use of resources.* Because the server, rather than the user, accesses the data, the user needs fewer resources. This means less computer time on the mainframe, fewer information systems staff on the host computer, and more reliance on the user's computers to do processing that once was dominated by the central mainframe.
- *More effective use of the graphic user interface.* The graphic user interface (GUI) is a money saver and an effective front end. GUI can ensure consistent user interface and improve the quality of finished documents by making it easy to make changes in fonts or images.

Related to the user interface challenge is the use of natural language interfaces in multiple languages. As satellites and other means of communications are more extensively used in networks, it is becoming necessary to make a single database under a single DBMS available to globally scattered affiliates in their respective languages. Such interfaces require multilingual support, a concept still being researched. One problem with multilingual support is how to display information in languages that have unique font and display patterns, such as Chinese, which is read top to bottom and uses ideographs instead of an alphabet, and Arabic, which reads from right to left.

LONG-TERM DATABASE DIRECTIONS

A key question for the 1990s is "what must be built into a database as a technology to handle the next generation of applications?" According to a 1990 study,[3] the next generation of database applications will be more complex, many of the basic DBMS algorithms will change, and "federated" DBMSs will come into widespread use. In a FEDERATED DBMS, a layer on top of a distributed database provides transparent access to various independent databases at multiple sites. To preserve local autonomy in a federated system, the local DBMS must operate

[3] Herbert A. Edelstein, "Database world targets next-generation problems." *Software Magazine*, May 1991, 79.

independently of the distributed DBMS. For example, the local DBMS determines when to use the distributed DBMS, when it wants to do backup, and so forth.

Federated database processing may become more popular than distributed processing, if it can provide the proper mix of a larger degree of local autonomy coupled with shared access.

PC-Based Database Management System Directions

More and more DBMS products created specifically for the PC are concentrating on the user interface. These are front-end products—products that specialize in the database only have their origins in the mainframe DBMS model and are essentially back-end products. Market leaders in PC-based DBMS are forging a reliable path with an SQL server for LAN. For example, Ashton-Tate's dBASE has an SQL server that stores data for front-end network applications running on workstations that need the data, rather like a secretary who hands out paychecks prepared by the payroll department.

A DBMS based on an arrangement such as an SQL server could open up IBM's DB2, Oracle, Informix, and other database servers to provide openness on the server side. This means that dBASE could run as a front-end tool and process data from virtually anywhere in the corporate environment.

Another example of progress in SQL server toolkits is Fact, a CASE tool that first asks the user for his or her level of expertise and the nature of the application to be designed. Fact can then bring up or match the right tool for the application. To do so, the product must be able to access all data and incorporate a GUI and an expert system containing program rules into the server.

Disaster Recovery

With today's increasing reliance on databases, backup and disaster recovery technologies have become very important. Many of today's vendors are working on technologies for transporting vital data to backup sites electronically rather than physically. Among the new technologies are electronic vaulting, remote journaling, and database shadowing.

ELECTRONIC VAULTING involves transmitting the contents of a database to a remote site in batches, via data networks. As Figure 18-5 shows, unlike the traditional approach of physically trucking data away, electronic vaulting involves electronically transporting a copy of the database to another computer site for ready use. REMOTE JOURNALING involves capturing data updates at a remote data center as they occur.

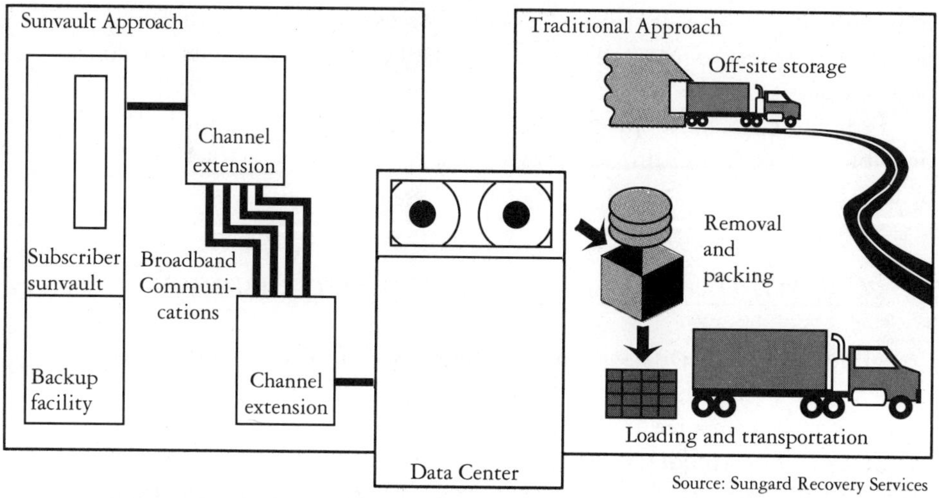

Source: Sungard Recovery Services

Figure 18-5 Traditional transportation and electronic vaulting

(See Figure 18-6.) This design reinforces the benefits of having multiple users share a common data resource and minimizes data redundancy. The main drawback to electronic vaulting and remote journaling is cost.

The most recent approach to DBMS disaster recovery is DATA SHADOWING. In this technology, the entire database is kept on-line at a remote data center. As shown in Figure 18-7, data shadowing recovers all data up to the moment of failure of the prime database and restores normal operation in a matter of minutes. Data shadowing is the most

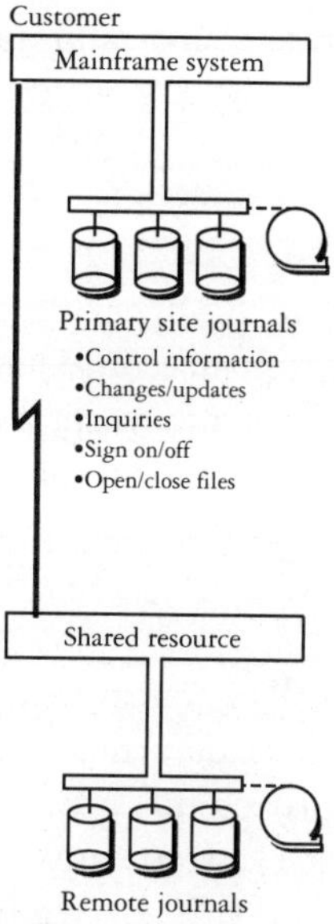

Figure 18-6 Remote journaling

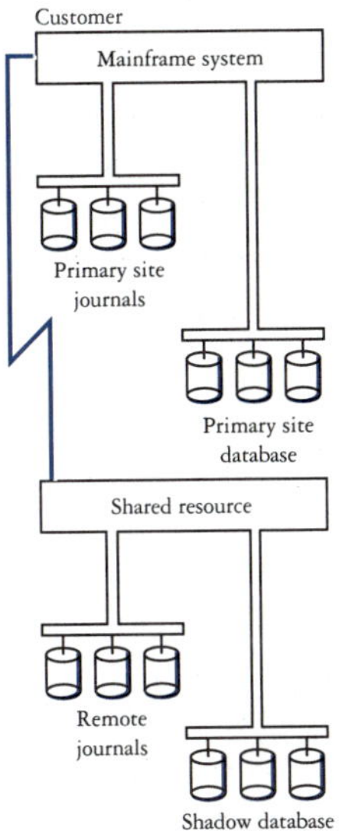

Figure 18-7 Data shadowing

comprehensive and expensive protection system designed to date—charges have been known to run up to $60,000 per month—and is beyond the means of most organizations.

LEGAL ISSUES

The proliferation of distributed databases and networks, as well as more vendor alliances and an upsurge in program code sharing, have created legal quandaries that have to be addressed.

Vendor Alliances

Many of today's vendors work together to provide software for complex database environments. For example, Santa Cruz Corporation's Open Desktop software for the Unix operating system includes programs from several vendors. The legal issue in cases like this is who owns the license and who is liable for performance. Contracts must clearly identify responsibilities (and liabilities) for changes.

Another area that is drawing attention is joint customer-vendor database packages. Who owns the copyright? What would happen if a customer modified customer-definable software developed by an outside vendor without that vendor's involvement? Who is liable for defects in the software? These issues are best handled through legislation, which is slowly beginning to explore methods of protecting the consumer from unfair vendor practices.

Intellectual Property

For over a decade, the computer industry has held that copyrights give software and database products legal protection. Unlike a PATENT, which is issued only for a new and useful machine or process invention, a COPYRIGHT protects "writing" and focuses on "expressions" which are descriptive of software. Yet, in recent years, a growing number of United States patents have been issued to protect program-related "inventions." But what appears original and "nonobvious" to one skilled person may seem derivative to another. If this trend continues, computer attorneys must look at the complex interaction between patent and copyright protection for software vendors.

Legal Status of Databases

Database technology is a $6 billion industry, yet the scope of legal protection offered to vendors and buyers is narrow. Recently, the United States Supreme Court ruled that the collection of data falls under copyright laws if the data shows at least a minimal level of organization and selection. Under this arrangement, for example, a telephone book would not be copyright protected, because it includes all individuals in a given town (no selection) arranged in alphabetic sequence (minimal organization). Enforcing application of these selection and organization criteria is difficult. Various DBMSs use different levels of organization, and the way data and records are organized in a given database frequently changes. In a recent case, the Supreme Court would not grant a database First Amendment protection as is given to traditional media such as newspapers.

Privacy Issues

As databases become larger and more accommodating, they also become subject to unauthorized tampering. The gathering and storage of data about individuals, especially on a large scale, as happens with credit rating systems, has raised privacy rights issues. For very little cost these days, almost anyone can learn almost anything about virtually any person. To illustrate, one superbureau gave a magazine editor open access to a large database in the belief that the editor was checking out a job applicant and needed his credit status. For a $500 initial fee, the editor had open access via his home computer to the database. He investigated the credit rating of his colleagues for $15 per report. Then he ran two prominent figures, one of whom was Vice President Quayle.[4]

With advanced, high-speed databases, it is possible to buy the names of virtually anyone—by location, income level, race, color, etc. It seems that our computers have outstripped the ability of our laws to

[4] Galen, Michele, "Is nothing private?" *Business Week*, September 4, 1989, 74.

Laws/Protection Offered	*Protection Failures*
Fair Credit Reporting Act (1970) Bars credit agencies from sharing credit information with anyone but authorized customers. Gives consumers the right to review their credit records and be notified of credit investigations for insurance and employment.	Lets credit agencies share information with anyone it reasonably believes has a "legitimate business need."
Privacy Act (1974) Bars federal agencies from letting information they collect for one purpose be used for a different purpose.	Exceptions let agencies share data too broadly.
Right to Financial Privacy Act (1978) Sets strict procedures when federal agencies want to access customer records in banks.	Doesn't cover state and local governments. And a growing list of exceptions let the FBI and federal attorneys grab files.
Video Privacy Protection Act (1988) Prevents retailers from disclosing video-rental records without the customers' consent or a court order. Also forbids sale of the records.	Medical and insurance files not covered.
Computer Matching and Privacy Protection Act (1988) Regulates computer matching of federal data for verifying eligibility for federal benefits programs or for recouping delinquent debts. Requires the government to give individuals a chance to respond before taking adverse action.	Limited in scope. Leaves many potential matches unaffected, including those done for law enforcement and tax purposes.

Table 18-2 Major laws governing privacy

Source: *Business Week*, September 4, 1989, 77.

safeguard privacy. Of all the federal laws designed to protect individual privacy, most are compromised by loopholes. Today, sadly, almost no information is private. Table 18-2 summarizes the major laws on privacy.

According to Radcliffe,[5] Lotus and Equifax, Inc. terminated their "Lotus Marketplace Database of Consumer Credit History" after 30,000 complaints. No real guidelines exist to determine the level of responsibility an information provider has in the information dissemination business, but this issue must be decided soon.

---

[5] Radcliffe, Mark, "Legal writes," *Computerworld*, June 17, 1991, 67.

CONCLUSIONS

Database technology began as a response to the problems of file processing. The first main database applications were in business data processing—inventory control, payroll, accounts receivable, and order processing, among others. During the late 1970s, the technology began to be used in other application areas, especially in producing summarized information for strategic planning and, in the 1980s, decision support information via ad hoc queries. From the late 1980s to the early 1990s, DBMSs have become a resource of centralized corporate information and can be distributed through various sites through data communications and local area networks.

There is no doubt that database applications are always faster than alternative data organization methods. One factor working against them, though, is the numerous extra layers of software that must be added to an already large operating system. Skilled implementation procedures can minimize this problem. The performance issue is only one factor in deciding on a DBMS installation, however. Other factors include data independence and immediate data access. Users simply cannot expect the DBMS to address all performance problems.

Most database systems are user friendly and are relatively easy to implement, especially for the PC and a first-time user. A well-designed database will also contain no redundancy and will have independent, comprehensive logical and physical designs. In the end, the people who know the data best are those who use it. To ensure database viability for the user, the database administrator must develop a common terminology so that end-users can tap the database without much background in the technology. When the end-user begins to feel that the database is an extension of his or her mind, the database becomes an indispensable tool for decision making and for successful management of the business. We are already experiencing this level of confidence in many applications and organizations.

Circulating among database designers today is the notion that the study of data is more important than the study of processes. Proponents of such data-driven designs look at data structures before they define the processes. In contrast, traditional database system development tries to determine what the system must do before defining the data. There is a reasonable rationale for either approach. For example, one could argue that unless we decide what we want to do, we cannot know what data we need. The data-driven approach assumes that the structure of data needed to run an organization changes very little, but processes change constantly, reflecting new products and technology. Data-driven design may be right in emphasizing data, but it cannot eliminate the need for structured and orderly analysis of processes.

Of the emerging database technologies summarized in this chapter, the area that poses the most challenge to new designers is knowledge processing, in which the role of the DBMS extends beyond that of information custodian or information provider to decision-maker and information producer. More friendly and understandable intelligent user interfaces should make information available to more users with less pain. Expert systems and intelligent front-end products are the trend and will be the direction databases take in industry.

SUMMARY

1 Database technology has a rich history of change and upgrade. The trend in hardware is away from the mainframe toward distributed networks that combine mainframes and PCs. The trend in processing is also toward a more distributed and cooperative environment. The user interface will continue to be highlighted by today's graphic user interface or GUI.

2 The intelligent database is already here. Knowledge-based systems are becoming integrated elements of complex applications, and successful knowledge-base/database combinations may be just around the corner.

3 CASE tools are beginning to be used to integrate database and process design. Many CASE tools have a repository about the database and the application under design. A relatively new tool in this area uses an expert system to look for inconsistencies in the data structure and to come up with alternative solutions.

4 Object-oriented programming (OOP) is a new programming methodology that defines data, called objects, by the way it will be used rather than by what it is. Objects are organized into classes, and classes into a hierarchy to allow methods or operations to be inherited from class to class or class to object.

5 Object-oriented programming allows complex systems to be built as sets of related objects with related attributes and behaviors. The hierarchical structure makes it possible to create generic components that can be reused in various parts of the system. Efficient management of working storage and the ability to allow multiple inheritance are additional features of OOP.

6 In cooperative processing, portions of an application run on different computers while data resides at one or multiple sites. The benefits of this approach include more effective use of the existing network and graphic user interface as a money saver and an effective front end.

7 The next generation of database applications is expected to be more complex with many of the basic DBMS algorithms changing and a trend toward "federated" DBMSs. This means providing transparent access to independent, multiple databases. Another trend is integrating large volumes of data in a distributed, heterogeneous environment where security, consistency, and integrity are not so easy to manage.

8 In the area of PC-based DBMSs, more and more DBMS products created specifically for the PC are concentrating on the user interface. Market leaders in PC-based DBMS are forging a reliable path with SQL servers for LANs.

9 Among the new backup and disaster recovery technologies are electronic vaulting, remote journaling, and database shadowing. Although each technology has much to offer the database environment, their cost is a major constraint.

10 The proliferation of databases with multiple users raises legal issues concerning vendor alliances, intellectual property, and privacy. The key questions have to do with who is liable, what is copyright-protected, and who should have authorized access to data.

11 Database applications are faster and more efficient than alternative data organization methods. A well-designed database will contain no redundancy, have independent, comprehensive logical and physical design, and reflect all the relationships among data. In the end, people who know data best are those who use it.

KEY WORDS

Artificial intelligence
Attributes
Behavior
Class
Cooperative processing
Copyright
Data shadowing
Electronic vaulting
Fair Credit Reporting Act
Federated database management systems
Inheritance
Objects
Object-oriented programming (OOP)
Patent
Remote journaling

REVIEW QUESTIONS

1 Review the past ten issues of *Computerworld, Datamation, DBMS*, or another computer journal in your library and write a report detailing the issues and developments in database processing.

2 In what ways are knowledge-based systems involved in database processing? Illustrate this relationship by describing a case in the technical literature.

3 Elaborate on the trends in database technology to date. Which change or trend do you consider the most important? Why?

4 Which of the emerging issues in Figure 18-1 do you consider the most promising? Discuss.

5 In what ways are CASE tools making a contribution to database application development?

6 Distinguish between the following pairs:
   a. cooperative processing and distributed processing
   b. copyright and patent
   c. electronic vaulting and data shadowing
   d. class and object

7 What is object-oriented programming? What are its main features?

8 What are some of the benefits of cooperative processing? How does cooperative processing make more effective use of existing networks? Explain.

9 In your opinion, how promising is the use of a natural language interface in multiple languages as a way to make a database available to multiple users?

10 What is unique about federated DBMSs, compared to a distributed, heterogeneous environment? Be specific.

11 How important do you think disaster recovery is? Under what circumstances would you not strongly recommend it? When does it become critical to adopt a disaster recovery program or technology?

12 In what way does data shadowing have an edge over other disaster recovery technologies?

13 Do you believe vendor alliances are ethical? Why? Discuss.

14 Should software and DBMS packages be copyright-protected or patented? Why?

15 "For very little cost, almost anyone can learn almost anything about virtually any person." Do you agree? If so, what do you think should be done to address the privacy issue? Be specific.

16 What conclusions can you draw regarding
   a. the database as a viable technology to operate a business.
   b. the kind of users who would benefit the most from a database environment.
   c. the role of networking in database design.

APPENDIX A

*USING EXCELERATOR/IS: A TUTORIAL**

PREFACE

Excelerator is a Computer-Aided Software Engineering (CASE) tool. Since their introduction to the market in the mid-1980s, CASE tools have been used by information systems personnel to automate tasks throughout the systems development life cycle. For example, Excelerator can be used to define, verify, and document a system prior to coding. It lets you create graphical models, describe their contents to a centralized data dictionary, and then analyze and document your system model.

This tutorial provides an introduction to the various features of Excelerator/IS. It is not meant to be inclusive, but rather representative of the capabilities. The "user interface" is consistent across all of Excelerator's features, which makes it feasible to use representative examples.

The tutorial consists of four parts which can be completed in approximately one to three hours each. After completing the tutorial, students are expected to use Excelerator on other projects in their courses.

As a user of Excelerator, you will be required to define your individual projects. Given that these instructions are contingent upon your specific computer environment, please disregard any environmentally specific instructions included within this tutorial.

CONTENTS

USING EXCELERATOR—PART I: MAKING DIAGRAMS

INTRODUCTION

This is Part I of a four-part tutorial. Your main goal is to learn the basics of Excelerator/IS, a CASE tool created by Index Technology Corporation in 1984 and updated in 1989. This software package provides all the capabilities necessary to design and document information systems. Readers should refer to the manuals accompanying the Excelerator/IS software, entitled *Excelerator Application Guide*, *Facilities and Functions Reference Guide*, and *Data and Reports Reference Guide*.

THE INFORMATION SYSTEM

For this assignment you will be using Excelerator to create and print flow diagrams for a simple information system. The drawing of each diagram is included within this tutorial. Your job is to reproduce them using Excelerator. Later you will use the dictionary facility to describe each element (e.g., processes, data stores, and data flows) in the diagrams.

Wahoos, Inc.

Wahoos, Inc. is a mail-order catalog business that sells souvenirs and other assorted items. The company receives orders from customers through the mail. Upon receiving the purchase order form and a check, a clerk at Wahoos, Inc. places the check in a check file which is later deposited at the bank. The purchase order form contains the item number, quantity ordered, amount enclosed, customer name, address, and phone number. When the check is received, the purchase order form is verified with the stock room inventory. If there are enough items to cover the order, a shipping order is sent to the warehouse where the merchandise is packaged and sent to the customer along with the invoice. For any items not in stock, a notification of backorder is sent to the customer.

Documenting the System

The mail-order system at Wahoos can be shown in three levels:

1 the context diagram which characterizes the system's interaction with its environment (see Figure A1-1).

2 diagram 0, which gives the general flow of information within the system (see Figure A1-2).

3 the lower-level diagrams which detail each process within Diagram 0 (in our case, only one process needs to be broken down further, see Figure A1-3).

Naming Conventions

In the interest of uniformity, please use the following naming conventions for your diagrams.

1 For the name of a data flow diagram, use either **context diagram** if it is a context diagram or the format **diagram #: name**, where the diagram number is the number of the diagram immediately above it in the hierarchy and the diagram name is the same name as the "bubble" from whence the diagram **explodes** (e.g., diagram 3.0: verify inventory).

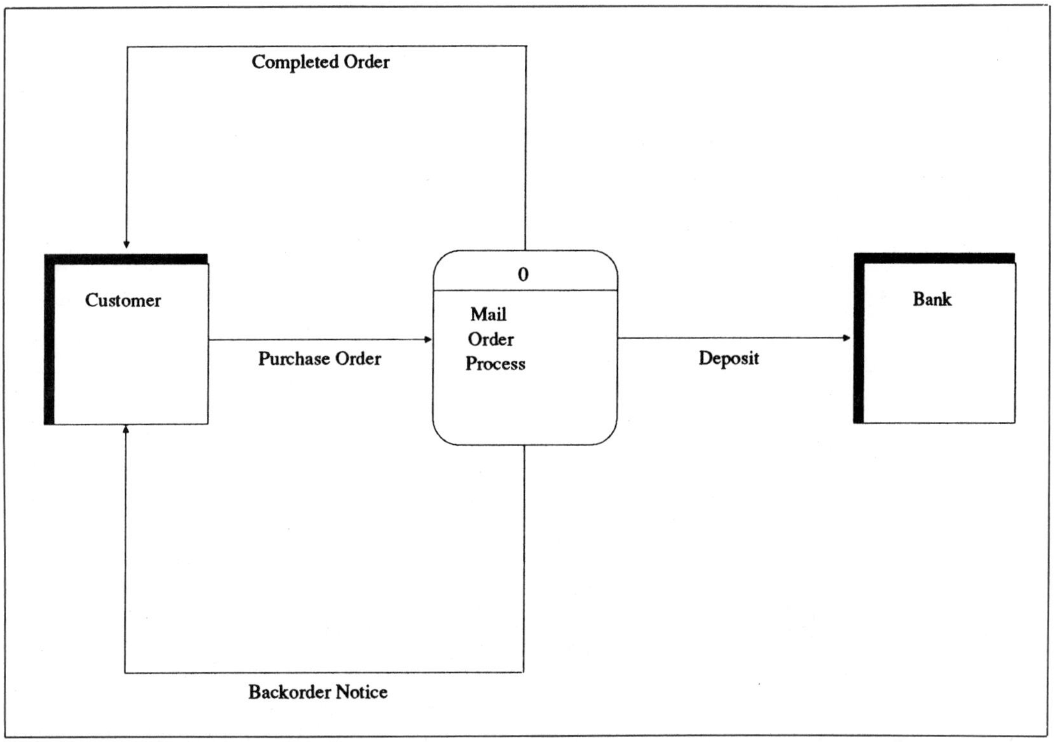

Figure A1-1 Context diagram Excelerator: Level 1

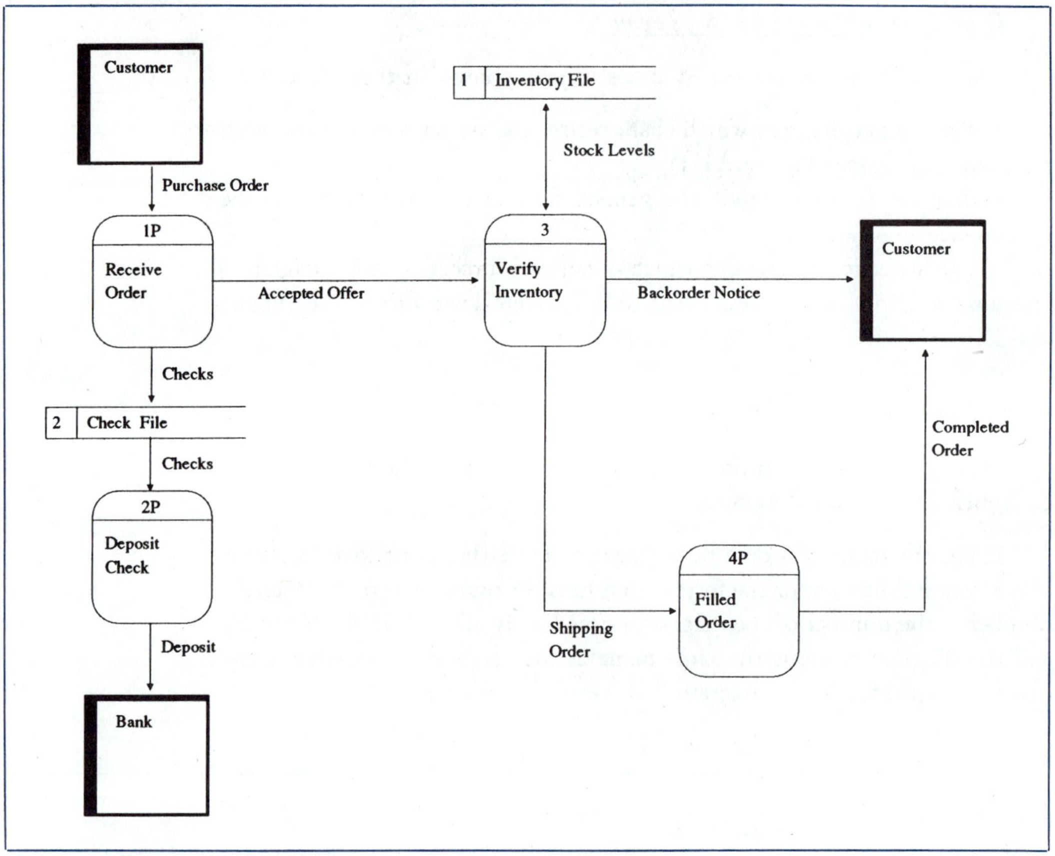

Figure A1-2 Diagram 0: mail-order process [Excelerator: Level 2]

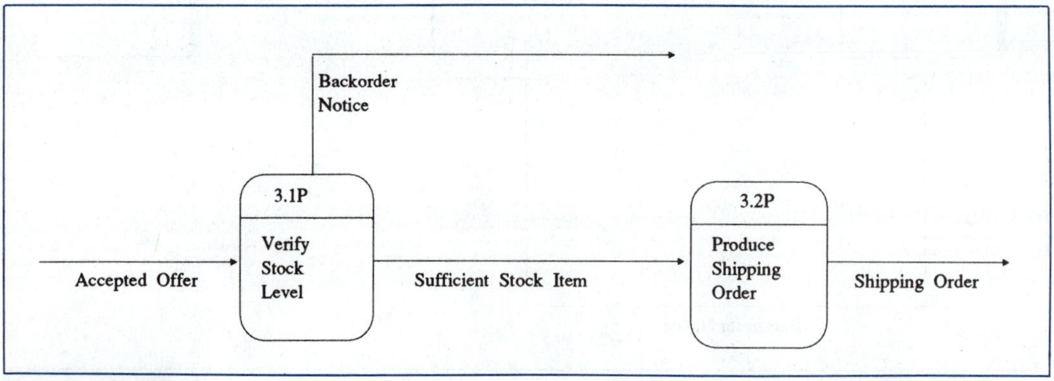

Figure A1-3 Diagram 3.0: Verify inventory [Excelerator: Level 3]

2 When you DESCRIBE (an Excelerator command) a process, you will be asked to give each process an ID. Use **0** for the context diagram; **1**, **2**, **3**, etc., for the level beneath the context diagram; and **1.1**, **1.2**, **2.1**, etc.,for the third level of diagrams and so on. If a process is **primitive**, that is, if it will not be broken down, add a **P** after the number (e.g., **1.1P**).

Note the use of the naming conventions in Figures A1-1 through A1-3. The need for a consistent vocabulary will become evident as you begin to work with Excelerator.

USING EXCELERATOR

As previously noted, Excelerator is a software package created specifically for systems analysis and design.[1] Excelerator's features and facilities are integrated to facilitate a complete and consistent analysis. An explanation of each Excelerator facility is given at the end of this tutorial.

Logging On to Your Project and Starting Excelerator

Although the directions for using Excelerator are system-specific, the following is a general guide for using Excelerator on the McIntire Computer Lab Novell Network:

1 Log on to the network.

2 Pick the Applications Development Tools Menu from the Main Menu, and then choose the Excelerator Menu. Pick Excelerator to begin your session. Excelerator will ask which disk drive your project is located on. After you type in the drive letter, the Excelerator logo will appear on the screen. Press **<Enter>**, and the Excelerator log-on screen appears.

3 Enter your Excelerator user name **<Enter>**, and your Excelerator password **<Enter>**. The default for the McIntire Lab is user **student** and no password. Use lowercase letters as Excelerator is case sensitive, which means you cannot use capital and lowercase letters interchangeably. A list of possible projects will appear. (See Part E of **Creating and Fixing Excelerator Projects.)**

Note: Excelerator is a "mouse-oriented" software package. Get accustomed to using the mouse since you will use it extensively to create charts and diagrams and to select and execute commands. Most mice have two buttons on them, a left and a right (see Figure A1-4). Some mice have three buttons

---

[1] Please refer to earlier chapters for a more detailed description of the concepts associated with systems analysis and design (e.g., data flow diagrams, data dictionaries, etc.).

(only use the left and right buttons in this case). To select a command, hold the mouse as shown in the figure and move it across the surface of the table until the cursor or arrow rests on the desired block. Press or "click" the left button to select it. The right button cancels noncompleted actions. When you are prompted for a name (e.g., data flow diagram name), clicking both buttons at the same time at a **Name** prompt will bring up a list of viable names.

4 Select the desired project using the mouse. If you are just beginning to work with Excelerator, you will probably only have one project named **project.** After selecting the project, the new menu display shows eight possible options. Select **GRAPHICS**. Another list will appear.

5 Select **DATA FLOW DIAGRAM**. Now select **ADD**.

6 Give your first graph the name **context diagram** and press **<Enter>**.

Using Excelerator to Create Diagrams

A screen will appear as shown in Figure A1-5. Note the different parts of the screen and their functions.

The first graph you will draw is the **context diagram**, or **level 1** in Excelerator (see Figure A1-1). Begin by selecting **OBJECT** from the command list. Now select **PROCESS** from the list of possible objects that appears below the regular commands. Note that the status line indicates to **TOUCH LOCATION**. This means to place your pointer on the part of the drawing screen where you want the **PROCESS** symbol to go and to click the left mouse button.

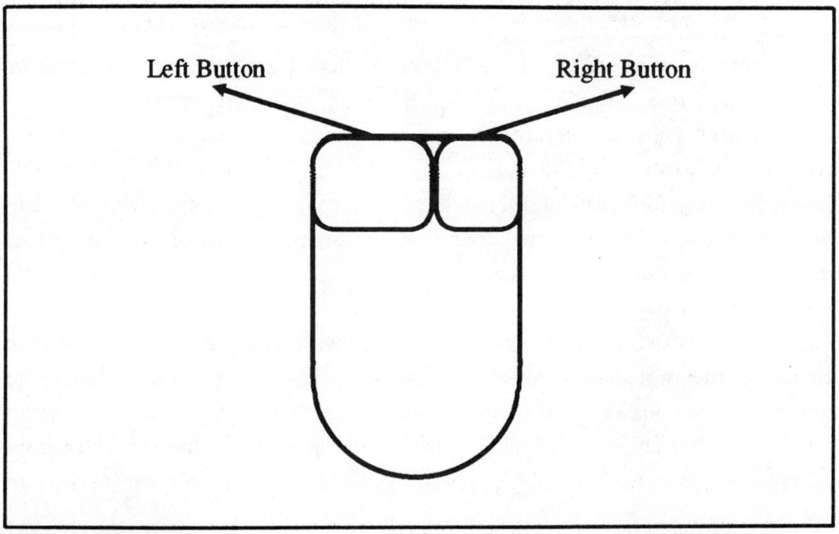

Figure A1-4 The mouse

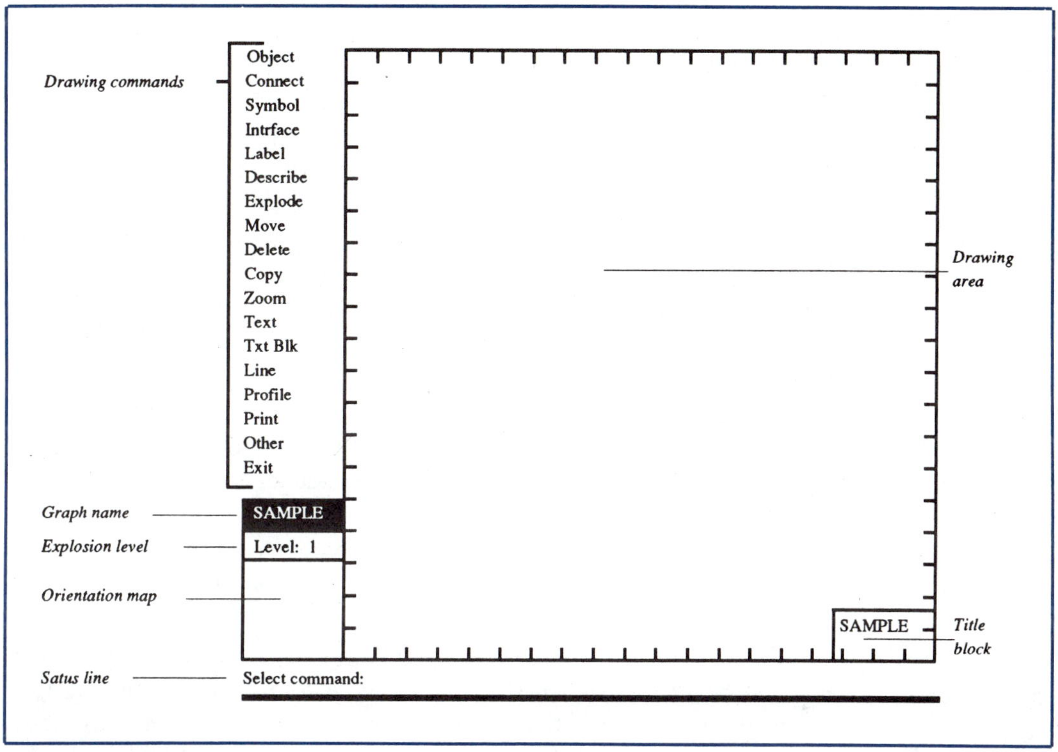

Figure A1-5 The drawing area

After you have done this, select **X-ENTITY** (external entity) from the list, and put one on both sides of the process as shown in Figure A1-1. Do this by pointing once to the left of the process symbol, clicking the left mouse button, and once to the right of the process symbol, clicking again. You need not select **X-ENTITY** twice—Excelerator keeps the previous command active until you select a new one.

Label each object by selecting **LABEL**, selecting the object to label, and then typing in the text for the label (e.g., for the process symbol, the label is **mail order process**).

Note: Use the **<Tab>** key to move down to the next line. DO NOT press **<Enter>** until you are finished typing in the label. To erase characters, use the **<Backspace>** or **<Delete>** keys. If you need to move to the line above, use **<Shift>** and **<Tab>** simultaneously. Finally, if you want to insert or move characters, press the **<Insert>** key and the cursor will move one space to the right each time.

Notice that the label has been abbreviated to fit in the object you are labeling. To show the whole label, select the following commands in order:

```
PROFILE
LABEL MD
COMPLETE
```

The complete label should now appear. Click your right mouse button twice to return to the main diagram menu.

Next, draw the data flows (arrows) between the objects by selecting **CONNECT**, followed by **DAT FLOW**. Note that the status line message is **TOUCH FIRST OBJECT**. First, point to the customer entity, click, and then point to the mail order process symbol and click. The little box in the center of the data flow is referred to as a **handle.** It allows you to easily select the data flow at a later time. Now, connect the **mail order process** to the **bank entity**.

Temporarily place another process (select **OBJECT**, **PROCESS**) on your screen in the lower righthand corner. Connect the two processes together. Notice how the system chooses a connection path. You can have some control over this path by using the following trick. First, **DELETE** the process and connection you just added. Select **DELETE**, then click on the connection and the process.

To draw the connections *from* the mail-order process to the customer entity, select **CONNECT**, followed by **DAT FLOW**. Then point to the mail-order process symbol and click. Now, point and click the mouse about an inch above the mail-order process, click again an inch above the customer entity, and click finally on the customer entity. Notice how you have determined the path of the connection. Draw the last connection and LABEL all of them. To label a data flow, point to the *handle* of a data flow. These handles are used to select the entity and are not part of your final graph.

Exploding Objects: Adding in the Details

Excelerator allows you to **explode** any part of a graph to the next level of detail. It keeps track of the relationships between graphs as well as the entities on those graphs.

Select **DESCRIBE** and then select the mail-order process. The status line requests an ID. Since this is the context diagram, the ID is 0 and you must erase the default ID. Enter **0 <Enter>**. A new screen appears similar to Figure A1-6.

The label **mail order process** is already in the label box. Put the cursor in the box labeled **Type** underneath **EXPLODES TO**. You can do this in one of two ways: by using the **<Tab>** key to move the cursor to the next box or by pointing and selecting with the mouse. Type in **DFD** for Data Flow Diagram, and type in the name **diagram 0: mail order process.** This will be the name of the data flow diagram to which the context diagram explodes. Review the naming conventions mentioned earlier. By naming this now, you will be able to access it later using the EXPLODE command. Once again, this will become clearer to you as you become more experienced with Excelerator.

After naming the data flow diagram, press the **<PgDn>** key (for the time being, we will skip the other items on this screen). You will again see a screen asking for **Satisfies Requirements** and **Associated**

Process

Label

EXPLODES TO: {DFD-STC-STD-PPS-PRG}

Type ______ Name ____________________

Location

Process Category

Duration Value
Duration Type

Manual or Computer

Figure A1-6 DESCRIBE screen

Entities. Press **<PgDn>** again until you see the description screen. Enter a brief description of your own for the mail-order process as it relates to the external entities shown on the diagram. When you are finished, press **<F3>**.

Before you go any further, **SAVE** your current graph. If **SAVE** is not one of your current choices, select **OTHER**, then **SAVE**.

If you would like to change the layout, you can **DELETE** or **MOVE** any part of your graph. Try moving one of the external entities and see what happens. For a fresh picture, select **OTHER**, then **REFRESH**.

Creating the Next Level Diagrams

Now create the next level DFD. Select **EXPLODE**, then select the **mail order process**. You will see four processes, one with an input interface, and three with output interfaces. Excelerator has transferred these from your top level diagram. Look closely at the four processes in Figure A1-2. Try to use what Excelerator has created for you on the exploded diagram to save time. You will need to delete the interfaces from the default processes to make the diagram connections appear correctly. Using Figure A1-2 as a model, put in the different entities the same as you did with the context diagram. The **check file** and **inventory file** are data stores. Notice the two-way arrow between the **verify inventory** process and the **inventory file**. Currently, all connections are set for one-way arrows. To change this setting, select **PROFILE, TWO-WAY**, and then click the right mouse button. Once you have connected the two entities, change the setting back to **ONE-WAY**. Label everything as shown. The numbers on the processes will be done next.

Excelerator keeps track of all the relationships between entities and diagrams. It is important to use the same names for data flows and other entities that are on different levels so that you do not define an entity twice with two different names. Observe closely the entity names in Figures A1-1 through A1-3.

To add the numbers to the processes, select **DESCRIBE** and enter the number as the ID: all of the processes except for verify inventory are **primitives**. As mentioned in the naming conventions, this means they are not detailed further. In Figure A1-2, only one process will explode into further detail—i.e., is not primitive. Therefore, when describing the primitive processes, you will not indicate anything in the **EXPLODES TO** section. Simply **<PgDn>** to enter a description. When you **DESCRIBE** the "verify inventory" process, be sure to give the diagram a name using the appropriate naming conventions. **SAVE** your diagram and use the **EXPLODE** command to create the next level diagram.

The third, and last, diagram is quite simple (see Figure A1-3). The arrows that appear to lead out of or into the picture are called **interfaces**. That is, instead of connecting to two objects, an interface points to or from an unseen destination from a higher level diagram.

To make the leftmost interface, select **INTERFACE, DAT FLOW**, and then **INPUT**. Point to a spot about two inches to the left of the **verify stock level** process and click. Finish the interface by selecting **verify stock level**.

For the shipping order arrow, select **INTERFACE, DAT FLOW**, and then **OUTPUT**. Then click a spot two inches to the right of **produce shipping order** and again on the process symbol.

Now create the backorder notice interface yourself. After you finish this final diagram, make sure you **SAVE** it.

Printing

There are three different ways to print a diagram. The three options are

1 **FULL GRAPH**—prints the full-size, final version of an entire graph using several pages of paper

2 **WINDOW**—prints full-size, but selected, portions of a graph. This printout may use one or several pages, depending on the window chosen

3 **DRAFT**—prints a reduced-size, one-page draft of a graph

Using DRAFT

At this point, your screen should still show the Diagram 3.0. Select **OTHER** and **RETRNTOP** to return to the highest level diagram. **Context diagram** should appear. Now select

```
PRINT
DRAFT
YES
PRINTER
```

Using FULL GRAPH

Although not used in this exercise, the commands for using FULL GRAPH are

```
PRINT, FULL GPH, YES, PRINTER
```

These commands will produce several pages of printout and should be used only if absolutely necessary.

Using WINDOW

Printing a window is a little more difficult. **EXPLODE** the **mail order process**, then the **verify inventory** process and select

```
PRINT, FULL GPH
```

A grid will appear on the screen which shows how the full graph would be printed on different pages of paper. Select **NO** to cancel the print request.

Notice that the grids remain. For our purposes, you only want to print a window, or a portion of the screen. At this point, your graph is probably divided among four pages. To get the diagram printed on only one page, you must move the objects close enough to each other so that they will all fit within a single grid section.

Use the **MOVE** command to move the objects so that they fit into one of the boxes. Do this by selecting **MOVE** and pointing to a process and then pointing again to where you want to move the process. Notice how the connect arrows move automatically. You will, however, have to **MOVE** each interface individually by touching the end handle and pointing to the new location. When you have moved the whole diagram into the box, select **PRINT** again, then **WINDOW**.

The status line says **Touch upper left corner**. Point and click the upper left corner of the box. Now the status line says **Touch lower right corner**. Touch the lower right corner of the box. The grids disappear and leave only the window outlined. The status line says **Print this window?** Select **YES** and **PRINTER**.

Finishing Up

To leave Excelerator, select **EXIT** on each level, and **RETURN TO DOS** at the main Excelerator Menu. At the drawing area level, you may be asked to **SAVE** before you can **EXIT**. You have completed Part I. Turn in the printouts of all three data flow diagrams.

USING EXCELERATOR—PART II: BUILDING THE DATA DICTIONARY

INTRODUCTION

In Part II you will work with a different facility within Excelerator called the XLDictionary (XLD). The XLD serves as a repository for all definitions created while using any Excelerator facility.

The XLD keeps track of every entity in the data flow diagrams you create and how each entity and each graph relates to the others in the project. Figure A2-1 shows the relationship among the components of a data flow diagram. Definitions of processes, data stores, data flows, and external entities link to the XLD through GRAPHICS. Data stores and data flows break down into records and/or elements within the XLD.

Linking the XLD with the Graphics Facility

As you will see, definitions can be entered into the dictionary through either the XLDictionary or other facilities. For example, in Part I of the tutorial you defined several processes from the GRAPHICS facility. These definitions are stored in the dictionary and are associated with a specific process bubble in your graphs. You can also enter definitions directly from the XLD facility. The difference is that the definition is not associated with a specific bubble (or other entity). The only way to link (create the association) between a specific object and its definition is from the other facilities (e.g., from GRAPHICS using the DESCRIBE command). However, when linking definitions with objects, you do not need to reenter the definition since it is already stored. The following paragraphs will lead you through both alternatives of defining and linking objects.

XLDICTIONARY LINK

To begin, log on to Excelerator and select **XLDICTIONARY**, **PROCESS**, **PROCESS**, and **MODIFY**. Click both of the mouse buttons when the **Name** prompt appears (double-clicking the mouse allows you

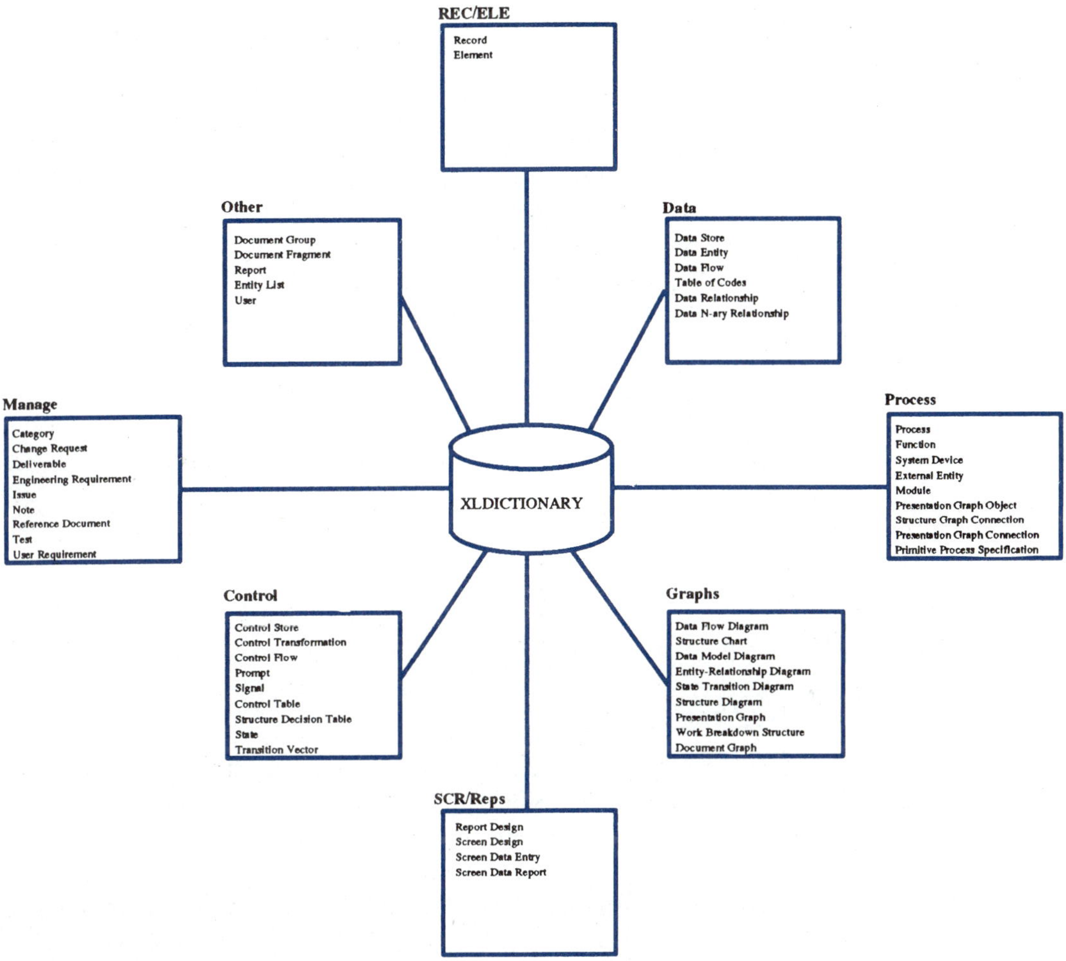

Figure A2-1 Dictionary relationships

to get a list of the processes that are currently stored). Select Entity **0** for **mail order process**.

The screen now shows the same layout used in the GRAPHICS facility when you DESCRIBEd the process. Press **<PgDn> twice** and notice the description you previously entered from the GRAPHICS facility. Press **<F3>** to return to the menu.

Select **DATA**, **DATA STORE**, **MODIFY**, and double-click. A message at the bottom of the screen should say **Could not find any items with that name.** You have just requested a listing of the defined data stores that you created in your diagrams in **Part I** (just like the listing of processes). The reason that none exist is that although you put them on your diagrams, you never DESCRIBEd them, whereas you did DESCRIBE your processes.

DESCRIBing an entity links it to the XLD. Press the right mouse button to Cancel before you proceed.

Defining a Data Store

To illustrate this notion of linking the XLD and GRAPHICS through the use of the DESCRIBE command, return to GRAPHICS by selecting **EXIT**, **GRAPHICS**, **DATA FLOW DIAGRAM**, **MODIFY**, and double-click. Select **Diagram 0: mail order process**. DESCRIBE the **inventory file**. For an ID, use 1 **<Enter>**. **<Tab>** (or **<Enter>**) to the **Explodes to . . .** and enter **inventory record**. Then, in the **Index Elements** field, enter the following two elements within the inventory record:

```
item name
item number
```

Now press **<PgDn> twice** and enter the following description:

```
The inventory file contains a complete list of
every item in stock. Each record includes, among
other data, both the item name and item number.
<Enter>
```

Press **F3** when you are finished with the description.

Defining a Data Flow

Similarly, DESCRIBE the **purchase order** data flow. Use 1 for the ID. Since the **inventory file** data store and the **purchase order** data flow are different types of entities, using the same ID will not cause a conflict within the XLD. Enter **REC** below **Explodes to...** and the name **purchase order record**. Press **<PgDn>** and enter the following description:

```
The purchase order is sent to Wahoos, Inc. from
the customer. The information includes customer
information, items ordered, and amount paid.
<Enter>
```

Press **F3** when you are finished with the description.

Select **EXIT**, **SAVE**, and **EXIT** (to leave GRAPHICS) and enter the XLDictionary. To verify that the definitions you just entered are in the data dictionary, select **DATA**, **DATA STORE**, **MODIFY**, double-click, **1...inventory file**. The description is the same one you entered through GRAPHICS. Do the same for the **purchase order** data flow: select **DATA FLOW**, **MODIFY**, double-click, **1...purchase order**. As you can see, when you DESCRIBE an entity in GRAPHICS, it automatically becomes part of the project dictionary.

DEFINING FROM WITHIN THE XLDICTIONARY

Another way of entering a definition of an entity into the dictionary is to ADD it while you are in the XLD facility. To illustrate, you will

ADD another data store, the **check file**. Start by selecting **DATA STORE**, **ADD**, and enter **2** for the Name (the Name in XLD is the same as the ID of DESCRIBE in GRAPHICS). Enter the following information and **<Tab>** over any of the fields not specified (use lowercase letters):

```
LABEL:                    check file
EXPLODES TO ONE OF:       check record
MANUAL OR COMPUTER:       m
```

Press **<PgDn> twice** and type the following:

```
The check file contains all the checks that
customers send with their purchase order forms.
This file is kept manually in an envelope and
taken to the bank for deposit daily. <Enter>
```

Press **F3** when you are finished entering the description.

Linking XLD Definitions with Specific Objects

Exit from the XLD and enter GRAPHICS. Select **DATA FLOW DIAGRAM**, and **MODIFY**. Next select the **mail order process** and DESCRIBE the check file. Notice how the ID prompt pops up at the bottom of the screen. Enter 2 **<Enter>** (the same ID or name you gave this data store in XLD). The **check file** (from GRAPHICS) is now linked with the definition entered from the XLD. This link is created by using the same Name and ID. Note that the definition is the same as entered from the XLD. Press **<F3>** to exit.

As a review, there are two ways to link entities between the GRAPHICS and the XLD facility. The first, and most efficient way, is to use the DESCRIBE command in GRAPHICS to directly link each entity in the diagram to the XLD. The second way to link entities is to ADD the definition of a process, data store, or data flow to the XLD, and then, using the DESCRIBE command through GRAPHICS, link the definition of a specific object.

Defining Data

You have seen how the XLD keeps track of entities in the diagrams. Some of these entities break down into smaller parts. For example, a data store generally consists of records. In turn, these records may either break down into more detailed records or into single elements.

Technically, this is not a correct definition of record-element relationships. However, to simplify the discussion and until you have discussed data models in a database course, we will use these relationships.

In this exercise, you will break the **purchase order record** into its basic elements. A visual breakdown of this record is given in Figure A2-2.

You will begin by defining the field composition of the **purchase**

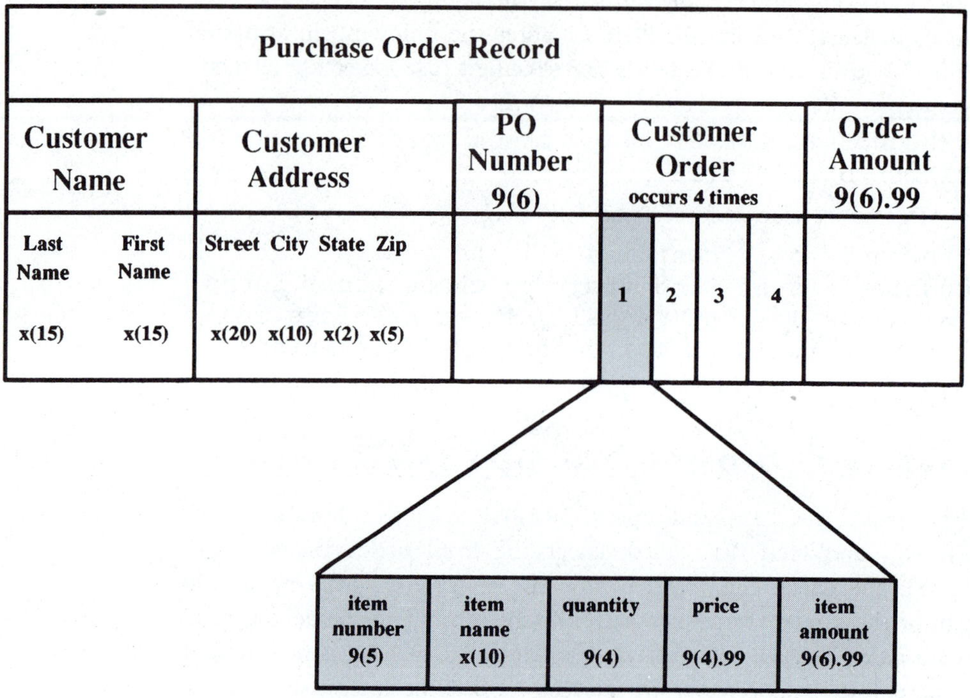

Figure A2-2 Purchase order record

order record. This record consists of three levels of subrecords and elements. Each part must be defined. To begin, you will have to **EXIT** from GRAPHICS and enter the XLD. Select **DATA**, **DATA FLOW**, **MODIFY**, double-click, **1...purchase order**. Notice that the **purchase order** data flow explodes to the **purchase order record**. Return to the menu and select **REC/ELE**, **RECORD**, **ADD**, and enter: **purchase order record <Enter>**.

For an Alternate Name, enter **PO**. <Tab> to Definition and enter **customer order information**. <Tab> to Normalized, and enter **Y**. <Tab> to the next field. This is where you detail each element or subrecord of the purchase order record (records can consist of other records as well as elements). Definitions for the headings on this part of the screen are as follows:

- The **Name** of element or record is the name of the item that you are defining.
- **Occ** stands for the number of times this item occurs within the record.
- **Seq** is the sequential order of the element or the record in its "parent record."

- **Type** means whether the item is an element (**e**) or another record (**r**).
- **Sec-Keys** will not be used for this exercise.

From Figure A2-2, we see that the first item within the purchase order record is the **customer name**, which we will treat as a record. To begin, enter **customer name**, **<Tab>**, **<Tab>**(skip **Occ** since it is already 1), 1 for the sequence, **<Tab>**, **r** for record **<Tab>**, and **<Tab>** twice for **Sec-Keys**.

- The second item is the **customer address**, it occurs once, is second in sequence, and is a record. Enter this information.
- The third item is the **po number**, it occurs once, is third in sequence, and is the Key element for this record. Enter this item.
- The fourth item is the **customer order**. It occurs four times (since the customer may order more than one product), is fourth in sequence, and is a record.
- The fifth and final item is the **order amount** which is a single element and occurs only once.

After you define the purchase order record, you must *define each record within that record and then each single element*. Press **<F3>** to accept the definition of the purchase order.

Return to the XLD main menu and select **RECORD**, **ADD**, and enter **customer name**. Remember, this record is the first item in the **purchase order record** you just defined. To define the **customer name record**, enter only the following information:

Name of element or record	Occ	Seq	Type
last name	1	1	e
first name	1	2	e

Press **<F3>** to accept your completed definition.

Defining Elements

Return to the menu and select **ELEMENT**, **ADD**, and enter **last name**. **<Tab>** to definition and enter **customer's last name.** **<Tab>** again to **Input Format**. Using COBOL syntax, define the **picture**. For the **last name**, the picture is **X(15)**. The **Output Format** is the same.

In the **Storage type** field, press the **F2** (Help) key, which gives a key for which letter to enter. Since the characters in the name are all alphanumeric, leave **C** in this field. Finally, **<Tab>** to the field labeled **Characters left of decimal** and enter 15. Make sure that the field **Characters right of decimal** contains a 0. Notice the field labeled **Base or Derived**. This field represents whether the element is actually entered by the user (B) or it is calculated from other data (D). Again, press **<F3>** to accept your completed definition.

Now that you have defined one element and one record, it should be fairly easy to define the rest of the records and elements. The remaining records in the **purchase order record** are given with the necessary information in Figure A2-2. Be sure to use the names exactly as shown.

You only need to be concerned with the following fields in the element description screen:

1 definition
2 input picture
3 output picture
4 storage type—use "C" for words and "P" for numbers
5 characters left of decimal—use for words and numbers
6 characters right of decimal—only necessary for numbers
7 base or derived

Code Generation

Excelerator has the capability to generate data description code in several different computer languages. Excelerator generates the detailed, time-consuming record layouts, provided your records and elements are all defined.

Generate code by selecting **RECORD**, **GENERATE**, double-click, **PURCHASE ORDER RECORD**. **<Tab>** to the Prefix field and enter **PO-**. **<Tab>** to the **Language Generated** field. Press **<F2>** to see a list of available languages. Enter **COBOL** and press **<F3>**. Select **PRINTER** from the bottom righthand corner of the screen and the code will appear. Figure A2-3 shows the COBOL code generated for the purchase order record.

```
*Record purchase-order-r   Compiled:   20-AU-1991 15:44
01         purchase-order-r.
     05    po-customer-name.
           10  po-last-name          PIC X(15).
           10  po-first-name         PIC X(15).
     05    po-customer-address.
           10  po-street             PIC X(20).
           10  po-city               PIC X(10).
           10  po-state              PIC X(2).
           10  po-zip                PIC X(5).
     05    po-po-number              PIC S9(6)          COMP-3.
     05    po-customer-order      OCCURS 4 TIMES.
           10  po-item-number        PIC S9(5)          COMP-3
           10  po-item-name          PIC X(10).
           10  po-quantity           PIC S9999          COMP-3.
           10  po-price              PIC S9999V99       COMP-3.
           10  po-item-amount        PIC S9(6)V99       COMP-3.
     05    po-order-amount           PIC S9(6)V99       COMP-3.
```

Figure A2-3 COBOL-generated code

Finishing Up

This is the end of Part II. Be sure to exit properly out of the XLD. Select **EXIT**, **EXIT**, **Return to DOS**. Turn in the output from the COBOL code generation.

USING EXCELERATOR—PART III: SCREEN AND REPORT DESIGN

INTRODUCTION

In Part III of the Excelerator assignment, you will create mockup screen and report designs. These designs are used for testing the design, not for actual input/output; i.e., you will still have to write code that generates the screen or report. It is suggested that you see the tutorials from Parts I and II as reference.

The difference between report design and screen design is that a report is an output document in hard copy form, while a screen is used to enter data at a terminal or provide a soft copy of information.

For this assignment you will create a report that serves as the invoice that Wahoos, Inc. sends to each customer along with the actual merchandise. Look at Diagram 0 from Part I. The data flow labeled **shipping order** represents the report you will create.

You will also create an input screen design for the **accepted order** information. At Wahoos, Inc., this screen would be used by a data entry clerk to enter information from the purchase order sent by the customer. In this case, the screen and the report designs contain basically the same information. However, this may not always be the case.

Before starting, get a list of the variable names that you have already defined in Excelerator. To do this, access Excelerator and select **XLDICTIONARY**, **REC/ ELE**, **ELEMENT**, **SUMMARY OUTPUT**, double-click, and **PRINTER**. **EXIT** from the XLDictionary facility.

CREATING REPORTS

Select **SCREENS AND REPORTS**, **REPORT DESIGN**, **ADD**. Enter **shipping order** for the name. When the report design screen appears, enter **Invoice sent to the customer** **<Enter>** as the description, and press **<F3>** to continue.

Using Figure A3-1 as a guide for the report design, point to row 2, col 30, and click the mouse. Enter the three lines of the report heading.

Move down the screen to row 6, col 5, and enter **Purchase Order Number**. Move the cursor over two columns where the 9s appear. These

Wahoos, Inc.

Kawabonga St.

Flemington, NJ 12345

Purchase Order Number: 99999

First name: XXXXXXXXXXXX Last name: XXXXXXXXXXXXXXXX

Street: XXXXXXXXXXXXXXXXXXXX

City: XXXXXXXXXX State: XX Zip: XXXXX

ITEM NUMBER	ITEM DESCRIPTION	QUANTITY	PRICE	NET PRICE
99999	XXXXXXXXXXX	9999	9999.99	999999.99
99999	XXXXXXXXXXX	9999	9999.99	999999.99
99999	XXXXXXXXXXX	9999	9999.99	999999.99
99999	XXXXXXXXXXX	9999	9999.99	999999.99
99999	XXXXXXXXXXX	9999	9999.99	999999.99

TOTAL : 999999.99

AMOUNT PAID : 999999.99

NET DUE : 999999.99

Figure A3-1 Invoice layout

are entered as a field. To do this, select the block in the lower righthand corner labeled **field** (or simply use the **<F10>** key). Excelerator asks for the name of the **Purchase Order Record** layout from Part II. This particular element was called **po number**. Enter **po number** and press **<F3>** (use lowercase letters—just as the element was defined within the XLD). Five 9s should appear on your screen. This is the **output picture** you specified in the XLD for this particular element.

As you can see, you are using previously defined definitions to build report layouts by simply using the defined name. Repeat the above steps for

1 first name
2 last name
3 street
4 city
5 state
6 zip

Then enter the column headings shown below and in Figure A3-1.

```
ITEM     ITEM                                NET
NUMBER   DESCRIPTION   QUANTITY   PRICE     PRICE
```

Repeating Fields

Place the cursor in a space below **item number** and select the **<FIELD>** block (alternatively, the **F10** key). Enter **item number** and press **<F3>**. Now, without moving the cursor from the field you just entered, select the block labeled **REPEAT**. The message **Repeat key now refers to current field** should appear.

Press **<Enter>** and move the cursor two rows below its current portion (for double spacing) and select **REPEAT** again. The repeat function duplicates the same field definition to other parts of the report design. Move down two more rows and select **REPEAT** again. Notice the most previous **current field** definition is used again. Repeat for the fourth item number field.

Complete the rest of the chart in a similar manner. You can add the = = = = as dividers or separators on the report design.

Finally, at the bottom of the report design, enter the payment labels **TOTAL, AMOUNT PAID,** and **NET DUE.**

Since we have not defined the elements **amount paid** and **net due** you can use the **total payment** element as the element name for all three or you can type in the 9s as shown.

When you are finished, select the **EXIT** block or the **<F3>** key. This command saves the report design (QUIT would exit without saving the changes).

Getting a Hard Copy of the Report Design

From the Report Design Menu, select **OUTPUT**, double-click at **Name or Name Range**, select **shipping order** and select **PRINTER**. Finally, **EXIT** from Report Design.

CREATING SCREENS

The creation of screen designs is similar to report designs. However, because screens can be used for both input and output, additional options are available to you as a designer. We will be designing the **accepted order** data entry screen from Diagram 0 in Part I.

Select **SCREEN DESIGN**, **ADD**, and enter **accepted order <Enter>**. **<Tab>** to the Description field and enter **Purchase order information data is keyed in by clerk**. Press **<F3>** to continue.

Enter **Accepted Order Form** at the top of the screen as shown in Figure A3-2. Note that the top and bottom lines in the file represent the top and bottom of the screen—do not include these in your screen design. The dashed lines under **Quantity** are for appearance only, and are meant to be an underscore of the column headings.

Place the cursor on the left side of the screen about three rows below the top. Enter **First Name:** and space over twice. Select **FIELD**.

Accepted Order Form

First Name: ____________________
Last Name: ____________________
Street: ________________________________
City: ____________
State: ____
Zip: __________

Amount enclosed: ____________

Quantity	Item Number	Item Description	Price
______	________	____________________	________
______	________	____________________	________
______	________	____________________	________
______	________	____________________	________

***Figure* A3-2** Screen layout

A field definition screen appears. Among the requested options are a field name and a related element name. A field is associated with a particular screen whereas an element is stored in the dictionary and can be referenced from a variety of facilities. Frequently, a field is conceptually the same as an element. In our case, we want to call the field first name, which is also the name of the element of interest. Enter **first name** as the field name and press the **<F10>** key. The **<F10>** key indicates that we want the same name for the related element and to access the dictionary for specific values. Look closely at the field definition screen for these values. Any of these values can be overridden by entering new values. At this point, we want to use these specific values. Indicate so by pressing **<F3>**.

In a similar manner, position **last name**, **street**, **city**, **state**, and **zip**. Use **FIELD** or the **<F10>** key to bring up the field definition screen in each case. Use the appropriate name for the field name and default name **amount encloses** and **<Tab>** over to the related element and enter **order amount. Order amount** is the name of the related element as it was defined in Part II. Pressing **<F10>** will retrieve the definition to order amount. Pressing **<F3>** will accept these values.

Next enter the column headings as shown in Figure A3-2. The dashed line under the column headings should also be put in.

Duplicating Fields in Screen Design

Position the cursor underneath the **Quantity** column heading. Press the **<F10>** key to bring up the field definition screen. Enter quantity as the field name and press **<F10>** again to retrieve the appropriate definitions followed by <F3> to accept these. To duplicate this field for the other three lines as shown we will use a **CUT** and **PASTE** procedure. Unlike report design we cannot use the **REPEAT** procedure on screens.

To do **CUT** and **PASTE**, position the cursor on the field to duplicate. Press the <F5> key. Notice that the field has disappeared from the screen. To **PASTE** it, simply press the <F6> key. Move your cursor down to the next line and press the <F6> key again. The most previously **CUT** field is duplicated at this new location. Duplicate the field for the rest of the rows.

Follow this procedure for **item number**, **item description**, and **price**, being sure to use the correct field name initially. Once the screen design is complete, exit by selecting <F3>.

Getting a Hard Copy of the Screen Design

To get a hard copy representation of your screen design, select **OUTPUT**, double-click, select **accepted order**, and select **PRINTER**. A screen will appear with some other options. Accept the default for these by just pressing <F3>. The output that you get will contain a copy of the screen design among other reports. What do these reports tell you?

In addition to getting a hard copy of the screen design, you can test the way the screen works. Select **INSPECT**, double-click, and select **accepted order.** You can then enter data as if you were actually using the screen. Simply enter data and <Tab> to the next input field. Try this on your own. Press <F3> when you are finished testing the screen.

You have now completed Part III of the Excelerator Tutorial. Exit from all levels of Excelerator.

The items to turn in for this section include the following:

1 a listing of defined elements
2 the report design
3 the screen design

Using Excelerator-Part IV: Analyzing and Documenting the System

Introduction

Two additional capabilities of Excelerator will be explored in the final assignment of the tutorial: ANALYSIS and DOCUMENTATION. The ANALYSIS capability checks the data flow diagrams for consistency and completeness. The DOCUMENTATION facility allows the user to define and generate reports. The reports can include a variety of things: hard copy graphics, lists of records, specific data definitions, etc. Report contents can be specified in advance and the report generated whenever it is needed.

Using Analysis

In order to appreciate the value of the ANALYSIS capability, we need to create another small system which has several errors in it. We could run the analysis on the mail-order process that was used in Parts I through III, but the analysis would not detect any problems.

Using the diagram in Figure A4-1, create another data flow diagram. When ADDing the new diagram, call it **errors**. DESCRIBE the different elements as indicated. The numbers on the graph are the IDs and the words are the labels. Indicate that all of the data flows explode to a record of the same name, i.e., the **student information** data flow explodes to the **student information** record. In addition, use the numbers 10, 20, 30, etc. for the IDs for the data flows. Do not explode the data store at this time.

Next, using the XLDictionary facility, define the records you have just indicated existed. Once the records are defined, you must also define

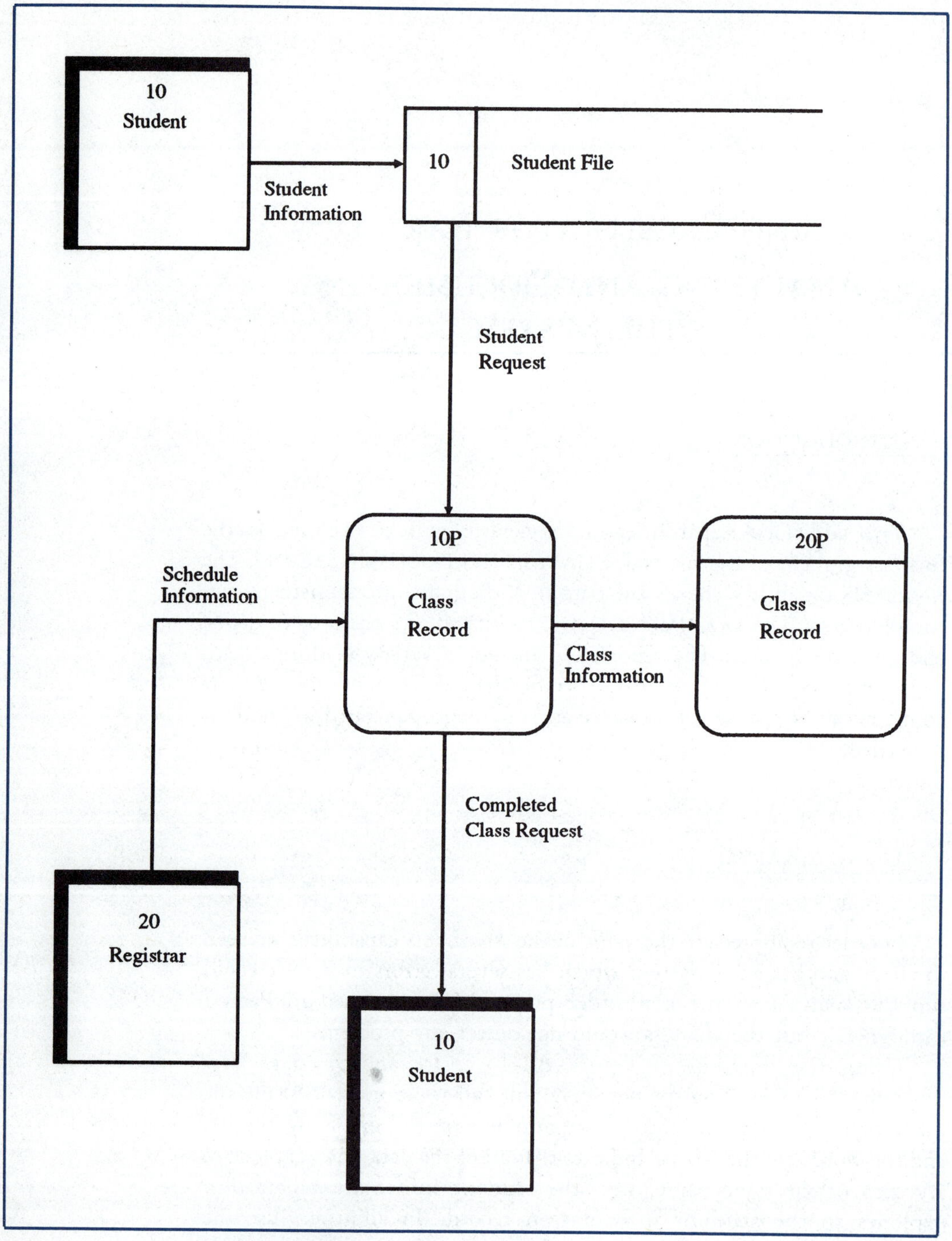

Figure A4-1 Sample system

the elements themselves. Use the packed format as the data type. Use the following definitions for both the records and elements:

student information	
name	X(20)
address	record
ssn	X(10)
student request	
course name	X(4)
course number	9(3)
class information	
name	
ssn	
course name	
course number	
completed class request	
course name	
course number	
class location	X(15)

Exit out of the XLDictionary facility.

Analysis of Graphs

Select ANALYSIS, **Graph Verification**, and **Data Flow Diagram**. Enter **errors** as the name of the graph to analyze and select **Printer.** The output generated is in two sections. The first is a list of free-standing objects. All must be connected to some other object to be a valid component of the system. Notice that the registrar, which is an EXTernal, is not connected to any other object. On simple diagrams it is easy to visually check for free-standing objects, but as diagrams become more complex, and often are created in portions at a time, this completeness check is a useful feature.

The second section of the Verification Report is a list of data store inconsistencies. Notice that Excelerator does not identify black holes or miracles. Is this a weakness? Let's see.

Select **Graph Summary Reports, Analysis Report**, and enter **errors** as the name of the diagram and **Printer** for output. The Analysis Report checks the processes and data stores for input/output consistencies. The output generated lists the processes and data stores identifying the inputs and outputs to each. Where records (and/or elements) are common to both the inputs and outputs, lines (a series of . . .) are drawn to show that the element is contained in both.

Notice that the register process has only two data elements going in (student request consists of course name and course number) and several elements coming out that were not input. Where does this information come from? There is no way that the process, using the defined inputs, could generate the desired outputs. Therefore the diagram and/or data definitions are incomplete.

The black hole created by the class record process is easy to spot: there are not any outputs shown. Also notice that the data store student file has inconsistent inputs and outputs. The information that goes into the file is nothing like the information coming out of it. There is probably an error here too.

Both of these reports demonstrate the usefulness of the ANALYSIS facility in Excelerator. Another option available in the **Graph Verification** facility is **Undescribed Graph Entities**, which reports any entities that do not have descriptions in the XLD. **Level Balancing**, another option, checks that the inputs and outputs from a process are consistent between levels of data flow diagrams. For example, if the register process exploded into a lower level diagram, Excelerator would verify that the same data inputs and outputs (elements, records, or data flows) exist and are consistent on both levels. The last option simply provides a list of all items that explode and what they explode to.

CREATING DOCUMENTATION

The final part of the tutorial project is to generate a rather complete set of documentation for your mail-order process system. The DOCUMENTATION capability provides you with a method of defining your hard copy requirements. For the most part, you could, either through GRAPHICS or XLDictionary, produce the equivalent documentation one piece at a time. DOCUMENTATION allows you to define all pieces to include and then produce them all at one time.

Creating Documentation Graphs

To generate DOCUMENTATION, you first create a Documentation Graph, which visually shows the contents and organization of the desired documentation. Figure A4-2 depicts the desired contents for the final report that you will turn in. The graph reads from left to right, and top to bottom. Figure A4-2 indicates that the final report consists of a section called entity lists, which contains an element list and a record list. The next section is called data dictionary and consists of element descriptions, etc. Any of the objects that break into other objects are called **docgroups**, and objects that do not break down are called

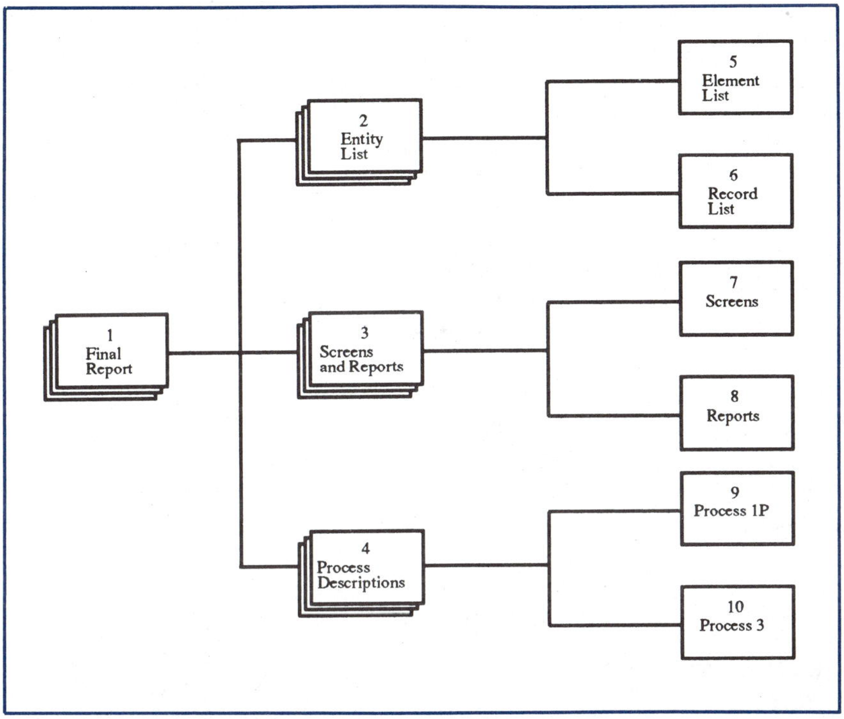

Figure A4-2 Document graph

fragments. Notice that the symbol for docgroups has overlaid fragment symbols.

To create the Documentation Graph, select **DOCUMENTATION, Document Graph, ADD**, and enter the name **final**. Select **OBJECT** and **Docgroup**. Place four document groups in the drawing areas as shown in Figure A4-2. Select **Fragment** and place these in the drawing area. Connect the document group and fragment symbols as shown.

The objects must now be defined. First DESCRIBE the document groups. Use the numbers (e.g., 1, 2) as the ID and the name (e.g., final report, data dictionary) as the label. You can enter a verbal description if you like. Leave the suppress output and produce outline fields with the defaulted values.

Defining the fragments is more involved. When describing fragments, use the number as the ID and enter the label as shown in Figure A4-2. DESCRIBE the element list fragment. Use **5** as the ID and enter the label. Tab to the **Fragment Type** field. One of the three-letter codes from Figure A4-3 must be entered here. For this fragment enter the code for an **Element Access and Derivation Analysis**, specifically **EAA**.

Fragment Type	Code	Output Options
All entity types not listed	Three-letter code	N,O,S,U,W
All relationship types	Up to 40-letter name of relationship	M,S
Analysis Report	SAR*	R
Block Diagram	BLD	I,N,O,S,U,W
Data Flow Diagram	DFD	I,N,O,S,U,W
Data Flow Diagram Verification	DFR*	R
Data Model Diagram	DMD	I,N,O,S,U,W
DMD Validation Analysis	DVA*	R,X
Data Normalization Analysis	DNA*	R,X
Document Graph	DCG	I,N,O,S,U,W
Element Access & Derivation Analysis	EAA*	R,X
Entity-Relationship Diagram	ERA	I,N,O,S,U,W
E-R Diagram Validation Analysis	EVA	R,X
Expansion Document Graph	EXP	I
Graph Explosion Report	GER*	R
Key Validation Analysis	KVA*	R,X
Level Balancing	LLB*	R
Matrix Graph	MTR	I,N,O,S,U,W
Presentation Graph	PRG	I,N,O,S,U,W
Record Content Analysis	RCA*	R,X
Report Design	RED	N,O,R,S,U,W
Report Writer Report	REP	N,O,R,S,U,W
Screen Data Report	SDR	N,O,R,S,U,W
Screen Design	SCD*	I,N,O,R,S,U,W
Screen/Report Usage Analysis	SRA*	R,X
State Transition Diagram	TRD	I,N,O,S,U,W
STD Verification	STR*	R
Structure Chart	STC	I,N,O,S,U,W
Structure Diagram	STD	I,N,O,S,U,W
Text File	TXF	I
Undescribed Graph Entities	UER*	R
Work Breakdown Structure	WBS	I,N,O,S,U,W

* This Fragment Type also requires a parameter.

Figure A4-3 Document production output options

Output Actions depend on the fragment type. Look at Figures A4-3 and A4-4 for descriptions of the fragment type, codes, output action, and description of output. Enter **R** for **Report** as the output action. Enter an * for the **Name**, and specify **A** as the **Parameter**.

Code	Output Option	Description
I	Image	Produces Excelerator/IS graphs, Screen Designs, Report Designs, and ASCII text files
N	Expanded Output	Traces all XLDictionary relationships going forward
M	Missing Entities	Identifies entities that are not yet defined in the XLDictionary
O	Output	Prints the description screen data for the entities you specify
S	Summary	Prints lists of entities or relationships
R	Report	Produces Entity Lists and all Excelerator/IS reports
U	Audit	Prints system-maintained control information
W	Where Used	Lists the entities directly associated with the ones you specify
X	Extended Analysis Matrix	Prints the matrices produced by Extended Analysis

Figure A4-4 Document production output options

DESCRIBE the rest of the fragments using the following information. Enter your own description if desired.

ID	*Label*	*Fragment Type*	*Output Action*	*Name*	*Param*
6	record list	RCA	R	*	A, 50
7	screens	SCD	R	*	
8	reports	RED	S	*	
9	process 1P	DFR	R	*	
10	process 3	DFR	R	*	

Note: An * indicates all names.

Generating the Documentation

Once the Document contents have been defined, two steps are needed to actually produce the documentation. Exit from the Document Graph drawing facility (be sure to save your work!). Select **Document Production** and **Doc Graph**. Before you can generate any hard copy output you must verify that all of the fragments from your document graph actually exist. Select **Verify** and use the name **final.** You should get a message that indicates that verification has been completed.

If you do not get an error-free verification, see a lab consultant or your instructor before proceeding.

Note: At this point, because the actual documentation is so extensive (approximately 30 to 40 pages) you should perform the next step in groups of two or three. This will reduce the unnecessary use of large quantities of paper.

Finally, select **Execute** from the menu. Use the name **final** and select **Printer.** Excelerator will go to work developing your documentation. Examine your output carefully and see where your project is incomplete and/or inconsistent.

SUMMARY

The documentation facility in Excelerator allows you to define fragments to include in a documentation package. You could get the individual fragments printed from the various other facilities in Excelerator with some effort. We did not include diagrams in our documentation because a full graph is produced which would mean voluminous amounts of paper (mostly blank sheets because of the way we positioned our graphs in the drawing area).

Once a document graph has been defined and verified, you can simply execute the graph from the Document Production Menu and generate a complete, updated set of documentation.

For this part of the assignment you should turn in the following as two separate documents:

1. Turn in individually:
   a. the analysis report for the error diagram,
   b. the verification report for the error diagram, and
   c. a hardcopy of the error diagram (go back and print this)
2. Turn in as a group of two or three:
   the set of generated documentation for your mail-order process system

EXCELERATOR FACILITIES

GRAPHICS:	Allows you to draw six different types of diagrams and charts for your systems design. This facility replaces the manual drawing and redrawing of systems logic diagrams and presentations.
XLDICTIONARY:	Allows you direct access into the Excelerator dictionary so that you can produce reports on its contents or create and update entries in the dictionary.
SCREENS AND REPORTS:	Allows you to create application screens and report designs for the systems you are designing or documenting. Screens created in Excelerator can actually be run in the screen data reporting facility as prototypes or as workstation-based applications.
ANALYSIS:	Provides validation of graphs, the ability to create and manipulate entity lists, and a report writing capability that lets you generate dictionary reports.
DICTIONARY INTERFACE:	Permits project sharing between Excelerator users and between Excelerator workstations and a mainframe dictionary. The facility manages the import, export, and locking of project files.
DOCUMENTATION:	Allows you to create and print an entire system specification document, including all the diagrams, dictionary entries, and report and screen specifications, as well as systems narratives. Documentation also allows you direct access to your favorite word processing program.
HOUSEKEEPING:	Includes a variety of facilities for maintaining the Excelerator environment, including backup and restoring of files, password changes, output device settings, and diagram default selections.

APPENDIX B

COMPREHENSIVE GLOSSARY

@ commands: Commands that allow for precise location of specific input and output information on the screen.

ACCEPT: A command that stores an entry as a character variable.

Access control: An area of data control that identifies which individuals may have access to which data.

Address: (1) An identification, as represented by a name, label, or number, for a register, location in storage, or any other data source or destination such as the location of a station in a communications network. (2) Loosely, any part of an instruction that specifies the location of an operand for the instruction.

After image: The image of a record in the database after fields on the record, a row, or a page have been modified.

Aggregate function: In SQL, an aggregate function makes it possible to perform summation, averaging, counting, and determining maximum and minimum values for a column; produces a single value which in some way summarizes the subject rows of the table.

Aggregation: Combining data into a question-answer format; an aggregation object is an object that represents groups of objects and provides inheritance.

Alias: Alternate name for a given table (used in SQL); a synonym for an already defined data item; a name variation to avoid ambiguity. Alias names make it easy to work with familiar names. For example, *production order* might have the alias names PO and PUR_ORD.

Alpha test: Verifying and studying software errors and failures based on simulated user requirements.

Alter: Modify a previously defined file; used to add or delete a column or to change the data type for a column.

Alternate key: A secondary attribute that can also serve as a primary key; one or more fields of a record used to directly access the record. For example, an employee record may be accessed using the alternative key of *employee name*. *Alternate key* is distinct from *primary* and *foreign keys*.

Anomaly: An irregularity stemming from updating a record; an operation on a database that has unwanted secondary effects, such as loss of data or data inconsistency. Anomalies result from poor design.

Application: A software package or a computer system that processes a portion of a database to meet a user's requirements.

Application development environment: Part of the information repository, in which specialists use special tools to develop new applications.

Application expert: A programmer proficient in physical database design, conversion, and operations.

Application program: A program that performs user-operated functions. It is written by a programmer, hardware vendor, or software house.

Artificial intelligence (AI): Doing on computers what, if done by humans, would be called intelligent; the capability of a computer to learn from experience, understand natural language, access information, and draw conclusions.

Asynchronous transmission: An operation initiated by a signal that a preceding operation has been completed and a new one can begin. Also, one bit at a time of transmission.

Attribute: A data item that characterizes an object; a field in a relational model; a column of a relation; a particular quality associated with an entity-type. Also called *column, field*, or *data item*; a property of an object.

Audit trail: Using documents to retrace the processing of data by changing or modifying records in a file.

Authentification: A security procedure that asks for information, such as a password, that should be known only to an assigned user.

Authorization rule: A rule specifying the conditions under which a subject (a person or a group) can take a specific action on a set of database entities.

Average function: An SQL function that produces the average for the values contained in the rows selected in the table, ignoring all null values.

AVG: See *Average function*.

Back end: In database design, the design and coding part of an application project life cycle; in expert systems, a back-end expert system evaluates the results of a query according to set rules before making a recommendation.

Balanced tree: A tree that has the same number of branches in each node.

Bandwidth: The frequency range of the communications channel that determines the maximum transmission rate, measured in bits per second or bps.

Baud: A unit of signaling speed that amounts to 1 bit per second.

Before image: The image of a record before modifying its fields. Before image is used in database recovery to roll a database back to a point following a failure.

Behavior: Function(s) performed by an object.

Benchmark test: In system testing, a test run on a candidate system to measure how long it takes to run a selected application; a processing procedure that verifies the performance level of the DBMS under full load.

Beta test: Subjecting modified software to the actual (live) user site environment; giving the program to a limited number of prospective users; the final test to ensure that the program runs according to specifications.

Boss module: A module that is not called on by any other module but calls on other modules to do work.

Bubble chart: See *Bubble diagram*.

Bubble diagram: A graphical representation of entities, attributes, and their relationships to form a data model; a useful way for the database administrator to communicate representations of data structures or logical schemas to the end-user.

Buffer: An area in memory for temporary storage of data.

Built-in function: In SQL, any of the functions AVG, SUM, COUNT, MAX, or MIN.

Bus network: LAN layout in which all functional devices are connected to a length of passive coaxial cable, called a *bus*.

Called module: Also called *worker module*; a module that contains a subroutine and is called on by another module.

Calling module: See *Boss module*.

Candidate key: A field or a group of fields that uniquely identify a unique row in a relation.

Carrier-sense and multiple access with collision detection: See *CSMA/CD*.

CASE: (1) A command that specifies a condition and the corresponding action to be taken if the condition is met. (2) See *Computer-Aided Software Engineering*.

Case construct: A nested series of conditional constructs that identifies the action to be taken for each possible, and mutually exclusive, set of conditions.

Chain: Records connected by means of pointers.

Chained list: A field that holds the address of the next record in the sequence; used to keep records in logical order.

Change log: A way of capturing the before and after images of each transaction on a storage device other than the one that has the database in residence.

Child: An owned entity. In a hierarchical structure, node B is the child of node A if A is directly above B in the hierarchy and B is related to A. Node B is called the *child* and node A is called the *parent*.

Class: A set of similar objects such as a group of employees; a template that permits objects to be created.

Clause: In a contract, a condition or a statement of understanding; in programming, a section of a command.

Client: Requester; the user of a server.

Client computer: A personal computer on a local area network with client/server architecture.

Client/server architecture: A LAN structure in which one personal computer performs services on behalf of other personal computers.

CODASYL: Conference on Data Systems Languages, developed in 1959 to set specifications for COBOL.

Column: A logical group of bytes in a row of a table; in a relational model, a column represents a field.

Column variable: A variable in a computer program containing embedded SQL commands used by SQL tables.

Command: A computer-oriented statement input to a database specifying the activity the user wants the system to perform.

Command-driven mode: An environment in which users enter commands to the database management system interactively for data access or problem solution.

Commit: Posting a completed transaction to the database; completing all updates for a logical transaction.

Commit work: A command input to the DBMS to make database modifications permanent; an SQL command that permits the user to control when tables should be updated.

Comparison operator: In SQL, an equality sign (=) in the WHERE clause.

Complex network model: A network model, in which lines with double-headed arrows join records in both directions. (See *Complex network model* for contrast.)

Computer-Aided Software Engineering (CASE): Software tools that automate the design of software. For example, CASE can draw data flow diagrams, entity-relationship diagrams, and structure charts.

Computer Matching and Privacy Protection Act: A law that regulates computer matching of federal data for verifying eligibility for federal benefits programs or for recouping delinquent debts.

Concatenated key: Two or more keys linked together to identify or access a record; two data elements taken together to produce a primary key.

Conceptual data model: See *Conceptual schema*.

Conceptual schema: The global organizational view of data. See *schema*.

Concurrency control: Ability of the DBMS to deal with several users as they modify the same data at the same time.

Concurrency threats: The possibility of a database allowing several users to access the same data at the same time; occur when two or more data modification entries work well separately, but produce invalid results when used together.

Concurrency transparency: In a distributed database environment, a situation in which an application program does not know if data is being concurrently processed.

Condition construct: A construct that specifies that IF a specific condition exists, THEN a certain action follows or ELSE a different action must be taken.

Connection: Lines linking modules together in a structure chart.

Connective: Operator signal; in expert systems, used to link predicates into large expressions.

Connectivity: The ability to connect PC-based database applications to a mainframe database or to a PC acting as a server.

Constraint: A limit placed on entities or their attributes.

Cooperative processing: Running the user interface on the client system (PC) and the database operations on the database server.

Coordinate: The intersection of a specific column and row created by lines on a screen grid.

Copyright: Official registration of software and database products to give them legal protection. A copyright protects "writing" and focuses on "expressions" that are descriptive of software.

COUNT: An SQL function that produces the number of items in the column specified.

Counter: A space in memory reserved to accumulate numeric values.

Couple: A connection between modules; a symbol representing data items moved from one module to another.

Create: The act of creating files, indexes, or views.

Cross-reference report: In a data dictionary, a report that shows where every variable is used in the application system program.

CSMA/CD: A detection device that looks at the transmitting device for a signal on the line to avoid a collision with another device already transmitting.

Cursor: On a computer screen, an indicator (a blinking dash or a box) of the current position; in embedded SQL, a pointer to a group of rows returned by the query that defines the cursor.

DA: See *Data administrator.*

Data: Facts; unprocessed information; facts about objects, people, or entities.

Data administrator (DA): A high-level manager responsible for maintaining corporate-wide standards, enforcing naming conventions for data elements, and tracking data contents of corporate databases.

Data analysis: Collecting information about present and future user requirements for data in a technology-independent manner.

Data base: See *Database.*

Data decryption: See *Decryption.*

Data definition language (DDL): The language used to describe how data is structured in the database, views, and subschemas; allows users to describe fields, records, and tables in the database; describes the schema to the DBMS; converts requests for data generated at terminals or by application programs from the logical view into the physical view.

Data dictionary: A structured repository of data about data; a list of terms and their definitions for all data items and data stores of a system; a set of definitions of all data flow diagram data elements and data structures (represented by arrows).

Data directory: A repository of information about where the data defined by the dictionary is stored; stores internal schema and programs.

Data element: The smallest unit of data where no further breakdown is provided. Also known as a *primitive.*

Data encryption: See *Encryption.*

Data field: Data item; a logical group of bytes in a record; in a relational model, it is equivalent to a column in a table and is synonymous with *attribute.*

Data flow diagram (DFD): Graphic representation of data movement, processes, and files (data stores) used in support of an information system; a picture of how data moves through a system, usually a series of "bubbles" joined by lines.

Data fragmentation: Dividing a group of related data elements into logical units for storage; dividing into chunks certain data to be stored closest to the site where it is used the most.

Data independence: Changing hardware and storage procedures or adding new data without having to rewrite application programs; The DBMS locates and retrieves the data requested, apart from the application program.

Data integration: Data in a DBMS is pooled to cut down on data redundancy.

Data integrity: Data reliability. Data that is logically inconsistent lacks integrity because it cannot be depended on.

Data item: See *Data field*.

Data manipulation language (DML): A language that specifies for the DBMS the data required in the database; the techniques used to process data; a host language that manages the data in the database, as defined by the DDL.

Data migration: Moving data from one device to another; for instance, transferring infrequently used data to archival storage.

Data model: A framework or mental image of how the user's data requirements look, expressed generally in terms of the E-R diagram.

Data model diagram: A graphical representation of entities and their relationships. See *Entity-relationship diagram*.

Data operations expert: A specialist whose main job is to maintain good communications between the database administration and MIS operations personnel.

Data redundancy: Data duplication; same data stored in different files.

Data relationship: Types of relationships among entities. There are three types of relationships: one-to-one, one-to-many, and many-to-many. Entities and their relationships make up a data model.

Data shadowing: Keeping the entire database on-line at a remote data center.

Data shareability: A database, as a single repository of data, can be shared by many people, each of whom may use it for different reasons.

Data store: In a data flow diagram, a storage area usually representing a file; symbolized by an open rectangle.

Data structure: A logically related set of data that can be decomposed into lower-level data elements; a group of data elements handled as a unit.

Data structure design: Developing the conceptual schema of the database; a DBMS-independent structure derived from the user requirement specifications.

Data structure diagram: A graphic display of tables and their relationships. Relationships are shown by lines connecting tables, which are represented by rectangles.

Data structure refinement: Transforming the DBMS-independent logical design into a data model compatible with the chosen DBMS.

Database: A store of integrated data capable of being directly addressed for multiple uses; it is organized so that various files can be accessed through a single reference based on the relationship among records in the file rather than the physical location.

Database administrator (DBA): A technical person responsible for designing and maintaining the physical database and the DBMS, enforcing security standards, maintaining database performance, and ensuring backup and recovery.

Database design: Organizing data into tables and identifying relationships and access keys; identifying user data requirements and determining how the data should be structured from the requirements; transforming unstructured information and the processing requirements of an application into representations that define the functional specifications.

Database designer: Database developer; a person in charge of the actual design of the database; an expert in database design and procedures.

Database environment: Includes the database software, the computer that operates the database, and the staff in charge of maintaining the database on a regular basis.

Database server: On a local area network with client/server architecture, the personal computer that processes activities against the database on request of the client computer.

Database management system (DBMS): A set of powerful, comprehensive programs that serves as an interface between the users and the physical database; the software that determines how data must be structured to produce the user's view; manages, stores, and retrieves data and enforces procedures.

DBA: See *Database administrator.*

DBMS: See *Database management system.*

DDBMS: See *Distributed database management system.*

DDL: See *Data definition language.*

Deadlock: Also called *deadly embrace*, a condition during concurrent processing in which each of two or more transactions is waiting to access data the other transaction has locked.

Debug: Remove errors (bugs) from an application program.

Decision tree: Graphic representation of conditions and outcomes resembling the branches of a tree; a graphical view or a model of the decision logic in a program.

Decryption: Restoring encrypted data to intelligible text form.

Delete: In SQL, remove rows from a table.

Deletion anomaly: A type of anomaly that triggers an unintended deletion of data about another record of a different type.

Derived knowledge: Makes use of intentional and extensional knowledge.

Determinant: An attribute that determines at least one other attribute.

DFD: See *Data flow diagram*.

Disclaimer: Related to a warranty; means that the vendor makes no promise about the quality of the software.

Distributed database management system (DDBMS): A system with multiple computer sites within a communication network; each site has its own database with its own DBMS, CPU, and terminals; or, a DBMS capable of manipulating distributed databases.

Distributed database systems: Usually, portions of a database maintained at remote physical locations or sites, each of which is responsible for maintaining the part of the database that is proprietary to its users.

Distributed processing: Availability of a computerized environment at the user's level, with control at the organization's host computer.

DML: See *Data manipulation language*.

DO CASE: A command that tells the program that a number of possibilities follow.

Domain: A set of values an attribute can have; in expert systems, the environment in which a problem resides.

DO-WHILE: A control structure that executes the statements bracketed between the words DO-WHILE and ENDDO a fixed number of times, or for as long as the statement on the DO-WHILE is a repeating IF.

Drop: In SQL, a term that means "delete the designated table, index, or view from the database."

Dynamic application: An application that requires frequent design changes to keep it up to user standards.

Dynamic SQL: A way in which the system can respond to unanticipated queries.

Eject: A command that causes the paper on the printer to move to the top of the next page and resets the *x,y* positions to zero.

Electronic vaulting: Transmitting the contents of a database to a remote site in batches, via data networks.

Embedded SQL: Embedding SQL statements in computer programs written in third-generation programming languages such as COBOL, C, PL/1, and Ada.

Encryption: Using encryption algorithms to scramble data and make it unintelligible to unauthorized users or those without the proper key and algorithm.

ENDCASE: Part of DO CASE...ENDCASE command structure; signals that end-of-program commands are to be executed.

ENDDO: Part of DO WHILE...ENDDO command structure; signals that end-of-program commands are to be executed.

ENDIF: Part of IF...ENDIF construction; terminates the performance of the commands tagged to the IF statement.

End-user: See *User*.

English-language description: In a data dictionary, description of information about data is presented in plain English.

Enhancement: Incorporating changes into the database application to reflect new user requirements; modifying the programs to respond to the user's additional or changing needs.

Entity: An object about which data is collected. In an E-R model, an entity is a thing that can be represented by a single table; a conceptual representation of a thing, event, or person about which data is collected, and is identified by its attributes.

Entity-relationship (E-R) diagram: A graphic representation of the conceptual database design; a nontechnical way of representing the data structure. Emphasizes entities and relationships that help the designer analyze the data and organize his or her ideas.

Entity type: A group of similar objects or events, such as customer.

Ergonomics: The science of adjusting machine specifications to match human comfort.

ESE: See *Expert System Environment*.

Evolvability: A database feature that makes it easy to modify the system when necessary.

Expert system: A system that uses symbolic knowledge to mimic the decision-making and problem-solving thought processes of human experts; an extension of artificial intelligence.

Expert System Environment (ESE): An IBM expert system shell that is able to access the relational database SQL/DS by creating SQL queries and passing data through import/export facilities.

External data model: The user's view of the data or of a specific processing application; a subset of the conceptual data model, necessary for supporting a particular user view.

External schema: The application program's view of the database.

Fair Credit Reporting Act: A law that bars credit agencies from sharing credit information with anyone but authorized customers; gives consumers the right to review their credit records and be notified of credit investigations for insurance and employment.

Federated database: A structure in which a layer on top of a distributed database provides transparent access to various independent databases at multiple sites.

Field: A group of bytes that represent a basic unit of information, such as an employee's last name.

File: A collection of records of the same type; for example, a customer file.

File processing system: Storing groups of records in separate files; descriptive of early computer processing systems such as accounts receivable, inventory control, and demand deposit systems.

File server: In a local area network, a personal computer that has a file that it processes on behalf of other personal computers on the network.

First normal form: In a relational model, a table is in first normal form if it contains no repeating groups or if and only if every attribute is single-valued for each record.

Fitness: The principle of determining that a system is appropriate for a user's needs; can be used as grounds for litigation.

Flow of control: Controlling the flow of a program by using commands that determine the action to be taken, the time when the action should be taken, and the next step to be taken after the action.

Foreign key: An attribute that is a key of one or more relations other than the relation in which it is a part.

Fourth normal form: A relation in third normal form, in which every multivalued dependency is a functional dependency.

Fragment: A row in a table in which a required parent or child is absent.

Fragmentation transparency: In distributed databases, splitting a file over multiple nodes without disrupting users or application programs.

Frame: A knowledge carrier that helps describe the syntax of a knowledge base; a set of slots and their associated entries; associates an object with facts, rules, or values.

Front-end development: In database design, determining user's requirements, data analysis, and data modeling that precedes actual design and programming of the application program. An expert system can be used as a front end to a database, asking questions and then initiating a database query.

Functional dependency: Field B is functionally dependent on field A if the value of A determines uniquely the value of B; occurs when a unique value of one attribute can always be determined if we know the value of another.

Gateway: An interface that connects one local area network to another.

Generalization: Combining objects into one category.

GET: A command that displays a blank for user input at the screen location indicated by the variables *(x,y)*.

Grant: In SQL, assign designated database privileges to a user or group of users.

Granularity: The size of the database that can be locked. For example, locking a column of a row is small granularity, whereas locking the entire database is large granularity.

Graphic user interface (GUI): An interface with pull-down menus, windows, and other features that are generally activated with a mouse.

GUI: See *Graphic user interface*.

Hardware: Physical equipment such as mechanical, magnetic, electrical, or electronic devices; includes the DBMS, an operating system, and one or more application programs.

Height: In a tree structure, the number of levels a tree contains.

Heterogeneous DDBMS: A distributed DBMS in which at least two of the local DBMSs are different from each other.

Heuristics: In expert systems, a rule of thumb or experiential reasoning, as opposed to textbook knowledge.

Hierarchical file: A file with a tree-structure relationship among its records.

Hierarchical model: A data model that represents all relationships using hierarchies or trees. See *hierarchical structure*.

Hierarchical structure: Also called *tree structure*; breaking down a large project into a series of successively smaller, manageable parts through iteration and according to a logical sequence; a hierarchy of groups of data such that the highest in the hierarchy has only one group, called a *root*, and all groups except the root are related to only one group on a higher level than themselves.

Hierarchy: A common word for a superior-subordinate relationship; in a database structure, a tree that has been turned upside down.

Homogeneity assumption: Expecting data to be exchanged between two DBMSs—for example, between IBM's DB2 at one site and ORACLE at another site. A gateway that runs on one DBMS should make that DBMS resemble another DBMS in residence.

Homogeneous DDBMS: A distributed DBMS in which all of the local DBMSs are the same.

Horizontal fragmentation: A type of fragmentation that occurs when a database file is divided "horizontally" to allow storage of data in different locations. That is, a table can be broken up into multiple tables by selecting rows.

Host language interface: A DBMS interface that allows DML commands to be embedded in a standard high-level language such as COBOL, C, and FORTRAN.

Host variable: A value placed by a DBMS in a variable in an application program.

IDBS: See *Intelligent database system.*

IF...ENDIF: A command structure that controls a conditional choice.

Implementation: Actual testing and installation of the database, developing a conversion plan, converting the existing application, converting the existing data to the new database environment, writing documentation, and training users.

IMS: See *Information Management System.*

Inference: In expert systems, the process of inferring new facts from current information; logical conclusions based on the data.

Inference engine: Part of an expert system that stands between the user and the knowledge base; contains the inference strategies and controls required for manipulating the facts and rules.

Information: Processed data; the product of the analysis and synthesis of data; data that has been organized in a form suitable for use by employees at all levels of an organization.

Information Management System: A project developed by IBM and Rockwell International Corporation in the early 1970s.

Information repository: The metadata that defines the organization's data and processing resources.

Inheritance: In a semantic network, instances of one class are assumed to have all the properties of more general classes of which they are members.

Input: The data to be processed; the process of transferring data from external storage to internal storage; a command that works like the ACCEPT command, except that it stores an entry as either a character or a numeric variable.

Insert: A command to add a row to a table.

Insertion anomaly: A type of anomaly that occurs when we try to add a record to a file and it is rejected because it is missing a value or because the data needed for a complete primary key is not available.

Integrity: Measures designed to ensure accuracy of data in a database.

Integrity violation: Adjusting one record or account in a database without a corresponding adjustment to another record, which results in invalid update; for example, in a funds transfer, debiting a savings account without a corresponding credit to a person's checking account.

Intelligent database system (IDBS): A tool for developing applications requiring both a DBMS and one or more expert system and CASE tools; a system for developing applications requiring knowledge-directed intelligent processing of shared information.

Internal data model: Shows how the data is internally or physically represented in the database; includes the data structures and file organizations used to store the data on a hard disk or another physical storage device.

Intersection: A relational algebra operation performed on two union-compatible relations (e.g., *A* and *B*), resulting in a third relation, *C*, which contains only rows that are present in *A* and *B*.

Intersection record: A record that is owned by two different records and that represents a M:N relationship.

Interview: A data-gathering or data-verification approach; talking with people in an organized manner and with a purpose (to gather information).

Inverted list: A copy of a list that has been inverted into a given sequence; the duplicated data is replaced by pointers to the original list.

IS-A relationship: In an entity-relationship diagram, a relationship between two entities of the same logical type.

Iteration operator: An operator represented by a pair of brackets that indicate that the contents of the brackets are to be repeated the designated number of times.

Join: A relational operation that produces a new relation, which includes all the combinations of tuples from two given relations that meet a specified condition; logically connecting multiple tables through a column with data common to both, then dealing with the combined data as though it were a column.

Journaling: The process of maintaining a log or a journal.

Key: An attribute or set of attributes that identifies a record; a field used to access a record; a unique identifier of an entity.

Knowledge: The thought process and experience of an expert; information at a high level of abstraction.

Knowledge acquisition: The process of using special tools to elicit or tap the knowledge of the domain expert.

Knowledge base: A part of expert system architecture that contains an unstructured set of facts and inference rules for determining new facts; contains the rules and heuristics that make possible the emulation of human thought and activity.

Knowledge engineer: A specialist who builds expert systems; a person specialized in knowledge acquisition and representation.

Knowledge engineering: Building expert systems; replicating the behavior of a specific expert in solving a narrowly defined problem.

Knowledge representation: Representing (in symbolic form) the knowledge acquired from the expert system that is used by the inference engine, which is the built-in software; similar to programming the expert system.

LAN: See *Local area network*.

Leaf: In a tree structure, a node at the end of the branch.

Link: Symbolic reference in memory used to associate an object with other objects; an association between two records made possible via pointers.

Linked list: A data structure that links records in a logical sequence via pointers.

Local area network (LAN): An electronic communication linkage in which all sources and recipients are in one office, in a single building, or on a single work site, typically less than one mile in radius.

Local autonomy: Being able to access data from multiple sites in a transparent fashion, while controlling the data local to the site that actually uses it.

Location transparency: In a distributed database environment, a situation in which a table can be located or relocated on any network node without disrupting users or application programs.

Locking: A routine that places a lock on a portion of a database or a file, which prevents other users from accessing that portion.

Log: A file that contains an accounting of database changes; a record of before images and after images.

Logic: (1) The science dealing with the criteria or formal principles of reasoning and thought. (2) The systematic scheme that defines the interactions of signals in the design of an automatic data processing system. (3) The basic principles and application of truth tables and interconnection between logical elements required for arithmetic computation in an automatic data processing system.

Logic error: Deviation from a range of acceptability.

Logical data independence: Capacity to change the conceptual data model without having to change the external data model or the application program.

Logical design: In developing a system, laying down specifications and depicting the system's logical flow through a data flow diagram; the first step in actually designing a database.

Logical record: In a database structure, a hierarchy of segments as perceived by an application program. Such a hierarchy may or may not exist physically.

Logical transaction: A series of specific steps that must be fully executed; otherwise, the database remains unaltered.

Logical view: What the data looks like, regardless of how it is stored in the database; the view perceived by the programmer.

Loop counter: A variable that keeps track of the number of times the DO-WHILE executes.

Machine-oriented description: In a data dictionary, the description of various types of information represented in machine-oriented language.

Mainframe-based database system: Database systems designed to run on large computers for large firms. These systems require large storage capacities and an environment dedicated to serving multiple users in real time.

Maintenance: Monitoring the database application and making the necessary modifications to ensure that the system meets initial user requirements.

Manual processing system: A collection of records stored in filing cabinets or similar containers; for example, a manila file folder containing sheets of paper.

Many-to-many relationship: Many objects are related to many other objects. For example, student and class relations are many-to-many relationships; each student can enroll in many classes and each class can be taken by many students.

MAX: See *Maximum function*.

Maximal path: In a tree structure, a path that originates at the root and picks up one branch of the tree all the way to the leaf.

Maximum function (MAX): An SQL function that returns the highest value in the specified column of the table.

Memory variable: A memory space set aside for specific data.

Menu: A selected list of options that the user chooses from, then types an option for a computer operation.

Menu-driven mode: A list of applications or options displayed on the screen, from which the user can select. The user selects one option at a time, such as *enter data, revise a record*, or *print a report*.

Merchantability: An implied warranty ensuring that a system or a piece of software functions properly within realistic guidelines.

Message: Data sent from one computer to another.

Metadata: Data about data. In a database, metadata includes items such as field names, field lengths, and data types.

Method: A program linked to object-oriented programming (OOP).

Microcomputer-based database systems: Database systems designed to run on microcomputers for medium-sized and small firms. These systems tend to be easy to use and easy to learn.

MIN: See *Minimum function*.

Minimum function (MIN): An SQL function that produces the lowest value in the specified column.

Modularity: In systems maintenance, a situation in which a system is constructed in modular units of a limited size to simplify maintenance, when necessary; in software reliability, the ease with which a package can be modified.

Module: A group of instructions with a single entry point and a single exit point.

Moment: In a tree structure, the number of nodes a tree contains.

Multiple join: Dealing with data from more than two tables. The multiple clauses in the WHERE clause are joined by AND, OR connectors.

Multivalued dependency: In a relation with three attributes, A, B, and C, there is multivalued dependency of attribute B on A if a value for A is related to a specific set of values for B independently of any values for C.

Natural join: A type of join in which only one of the columns used appears in the result.

Natural language: Computer programs capable of reading, speaking, or understanding human language; using the conceptual structure of English to match the user's conceptualization of the problem.

Natural user interface: The function of a DBMS that expresses system functions in terms that are natural to an application or a user.

Nested normal forms: Each level of normalization is dependent on the previous level. For example, the third normal form depends on the second, and the second normal form on the first.

Nested query: See *Subquery*.

Network: Events and activities in PERT/CPM; in a database, a data structure that allows 1:1, 1:M, or M:N relationships between entities.

Network-based database system: A database system linked to a network; physically linking two or more computers so that users can share common resources such as software packages and printers as well as databases.

Network model: A data model that describes relationships between records in which one item can be linked to any other item; a data model that supports at least simple network relationships. The nature of the relationship is many-to-many or M:N.

Node: An element; a part of a network structure; a record in a hierarchical data structure; an entity in a tree; in expert systems, a beginning or an ending point of an activity.

Nonkey identifier: Data items that cannot be used as identifiers because they are not unique.

Nonprocedural language: A programming language in which the user specifies the tasks to be carried out rather than the steps to accomplish the tasks.

Normal form: A class of relational schemas that conform to some set of rules; sets of increasingly stringent rules that govern the design of a table; used to successfully examine specific aspects of data relationships in order to reduce the complexity, redundancy, or inconsistency of these relations.

Normalization: A process of evaluating a relation to decide if it is in a specified normal form and transforming it into relations that are in that specified normal form; organizing data into tables so as to remove update anomalies.

Not null: A case in which the actual value is known and applicable.

Null value: A value assigned by the DBMS to fields that have not been assigned a value by users; a value that is either unknown or not applicable.

Object: A representation of knowledge in symbolic form that can be efficiently used by an inference engine; a representation of a real-world entity. In object-oriented programming, objects are defined based on how they will be used rather than by what they are.

Object-oriented programming: Data abstractions, called *objects* rather than *data entities*, are the basis of the program. Functionality and data are not separated into programs and databases, but are encapsulated into a single whole called an *object*.

Object program: The program that is the output of a compiler. Often the object program is a machine language program ready for execution, but it may well be in an intermediate language.

Occurrence: A specific example of a structure; for example, the record for employee Mal Jones.

One-to-many relationship: A relationship in which one record is related to one or many records. For example, the relationship between customer and invoice is a one-to-many relationship in that a customer may receive more than one invoice.

One-to-one relationship: A relationship in which every occurrence of a given entity is related to one and only one occurrence of another specific entity. For example, an employee has one and only one supervisor.

Open architecture: Making minor changes in the software so that it can run on a variety of types of vendor hardware.

Operating system: A collection of programs that control and manage the activities of a computer system.

Optimizer: The component of a DBMS that will select the best way to handle a query.

Optional operator: An operator with a pair of bars notation represents phrases that may or may not be included in the data elements definition of a data dictionary.

Outer join: Used when the data required meets one but not both of the conditions specified in the WHERE clause of the SELECT statement; a type of join in which rows in one table that do not match the rows in another table are still included in the result.

Owner: In SQL, when a table is created, a record may be kept of the person (owner) who created it.

Parallel run: A processing routine in which the new and the old systems are run simultaneously for a designated time period.

Parent: An owning entity that can have more than child.

Password: A unique word that must be entered before a user can access a predetermined area in the computer, application, or file.

Patent: A legal registration of new and useful machines or process inventions.

Path: The direction of a specific set of nodes in a tree structure.

Performance monitor routines: Special utilities that keep track of the number of times the disk has been accessed, the CPU time used by each user or workstation, the amount of memory used by each application, and so forth.

Physical data independence: Separating physical data storage details from database use; ability to change the internal data model without having to change the external or conceptual data models.

Physical design: In systems design, the stage after logical design that develops program software—the working system; the logical model mapped to physical storage, normally on hard disk.

Physical pointer: A pointer that points to the absolute location of the next record in the chain of records by specifying the cylinder, track, and position of that record on the hard disk.

Physical record: A hierarchy of segments that is stored in database files, etched electronically on designated sectors of a hard disk.

Physical schema: A schema that defines the physical specifications of the conceptual design of a database.

Physical view: What the data actually looks like in storage or on the disk.

Pointer: A data item in a record that contains the storage address of another record; an address of a record in a directly addressed file.

Predicate: In logic programming, an expression with a true or false condition.

Premise: A situation; in expert systems, a *premise* is combined with a *conclusion* to form a *rule*.

Preorder traversal: A procedure for decomposing a tree by starting with the root and working downward along the extreme left branches of the tree, listing each node on the way. At the bottom, the next level continues to the bottom of that level, and so on until we have scanned the rightmost level of branches; top-to-bottom and left-to-right hierarchical path followed through a tree structure; commonly done when a backup copy of a database is desired.

Primary key: An attribute that uniquely defines a record in a table; a candidate key selected to be the key of a relation.

Primitive: See *Data element*.

Print server: A common local area network feature that makes remote printing devices available so that, for example, the user with a short-term need for high-quality graphics may share another user's laser printer.

Privacy Act: A law that bars federal agencies from letting information they collect for one purpose be used for a different purpose.

Procedural language: A programming language in which the user specifies the steps to accomplish a task rather than specifying the task itself.

Production environment: A component of the information repository, in which people use applications to build or update databases.

Program logical view: See *Subschema*.

Projection: A relational database operation that results in a new table containing one or more columns from a base table.

PROLOG: PROgramming language for LOGic; a logic programming dialect that is suitable as an implementation language for expert systems.

Prompt: A symbol on a computer screen that asks the user for a command or response.

PROSQL: A new DML that combines the intelligence of PROLOG with the strength of SQL.

Protocol: Refers to the rules that both the sender and the receiver use; a standardized use of certain characters for control of the communications procedure and error-handling rules.

Prototype: A working system to explore implementation or processing alternatives and evaluate results.

Pseudocode: A design tool that produces a highly readable program design; uses more formal notation and is geared more to database designers and professionals than to end-users.

Public: In SQL, the designated privileges of anyone on the system.

Quality assurance: Developing controls to ensure a quality product; defining factors that determine system quality and the criteria that the software must meet to contain these factors.

Query language: A language used to specify characteristics of data to be retrieved from a database; English-language facility that allows users with limited or no computer experience to query the database for information via a display terminal.

Query languages expert: A specialist in on-line query management whose responsibilities include design, conversion, and operations.

Query optimizer: A DDBMS software that decides on the best route and gets data for processing a query.

Questionnaire: A self-administered data-gathering tool used in situations in which standard information must be gathered from a large group within a short time frame.

Ranking scales question: A question that asks the respondent to determine preferences for the importance of a set of items.

Rapid prototyping: An interactive technique that allows the knowledge engineer to quickly incorporate changes suggested from the domain expert for building the expert system.

Rating scales question: A multiple-choice item that offers a range of responses along a given dimension.

READ: A command that stores screen input into a memory variable. It is used in a program file when a GET form of the @ command is used.

Record: A group of fields belonging to the same entity; in a relational model, synonymous with *row* and *tuple*.

Recovery: An integrity-protecting procedure that reacts to hardware or software malfunction by returning the data to its original condition; restoring to a correct state a database that has been damaged or destroyed.

Redundancy: A situation in which two or more pieces of information in a file are the same.

Referential integrity: Integrity constraints to ensure that references or associations between records are valid; accurate relationships or matches between the rows of one table and those of another.

Relation: A two-dimensional table in which all entries are single-valued.

Relational algebra: A set of operations that acts on relations to produce new relations.

Relational model: Data and relationships represented in a flat, two-dimensional table.

Relationship: An association between entity-types, objects, or other data items.

Relative address: The location of a record relative to the beginning of a file.

Relative pointer: A pointer that specifies the relative position of the next record within a file.

Remote journaling: Capturing data updates at a remote data center as they occur.

Repeat-until construct: A construct that allows a specific set of operations to be repeated at least once until a condition is met.

Repeating field: A collection of logically related attributes that occur many times within a record or row; one or more data items that are repeated. For example, on a student registration form, multiple classes may be selected.

Repetition construct: A construct that deals with a set of operations that are repeated over and over again until a condition is met that terminates the repetition.

Replication transparency: Redundant data are transparently updated. A data object may be duplicated at various sites to minimize traffic, but the duplication, or replication, is transparent to the user.

Report: A formal function useful for decision making; an extraction of data from an existing database; reports on paper can be generated on a daily basis, on an ad hoc basis, or when exceptions to a routine occur.

Report generator: Software that allows the user to interactively define the data files and produce reports.

Representational knowledge: An expert system using two facts to perform deductive reasoning from the two structures.

Request for proposal (RFP): A user's report requesting selected vendors to bid on a proposed system.

Requirements costing: An evaluation method in which the cost of the DBMS is the vendor's price plus the cost to incorporate features the DBMS does not provide.

Revoke: In SQL, a command that cancels previously granted database privileges.

RFP: See *Request for proposal*.

Right to Financial Privacy Act: A law that sets strict procedures when federal agencies want to access customer records in banks.

Ring network: LAN layout in which several processors or microcomputers are linked to form the equivalent of a ring, so that data lines connect each unit only to adjacent ones.

Rollback: A process that reverses changes made to a database, typically affected by use of before images; in the event a transaction is not completed, returns the database to its original state.

Rollback work: An SQL command that rolls back incomplete work when an error occurs in database operations to maintain database integrity.

Rollforward: Restoring a backup copy of the database and bringing the restored copy up to date; typically affected by use of after images.

Root: A parent with no owners; the topmost node in a tree structure.

Row: In a relational table, a *row* corresponds to a *record*.

Rule: In expert systems, a conditional statement that specifies an action to be taken, if a certain condition is true.

Schema: A map of the overall logical structure of a database; the global plan that controls the organization and use of data; the logical representation of the physical database or a complete description of all records, fields, and data relationships.

Scope: In a database application, a setting of the boundary of the project or problem.

Screen grid: An evenly spaced set of horizontal and vertical lines on a VDT screen.

Second normal form: Ensures that all fields on a row are fully functionally dependent on the primary key. An entity is in second normal form if it has been placed in first normal form, and if every field in the entity is fully functionally dependent on the primary key.

Secondary key: A field that is not unique but is used as an alternative search path. Same as *alternate key*.

Secondary storage: Storage media such as magnetic tape or magnetic disk.

Select: In SQL, a command used to extract information from a table; a relational operation that takes horizontal rows in a relation or identifies the tuples to be included in a new relation; a command that allows the user to work with information in two or more databases at the same time.

Selection operator: A relational operator that selects or displays only those rows that meet a specified set of conditions; for example, select all customers with a balance outstanding of $150 or greater. In a data dictionary, an operator that represents a choice between two or more alternatives.

Self-join: A query that requires that the table be joined with itself. The combined result of a self-join consists of two rows from the same table.

Semantic data model: A conceptual modeling tool that uses words rather than graphic symbols to classify data.

Semantic integrity threats: Threats to database integrity resulting from miskeyed input data, program errors, or user misunderstanding of what is supposed to be entered.

Semantic knowledge: In expert systems, a semantic network or a collection of nodes linked together to form a net.

Sequence: In a data dictionary, an instruction that is executed after its predecessor; the concatenation of two or more components in a sequence.

Sequence construct: A construct that applies simple top-to-bottom ordering of subordinate descriptions in a logical program. The sequence is ended with the word EXIT, followed by an optional sequence title.

Server: A PC with large hard-disk capacity used to store common files in a network.

SET FORMAT TO PRINT: A command that sends the results of the @ command to the printer and then resets control to the screen display.

Shell: An expert system stripped of its specific knowledge; an expert system with a rule set manager and an inference engine.

Sibling: In a hierarchical database, the relationship of the children of one parent; two records or nodes that have the same parent record.

Simple join: See *Join*.

Simple network model: A network model in which lines joining records indicate 1:1 or 1:M relationships. (See *Complex network model* for contrast.)

Singleton select: The simplest form of the embedded SELECT command, in which only one row is selected in response to the query and, because something must be done with the row, the column variable data is moved into host variable data.

Slot: Part of a frame in which facts and values related to a specific object are stored.

Software: (1) The collection of programs and routines associated with a computer; for example, compilers and library routines. (2) All the documents associated with a computer; for example, manuals and circuit diagrams.

SQL: See *Structured query language*.

SQL communications area: An area in which SQL provides feedback information regarding the proper performance of commands in embedded SQL.

SQL database server: A computer that houses an SQL database application.

SQLCA: See *SQL communications area*.

Star network: LAN layout in which each terminal is linked by a separate line to a central host computer.

Static application: An application that requires only minor changes to keep it up to date. For example, a bills of materials application for a lumber yard written closely to the DBMS can be expected to run for a long time with only minor changes to keep it current.

Store: In data flow diagrams, a file or a repository of data; in programming, used to put user input into a memory variable, keep a running total of values, or reserve space for later input.

Structural knowledge: Knowledge that deals with constraints and dependencies among data. For example, the statement "insertion into a Supersaver fare is subject to reservations 14 days in advance of departure date" contains a familiar constraint, cued by the words "subject to."

Structure: The manner in which the system structures data.

Structure chart: Graphic representation of the control logic of processing functions or modules representing a system.

Structured English: Formal English statements used for communicating processing rules or describing the structure of a system.

Structured interview: Also called a *directive interview*; an approach in which the questions and the alternative responses are fixed.

Structured query language (SQL): A relational database language; a language for defining the structure and processing of a relational database; a nonprocedural and English-like language.

Structured walkthrough: A design procedure that helps systems analysts and database developers recognize various errors in system design; interchange of ideas among peers who review design work presented by the designer and agree on the validity of the design.

Subquery: In SQL, perming a query to obtain a result that will then be used as the basis of the WHERE clause in another query.

Subschema: A map of the programmer's view of data he or she uses; derived from the schema; the functional database.

SUM: See *Total function*.

Symbol: In expert systems, a group of characters that stands for real-life, such as *women* and *mother*. These symbols can combine to structure relationships between them.

Synonym: Two or more names used for the same data item; a hashed address that is not unique.

Syntax error: A program statement that violates one or more rules of the language in which it is written.

System specifications document: A document that identifies the user's problem and details what must be done to solve it properly; includes the necessary hardware and software requirements.

Table: Collection of records of the same type; in a relational model, a *table* is a two-dimensional arrangement of rows and columns. The rows represent records and the columns represent fields.

Teleprocessing (TP): Processing of data by an electronic transmission system among multiple sites; a long-haul processing system.

Teleprocessing (TP) monitor: Communications control software that resides in the host computer or in front-end computers to manage and control communications traffic.

Third normal form: Ensures that all data items on a record are dependent on the primary key of the record. An entity is in third normal form if it is in second normal form and if all fields that are not a part of the primary key have no transitive dependencies; is violated if a nonkey field is dependent on another nonkey field.

Token passing: A procedure that allows a terminal to transmit only while it holds a logical "token" that is passed from one terminal to another in a predefined manner.

Total function (SUM): An SQL function that produces the total for the values in the specified column.

Transaction: A user-defined set of work that requires all the work of the transaction be completed; a unit of work.

Transaction control: A basic area of data control that maintains the accuracy of the database by preventing partial transactions from being posted to the tables.

Transaction log: A way of keeping track of all transactions processed against the database.

Transaction transparency: A coordinating process in which all the statements representing a transaction must be executed or all must fail. Each local DBMS must be able to correctly process the transaction in question.

Transitive dependency: A relation having three or more attributes, $X(A,B,C)$, where A determines B, B determines C, and B does not determine A.

Transparency: In a distributed database, users should be able to use the database as though it is completely located on the user's premise; in expert systems, developing a system that employs similar knowledge and inference strategy to simulate the behavior of the human expert.

Tree: A hierarchy of nodes or records; in a database language, synonymous with a hierarchy.

Tree structure: See *Hierarchical structure*.

Triggers: Procedures stored in a server that are automatically executed every time a record is updated.

Tuning: Adjusting a database to improve its performance.

Tuple: A group of related fields; synonym for *row*.

Two-phase commit: A coordinating process that ensures that a logical transaction in a physically distributed computer environment is either completely successful or rolled back (aborted).

Unbalanced tree: A tree that has an uneven number of branches in each node.

Union: A relational algebra operation that combines the tuples of one relation to the tuples of another relation to form a third relation.

Unique: One of a kind; for example, a Social Security number is unique.

Unit of work: See *Transaction*.

Unnormalized relation: A relation in which there are repeating fields or fields that are not the key or partial key for the data set.

Unstructured interview: An approach in which the questions and the alternative responses are open-ended or not specified in advance.

Update: Any changes made in an existing file. This includes adding data to, deleting data from, or changing existing data in the database; changing the value of data in a row.

Update anomaly: A type of anomaly that occurs when updating a file becomes unnecessarily complicated due to redundancy. For example, updating an attribute of a logical entity occurrence necessitates the updating of several other logical entity occurrences.

User: Person who uses a computer (e.g., a manager entering an inquiry via a keyboard); anyone who employs a database to solve a problem or compile information; a person who enters and accesses data.

User view: See *View*.

Values: In SQL, a clause that specifies the data to be added, in the order the columns appear in the table.

Vertical fragmentation: A type of fragmentation that occurs when a file is split "vertically" and various attributes are stored at different sites. That is, we break up a table into multiple tables by selecting columns.

Video Privacy Protection Act: A law that prevents retailers from disclosing video-rental records without the customers' consent or a court order. Also forbids sale of the records.

View: A logically derived data field from one or more tables; provides the user with the data needed to do a job; a restricted set of columns from one or more tables.

WAIT: A command that appears at the end of a file to allow the user to view the records selected for display by the program.

Walkthrough: A peer group meeting in which the database design or systems development documentation is reviewed.

WAN: See *Wide area network*.

WHERE clause: In SQL, a clause that limits the scope of the command to only those rows that meet the conditions specified.

Wide area network (WAN): A network of computing environments, typically covering a wide geographical area; long-haul network.

Window: A screen divided into a number of rectangular areas, making up a split screen.

Workstation: An area set aside for users, equipped with office furniture, a "smart" terminal, voice transfer devices, and other computer-oriented equipment; a man-machine interface—a device through which a user can communicate with a database.

WYSIWIG: "What you see is what you get"; a term used with report generators, in which the DBMS repeats exactly what the designer types on the screen during report development.

Index

D

E

F

G

M

N

O

P

Q

R

S

T

U

V

W

X

Y

PHOTO CREDITS

Figure 1-1: The Image Bank, David W. Hamilton
Figure 1-3: The Image Bank, Flip Chalfant
Figure 1-4: The Image Bank, Chuck Mason
Figure 3-1: The Image Bank, Jeff Smith
Figure 3-2: The Image Bank, Bill Varie